"This impressive book covers an important and highly complex area of quantitative finance dealing with counterparty credit risk. It covers many vital topics and demonstrates in great detail how to compute Credit, Debt, and Funding Value Adjustments. Written by some of the best experts in the field, it provides important insights in its subject matter, which will be of great value for practitioners, academics, and regulators."

Alexander Lipton, Co-Head of Global Quantitative Group at Bank of America Merrill Lynch and Honorary Professor at Imperial College

"This book could rightly be called The Encyclopaedia of Credit Value Adjustments, *although it is both more detailed and more pleasantly readable than an encyclopaedia. It is the one-stop CVA (and more) reference for practitioners and academics alike."*

(This endorsement is a personal opinion and does not represent the view of the Financial Services Authority)

Dirk Tasche, Technical Specialist, Risk Specialists Division, Financial Services Authority

"There are many books in Finance. This one is different. It focuses on CVA (Credit Valuation Adjustment), a topic related to counterparty risk. The first chapter alone is worth the price of the book. This chapter is an 'extended dialogue,' where Brigo uses a question and answer format to teach, in an entertaining manner, a lot of the fundamental ideas, as well as the jargon with its alphabet-city innumerable acronyms, of modern financial mathematics, both as it is practiced in industry and in academia. His approach is creative and original; it could be acted out by two performers in front of a live audience. The book is urgently needed at a time when credit risk has emerged as the issue of the times."

Professor Philip Protter, Professor of Statistics, Statistics Department, Columbia University

Counterparty Credit Risk, Collateral and Funding

For other titles in the Wiley Finance series
please see www.wiley.com/finance

Counterparty Credit Risk, Collateral and Funding

With Pricing Cases for All Asset Classes

Damiano Brigo
Massimo Morini
Andrea Pallavicini

WILEY
A John Wiley & Sons, Ltd., Publication

Registered office
John Wiley & Sons Ltd, The Atrium, Southern Gate, Chichester, West Sussex, PO19 8SQ, United Kingdom

For details of our global editorial offices, for customer services and for information about how to apply for permission to reuse the copyright material in this book please see our website at www.wiley.com.

Library of Congress Cataloging-in-Publication Data

Brigo, Damiano, 1966–
Counterparty credit risk, collateral and funding : with pricing cases for all asset classes / Damiano Brigo, Massimo Morini, Andrea Pallavicini.
1 online resource.
Includes bibliographical references and index.
Description based on print version record and CIP data provided by publisher; resource not viewed.
ISBN 978-0-470-66167-3 (ebk) – ISBN 978-0-470-66178-9 (ebk) – ISBN 978-0-470-66249-6 (ebk) – ISBN 978-0-470-74846-6 (cloth) 1. Finance–Mathematical models. 2. Credit–Mathematical models. 3. Credit derivatives–Mathematical models. 4. Financial risk–Mathematical models. I. Morini, Massimo. II. Pallavicini, Andrea. III. Title.
HG106
332.701′5195–dc23

2013001506

A catalogue record for this book is available from the British Library.

ISBN 978-0-470-74846-6 (hbk) ISBN 978-0-470-66249-6 (ebk)
ISBN 978-0-470-66167-3 (ebk) ISBN 978-0-470-66178-9 (ebk)

Cover images reproduced by permission of Shutterstock.com

Set in 10/12pt Times by Aptara, Inc., New Delhi, India
Printed in Great Britain by CPI Group (UK) Ltd, Croydon, CR0 4YY

Contents

PART II PRICING COUNTERPARTY RISK: UNILATERAL CVA

Ignition

TIMELINE

This book has been planned and should have been published years ago. We apologize for the delay, but every time we thought we had it completed, some new counterparty risk-related topic would show up. The original version was only a portion of the first two parts of the present book. None of the advanced topics had been developed or even thought of. Moreover, the inclusion of these new topics has forced us to redesign the theory almost from scratch a few times.

Credit Valuation Adjustment, CVA

First we had unilateral Credit Valuation Adjustments, namely the reduction in price an investor requires in order to trade a product with a default-risky counterparty as opposed to a default-free one, with which the investor would pay the full price. We studied this across asset classes, and under netting and wrong way risk. Many examples were performed by means of least-squares Monte Carlo techniques applied to CVA, the now so-called "American Monte Carlo", first used in CVA pricing by Brigo and Pallavicini (2007) [57].

Bilateral Risk: Credit and Debit Valuation Adjustment, CVA and DVA

When we were done with unilateral CVA across asset classes, the paper by Brigo and Capponi (2008) [39] introduced a detailed account of bilateral counterparty credit and debit risk for Credit Default Swaps, and we had to include it, with all the nuisances and the debate on the Debit Valuation Adjustment (DVA) – namely the increase in price one party would accept for a product for the fact that this party itself is default-risky and would thus expect to be charged more with respect to the case where it was default-free.

Collateral

Once we included DVA, the issue of collateral modelling exploded. So far we had been able to build a satisfactory picture for trades between banks and corporates, given that often the latter do not post collateral (see [192] and the interview with the CFO of Lufthansa, for example). Now, however, for trades between banks, collateral and the Credit Support Annex (CSA) regulation has become fundamental. We had therefore to derive a consistent theory of credit, debit and collateral, where we would look at the impact of margining, Gap risk, re-hypothecation, and the rigorous interaction of this with default risk. To the best of our knowledge, Brigo, Capponi, Pallavicini and Papatheodorou (2011) [41] were the first to do so in full so we had to also add this to the book.

Funding

Then we had the emergency of funding costs showing up. This was so relevant that we could not have a book without this fundamental aspect joining default modelling. We looked first at the paper by Morini and Prampolini (2010) [157], then at the the paper by Pallavicini, Perini and Brigo (2011) [165], one of the most general papers on the topic, and decided to include this aspect too.

Emerging Asset Classes: Longevity Risk

Finally, although the core work in the book concerns the most standard asset classes, namely interest rates, credit, equity, FX and commodities, emerging asset classes are also heavily affected by counterparty credit and funding risk. To make an example we decided to include Longevity Risk, that is hedged occasionally in the market through longevity swaps. Such instruments have typically very long maturities, and as such they are subject to important counterparty risk. We decided to include an analysis of counterparty risk for longevity swaps based on Biffis, Blake, Pitotti and Sun [21].

These subsequent inclusions forced us to postpone publishing a few times but, finally, we are ready to talk about this new book.

THIS BOOK AND NEW-GENERATION FINANCIAL MODELLING

The financial modelling landscape has changed completely, as has the job of quantitative analysts. In the old days, pre-2007, front-office quants would be typically busy pricing and hedging new products, more and more complex functionals of simple underlying assets. This used to happen in a world where collateral, funding and trading liquidity, and counterparty credit risk were secondary aspects, often left to other areas of the bank to manage with much simpler methodologies than those used for the exotic derivatives themselves.

With the development of the crisis it became clear that derivatives are not entities living in a platonic world: they are affected, quite heavily, by liquidity, credit risk, collateral modelling, funding costs, and all the related subtleties. We witnessed:

- The disappearance of the "unique-objective" price for a financial payoff.
- Multiple discount curves.
- The impossibility to standardize and regulate complex risks with simplistic formulas, tables, multipliers and so on.
- The necessity to invest more in modelling, not less, and the necessity to do the hard work without trying to bypass it with simplistic rules and regulation.
- The emerging holistic nature of risks, that cannot be modelled and analyzed separately any longer.

Part of the quant intelligentsia tried to deny these problems and the world of multiple curves, CVA-DVA-FVA (Funding Valuation Adjustment) and so on, coming out of this, either by denying these were really quant problems, claiming they were easily and trivially solvable and going back to their dream world of more and more complex instruments without additional risks, or by pretending that such effects were just temporary. It is amazing how even celebrated or industry-awarded quants, who should know better, fell for this trap of wishful thinking.

We will be honest here and state this possibly uncomfortable fact very clearly from the start. *It does not make sense to consider derivatives as platonic instruments living in a world of their own without being affected by credit, default, liquidity, funding, close-out, netting and collateral. This would be, once upon a time, the attitude of derivatives quants, who had better to do than model quantities such as collateral. However, when even a vanilla instruments portfolio is properly embedded in such risks, it suddenly becomes the most formidable derivative to be priced or managed. It is not an easy problem at all and the difficulty in modelling such aspects consistently far exceeds the difficulties of coming up with a new stochastic volatility model for the smile, for example, or with a new stochastic volatility extension of the LIBOR(!!) market model. Even the implications on global modelling, on the bank systems architecture and on the mathematical tools to be used are important and at times revolutionary in scope and scale, compared to past quant themes. This will be obvious once the reader has gone through the book.*

The reader will have a better understanding after reading the dialogue in Chapter 1, which summarizes the book's themes without a single formula. Chapter 10 represents a more advanced summary of the book's themes.

We will say many times that the pricing and management of counterparty credit and funding risk is a very complex, model-dependent task and requires a holistic approach to modelling that goes against much of the ingrained culture in most of the financial industry and regulators, and even of most traditional western science to some extent. Regulators and part of the industry are desperately trying to standardize the related calculations in the simplest possible ways but our conclusion will be that such effects are complex and need to remain so to be properly accounted for. The attempt to standardize every risk to simple formulas is misleading and may result in the relevant risks not being addressed at all. Instead, industry and regulators should acknowledge the complexity of this problem and work to attain the necessary methodological and technological prowess to handle it, rather than trying to bypass it. Until the methodology is sufficiently good, we should refrain from proposing inadequate solutions that may only make the situation worse. This book is a beginning in such a direction, in that it is more advanced and consistent than most of the Credit Valuation Adjustment (CVA) literature available, although it is far from being perfect or even fully adequate.

There is no easy way out.

THE STRUCTURE OF THE BOOK

The book is structured in three parts, each divided in chapters.

Part I

Part I sets up the context for counterparty risk pricing and measurement, collateral and funding costs.

Chapter 1 presents a long, and hopefully, entertaining dialogue between two colleagues on all the aspects of counterparty risk dealt with in the book.

Chapter 2 sets the context for the book, introducing technical definitions for counterparty risk, exposures, credit Value at Risk (VaR), CVA, CVA VaR in relation to Basel III, and other related concepts, including collateral, netting and funding.

Chapter 3 illustrates credit modelling, a clearly necessary tool for the development of satisfactory counterparty credit risk pricing. Both intensity models and firm value models are covered, with a discussion also of multivariate credit modelling. Arbitrage-free credit spread models with volatility (very important in CVA calculations) and possibly jumps are introduced. Such models can be easily calibrated to market credit data.

Part II

Part II deals with pricing of unilateral CVA across asset classes. Here unilateral means that only the counterparty may default, whereas the calculating party, typically the bank, is considered as default free and its credit risk does not enter valuation. This used to be the prevailing paradigm at the time banks were considered to be default free, or much safer than corporates. After the eight credit events that happened to financial institutions in one month of 2008 this was no longer considered to be a realistic assumption, and Part III will deal with that and many other aspects. Part II keeps the unilateral assumption and shows how CVA with wrong way risk works across asset classes. Wrong way risk is the additional risk when the default of the counterparty and the underlying portfolio are correlated in the worst possible way for the calculating agent.

Chapter 4 illustrates unilateral CVA for interest rate swap portfolios with possible netting. There is no wrong way risk in this chapter, but despite this simplifying assumption we show that the option nature of CVA makes valuation of the pure interest rate part complicated, especially because of the netting clause.

Chapter 5 focuses again on interest rate portfolios and exotics, this time allowing for wrong way risk. Correlation between credit risk of the counterparty and interest rates is modelled explicitly and properly accounted for. Wrong way risk patterns and the impact of correlation are investigated, and exclude the use of simple multipliers applied to the zero correlation case. This is already enough to show that "bond equivalent approaches" that try to account for correlation through standardized multipliers are destined to fail. In this chapter we also introduce contingent Credit Default Swap (CDS) briefly, as a tool to hedge unilateral CVA perfectly.

Chapter 6 illustrates unilateral CVA for oil swaps, showing again the detailed impact of volatilities and correlations on valuation.

Chapter 7 illustrates unilateral CVA for credit default swaps. This is particularly relevant, since we add the default of the underlying instrument to the default of the counterparty. The default correlation between the two will be a key driver of our analysis. A special role is played here by credit spread volatility. With low volatility, the wrong way risk becomes completely unrealistic, and we explain why.

Chapter 8 illustrates unilateral CVA for equity return swaps. This is the only chapter in this part to resort to firm value models rather than intensity models, a choice stemming from the difficulty to force equity to zero upon default in intensity models. The impact of wrong way risk in this case is huge.

Chapter 9 introduces unilateral CVA for FX and cross currency swaps in particular. This is done without wrong way risk, namely without modelling correlation between counterparty default and underlying FX and interest rates. Despite this simplification, as in Chapter 4 a lot of work is required for CVA valuation. In this chapter we also analyze the Novation, an alternative to contingent CDS for hedging counterparty risk.

Part III

Part III is the advanced section of the book and introduces new generation counterparty and funding risk problems. It is the part that most differentiates our book from previous and current competitor books such as [173], [76], [119], and [136]. While the recent book [136] deals with funding and credit jointly, we follow a more cash-flow oriented approach, reaching a final master equation in line with the paper [85] and more precisely with [165].

Chapter 10 presents a more advanced summary of the book, with formulas. The chapter also introduces unilateral Debit Valuation Adjustment, and bilateral CVA, DVA and bilateral total adjustment BVA. It highlights problems with DVA interpretation and hedging, and shows the current conflicting opinions of regulators on DVA. While bilateral CVA and DVA allow two parties to agree again on the price of the deal, contrary to unilateral CVA, DVA opens a Pandora's box of problems that we hint at in the chapter. We also consider whether an industry-used formula for BVA neglecting first-to-default risk is appropriate, and we introduce again the problem of funding costs, while looking at whether we should be using risk-free close-out or replacement close-out.

Chapter 11 introduces our first tackling of funding costs. We illustrate an interesting relationship between DVA and funding in situations where there is a clear distinction of a borrower and a lender in the deal.

Chapter 12 covers bilateral CVA and DVA more rigorously than in Chapter 10 and looks at a number of problems with the related definitions. Furthermore, this chapter shows numerical examples of bilateral CVA and DVA based on interest rate swap portfolios, analyzing the adjustments patterns in terms of dynamics parameters, namely volatilities and correlations.

Chapter 13 looks at collateral modelling, analyzing the residual CVA and DVA one faces even under collateralization. The possibility of Gap risk is introduced, and master equations for CVA and DVA under collateralization are derived, following legal Credit Support Annex (CSA) documentation and the International Swaps and Derivatives Association (ISDA) suggestions.

Chapter 14 returns to the close-out problem, first hinted at in Chapter 10, and described in Chapter 13. A detailed analysis is presented of different close-out formulations, mostly risk-free close-out and replacement close-out, with the related contagion. We find that contagion is important, and that the convenience of a close-out is also a matter of default correlation between the calculating party and the counterparty in the deal.

Chapter 15 is a continuation of Chapter 13, and looks at the application of the theory developed in Chapter 13 to interest rates and Credit Default Swap (CDS) portfolios. We see that in the case of interest rate swaps' collateralization is quite effective in reducing CVA, even for relatively long margining periods, whereas we will see that for the case of a CDS as an underlying trade the Gap risk may become so extreme as to make even daily collateralization completely useless. This goes against the folklore myth that collateral completely kills counterparty risk.

Chapter 16 adds collateral costs to the picture, extending the formula obtained in Chapter 13 by adding margining costs for collateral.

Chapter 17 develops a complete theory of funding costs, based on possibly different models of treasury policy, that is consistent with the earlier theory of CVA, DVA and collateral. This leads, however, to a recursive equation that is no longer additive. This is the main feature stemming from the inclusion of funding costs, and is confirmed by recent works in the literature, for example [85] and [165]. We also re-derive previous funding literature as special cases for our general framework.

Chapter 18 introduces a "non-standard" asset class for which counterparty risk, collateral and funding are crucial. This is the area of longevity risk, roughly speaking the risk that an annuity or pension provider may have to pay benefits to clients longer than expected. Pension funds and annuity providers are known to hedge this risk by resorting to longevity swaps. These are, however, quite opaque in the pricing technique and furthermore tend to have quite long maturities, so that their valuation is not easy. We resort to the work of Biffis, Blake, Pitotti and Sun (2011) [21] combined with our master formulas developed in the funding chapters to illustrate how counterparty credit and debit risk, collateral and funding impact the valuation of longevity swaps, and to derive the endogenous swap rate of such instruments.

Chapter 19 concludes the book by providing our main message and analyzing the situation from a broad point of view after the start of the global financial crisis in 2007.

ACKNOWLEDGMENTS

We are grateful to a number of colleagues and co-authors with whom we discussed counterparty risk, collateral and funding over the years. We have benefited from countless panels, round-tables, informal conversations, trattorie, pub and bacari toasts, conference dinners, press interviews, industry meetings, correspondence messages, letters, and many other forms of debate. It is impossible to thank all colleagues and friends who enriched our understanding of this area, but here we would like to mention explicitly Claudio Albanese, Emilio Barucci, Tom Bielecki, Stéphane Crépey, Mark Davis, Diego Di Grado, Cyril Durand, Naoufel El-Bachir, Andrea Germani, Patrick Haener, Alexander Herbertsson, Jeroen Kerkhof, Claudio Nordio, Frank Oertel, Giacomo Pietronero, Dan Rosen, Marek Rutkowski, Gary Wong.

Special thanks to our co-authors: Agostino Capponi, who is virtually a co-author of the second part of this book; Vasileios Papatheodorou who co-authored bilateral CVA applications to rates with collateral; Daniele Perini who helped us considerably with funding costs modelling; Enrico Biffis, who helped us and virtually co-authored the longevity chapter; Cristin Buescu, Kyriakos Chourdakis, Massimo Masetti, Andrea Prampolini, Marco Tarenghi who co-authored other works on counterparty risk with us. Massimo and Andrea are also thankful to their current and past Banca IMI and Banca Intesa colleagues supporting their work, with a special thank you to Aleardo Adotti, Nando Ametrano, Marco Bianchetti, Sebastiano Chirigoni, Giorgio Facchinetti, Diego Giovannini, Fabio Mercurio, Nicola Moreni, Paola Mosconi, Giulio Sartirana, Giulio Sartorelli, Roberto Torresetti and Michele Trapletti.

Damiano is grateful to his family for support, since it is very hard to write a book while raising twin babies, and special thanks go in particular to babies Giacomo and Lorenzo for their emotional support and their sense of wonder, and to mum Valeria. This book is for Damiano's mother Anna and father Francesco. Damiano would also like to dedicate this book to the memory of his friend and colleague, Professor Renato Maino (1953–2012).

Massimo is grateful to his family, his students, his closest colleagues and his friends, particularly for keeping from saying "What? Another book!?!" and being, instead, always helpful and collaborative. This book is for Giulia and Vittorio and all those like them, who are still curious about everything in of life.

Andrea is grateful to all his friends who suffered him speaking in strange acronyms such as DVA or CFBVA, not only when working at the office, but also when cooking dinner or drinking a beer. This book is for Andrea's father Sergio and in memory of his mother Pierluigia.

Finally, we all dedicate this book to our readers. We imagine our readers as curious, with a sense of wonder, with a passion to look at problems in depth, and willing to do the hard work. This book is for you.

London and Venice, Milan and Pavia, 1 October 2012.

Abbreviations and Notation

ACRONYMS:

- AMC = American Monte Carlo
- AT1P = Analytically Tractable 1st Passage Model
- ATM = At-the-money
- BC = Black Cox model
- BID, ASK, MID = Bid, ask, mid prices
- BIS = Bank of International Settlements, BASEL I, II, III
- bps = Basis Point ($1bps = 10^{-4} = 1E - 4 = 0.0001$)
- BSDE = Backwards Stochastic Differential Equation
- BVA = Bilateral Valuation Adjustment
- BVAS = Bilateral Valuation Adjustment Simplified (without first to default times)
- CBVA = Collateral-inclusive Bilateral Valuation Adjustment
- CCDS = Contingent Credit Default Swap
- CCP = Central Counterparty Clearing House
- CCS = Cross Currency Swap
- CCVA = Collateral-inclusive Credit Valuation Adjustment
- CDF = Cumulative Distribution Function
- CDO = Collateralized Debt Obligation
- CDS = Credit Default Swap
- CDVA = Collateral-inclusive Debit Valuation Adjustment
- CE = Current Exposure
- CEO = Chief Executive Officer
- CFBVA = Collateral- and Funding-inclusive Bilateral Valuation Adjustment
- CFO = Chief Financial Officer
- CIR = Cox-Ingersoll-Ross model
- CIR++ = Shifted Cox-Ingersoll-Ross model
- CMCDS = Constant-Maturity Credit Default Swap
- Corr = Correlation
- Cov = Covariance
- CR, CCR = Counterparty (Credit) Risk
- CrVaR = Credit Value at Risk, Credit VaR
- CSA = Credit Support Annex
- CVA = Credit Valuation Adjustment

- DVA = Debit Valuation Adjustment
- EAD = Exposure at Default
- EE = Expected Exposure
- ENE = Expected Negative Exposure
- EPE = Expected Positive Exposure
- ERS = Equity Return Swap
- ES = Expected Shortfall
- Ex = Exposure
- Exs = Exposure with sign
- FAS(B) = Financial Accounting Standard (Board)
- FRA = Forward Rate Agreement
- FRCVA = Floating Rate Credit Valuation Adjustment
- FT = *Financial Times*
- FtD = First-to-Default
- FTP = Funds Transfer Pricing
- FVA = Funding Valuation Adjustment
- FX = Foreign Exchange
- G2++ = Shifted two-factor Gaussian short rate model
- GBM = Geometric Brownian Motion
- GPL = Generalized Poisson Loss model
- HMD = Human Mortality Database
- IAS = International Accounting Standards
- ILVAA = Independence-based Liquidity Valuation Adjustment Approximation
- IMF = International Monetary Fund
- IRS = Interest Rate Swap (either payer or receiver)
- ISDA = International Swaps and Derivatives Association
- ITM = In-the-money
- JCIR(++) = Jump CIR model (with shift)
- LCH = London Clearing House
- LGD = Loss Given Default
- LLMA = Life and Longevity Markets Association
- LMM = LIBOR Market Model (BGM model)
- LSMC = Least-Squares Monte Carlo
- MC = Monte Carlo
- MPFE = Maximum Potential Future Exposure
- MTM = Mark-to-Market
- NPV = Net Present Value
- OECD = Organisation for Economic Co-operation and Development
- OTC = Over-the-counter
- OTM = Out-of-the-money
- PDE = Partial Differential Equation
- PDF = Probability Density Function
- PFE = Potential Future Exposure
- RWR = Right Way Risk
- SBTV = Scenario Barrier Time-Varying Volatility AT1P model
- SDE = Stochastic Differential Equation
- SSRD = Shifted Square Root Diffusion

- TED = Interbank Treasury Spread
- UCVA = Unilateral Credit Valuation Adjustment
- UCVAB = Bucketed UCVA
- UCVABI = Bucketed UCVA under Independence
- UDA = Unilateral Default Assumption
- UDVA = Unilateral Debit Valuation Adjustment
- VaR = Value at Risk
- VAR = Variance
- WTI = West Texas Intermediate (Oil futures market)
- WWR = Wrong Way Risk

PROBABILITY MEASURES, EXPECTATIONS, FILTRATIONS

- $\mathbb{P}$: Physical/Objective/Real-World measure
- $\mathbb{Q}, \mathbb{E}$: Risk-neutral measure (equivalent martingale measure, risk-adjusted measure), and related expectation
- $\mathcal{F}_t$: Default-free market information up to time t
- $\mathcal{G}_t$: Complete market filtration, i.e. default-free market information plus explicit monitoring of default, up to time t
- $\mathbb{E}\{\cdot|\mathcal{F}_t\}, \mathbb{E}[\cdot|\mathcal{F}_t], \mathbb{E}(\cdot|\mathcal{F}_t)$: Expectation conditional on the $\mathcal{F}_t$ σ–field; $\mathbb{E}_t$ denotes expectation with respect to the complete sigma-field $\mathcal{G}_t$
- $\mathbb{Q}^U, \mathbb{E}^U$: Measure and expectation associated with the numeraire U when U is a positive non-dividend-paying asset
- $\mathbb{Q}^T$: T–forward adjusted measure, i.e. measure associated with the numeraire $P(\cdot, T)$
- $\mathbb{Q}^i$: T_i–forward adjusted measure
- $p_X^U(x)$: Probability density function at point x for the random vector X under the $\mathbb{Q}^U$ measure; U can be omitted if clear from the context or under the risk-neutral measure
- $F_X^U(x)$: Cumulative probability distribution function at point x for the random vector X under the $\mathbb{Q}^U$ measure; U can be omitted if clear from the context or under the risk-neutral measure
- φ_X^U: Characteristic function of the random vector X (Fourier transform of its probability density) under the $\mathbb{Q}^U$ measure; U can be omitted if clear from the context or under the risk-neutral measure
- M_X^U: Moment generating function of the random vector X (Laplace transform of its probability density) under the $\mathbb{Q}^U$ measure; U can be omitted if clear from the context or under the risk-neutral measure
- $C_X(u_1, u_2 \ldots, u_n) = C_{X_1,X_2,\ldots,X_n}(u_1, u_2, \ldots, u_n)$: Copula function for the random variables $X_1, X_2, \ldots, X_n$. When clear from the context we write simply $C(u_1, u_2 \ldots, u_n)$
- τ^C, ρ^C: Kendall's tau and Spearman's rho associated with the copula C
- $\sim$: distributed as
- $\mathcal{N}(\mu, V)$: Multivariate normal distribution with mean vector μ and covariance matrix V; Its density at x is at times denoted by $p_{\mathcal{N}(\mu,V)}(x)$
- Φ: Cumulative distribution function of the standard Gaussian distribution
- Φ_R^n: Cumulative distribution function of the n-dimensional Gaussian random vector with standard Gaussian margins and $n \times n$ correlation matrix R
- χ_ν^2: chi-squared distribution with ν degrees of freedom

- $\chi^2(\cdot; r, \rho)$: Cumulative distribution function of the noncentral chi-squared distribution with r degrees of freedom and noncentrality parameter ρ
- W_t: (Vector) Brownian motion under the risk-neutral measure
- $J_t^{F,\gamma}$: Compound Poisson process under $\mathbb{Q}$ given by $\sum_{i=1}^{M_t} Y_i$ with Y_i i.i.d. $\sim F$ and M Poisson with intensity γ

PRODUCTS PAYOFFS, TERMS, VARIABLES AND PRICES

- $B(t)$, B_t: Money market account at time t, bank account at time t
- $D(t, T)$: Default-free Stochastic discount factor at time t for the maturity T
- $P(t, T)$: Default-free zero-coupon bond price at time t for the maturity T
- $r(t)$, r_t: Default-free instantaneous spot interest rate at time t
- $R(t, T)$: Default-free Continuously compounded spot rate at time t for the maturity T
- $L(t, T)$: Default-free Simply compounded (LIBOR) spot rate at time t for the maturity T
- $f(t, T)$: Default-free Instantaneous forward rate at time t for the maturity T
- $F(t; T, S)$: Default-free Simply compounded forward (LIBOR) rate at time t for the expiry–maturity pair T, S
  $T_1, T_2, \ldots, T_{i-1}, T_i, \ldots$: An increasing set of maturities
- α_i: The year fraction between T_{i-1} and T_i
- $F_i(t)$: $F(t; T_{i-1}, T_i)$
- $S(t; T_i, T_j)$, $S_{i,j}(t)$: Forward swap rate at time t for a swap with first reset date T_i and payment dates $T_{i+1}, \ldots, T_j$
- $A_{i,j}(t)$: Annuity (or Present value of a basis point (PVBP)) associated to the forward swap rate $S_{i,j}(t)$, i.e. $\sum_{k=i+1}^{j} \alpha_k P(t, T_k)$
- $\tau = \tau_C$: Default time of the reference entity "C"
- $\tau_1, \tau_2, \ldots, \tau_n$: Default times of names $1, 2, \ldots, n$
- $\tau^1, \tau^2, \ldots, \tau^n$: First, second... and n-th default times in the pool
- REC: Recovery fraction on a unit notional
- LGD $= 1 -$ REC: CDS Protection payment against a Loss (given default of the reference entity in the protection interval). More generally, Loss Given Default
- $T_a, (T_{a+1}, \ldots, T_{b-1}), T_b$: Initial and final dates in the protection schedule of the premium leg in the CDS
- α_i: Year fraction between T_{i-1} and T_i
- $T_{\beta(t)}$: First of the T_i's following t
- $\mathrm{CDS}_{a,b}(t, S, \mathrm{LGD})$: Price of a running CDS to the protection seller, protecting against default of the reference entity in $[T_a, T_b]$ with a premium spread S. This is also called "price of a receiver CDS". The corresponding payer CDS price, i.e. the CDS price seen from the point of view of the protection buyer, is $-\mathrm{CDS}_{a,b}(t, S, \mathrm{LGD})$
- $-\mathrm{CDS}_{a,b}(t, S, \mathrm{LGD})$: Price of a running CDS to the protection buyer, also called "price of a payer CDS"
- $S_{a,b}(t)$: Fair rate (spread) at time t in the premium leg of a CDS protecting in $[T_a, T_b]$

Intensity Models:

- $\gamma(t)$: Deterministic default intensity (and then hazard rate) for the default time at time t
- $\lambda(t)$: Possibly stochastic default intensity (and then hazard rate) for the default time at time t

- $\Gamma(t) = \int_0^t \gamma(s)ds$: Deterministic cumulated default intensity (and then hazard function) for the default time at time t
- $\Lambda(t) = \int_0^t \lambda(s)ds$: Possibly stochastic cumulated default intensity (and then hazard function) for the default time
- ξ: Transformation of the default time by its cumulated intensity, $\xi = \Lambda(\tau)$ or $\Gamma(\tau)$; it is exponentially distributed and independent of default free quantities. The default time can be expressed, if intensity is strictly positive, as $\tau = \Lambda^{-1}(\xi)$, otherwise we need to introduce a pseudo-inverse

Structural Models, First Passage Time Models:

- $V_C(t)$: Firm value (of assets) for name "C". "C" can be omitted and we write V_t
- $D_C(t)$: Debt value for name "C". "C" can be omitted and we write D_t
- $S_C(t)$, $E_C(t)$: Equity value for name "C". "C" can be omitted and we write S_t or E_t
- L: Zero coupon debt level at maturity. In Merton's model there is default at debt maturity $\bar{T}$ if $V_C(\bar{T}) < L$
- $H(t)$: Early default barrier, or safety covenant barrier; Default is the first time V hits H from above

VECTOR/MATRIX NOTATION ET AL.

- I_n: the $n \times n$ identity matrix
- e_i: i-th canonical vector of $\mathbb{R}^n$, a vector with all zeros except in the i-th entry, where a "1" is found
- $[x_1, \ldots, x_m]$: row vector with i-th component x_i
- $[x_1, \ldots, x_m]'$: column vector with i-th component x_i
- $'$: Transposition
- 1_A, $1\{A\}$: Indicator function of the set A
- $\#\{A\}$: Number of elements of the finite set A

Part I

COUNTERPARTY CREDIT RISK, COLLATERAL AND FUNDING

1 Introduction

This chapter is based on the summary given in Brigo (2011b) [34].

In this introductory chapter we present a dialogue that clarifies the main issues dealt with in the book. This chapter is also a stand-alone informal guide to problems in counterparty risk valuation and measurement, with references for readers who may wish to pursue further the different aspects of this type of credit risk. Later chapters in the book will provide in-depth studies of all aspects of counterparty risk.

1.1 A DIALOGUE ON CVA

Although research on counterparty risk pricing started way back in the nineties, with us joining the effort back in 2002, the different aspects of counterparty credit risk exploded after the start of the global financial crisis in 2007. In less than four years we have seen the emergence of a number of features that the market operators are struggling to account for with consistency. Further, the several possible definitions and methodologies for counterparty risk may create confusion. This dialogue is meant to provide an informal guide to the different aspects of counterparty risk. It is in the form of questions and answers between a CVA expert and a newly hired colleague, and provides detailed references for investigating the different areas sketched here in more detail.

1.2 RISK MEASUREMENT: CREDIT VaR

Q: [Junior colleague, he is looking a little worried] I am new in this area of counterparty risk, and I am struggling to understand the different measures and metrics. Could you start by explaining generally what counterparty risk is?

A: [Senior colleague, she is looking at the junior colleague reassuringly.] The risk taken on by an entity entering an Over-The-Counter (OTC) contract with one (or more) counterparty having a relevant default probability. As such, the counterparty might not respect its payment obligations.

Q: What kind of counterparty risk practices are present in the market?

A: Several, but most can be divided into two broad areas. Counterparty risk measurement for capital requirements, following Basel II, or counterparty risk from a pricing point of view, when updating the price of instruments to account for possible default of the counterparty. However, the distinction is now fading with the advent of Basel III.

Q: [Shifts nervously] Let us disentangle this a little, I am getting confused.

A: Fine. Where do we start from?

Q: Let us start from Counterparty Risk Measurement for Capital Requirements. What is that?

A: It is a risk that one bank faces in order to be able to lend money or invest towards a counterparty with relevant default risk. The bank needs to cover for that risk by setting capital aside, and this can be done after the risk has been measured.

Q: You are saying that we aim at measuring that risk?

A: Indeed, and this measurement will help the bank decide how much capital the bank should set aside (capital requirement) in order to be able to face losses coming from possible defaults of counterparties the bank is dealing with.

Q: Could you make an example of such a measure?

A: A popular measure is Value at Risk (VaR). It is basically a percentile on the loss distribution associated with the position held by the bank, over a given time horizon. More precisely, it is a percentile (say the 99.9th percentile) of the initial value of the position minus the final value at the risk horizon, across scenarios.

Q: Which horizon is usually taken?

A: When applied to default risk the horizon is usually one year and this is called "Credit VaR (CrVaR)". If this is taken at the 99.9-th percentile, then you have a loss that is exceeded only in 1 case out of 1,000. The Credit VaR is either the difference of the percentile from the mean, or the percentile itself. There is more than one possible definition.

Q: Is this a good definition of credit risk?

A: [Frowning] Well what does "good" really mean? It is not a universally good measure. It has often been criticized, especially in the context of pure market risk without default, for lack of sub-additivity. In other terms, it does not always acknowledge the benefits of diversification, in that in some paradoxical situations the risk of a total portfolio can be larger than the sum of the risks in a single position. A better measure from that point of view would be expected shortfall, known also as tail VaR, conditional VaR, etc.

Q: And what is that?

A: This is loosely defined as the expected value of the losses beyond the VaR point. But this need not concern us too much at present.

Q: Fine. How is Credit VaR typically calculated?

A: Credit VaR is calculated through a simulation of the basic financial variables underlying the portfolio under the historical probability measure, commonly referred to as P, up to the risk horizon. The simulation also includes the default of the counterparties. At the risk horizon, the portfolio is priced in every simulated scenario of the basic financial variables, including defaults, obtaining a number of scenarios for the portfolio value at the risk horizon.

Q: So if the risk horizon is one year, we obtain a number of scenarios for what will be the value of the portfolio in one year, based on the evolution of the underlying market variables and on the possible default of the counterparties.

A: Precisely. A distribution of the losses of the portfolio is built based on these scenarios of portfolio values. When we say "priced" we mean to say is that the discounted future cash flows of the portfolio, after the risk horizon, are averaged conditional on each scenario at the risk horizon but under another probability measure, the Pricing measure, or Risk-neutral measure, or Equivalent Martingale measure if you want to go technical, commonly referred as Q.

Q: Not so clear... [Looks confused]

A: [Sighing] All right, suppose your portfolio has a call option on equity, traded with a corporate client, with a final maturity of two years. Suppose for simplicity there is no interest rate risk, so discounting is deterministic. To get the Credit VaR, roughly, you simulate the underlying equity under the P measure up to one year, and obtain a number of scenarios for the underlying equity in one year. Also, you need to simulate the default scenarios up to one year, to know in each scenario whether the counterparties have defaulted or not. This default simulation up to one year is under the measure P as well. And you may want to include the "correlation" between default of the counterparty and underlying equity, that would allow you to model Wrong Way Risk (WWR). But let us leave WWR aside for a moment.

Q: OK. We simulate under P because we want the risk statistics of the portfolio in the real world, under the physical probability measure, and not under the so-called pricing measure Q.

A: That's right. And then in each scenario at one year, if the counterparty has defaulted there will be a recovery value and all else will be lost. Otherwise, we price the call option over the remaining year using, for example, a Black-Scholes formula. But this price is like taking the expected value of the call option payoff in two years, conditional on each scenario for the underlying equity in one year. Because this is pricing, this expected value will be taken under the pricing measure Q, not P. This gives the Black-Scholes formula if the underlying equity follows a Geometric Brownian Motion (GMB) under Q.

Q: So default needs to be simulated only under P? Where do you find such probabilities?

A: [Frowning] This is a very difficult question. Often one uses probabilities obtained through aggregation, like the probability associated to the rating of the counterparty, for example. But this is not very precise. Default of a single firm occurs only once, so determining the P probability through direct historical observation is not possible...

Q: [Shifts nervously on the chair]...

A: [Concentrating] Notice also that in a more refined valuation, you may also want to take into account the default probability of the counterparty between 1 and 2 years in valuing the call option. But this would now be the default probability under Q, not under P, because this is pricing. But let us leave this aside for the time being, because this leads directly to Credit Valuation Adjustments (CVA) which we will address later. It would be like saying that in one year you compute the option price value by taking into account its CVA.

Q: [Frowning] I think I need to understand this P and Q thing better. For example, how are the default probabilities under P and Q different?

A: The ones under Q, typically inferred from market prices of credit default swaps (CDS) or corporate bonds, are typically larger than those under the measure P. This has been observed a number of times. A comparison of the P and Q loss distributions involved in Collateralized Debt Obligations (CDOs) is carried out in [190].

Q: Some more acronyms ... In the meantime, where can I read more about VaR and Expected Shortfall (ES)?

A: On a basic technical level you have books like [133], whereas at a higher technical level you have books like [147]. For the original Credit VaR framework it is a good idea to have a look at the original "Credit Metrics Technical Document" [121], which is available at defaultrisk.com.

1.3 EXPOSURE, CE, PFE, EPE, EE, EAD

Q: OK, I have more or less understood Credit VaR and ES. But I also keep hearing the word "Exposure" in a lot of meetings. What is that, precisely?

A: Let me borrow [69]. [Calls up a paper on the screen of her tablet] These are not exactly the definitions and calculations used in Basel, we would need to go into much more detail for that, but they are enough to give you a good idea of what's going on.

Q: Hopefully . . . [Looks at his senior colleague skeptically]

A: [Rolls her eyes] Counterparty exposure at any given future time is the larger figure between zero and the market value of the portfolio of derivative positions with a counterparty that would be lost if the counterparty were to default with zero recovery at that time.

Q: This is clear.

A: Current Exposure (CE) is, obviously enough, the current value of the exposure to a counterparty. This is simply the current value of the portfolio if positive, and zero otherwise. This is typically the expected value under the pricing measure Q of future cashflows, discounted back at the present time and added up, as seen from the present time, if positive, and zero otherwise.

Q: OK, I see.

A: Potential Future Exposure (PFE) for a given date is the maximum exposure at that date, with a high degree of statistical confidence. For example, the 95% PFE is the level of potential exposure that is exceeded with only 5% P-probability. The curve of PFE in time is the potential exposure profile, up to the final maturity of the portfolio of trades with the counterparty.

Q: Why 95? And what about P and Q.

A: Just because [Amused]. On P and Q, let's talk about that later.

Q: . . . .

A: PFE is usually computed via simulation: for each future date, the price of the portfolio of trades with a counterparty is simulated. A P-percentile of the distribution of exposures is chosen to represent the PFE at the future date. The peak of PFE over the life of the portfolio is called Maximum Potential Future Exposure (MPFE). PFE and MPFE are usually compared with credit limits in the process of permissioning trades.

Q: But wait . . . isn't this what you said about Credit VaR? Because earlier you said..

A: [Raising her hand] No, be careful . . . here there is no default simulation involved, only the portfolio is simulated, not the default of the counterparty. With exposure we answer the question: IF default happens, what is going to be the loss?

Q: So in a way we assume that default happens for sure and we check what would be the loss in that case. I see. No default simulation or probabilities here.

A: Good. As we have seen above, with Credit VaR instead we answer the question: what is the final loss that is not exceeded with a given P probability, over a given time horizon? This second question obviously involves the inclusion of the default event of the counterparty in generating the loss.

Q: OK I understand. And that's it about exposure, isn't it? [Smiling hopefully]

A: By no means! [Amused]

Q: How many more acronyms do I have to learn???

A: Here you go. Expected Exposure (EE) is the average exposure under the P-measure on a future date. The curve of EE in time, as the future date varies, provides the expected exposure profile. Expected Positive Exposure (EPE) is the average EE in time up to a given future date (for example, for dates during a given year).

Q: Gosh. . .

A: And did I mention Exposure at Default (EAD)? This is simply defined as the exposure valued at the (random future) default time of the counterparty.

Q: That's quite enough! [pulling his hair]

1.4 EXPOSURE AND CREDIT VaR

A: [Looking at the junior colleague in a motherly fashion] OK let's stop there. Basel II provided some rules and approximations explaining how such exposures could be approximated and calculated. Notice that the default probabilities are not part of this picture. There is no default simulation here, contrary to Credit VaR.

Q: That's right, you never mentioned default modelling here.

A: Essentially exposure measures how much you are likely to lose if the counterparty defaults. With Credit VaR we also add the default probability to the picture and get a final value for the possible loss inclusive of default probability information.

Q: And why is exposure important?

A: Banks use to measure counterparty risk internally using mainly two measures: PFE, which is mainly used internally to monitor when the credit limits with the counterparties are breached, and EE, which is used, when combined with other quantities, for the calculation of EAD and the capital requirements due to counterparty risk. This last calculation may combine exposures with default probabilities and recovery estimates, and it produces an approximation to Credit VaR, which is used as a capital requirement.

Q: So we go back again to a percentile of the loss under a given risk horizon. What is the percentile and what is the risk horizon?

A: The risk horizon for this approximation of Credit VaR is typically one year and the confidence level is 99.9%.

Q: That would seem to be quite safe.

A: That seems safe, but the approximations and the assumptions introduced by Basel II to compute the approximated Credit VaR are not realistic and have been heavily criticized. See the Organization for Economic Co-Operation and Development (OECD) paper [27] for an overview of the problems, some of them also affecting Basel III.

1.5 INTERLUDE: P AND Q

Q: More on P and Q? You keep mentioning these two probability measures as if they were obvious, but I don't think they are . . . [Looking worriedly at his senior colleague]

A: [Frowning again] Statistical properties of random objects such as future losses depend on the probability measure we are using. Under two different probabilities a random variable will usually have two different expected values, variances, medians, modes, etc.

Q: [Frowning in turn] So you are saying that a future random loss can have a different distribution under two different measures, such as P and Q? But what is P and what is Q, and why do they differ?

A: P, the historical or physical probability measure, also called real world probability measure, is the probability measure under which we do historical estimation of financial variables, econometrics, historical volatility estimation, maximum likelihood estimation, and so forth. When we need to simulate the financial variables up to the risk horizon we are using statistical techniques under P. When we try to make a prediction of future market variables, again, we do it under P.

Q: I guess this is because prediction and risk measurement need to be done with the statistics of the observed world. But why introduce another probability measure Q? Why is it needed? [Looking puzzled]

A: If instead of simulating financial variables for prediction or risk measurement we are trying to price an option or a financial product, when we price products in a no-arbitrage framework, the no-arbitrage theory tells us that we need to take expected values of discounted future cash flows under a different probability measure, namely Q.

Q: And how is this Q related to P? [Still puzzled]

A: The two measures are related by a mathematical relationship that depends on risk aversion, or market price of risk. In the simplest models the real expected rate of return is given by the risk-free rate plus the market price of risk times the volatility. Indeed the "expected" return of an asset depends on the probability measure that is used. For example, under P the average rate of return of an asset is hard to estimate, whereas under Q one knows that the rate of return will be the risk-free rate, since dependence on the real rate of return can be hedged away through replication techniques. [Starts looking tired]

Q: And why should this be interesting? [Ironic]

A: Well, maybe it's not string theory or non-commutative topology (what did you say you studied for your PhD?), but the fact that arbitrage-free theory removes uncertainty about the expected rate of return by substituting it with the risk-free rate has been a big incentive in developing derivatives.

Q: Why is working under P so difficult? [Puzzled]

A: Determining the real world or P expected return of an asset is difficult, and rightly so, or else we would all be rich by knowing good estimates of expected returns of all stocks in the future. [Looks at the window dreamingly]

A: This is a lot to take in...

Q: Let us say that you use P to the risk horizon and then Q to price the portfolio at the risk horizon.

A: I think I am starting to get a grip on this. So let me ask: What is "Basel"?

Q: A city in Switzerland?

A: Ha ha, very funny...

1.6 BASEL

A: OK seriously . . . [pulls her tablet and visualizes a PDF document, handing the tablet to her junior colleague] "Basel II" is a set of recommendations on banking regulations issued by the Basel Committee on Banking Supervision. The "II" is because this is a second set of rules, issued in 2004 and later on updated, following Basel I, the first set, issued in 1998. Basel II was introduced to create a standard that regulators could use to establish how much capital a bank needs to set aside to cover financial and operational risks connected to its lending and investing activities. Banks are often willing to employ as much capital as possible, and so the more the reserves can be reduced while still covering the risks, the better for the banks. In other words, banks often aim at reducing the capital requirements (i.e. the amounts to be set aside) to the minimum. Among Basel II purposes, the two most interesting for us are:

- Improve capital requirements by aligning them more with risks and by making them more risk sensitive;
- Split operational risk and credit risk, quantifying both;

The capital requirements concern overall the three areas of credit – or counterparty – risk, market risk, and operational risks. Here we deal mostly with the first two and in particular with the first. From this capital adequacy point of view, the counterparty risk component can be measured in three different frameworks of increasing complexity, the "standardized approach", the foundation Internal Rating-Based Approach (IRBA) and the advanced IRBA. The standardized approach employs conservative measures of capital requirements based on very simple calculations and quantities, so that if a bank follows that approach it is likely to find higher capital requirements than with the IRBA's. This is an incentive for banks to develop internal models for counterparty risk and credit rating, although the credit crisis that started in 2007 is generating a lot of doubt and debate on the effectiveness of Basel II and of banking regulation more generally. Basel regulation is currently under revision in view of a new set of rules commonly referred to as Basel III. We will get to Basel III later.

Q: Is the Basel accord considered to be effective? Has there been any criticism?

A: You really are a rookie, aren't you? Of course there has been a lot of criticism. Have a look again at the OECD paper [27], for example.

Q: I'll do that. So, we mentioned above two broad areas: (i) Counterparty risk measurement for capital requirements, following Basel II, and the related Credit VaR risk measure, or (ii) counterparty risk from a pricing point of view. Basel II then is concerned with the capital one bank has to set aside in order to lend money or invest towards a counterparty with relevant default risk, to cover for that risk, and is related to Credit VaR. What about the other area, i.e. pricing?

A: Pricing concerns updating the value of a specific instrument or portfolio, traded with a counterparty, by altering the price to be charged to the counterparty. This modification in price is done to account for the default risk of the counterparty. Clearly, all things being equal, we would always prefer entering a trade with a default-free counterparty than with a default-risky one. Therefore we charge the default-risky one a supplementary amount besides the default-free cost of the contract. This is often called Credit Valuation Adjustment, or CVA. Since it is a price, it is computed entirely under the Q probability measure, the pricing measure. In principle, the P probability measure does not play a role here. We are computing a price, not measuring risk statistics.

Q: Has this concept been around for a long time or is it recent?

A: It has been around for a while see, for example, [101], [18], [47]. However, it became more and more important after the 2008 defaults.

1.7 CVA AND MODEL DEPENDENCE

Q: But this CVA term, what does it look like?

A: It looks like an option on the residual value of the portfolio, with a random maturity given by the default time of the counterparty.

Q: Why an option? How does it originate?

A: If the counterparty defaults and the present value of the portfolio at default is positive to the surviving party, then the surviving party only gets a recovery fraction of the portfolio value from the defaulted entity. If, however, the present value is negative to the surviving party, the surviving party has to pay it in full to the liquidators of the defaulted entity. This creates an asymmetry that, once one has done all calculations, says that the value of the deal under counterparty risk is the value without counterparty risk minus a positive adjustment, called CVA. This adjustment is the price of an option in the above sense. See again [47] for details and a discussion.

Q: A price of an option with random maturity? Looks like a complicated object . . . [frowning]
A: [Smiling] It is, and it is good that you realize it. Indeed, it is quite complicated. First of all, this is complicated because it introduces model dependence, even in products that were model independent to start with. Take, for example, a portfolio of plain vanilla swaps. You don't need a dynamic term structure model to price those, but only the curves at the initial time.
Q: And what happens with CVA?
A: Now you have to price an option on the residual value of the portfolio at default of the counterparty. To price an option on a swap portfolio you need an interest rate option model. Therefore, even if you portfolio valuation was model independent before including counterparty risk, now it is model dependent. This means that quick fixes to pricing libraries are quite difficult to obtain.
Q: I see . . . model dependence . . . and model risk. So, anyway, volatilities and correlations would impact this calculation?
A: Yes, and dynamics features more generally. Volatilities of the underlying portfolio variables and also of the counterparty credit spreads all impact valuation importantly. But also the statistical dependence (or "correlation") between default of the counterparty and underlying financial variables, leading to so-called Wrong Way Risk, can be very important.
Q: Wrong Way Risk? WWR?
A: Yes, I am sure you have heard this before.
Q: Well I am not sure about WWR, but before we go there hold on a minute, I have another question.
A: [Sighing] Go ahead.

1.8 INPUT AND DATA ISSUES ON CVA

Q: You mentioned volatilities a correlations, but are they easy to measure?
A: That is both a very good and important question. No, they are not easy to measure. We are pricing under the measure Q, so we would need volatilities and correlation extracted from traded prices of products that depend on such parameters.
Q: But where can I extract the correlation between a specific corporate counterparty default and the underlying of the trade, for example, oil or a specific Foreign Exchange (FX) rate? And where do I extract credit spread volatilities from?
A: [Looks at the young colleague with increased attention] You are not a rookie then if you ask such questions, you must have some experience.
Q: [Sighing] Not really . . . I heard such questions at a meeting of the new products committee yesterday, I was sitting in a corner as the resident newbie, and started thinking about these issues.
A: [Sighing in turn] Well at least you learn fast. Let me tell you that the situation is actually worse. For some counterparties it is even difficult to find levels for their default probabilities, not to mention expected recoveries.
Q: Aren't Q default probabilities deduced from Credit Default Swap (CDS) or corporate bond counterparty data?
A: Yes they are . . . in principle. But for many counterparties we do not have a liquid CDS or even a bond, written on them, that is traded. What if your counterparty is the airport

of Duckburg? Where are you going to imply default probabilities from, let alone credit volatilities and credit-underlying "correlations"? And recoveries?

Q: Recoveries, indeed, aren't those just 0.4? [Grinning]

A: [Rolling eyes] Right. Just like that. However, let me mention that when the Q statistics are not available, a first attempt one can consider is using P-statistics instead. One can estimate credit spread volatility historically if no CDS or corporate bond option implied volatility is available. Also historical correlations between the counterparty credit spreads and the underlying portfolio of the trade can be much easier to access than implied ones. It is clearly an approximation but it is better than no idea at all. Even default probabilities, when not available under Q, may be considered under P and then perhaps adjusted for an aggregate estimate of credit risk premia. Rating information can provide rough aggregate default probabilities for entities such as the airport of Duckburg if one has either an internal or external rating for small medium enterprises (SME).

Q: Aren't there a lot of problems with rating agencies?

A: Yes there are, and I am open to better ideas if you have anything to propose.

Q: Not easy... But leaving aside default probabilities, credit correlations, credit-underlying correlations, and recoveries...

A: You are leaving aside quite a lot of material...

Q: ... what about the underlying contract Q dynamics, is that clear for all asset classes?

A: For a number of asset classes, traditional derivatives markets provide you with underlying market levels, volatilities and market-market "correlations". But not always.

Q: Can you provide an example where this does not work?

1.9 EMERGING ASSET CLASSES: LONGEVITY RISK

A: Let me think... yes, that could be a good example, Longevity Risk.

Q: I was never sure how to pronounce that in English.

A: It is longevity, [lon-jev-i-tee], as I pronounced it, "ge" like in "George" rather than "get".

Q: Longevity... but what kind of risk is that? I wouldn't mind living a long time, provided the quality of life is good.

A: It is not a risk for you, it is a risk for your pension provider. If you live longer than expected then the pension fund needs extra funding to keep your pension going.

Q: Right [touching the wooden table].

A: [Laughing] If you find the name disturbing, we may call it mortality risk. Anyway with longevity swaps the problem is also finding the underlying Q-dynamics, both in levels and volatilities, namely levels and volatilities of mortality rates...

Q: Wait a minute. Longevity *swaps*? What is a longevity swap? Sounds like a pact with the devil for longer life in exchange for your soul or...

A: [Raising her hand] Can't you be professional for a minute? A longevity swap is a contract where one party (typically a pension fund) pays a pre-assigned interest rate in exchange for a floating rate linked to the realized mortality rate in a given country, or area, over a past window of time.

Q: Sorry for the interruptions, OK this makes sense. So I guess the problem is the calibration of the mortality rate dynamics in pricing the future cash flows of the swap?

A: Indeed, the problem is that for this product there is basically almost no information from which one can deduce the Q dynamics... I wonder actually if it even makes sense to talk about Q-dynamics. If swaps were very liquid we could imply a term structure of mortality rates from the prices, and also possibly implied volatilities if options on these swaps became liquid.

Q: And I imagine that, being linked to pensions, these contracts have large maturities, so that counterparty risk is relevant?

A: Precisely. Now this is an emerging area for counterparty risk, with almost no literature, except the excellent initial paper [21]. In terms of Q-dynamics, a first approach could be to use the P-dynamics and assume there is no market price of risk, at least until the market develops a little further.

Q: Here I think it may be really hard to find data for the statistical dependence between the underlying mortality rates and the default of the counterparty, which brings us back to the subject of Wrong Way Risk, on which I have many general questions.

1.10 CVA AND WRONG WAY RISK

A: [Shifting on the chair] Oh I'm sure you do! Let me try and anticipate a few of them. WWR is the additional risk you have when the underlying portfolio and the default of the counterparty are "correlated" in the worst possible way for you.

Q: For example?

A: Suppose you are trading an oil swap with an airline and you are receiving floating (variable) oil and paying fixed. We may envisage a positive correlation between the default of the airline and the price of oil, since higher prices of oil will put the airline under more stress to finance its operations. When the correlation is extremely high, so that at a marked increase of oil there is a corresponding marked increase in the airline default probability, we have the worst possible loss at default of the airline. Indeed, with high oil price increases the oil swap now has a much larger value for us, and there is a higher probability of default from the airline due to the correlation. If the airline defaults now, it will do so in a state where the mark-to-market is quite high in our favour, so that we face a large loss. This is an example of wrong way risk.

Q: Has Wrong Way Risk been studied?

A: Yes, see, for example, the following references for such issues in different asset classes: [47], [55], [61], [62] for equity, [57], [58] for interest rates, [36] for commodities (Oil), [43] for Credit Default Swap (CDS).

Q: So there has been literature available on wrong way risk. Going back to the option structure of Credit Valuation Adjustment (CVA), since options are priced under Q, I would guess that CVA calculations occur mostly under Q. But can one really work only under Q?

A: Before the crisis started in 2007, in a front office environment it had been relatively common to work under Q, forgetting about P. One would postulate models for market processes and then calibrate them to prices that are expectations under Q. At that point simulations to compute prices of other products as expected values would still be done under Q. Similarly, to compute hedge ratios Q used to be enough. P used to be ignored except for risk measurement and possibly stress testing and model validation.

Q: And was this a good thing? [Perplexed]

A: [Frowning] It was good because it allowed you to avoid modelling the same processes under two probability measures, which could be rather tricky, since the real world P statistics are often hard to obtain, as we explained above. But on the other hand one should really do a combined estimation of a pricing model based on the observed history of prices. The prices are Q expectations but they move in time, following the evolution of basic market variables under the P measure. Kalman and more generally non-linear filtering techniques can be used to obtain a joint estimation of the underlying market processes, which would incorporate market history (P) AND risk-neutral expectations (Q) at the same time. This implicitly estimates also market aversion, connecting P and Q.

Q: So all the attention to counterparty risk now is about P (Credit VaR) or Q (CVA)?

A: [Looking at the ceiling] At the moment most attention is on CVA, but now with Basel III the distinction is blurring.

1.11 BASEL III: VaR OF CVA AND WRONG WAY RISK

Q: What do you mean? Give me a break! It is already complicated enough!

A: Relax. Let us say that Credit VaR measures the risk of losses you face due to the possible default of some counterparties you are doing business with. CVA measures the pricing component of this risk, i.e. the adjustment to the price of a product due to this risk.

Q: This is clear.

A: But now suppose you revalue and mark-to-market CVA in time. Suppose that CVA moves in time and moves against you, so that you have to book negative losses NOT because the counterparty actually defaults, but because the pricing of this risk has changed for the worse for you. So in this sense you are being affected by CVA volatility.

Q: Ah...

A: To quote Basel III: [Visualizes a document on her tablet]

> Under Basel II, the risk of counterparty default and credit migration risk were addressed but mark-to-market losses due to credit valuation adjustments (CVA) were not. During the global financial crisis, however, roughly two-thirds of losses attributed to counterparty credit risk were due to CVA losses and only about one-third were due to actual defaults.

Q: So in a way the variability of the price of this risk over time has made more damage than the risk itself?

A: I guess you could put it that way, yes. This is why Basel is considering setting up quite severe capital charges against CVA.

Q: And why did you say that this blurs the picture?

A: Because, now, you may decide that you need a VaR estimate for your CVA, especially after the above Basel III statement.

Q: How would this be computed?

A: You could simulate basic market variables under P, up to the risk horizon. Then, in each scenario, you price the residual CVA until final maturity using a Q expectation. You put all the prices at the horizon time together in a histogram and obtain a profit and loss distribution for CVA at the risk horizon. On this P distribution you select a quantile at the chosen confidence level and now you will have computed VaR of CVA. But this does not measure the default risk directly, it measures the risk to have a mark-to-market loss due either to default or to adverse CVA change in value over time.

Q: ... while Credit VaR only measures the default risk, i.e. the risk of a loss due to a direct default of the counterparty. Let's go back to counterparty risk as a whole now. Where is our focus in all of this?

A: Here we are dealing mostly with CVA valuation. So we give more relevance to Q than P, but we'll have a number of comments on P as well.

Q: So what is Basel III saying about CVA, specifically?

A: Well the framework has changed several times: Bond Equivalent formula, multipliers... One of the main issues has to do with Wrong Way Risk (WWR).

Q: What do you mean?

A: In some part of the Basel regulation it had been argued that you could calculate CVA as if there were no wrong way risk, and then use a standard multiplier to account for wrong way risk.

Q: So I should assume independence between default of the counterparty and underlying portfolio, compute CVA, and then multiply for a given number to account for correlation risk?

A: Something like that. However, this does not work. Depending on the specific dynamics of the underlying financial variables, on volatilities and correlations, and on the chosen models, the multipliers vary a lot. See again [55], [57], [36] and [43] for examples from several asset classes. The multipliers are very volatile and fixing them is not a good idea. Even if one were to use this idea only for setting capital requirements of well diversified portfolios, this could lead to bitter surprises in situations of systemic risk. And there is a further problem...

Q: What else???!!? [Looking desperate]

1.12 DISCREPANCIES IN CVA VALUATION: MODEL RISK AND PAYOFF RISK

A: Relax, relax... Look, we can take a break, you look too distressed.

Q: OK let's have a coffee.

A: I would advise a Chamomile tea.
[Twenty minutes later]

A: Let's go on. Basel III recognizes CVA risk but does not recognize Debit Valuation Adjustment (DVA) risk, the quantity one needs to introduce to make counterparty risk work from an accounting perspective. This creates a misalignment between CVA calculations for capital adequacy purposes and CVA calculations for accounting and mark-to-market. This is part of a more general problem.

Q: Really? Sounds unbelievable that two bits of regulation can be at odds like that!

A: I can show you. Look at this:

> This CVA loss is calculated without taking into account any offsetting debit valuation adjustments which have been deducted from capital under paragraph 75. (Basel III, page 37, July 2011 release.)

> Because nonperformance risk (the risk that the obligation will not be fulfilled) includes the reporting entity's credit risk, the reporting entity should consider the effect of its credit risk (credit standing) on the fair value of the liability in all periods in which the liability is measured at fair value under other accounting pronouncements. (FAS 157, http://www.fasb.org/summary/stsum157.shtml).

Q: Surprisingly clear and at odds.

A: Well since you seem to enjoy it, here is what the former secretary general of the Basel Committee said:

> The potential for perverse incentives resulting from profit being linked to decreasing creditworthiness means capital requirements cannot recognise it. The main reason for not recognising DVA as an offset is that it would be inconsistent with the overarching supervisory prudence principle under which we do not give credit for increases in regulatory capital arising from a deterioration in the firm's own credit quality. (Stefan Walter)

Q: I am quite confused. Should I compute DVA or not?

A: It depends on the purpose you are computing it for. However, the situation is not that clear, there are a number of issues more generally with counterparty risk pricing.

Q: You mean objectivity on CVA valuation?

A: I mean that there is a lot of model risk and of "payoff risk" if we want to call it that.

Q: I understand model risk, since this is highly model dependent, but what do you mean by payoff risk?

A: There are a lot of choices to be made when computing CVA, both on the models used, and on the type of CVA to be computed. We will see that there are choices to be made on whether it is unilateral or bilateral, on the close-out formulation; on how you account for collateral and re-hypothecation, on whether you include first to default, and on how you account for funding costs and so on. Owing to the variety of possible definitions for CVA and modelling choices, there appear to be material discrepancies in CVA valuation across financial institutions, as pointed out in the recent article [192].

1.13 BILATERAL COUNTERPARTY RISK: CVA AND DVA

Q: Wait, you're going too fast. You mentioned DVA and I don't even know what it is. What is DVA?

A: Debit Valuation Adjustment. It has to do with both parties in a deal agreeing on the counterparty risk charge.

Q: Let me get this straight. Let's say that we are doing pricing, at a point in time, of the risk that the counterparty defaults before the final maturity of the deal, on a specific portfolio. This is the CVA. It is a positive quantity, an adjustment to be subtracted from the default risk-free price in order to account for the counterparty default risk in the valuation. Clearly, having the choice, and all things being equal, one would prefer to trade a deal with a default risk-free counterparty rather than with a risky one. So I understand the risk-free price needs to be decreased through a negative adjustment, i.e. the subtraction of a positive term called CVA. Now you are implicitly raising the question: since it is an adjustment and it is always negative, what happens from the point of view of the other party?

A: Indeed, that's what I am saying. In this setup there is no possibility for both parties to agree, unless they both recognize that one of the calculating parties is default free. Suppose we have two parties in the deal, a bank and a corporate counterparty. If they both agree that the bank can be treated as default free, then the bank will mark a negative adjustment on the risk-free price of the deal with the corporate client, and the corporate client will mark a corresponding positive adjustment (the opposite of the negative one) to the risk-free price. This way both parties will agree on the price.

Q: The adjustment for the corporate client is positive because the client needs to compensate the bank for the client default risk?

A: Indeed, this is the case. The adjustment seen from the point of view of the corporate client is positive, and is called Debit Valuation Adjustment, DVA. It is positive because the early default of the client itself would imply a discount on the client payment obligations, and this means a gain in a way. So the client marks a positive adjustment over the risk-free price by adding the positive amount called DVA. In this case, where the bank is default free, the DVA is also called Unilateral DVA (UDVA), since only the default risk of the client is included. Similarly, the adjustment marked by the bank by subtraction is called Unilateral CVA (UCVA). In this case UCVA(bank) = UDVA(corporate), i.e. the adjustment to the risk-free price is the same, but it is added by the corporate client and subtracted by the bank.

Q: But then the UCVA(corporate) must be zero, because the bank is default free.

A: Correct, and similarly UDVA(bank) = UCVA(corporate) = 0.

Q: But what happens when the two firms do not agree on one of them being default free? Say that in your example the corporate client does not accept the bank as default free (a reasonable objection after Lehman. . .)

A: Well in this case then the only possibility to agree on a price is for both parties to consistently include both defaults into the valuation. Hence every party needs to include its own default besides the default of the counterparty into the valuation. Now both parties will mark a positive CVA to be subtracted and a positive DVA to be added to the default risk-free price of the deal. The CVA of one party will be the DVA of the other one and viceversa.

Q: So every party will compute the final price as [writes on a notebook]

$$\text{DEFAULT RISK-FREE PRICE} + \text{DVA} - \text{CVA?}$$

A: Indeed. In our example when the bank does the calculation,

$$\begin{aligned}\text{Price To Bank} &= \text{DEFAULT RISK-FREE PRICE to Bank}\\ &\quad + \text{DVA Bank} - \text{CVA Bank}\end{aligned}$$

whereas when the corporate does the calculation one has a similar formula. Now, since

$$\begin{aligned}&\text{DEFAULT RISK-FREE PRICE to Bank}\\ &\quad = -\text{DEFAULT RISK-FREE PRICE to Corporate}\\ &\text{DVA Bank} = \text{CVA Corporate}\\ &\text{DVA Corporate} = \text{CVA Bank}\end{aligned}$$

we get that eventually

$$\text{Price To Bank} = -\text{Price To Corporate}$$

so that both parties agree on the price, or, we could say, there is money conservation.

We may define "Bilateral Valuation Adjustment (BVA)" (to one party) to be the difference DVA − CVA (as seen from that party),

$$\begin{aligned}&\text{BVA} = \text{DVA} - \text{CVA}\\ &\text{Clearly BVA to Bank} = -\text{BVA to corporate.}\end{aligned}$$

Q: Clear enough . . . so what is meant usually by "bilateral CVA"?

A: Good question. By looking at the formula

$$\text{BVA} = \text{DVA} - \text{CVA}$$

bilateral CVA could refer both to BVA, or just to the CVA component of BVA on the right-hand side. Usually the industry uses the term to denote BVA, and we will do so similarly, except when explicitly countered.

Q: OK, summarizing... if we ask when valuation of counterparty risk is symmetric, meaning that if the other party computes the counterparty risk adjustment towards us she finds the opposite number, so that both parties agree on the charge, the answer is... [hesitating]

A: The answer is that this happens when we include the possibility that also the entity computing the counterparty risk adjustment (i.e. us in the above example) may default, besides the counterparty itself.

Q: Is there any technical literature on Bilateral CVA and on DVA?

A: Yes, the first calculations are probably again in Duffie and Huang (1996) [101], who, however, resort to specific modelling choices where credit risk is purely accounted for by spreads and it is hard to create a strong dependence between underlying and default, so that wrong way risk is hard to model. Furthermore, that paper deals mostly with swaps. Again, swaps with bilateral default risk are dealt with in [18], but the paper where bilateral risk is examined in detail and DVA derived is [39], where bilateral risk is introduced in general and then analyzed for CDS. In the following works [59], [40], and [41] several other features of bilateral risk are carefully examined, also in relationship with wrong way risk, collateral and extreme contagion, and Gap risk, showing up when default happens between margining dates and a relevant mark-to-market change for the worse has occurred. In this respect, [40] shows a case of an underlying CDS with strong default contagion where even frequent margining in collateralization is quite ineffective. For a basic introduction to bilateral CVA see [118].

Q: There's too much material to read already!

A: Well, that's why I'm trying to give you a summary here.

Q: OK thanks, at least now I have an idea of what Bilateral CVA and DVA are about.

1.14 FIRST-TO-DEFAULT IN CVA AND DVA

A: Yes, but you have to be careful. Bilateral Valuation Adjustment (BVA) is not just the difference of DVA and CVA computed each as if in a universe where only one name can default. In computing DVA and CVA in the difference you need to account for both defaults of bank and corporate in both terms. This means that effectively there is a first to default check. If the bank is doing the calculations, in scenarios where the bank defaults first the DVA term will be activated and the CVA term vanishes, whereas in scenarios where the corporate defaults first then the bank DVA vanishes and the bank CVA payoff activates. So we need to check who defaults first.

Q: Indeed, I heard "first to default risk" in connection with bilateral CVA. Now, in computing the CVA and DVA terms, we should know who defaults first, that's what you are saying. That makes sense: to close the position in the right way and at the right time, I need to know who defaults first and when.

A: Correct. However, some practitioners implemented a version of BVA that ignores first to default times. Suppose you are the bank. Then for you

$$\text{BVABank} = \text{DVABank} - \text{CVABank}$$

See [167]. What you do now is compute DVABank as if in a world where only you may default, and then compute CVABank as if in a world where only the corporate client may default. But you do not kill the other term as soon as there is a first default. So in a sense you are double counting, because if you do as we just said, you are not really closing the deal at the first default. The correct BVA includes a first to default check.

Q: My head is spinning... let me try to summarize.

A: Go ahead

Q: You have to be careful with bilateral CVA. BVA is not just the difference of DVA and CVA computed each as if in a world where only one name can default. In computing DVA and CVA in the difference you need to account for both defaults of bank and corporate *in both terms*. This means that, effectively, there is a first to default check. If the bank is doing the calculations, in scenarios where the bank defaults first the DVA term will be activated and the CVA term vanishes, whereas in scenarios where the corporate defaults first then the bank DVA vanishes and the bank CVA payoff activates. So we need to check who defaults first.

A: Excellent, even better than my original explanation. More than a summary it looks like an essay!

Q: Well, not that I am going to write a paper on this.

A: Someone did already, see [37]. The error in neglecting the first to default risk can be quite sizeable even in simple examples.

1.15 DVA MARK-TO-MARKET AND DVA HEDGING

Q: I don't know, even with everything you have told me I am not at ease with this idea of DVA. It is a reduction on my debt due to the fact that I may default, and if I default I won't pay all my debt, so it is like a gain, but I can only realize this gain as a cash flow if I default!!

A: I agree it can be disconcerting. And consider this: if your credit quality worsens and you recompute your DVA, you mark a gain.

Q: Has this really happened?

A: Citigroup in its press release on the first quarter revenues of 2009 reported a *positive* mark-to-market due to its *worsened* credit quality: [pulls out her tablet] "Revenues also included [...] a net $2.5 billion positive CVA on derivative positions, excluding monolines, mainly due to the widening of Citi's CDS spreads."

Q: Ah...

A: More recently, from the *Wall Street Journal*:

> October 18, 2011, 3:59 PM ET. *Goldman Sachs Hedges Its Way to Less Volatile Earnings.* Goldman's DVA gains in the third quarter totaled $450 million, about $300 million of which was recorded under its fixed-income, currency and commodities trading segment and another $150 million recorded under equities trading. That amount is comparatively smaller than the $1.9 billion in DVA gains that J.P. Morgan Chase and Citigroup each recorded for the third quarter. Bank of America reported $1.7 billion of DVA gains in its investment

> bank. Analysts estimated that Morgan Stanley will record $1.5 billion of net DVA gains when it reports earnings on Wednesday [. . .]

Q: Sounds strange, you gain from the deterioration of your credit quality . . . and you lose from improvement of your credit quality. So how could DVA be hedged? One should sell protection on oneself, an impossible feat, unless one buys back bonds that one had issued earlier. This may be hard to implement, though. [looking more and more puzzled]

A: It seems that most times DVA is hedged by proxying. Instead of selling protection on oneself, one sells protection on a number of names that one thinks are highly correlated to oneself. Again [waving her tablet at her junior colleague] from the *Wall Street Journal* article:

> [. . .] Goldman Sachs CFO David Viniar said Tuesday that the company attempts to hedge [DVA] using a basket of different financials. A Goldman spokesman confirmed that the company did this by selling CDS on a range of financial firms. [. . .] Goldman wouldn't say what specific financials were in the basket, but Viniar confirmed [. . .] that the basket contained a peer group. Most would consider peers to Goldman to be other large banks with big investment-banking divisions, including Morgan Stanley, J.P. Morgan Chase, Bank of America, Citigroup and others. The performance of these companies' bonds would be highly correlated to Goldman's.

Q: It seems to be relatively common practice then. Mmmmmm . . . isn't it risky? Proxying can be misleading. [Shaking his head]

A: [Shrugging] Admittedly . . . This can approximately hedge the spread risk of DVA, but not the jump to default risk. Merrill hedging DVA risk by selling protection on Lehman would not have been a good idea. In fact this attitude, in the presence of jump to default risk, can worsen systemic risk.

Q: Indeed, I can see that. If I sell protection on a firm that is correlated to me to hedge my DVA, and then that firm not only has its credit quality worsen (which would hedge my DVA changes due to spread movements) but actually defaults, then I have to make the protection payments and, paradoxically, that could push me into default! [Looking at the senior colleague excitedly]

A: Sounds crazy, doesn't it? [Grinning]

1.16 IMPACT OF CLOSE-OUT IN CVA AND DVA

Q: Well, to be perfectly honest, it does, but maybe it's just you and me being unsophisticated enough. However, there seem to be other matters that are as pressing. I am having a hard time figuring out what this other problem with close-out is, for example.

A: [Sighs] Close-out is basically what happens when one name defaults. So suppose in our example the corporate client defaults. Close-out proceedings are then started according to regulations and ISDA[1] documentation. The close-out procedure establishes the residual value of the contract to the bank, and how much of that is going to be paid to the bank party, provided it is positive. If it is negative then the bank will have to pay the whole amount to the corporate.

Q: Well this seems simply the definition of CVA payout.

[1] International Swaps and Derivatives Association.

A: Ah, but let me ask you a question. At the default time of the corporate, you are the bank. Do you value the remaining contract by taking into account your own credit quality (in other words your now unilateral DVA, "replacement close-out") or by using the risk-free price ("risk-free close-out")? The replacement close-out argues that if you are now going to re-open the deal with a risk-free party, the risk-free party will charge you your unilateral CVA, which, seen from your point of view, is your unilateral DVA. Hence, in computing the replacement value you should include your DVA to avoid discontinuity in valuation. If you always used DVA to value the deal prior to the corporate's default, you should not stop doing so at default if you aim at being consistent.

Q: But there seem to be two choices here, risk-free or replacement close-out. What is the difference? Is it just consistency and continuity of valuation?

A: The counterparty risk adjustments change strongly depending on which assumption is chosen in the computation of the close-out amount, and the choice has important consequences on default contagion.

Q: I would naively think that risk-free close-out is simpler and more "objective".

A: Well in [54], [52] and [53] it is shown that a risk-free close-out has implications that are very different from what we expect in case of a default in standardized markets, such as the bond or loan markets. Let us take a case of BVA where the valuation is always in the same direction, such as a loan or a bond. Suppose the bank owns the bond. If the owner of a bond defaults, or if the lender of a loan defaults, this means no losses to the bond issuer (the corporate in our example) or to the loan borrower. Instead, if the risk-free default close-out applies, when there is default of the party which is a net creditor in a derivative (thus in a position similar to a bond owner or loan lender, the bank), the value of the liability of the net debtor will suddenly jump up. In fact, before the default, the liability of the net debtor had a mark-to-market that took into account the risk of default of the debtor itself. After the default of the creditor, if a risk-free close-out applies, this mark-to-market transforms into a risk-free one, surely larger in absolute value than the pre-default mark-to-market.

Q: This appears to be definitely wrong. [Shaking his head again]

1.17 CLOSE-OUT CONTAGION

A: You are taking it too personally. Calm down. It's actually worse: the larger the credit spreads of the debtor, the larger the increase. This is a dramatic surprise for the debtor who will soon have to pay this increased amount of money to the liquidators of the defaulted party. There is a true contagion of a default event towards the debtors of a defaulted entity, that does not exist in the bond or loan market. Net debtors at default will not like a risk-free close-out. They will prefer a replacement close-out, which does not imply a necessary increase of the liabilities since it continues taking into account the creditworthiness of the debtor after the default of the creditor.

Q: You are saying that the replacement close-out inherits one property typical of fundamental markets: if one of the two parties in the deal has no future obligations, like a bond or option holder, his default probability does not influence the value of the deal at inception.

A: Correct. One could, based on this, decide to use replacement close-out all the time, since it is consistent with this basic principle. The replacement close-out, however, has shortcomings opposite to those of the risk-free close-out. While the replacement close-out

Table 1.1 Impact of the default of the lender (bank) under risk-free or replacement close-out and under independence or co-monotonicity between default of the lender and of the borrower (corporate)

Dependence→ Close-out↓	Independence	Co-monotonicity
Risk free	Negatively affects borrower	No contagion
Replacement	No contagion	Further negatively affects lender

is preferred by debtors of a defaulted company, symmetrically a risk-free close-out will be preferred by the creditors. The more money debtors pay, the higher the recovery will be. The replacement close-out, while protecting debtors, can in some situations worryingly penalize the creditors by abating the recovery.

Q: What are such cases?

A: Consider the case where the defaulted entity is a company with high systemic impact, so that when it defaults the credit spreads of its counterparties are expected to jump high. Lehman's default would be a good example of such a situation. If the credit spreads of the counterparties increase at default, under a replacement close-out the market value of their liabilities will be strongly reduced, since it will take into account the reduced credit-worthiness of the debtors themselves. All the claims of the liquidators towards the debtors of the defaulted company will be deflated, and the low level of the recovery may be again a dramatic surprise, but this time for the creditors of the defaulted company.

Q: [Baffled] It seems unbelievable that no clear regulation was available for this issue.

A: [Sighing] Well this is because there is no ideal solution. You may summarize the choice according to this table, let me draw it for you [draws Table 1.1 on her tablet]. As you see, there is no optimal choice guaranteeing no contagion. Depending on the "correlation" structure between default of the borrower and the lender party in the transaction, the optimal choice is different. ISDA cannot set a standard that is correlation dependent, so it is understandable that there are difficulties in standardizing close-out issues.

Q: It looks more and more complicated. So many choices...

A: It's not over yet in terms of issues. But it's not that bad that it will keep us working for a long time [sarcastically].

Q: So what are the next issues that are keeping CVA people busy?

A: Collateral modelling, possible re-hypothecation, netting, capital requirements around CVA for Basel III and possibilities to reduce them through restructuring, collateral or margin lending. Finally, consistent inclusion of funding costs...

Q: [Rolling his eyes] That's quite enough. Let's start from collateral.

1.18 COLLATERAL MODELLING IN CVA AND DVA

A: Collateral is an asset (say cash for simplicity) that is posted frequently as a guarantee for due payments following mark-to-market, by the party to whom mark-to-market is negative. The guarantee is to be used by the party to whom mark-to-market is positive in case the other party defaults.

Q: That seems the end of counterparty risk then.

A: Indeed, collateral would be the main and most effective tool against counterparty risk, with two caveats. It is not always effective, even under frequent margining, and it can be expensive. It is shown in [40] and [41] that even very frequent margining may not be enough to fully protect from counterparty risk. The fact is that in extreme scenarios, the portfolio value may have moved a lot from the last margining date, even if this was a few moments ago. In [40] an example is given, with Credit Default Swaps (CDS) as underlying instruments, where the default of the counterparty triggers an immediate jump in the underlying CDS by contagion, so that the collateral that was posted an instant earlier is not enough to cover the loss.

Q: Is this a rather abstract case?

A: I wouldn't think so, given what happened in 2008 after Lehman's default, and also keeping in mind that we had seven credit events on financials that happened in one month during the period from 7 September 2008 to 8 October 2008, namely the credit events on Fannie Mae, Freddie Mac, Lehman Brothers, Washington Mutual, Landsbanki, Glitnir and Kaupthing.

Q: And what is re-hypothecation then?

1.19 RE-HYPOTHECATION

A: Re-hypothecation means that the collateral received as a guarantee can be utilized as an investment or as further collateral. Suppose we are again as in the previous example with a bank and a corporate client. Suppose that at a margining date the mark-to-market of the portfolio is in favour of the bank, i.e. positive to the bank, so that the corporate client is posting collateral. If re-hypothecation is allowed, the bank is free to re-invest the collateral. Now suppose that there is an extreme movement in the market, such that the mark-to-market of the portfolio turns in favour of the corporate, and before the next collateral adjustment margining date arrives, the bank (and not the corporate) defaults.

Q: Uh-oh

A: Indeed, 'uh-oh', but as I said don't take it personally. The bank defaults while the mark-to-market of the portfolio is in favour of the corporate. Also, the bank had reinvested the collateral that had been posted by the corporate earlier. So the corporate client takes a double punishment: a loss of mark-to-market, and a loss of collateral.

Q: This sounds like a problem

A: It is, and parts of the industry have applied pressure to forbid re-hypothecation. While this is reasonable, the impossibility to re-invest collateral makes it particularly expensive, since the collateral taker needs to remunerate the interest on collateral to the collateral provider, now without the possibility to re-invest collateral.

Q: What is the extent of the impact of re-hypothecation on CVA?

A: This has been studied in a few papers see, for example, again [40] and [41].

Q: So many things to read... what about netting then?

1.20 NETTING

A: Netting is an agreement where, upon default of your counterparty, you do not check the losses at single-deal level but rather at the netted portfolio level.

Q: Could you provide an example please?

A: Suppose you are the bank and you are trading two interest rate swaps with the same corporate, whose recovery rate is 0.4. Suppose at a point in time the two swaps have exactly the opposite value to the bank, say +1M USD and −1M USD respectively. Now assume that the corporate client defaults. In the case with netting, the two swaps are netted, so that we compute 1M - 1M = 0 and there is no loss to account for. In the case without netting, the two deals are treated separately. In the first swap, the bank loses (1-REC)1M = 0.6 M. In the second swap, the bank loses nothing.

Q: I see...

A: Now in view of charging a fair CVA to the corporate, the bank needs to know whether there is netting or not since, as you have seen, the difference can be rather important. In general, unilateral CVA with netting is always smaller than without netting.

Q: And why is that?

A: This is because CVA is like a call option with zero strike on the residual value of the deal, and an option on a sum is smaller than the sum of options.

Q: Has netting been studied?

A: There is a paper on netting for interest rate swaps where an approximate formula has also been derived, see [47], but there is no wrong way risk. Netting with wrong way risk has been examined in [57].

1.21 FUNDING

Q: OK, we have covered quite a lot of stuff. There is a further topic I keep hearing. It's the inclusion of cost of funding into the valuation framework. Is this actually happening?

A: Yes, that's all the rage now. If you attend a practitioner conference, a lot of talks will be on consistent inclusion of funding costs. However, very few works try to build a consistent picture where funding costs are consistently included together with CVA, DVA, collateral, close-out etc.

Q: Can you give me some examples?

A: The working paper [85], then published in [86] and [87], is the most comprehensive treatment I have seen so far. The only limitation is that it does not allow for underlying credit instruments in the portfolio, and has possible issues with FX. It is a very technical paper. A related framework that is more general and includes most recent literature as a special case is in Pallavicini, Perini and Brigo (2011a) [165]. Earlier works are partial but still quite important.

Q: For example?

A: The influential industry paper [168] considers the problem of replication of derivative transactions under collateralization but without default risk and in a purely classical Black-Scholes framework, considering two relatively basic special cases. That paper is quite well known here in the industry (the author was awarded the Quant of the Year 2011 title by *Risk* magazine largely for that paper). However, a professor at the University of London told me there are some important problems with the way the self-financing condition is formulated, although the final result is in his opinion still correct, see [38]

Q: A wrong formulation of the self-*financing* condition in one of the influential (and somehow "decorated") industry papers on *funding/financing* costs in *Risk* magazine? Is *Risk* magazine peer reviewed?

A: Well it is quite a common wrong formulation, but I think it is particularly unfortunate in a work on funding costs, as you are implying. *Risk* magazine is peer reviewed and it is quite a good and influential publication on the technical side, however, it is not read much in academia, since I heard that it does not usually count as a relevant publication when you compete for a position. Academia is a funny place: some of the top-ranked academic journals on finance I have never seen inside a bank, but they are considered to have large impact. This impact factor is sometimes a little self-referential and does not reflect reality. This is a pity because it leads to some academics not reading journals like *Risk* magazine I think. Otherwise the problem would have been found earlier, this is the kind of thing where academics are good, I'd tend to think.

Q: Fascinating, but let us leave aside the sociology of the practitioner's industry awards, technical communications and interaction with academia. Besides this technical glitch with the self-financing condition, there is something else that caught my attention in what you said on this paper. What is the point of collateral without default risk? What is it used for then?

A: Well, there is not only default risk in collateral, there is also liquidity risk, transaction costs... and you might be still modelling credit spread risk but not jump to default risk, a distinction that is natural in intensity models.

Q: You mean Cox processes used for credit risk?

A: Indeed. However, it is true that the main reason for having collateral is default risk, otherwise one would not have collateral in the first place. In fact, the fundamental funding implications in the presence of default risk have been considered in simple settings first in [157], see also [74]. These works focus on particularly simple products, such as zero coupon bonds or loans, in order to highlight some essential features of funding costs. [109] analyses the implications of currency risk for collateral modelling. [65] resort to a Partial Differential Equation (PDE) approach to funding costs (and have the same problem on the self-financing condition as mentioned before). As I mentioned previously [85], then published in [86] and [87], and [165] remain the most general treatments of funding costs to date. These papers show how complicated it is to formulate a proper general framework with collateral and funding but inclusive of default risk.

Q: What are the findings in Morini and Prampolini [157]? I heard about this paper when it was still a preprint.

A: One important point in Morini and Prampolini [157] is that in simple payoffs such as bonds, DVA can be interpreted as funding, in order to avoid double counting. However, this result does not extend to general payoffs, where different aspects interact in a more complex way and the general approach of Crepey [85] or Pallavicini et al. [165] is needed.

Q: All right, ten more papers to read, but what is the funding problem, basically?

A: To put it in a nutshell, when you need to manage a trading position, you may need to obtain cash in order to do a number of operations: hedging the position, posting collateral, and so on. This is cash you may obtain from your treasury department or in the market. You may also receive cash as a consequence of holding the position: a coupon, a notional reimbursement, a positive mark-to-market move, getting some collateral, a close-out payment. All such flows need to be remunerated: if you are borrowing, this will have a cost, and if you are lending, this will provide you with some revenues. Including the cost of funding into your valuation framework means to properly account for such features.

Q: Well looks like accounting to me.

A: [Sighing] The trick is doing this consistently with all other aspects, especially counterparty risk. A number of practitioners advocate a "Funding Valuation Adjustment", or FVA, that would be additive so that the total price of the portfolio would be

$$\text{RISK-FREE PRICE} + \text{DVA} - \text{CVA} + \text{FVA}$$

However, it is not that simple. Proper inclusion of funding costs leads to a recursive pricing problem that may be formulated as a backwards stochastic differential equation (BSDE, as in [85]) or to a discrete time backward induction equation (as in [165]). The simple additive structure above is not there in general.

Q: I doubt the banks will be willing to implement BSDEs, and I also doubt the regulators will prescribe that. We need something simple coming out of this.

A: All of a sudden you have become reasonable and moderate? That's good [smiling]. However, sometimes it isn't possible to simplify dramatically.

1.22 HEDGING COUNTERPARTY RISK: CCDS

Q: My last question is this. From what you have said, it looks like Basel III may impose quite some heavy capital requirements for CVA. Collateralization is a possible way out, but it may become expensive for some firms and lead to a liquidity strain, while firms that are not organized for posting collateral may be in troubles. [192] reports the case of the leading German airline: bear with me, I am low-tech compared to you [pulls out a piece of paper with part of an article]:

> The airline's Cologne-based head of finance, Roland Kern, expects its earnings to become more volatile not because of unpredictable passenger numbers, interest rates or jet fuel prices, but because it does not post collateral in its derivatives transactions.

Indeed, without the possibility to post collateral, the firms would be subject to heavy CVA capital requirements. Is there a third way?

A: There have been proposals for market instruments that can hedge CVA away, or reduce its capital requirements in principle. One such instrument, for example, is the Contingent Credit Default Swap (CCDS).

Q: What is a CCDS? Anything to do with a standard CDS?

A: It is similar to a CDS, but when the reference credit defaults, the protection seller pays protection on a notional that is not fixed but is rather given by the loss given default fraction (1 - recovery) of the residual value of a reference portfolio at that time, if positive.

Q: So there is both a reference credit, against whose default protection is traded, and a reference portfolio?

A: Consider this example. Suppose Bank 1 buys a contingent CDS, offering protection against default of her corporate client, which is the reference credit. Protection is bought by the bank on the portfolio the bank is trading with the client. The bank buys this protection from another bank, say Bank 2. The payoff of the default leg of the CCDS to Bank 1 is exactly the unilateral CVA Bank 1 would measure against the corporate client on the traded portfolio. So if Bank 2 is default-free, with the CCDS Bank1 is perfectly hedged against CVA on the reference portfolio traded with the corporate client, since the CVA payoff will be matched exactly by the CCDS protection leg.

Q: Have these products been popular in the past?

A: Not really. [Visualizes on the tablet the scan of a newspaper page.] The *Financial Times* was commenting back in 2008:

> [. . .] Rudimentary and idiosyncraic versions of these so-called CCDS have existed for five years, but they have been rarely traded due to high costs, low liquidity and limited scope. [. . .] Counterparty risk has become a particular concern in the markets for interest rate, currency, and commodity swaps – because these trades are not always backed by collateral.[. . .] Many of these institutions – such as hedge funds and companies that do not issue debt – are beyond the scope of cheaper and more liquid hedging tools such as normal CDS. The new CCDS was developed to target these institutions (*Financial Times*, 10 April 2008).

Interest in CCDS came back in 2011 now that CVA capital charges risk to become punitive. However, CCDS do not fully solve the problem of CVA capital requirements. First of all, there is no default-free Bank 2, so the CCDS itself would be subject to counterparty risk. Also, it is not clear how CCDS would work in the bilateral case. And the hedging problem of a possible bilateral CCDS (with all the DVA problems seen above) would fall on Bank 2, so that the problem is only moved. While CCDS can be helpful in limited contexts, it is probably worth looking for alternatives.

Q: So the market forgot about CCDS?

A: Not really. In fact, CCDS are now finally standardized on index portfolios by ISDA. ISDA came out with templates and documentation for CCDS, you may find those on the ISDA website. Still, most of the problems I mentioned above are still there. This is prompting the industry to look for other solutions that may be effective also across several counterparties at the same time.

Q: For example?

A: CVA securitization could be considered, although the word "securitization" is not very popular these days.

Q: Is there any proposed form of CVA restructuring, or securitization?

1.23 RESTRUCTURING COUNTERPARTY RISK: CVA-CDOs AND MARGIN LENDING

A: [Concentrating, looking tired] There are a few. I am familiar with a few deals that have been discussed in the press, and in the *Financial Times* blog Alphaville in particular [170].

Q: The FT? Looks like this made the mainstream media

A: Yes. Let me show you: [Connects with the *FT* Alphaville website.]

> In short, Barclays has taken a pool of loans and securitized them, but retained all but the riskiest piece. On that riskiest 300 million euros, Barclays has bought protection from an outside investor, e.g. hedge fund. That investor will get paid coupons over time for their trouble, but will also be hit with any losses on the loans, up to the total amount of their investment. To ensure that the investor can actually absorb these losses, collateral is posted with Barclays.

Q: Looks like a CDO from the little I know? Looks like an equity tranche backed by collateral.

A: Yes, collateral is key here. The blog continues:

> This point about collateral means that, at least in theory, Barclays is not exposed to the counterparty risk of the hedge fund. This is especially important because the hedge fund is outside the normal sphere of regulation, i.e. they aren't required to hold capital against risk-weighted assets in the way banks are.

Notice this point of transferring risk outside the regulated system. This is a point that is stressed also in the OECD paper [27]. The blog continues:

> [. . .] And then there is the over-engineering element whereby some deals were, and maybe still are, done where the premiums paid over time to the hedge fund are actually equal to or above the expected loss of the transaction. That the Fed and Basel Committee were concerned enough to issue guidance on this is noteworthy. It'll be down to individual national regulators to prevent "over-engineering", and some regulators are more hands-on than others.

So there you have it.

Q: Interesting, are you aware of any other such deals?

A: I know of a different one called SCORE. Again *FT* Alphaville, this time from [171]:

RBS had a good go at securitising these exposures, but the deal didn't quite make it over the line. However, Euroweek reports that banks are still looking into it:

> Royal Bank of Scotlands securitisation of counterparty credit risk, dubbed Score 2011, was pulled earlier this year, but other banks are said to be undeterred by the difficulties of the asset class, and are still looking at the market. However, other hedging options for counterparty risk may have dulled the economics of securitising this risk since the end of last year.

So this has not been that successful.

A: Not really. The latest I heard of is Credit Suisse [173]:

> Last week Credit Suisse announced it had bought protection on the senior slice of its unusual employee compensation plan. The Swiss bank pays some of its senior bankers using a bond referencing counterparty risk, which also involves shifting some counterparty credit risk from the bank to its workers.

So that is like buying protection from your own employees. Interesting concept if you think about it. That way the employee, in theory, is incentivized to improve the risk profile of the company.

Q: Maybe I'm a rookie, but to be honest I wouldn't be too happy if I were paid that kind of bonus. It may work for super-senior employees, like you, but for me . . . well . . . I don't participate in the important decisions of the company, I'm not a decision maker.

A: You overestimate my importance, I'm not the CEO, CFO, CRO, CIO, or C∗O, I'm just your average risk manager!!

Q: But is this all about counterparty risk restructuring? No other idea? No new idea?

A: There are actually more innovative ideas. On CVA securitization, see [2], which advocates a global valuation model. The more model-agnostic [3] explains how margin lending through quadripartite or penta-partite structures involving clearing houses would be effective in establishing a third way.

Q: [Excitedly] Can you tell me more? This sounds intriguing.

A: Let me borrow from [2] and [3], to which I refer for the full details. If I understood correctly, the structure is like this. [Draws Figure 1.1 on her tablet]

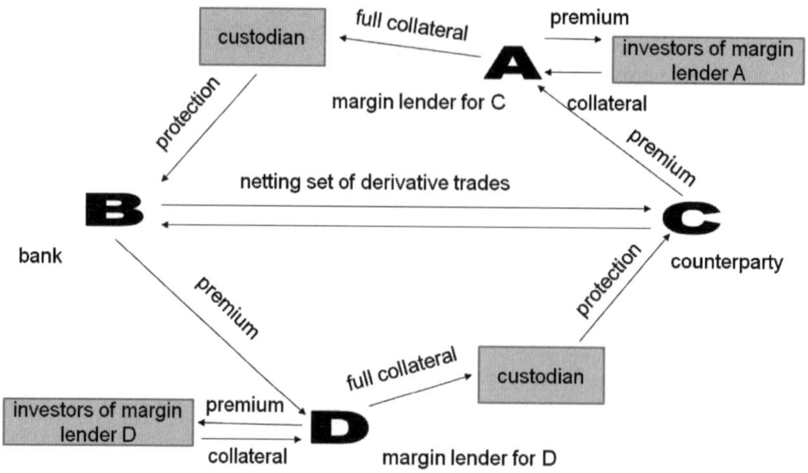

Figure 1.1 General counterparty scheme including quadripartite structure.

Q: How does this picture work?

A: Traditionally, the CVA is typically charged by the structuring bank B either on an upfront basis or it is built into the structure as a fixed coupon stream. The deals we discussed above, such as Papillon and Score, are probably of this type too. Margin lending instead is predicated on the notion of floating rate CVA payments with periodic resets...

Q: What is "floating rate CVA"?

A: Whichever formulation of CVA and DVA is chosen, one could postulate that CVA and DVA are paid periodically on rolling protection intervals. The related CVA is termed "Floating Rate CVA" (FRCVA), and similarly for DVA. Assume for simplicity that we are in a bipartite transaction between the default-free bank B and the defaultable counterparty (say a corporate client) C. In principle, instead of charging CVA upfront at time zero for the whole maturity of the portfolio, the bank may require a CVA payment at time zero for protection on the exposure for up to six months. Then in six months the bank will require a CVA payment for protection for a further six months on what will be the exposure for up to one year, and on and on, up to the final maturity of the deal. Such a CVA would be an example of FRCVA.

Q: OK, back to Figure 1.1.

A: I was saying that margin lending is based on the notion of floating rate CVA payments with periodic resets, and is designed in such a way to transfer the conditional credit spread volatility risk and the mark-to-market volatility risk from the bank to the counterparties. We may explain this more in detail by following the arrows in the Figure 1.1.

Q: OK, I'm ready, looking at Figure 1.1. [Excited]

A: Relax a second. The counterparty C, a corporate client, has problems with posting collateral periodically in order to trade derivatives with bank B. To avoid posting collateral, C enters into a margin lending transaction. C pays periodically (say semi-annually) a floating rate CVA to the margin lender A ('premium' arrow connecting C to A), which the margin lender A pays to investors (premium arrow connecting A to investors). This latest payment can have a seniority structure similar to that of a cash CDO.

Q: Dangerous territory there . . . [Grinning]

A: [Flashing an irritated look] Let me finish. In exchange for this premium, for six months the investors provide the margin lender A with daily collateral posting ('collateral' arrow connecting Investors to A) and A passes the collateral to a custodian ('collateral' arrow connecting A to the custodian). This way, if C defaults within the semi-annual period, the collateral is paid to B to provide protection ('protection' arrow connecting the custodian to B) and the loss in taken by the investors who provided the collateral.

Q: OK, so far it's clear.

A: At the end of the six-month period, the margin lender may decide whether to continue with the deal or to back off. With this mechanism C is bearing the CVA volatility risk, whereas B is not exposed to CVA volatility risk, which is the opposite of what happens with traditional upfront CVA charges.

Q: So one of the big differences with traditional CVA is that in this structure the CVA volatility stays with the counterparty C that is generating it, and does not go to the bank.

A: Indeed, [3] argue that whenever an entity's credit worsens, it receives a subsidy from its counterparties in the form of a DVA positive mark-to-market which can be monetized by the entity's bond holders only upon their own default. Whenever an entity's credit improves, it is effectively taxed as its DVA depreciates. Wealth is thus transferred from the equity holders of successful companies to the bond holders of failing ones, the transfer being mediated by banks acting as financial intermediaries and implementing the traditional CVA/DVA mechanics.

Q: Whoa!

A: [Smiling] It's good to see someone still so refreshingly enthusiastic. Rewarding failing firms with a cash subsidy may be a practice of debatable merit as it skews competition. But rewarding failing firms with a DVA benefit is without question suboptimal from an economic standpoint: the DVA benefit they receive is paid in cash from their counterparties but, once received in this form, it cannot be invested and can only be monetized by bond holders upon default.

Q: I see. . .

A: Again, [3] submit that margin lending structures may help reversing the macroeconomic effect by eliminating long term counterparty credit risk insurance and avoiding the wealth transfer that benefits the bond holders of defaulted entities.

Q: I can see a number of problems with this. First, proper valuation and hedging of this to the investors who are providing collateral to the lender is going to be tough. I recall there is no satisfactory standard for even simple synthetic CDOs. One would need an improved methodology.

A: Weren't you the one complaining about the situation being already too complicated? But indeed, the modelling problems have been highlighted for example in Brigo, Pallavicini and Torresetti (2010) [60]. Admittedly this requires an effective global valuation framework, see, for example, the discussion in [2].

Q: The other problem is: what if all margin lenders pull off at some point due to a systemic crisis?

A: That would be a problem, indeed, but [3] submit that the market is less likely to arrive in such a situation in the first place if the wrong incentives to defaulting firms are stopped and an opposite structure, such as the one in Figure 1.1, is implemented. There is also a pentapartite version including a clearing house.

Q: Mmmm.... I understand that if the counterparty credit risk deteriorates, the counterparty will be charged more. Isn't this something that could compromise the relationship of a bank with an important client?

A: It is. One could diminish this by putting a cap and a floor on the floating CVA. However, the task of pricing and hedging this cap risk would bring us back to part of the original problems. Part of the volatility would be still neutralized, however.

Q: But I can see the appeal of floating CVA. It's like car insurance. If you drive well, you expect to be rewarded with less premium next year. If you drive poorly and have an accident, you may expect your premium to go up. Everyone accepts this. So I think it could work for banks.

A: Well the client relationship is more complex with banks, but yes, that is an initial analogy. In any case there is much more work to do to assess this framework properly, and it is evolving continually.

Q: This looks like a good place to stop then.

A: Indeed. [Smiling but looking tired]

Q: Thanks for your time and patience. [Smiling gratefully but still a little puzzled]

2
Context

In this chapter we deal with counterparty risk definitions and concepts in a broad sense. Counterparty risk can be considered broadly from two different points of view. The first point of view is risk measurement, leading to capital requirements revision, trading limits discussions and so on. The second point of view is valuation or pricing, leading to amounts called Credit Valuation Adjustment (CVA) and extensions thereof, including netting, collateral, re-hypothecation, close-out specification, wrong way risk and funding costs. We have seen in an earlier chapter a dialogue trying to clarify such issues. Here we present a more formal introduction. The master formula including consistently all such aspects will be given in Chapter 17 and is based on Pallavicini, Perini and Brigo (2011) [165]. In this chapter we only describe the qualitative features of such master formula.

More generally, in this chapter we introduce definitions that pertain to both the "measurement" and "pricing" points of view, and will explain how the concepts diverge depending on the intended point of view. We will also explain how Basel III and the problem of computing VaR of CVA brings both points of view together. We also point out that the Canabarro and Duffie (2004) [69] field reference paper is not always fully consistent with the Basel methodology on the fine details, but it is nonetheless an excellent introduction. We follow it fully here, although we update its exposition to include the most recent developments.

2.1 DEFINITION OF DEFAULT: SIX BASIC CASES

This book is about counterparty risk, which is the risk of losses due to the default of a counterparty. Thus default is a concept of paramount importance, and yet defining it is not trivial. Intuitively, it is a simple concept: a company defaults when it fails to fulfil some important obligations arising from a debt contract. The paradigmatic case is missing a scheduled debt payment, either an interest or principal payment. However, missing a scheduled debt payment does not immediately translate into a default: usually debt contracts allow a grace period. This is the maximum payment delay which is allowed before the creditor takes any action against the debtor. A typical grace period is 15 days.

On the other hand, we can have a default even without any missed payment. This was the case for Lehman Brothers, for example. In fact, the bank filed for bankruptcy simply based on the recognition of an unsustainable financial condition. In some other cases, the bankruptcy petition has been initiated by worried creditors.

We have just come across another interesting term related to default: bankruptcy. This is when a law court declares with an official act that a company cannot repay its debts; so it is a sort of official recognition of a default. There are different types of bankruptcy, details of which we do not give. They are relevant, however, because they define what happens in the process of the recovery payment.

Beyond the classical definition of default given above, in today's financial world there can be different concepts of default that are relevant for market operators. For example, a credit default swap is usually defined as a derivative paying protection when the reference entity defaults, but in reality the payment is triggered every time a "credit event" is recognized by ISDA, and this concept of credit event goes beyond the above definition of default. ISDA defined in 1999 six types of credit events that can be incorporated in a CDS. They are:

1. **Bankruptcy**: ISDA will declare a credit event when there is a court bankruptcy sentence.
2. **Failure to pay**: even without an official bankruptcy sentence, a missed payment can be a credit event, but not in all cases. It must be material, namely failure to pay a trivial amount is not default. Additionally, a company may decide not to pay a bill for reasons other than credit, for example the bill may be disputed. In all such cases there is no default. So, a missed payment will be recognized as a credit event by ISDA only if some other conditions hold.
3. **Restructuring**: this is when the debt of a company gets redefined, for example, proposing to creditors a later payment than originally prescribed. For example, in 2000 Conseco's bank deferred its loans' maturity by three months, and this was considered a credit event by ISDA. On the other hand Moody's did not consider this a default, because simultaneously Conseco increased the coupon, compensating the creditors. Thus, in this case we can have a credit default swap where a protection payment is triggered even when, according to some other institutions like rating agencies, there has been no default of the reference name and no credit loss.
4. **Repudation/moratorium**: this is the equivalent of bankruptcy for sovereigns. Clearly, sovereigns are not subject to court sentences, however, they can issue statements repudiating debts or declaring moratoria (postponements) of their debts. This is the typical credit event for sovereigns.

5. & 6. **Obligation and acceleration default**: this case is at times called technical default. It is the violation of some covenants (conditions) written in the debt contract. For example, some covenants may require a company to keep certain levels of capital (a typical affirmative covenant) or may prohibit a company to distribute dividends (a typical negative convenant). When the covenant is violated, the lender has the right to ask for immediate liquidation of the debt or for acceleration of repayment. Again, this can trigger a missed payment or some attempt to restructuring, leading to losses for creditors, but it may also be that no losses emerge from this acceleration. Yet it can be included in a CDS as a credit event, thus triggering the protection payment.

In this book we will be mostly denoting the default time by τ, modelling it as a random time and without going into details on the above distinctions among defaults. Thus, we do not discuss in detail the legal and administrative aspects of defaults, except in the cases where this is needed for the discussion. We try to stay on the modelling side as much as possible, although in credit markets one needs to pay attention to legal and administrative details, and we will do so when needed.

2.2 DEFINITION OF EXPOSURES

In the industry, counterparty risk is based on the following definitions.

Definition 2.2.1 ***Exposure at time*** t. *Exposure at time t for a position with final maturity T and whose discounted and added random cash flows at time $t \le T$ are denoted by $\Pi(t, T)$, is defined as*

$$Ex(t) = (\mathbb{E}_t[\Pi(t, T)])^+.$$

Although typically in counterparty risk pricing and measurement one is concerned with the exposure as we defined it above, occasionally it is relevant to consider the exposure with sign, namely the above definition but without the positive part.

Definition 2.2.2 ***Exposure with sign at time*** t. *Exposure with sign at time t for a position with final maturity T and whose discounted and added random cash flows at time $t \le T$ are denoted by $\Pi(t, T)$, is defined as*

$$Exs(t) = \mathbb{E}_t[\Pi(t, T)].$$

We will use the notation ε_t later on in the book to denote Exs(t) and $(\varepsilon_t)^+$ to denote Ex(t).

As usual, $\mathbb{E}_t$ denotes the risk-neutral expectation conditional on market information at time t. Exposure for a position at a given time is thus simply the price, value or "mark to market" of the position at that time if this is positive, or zero otherwise. As prices are computed as expectation under the risk-neutral measure, the above definition follows as a sensible framework. Exposure with sign at a given time is thus simply the price, value or mark-to-market of the position at that time, whether it is positive or negative.

If $t = 0$ is the current time, Ex is called the *current exposure* and Exs current exposure with sign.

Definition 2.2.3 ***Potential Future Exposure (PFE) at time*** t ***at confidence level*** q. *Potential Future Exposure $PFE_q(t)$ for a position $\Pi(t, T)$ is defined as the q-quantile as seen from current time 0 of the random variable $Ex(t) = (\mathbb{E}_t[\Pi(t, T)])^+$ under the physical measure $\mathbb{P}$.*

Typically $q = 0.95$, so that $\text{PFE}_q(t)$ is the 95 percentile of the future value distribution at time t as seen from time 0 (and as such random). When $q = 0.95$ the parameter q is omitted from the notation.

The *PFE profile* is the curve $t \mapsto \text{PFE}_q(t, T)$.

Definition 2.2.4 ***Maximum (or Peak) Potential Future Exposure (MPFE) at confidence level*** q ***in the time interval*** $[0, t]$. *Maximum Potential Future Exposure $MPFE_q(t)$ for a position $\Pi(s, T)$ over an interval $[0, t]$ is defined as the supremum of the q-quantile as seen from current time 0 of the random variables $Ex(s) = (\mathbb{E}_s[\Pi(s, T)])^+$ for $s \in [0, t]$:*

$$MPFE_q(t) = \sup_{s\in[0,t]} \textit{ q quantile under } \mathbb{P} \textit{ of } (\mathbb{E}_s[\Pi(s, T)])^+.$$

Definition 2.2.5 ***Expected Exposure at time*** t. *Expected Exposure for a position $\Pi(t, T)$ is defined as*

$$EEx(t) = \mathbb{E}_0^P(Ex(t)) = \mathbb{E}_0^P(\mathbb{E}_t[\Pi(t, T)])^+.$$

Notice the important point that here the external expectation is under the physical measure, not the risk-neutral one.

Definition 2.2.6 ***Expected Exposure Profile (EEP).*** *This is defined as the curve*

$$t \mapsto EEx(t).$$

It is also called, depending on the context, "credit equivalent exposure curve" or "loan equivalent exposure curve".

Definition 2.2.7 ***Averaged Expected Exposure (AEE) in the time interval*** $[t_1, t_2]$. *This is defined as the time-average of the expected exposure in the interval* $[t_1, t_2]$,

$$AEE(t_1, t_2) = \frac{1}{t_2 - t_1} \int_{t_1}^{t_2} EEx(t)dt.$$

This is often called *Expected Positive Exposure* in the industry, but this terminology is misleading, as it confuses the mean in time with the mean over the states. We therefore use "Expectation" to denote the mean in the states and "Average" to denote the mean in time.

Before moving to Credit Valuation Adjustment, i.e. the main theme of this book, we deal with the definition of Exposure at Default (EAD) and Credit Value at Risk (CrVaR). EAD is simply defined as

Definition 2.2.8 ***Exposure at default (EAD).*** *Exposure at default is simply the exposure valued at the (usually random) default time* τ *of the counterparty,*

$$EAD = Ex(\tau) = (\mathbb{E}_\tau[\Pi(\tau, T)])^+$$

We may define now the loss associated with the portfolio. Once again, if there is a default at τ, before the final maturity T, what is lost by the surviving party is all but the recovery on the portfolio if this is positive, and nothing if the portfolio is negative. Indeed, in the latter case the surviving party would have to pay upon unwinding the position whether the counterparty defaulted or not, and hence would face no further loss due to a possible default. Instead, in the former case, upon unwinding the position the surviving party would have had the right to receive the positive value of the portfolio, and receives instead only the recovery value. The loss random variable for the risk horizon $\bar{T} \leq T$, for default induced losses up to time $\bar{T}$ (T is the final maturity of the portfolio as usual) is therefore

$$L_{\tau,\bar{T},T} := 1_{\{\tau \leq \bar{T}\}}(1 - \text{Rec})\text{Ex}(\tau) = 1_{\{\tau \leq \bar{T}\}}\text{Lgd}(\mathbb{E}_\tau[\Pi(\tau, T)])^+$$

and is non-zero only in scenarios of early default of the counterparty. Here the default risk that we consider is that due to a single counterparty in a specific portfolio, but in general CrVaR is defined on the overall exposure to all counterparties. Furthermore, although we monitor default until the final maturity T, CrVaR assumes typically that default is monitored up to 1y. Our specific definition of CrVaR for a single counterparty will be useful for highlighting analogies and differences with CVA.

Credit VaR is defined in the usual way Value at Risk measures are defined. It is a percentile on the Loss above.

Definition 2.2.9 ***Credit Value at Risk (CrVaR).*** *Given a confidence level* q *and a risk horizon* $\bar{T}$, *Credit Value at Risk is simply the* q *percentile of the loss* $L_{\tau,\bar{T},T}$ *under the physical measure* P.

$$\begin{aligned} CrVaR_{q,\bar{T},T} &= q\text{quantile under } \mathbb{P} \text{ of } L_{\tau,\bar{T},T} = q\text{quantile under } \mathbb{P} \text{ of } 1_{\{\tau \leq \bar{T}\}}\text{Lgd}Ex(\tau) \\ &= q\text{quantile under } \mathbb{P} \text{ of } 1_{\{\tau \leq \bar{T}\}}\text{Lgd}(\mathbb{E}_\tau[\Pi(\tau, T)])^+. \end{aligned}$$

Notice that, differently from exposures, this quantity does contain the default flag $\{\tau \leq \bar{T}\}$. Hence CrVaR weights the scenarios on which the percentile is to be taken with the default event. If there is no default, the loss scenario is 0, and similarly if there is default before the risk horizon but the portfolio is negative, there is no loss due to default risk.

VaR-type measures are often criticized on the grounds of being not sub-additive (e.g. [147]). An alternative risk measure is expected shortfall. We may define it as follows:

Definition 2.2.10 ***Credit Expected Shortfall (CrES).*** *Given a confidence level q and a risk horizon $\bar{T}$, Credit Expected Shortfall is simply the expected value beyond the q percentile of the loss L_τ under the physical measure P:*

$$CrES_{q,\bar{T},T} = \mathbb{E}_0^P[L_{\tau,\bar{T},T} | L_{\tau,\bar{T},T} \geq CrVaR_{q,\bar{T},T}].$$

This risk measure is sub-additive and depends on the whole tail beyond the percentile. However, the reader should keep in mind the fact that despite being sub-additive, Expected Shortfall does not answer the question "Where does the tail really begin for this portfolio"? In fact tabulating percentiles at different confidence levels or inspecting the tail of the loss distribution as a whole can lead to a better risk analysis than taking a single number like VaR or ES. The concept of fat tail is not necessarily helpful for a portfolio with finite notional. Rather, it is more important to inspect how the probability mass is distributed in the *finite* tail up to that notional. The importance of the structure of the tail of the loss distribution as a whole has been highlighted in different contexts such as CDOs for example, in [60].

2.3 DEFINITION OF CREDIT VALUATION ADJUSTMENT (CVA)

The detailed definition of CVA will be given in Chapter 4. We repeat the (asymmetric or unilateral) definition here because we aim at pointing out the connections with the risk-measurement notions we have already mentioned. For the sake of clarity, we present the basic CVA formula with risk-free close-out, without collateral, re-hypothecation and funding costs. Even this simplified case will be enough to highlight the intricacies of proper CVA valuation.

Definition 2.3.1 ***Counterparty Credit Valuation Adjustment (CVA).*** *This is defined as the difference between the value of a position traded with a default-free counterparty and the value of the same position when traded with a given counterparty. Formally, if τ is the default time of the counterparty, the CVA is written as*

$$\begin{aligned} CVA &= \mathbb{E}_0[(1 - \text{Rec})D(0,\tau)1_{\{\tau<T\}}(\mathbb{E}_\tau[\Pi(\tau,T)])^+] \\ &= \mathbb{E}_0[(1 - \text{Rec})D(0,\tau)1_{\{\tau<T\}}Ex(\tau)] = \mathbb{E}_0[(1 - \text{Rec})D(0,\tau)1_{\{\tau<T\}}EAD] \\ &= \mathbb{Q}\{\tau < T\}\mathbb{E}_0[(1 - \text{Rec})D(0,\tau)EAD | \tau < T]. \end{aligned}$$

Since we are talking about values or prices here, also the external expectation is under the risk-neutral measure, rather than the physical one as above.

It is common, although not realistic, to assume the recovery rate to be deterministic and to take the factor $1 - \text{Rec}$ out of the expectation.

The above formula may read: The credit valuation adjustment is given by the loss given default rate $(1 - \text{Rec})$ times the default probability of the counterparty for the final maturity $(\mathbb{Q}\{\tau < T\})$ times the value at time 0 of the discounted exposure at default conditional on early default of the counterparty (before the deal maturity).

We also notice that we may bucket the default time τ in a set of intervals

$$(0 = t_0, t_1], (t_1, t_2], \ldots, (t_{n-2}, t_{n-1}], (t_{n-1}, t_n = T]$$

forming a partition of $(0, T]$, i.e.

$$\begin{aligned}\mathrm{CVA} &= (1 - \mathrm{REC}) \sum_{i=1}^{n} \mathbb{E}_0[D(0, \tau) 1_{\{\tau \in (t_{i-1}, t_i]\}} (\mathbb{E}_\tau[\Pi(\tau, T)])^+] \\ &= (1 - \mathrm{REC}) \sum_{i=1}^{n} \mathbb{E}_0[D(0, \tau) 1_{\{\tau \in (t_{i-1}, t_i]\}} \mathrm{Ex}(\tau)].\end{aligned}$$

Now if we adopt the approximation given by substituting τ with t_i whenever τ is in $(t_{i-1}, t_i]$ we have the bucketed approximated CVA (CVAB)

$$\begin{aligned}\mathrm{CVAB} &= (1 - \mathrm{REC}) \sum_{i=1}^{n} \mathbb{E}_0[D(0, t_i) 1_{\{\tau \in (t_{i-1}, t_i]\}} (\mathbb{E}_{t_i}[\Pi(t_i, T)])^+] \\ &= (1 - \mathrm{REC}) \sum_{i=1}^{n} \mathbb{E}_0[D(0, t_i) 1_{\{\tau \in (t_{i-1}, t_i]\}} \mathrm{Ex}(t_i)] \\ &= (1 - \mathrm{REC}) \sum_{i=1}^{n} \mathbb{Q}\{\tau \in [t_{i-1}, t_i]\}\ \mathbb{E}_0[D(0, t_i) \mathrm{Ex}(t_i) | \{\tau \in (t_{i-1}, t_i]\}].\end{aligned}$$

There is a final but quite heavy further simplification that is possible. If we assume the default flag $\{\tau \in (t_{i-1}, t_i]\}$ to be independent of the market value at time t_i, $\mathbb{E}_{t_i}[\Pi(t_i, T)]$ for all i, then we can factor the expectation into the Independence based CVA (ICVAA)

$$\begin{aligned}\mathrm{ICVAA} &= (1 - \mathrm{REC}) \sum_{i=1}^{n} \mathbb{E}_0[D(0, t_i) 1_{\{\tau \in (t_{i-1}, t_i]\}} (\mathbb{E}_{t_i}[\Pi(t_i, T)])^+] \\ &= (1 - \mathrm{REC}) \sum_{i=1}^{n} \mathbb{Q}\{\tau \in (t_{i-1}, t_i]\} \mathbb{E}_0[D(0, t_i) (\mathbb{E}_{t_i}[\Pi(t_i, T)])^+] \\ &= (1 - \mathrm{REC}) \sum_{i=1}^{n} \mathbb{Q}\{\tau \in (t_{i-1}, t_i]\} \mathbb{E}_0[D(0, t_i) \mathrm{Ex}(t_i)].\end{aligned}$$

Under this independence assumption plus bucketing, the CVA is therefore a weighted sum of expected discounted exposures, the weights being the default probabilities in the buckets. Notice that if we take out the discount factor and replace the risk-neutral expectation with the physical one, we would obtain a corresponding weighted sum of expected exposures,

$$\sum_{i=1}^{n} \mathbb{Q}\{\tau \in (t_{i-1}, t_i]\} P(0, t_i) \mathbb{E}_0^P[\mathrm{Ex}(t_i)] = \sum_{i=1}^{n} \mathbb{Q}\{\tau \in (t_{i-1}, t_i]\} P(0, t_i) \mathrm{EEx}(t_i).$$

Therefore if one is willing to approximate risk-neutral expectations with physical ones, the CVA is a weighted sum of discounted expected exposures, the weights being given by probability of defaults in buckets.

Remark 2.3.2 *IMPORTANT. This is the right moment to point out that this book deals mostly with the counterparty risk problem as seen from the valuation point of view, i.e. with* *the problem of computing CVA. From the previous definitions it is clear that this may help also in the risk measurement arena, but the main focus of the book is on valuation. It is also worth noticing that with CVA Value at Risk (CVA VaR) becoming important following Basel III, the two aspects are coming together. We will say more on this below.*

2.4 COUNTERPARTY RISK MITIGANTS: NETTING

In computing any of the above measures, be it EE, PFE, MPFE, or CVA, one may have to take into account counterparty risk mitigants. These are clauses that, when agreed and enforced, may reduce the counterparty risk considerably. We consider two of them here, starting from netting. Netting occurs when the residual net present values of several positions of an investor towards a counterparty add up to form a total NPV that is considered as a single amount. This is not always the case. Let us illustrate this difference with a toy example.

Example 2.4.1 *Consider an investor having two positions towards a counterparty, whose net present values at future time t are given by the normal random variables X_1 and X_2 respectively, where X_1 and X_2 are jointly normal, with means μ_1 and μ_2, standard deviations σ_1 and σ_2, and correlation ρ. We denote $\mu = \mu_1 + \mu_2$ and $\sigma^2 = \sigma_1^2 + \sigma_2^2 + 2\rho\sigma_1\sigma_2$ mean and variance of the sum of the two random variables. The related exposures at time t will be X_1^+ and X_2^+.*

As for the exposure of the portfolio comprising X_1 and X_2, without netting, if the counterparty were to default in t, the investor would lose $(1 - \text{REC})X_1^+$ from the first position and $(1 - \text{REC})X_2^+$ from the second one. With netting, the investor would lose $(1 - \text{REC})(X_1 + X_2)^+$ from the whole position, as the check on positivity would be applied to the whole netted portfolio. It is well known that in general

$$(X_1 + X_2)^+ \leq X_1^+ + X_2^+$$

for any two real numbers, and in particular for our two random variable realizations. Therefore, netting diminishes the counterparty risk adjustment.

In the Gaussian case above, we can even compute the expected exposures in the netted case:

$$EEx_{Net} = \mathbb{E}[(X_1 + X_2)^+] = \sigma\varphi(\mu/\sigma) + \mu\Phi(\mu/\sigma)$$

and in the non-netted one

$$EEx_{NoNet} = \mathbb{E}[X_1^+ + X_2^+] = \sigma_1\varphi(\mu_1/\sigma_1) + \mu_1\Phi(\mu_1/\sigma_1) + \sigma_2\varphi(\mu_2/\sigma_2) + \mu_2\Phi(\mu_2/\sigma_2)$$

where as usual Φ is the standard normal cumulative distribution function and φ is its density. There is a clear benefit in the netted case, as the correlation, if negative, can diminish the value of the expectation. Indeed, as a basic example we may show the difference between the expected exposure without and with netting as a function of correlation, assuming for simplicity $\mu_1 = \mu_2 = 0$ and $\sigma_1 = \sigma_2$. We get

$$EEx_{NoNet} - EEx_{Net}(\rho) = \frac{\sigma_1}{\sqrt{\pi}}(\sqrt{2} - \sqrt{1+\rho}).$$

We see clearly that in this toy example the case with correlation 1 leads to no difference between netting and no netting, whereas the case with correlation −1 is the one resulting in the largest difference. This is obvious: two Gaussians with the same mean and variance and with the correlation 1 basically coincide, so it is like computing $(X_1 + X_1)^+ = (2X_1)^+ = 2X_1^+$ *which is the same as the non-netted case* $X_1^+ + X_1^+ = 2X_1^+$. *Instead, if the correlation is* -1*, it is like saying that one Gaussian is the opposite of the other one, leading to* $(X_1 - X_1)^+ = (0)^+ = 0$ *in the netted case and* $X_1^+ + (-X_1)^+ = |X_1|$ *in the non-netted case. Take, for example, a* 20% *volatility in each single position for the two positions. The difference between the non-netted and netted credit exposures is about* 4.7% *of the notional if the correlation is* 0 *(independence of the two positions) and is* 0 *if the correlation is* 1 *(total dependence). This is clearly a very large variation that points out the importance of netting in environments with correlation smaller than one.*

Even in this simple case it is clear that correlation plays a key role in showing the benefits of netting. People who are familiar with interest rate derivatives will recognize an analogy in valuing caps as opposed to swaptions. The latter valuation depends on correlation but the former does not.

As the portfolio size increases and the assets distributions become more complex the patterns can be less simple, but even our simple example above points out the importance of netting.

2.5 COUNTERPARTY RISK MITIGANTS: COLLATERAL

Informally, in loans and lending transactions, collateral is an asset of the borrower that is transferred to the lender if the borrower defaults, and in particular this happens if the borrower cannot pay back the principal and interest on the loan. After default the lender becomes the owner of the collateral. In a mortgage the typical collateral is the real estate property being acquired with the help of the loan.

In banking, there are two different contexts for collateral. One is the traditional practice of giving some assets (bonds, equity, physical assets) as a guarantee for a specific lending transaction, the other context is more recent and is based on signing complex bilateral collateralization arrangements, involving usually liquid collateral, in particular cash, for securing derivative transactions. This is sometimes referred to as capital market collateralization, and in this case the securing material is often called margin.

Collateral is an important topic for this book, since its use as a mitigation of counterparty risk is one of the main answers of the financial markets to the explosion of such risk after the start of the global financial crisis. The regular exchange of liquid collateral to minimize counterparty risk is typical in interbank derivative transactions, because usually only banks have the necessary infrastructure. In fact, maintaining a bilateral collateral account requires the capability to re-evaluate frequently and precisely the entire portfolio of financial transactions with a counterparty, and the availability of cash to be posted or withdrawn regularly every time there is a change in the value of the portfolio and every time there is an interest payment. This highlights two important features of modern collateralization: collateral must be kept in line with the mark-to-market of the portfolio of deals with the counterparty (if the mark-to-market is negative to me I will have to post collateral, while I will receive it when the mark-to-market is positive). Secondly, the collateral that a party posts to the other earns an interest, usually settled daily (in fact posting collateral is just a guarantee, the property will be transferred only upon default). Recently some large corporate counterparties have also been setting up a framework for regular collateralization, but this remains unfeasible for small corporates.

2.5.1 The Credit Support Annex (CSA)

Two counterparties who are willing to exchange collateral usually sign a Credit Support Annex, or CSA, a legal document which regulates the credit risk mitigation for derivative transactions, in particular collateral. It is one of the four parts that make up an ISDA Master Agreement, a framework of documents designed to enable OTC derivative trading to be regulated fully and flexibly.

A CSA defines the terms or rules under which collateral is posted or transferred between counterparties. It includes crucial aspects such as the *Threshold*, the amount of mark-to-market above which collateralization must begin, the *Minimum Transfer Amount* (another threshold defining the minimum mismatch between collateral and mark-to-market that actually triggers an adjustment), the *Eligible collateral* (which securities can be used as collateral), the haircuts that apply to securities used as collateral (a bond having a 20% haircut means that one must post bonds for a current value of \$120 in order to secure \$100 exposure) and the frequency of portfolio revaluation and collateral rebalancing. The last feature contributes to determining the *Margin Period of Risk*, namely the time period from the last exchange of collateral with a defaulting counterpart and the time when the default close-out amount is computed.

Two parties have the possibility to set such features as desired, but in practice there are some very standardized choices. ISDA strongly encourages harmonisation in collateral agreements, and for this purpose they issued a document called "Best Practices for the OTC Derivatives Collateral Process". Let's see some interesting points about this document.

The document points out first of all the importance of precision and timeliness in collateral management. Collateral, when it is not cash, should be revalued daily, and also the exposure should be calculated on a timely basis consistently with standard market practices, so that margin calls can be based on the precise mark-to-market of the trades covered by the agreement (a number called variation margin), on the correct valuation of the collateral previously held or posted, and on the possible presence of independent amounts (amounts of collateral which are fixed at the beginning of a transaction usually in excess of the variation margin). The document also stresses the need for automation of collateral management, in particular "parties should have the system capability and the procedural framework in place allowing for delivery of collateral within the time-frames agreed upon in the CSA".

The main goal is minimizing collateral disputes that can naturally arise from differences in the valuation of the exposures. In such a case, the "ISDA Collateral Dispute Resolution Procedure" highlights that "Firms should have the ability to easily extract a trade file from their collateral system, on a regular or ad-hoc basis, to facilitate a portfolio reconciliation in the event of a collateral dispute", so that parties can see which trades are generating differences in valuation. Additionally, firms should establish internal processes, involving front, middle and back office, for the investigation of the causes of collateral disputes. To avoid such disputes to arise too often, paralyzing the process, "Parties should discuss and agree tolerances between themselves in order to determine what they judge to be significant mark-to-market differences, as well as material trade booking discrepancies and any other differences that may arise". In any case, parties need to have effective channels of communication to raise and resolve relevant disputes that can be due to time discrepancies in valuation, different parameters used, or different valuation models. One final curiosity. ISDA acknowledges that in the recent years the interest rates on which collateral interest is based have reached historical lows, so much so that analysts and modellers have started to allow for the possibility of negative rates in the future. Yet, ISDA recommends that at no point interest accrual should drop into a negative figure. To avoid this, a floor on the interest rate applying to collateral should be set.

2.5.2 The ISDA Proposal for a New Standard CSA

On 3 November 2011, ISDA released a presentation outlining its plans for a new Standard Credit Support Annex (SCSA). The SCSA is intended to align the collateral mechanics of bilateral OTC derivatives with collateralization of cleared derivatives transactions, and to mimic the collateral mechanics at certain major clearing-houses, most notably London Clearing House (LCH), one of the world's largest clearers of interest rate swaps.

ISDA suggests to fix and standardize under the SCSA the following variables that parties may modify under the current CSA:

- → collateral eligibility,
- → threshold amounts,
- → interest on posted collateral,
- → initial margin requirements based on counterparty credit ratings.

The main features of new SCSA contracts are removing the optionality found in the existing ISDA Credit Support Annex (CSA); promoting the adoption of Overnight Index Swap (OIS) discounting for derivatives, which would align interest accruals on cash collateral with discount rates for the underlying derivatives transactions; creating a homogeneous collateral valuation framework designed to reduce Novation and valuation disputes.

The SCSA retains the operational mechanics of the current CSA, but amends collateral calculations so that derivatives exposures and their offsetting collateral positions are grouped by currency (silo), and evaluated independently. See [111] to include silos into curve bootstrapping.

2.5.3 Collateral Effectiveness as a Mitigant

Counterparty risk is clearly mitigated by the presence of collateral, to the point that it can be almost completely offset leaving only some sort of Gap risk. Gap risk can be one of two types.

First, in case securities are posted as collateral (instead of cash), the collateral value can move against the net creditor during the margin period of risk. The second case is the following. Even if collateral is cash, between two collateral margining dates the mark-to-market of the position may change dramatically, due to a systemic event or to a strong contagion following the default of the counterparty. The cash-collateral that had been posted by the counterparty at the last margin call may then be quite inadequate as a guarantee for the surviving party, whose exposure is now quite different from the one at the earlier margin call.

In the initial part of our CVA analysis we will price counterparty risk assuming there is no collateral posted. This is a relatively common scenario when the counterparty is a corporate. Let us recall the interview in [192], that reports the case of the leading German airline:

> The airline [. . .] does not post collateral in its derivatives transactions.

For cases where collateral is posted, typically a derivative transaction between banks, the inclusion of collateral and margin calls will be added consistently later on in the book, showing that collateral is not always effective in reducing CVA risk significantly. Indeed, as just mentioned, in cases of strong contagion, even frequent margining can have limited effectiveness in reducing counterparty risk. We will see such a case based on Credit Default Swaps as underlying instruments. We will also see different cases where collateral is very effective.

One more issue concerning collateral is rehypothecation, namely the right of a firm with a positive mark-to-market with respect to a counterparty, to re-use the collateral received from this counterparty for securing borrowing with a different counterparty. We will include it explicitly in our master formula, although a debate is currently occurring in the industry on whether collateral rehypothecation should be allowed. With this respect, ISDA say that rehypothecation and substitution of collateral are "standard elements of collateralization where appropriate, but have been under close inspection recently due to issues in other product sets". They point out that, in any case, the decision to grant rehypothecation rights is usually on a reciprocal basis, and in any case must be "a decision made by both sides to the agreement". Other features such as minimum transfer amounts and thresholds will be briefly considered.

2.6 FUNDING

As we observed in the introductory dialogue in Chapter 1, when one manages a trading position, one needs to obtain cash in order to do a number of operations:

- hedging the position
- posting collateral
- paying coupons or notionals
- set reserves in place
- paying interest on collateral received
- managing Novation costs

and so on. One may obtain cash from one's treasury department or in the market. One may also receive cash as a consequence of being in the position: a coupon, a notional reimbursement, a positive mark-to-market move, getting some collateral, a close-out payment, receiving interest on collateral posted, and so on. In short, and loosely speaking, if one is borrowing, this will have a cost, and if one is lending, this will provide some revenues. Including the cost of funding in a valuation framework means to properly account for such features.

Before the credit crunch started in 2007, the funding costs of banks were fairly homogeneous across banks, and, internally to each bank, the different sources of funding happened at similar rates, usually approximated by the concept of a unique risk-free rate. In this context, simple pure discounting of payoff's cash flows provided an acceptable approximation of the value of a derivatives transaction. Nowadays, instead, a much more precise approach is required.

The debate about the inclusion of funding costs in pricing was, in recent times, considered in [168]. This paper considers an initial analysis of the problem of replication of derivative transactions taking funding costs into account. The derivation there, however, has two problems. First, a technical problem is that the self-financing condition is simplified in such a way that it implies that equity would fund itself as a stand-alone position. This issue is addressed in [38]. Secondly, there is a more fundamental issue: the approach does not extend to the inclusion of default risk.

2.6.1 A First Attack on Funding Cost Modelling

This was pointed out in [157] and [158]. This is the first work that introduces explicitly the possibility of a default in the funding strategy. Focusing only on simple products, such as zero coupon bonds or loans, it highlights some essential features of funding costs. First of all, it shows that the advantage associated to borrowing money in a derivative transaction can in part be identified with Debit Valuation Adjustments (DVA), pointing out the risk of double counting if this is not taken into account. Then it points out that there are two alternatives in computing the funding cost associated to lending money: either by taking into account DVA, or without taking it into account. The first approach seems more consistent with the computation of precise expected cash-flows, but the second one seems more consistent with a prudent management of the liquidity resources of an institution.

While for the part regarding the funding adjustment for borrowed money, the approach of this paper has been generally accepted and included in the subsequent literature, with a number of extensions to more realistic contexts, it sparked a debate for the part regarding lending. The possibility to take funding DVA into account in charging funding costs has been criticized in [74], who reasons on the balance sheet implications of DVA and funding, while it has been strongly advocated in [125] who reason on the implications of investment choices on the financial perspectives of an institution. Other literature on funding includes [111] that analyzes implications of currency risk for collateral modelling [65], that resorts to a PDE approach, with the same difficulties in the self-financing condition as [168] (see again [38]), and [85], [165].

In the following chapters, and mainly in Chapter 11, we present the main results of the seminal paper by Morini and Prampolini (2011) [157]. This is the first step in the fundamental challenge of accounting for funding costs consistently with counterparty risk.

2.6.2 The General Funding Theory and its Recursive Nature

Further on, in Chapter 17 we follow Pallavicini, Perini and Brigo (2011) [165] that, with [85], is the first attempt to a really comprehensive framework where cash flows can be both positive and negative in different scenarios and where collateral is also modelled with a number of realistic features.

One final observation is in order in closing this introduction to funding. A number of practitioners advocate a "Funding Valuation Adjustment", or FVA, that would be additive so that the total price of the portfolio would be something like

$$AdjustedPrice = RiskFreePrice + DVA - CVA + FVA.$$

However, it is not that simple. Proper inclusion of funding costs leads to a recursive pricing problem, since the funding adjustment is a function of the price, that in turns depends on the funding adjustment itself. Such a problem may be formulated as a backwards stochastic differential equation (BSDE, as in [85], but also in [65]) or as a discrete time backward induction equation (as in [165]). The simple additive structure above is not there in general. The problem is inherently recursive because the value of the cash and collateral processes and the cost of their funding may depend on the future price patterns of the derivative, which, in turn, depends on the future management of funding processes. This transforms the pricing equation into a recursive equation.

Thus, in full generality, funding and investing costs cannot be considered as a simple additive term to other adjustments such as DVA, CVA and a credit-and-funding free price.

Additionally, we will see that in a general context the relation between DVA and funding is more complex than in the simple setting of [157]. We will illustrate a consistent theory and practice of funding costs in Chapter 17, drawing on the work of [165].

2.7 VALUE AT RISK (VaR) AND EXPECTED SHORTFALL (ES) OF CVA

We close this chapter by mentioning a problem that is currently bringing together the pricing and risk measurement aspects of counterparty risk: VaR or ES of CVA. We have already discussed this briefly in the dialogue in Chapter 1.

We have specified earlier in this chapter that Credit VaR measures the risk of losses one faces due to the possible default of some counterparties one is having business with. CVA measures the pricing component of this risk, i.e. the adjustment to the price of a product due to this risk.

Now one may need to revalue and mark-to-market CVA in time. When CVA moves in time and moves against the calculating party, the calculating party books negative mark-to-market and hence losses NOT because the counterparty actually defaults, but because the pricing of this default risk has changed for the worse. So in this sense the calculating party is being affected by CVA volatility.

It is interesting that CVA volatility does not affect the party that generates it but rather the opposite one. This relates with the discussion, see the dialogue in Chapter 1, on possible Floating Rate CVA and margin lending. With the traditional upfront or fixed premium CVA mechanics one has, to quote Basel III:

> Under Basel II, the risk of counterparty default and credit migration risk were addressed but mark-to-market losses due to credit valuation adjustments (CVA) were not. During the financial crisis, however, roughly two-thirds of losses attributed to counterparty credit risk were due to CVA losses and only about one-third were due to actual defaults.

In other terms, the variability of the price of default and market risk over time has caused more damage than the direct risks themselves. This is why Basel is considering risk measuring CVA with a VaR- or ES-type measure and setting up quite severe capital charges against CVA. It follows that most institutions will need a VaR estimate for their CVA.

This is very hard to compute accurately. One could simulate basic market variables under the measure P, up to the risk horizon, say h years. Then, in each scenario, one would have to price the residual CVA, conditional on that scenario, until the final maturity using a Q expectation.

This would be, in each scenario for $\mathcal{G}_h$, i.e. the market information up to h years:

$$\mathrm{CVA}_h(\omega) = \mathbb{E}\{(1-\mathrm{Rec})D(h,\tau)1_{\{h\le\tau<T\}}(\mathbb{E}[\Pi(\tau,T)|\mathcal{G}_\tau])^+|\mathcal{G}_h(\omega)\}.$$

One puts all the prices at the horizon time together in a histogram and obtains a profit and loss distribution for $\mathrm{CVA}_h(\omega)$. On the distribution of this random variable one would have to select a $\mathbb{P}$-quantile at the chosen confidence level and this way one would have computed VaR of CVA.

Definition 2.7.1 ***Value at Risk of CVA (CVAVaR).*** *Given a confidence level q and a risk horizon h, Value at Risk of CVA is simply the q percentile of the CVA mark to market random loss $CVA_0 - CVA_h$ under the physical measure P.*

$$CVAVaR_{q,h,T} = q\,quantile\ under\ \mathbb{P}\ of\,(CVA_0 - CVA_h(\omega)).$$

This may require sub-simulations or even sub-sub simulations, and is therefore very difficult computationally:

- First one has to simulate risk factors scenarios ω under $\mathbb{P}$ up to h years, first simulation.
- Then, in each obtained scenario ω, one has to simulate default and market risk factors conditional on $\mathcal{G}_h(\omega)$ and up to the default times τ, second simulation.
- Third, at each τ scenario the portfolio is to be priced to determine $\mathbb{E}[\Pi(\tau, T)|\mathcal{G}_\tau]$, third simulation.
- At this point one may build the loss distribution, namely the $\mathbb{P}$ distribution of the random variable

$$\text{CVA}_0 - \text{CVA}_h(\omega)$$

and take VaR as a percentile of that.

Definition 2.7.2 ***Expected Shortfall of CVA (CVAES).*** *Given a confidence level q and a risk horizon h, Expected Shortfall of CVA is simply the expectation of the CVA loss beyond the q percentile under the physical measure P.*

$$CVAES_{q,h,T} = \mathbb{E}^P[CVA_0 - CVA_h(\omega)|CVA_0 - CVA_h(\omega) \geq CVAVaR_{q,h,T}].$$

It is important to stress again that CVA VaR and ES do not measure the default risk directly, they measure the risk to have a mark to market loss due to adverse CVA change in value over time.

Finally, we need to specify that the real CVA and ES VaR calculation is done on a pool of several counterparties at the same time and not on a single one. In this sense one has to add up the CVA losses across counterparties, generalizing the above definition in the obvious way by taking the relevant percentile, or expectation beyond the percentile, of

$$\sum_{i \in \text{Counterparties}} (\text{CVA}_0^i - \text{CVA}_h^i(\omega))$$

where the upper script i refers to CVA for the counterparty i.

2.8 THE DILEMMA OF REGULATORS AND BASEL III

Regulators would like to recommend a methodology for the measurement of CVA risk that is standard, objective, fully determined methodologically and relatively easy to implement. However, even from our initial discussion in this chapter, and this will be even clearer later in the book, it is evident that CVA can be quite complex, extremely model dependent and difficult to value, especially when including advanced features. As we have seen CVA VaR may require sub simulations or even sub-sub simulations, limiting the number of scenarios, for most systems, to a ridiculous low. There are ways to avoid this but they are based on heroic assumptions that, in a number of cases, imply quite relevant errors in the way CVA is approximated. These approximations concern mostly wrong way risk, namely the impact of statistical dependence between counterparties defaults and underlying contract values. We will explore this feature extensively in the following chapters, showing that it is indeed quite model dependent and complex to model. Chapter 5 looks at wrong way risk for interest rates and is based on [57] and [58]. Chapter 6 shows wrong way risk modelling for commodities (Oil), and is based on [36]. Chapter 7 looks at wrong way risk for credit instruments and CDS specifically, based on [43]. Chapter 8 looks at wrong way risk for equity, and is based on [47], [55], [61], [62]. The following chapters look at advanced features of CVA that make the calculation of CVA VaR even more complicated. In a way it is very difficult to standardize this quite complex object, given that proper implementation with a suitable number of scenarios is almost beyond the capabilities of available commercial (and to the best of our knowledge, internal) CVA systems. In this sense regulators may consider an advanced approach, allowing institutions to implement these measures the best way they can, resorting to inspections and controls a posteriori. This can be an effective approach. Trying instead to impose a simplistic and potentially inadequate methodology top-down to all institutions would result in undesirable consequences that are easy to imagine.

3

Modelling the Counterparty Default

This chapter re-elaborates and expands material originally presented in Brigo (2010) [33], Brigo and Mercurio (2006) [48], Brigo and Pallavicini (2006, 2007, 2008) [56] [57] and [58], Brigo, Morini and Tarenghi (2011) [55], Brigo and Alfonsi (2005) [35] and Brigo and El-Bachir (2010) [46]. In this chapter we address modelling of the counterparties' defaults.

Our discussion has to begin with the default event of the counterparty. A default event is an event where a firm cannot face its obligation on the payments owed to some entity.

Mathematically, default is represented by means of the default time. The default time, typically denoted by τ, is a random time that can be modelled in several ways. There are essentially two paradigms that emerged over the years,

- Structural/Firm Value Models, and
- Reduced Form/Intensity/Hazard Rate models

We will start from Firm Value Models.

3.1 FIRM VALUE (OR STRUCTURAL) MODELS

Structural models are based on the work by Merton (1974), in which a firm life is linked to its ability to pay back its debt. Let us suppose that a firm issues a bond to finance its activities and also that this bond has maturity T. At final time T, if the firm is not able to reimburse all the bondholders we can say that there has been a default event. In this context default may occur only at final time T and is triggered by the value of the firm being below the debt level. In a more realistic and sophisticated structural model Black and Cox (1976) [24], part of the family of *first passage time models*, default can happen also before maturity T. In first passage time models, the default time is the first instant where the firm value hits from above either a deterministic (possibly time varying) or a stochastic barrier, ideally associated with safety covenants, forcing the firm to early bankruptcy in case of important credit deterioration. In this sense the firm value is seen as a generic asset and these models use the same mathematics of barrier options pricing models.

3.1.1 The Geometric Brownian Assumption

More in detail, the fundamental hypothesis of the standard structural models is that the underlying process is a Geometric Brownian Motion (GBM), which is also the kind of process commonly used for equity stocks in the Black-Scholes model. Classical structural models (Merton, Black Cox) postulate a GBM (Black-Scholes) lognormal dynamics for the value of the firm V. This lognormality assumption is considered to be acceptable. [88] report that "this assumption [lognormal V] is quite robust and, according to KMV's own empirical studies, actual data conform quite well to this hypothesis.". The GBM for the firm value V, under the risk-neutral measure, reads

$$dV_t = (r - k)V_t dt + \sigma V_t dW_t$$

where r is the risk-free rate, k is a payout ratio, and σ is the volatility. We assume such parameters to be positive constants for simplicity, and we will extend the model to time dependent parameters later on.

In these models the value of the firm V is the sum of the firm equity value S, and of the firm debt value D. The firm equity value S, in particular, can be seen as a kind of (vanilla or barrier-like) option on the value of the firm V. Merton typically assumes a zero-coupon debt at a terminal maturity T. Black and Cox assume, besides a possible zero coupon debt, safety covenants forcing the firm to declare bankruptcy and pay back its debt with what is left as soon as the value of the firm itself goes below a "safety level" barrier. This is what introduces the barrier option technology in structural models for default.

3.1.2 Merton's Model

In Merton's model there is a debt maturity T, a debt face value L and the company defaults at final maturity (and only then) if the value of the firm V_T is below the debt L to be paid. We present some quick calculations in Merton's model, taken by [33].

Default probability. We know that the solution for the equation of V satisfies

$$\log V(T) = \log V(0) + (r - k - \sigma^2/2)T + \sigma W(T)$$

so that

$$\log V(T) = \log V(0) + (r - k - \sigma^2/2)T + \sigma\sqrt{T}N(0, 1)$$

where $N(0, 1)$ is a standard normal random variable. This implies that the default event, which in the Merton model can only happen at maturity, is written as $\{V(T) \leq L\}$, i.e. the final firm value went below the debt L to be paid. We have that $\{V(T) \leq L\} = \{\log V(T) \leq \log L\}$ since log is an increasing function. Given the above equation for $V(T)$ this translates into

$$\{\log V(T) \leq \log L\} = \left\{ N(0, 1) \leq \frac{\log(L/V(0)) - (r - k - \sigma^2/2)T}{\sigma\sqrt{T}} \right\}$$

whose probability is

$$\mathbb{Q}\left\{ N(0, 1) \leq \frac{\log \frac{L}{V(0)} - (r - k - \frac{\sigma^2}{2})T}{\sigma\sqrt{T}} \right\} = \Phi\left(\frac{\log \frac{L}{V(0)} - (r - k - \frac{\sigma^2}{2})T}{\sigma\sqrt{T}} \right)$$

where Φ is the cumulative distribution function of a $N(0, 1)$ standard normal random variable.

Since Φ is increasing, being a cdf, and log is increasing, it follows that $\log(L/V(0)) = \log L - \log V(0)$ is increasing in L and decreasing in $V(0)$, so that we can say the same for the default probability formula above.

If $V(0) \to +\infty$ then $\log(L/V(0)) \to -\infty$ and therefore since $\lim_{x \to -\infty} \Phi(x) = 0$ we have that the default probability formula above tends to zero. This is intuitive: if $V(0)$ is infinitely far away from the final debt level L then default will never happen, so that its probability will tend to zero.

To compute the hazard rate in Merton model, defined as

$$\lim_{T \downarrow 0} \frac{\mathbb{Q}\{\tau \leq T\}}{T},$$

we need to compute the limit of the above default probability formula, after assuming for simplicity $r - k - \sigma^2/2 = 0$. We have

$$\lim_{T\downarrow 0} \frac{\mathbb{Q}\{\tau \leq T\}}{T} = \lim_{T\downarrow 0} \frac{\Phi\left(\frac{\log \frac{L}{V(0)}}{\sigma\sqrt{T}}\right)}{T} =$$

This would lead to a limit of the type zero over zero. This is because in the numerator, the denominator term tends to zero from the positive side, so that the fraction, with negative numerator, tends to minus infinity. Taking into account that the normal cdf Φ tends to zero when the argument of the numerator tends towards minus infinity, we have a limit of the type zero over zero. We apply the limit theorem of De L'Hopital, and we get

$$= \lim_{T\downarrow 0} \frac{p\left(\frac{\log \frac{L}{V(0)}}{\sigma\sqrt{T}}\right)\left(-\frac{1}{2T\sqrt{T}}\frac{\log \frac{L}{V(0)}}{\sigma}\right)}{1} =$$

where p is the normal density function,

$$p(x) = \frac{1}{\sqrt{2\pi}} e^{-\frac{x^2}{2}}.$$

If we set $1/\sqrt{T} = y$, the limit becomes:

$$= \lim_{y\uparrow +\infty} -y^3 \frac{\log \frac{L}{V(0)}}{2\sigma} p\left(y\frac{\log \frac{L}{V(0)}}{\sigma}\right) = A \lim_{y\uparrow+\infty} \frac{y^3}{\exp[(y^2(\log(L/V(0))/\sigma)^2)/2]} = 0$$

(for some constant A), since the exponential goes to infinity faster than any polynomial.

So we obtained in the Merton model

$$\lim_{T\downarrow 0} \frac{\mathbb{Q}(\tau \leq T)}{T} = 0.$$

Compare with a standard constant hazard rate model, with deterministic intensity $\lambda > 0$ that is constant in time where, as we shall see later in the book, one has

$$\mathbb{Q}(\tau \leq T) - 1 - e^{-\lambda T}$$

In this case we can see that the analogous limit gives

$$\lim_{T\downarrow 0} \frac{\mathbb{Q}\{\tau \leq T\}}{T} = \lambda > 0.$$

This is an important difference: basic structural models like Merton have no short-term credit spreads (the limit is zero). Intensity models instead have non-zero short-term credit spread. This is a modelling advantage of intensity models. It means that for very short maturities the Merton model will have great difficulty in fitting non-zero spreads, whereas the intensity model will have no problem.

Continuing with the calculations in Merton's model, the debt value at time $t < T$ is thus

$$D_t = \mathbb{E}_t[D(t,T)\min(V_T, L)] = \mathbb{E}_t[D(t,T)[V_T - (V_T - L)^+]] =$$
$$= \mathbb{E}_t[D(t,T)[L - (L - V_T)^+]] = P(t,T)L - \text{Put}(t,T; V_t, L)$$

where Put(time, maturity, underlying, strike) is a put option price and one assumes deterministic interest rates ($D(t, T) = P(t, T) = \exp(-r(T - t))$).

The equity value can be derived as a difference between the value of the firm and the debt:

$$S_t = V_t - D_t = V_t - P(t, T)L + \text{Put}(t, T; V_t, L) = \text{Call}(t, T; V_t, L)$$

(by put-call parity) so that, as is well known, in Merton's model the equity can be interpreted as a call option on the value of the firm.

3.1.3 Black and Cox's (1976) Model

Let us now move to the Black and Cox (BC) model [24]. In this model we have safety covenants in place, in that the firm is forced to reimburse its debt as soon as its value V_t hits a low enough "safety level" $H(t)$. Hitting this barrier is considered to represent an earlier default. Assuming a debt face value of L at final maturity T, as before, an obvious candidate for this "safety level" is the final debt present value discounted back at time t, i.e. $LP(t, T)$. However, one may want to cut some slack to the counterparty, giving it some time to recover even if the level goes below $LP(t, T)$, and the "safety level" can be chosen to be lower than $LP(t, T)$.

In any case, once the barrier is chosen, the price of a zero coupon corporate bond with maturity $T_B < T$ is the risk-neutral expectation of a final payoff at T_B that is one in all scenarios where the barrier has not been touched (no early default) and zero (or a recovery amount) in all scenarios where the barrier has been touched. Clearly, pricing this bond is solving a barrier option pricing problem, and first passage time models make use of barrier options techniques. Notice also the different nature of the default time in a stylized case: now τ can be defined as

$$\inf\{t \geq 0 : \; V_t \leq H(t)\}$$

if this quantity is smaller than the final debt maturity T, and by T in the other case if further $V_T < L$. In all other cases there is no default. Notice that the "inf" quantity is the first time V hits the barrier H, hence the term "first passage models".

Let $H(t; T)$ be the barrier with time dependence on t and final zero coupon debt maturity T.

Black and Cox assume a constant parameters Geometric Brownian Motion

$$dV(t) = (r - k)V(t)dt + \sigma_V V(t)dW(t) \tag{3.1}$$

as above, and an exponential barrier (we omit the T dependence in H)

$$H(t) = \begin{cases} L & t = T \\ Ke^{-\gamma(T-t)} & t < T \end{cases} \tag{3.2}$$

where γ and K are positive parameters. Black and Cox assume also that $Ke^{-\gamma(T-t)} < Le^{-r(T-t)}$.

This second assumption means that, following the possibility we mentioned above, the safety covenants are lower than the final debt present value. In this framework the default time τ is defined as follows:

Definition 3.1.1 *Let the firm value dynamics follow Equation 3.1. Let the debt maturity be T, let the final debt face value be $L > 0$, with $V_0 > L$, and let the safety covenants early default barrier $H(t, T)$ be given by Eq 3.2, where $K \geq 0$ and $\gamma \geq 0$ are barrier parameters. Assume*

$V_0 > H(0, T)$. *Then the default time is defined as*

$$\tau = \inf\{t \in (0, T] : V_t \le H(t, T)\} \quad (\inf \emptyset = \infty).$$

Notice that if we set $\gamma = 0$ we have the particular case of a flat barrier.

If the dynamics parameters are constant, the default/survival probabilities can be directly computed (for example, [18]):

$$\mathbb{Q}\{\tau > U\} = \Phi\left(\frac{\ln\left(\frac{V_0}{H(0)}\right) + \tilde{\nu}S}{\sigma_V\sqrt{U}}\right) - \left(\frac{H(0)}{V_0}\right)^{2\tilde{a}} \Phi\left(\frac{\ln\left(\frac{H(0)}{V_0}\right) + \tilde{\nu}U}{\sigma_V\sqrt{U}}\right)$$

for $U < T$, where $\tilde{\nu} = r - k - \gamma - \frac{1}{2}\sigma_V^2$ and $\tilde{a} = \frac{\tilde{\nu}}{\sigma_V^2}$. We will see shortly that given survival probabilities, under some assumption on interest rates one can compute CDS prices. This allows one to calibrate the model to CDS data, as we will illustrate below.

At this point, one may wonder whether the additional complication of barrier options techniques is absolutely necessary. Could one use Merton's model, check for default only at the final debt maturity T, and forget about early default? In comparing the Merton and Black and Cox models, one legitimate question is whether including early default, as in Black and Cox, is making a relevant difference from a numerical point of view.

To illustrate that this is indeed the case, we follow [33] and consider the comparison between Merton and Black and Cox when they both have the same parameters. In Black and Cox we take a flat barrier equal to L with $\gamma = r$ and $L = K$ so as to be closest to Merton's parameters. For simplicity we assume $r = k = 0$ and take two possible parameter sets:

$$P1: \quad L/V_0 = 0.9; \quad \sigma_1 = 0.2;$$
$$P2: \quad L/V_0 = 0.2; \quad \sigma_2 = 0.6.$$

In Figure 3.1 we compare the default probability curves in the Merton model with two different parameter sets "P1" and "P2" given above. In Figure 3.2 we compare the default probability curves in the Black and Cox model with two different parameter sets "P1" and "P2".

In Figure 3.3 we compare the default probability curves using the parameter set "P1" in the two different models, Merton and Black and Cox, and we can see that the difference is quite relevant. Similarly, in Figure 3.4 we compare the default probability curves under the parameter set "P2" in the two different models. Again, the difference is still relevant, although less so than in the previous case with parameters "P1".

Having clarified that the difference between Black and Cox and Merton is relevant, we may continue with the Black and Cox model. Black and Cox devoted part of their work to further describing the capital structure of the firm, looking for the best way to express debt.

In fact, the zero coupon bond debt assumption is not always satisfying. Black and Cox alternatively derived a closed form expression for the debt seen as a consol bond, i.e. a bond paying a continuous coupon for all the life of the firm. The value of the equity can be derived by subtraction as the firm value minus the present value of the debt. As we are going to show later on, the model can be potentially interesting for hybrid equity/credit products with structural models, in the valuation of equity options and equity return swaps under counterparty risk.

We now turn to the model calibration of market data, and Credit Default Swaps in particular. In doing so we will highlight some important limits of the Black and Cox model, which will prompt us to introduce extensions of the same model, called AT1P and SBTV.

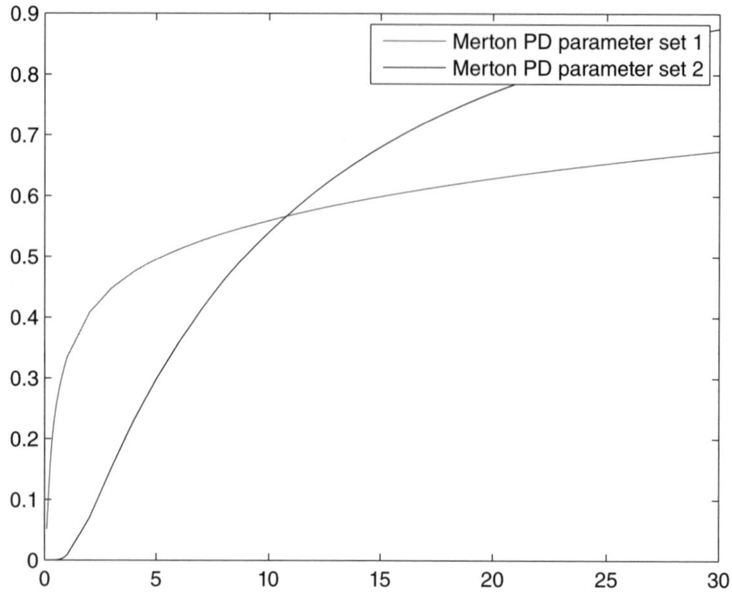

Figure 3.1 Merton model default probabilities in T with the two parameter sets

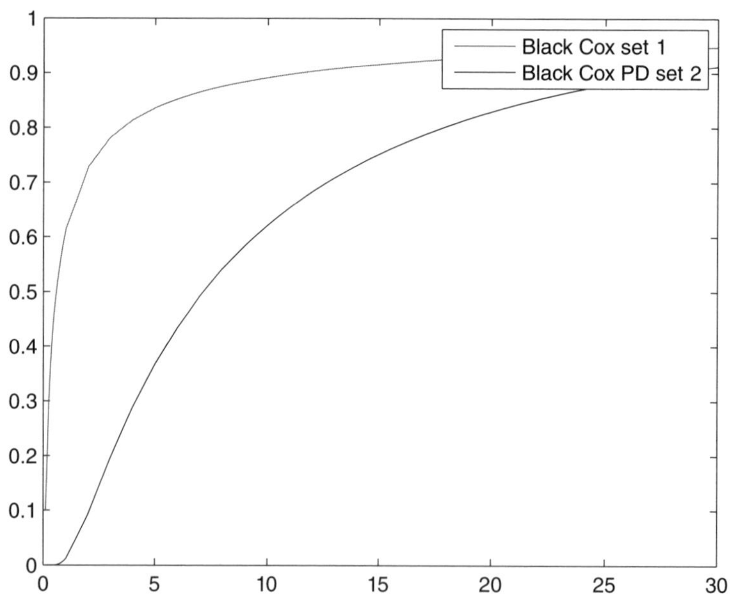

Figure 3.2 Black and Cox model default probabilities in T with the two parameter sets

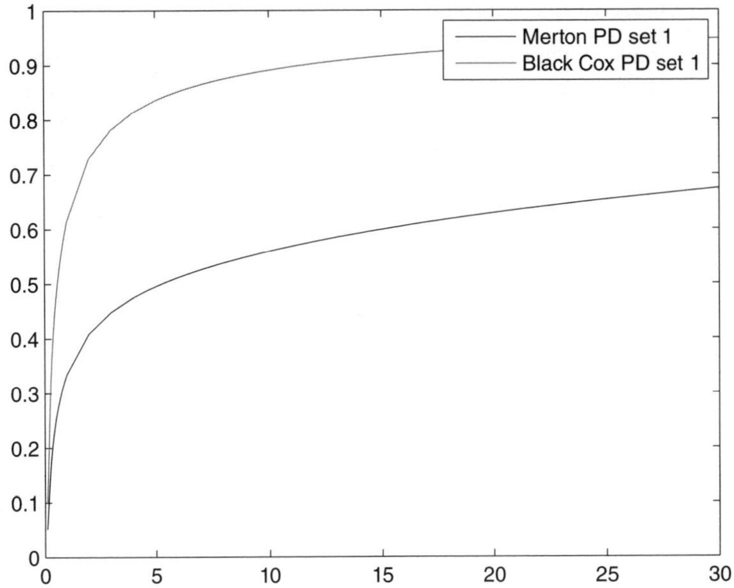

Figure 3.3 Merton vs Black and Cox default probabilities in T with the first parameter set

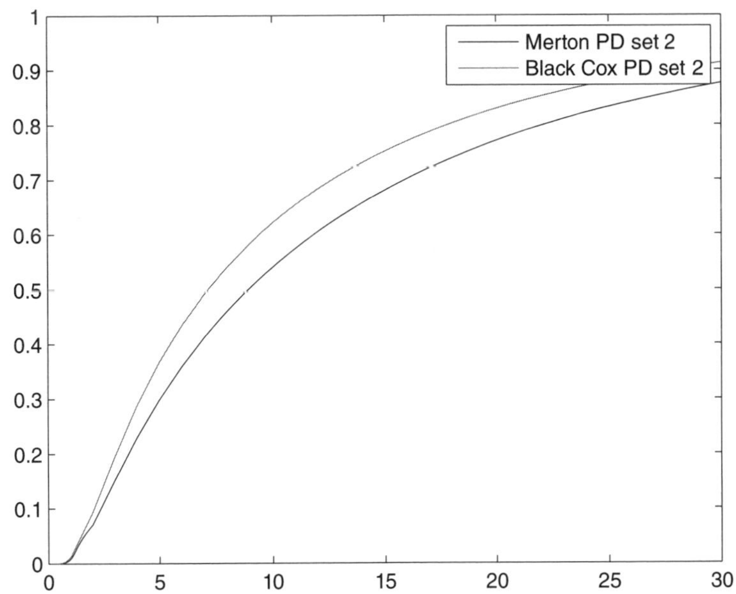

Figure 3.4 Merton vs Black and Cox default probabilities in T with the second parameter set

3.1.4 Credit Default Swaps and Default Probabilities

Since we are dealing with the default probabilities of firms, it is straightforward to think of financial instruments depending on these probabilities whose final aim it is to protect against the default event. One of the most representative protection instruments is the Credit Default Swap (CDS). CDSs are contracts that have been designed to offer protection against default in exchange for a periodic premium. Here we introduce CDS in their traditional "running" form. For a methodology for converting running CDS to upfront CDS, as from the so-called ISDA Big Bang, see [28].

Consider two companies "A" (the *protection buyer*) and "B" (the *protection seller*) who agree on the following. Consider a protection time window $(T_a, T_b]$, meaning that protection will be negotiated for defaults happening between times T_a and T_b. If a third reference company "C" (the *reference credit*) defaults at a time $\tau_C \in (T_a, T_b]$, "B" pays to "A" at time $\tau = \tau_C$ a certain "protection" cash amount LGD (Loss Given the Default of "C"), supposed to be deterministic in the present section. This cash amount is a *protection* for "A" in case "C" defaults. A typical stylized case occurs when "A" is strongly exposed to "C". For example, "A" has bought several corporate bonds issued from "C" and is waiting for the coupons and final notional payment from this bond: If "C" defaults before the corporate bonds maturities, "A" does not receive such payments. "A" then goes to "B" and buys some protection against this risk, asking "B" for a payment that roughly amounts to the bonds notional in case "C" defaults.

Typically LGD is equal to a notional amount, or to a notional amount minus a recovery. We denote the recovery rate by "REC".

In exchange for this protection, company "A" agrees to pay periodically to "B" a fixed "running" amount R (sometimes denoted also by S for "Spread"), called "CDS spread", at a set of times $\{T_{a+1}, \ldots, T_b\}$, $\alpha_i = T_i - T_{i-1}$, $T_0 = 0$. These payments constitute the "premium leg" of the CDS (as opposed to the LGD payment, which is termed the "protection leg" or "default leg"), and R is fixed in advance at time 0; the premium payments go on up to default time τ if this occurs before maturity T_b, or until maturity T_b if no default occurs.

Protection Seller B	→	protection $\mathrm{L_{GD}}$ at default τ_C if $T_a < \tau_C \le T_b$	→	Protection Buyer A
	←	rate R at $T_{a+1}, \ldots, T_b$ or until default τ_C	←	

Formally, we may write the RCDS ("R" stands for running) future cash flows discounted back at time t seen from "A" as

$$\Pi\mathrm{RCDS}_{a,b}(t) := -D(t,\tau)(\tau - T_{\beta(\tau)-1}) R \mathbf{1}_{\{T_a<\tau<T_b\}} - \sum_{i=a+1}^{b} D(t,T_i)\alpha_i R \mathbf{1}_{\{\tau \ge T_i\}} + \mathbf{1}_{\{T_a<\tau\le T_b\}} D(t,\tau)\,\mathrm{LGD} \quad (3.3)$$

where $t \in [T_{\beta(t)-1}, T_{\beta(t)})$, i.e. $T_{\beta(t)}$ is the first date among the T_i's that follows t, and where α_i is the year fraction between T_{i-1} and T_i.

This is a sum of discounted cash flows, and not yet a price. To obtain the price we need to take the expectation of this discounted payout. The pricing formula for this payoff depends on the assumptions on the interest rate dynamics and on the default time τ. Let $\mathcal{F}_t$ denote the basic filtration without default, typically representing the information flow of interest rates and possibly other default-free market quantities (and also intensities in the case of reduced form models), and $\mathcal{G}_t = \mathcal{F}_t \vee \sigma(\{\tau < u\}, u \le t)$ the extended filtration including explicit default information. In our current "structural model" framework with deterministic default barrier the two sigma-algebras coincide by construction, i.e. $\mathcal{G}_t = \mathcal{F}_t$, because here the default is completely driven by default-free market information. This is not the case with intensity models, where the default is governed by an external random variable and $\mathcal{F}_t$ is strictly included in $\mathcal{G}_t$, i.e. $\mathcal{F}_t \subset \mathcal{G}_t$.

We denote by $\mathrm{CDS}(t, [T_{a+1}, \ldots, T_b], T_a, T_b, R, \mathrm{LGD})$ or $\mathrm{CDS}_{a,b}(t, R, \mathrm{LGD})$ the price at time t of the above standard running CDS. At times some terms are omitted, such as, for example, the list of payment dates $[T_{a+1}, \ldots, T_b]$. In general, we can compute the CDS price according to risk-neutral valuation (for example, [18]):

$$\mathrm{CDS}_{a,b}(t, R, \mathrm{LGD}) = \mathbb{E}\{\Pi\mathrm{RCDS}_{a,b}(t)|\mathcal{G}_t\} = \mathbb{E}\{\Pi\mathrm{RCDS}_{a,b}(t)|\mathcal{F}_t\} =: \mathbb{E}_t\{\Pi\mathrm{RCDS}_{a,b}(t)\} \tag{3.4}$$

and we may apply this formula also to our structural model setup.

In the market, a CDS is quoted through its "fair" R, in that the rate R that is quoted by the market at time t satisfies $\mathrm{CDS}_{a,b}(t, R, \mathrm{LGD}) = 0$. Let us assume, for simplicity, deterministic interest rates; then we have

$$\begin{aligned}
\mathrm{CDS}_{a,b}(t, R, \mathrm{LGD}) &:= -R\,\mathbb{E}_t\{P(t,\tau)(\tau - T_{\beta(\tau)-1})\mathbf{1}_{\{T_a<\tau<T_b\}}\} \\
&\quad - \sum_{i=a+1}^{b} P(t,T_i)\alpha_i R\,\mathbb{E}_t\{\mathbf{1}_{\{\tau\geq T_i\}}\} + \mathrm{LGD}\,\mathbb{E}_t\{\mathbf{1}_{\{T_a<\tau\leq T_b\}}P(t,\tau)\} \\
&= -R\left[\sum_{i=a+1}^{b}\left(P(t,T_i)\alpha_i\,\mathbb{Q}\{\tau\geq T_i\} + \int_{T_{i-1}}^{T_i}(u - T_{i-1})P(t,u)d\mathbb{Q}(\tau\leq u)\right)\right] \\
&\quad + \mathrm{LGD}\int_{T_a}^{T_b} P(t,u)d\mathbb{Q}(\tau\leq u).
\end{aligned} \tag{3.5}$$

From our earlier definitions, straightforward computations lead to the price at initial time 0 of a CDS, under deterministic interest rates, as

$$\begin{aligned}
\mathrm{CDS}_{a,b}(0, R, \mathrm{LGD}) = -R\int_{T_a}^{T_b} P(0,t)(t - T_{\beta(t)-1})d\mathbb{Q}(\tau<t) \\
- R\sum_{i=a+1}^{b} P(0,T_i)\alpha_i\mathbb{Q}(\tau\geq T_i) + \mathrm{LGD}\int_{T_a}^{T_b} P(0,t)d\mathbb{Q}(\tau<t)
\end{aligned} \tag{3.6}$$

so that if one has a formula for the curve of survival probabilities $t \mapsto \mathbb{Q}(\tau \geq t)$, or default probabilities $t \mapsto \mathbb{Q}(\tau < t)$, as in the Black and Cox model, one also has a formula for CDS. It is clear that the fair rate R strongly depends on the default probabilities. The idea is to use, at initial time 0, quoted values of these fair Rs with $T_a = 0$ and with increasing maturities T_b to derive the default probabilities assessed by the market at time 0 and to calibrate the firm value model to such probabilities.

3.1.5 Black and Cox (B&C) Model Calibration to CDS: Problems

We now turn to the model calibration. How can the parameters in the model be obtained from market data? Despite the model positive features we have seen so far, the Black and Cox model is not easily calibrated to CDS data. The question is whether one can make the model consistent with liquid CDS data by inverting the model formula to correspond to the market quotes, so as to obtain the model parameters that reproduce the market CDS quotes. This would amount to a perfect CDS calibration.

What we are trying to do can be summarized as:

$$\left.\begin{array}{l} R_{0,1y}^{\text{MktCDS}} \\ R_{0,2y}^{\text{MktCDS}} \\ \vdots \\ R_{0,10y}^{\text{MktCDS}} \end{array}\right\} \longleftrightarrow \left\{\begin{array}{l} dV(t) = (r-k)V(t)dt + \sigma_V V(t)dW(t) \\ H(t) = \begin{cases} L & t = \bar{T} \\ Ke^{-\gamma(\bar{T}-t)} & t < \bar{T} \end{cases} \\ \text{modelparameters}: \ \sigma_V, \ L, \ K, \ \gamma \end{array}\right.$$

Typically one has from 5 to 10 CDS market quotes and only 4 parameters in the B&C model to calibrate them. Furthermore, even if there were only 4 CDS quotes, the 4 parameters

$$\sigma_V, \ L, \ K, \ \gamma$$

would not be flexible enough to produce survival probability patterns. A natural question is whether one can extend the model to make it more flexible and capable of exactly retrieving any number of quoted CDSs. The answer is in the affirmative and we present it below. Our strategy can be summarized as follows:

$$\left.\begin{array}{l} R_{0,1y}^{\text{MktCDS}} \\ R_{0,2y}^{\text{MktCDS}} \\ \vdots \\ R_{0,10y}^{\text{MktCDS}} \end{array}\right\} \longleftrightarrow \left\{\begin{array}{l} dV(t) = (r-k)V(t)dt + \boxed{\sigma_V(t)}\, V(t)dW(t) \\ H(t) = \ldots \\ \text{model parameters}: \ t \mapsto \sigma_V(t), \ \ t \mapsto H(t) \end{array}\right.$$

Now we would have infinite parameters (all the values of $\sigma_V(t)$, for example) to account for 10 CDS quotes.

The problem is: can we insert a time-dependent V dynamics and preserve barrier-like analytical formulae for survival probabilities $\mathbb{Q}(\tau > t)$ (and thus CDS and so forth?).

The difficulties in formulating such a model (like the following AT1P) are that, in general, barrier option problems are difficult, or impossible, in presence of time-dependent volatilities or general curved barriers.

However, there are works in the literature that show that it is possible to find analytical barrier option prices when the barrier has a particular curved shape, depending partly on the time-dependent volatility (see [142], [175]).

Our AT1P model builds on these results: indeed, our curved barrier $\widehat{H}(t)$ will depend on $\sigma_V(t)$.

Before turning to the AT1P model in detail, it is worth mentioning that for a summary of the literature on structural models, possibly with stochastic interest rates and default barriers, we refer, for example, to Chapter 3 of [18]. It is important to notice that structural models make some implicit but important assumptions. As we have just seen, they assume that the firm value follows a random process similar to the one used to describe generic stocks in equity markets, and that it is possible to observe this value at any time. This assumption is often debated, but in basic structural models it is usually maintained. Therefore, unlike the intensity models we are going to see later, here the default process can be completely monitored, based on default-free market information and comes as less of a surprise. Also, structural models in their basic formulations and with standard barriers (Merton, BC) have few parameters in their dynamics and cannot be calibrated exactly to structured data, such as CDS quotes along different maturities. Brigo and Tarenghi (2004, 2005) [61] [62] have extended the Black and Cox first passage model first by means of the time-varying volatility and curved barrier techniques, which we will explore now, and then further by random barrier and volatility scenarios. Brigo and Tarenghi's approach maintains the model tractability and illustrates the calibration to the term structure of CDS rates, showing also a calibration case study based on Parmalat and Vodafone data. Results are refined with different parameterizations in [49].

In the following text, we present the summary of such a model from [55], showing the history of the calibration to Lehman Brothers CDS.

3.1.6 The AT1P Model

Proposition 3.1.2 ***(Analytically-Tractable First Passage (AT1P) Model)*** *Assume the risk-neutral dynamics for the value of the firm V is characterized by a risk-free rate r_t, a payout ratio k_t and an instantaneous volatility σ_t, according to the equation:*

$$dV_t = V_t\,(r_t - k_t)\,dt + V_t\,\sigma_t\,dW_t \tag{3.7}$$

and assume a default barrier $H(t)$ (depending on the parameters H and B) of the form

$$H(t) = H\exp\left(\int_0^t \left(r_u - k_u - B\sigma_u^2\right)du\right)$$

and let τ be defined as the first time where $V(t)$ hits $H(t)$ from above, starting from $V_0 > H$,

$$\tau = \inf\{t \geq 0 : V_t \leq H(t)\}.$$

Then the survival probability is given analytically by

$$\mathbb{Q}(\tau > T) = \left[\Phi\left(\frac{\log\frac{V_0}{H} + \frac{2B-1}{2}\int_0^T \sigma_u^2 du}{\sqrt{\int_0^T \sigma_u^2 du}}\right) - \left(\frac{H}{V_0}\right)^{2B-1}\Phi\left(\frac{\log\frac{H}{V_0} + \frac{2B-1}{2}\int_0^T \sigma_u^2 du}{\sqrt{\int_0^T \sigma_u^2 du}}\right)\right] \tag{3.8}$$

For a proof, see [61] or [55].

A couple of remarks are in order. First of all, we notice that in the formula for the survival probability in Proposition 3.1.2, H and V never appear alone, but always in ratios like V/H; this homogeneity property allows us to rescale the initial value of the firm $V_0 = 1$, and express the barrier parameter H as a fraction of it. In this case we do not need to know the real value of the firm, or its real debt situation. Also, we can re-write the barrier as

$$H(t) = \frac{H}{V_0}\mathbb{E}_0\left[V_t\right]\exp\left(-B\int_0^t \sigma_u^2 du\right).$$

Therefore the behaviour of $H(t)$ has a simple economic interpretation. The backbone of the default barrier at t is a proportion, controlled by the parameter H, of the expected value of the company assets at t. H may depend on the level of liabilities, on safety covenants, and in general on the characteristics of the capital structure of the company. This is in line with observations in Giesecke (2004), pointing out that some discrepancies between the Black and Cox model and empirical regularities may be addressed with the realistic assumption that, like the firm value, the total debt grows at a positive rate, or that firms maintain some target leverage ratio as in Collin-Dufresne and Goldstein (2001) [80].

Also, depending on the value of the parameter B, it is possible that this backbone is modified by accounting for the volatility of the company's assets. For example, $B > 0$ corresponds to the interpretation that when volatility increases – which can be independent of credit quality – the barrier is slightly lowered to cut some more slack to the company before going bankrupt. In the following tests we simply assume $B = 0$, corresponding to a case where the barrier does not depend on volatility and the "distance to default" is simply modelled through the barrier parameter H.

3.1.7 A Case Study with AT1P: Lehman Brothers Default History

The above AT1P Formula 3.8 can be used to fit model parameters to market data. If we aim at creating a one-to-one correspondence between volatility parameters and CDS quotes, we can exogenously choose the value H and B, leaving all the unknown information in the calibration of the volatility. If we do so, we find exactly one volatility parameter for each CDS maturity, including the first one. In our tests we have followed this approach, where H has been chosen externally before calibration. In [61], [49] and [55] we also suggest a methodology that takes equity volatilities into account in the calibration.

In general, the preceding CDS calibration procedures are justified by the fact that in the end we are not interested in estimating the real process of the firm value underlying the contract, but only in reproducing risk-neutral default probabilities with a model that makes economic sense. While it is important that the underlying processes have an economic interpretation, we are not interested in sharply estimating them or the capital structure of the firm, but rather we appreciate the structural model interpretation as a tool for assessing the realism of calibration outputs, and as an instrument to check economic consequences and possible diagnostics.

In this section we analyze how the AT1P model works in practice, in particular we consider the case of Lehman Brothers, one of the major world banks that incurred a deep crisis, ending with the bank's default. For simplicity our tests have been performed using the approximated postponed payoff for CDS (see [55] or Brigo and Mercurio (2006) [48] for the details). An analysis of the same model on the Parmalat crisis, terminating in default in 2003, is available in [61] and [49].

The history of Lehman's default can be summarized as follows:

- **23 August 2007**: Lehman announces that it is going to shut one of its home lending units (*BNC Mortgage*) and lay off 1,200 employees. The bank says it would take a \$52 million charge to third-quarter earnings.
- **18 March 2008**: Lehman announces better than expected first-quarter results (but profits have more than halved).
- **9 June 2008**: Lehman confirms the booking of a \$2.8 billion loss and announces plans to raise \$6 billion in fresh capital by selling stock. Lehman shares lose more than 9% in afternoon trade.
- **12 June 2008**: Lehman shakes up its management; its chief operating officer and president, and its chief financial officer are removed from their posts.
- **28 August 2008**: Lehman prepares to lay off 1,500 people. The Lehman executives have been knocking on doors all over the world seeking a capital infusion.
- **9 September 2008**: Lehman shares fall 45%.
- **14 September 2008**: Lehman files for bankruptcy protection and hurtles toward liquidation after it failed to find a buyer.

Table 3.1 Results of calibration for 10 July 2007. The σ_i's are AT1P volatilities that are constant in $(T_{i-1}, T_i]$. The $\lambda_i = \gamma(t)$ are deterministic intensities that are constant in $(T_{i-1}, T_i]$, see Section 3.3.1

T_i	R_i (bps)	λ_i	Surv (Int)	σ_i	Surv (AT1P)
10 Jul 2007			100.0%		100.0%
1y	16	0.267%	99.7%	29.2%	99.7%
3y	29	0.601%	98.5%	14.0%	98.5%
5y	45	1.217%	96.2%	14.5%	96.1%
7y	50	1.096%	94.1%	12.0%	94.1%
10y	58	1.407%	90.2%	12.7%	90.2%

Here we show how the AT1P model calibration behaves when the credit quality of the considered company deteriorates in time (perceived as a widening of CDS spreads[1]). We are going to analyze three different situations: i) a case of relatively stable situation, before the beginning of the crisis, ii) a case in the midst of the crisis and iii) and a case just before the default.

During our calibration we fix REC $= 40\%$, $B = 0$ and $H = 0.4$; this last choice is a completely arbitrary choice and has been suggested by the analogy with the CDS recovery rate. Also, as a comparison, we report the results of the calibration obtained using an intensity model. In simple intensity models, the survival probability can be computed as $\mathbb{Q}(\tau > t) = \exp(-\int_0^t \lambda(u)du)$, where λ is the *intensity function* or *hazard rate* (assumed here to be deterministic). We choose a piecewise constant shape for $\lambda(t)$ and calibrate it to CDS quotes through a boostrapping algorithm that we will clarify in detail later on.

3.1.7.1 Lehman Brothers CDS Calibration: 10 July 2007

On the left of Table 3.1 are the values of the quoted CDS spreads on 10 July 2007, before the beginning of the crisis. We see that the spreads are very low, indicating a stable situation for Lehman. In the middle of Table 3.1 are the results of the calibration obtained using an intensity model, while on the to the right of the Table are the results of the calibration obtained using the AT1P model.

It is important to stress the fact that the AT1P model is flexible enough to achieve exact calibration.

3.1.7.2 Lehman Brothers CDS Calibration: 12 June 2008

In Table 3.2 we report the results of the calibration on 12 June 2008, in the middle of the crisis. We see that the CDS spreads R_i have increased with respect to the previous case, but are not very high, indicating that the market is aware of the Lehman's difficulties but thinks that it can come out of the crisis. The survival probability resulting from calibration is lower than in the previous case; since the barrier parameter H has not changed, this translates into higher volatilities.

[1] It is market practice for CDS of names with deteriorating credit quality to quote an upfront premium rather than a running spread. After the so-called ISDA Big Bang, it is likely that several names will quote an upfront on top of a fixed pre-specified running spread, even when the credit quality has not deteriorated. In our tests we deal directly with the equivalent running spread alone, which can be obtained by up-front premia by means of standard techniques, for example, [28].

Table 3.2 Results of calibration for June 12th, 2008. The σ_i's are AT1P volatilities that are constant in $(T_{i-1}, T_i]$. The $\lambda_i = \gamma(t)$ are deterministic intensities that are constant in $(T_{i-1}, T_i]$, see Section 3.3.1 below

T_i	R_i (bps)	λ_i	Surv (Int)	σ_i	Surv (AT1P)
12 Jun 2008			100.0%		100.0%
1y	397	6.563%	93.6%	45.0%	93.5%
3y	315	4.440%	85.7%	21.9%	85.6%
5y	277	3.411%	80.0%	18.6%	79.9%
7y	258	3.207%	75.1%	18.1%	75.0%
10y	240	2.907%	68.8%	17.5%	68.7%

3.1.7.3 *Lehman Brothers CDS Calibration: 12 September 2008*

In Table 3.3 we report the results of the calibration on 12 September 2008, just before Lehman's default. We see that the spreads are now very high, corresponding to lower survival probability and higher volatilities than before.

3.1.8 Comments

We have seen that the AT1P model can calibrate exactly CDS market quotes, and the survival probabilities obtained are in accordance with those obtained using an intensity model. This confirms the well-known fact that when interest rates are assumed independent of default, survival probabilities can be implied from CDS in a model-independent way (Formula 3.6). Anyway, after a deeper analysis of the results, we find:

- *Scarce relevance of the barrier in calibration*: the barrier parameter H has been fixed before calibration and everything is left to the volatility calibration;
- *High discrepancy between first volatility bucket and the following values.*

The problem is that when the default boundary is deterministic, diffusion models tend to calibrate a relevant probability of default by one year (the shortest horizon credit spread) only by supposing particularly high one-year volatility. This is because, initially, with low volatilities the trajectories of a model like (3.7) do not widen fast enough to hit a deterministic

Table 3.3 Results of calibration for 12 September 2008. The σ_i's are AT1P volatilities that are constant in $(T_{i-1}, T_i]$. The $\lambda_i = \gamma(t)$ are deterministic intensities that are constant in $(T_{i-1}, T_i]$, see Section 3.3.1

T_i	R_i (bps)	λ_i	Surv (Int)	σ_i	Surv (AT1P)
12 Sep 2008			100.0%		100.0%
1y	1437	23.260%	79.2%	62.2%	78.4%
3y	902	9.248%	65.9%	30.8%	65.5%
5y	710	5.245%	59.3%	24.3%	59.1%
7y	636	5.947%	52.7%	26.9%	52.5%
10y	588	6.422%	43.4%	29.5%	43.4%

barrier frequently enough to generate relevant default probabilities. One has to choose a high initial volatility to achieve this. The problem is also related to the basic assumption that the default threshold is a deterministic, known function of time, based on reliable accounting data. This very strong assumption is usually not true: balance-sheet information is not certain, possibly because the company is hiding information, or because a real valuation of the firm's assets is not easy (for example, in case of derivative instruments). Public investors may have incomplete information about the true value of the firm's assets or its related liability-dependent condition that would trigger default.

In the AT1P model, H is the ratio between the initial level of the default barrier and the initial value of the company assets. To take market uncertainty into account in a realistic, albeit simple manner, H can be replaced by a random variable assuming different values in different scenarios. This is the main idea that leads us to the SBTV model.

3.1.9 SBTV Model

How can one consider explicitly market uncertainty on the firm's situation when the balance sheet information is not always reliable or easy to value? This is the case if the company is hiding information, or in the case of illiquidity causing the valuation of the firm's assets and liabilities to be uncertain. In the first case, following, for example, [116] who refers to such scandals as Enron, Tyco and WorldCom, a crucial aspect in market uncertainty is that public investors have only incomplete information about the true value of the firm's assets or the related liability-dependent firm condition that would trigger default. This motivated us to introduce randomness in H when we dealt with Parmalat in [62] and [49]. In particular, randomness in the initial level H of the barrier was used in [49] to represent the uncertainty of market operators on the real financial situation of Parmalat, due to lack of transparency and actual fraud in Parmalat's accounting. Here it can represent equally well the uncertainty of market operators on the real financial situation of Lehman. But in this case the uncertainty is related to an objective difficulty in assigning a fair value to a large part of the assets and liabilities of Lehman (illiquid mortgage-related portfolio credit derivatives) and to the intrinsic complexity of the links between the bank and the related SIVs and conduits.

Therefore, in order to take market uncertainty into account in a realistic, albeit simple manner, in the following H is replaced by a random variable assuming different values in different scenarios, each scenario with a different probability.

As in [49], we judge scenarios on the barrier to be an efficient representation of the uncertainty on the firm's balance sheet, while deterministic time-varying volatility may be required for precise and efficient calibration of CDS quotes. The resulting model is called Scenario Barrier Time-Varying Volatility AT1P Model (SBTV). In this way we can achieve exact calibration to all market quotes. Let the assets value V risk-neutral dynamics be given by (3.7). The default time τ is again the first time where V hits the barrier from above, but now we have a scenario barrier

$$H^I(t) = H^I \exp\left(\int_0^t (r_u - k_u - B\sigma_u^2)du\right) = \frac{H^I}{V_0}\mathbb{E}[V_t] \exp\left(-B\int_0^t \sigma_u^2 du\right)$$

where H^I assumes scenarios $H^1, H^2, \ldots, H^N$ with $\mathbb{Q}$ probabilities $p^1, p^2, \ldots, p^N$. All probabilities are in $[0, 1]$ and add up to one, and H^I is independent of W. Thus now the ratio H^I/V_0 depends on the scenario I. If we are to price a default-sensitive discounted payoff Π, by iterated expectation we have

$$\mathbb{E}[\Pi] = \mathbb{E}\left[\mathbb{E}\left[\Pi|H^I\right]\right] = \sum_{i=1}^{N} p^i\, \mathbb{E}\left[\Pi|H^I = H^i\right]$$

so that the price of a security is a weighted average of the security prices in the different scenarios, with weights equal to the probabilities of the different scenarios. For CDS, the price with the SBTV model is

$$\text{SBTVCDS}_{a,b} = \sum_{i=1}^{N} p^i \cdot \text{AT1PCDS}_{a,b}(H^i) \tag{3.9}$$

where $AT1PCDS_{a,b}(H^i)$ is the CDS price computed according to the AT1P survival probability formula 3.8 when $H = H^i$. Hence, the SBTV model acts like a mixture of AT1P scenarios.

3.1.10 A Case Study with SBTV: Lehman Brothers Default History

Here we show how the SBTV model calibration behaves with respect to the AT1P model. We consider the Lehman Brothers example as before. We limit our analysis to only two barrier scenarios (H^1 with probability p^1 and H^2 with probability $p^2 = 1 - p^1$), since, according to our experience, further scenarios do not increase the calibration power.

In the calibration, we set the lower barrier parameter $H^1 = 0.4$. If we consider M CDS quotes, we have $M + 2$ unknown parameters: H^2, p^1 ($p^2 = 1 - p^1$) and all the volatilities σ_j corresponding to the M buckets. It is clear that a direct fit like in the AT1P case (where we have one unknown volatility σ_j for each CDS quote R_j) is not possible. Exact calibration could be achieved using a two-step approach:

1. We limit our attention to the first three CDS quotes, and set $\sigma_1 = \sigma_2 = \sigma_3 = \bar{\sigma}$. Now we have three quotes for three unknowns (H^2, p^1 and $\bar{\sigma}$) and can run a best-fit on these parameters (not exact calibration, since the model would not be flexible enough to attain it).
2. At this point we go back to consider all the M CDS quotes and, using H^2 and the p's just obtained, we can run a second calibration on the M volatilities σ_j to get an exact fit. Notice that if the first calibration is good enough, then the refinement to $\sigma_{1,2,3}$ due to second calibration is negligible.

3.1.10.1 Lehman Brothers CDS Calibration: 10 July 2007

In Table 3.4 we report the values of the calibrated barrier parameters with their corresponding probabilities, while in Table 3.5 we show the results of the calibration.

Table 3.4 Scenario barriers and probabilities

Scenario	H	p
1	0.4000	96.2%
2	0.7313	3.8%

Table 3.5 Results of calibration for 10 July 2007

T_j	R_j (bps)	σ_j	Surv (SBTV)	σ_j	Surv (AT1P)
10 Jul 2007			100.0%		100.0%
1y	16	16.6%	99.7%	29.2%	99.7%
3y	29	16.6%	98.5%	14.0%	98.5%
5y	45	16.6%	96.1%	14.5%	96.1%
7y	50	12.6%	94.1%	12.0%	94.1%
10y	58	12.9%	90.2%	12.7%	90.2%

Looking at the results in Tables 3.4 and 3.5 we see that, in the case of the quite stable situation for Lehman, we have a lower barrier scenario (better credit quality) with very high probability, and a higher barrier scenario (lower credit quality) with low probability. Also, when comparing the results with the AT1P calibration, we see that now the calibrated volatility is nearly constant on all maturity buckets, which is a desirable feature for the firm value dynamics.

3.1.10.2 Lehman Brothers CDS Calibration: 12 June 2008

Looking at the results in Tables 3.6 and 3.7 we see that the (worse credit quality) barrier parameter H^2 has both a higher value (higher proximity to default) and a much higher probability with respect to the calibration case of 10 July 2007. This is due to the higher CDS spread values. Moreover, by noticing that the fitted volatility has not increased too much, we can argue that the worsened credit quality can be reflected in to a higher probability of being in the scenario with higher default barrier (worsened credit quality).

3.1.10.3 Lehman Brothers CDS Calibration: 12 September 2008

Here we have a large increase in CDS spreads, which can be explained by a very large probability of 50% for the higher barrier scenario and a higher value for the scenario itself,

Table 3.6 Scenario barriers and probabilities

Scenario	H	p
1	0.4000	74.6%
2	0.7971	25.4%

Table 3.7 Results of calibration for 12 June 2008

T_j	R_j (bps)	σ_j	Surv (SBTV)	σ_j	Surv (AT1P)
12 Jun 2008			100.0%		100.0%
1y	397	18.7%	93.6%	45.0%	93.5%
3y	315	18.7%	85.7%	21.9%	85.6%
5y	277	18.7%	80.1%	18.6%	79.9%
7y	258	17.4%	75.1%	18.1%	75.0%
10y	240	16.4%	68.8%	17.5%	68.7%

Table 3.8 Scenario barriers and probabilities

Scenario	H	p
1	0.4000	50.0%
2	0.8427	50.0%

which moves to 0.84 from the preceding cases of 0.79 and 0.73. Tables 3.8 and 3.9 show the results of calibration. We see that there are no greater differences in volatilities than before, and the larger default probability can be explained by a higher level of proximity to default and high probability of being in that proximity (high H scenario). In this particular case we have equal probability of being in either the risky or the stable scenario.

3.1.11 Comments

We have seen that the calibration performed with the SBTV model is comparable, in terms of survival probabilities, with the calibration obtained using the AT1P model, and the calibration is exact in both cases. However, we have seen that the SBTV model returns a more stable volatility term structure, and also has a more robust economic interpretation.

One of the main drawbacks with structural models is that usually they are not able to explain short-term credit spreads; in fact, usually the diffusion part of the GBM is not enough to explain a non-null default probability in very small time intervals. The introduction of default barrier scenarios could be a way to overcome this problem; in fact, a very high scenario barrier could be enough to account for short term default probabilities.

At this point, a natural extension of the family of structural models we have presented here is the valuation of hybrid equity/credit products. In this sense we will price counterparty risk in Equity Return Swaps, and then in Equity Options, in later chapters.

3.2 FIRM VALUE MODELS: HINTS AT THE MULTINAME PICTURE

With firm value models the extension to more names is straightforward, although calculations, in case of the Black and Cox model, can become quite complicated.

Suppose we have names $1, 2, \ldots, n$, each with a firm value V_i.

Table 3.9 Results of calibration for 12 September 2008

T_j	R_j (bps)	σ_j	Surv (SBTV)	σ_j	Surv (AT1P)
12 Sep 2008			100.0%		100.0%
1y	1437	19.6%	79.3%	62.2%	78.4%
3y	902	19.6%	66.2%	30.8%	65.5%
5y	710	19.6%	59.6%	24.3%	59.1%
7y	636	21.8%	52.9%	26.9%	52.5%
10y	588	23.7%	43.6%	29.5%	43.4%

The simplest choice to model all defaults is to consider Merton's model for all names. This way each named firm value V_i follows a geometric Brownian motion

$$dV_i(t) = (r - k_i)V_i(t)dt + \sigma_i V_i(t)dW_i(t), \quad V_i(0)$$

(assuming for simplicity all names to be under the same currency), driven by a standard Brownian motion W_i. Each name has its own debt face value L_i to be paid at a common final maturity T. The key issue is modelling the statistical dependence or "correlation" among the different defaults. This can be done simply by introducing a instantaneous correlation ρ on the firm values

$$d\langle W_i, W_j\rangle_t = dW_i\, dW_j = \rho_{i,j}dt.$$

A related approach is at the basis of the Credit Metrics approach [121].

Estimating ρ can be a difficult task, since the firm value is not directly observable. However, since equity is an option on firm value and is observable, in principle we could link the firm value correlations to the equity correlations in this model, and estimate the firm value correlations from equity ones. This approach needs to be considered very carefully: the equity market is providing information on the credit market mostly when credit quality is poor, i.e. when equity is near zero. Otherwise the two markets are not necessarily strongly correlated.

To improve on Merton's model and allow for early default, we could simply model the different firm values as in Black and Cox or AT1P, and correlate the firm values as above. However, when trying to price a multi-name payoff (such as a CDO or a default basket, see [60] or [33] for the mathematics of such products) with such a model we woud have to manage multiple barrier events. In general, multiple barrier events are not analytically tractable and therefore the use of this model in a multiname context would have to rely on numerical techniques. In dimensions larger than 3 it is difficult to use Partial Differential Equation (PDE) methods, so that for a large number of names simulation would be necessary, which is expensive when combined with barrier monitoring. This is one of the reasons why multiname first passage firm value models are rarely used in the industry for CDO's or default baskets. To compute the CVA and DVA in a deal between two parties where the underlying is not a credit product, one would have to model only two defaults so that this task becomes more feasible.

For more discussion on multi-name credit modelling see Section 3.4.

3.3 REDUCED FORM (INTENSITY) MODELS

Reduced form models (also called *intensity models* when a suitable context is present) describe default through an exogenous jump process; more precisely, the default time τ is the first jump time of a Poisson process, with deterministic or stochastic (Cox process) intensity. Default is not triggered by basic market observables but has an exogenous component, independent of all the default-free market information. Monitoring the default-free market with its interest rates, exchange rates and so forth, does not give complete information on the default process, and there is no economic rationale behind default, contrary to structural models where default arrives because the firm value hits a default barrier associated with the debt level. This reduced form family of models is particularly suited to model credit spreads and in its basic formulation is easy to calibrate to corporate bond data or Credit Default Swap (CDS). See also references at the beginning of Chapter 8 in [18] for a summary of the literature on intensity models. We cite here [103] and [139] as general references, and refer to [35], [45] and [46] as references for explicit CDS calibration and CDS option formulas with tractable stochastic intensity models. The reference [46] introduces jumps into the credit spread intensity model while keeping the model tractable for survival probabilities, CDS and CDS options prices.

While introducing intensity models, one of the crucial points we would like to explain is why these models are well suited for credit spreads.

In basic reduced form or intensity models, the default time τ is the first jump of a Poisson process. Recall that the first jump time of a (time-inhomogeneous) Poisson process obeys roughly the following:

Having not defaulted (jumped) before t, the (risk-neutral) probability of defaulting (jumping) in the next dt instants is

$$\mathbb{Q}(\tau \in [t, t+dt) | \tau > t, \text{market info up to } t) = \lambda(t)dt$$

where the "probability" dt factor λ is assumed here, for simplicity, to be strictly positive and is generally called *intensity* or *hazard rate*.

Define also the further quantity

$$\Lambda(t) := \int_0^t \lambda(u)du,$$

i.e. the *cumulated intensity, cumulated hazard rate,* or also *Hazard function*. Now, assume for simplicity λ to be deterministic; since it is positive, its integral Λ will be strictly increasing. One of the key facts about Poisson processes is that transformation of the jump time τ according to its own cumulated intensity Λ leads to an exponential random variable. We have

$$\Lambda(\tau) =: \xi \sim \text{standard exponential random variable with mean 1}$$

and ξ is independent of all other variables (interest rates, equities, intensities themselves in case these are stochastic, etc.). By inverting this last equation we see that

$$\tau = \Lambda^{-1}(\xi).$$

But if we recall for a second the cumulative distribution function of a standard exponential random variable, leading to $\mathbb{Q}(\xi \geq x) = e^{-x}$, we can show immediately that

$$\mathbb{Q}\{\tau > t\} = \mathbb{Q}\{\Lambda(\tau) > \Lambda(t)\} = \mathbb{Q}\{\xi > \Lambda(t)\} = e^{-\int_0^t \lambda(u)du}.$$

The last term is structurally identical to a discount factor under continuous compounding.

3.3.1 CDS Calibration and Intensity Models

Now is a good point to go a little more into detail on how the market quotes running and upfront CDS prices. First we have to notice that typically the T's are quarterly spaced. Let us begin with running CDSs. Usually at the inception time or at a coupon time of the CDS contract, say time $t = 0$, provided default has not yet occurred, the market sets R to a value $R_{a,b}^{\text{MID}}(0)$ that makes the CDS fair at time 0, i.e. such that $\text{CDS}_{a,b}(0, R_{a,b}^{\text{MID}}(0), \text{LGD}) = 0$. In fact, in the market running CDS's can be quoted at a time 0 through a bid and an ask value for this "fair" $R^{\text{MID}}_{a,b}(0)$, for CDS's with $T_a = 0$ and with T_b spanning a set of canonical final maturities, $T_b = 1y$ up to $T_b = 10y$.

We now present a model independent valuation formula for CDS that assumes independence between interest rates and the default time.

Assume the stochastic discount factors $D(s,t)$ to be independent of the default time τ for all possible $0 < s < t$.

The premium leg of the CDS at time 0 for a premium rate R can be valued as follows:

$$\begin{aligned}
\text{PremiumLeg}_{a,b}(0;R) &= \mathbb{E}[D(0,\tau)(\tau - T_{\beta(\tau)-1})R\mathbf{1}_{\{T_a<\tau<T_b\}}] + \sum_{i=a+1}^{b} \mathbb{E}[D(0,T_i)\alpha_i R\mathbf{1}_{\{\tau\ge T_i\}}] \\
&= \mathbb{E}\left[\int_{t=0}^{\infty} D(0,t)(t - T_{\beta(t)-1})R\mathbf{1}_{\{T_a<t<T_b\}}\text{“}\mathbf{1}\text{”}_{\{\tau\in[t,t+dt]''\}}\right] + \sum_{i=a+1}^{b} \mathbb{E}[D(0,T_i)]\alpha_i R\,\mathbb{E}[\mathbf{1}_{\{\tau\ge T_i\}}] \\
&= \int_{t=T_a}^{T_b} \mathbb{E}[D(0,t)(t - T_{\beta(t)-1})R\,\text{“}\mathbf{1}\text{”}_{\{\tau\in[t,t+dt)\}}] + \sum_{i=a+1}^{b} P(0,T_i)\alpha_i R\,\mathbb{Q}(\tau\ge T_i) \\
&= \int_{t=T_a}^{T_b} \mathbb{E}[D(0,t)](t - T_{\beta(t)-1})R\,\mathbb{E}[\mathbf{1}_{\{\tau\in[t,t+dt)\}}] + \sum_{i=a+1}^{b} P(0,T_i)\alpha_i R\,\mathbb{Q}(\tau\ge T_i) \\
&= R\int_{t=T_a}^{T_b} P(0,t)(t - T_{\beta(t)-1})\mathbb{Q}(\tau\in[t,t+dt)) + R\sum_{i=a+1}^{b} P(0,T_i)\alpha_i\mathbb{Q}(\tau\ge T_i),
\end{aligned}$$

where we have first distributed the default on $[0,T_b]$ as a sum of defaults in all disjoint small intervals $[t,t+dt)$ spanning $[0,T_b]$, and secondly we used independence in factoring the above expectations. Notice that the terms

$$\text{“}\mathbf{1}\text{”}_{\{\tau\in[t,t+dt)\}}$$

are an informal notation for the Dirac delta function

$$\delta(t-\tau)\,dt$$

that we will use now. We have thus, by rearranging terms and introducing a "unit-premium" premium leg:

$$\begin{aligned}
\text{PremiumLeg}_{a,b}(R;P(0,\cdot),\mathbb{Q}(\tau>\cdot)) &= R\ \text{PremiumLeg1}_{a,b}(P(0,\cdot),\mathbb{Q}(\tau>\cdot)), \\
\text{PremiumLeg1}_{a,b}(P(0,\cdot),\mathbb{Q}(\tau>\cdot)) &:= -\int_{T_a}^{T_b} P(0,t)(t - T_{\beta(t)-1})d_t\boxed{\mathbb{Q}(\tau\ge t)} \\
&\quad + \sum_{i=a+1}^{b} P(0,T_i)\alpha_i\boxed{\mathbb{Q}(\tau\ge T_i)}
\end{aligned} \tag{3.10}$$

This formula is indeed model independent given the initial zero coupon curve (bonds) at time 0 observed in the market (i.e. $P(0,\cdot)$) and given the survival probabilities $\mathbb{Q}(\tau\ge\cdot)$ at time 0 (terms in the boxes).

A similar formula holds for the protection leg, again under independence between default τ and interest rates.

$$
\begin{aligned}
\text{ProtecLeg}_{a,b}(\text{LGD}) &= \mathbb{E}[\mathbf{1}_{\{T_a<\tau\le T_b\}} D(0,\tau)\,\text{LGD}] \\
&= \text{LGD}\,\mathbb{E}\left[\int_{t=0}^{\infty} \mathbf{1}_{\{T_a<t\le T_b\}} D(0,t)\delta(t-\tau)\,dt\right] \\
&= \text{LGD}\left[\int_{t=T_a}^{T_b} \mathbb{E}[D(0,t)\delta(t-\tau)\,dt]\right] \\
&= \text{LGD}\int_{t=T_a}^{T_b} \mathbb{E}[D(0,t)]\mathbb{E}[\delta(t-\tau)]dt \\
&= \text{LGD}\int_{t=T_a}^{T_b} P(0,t)\mathbb{Q}(\tau\in[t,t+dt))
\end{aligned}
$$

so that we have, by introducing a "unit notional" protection leg:

$$
\text{ProtecLeg}_{a,b}(\text{LGD}; P(0,\cdot), \mathbb{Q}(\tau>\cdot)) = \text{LGD ProtecLeg1}_{a,b}(P(0,\cdot),\mathbb{Q}(\tau>\cdot)),
$$

$$
\text{ProtecLeg1}_{a,b}(P(0,\cdot),\mathbb{Q}(\tau>\cdot)) := -\int_{T_a}^{T_b} P(0,t)\,d_t\boxed{\mathbb{Q}(\tau\ge t)} \tag{3.11}
$$

We have implicitly used a number of theorems in deriving this formula, including Fubini's theorem to switch the time integral with the expectation integral. This last formula too is model independent given the initial zero coupon curve (bonds $t\mapsto P(0,t)$) at time 0 observed in the market, and given the survival probabilities at time 0 (terms in the box).

The integrals in the survival probabilities given in the above formulas can be valued as Stieltjes integrals in the survival probabilities themselves, and can easily be approximated numerically by summations through Riemann-Stieltjes sums, considering a low enough discretization time step.

Now recall that the market quotes, at time 0, the fair $R = R_{0,b}^{\text{mktMID}}(0)$ (actually bid and ask quotes are available for this fair R) equating the two legs for a set of CDS with initial protection time $T_a = 0$ and final protection time $T_b \in \{1y, 2y, 3y, 4y, 5y, 6y.7y, 8y, 9y, 10y\}$, although often only a subset of the maturities $\{1y, 3y, 5y, 7y, 10y\}$ is available. Solve then

$$
\text{ProtecLeg}_{0,b}(\text{LGD}; P(0,\cdot), \mathbb{Q}(\tau>\cdot))) = \text{PremiumLeg}_{0,b}(0, R_{0,b}^{\text{mktMID}}(0); P(0,\cdot), \mathbb{Q}(\tau>\cdot))
$$

in portions of $\mathbb{Q}(\tau>\cdot)$ starting from $T_b = 1y$, finding the market implied survival $\{\mathbb{Q}(\tau\ge t), t\le 1y\}$; plugging this into the $T_b = 2y$ CDS legs formulas, and then solving the same equation with $T_b = 2y$, we find the market implied survival $\{\mathbb{Q}(\tau\ge t), t\in(1y,2y]\}$, and so on up to $T_b = 10y$.

This is a way to strip survival probabilities from CDS quotes in a model independent way. No need to assume an intensity or a structural model for default here.

The market in doing the above mentioned stripping typically resorts to hazard functions, assuming existence of hazard functions associated with the default time. We now assume existence of a deterministic intensity, as in deterministic intensity models above,

$$
\lambda_t = \gamma(t), \quad \Gamma(t) = \int_0^t \gamma(s)ds
$$

and briefly illustrate the notion of implied deterministic cumulated intensity (hazard function) Γ, satisfying

$$\mathbb{Q}\{\tau \geq t\} = \exp(-\Gamma(t)), \quad \mathbb{Q}\{s < \tau \leq t\} = \exp(-\Gamma(s)) - \exp(-\Gamma(t)).$$

As usual, the interpretation of this function $\gamma(t)dt$ is: probability of defaulting in $[t, t + dt)$ having not defaulted before t:

$$\mathbb{Q}(\tau \in [t, t + dt)|\tau > t, \mathcal{F}_t) = \gamma(t)dt.$$

In this case one can derive a formula for CDS prices based on integrals Γ of γ, and on the initial interest rate curve, resulting from the above expectation:

$$\mathrm{CDS}_{a,b}(t, R, \mathrm{LGD}; \Gamma(\cdot)) = \mathbf{1}_{\{\tau > t\}} \left[-R \int_{T_a}^{T_b} P(t, u)(u - T_{\beta(u)-1}) d_u(e^{-(\Gamma(u)-\Gamma(t))}) \right. \tag{3.12}$$
$$\left. + \sum_{i=a+1}^{b} P(t, T_i) R \alpha_i e^{\Gamma(t)-\Gamma(T_i)} + \mathrm{LGD} \int_{T_a}^{T_b} P(t, u) d_u(e^{-(\Gamma(u)-\Gamma(t))}) \right].$$

By equating to zero the above expression in γ for $t = 0$, $T_a = 0$, after plugging in the relevant market quotes for R, one can extract the γ's corresponding to CDS market quotes for increasing maturities T_b and obtain market implied γ^{mkt} and Γ^{mkt}'s.

More in detail, one finds the Γ^{mkt}'s solving

$$\mathrm{CDS}_{0,b}(0, R_{0,b}^{\mathrm{mktMID}}(0), \mathrm{LGD}; \Gamma^{\mathrm{mkt}}([0, T_b])) = 0, \quad T_b = 1y, 2y, 3y, 5y, 7y, 10y.$$

If we are given $R_{0,b}^{\mathrm{mktMID}}(0)$ for different maturities T_b, we can assume a *piecewise constant* (or at times linear or splines) γ, and invert prices in an iterative way as T_b increases, deriving each time the new part of γ that is consistent with the R for the new increased maturity.

It is important to point out that usually the actual model one assumes for τ is more complex and may involve stochastic intensity, as we will see shortly. Even so, the γ^{mkt}'s are retained as a mere quoting mechanism for CDS rate market quotes, and may be taken as inputs in the calibration of more complex models, as we will do in particular with the stochastic intensity model below.

Upfront CDS are simply quoted through the present value of the protection leg. Under deterministic hazard rates γ, we have

$$\mathrm{UCDS}(t, T_a, T_b, R, \mathrm{L_{GD}}; \Gamma(\cdot)) = -\mathbf{1}_{\{\tau > t\}} \mathrm{LGD} \int_{T_a}^{T_b} P(t, u) d_u(e^{-(\Gamma(u)-\Gamma(t))}).$$

As before, by equating to the corresponding upfront market quote the above expression in γ, one can extract the γ's corresponding to UCDS market quotes for increasing maturities and obtain again market implied γ^{mkt} and Γ^{mkt}'s.

Once the implied γ are estimated, it is easy to switch from the "running CDS quote" R to the "upfront CDS quote" UCDS, or vice versa. Indeed, we see that the two quotes are linked by

$$\mathrm{UCDS}(t, T_a, T_b, R, \mathrm{LGD}; \Gamma^{\mathrm{mkt}}(\cdot))$$
$$= R_{a,b}(t) \left[- \int_{T_a}^{T_b} P(t, u)(u - T_{\beta(u)-1}) d_u(e^{-(\Gamma^{\mathrm{mkt}}(u)-\Gamma^{\mathrm{mkt}}(t))}) + \sum_{i=a+1}^{n} P(t, T_i) \alpha_i e^{\Gamma^{\mathrm{mkt}}(t)-\Gamma^{\mathrm{mkt}}(T_i)} \right].$$

As mentioned in previous chapters, the so-called ISDA Big Bang introduced a different type of upfront CDS where there is a fixed running fee R that is standardized, and the remaining value of the protection is settled as an upfront price. See [28] for the details and a critique of this Big Bang paradigm.

We presented some concrete examples of calibrated hazard rates γ in Section 3.1.7. In Section 3.1.7, besides displaying the AT1P parameters σ, we also displayed the piecewise constant intensity parameters $\gamma(t) = \lambda_i$. Going back to that section, the reader can compare the output of the firm value model with the output of a piecewise constant intensity model.

3.3.2 A Simpler Formula for Calibrating Intensity to a Single CDS

The market makes intensive use of a simpler formula for calibrating a constant intensity (and thus hazard rate) $\gamma(t) = \gamma$ to a single CDS, say $\text{CDS}_{0,b}$. The formula is the following:

$$\boxed{\gamma = \frac{R_{0,b}(0)}{\text{LGD}}} \tag{3.13}$$

This Formula is very handy: one does not need the interest rate curve to apply it. Furthermore, if we recall what was anticipated in Section 3.3, i.e. that the intensity $\gamma = \lambda$ can be interpreted as an instantaneous credit spread, then the interpretation as credit spread extends to the CDS rate R.

In the present context, this simple formula shows us that, given a constant hazard rate (and subsequent independence between the default time and interest rates), *the CDS premium rate R can really be interpreted as a credit spread, or a default probability*. We derive this formula now.

Assume we have a stylized CDS contract for protection in $[0, T]$ under independence between interest rates ($D(0, t)$'s) and the default time τ. The premium leg pays continuously until default the premium rate R of the CDS: this means that in the interval $[t, t + dt]$ the premium leg pays "$R\,dt$". By discounting each premium flow "$R\,dt$" from the time t where it occurs to time 0, we obtain $D(0, t)R\,dt$, and by adding up all the premiums in different instants of the period $[0, T]$ where default has not yet occurred ($\tau > t$) we get

$$\int_0^T D(0, t)1_{\{\tau>t\}}R\,dt.$$

The protection leg is as usual. We can then write

$$\begin{aligned}
\text{PremiumLeg} &= \mathbb{E}\left[\int_0^T D(0, t)1_{\{\tau>t\}}R dt\right] = R\int_0^T \mathbb{E}[D(0, t)1_{\{\tau>t\}}]dt \\
&= R\int_0^T \mathbb{E}[D(0, t)]\mathbb{E}[1_{\{\tau>t\}}]dt = R\int_0^T P(0, t)\mathbb{Q}(\tau > t)dt
\end{aligned}$$

and

$$\begin{aligned}
\text{ProtectionLeg} &= \mathbb{E}[\text{LGD}D(0, \tau)1_{\{\tau\le T\}}] \\
&= \text{LGD}\int_0^T \mathbb{E}[D(0, t)\delta(t-\tau)]dt = \text{LGD}\int_0^T \mathbb{E}[D(0, t)]\mathbb{E}[\delta(t-\tau)]dt \\
&= \text{LGD}\int_0^T P(0, t)\mathbb{Q}(\tau\in[t, t+dt)) = -\text{LGD}\int_0^T P(0, t)d_t\mathbb{Q}(\tau > t).
\end{aligned}$$

Assume that the default curve comes from a constant intensity model, where default is the first jump of a time homogeneous Poisson process: $\mathbb{Q}(\tau > t) = e^{-\gamma t}$. Substitute

$$\mathbb{Q}(\tau > t) = e^{-\gamma t}, \quad d\,\mathbb{Q}(\tau > t) = -\gamma e^{-\gamma t}\,dt = -\gamma \mathbb{Q}(\tau > t)\,dt$$

to obtain

$$\text{ProtectionLeg} = -\text{LGD} \int_0^T P(0,t)\, d_t \mathbb{Q}(\tau > t) = \gamma \text{LGD} \int_0^T P(0,t)\mathbb{Q}(\tau > t)dt.$$

Now recall that the market quotes the fair R equating the two legs. Solve then

$$\text{ProtectionLeg} = \text{PremiumLeg}$$

i.e.

$$\gamma \text{LGD} \int_0^T P(0,t)\mathbb{Q}(\tau > t)dt = R \int_0^T P(0,t)\mathbb{Q}(\tau > t)dt$$

to obtain our initial formula above.

Clearly this formula is only approximated, due to the assumptions of continuous payments in the premium leg, and it does not take into account the term structure of CDS, since it is based on a single quote for R; however, it can be used in any situation where one needs a quick calibration of the default intensity or probability to a single (say, for example, 5y) CDS quote.

Remark 3.3.1 ***(Caution in interpreting deterministic intensities).*** *A word of caution is in order after we introduced the above formula and calibration, based on deterministic piecewise constant or even constant intensity. As we have seen, intensity is analogous to an instantaneous credit spread, and credit spread volatilities as from CDS/Bond historical or implied volatilities are very large, typically well above 50%, see [31] or Chapter 23 of [48]. When we assume deterministic intensities, we assume that the credit spread volatility is zero. Furthermore, CDS quotes incorporate liquidity premia and also, when applied to sovereign or to macro-economically relevant firms, FX risk. Finally, CDS may be subject themselves to counterparty default risk of the protection buyer or seller. Care must be taken in interpreting CDSs as instruments depending only on default probabilities of the reference credit.*

To account for credit spread volatility, which is typically large, we need to introduce Stochastic Intensity.

If intensity is stochastic, the probability to default after t, or to survive t, or *survival probability* at t, is

$$\mathbb{Q}\{\tau > t\} = \mathbb{E}[e^{-\int_0^t \lambda(u)du}],$$

which is just the price of a zero coupon bond in a stochastic interest rate model with short rate r replaced by λ. This is why survival probabilities are interpreted as zero coupon bonds and intensities λ as instantaneous credit spreads. Thus one can choose any (positive!) interest stochastic short-rate model for λ. We will see in particular what happens when choosing the CIR++ model with possible addition of jumps and some variants as a possible model for λ. Necessity to have positive intensity will eliminate the rich family of Gaussian models, leaving us with a choice between lognormal or CIR processes. Given the need for analytical tractability to speed up calibration, among other considerations, we will resort mostly to CIR and variants.

We will therefore focus now on the CIR model. For an overview of different short rate models with pros and cons and analytical formulas or numerical methods, the reader is referred to [48], from where we borrow our CIR model exposition.

3.3.3 Stochastic Intensity: The CIR Family

We start from the CIR model for the risk-free short-term insterest rate r_t. The CIR model for the intensity will be similarly formulated.

3.3.4 The Cox-Ingersoll-Ross Model (CIR) Short-Rate Model for *r*

The general equilibrium formulation adopted by Cox, Ingersoll and Ross (1985) [83] led to the introduction of a "square-root" term in the diffusion coefficient of the instantaneous short-rate $r_t = r(t)$ dynamics proposed by Vasicek (1977). Recall that stochastic default-free discount factors and default-free zero-coupon bond prices at time t for maturity T are written as

$$D(t,T) = \exp(-\int_t^T r_s ds), \quad P(t,T) = \mathbb{E}_t[\exp(-\int_t^T r_s ds)]$$

respectively.

The resulting r model (hereafter CIR) has been a benchmark for many years because of its analytical tractability and the fact that, contrary to the Vasicek (1977) model, the instantaneous short rate is always positive. It is one of the few short-rate models that can be straightforwardly adapted to credit modelling.

The model formulation under the risk-neutral measure Q is

$$dr(t) = k(\theta - r(t))dt + \sigma\sqrt{r(t)}\,dW(t), \quad r(0) = r_0, \tag{3.14}$$

with r_0, k, θ, σ positive constants. The condition

$$2k\theta > \sigma^2$$

has to be imposed to ensure that the origin is inaccessible to the process (3.14), so that we can grant that r remains positive. The CIR model is a particular case of an affine model see, for example [48].

We now consider a little digression on a tractable form for the market price of risk in this model. If we need to model the objective or physical measure P dynamics of the model, it is a good idea to adopt the following formulation:

$$dr(t) = [k\theta - (k + \zeta\sigma)r(t)]dt + \sigma\sqrt{r(t)}\,dW^0(t), \quad r(0) = r_0, \tag{3.15}$$

where W_0 is a Brownian motion under P. Notice that in moving from Q to P the drift has been modified in a special way that preserves the same structure under the two measures. The change of measure is designed so as to maintain a square-root-process structure. Since the diffusion coefficient is different, the change of measure is also different. In particular, we have

$$\left.\frac{dQ}{dP}\right|_{\mathcal{F}_t} = \exp\left(-\frac{1}{2}\int_0^t \zeta^2 r(s)ds + \int_0^t \zeta\sqrt{r(s)}dW^0(s)\right).$$

In other words we are assuming the market price of risk process $\zeta(t)$ to be of the particular functional form

$$\zeta(t) = \zeta\sqrt{r(t)}$$

in the short rate. In general, there is no reason why this should be the case, nevertheless, under this choice we obtain a short-rate process which is tractable under both measures. Tractability under the objective measure can be helpful for historical-estimation purposes and for Value at Risk-type calculations.

Notice that usually the formulation under the two measures is the opposite of the one presented here. Usually the dynamics without ζ is a P dynamics, and one adds one new parameter ζ to move under the Q measure, so that bond prices will depend on ζ. Because in pricing one uses mostly the risk-neutral measure, we started from the simplest dynamics under Q. So in a way our market price of risk is the opposite of the one usually considered.

Let us now move back to the risk-neutral measure Q. The process r features a noncentral chi-squared distribution. Precisely, denoting by p_Y the density function of the random variable Y,

$$\begin{aligned}
p_{r(t)}(x) &= p_{\chi^2(v,\,\lambda_t)/c_t}(x) = c_t\, p_{\chi^2(v,\,\lambda_t)}(c_t x),\\
c_t &= \frac{4k}{\sigma^2(1-\exp(-kt))},\\
v &= 4k\theta/\sigma^2,\\
\lambda_t &= c_t r_0 \exp(-kt),
\end{aligned}$$

where the noncentral chi-squared distribution function $\chi^2(\cdot, v, \lambda)$ with v degrees of freedom and non-centrality parameter λ has density

$$\begin{aligned}
p_{\chi^2(v,\,\lambda)}(z) &= \sum_{i=0}^{\infty} \frac{e^{-\lambda/2}(\lambda/2)^i}{i!} p_{\Gamma(i+v/2,\,1/2)}(z),\\
p_{\Gamma(i+v/2,\,1/2)}(z) &= \frac{(1/2)^{i+v/2}}{\Gamma(i+v/2)} z^{i-1+v/2} e^{-z/2} = p_{\chi^2(v+2i)}(z),
\end{aligned}$$

with $p_{\chi^2(v+2i)}(z)$ denoting the density of a (central) chi-squared distribution function with $v+2i$ degrees of freedom.[2]

The mean and the variance of $r(t)$ conditional on $\mathcal{F}_s$ are given by

$$\begin{aligned}
E\{r(t)|\mathcal{F}_s\} &= r(s)e^{-k(t-s)} + \theta\left(1-e^{-k(t-s)}\right),\\
\mathrm{Var}\{r(t)|\mathcal{F}_s\} &= r(s)\frac{\sigma^2}{k}\left(e^{-k(t-s)} - e^{-2k(t-s)}\right) + \theta\frac{\sigma^2}{2k}\left(1-e^{-k(t-s)}\right)^2.
\end{aligned} \tag{3.16}$$

The price at time t of a zero-coupon bond with maturity T is easily deduced by the moment generating function of the integrated CIR process. This is known to be

$$E_t\left[\exp\left(-u\int_t^T r_s ds\right)\right] = M_A(t,T,u)e^{-M_B(t,T,u)ur(t)}$$

---

[2] A useful identity concerning densities of χ^2 distributions is

$$p_{\chi^2(v,\,\lambda)}(bz) = \exp\left(\frac{1}{2}(1-b)(z-\lambda)\right) b^{v/2-1} p_{\chi^2(v,b\lambda)}(z).$$

where

$$M_A(t,T,u) = \left[\frac{2h_u \exp\{(k+h_u)(T-t)/2\}}{2h_u + (k+h_u)(\exp\{(T-t)h_u\}-1)}\right]^{2k\theta/\sigma^2}, \quad h_u = \sqrt{k^2 + 2u\sigma^2},$$

$$M_B(t,T,u) = \frac{2(\exp\{(T-t)h_u\}-1)}{2h_u + (k+h_u)(\exp\{(T-t)h_u\}-1)}.$$

As a consequence, for $u = 1$ we get the bond price

$$P(t,T) = A(t,T)e^{-B(t,T)r(t)}, \tag{3.17}$$

where

$$\begin{aligned} A(t,T) &= \left[\frac{2h \exp\{(k+h)(T-t)/2\}}{2h + (k+h)(\exp\{(T-t)h\}-1)}\right]^{2k\theta/\sigma^2}, \\ B(t,T) &= \frac{2(\exp\{(T-t)h\}-1)}{2h + (k+h)(\exp\{(T-t)h\}-1)}, \\ h &= \sqrt{k^2 + 2\sigma^2}. \end{aligned} \tag{3.18}$$

For the price at time t of a European call option with maturity $T > t$, strike price X, written on a zero-coupon bond maturing at $S > T$, and with the instantaneous rate at time t given by $r(t)$, see [83] or [48]. This is then used to derive the price of an interest rate caplet and cap.

See [48] for other properties, including the forward measure dynamics and the bond dynamics under this model.

3.3.5 Time-Inhomogeneous Case: CIR++ Model

For the following extension of the CIR [83] model, referred to as CIR++, see also [48]. In this case, the process x^α is defined as in (3.14), where the parameter vector is $\alpha = (k, \theta, \sigma)$. The short-rate dynamics is then given by:

$$\begin{aligned} dx(t) &= k(\theta - x(t))dt + \sigma\sqrt{x(t)}dW(t), \quad x(0) = x_0, \\ r(t) &= x(t) + \varphi(t), \end{aligned} \tag{3.19}$$

where x_0, k, θ and σ are positive constants such that $2k\theta > \sigma^2$, thus ensuring that the origin is inaccessible to x, and hence the process x remains positive. The deterministic positive time function φ is added to fit exactly the initial observed term structure of interest rates.

We have that $\varphi(t) = \varphi^{CIR}(t;\alpha)$ where

$$\begin{aligned} \varphi^{CIR}(t;\alpha) &= f^M(0,t) - f^{CIR}(0,t;\alpha), \\ f^{CIR}(0,t;\alpha) &= \frac{2k\theta(\exp\{th\}-1)}{2h + (k+h)(\exp\{th\}-1)} + x_0 \frac{4h^2 \exp\{th\}}{[2h + (k+h)(\exp\{th\}-1)]^2} \end{aligned} \tag{3.20}$$

with $h = \sqrt{k^2 + 2\sigma^2}$. Moreover, the price at time t of a zero-coupon bond maturing at time T is

$$P(t,T) = \bar{A}(t,T)e^{-B(t,T)r(t)},$$

where

$$\bar{A}(t,T) = \frac{P^M(0,T)A(0,t)\exp\{-B(0,t)x_0\}}{P^M(0,t)A(0,T)\exp\{-B(0,T)x_0\}} A(t,T)e^{B(t,T)\varphi^{CIR}(t;\alpha)},$$

and $A(t,T)$ and $B(t,T)$ are defined as in 3.18.

For a study of the positivity of $\varphi^{CIR}(t;\alpha)$ and for sufficient conditions for this to happen we refer the reader to [48].

3.3.6 Stochastic Diffusion Intensity is Not Enough: Adding Jumps. The JCIR(++) Model

There is a problem we should mention in closing this chapter. The CIR++ stochastic intensity model we introduced is not always capable of generating high levels of implied volatility. Indeed, the numerical experiments in Brigo and Cousot (2006) [45] point out that it is quite difficult to find implied volatilities with an order of magnitude of 30% with the CIR++. This is due essentially to two reasons. First, we need to keep the shift φ positive and this limits the configurations of parameters in a way that renders high implied volatilities hard to attain. Second, the problem is more fundamental and is related to the structure of the square root diffusion dynamics. Assume for a moment that we give up the shift and work with a time homogenous CIR model for r, or in other terms $r = x$, $\varphi = 0$, so that

$$dr_t = k(\theta - r_t)dt + \sigma\sqrt{r_t}dW_t.$$

Intuitively, high implied volatility for the option prices generated by this model corresponds to a high volatility parameter σ in the intensity dynamics. However, to restrict the values attainable by r in the positive domain, we need to ensure that the following condition is satisfied:

$$2k\theta > \sigma^2.$$

This condition implies that if σ is large, k and/or θ are also forced to assume large values. None of these possibilities is really desirable though. Drastically increasing θ means increasing the mean reversion level of the intensity process, so that r is supposed to tend to possibly very high values. Alternatively, increasing k drastically can counter the increase in σ as far as the CIR++ implied volatility is concerned. Indeed, large k means a large speed of mean reversion, which in turn means that the trajectories will tend to regroup around θ faster, so that the system will have less stochasticity, for a given value of σ. To sum up, we may increase θ to increase the implied volatility but this will force us, due to the positivity condition, to increase k, whose effect will counter the initial increase in σ. In practice, we have been able in realistic situations to go up to a 30% implied volatility. However, when used to model stochastic intensity λ_t rather than r_t, implied volatilities in credit, especially in the CDS markets, may easily exceed 50%, see for example [31] or again [48]. This means that we can easily find situations where no realistic configuration of the parameters of the CIR++ model can generate market implied volatilities.

This is particularly annoying as the square root diffusion is convenient to work with, since it restricts the intensity to positive values only and at the same time is relatively tractable.

For a more detailed account of these issues, see the discussion in [46], where it is suggested to introduce a jump component in the CIR++ process, as we do now.

3.3.7 The Jump-Diffusion CIR Model (JCIR)

We consider a special case of the class of Affine Jump Diffusions (AJD) (see, for example, [102], and [100]).

Here we express the model for a default intensity λ_t rather than for a short-term interest rate r_t, since jumps are mostly used in modelling intensity. The dynamics of λ_t under the risk-neutral measure would then satisfy

$$d\lambda_t = k(\mu - \lambda_t)dt + \nu\sqrt{\lambda_t}dZ_t + dJ_t$$

where J is a pure jump process with jumps arrival rate $\alpha > 0$ and jump sizes distribution π on $\mathbb{R}^+$.

Notice an important point: the jump process J we just introduced is a jump in the stochastic intensity dynamics, not the already introduced fundamental jump in the default process, related to ξ. Recall indeed that τ is the first jump of a suitable Cox process. This first jump is not a jump of J. When J alone jumps the intensity is affected by an increase but there is no default.

Notice also that we restrict the jumps to be positive, preserving the attractive feature of positive default intensity implied by the basic CIR dynamics. Further, assume that π is an exponential distribution with mean $\gamma > 0$, and that

$$J_t = \sum_{i=1}^{M_t} Y_i$$

where M is a time-homogeneous Poisson process with intensity α, the Ys being exponentially distributed with parameter γ. The larger α, the more frequent the jumps, and the larger γ, the larger the sizes of the occurring jumps. We denote the resulting jump process by $J^{\alpha,\gamma}$, to point out the parameters influencing its dynamics. We write:

$$d\lambda_t = \kappa(\mu - \lambda_t)dt + \nu\sqrt{\lambda_t}dZ_t + dJ_t^{\alpha,\gamma}, \tag{3.21}$$

so that we can see all the parameters in the dynamics.

3.3.7.1 *Bond (or Survival Probability) Formula*

Since this model belongs to the tractable affine jump diffusion (AJD) class of models, the survival probability has the typical "log-affine" shape

$$\mathbb{Q}\{\tau > T|\mathcal{G}_t\} = \mathbf{1}_{\{\tau>t\}}\bar{\alpha}(t,T)\exp(-\bar{\beta}(t,T)\lambda_t) =: \mathbf{1}_{\{\tau>t\}}P^{JCIR}(t,T,\lambda_t)$$

where the functional forms of the terms $\bar{\alpha}$ and $\bar{\beta}$ with respect to the parameters $\kappa, \mu, \nu, \alpha, \gamma$ [100] are obtained by solving the usual Riccati equations. These expressions for $\bar{\alpha}$ and $\bar{\beta}$ can be recast in a form that is similar to the classical terms A and B in the bond price formula for CIR as in Brigo and El Bachir [46]:

$$\bar{\alpha}(t,T) = A(t,T)\left(\frac{2h\exp\left(\frac{h+\kappa+2\gamma}{2}(T-t)\right)}{2h+(\kappa+h+2\gamma)(\exp^{h(T-t)}-1)}\right)^{\frac{2\alpha\gamma}{\nu^2-2\kappa\gamma-2\gamma^2}} \tag{3.22}$$

$$\bar{\beta}(t,T) = B(t,T) \tag{3.23}$$

where $A(t,T)$, $B(t,T)$ are the terms from the CIR model, and similarly $h = \sqrt{\kappa^2 + 2\nu^2}$.

In this expression one has to be careful. Given the denominator in the exponent of the large round brackets, one sees that this denominator can be rewritten as

$$\nu^2 - 2\kappa\gamma - 2\gamma^2 = \frac{1}{2}[h^2 - (\kappa + 2\gamma)^2],$$

and is zero if $h = \kappa + 2\gamma$. One can see through a limit, that when this happens the expression above for $\bar{\alpha}$ has to be substituted by the following one:

$$\bar{\alpha}(t, T) = A(t, T) \exp\left(-2\alpha\gamma \left[\frac{T-t}{\kappa + h + 2\gamma} + \frac{e^{-h(T-t)} - 1}{h(\kappa + h + 2\gamma)}\right]\right).$$

3.3.7.2 Exact calibration of CDS: The JCIR++ model

In general, our jump-diffusion square root process above could be shifted again according to the usual trick to obtain an exact calibration to credit default swaps. Indeed, all we need to compute the shift is the bond price formula for the homogenous model as given previously. The shift reproducing exactly CDS quotes would then be the following generalization of the CIR++ shift:

$$\Psi^J(t, \beta) = \Gamma^{mkt}(t) + \ln\left(\mathbb{E}\left[\exp^{-\int_0^t \lambda_s ds}\right]\right) = \Gamma^{mkt}(t) + \ln\left(P^{JCIR}(0, t, \lambda_0; \beta)\right) \quad (3.24)$$

where

$$\Gamma^{mkt}(t) = -\ln \mathbb{Q}(\tau > t)^{mkt}.$$

This leads to the Jump-diffusion CIR++ model (JCIR++). Still, the addition of the jump component makes it more difficult to find conditions guaranteeing the shift ψ^J to be positive (or, equivalently, its integral Ψ^J increasing). At the same time, it is good to notice that now the basic model without shift has six parameters

$$\kappa, \mu, \nu, \lambda_0, \alpha, \gamma$$

that we might try to use to calibrate 5 CDS quotes plus one option volatility.

More generally, once we have calibrated CDS or Corporate Bond data through the shift $\psi(\cdot, \beta)$, we are left with the parameters β, which can be used to calibrate further products. This will be interesting when single name option data on the credit derivatives market will become more liquid. Currently the bid-ask spreads for single name CDS options are large and suggest either considering these quotes with caution, or trying to deduce volatility parameters from more liquid index options through some ad-hoc single name re-scaling. At the moment we content ourselves calibrating only CDSs through the shift. To help specifying β without further data one may set some parameter values implying possible reasonable values for the implied volatility of hypothetical CDS options on the counterparty, which are in line with possible historical volatilities of credit spreads. Another possibility is to use the much more liquid implied volatility of options on CDS indices (iTraxx or CDX) with ad-hoc corrections accounting for the single name idiosyncrasies.

3.3.7.3 Simulating the JCIR++ model

As for simulation, simulating the (possibly shifted) J-CIR process is no more difficult than simulating only the diffusion part. Because the Brownian Z and the compound Poisson process

$J^{\alpha,\gamma}$ are independent, Mikulevicius and Platen (1988) [150] propose to generate jump times and jump amplitudes, then proceed with the diffusion discretization schemes adding the jumps at the times when they occur. To apply this method here, one only needs to be able to generate Poisson jump times and exponentially distributed jump sizes, in addition to one of the usual schemes discussed for CIR, see [48] for the details.

One can also develop Jamshidian's decomposition for the JCIR++ model in order to price Swaptions and CDS options in closed form, see [46] or [48].

3.3.8 Market Incompleteness and Default Unpredictability

The "out-of-the-blue" characteristic of the exponential core of randomness ξ in intensity models is not a cost we face without reward. The exogenous component, besides making the model incomplete, makes default unpredictable in an important technical sense, and allows for non-null instantaneous credit spreads, contrary to the other important family of (basic) firm value (or structural) models we have seen above.

3.3.9 Further Models

We should also say that the picture given here is a simple version of the credit models area: Hybrid models mixing structural and intensity characteristics have been introduced, although we will not go through them here.

Jump diffusion models are also proposed in lieu of the diffusions we used above, and the broad family of Levy processes. Jump diffusion dynamics may be considered both in the structural and reduced-form frameworks. We have hinted at examples of jump diffusion intensity models above earlier.

3.4 INTENSITY MODELS: THE MULTINAME PICTURE

When dealing with more counterparties or when analyzing symmetric counterparty risk in a single transaction, the notion of dependence between default times needs to go beyond linear correlation. Linear correlation is not suited to model dependence among variables that are not jointly instantaneous Gaussian shocks (Brownian motions), and more generally it is not a good parameter for measuring dependence outside elliptical distributions. Copula functions are then often used in conjunction with intensity models to deal with this task.

3.4.1 Choice of Variables for the Dependence Structure

Dependence is introduced across the default times $\tau_1, \tau_2, \tau_3 \ldots$ of different counterparties as follows.

We have seen above that in reduced form models, transforming the default time τ by its cumulated intensity $\Lambda(t) = \int_0^t \lambda(s)ds$ leads to an exponential random variable independent of any default-free quantity:

$$\Lambda(\tau) = \xi \sim \text{exponential}, \quad \mathcal{F} - \text{independent}.$$

If we assume λ to be positive, we may define τ as

$$\tau = \Lambda^{-1}(\xi).$$

If we have several names $1, 2, \ldots, n$, we may define dependence between the default times

$$\tau_1 = \Lambda_1^{-1}(\xi_1), \ldots, \tau_n = \Lambda_n^{-1}(\xi_n)$$

essentially in three ways:

1. Put dependence in (stochastic) intensities of the different names and keep the ξ of the different names independent;
2. Put dependence among the ξ of the different names and keep the (stochastic or trivially deterministic) intensities λ_i independent;
3. Put dependence both among (stochastic) intensities λ of the different names and among the ξ of the different names;

Let us look at these three possibilities in more detail.

3.4.1.1 *Dependence in (stochastic) intensities with independent ξ's*

With choice 1), one may induce dependence among the $\lambda_i(t)$ by taking diffusion dynamics for each of them and correlating the Brownian motions:

$$d\lambda_i(t) = \mu_i(t, \lambda_i(t))dt + \sigma_i(t, \lambda_i(t))dW_i(t),$$

$$d\lambda_j(t) = \mu_j(t, \lambda_j(t))dt + \sigma_j(t, \lambda_j(t))dW_j(t),$$

$$dW_i dW_j = \rho_{i,j}dt, \quad \xi_i, \xi_j \text{ independent.}$$

The advantages with this choice are possible partial tractability and ease of implementation; also, the default of one name does not affect the intensity of other names. The correlation can be estimated historically from time series of credit spreads and inserted into the model. Furthermore, with stochastic intensity we may model correlation between interest rates and credit spreads, that is considered to be an important feature in some situations.

The disadvantages consist in a non realistic (too low) level of dependence across default events $1_{\{\tau_i<T\}}, 1_{\{\tau_j<T\}}$. See [134]. This can be improved by adding jumps to the spreads and making the jumps common so as to create a strong dependence across spreads of different names. However, this leads to quite unnatural spread dynamics that often look artificial.

3.4.1.2 *Dependence on the ξ's with independent intensities λ's*

With choice 2) the advantages are: We can take even deterministic intensities, which makes life easier for stripping single name default probabilities. We can reproduce realistically large levels of dependence across default times of different names by putting dependence structures called "copula functions" on the ξ's.

Disadvantages: There is no natural and feasible historical source for estimating the copula, that is often calibrated by means of dubious considerations. Furthermore, default of one name affects the intensity of other names through partial derivatives of the imposed copula, see [181] or [43]. In case of deterministic intensities this approach ignores credit spreads volatilities, which can be rather large (besides ignoring credit spread correlations in general).

3.4.1.3 *Dependence both on stochastic intensities λ's and on ξ's*

Choice 3) leads to the most complicated framework. The advantages of this third solution are that it takes into account possible credit spread volatility, and can produce a sufficient amount of dependence among default times.

Disadvantages: there is no natural and feasible historical source for estimating the copula that is often calibrated by means of dubious considerations. Moreover, as before, default of one name affects the intensity of other names through partial derivatives of the copula. Calculations are quite complicated, due to the presence of stochasticity both in the intensities λ_i's and in the ξ's.

3.4.2 Firm Value Models?

A different situation arises if we use firm value models for the default times. In this case the default dependence can be driven by correlation in the Brownian motions of the different firm values. This brings us back to more traditional models, but if we use first passage models we would face barrier problems in high dimensions when a large number of counterparties is there, so that simulation of large numbers of default times may become rather cumbersome. This is the reason why for situations with several names and high dimensionality, intensity models with copula are still preferred to firm value models, notwithstanding their known drawbacks.

3.4.3 Copula Functions

Let us focus now on choice 2 above, namely inserting dependence on the ξ's with independent or even deterministic intensities λ's. This choice involves copula functions. What are copula functions and why are they introduced?

It is well known that linear correlation is not enough to express the dependence between two random variables in an efficient way.

Example: take X standard Gaussian and take $Y = X^5$. Y is a deterministic one-to-one transformation of X, so that the two variables give exactly the same information and should have maximum dependence. However, if we take the linear correlation between X and Y we easily get

$$(E(X^5X) - E(X^5)E(X))/(\mathrm{Std}(X^5)\mathrm{Std}(X)) = \sqrt{5/21} < \frac{1}{2}.$$

We obtain a dependence measure that is much smaller than 1 (1 corresponds to maximum dependence). So *correlation is not a good measure of dependence in this case.*

In standard financial models this problem with correlation as a dependence measure is usually absent because in standard modelling we are concerned with dependence between instantaneous Brownian shocks, which are jointly Gaussian. *Correlation works well for jointly Gaussian variables*, so that as long as we are concerned with instantaneous correlations in jointly Gaussian shocks we do not need to generalize our notion of dependence.

In credit derivatives with intensity models we may find ourselves in the situation where we need to introduce dependence between the *exponential* components $\xi = \Lambda(\tau)$ of Poisson processes for different names. This is usually done by means of copula functions.

Let us see how we arrive at the definition of copula function. A fundamental fact about transformation of random variables is the following. Given a random variable X, we may transform it in several ways through a deterministic function: $2X$, X^5, $\exp(X)$, ... A particularly interesting transformation function is the cumulative distribution function F_X of X. Set $U = F_X(X)$ and assume for simplicity F_X to be invertible (say strictly increasing and continuous). Let us compute F_U in a generic point $u \in [0, 1]$.

$$F_U(u) = \mathbb{Q}(U \leq u) = \mathbb{Q}(F_X(X) \leq u) = \mathbb{Q}(F_X(X) \leq F_X(F_X^{-1}(u)))$$
$$= \mathbb{Q}(X \leq F_X^{-1}(u))) = F_X(F_X^{-1}(u)) = u.$$

However, the identity distribution function $F_U(u) = u$ is characteristic of a uniform random variable in [0 1]. This means that $U = F_X(X)$ is a uniform random variable. Notice also that since F_X is one-to-one, U contains the same information as X.

The idea then is to transform all random variables X by their F_X obtaining all uniform variables that contain the same information as the starting X. This way we rid ourselves of marginal distributions, obtaining only uniform random variables, and can concentrate on introducing dependence directly for these standardized uniforms.

Indeed, let $(U_1, \ldots, U_n)$ be a random vector with uniform margins and joint distribution $C(u_1, \ldots, u_n)$. $C(u_1, \ldots, u_n)$ is the *copula* of the random vector. It can be characterized by a number of properties that we do not repeat here. See, for example [160], [131], [78] or [106]. For a discussion on how the Gaussian copula parameterization has been abused and on the dangers of improperly attributing dynamic properties to copulas see for example [60] and [43].

An important result is the following. We may intuitively write:

$$\begin{aligned}
H(x_1, \ldots, x_n) &= \mathbb{Q}(X_1 \leq x_1, \ldots, X_n \leq x_n) \\
&= \mathbb{Q}(F_1(X_1) \leq F_1(x_1), \ldots, F_n(X_n) \leq F_n(x_n)) \\
&= \mathbb{Q}(U_1 \leq F_1(x_1), \ldots, U_n \leq F_n(x_n)) = C(F_1(x_1), \ldots, F_n(x_n))
\end{aligned}$$

where C is the joint distribution function of uniforms $U_1, \ldots, U_n$.

This can be generalized: For any joint distribution function $H(x_1, \ldots, x_n)$ with margins $F_1, \ldots, F_n$ there exists a copula function $C(u_1, \ldots, u_n)$ (i.e. a joint distribution function on n uniforms) such that

$$H(x_1, \ldots, x_n) = C(F_1(x_1), \ldots, F_n(x_n)).$$

Notice that C contains the pure dependence information.

We may also write

$$C(u_1, \ldots, u_n) = H(F_1^{-1}(u_1), \ldots, F_n^{-1}(u_n)). \tag{3.25}$$

from which we see that we may use any known joint distribution H function to define a copula C.

Consider again our example with X standard Gaussian and $Y = X^5$, $Z = X$. The copula between X and Z is the copula expressing maximum dependence (also correlation works in this case: $\mathrm{Corr}(X, Z) = 1$). This copula is the joint distribution of $U_1 = F_X(X)$ and $U_2 = F_Z(Z) = F_X(X) = U_1$,

$$\mathbb{Q}(U_1 < u_1, U_1 < u_2) = \mathbb{Q}(U_1 < \min(u_1, u_2)) = \min(u_1, u_2).$$

So this "min" copula corresponds to maximum dependence. Now consider $Y = X^5$ and the dependence between X and Y. We have seen above that linear correlation fails to be an efficient measure of dependence in this case. Call $U_5 = F_Y(Y)$. Notice that

$$F_{X^5}(x^5) = \mathbb{Q}(X^5 \leq x^5) = \mathbb{Q}(X \leq x) = F_X(x) \text{ forall } x,$$

so that in particular

$$U_5 = F_Y(Y) = \boxed{F_{X^5}(X^5) = F_X(X)} = U_1.$$

Consider the copula between X and Y. Since $U_5 = U_1$, this copula is

$$\mathbb{Q}(U_1 < u_1, U_5 < u_2) = \mathbb{Q}(U_1 < u_1, U_1 < u_2) = \min(u_1, u_2),$$

the same as before. So with copulas also X and X^5 get maximum dependence, as should be the case.

This example actually has a more general version: if $g_1, \ldots, g_n$ are (say strictly increasing) one-to-one transformations, then the copula of some given $X_1, \ldots, X_n$ is the same as the copula for $g_1(X_1), \ldots, g_n(X_n)$ (not so for correlation). So *the copula is invariant for deterministic transformations that preserve the information*. This tells us again that copulas are really expressing the core of dependence.

Also, it can be proved that every copula C is bounded between two functions C^+ and C^-, which are known as the Fréchet-Hoeffding bounds:

$$C(u_1, u_2, \ldots, u_n)^- \leq C(u_1, u_2, \ldots, u_n) \leq C(u_1, u_2, \ldots, u_n)^+$$

where

$$C(u_1, u_2, \ldots, u_n)^- = \max(u_1 + u_2 + \ldots + u_n + 1 - n, 0)$$

and

$$C(u_1, u_2, \ldots, u_n)^+ = \min(u_1, u_2, \ldots, u_n)$$

as in our example above. While C^+ is a copula in general, C^- is a copula only in dimension 2. We can define also an "orthogonal" copula $C^\perp$ corresponding to independent variables:

$$C(u_1, u_2, \ldots, u_n)^\perp = u_1 \cdot u_2 \cdot \ldots \cdot u_n.$$

Then C^+ is the copula corresponding to the maximum dependence and C^- is (in dimension 2) the copula corresponding to the maximum negative dependence. $C^\perp$ corresponds to perfect independence between two variables.

We also recall the notion of *survival copula*: this is defined as

$$\mathbb{P}\big[X_1 > x_1, \ldots, X_n > x_n\big] = \check{C}(\bar{F}_1(x_1), \ldots, \bar{F}_n(x_n))$$

where the $\bar{F}$'s are the margin survival functions (i.e. for example $\bar{F}_1(x_1) = \mathbb{Q}(X_1 > x_1) = 1 - F_1(x_1)$). The survival copula is not linked to the copula in a simple way. It can be proved that in two dimensions the following relation holds:

$$\check{C}(u, v) = u + v - 1 + C(1 - u, 1 - v).$$

In general, if one is able to compute survival copulas from the original copula, one obtains yet one more family of copulas for each given copula family.

At this point it is important to point out an important fact.

Remark 3.4.1 ***(Expressing Statistical Dependence: Whole Copula vs single number)*** *We motivated the introduction of copula functions by noticing that, if X is a Gaussian standard random variable, the linear correlation between X and the informationally equivalent X^5 is strictly less than 1. Linear correlation failed to recognize that the dependence between X and X^5 is the maximum possible dependence. As a remedy to this problem we introduced the notion of copula. The copula between two random variables, however, is not a single number like 1, but a whole bivariate distribution, and hence a whole two-dimensional function. In some applications it is desirable to have a single number synthesizing the dependence information between two random variables. We would need something like an improved version of linear correlation, i.e. a number, but we need a number recognizing that the dependence between X and X^5 is maximum.*

Such numbers exist and are called Rank Correlations, or measures of Concordance. Two important examples are Kendall's tau and Spearman's rho, which we describe below.

We present now two important measures of concordance. They provide the perhaps best alternatives to the linear correlation coefficient as a measure of dependence for pairs of non-gaussian (and non-elliptical) distributions, for which the linear correlation coefficient is inappropriate and often misleading.

Definition 3.4.2 *Kendall's tau between two random variables X, Y is defined as the probability*

$$\tau(X, Y) = \mathbb{Q}\{(X - \tilde{X})(Y - \tilde{Y}) > 0\} - \mathbb{Q}\{(X - \tilde{X})(Y - \tilde{Y}) < 0\}$$

where $(\tilde{X},\tilde{Y})$ is an independent and identically distributed copy of (X,Y). It can be proved that if (X,Y) is a couple of continuous random variables with copula C, then

$$\tau(X, Y) = 4 \int\int_{[0,1]^2} C(u, v) dC(u, v) - 1.$$

Kendall's tau for a pair of random variables (X, Y) is invariant under strictly increasing component-wise transformations, so that the tau between X and X^5 is the same as the tau between X and X, i.e. 1.

Definition 3.4.3 *Spearman's rho between two random variables X, Y is defined as the probability*

$$\rho_S(X, Y) = 3\mathbb{Q}\{(X - \tilde{X})(Y - Y') > 0\} - \mathbb{Q}\{(X - \tilde{X})(Y - Y') < 0\}$$

where (X',Y') and $(\tilde{X},\tilde{Y})$ are independent and identically distributed copies of (X,Y). It can be proved that if (X,Y) is a couple of continuous random variables with copula C, then

$$\rho(X, Y) = 12 \int\int_{[0,1]^2} C(u, v) du\, dv - 3.$$

Spearman's rho for a pair of random variables (X,Y) is invariant under strictly increasing componentwise transformations, so that again the rho between X and X^5 is the same as the rho between X and X, i.e. 1.

As for special cases of copulas, we have the obvious properties: if (X,Y) is a pair of random variables with copula C, then

$$C = C^+ \rightarrow \tau_C = \rho_C = 1$$
$$C = C^\perp \rightarrow \tau_C = \rho_C = 0$$
$$C = C^- \rightarrow \tau_C = \rho_C = -1.$$

Before starting to introduce the most important families of copulas, let us define the concept of tail dependence.

The concept of tail dependence relates to the amount of dependence in the upper-right quadrant tail or lower-left quadrant tail of a bivariate distribution. It is a concept that is relevant for the study of dependence between extreme values. Roughly speaking, it is the idea of "fat tails" for the dependence structure.

It turns out that tail dependence between two continuous random variables X and Y is a copula property and hence the amount of tail dependence is invariant under strictly increasing transformations of X and Y.

Let (X,Y) be a pair of continuous random variables with marginal distribution functions F_X and F_Y. The coefficient of upper-tail dependence of (X,Y) is

$$\lim_{u \uparrow 1} \mathbb{Q}\{Y > F_Y^{-1}(u) | X > F_X^{-1}(u)\} = \lambda_U$$

provided that the limit $\lambda_U \in [0, 1]$ exists. If $\lambda_U \in (0, 1]$, X and Y are said to be asymptotically dependent in the upper tail; if $\lambda_U = 0$, X and Y are said to be asymptotically independent in the upper tail.

Since $\mathbb{Q}\{Y > F_Y^{-1}(u) | X > F_X^{-1}(u)\}$ can be rewritten as

$$\frac{1 - \mathbb{Q}\{X \leq F_X^{-1}(u)\} - \mathbb{Q}\{Y \leq F_Y^{-1}(u)\} + \mathbb{Q}\{X \leq F_X^{-1}(u), Y \leq F_Y^{-1}(u)\}}{1 - \mathbb{Q}\{X \leq F_X^{-1}(u)\}}$$

an alternative and equivalent definition (for continuous random variables), which shows that the concept of tail dependence is indeed a copula property, is the following:

$$\lim_{u \uparrow 1} (1 - 2u + C(u, u))/(1 - u) = \lambda_U.$$

A more compact characterization of upper tail dependence can be given in terms of the survival copula:

$$\lim_{v \downarrow 0} \breve{C}(v, v)/v = \lambda_U.$$

The concept of lower tail dependence can be defined in a similar way. If the limit

$$\lim_{u \downarrow 0} \mathbb{Q}\{Y \leq F_Y^{-1}(u) | X \leq F_X^{-1}(u)\} = \lim_{u \downarrow 0} C(u, u)/u = \lambda_L$$

exists, then C has lower tail dependence if $\lambda_L \in (0, 1]$, and lower tail independence if $\lambda_L = 0$.

We describe now what is the most known copula: the Gaussian copula. The Gaussian copula is obtained by using a multivariate n-dimensional normal distribution Φ_R^n with standard Gaussian margins and correlation matrix R as multivariate distribution H:

$$C_{\mathcal{N}(R)}(u_1, \ldots, u_n) = \Phi_R^n(\Phi^{-1}(u_1), \ldots, \Phi^{-1}(u_n)) \tag{3.26}$$

where Φ^{-1} is the inverse of the usual standard normal cumulative distribution function. Unfortunately this copula cannot be expressed in closed form. Indeed, in the 2-dimensional case we have:

$$C_{\mathcal{N}(R)}(u, v) = \int_{-\infty}^{\Phi^{-1}(u)} \int_{-\infty}^{\Phi^{-1}(v)} \frac{1}{2\pi(1-\rho^2)^{1/2}} \exp\left\{-\frac{s^2 - 2\rho st + t^2}{2(1-\rho^2)}\right\} ds\, dt, \quad (3.27)$$

ρ being the (only) correlation parameter in the 2×2 matrix R. Notice that in case we are modelling the dependence among n names, the correlation matrix R in principle has $n(n-1)/2$ free parameters.

Now some properties of the Gaussian copula for $\rho \in (-1, 1)$:

- Neither upper nor lower tail dependence;
- $C(u, v) = C(v, u)$ i.e. *exchangeable copula*.

There is then the family of Archimedean copulas, for which we refer to the literature.

An alternative to the Gaussian copula can be the family of t-Copulas. If the vector $\mathbf{X}$ of random variables has the stochastic representation $\mathbf{X} \sim \mu + \frac{\sqrt{\nu}}{\sqrt{S}}\mathbf{Z}$ where $\mu \in \mathbb{R}^n$, ν is a positive integer, $S \simeq \chi^2_\nu$ and $\mathbf{Z} \simeq \mathcal{N}(\mathbf{0}, \Sigma)$ are independent, where Σ is an $n \times n$ covariance matrix, then $\mathbf{X}$ has an n-variate t_ν -distribution with mean μ (for $\nu > 1$) and covariance matrix $\frac{\nu}{\nu-2}\Sigma$ (for $\nu > 2$). If $\nu \leq 2$ then Cov($\mathbf{X}$) is not defined. In this case we just interpret Σ as being the shape parameter of the distribution of $\mathbf{X}$.

The copula of $\mathbf{X}$ defined above can be written as

$$C^t_{\nu,R}(\mathbf{u}) = t^n_{\nu,R}(t_\nu^{-1}(u_1), \ldots, t_\nu^{-1}(u_n))$$

where $R_{ij} = \Sigma_{ij}/\sqrt{\Sigma_{ii}\Sigma_{jj}}$ for $i, j \in \{1, \ldots, n\}$ and where $t^n_{\nu,R}$ denotes the distribution function of $\sqrt{\nu}\mathbf{Y}/\sqrt{S}$ where $S \simeq \chi^2_\nu$ and $\mathbf{Y} \simeq \mathcal{N}(\mathbf{0}, R)$ are independent. Here t_ν denotes the (equal) margins of $t^n_{\nu,R}$, i.e. the distribution function of $\sqrt{\nu}Y_1/\sqrt{S}$.

In the bivariate case the copula expression can be written as

$$C^t_{\nu,R}(u, v) = \int_{-\infty}^{t_\nu^{-1}(u)} \int_{-\infty}^{t_\nu^{-1}(v)} \frac{1}{2\pi(1-R_{12}^2)^{1/2}} \left\{1 + \frac{s^2 - 2R_{12}st + t^2}{\nu(1-R_{12}^2)}\right\}^{-\frac{\nu+2}{2}} ds\, dt.$$

Note that R_{12} is simply the usual linear correlation coefficient of the corresponding bivariate t_ν-distribution if $\nu > 2$.

When we move to dimensions larger than 2, as is typical with multiname credit derivatives, we need to look at the copula across a large number of random variables. It is important to point out the following:

Remark 3.4.4 ***(Gaussian Copula: Decomposing block dependence in pairwise dependences)*** *A very important but often underappreciated property of the Gaussian, and in part of the t- copulas, is that the block dependence structure can be decomposed in pairwise dependence structure through the matrix parameterization of the copula itself. This is not at all the case for different copulas. For example, in general it is not possible to deduce the copula of a random vector $X_1, \ldots, X_n$, with $n > 2$, from a matrix of Kendall's tau or Spearman's rho's taken on each pair of random variables X_i, X_j. This is only possible with the Gaussian copula and, in case one knows the degree of freedom parameter, with the t copula.*

All the copulas we have introduced above are exchangeable. In some situations it is appropriate to have non-exchangeable copulas. We introduce one such family below. Before closing this digression on copula functions, we introduce a recent development. [5] introduced new families of copulas based on periodic functions. This was based on the observation that if f is a 1-periodic non-negative function that integrates to 1 over [0, 1] and φ is a double primitive of f, then both

$$\varphi(u+v)-\varphi(u)-\varphi(v) \quad \text{and} \quad -\varphi(u-v)+\varphi(u)+\varphi(-v)$$

are copulas, where the second one can be not exchangeable.

The resulting copulas do not feature tail dependence, can easily range from C^- to C^+, are relatively easy to simulate and can be extended to dimensions beyond two.

3.4.4 Copula Calibration, CDOs and Criticism of Copula Functions

Calibration of the copula parameters from market data is a difficult task. To see how the credit markets have used and also abused the notion of copula in calibrating Collateralized Debt Obligations (CDOs) Tranche data see [189] and [60]. The notion of implied and base correlation is discussed in such works, showing that it may lead to arbitrageable consequences such as negative losses.

Besides abusing the already limited and static copula notion, credit markets also typically assumed zero credit spread volatility, when actually credit spread volatility has always been found to be quite large and easily above 50% (see [31]). The dangers of assuming zero credit volatility in conjunction with copula default modelling have been highlighted in the context of counterparty risk on CDS in [43], see also CVA for CDS in Chapter 7, Section 7.5.

Besides the specific criticism above related to the application to CDOs, copula functions have been invested with more methodological criticism, see [149] and a response in [113]. Our opinion on this debate is that copulas should be neither demonized nor idolized. We believe copulas can be used properly in suitable contexts. In a way, copulas are nothing but multivariate distributions (after standardizing away marginal information) and as such are not sophisticated stochastic processes, but this does not mean they do not pose interesting problems. For example, one can study the extreme value properties of the copula or even generalize lack of memory to the multivariate case through copula functions, see [44].

In this book we will use copula functions only for low dimensional systems, so that the information flattening, calibration and arbitrage problems we described above for the CDO case will not affect our analysis. Despite this, the lack of dynamics and the artificial split between marginals and dependency may still pose problems, as we will argue in Chapter 7.

Part II

PRICING COUNTERPARTY RISK: UNILATERAL CVA

4

Unilateral CVA and Netting for Interest Rate Products

This chapter re-elaborates and expands material from Brigo and Masetti (2005) [47] and Brigo and Mercurio (2006) [48].

In this chapter we show how to handle counterparty risk when pricing some basic financial products in the interest rates asset class. In particular, we are analyzing in detail *counterparty-risky* (or default-risky) *Interest-Rate Swaps*. In doing so we will also establish the basic formula and framework for pricing of counterparty risk in general. It is somehow appropriate that we establish the general formula in the initial interest rate chapter, since interest rate swaps constitute the majority of instruments to which counterparty risk pricing is typically applied.

This chapter, therefore, starts considering the point of view of computing the credit valuation adjustment, or CVA.

In general, the reason to introduce counterparty risk when evaluating a contract is linked to the fact that many financial contracts are traded over the counter (OTC), outside exchanges, so that the credit quality of the counterparty can be important. To give the reader an idea of the size of the OTC derivatives market, the 2007 statistics on notional amounts outstanding of such instruments showed a figure of USD516 trillion in June 2007 (1 trillion $= 10^{12} =$ 1,000 billions). More significantly, gross market values, representing the cost of replacement for all open contracts at the prevailing market prices, have, again in June 2007 (see BIS Quarterly Review, December 2007 [23]), been estimated at USD11 trillion. To put such figures in context, one may consider that the gross domestic product of the USA in the same period was of the order of magnitude of USD13 trillion.

The staggering size of the OTC derivatives market clearly shows that counterparty risk is a very relevant issue. This is particularly poignant when thinking of the different defaults experienced by important financial companies and banks during the past years and the global financial crisis in particular. Regulatory issues related to the FASB and IAS accounting standards encourage the inclusion of counterparty risk in valuation practices, although not always in a way that is consistent with capital requirements regulation such as the forthcoming Basel III. We will say more about such a discrepancy later in the book, but see also Chapter 1.

4.1 FIRST STEPS TOWARDS A CVA PRICING FORMULA

We face the problem from the viewpoint of a safe (default-free) counterparty entering a financial contract with another counterparty that has a positive probability of defaulting before the maturity of the contract itself. This is a stylized situation and it is clearly not realistic, since default-free counterparties are hard to find these days, even among sovereigns.

We name the two parties in the deal "B" and "C". For example, "B" could be typically a bank, and "C" could be a corporate counterparty with whom the bank is trading a swap. In other parts of the book the bank "B" will be replaced by a more generic investor "I" but the idea is the same. The counterparty, besides being a corporate can also be, more generally, another bank or a buy side client "C". In this chapter "C" is not posting collateral and therefore CVA is relevant (we will see cases where, due to Gap risk, CVA is relevant even with daily collateral margining, later in the book) although our notation is completely general and the opposite may apply.

Usually we compute the contract value from the point of view of the default-free party, namely "B".

4.1.1 Symmetry versus Asymmetry

When is counterparty risk symmetric and when is it asymmetric? Symmetry involves a sort of local "money conservation" principle:

Definition 4.1.1 *The counterparty risk valuation problem is said to be symmetric for two parties B and C if the total price of the position for B as valued at a given time, including counterparty risk, is exactly the opposite of the total price of the position valued by C at the time and including, again, counterparty risk.*

We can define the asymmetric case as

Definition 4.1.2 *The counterparty risk valuation problem is said to be asymmetric for two parties A and B if it is not symmetric.*

Particular cases of interest in the above definitions regard the situation where at least one party, say B, is taken as default free. This is the point of view we take in this chapter.

Assumption 4.1.3 ***Unilateral Default Assumption (UDA): Assuming one party (B) to be default free.*** *In this chapter we assume that calculations are done considering "B" to be default free. Valuation of the contract is done usually from "B's" point of view.*

Under Assumption 4.1.3, the case will be symmetric if the fact that B is default free is recognized by C, the case will be asymmetric if C does not recognize B as default free. Indeed, if C does not recognize B as default free, it will charge a counterparty risk adjustment to B that B does not recognize, leading to an asymmetry in the valuation.

One context where the asymmetric case can work in practice is when it is an approximation for the symmetric case. Assume B has a much higher credit quality than C. In such a case, C may agree that B assumes to be default-free when valuing counterparty risk to C for practical purposes. This way C also assumes that, if C were to compute the counterparty risk valuation adjustment of the position towards B, this would be zero since B is considered as having null default probability for practical purposes (even if this is not really the case).

Remark 4.1.4 ***(On the realism of UDA Assumption 4.1.3 after the 8 credit events on Financials in 2008)*** *Since 2008 it is very difficult to accept the notion that market parties can be default free. Even sovereign debts have faced considerable credit problems during the global crisis which started in 2007. In the past, financial institutions were often considered of a higher credit quality than corporates, and they would often assume themselves to be default free in valuing CVA, thus following the UDA Assumption 4.1.3 above. This would be generally recognized by C, so that we are in the symmetric definition above. However, the 8 credit events on financial institutions that occurred in one month of 2008 (Fannie Mae, Freddie Mac, Lehman Brothers, Washington Mutual, Landsbanki, Glitnir, Kaupthing, and in a way* *also Merrill Lynch) clearly show that the assumption that important financial institutions are default free is not realistic.*

We will start by adopting the UDA Assumption 4.1.3, and explore the bilateral one with two defaultable parties later in the book. This is because the case with only one defaultable party is already sufficient to highlight a number of fundamental issues one faces when dealing with CVA calculations.

As we hinted above, we assume that there are no guarantees in place (such as collateral), and also that the default risk is charged upfront to counterparty C and has to be included in the risk-neutral pricing paradigm. From this point of view, when investing in default-risky assets one requires a premium as a reward for assuming the default risk. If we think, for example, of a corporate bond, we know that the yield is higher than the corresponding yield of a hypothetical risk-free bond, and this difference is usually called *credit spread*. The (positive) credit spread implies a lower price for the bond when compared to default-free bonds. This is a typical feature of every asset: the value of a generic claim traded with a counterparty subject to default risk is always smaller than the value of the same claim traded with a counterparty having a null default probability. This will imply that the price adjustment to the default-free party "B" will be negative, and indeed we will see that the Credit Valuation Adjustment (CVA) is a positive term to be subtracted from the risk-free price by "B" when marking to market the position towards "C". In this chapter we call such a term Unilateral Credit Valuation Adjustment (UCVA), Unilateral referring to the fact that default risk is only on one side, following the UDA Assumption 4.1.3.

In this chapter we focus on the following points in particular:

- Given the assumption of absence of guarantees, the counterparty risk for the payout has to be charged upfront, by including it in the risk-neutral valuation paradigm as a component of the price.
- Illustrate how the inclusion of counterparty risk in the valuation can make a payoff model dependent by adding one level of optionality.
- Use the risk-neutral default probability for the counterparty by extracting it from Credit Default Swap (CDS) or corporate bond data.
- Because of the previous point, the chosen default model will have to be calibrated to CDS data.
- When possible (later on in the book), we will take into account the correlation between the underlying of the contract and the default of the counterparty. This will allow us to model Wrong Way Risk (WWR).

4.1.2 Modelling the Counterparty Default Process

We have seen how to model the counterparty default in detail in Chapter 3. Here we give a brief summary of the relevant part of that chapter.

When evaluating default-risky assets, one has to introduce the default times and default probabilities in the pricing models. We consider Credit Default Swaps as liquid sources of market risk-neutral default probabilities. Another choice could be to use the credit spread in corporate bonds to calibrate the default probability, but the results would not be the same when applied to the same name, due to the CDS-Bond basis. The CDS bond basis has become a very relevant quantity and is discussed with possible interpretations in [157]. We stick to CDS but the mathematics would be exactly the same for bonds.

As we have seen in Chapter 3 different models can be used to calibrate CDS data and obtain default probabilities. Here we resort to intensity models, and use the structural models in connection with the equity market in Chapter 8. When dealing with the interest rate swap examples, we strip default probabilities from CDS data by resorting to basic intensity models in their simplest formulation. In this formulation default is modelled as the first jump of a Poisson process.

The chapter starts in Section 4.3 with a general formula for unilateral counterparty risk valuation. We show that the price in the presence of counterparty risk is just the default-free price minus a discounted option term in scenarios of early default multiplied by the loss given default. The option is on the residual present value at time of default, with zero strike. We notice that even payoffs where the valuation is model independent become model dependent due to counterparty risk. This aspect is rather dramatic when trying to incorporate counterparty risk in a way that does not destroy the default-free valuation models.

In this chapter, we compute upfront counterparty risk for portfolios of interest rate swaps, possibly in the presence of netting agreements. We will derive quick approximated formulas and test them against full Monte Carlo simulations of the price. The derivation will assume independence between interest rates and credit spreads (intensity), or more particularly deterministic intensity. The framework is also suited to computing counterparty risk on non-standard swap contracts such as zero coupon swaps, amortizing swaps and so on. With the independence assumption we are neglecting the important feature of wrong way risk. Wrong way risk will be analyzed in depth in Chapter 5.

Remark 4.1.5 ***(Overlap).*** *We would like to keep the chapters as self-contained as possible, so that readers interested in only specific asset classes will not need to read all the book. Therefore there will be a minium degree of overlap among chapters.*

4.2 THE PROBABILISTIC FRAMEWORK

This section contains our probabilistic assumptions.

We place ourselves in a probability space $(\Omega, \mathcal{G}, \mathcal{G}_t, \mathbb{Q})$. The usual interpretation of this space as an experiment can help intuition. We denote the generic experiment result by $\omega \in \Omega$; Ω represents the set of all possible outcomes of the random experiment, and the σ-field $\mathcal{G}$ represents the set of events $A \subset \Omega$ with which we shall work. The σ-field $\mathcal{G}_t$ represents the information available up to time t. We have $\mathcal{G}_t \subseteq \mathcal{G}_u \subseteq \mathcal{G}$ for all $t \leq u$, meaning that "the information increases in time", never exceeding the whole set of events $\mathcal{G}$. The family of σ-fields $(\mathcal{G}_t)_{t\geq 0}$ is called filtration.

If the experiment result is ω and $\omega \in A \in \mathcal{G}$, we say that the event A occurred. If $\omega \in A \in \mathcal{G}_t$, we say that the event A occurred at a time smaller or equal to t.

The probability measure $\mathbb{Q}$ is the risk-neutral measure, or the pricing measure. It is the measure associated with the locally risk-free bank account numeraire B_t, evolving according to the risk-free rate r

$$dB_t = r_t B_t dt, \quad B_0 = 1.$$

Under this measure all prices of tradable assets divided by B_t are martingales. We refer to Chapter 2 of [48] for more details, in a notation that is similar to the one used in this book. It is worth noticing that defaultable assets cannot be numeraires, which introduces problems in valuation of CDS options and defaultable claims generally. The interested reader is referred to Chapters 20–23 of [48], as they are friendly, in terms of notation, with this book, and to [156] for a discussion of multiname credit pricing under possibly vanishing "numeraires".

We use the symbol $\mathbb{E}$ to denote expectation with respect to the probability measure $\mathbb{Q}$.

The default time τ will be defined on this probability space.

This space is endowed with a right-continuous and complete sub-filtration $\mathcal{F}_t$ representing all the observable market quantities but the default event (hence $\mathcal{F}_t \subseteq \mathcal{G}_t := \mathcal{F}_t \vee \mathcal{H}_t$ where $\mathcal{H}_t = \sigma(\{\tau \leq u\} : u \leq t)$ is the right-continuous filtration generated by the default event). We set $\mathbb{E}_t[\cdot] := \mathbb{E}[\cdot|\mathcal{G}_t]$.

In more colloquial terms, throughout the chapter $\mathcal{G}_t$ is the filtration modelling the market information up to time t, including explicit default monitoring up to t, whereas $\mathcal{F}_t$ is the default-free market information up to t (FX, interest rates, etc), without default monitoring.

We use an intensity model for the default time of the counterparty. In (deterministic-) intensity models the default event is described by a jump process, in particular a Poisson process with intensity γ. The jumps are completely independent of other market-observable quantities and are introduced as an exogenous component. The default time τ of the counterparty is the first jump time of a time-inhomogeneous Poisson process with intensity $\gamma(t)$ (which we assume to be strictly positive), i.e. is defined as

$$\tau := \Gamma^{-1}(\xi) \tag{4.1}$$

where Γ is the cumulated intensity $\Gamma(t) = \int_0^t \gamma(s)ds$ and ξ is a $\mathcal{F}_t$-independent random variable, with a standard exponential distribution.

Remark 4.2.1 ***(Instantaneous Default Probability).*** *In these models, in general $\mathcal{F}_t \subset \mathcal{G}_t$. When the intensity is deterministic, the filtration $\mathcal{F}$ plays a trivial role: $\mathbb{Q}\{\tau \leq u|\mathcal{F}_t\} = \mathbb{Q}\{\tau \leq u\}$. Moreover, we recall the interpretation of γ for Poisson processes:*

$$\mathbb{Q}(\tau \in [t, t + dt)|\tau \geq t) = \gamma(t)dt$$

so that $\gamma(t)$ is associated with the probability of defaulting around time t.

The default probability is $\mathbb{Q}\{\tau \leq T\} = 1 - \mathbb{Q}\{\tau > T\}$ where, using the above exponential distribution, we have

$$\mathbb{Q}\{\tau > T\} = \mathbb{Q}\{\Gamma(\tau) > \Gamma(T)\} = \mathbb{Q}\{\xi > \Gamma(T)\} = \exp\left(-\int_0^T \gamma_s ds\right). \tag{4.2}$$

The intensity function can be stripped from market prices of credit derivatives actively traded in the market, for example, Credit Default Swaps. Usually a particular shape is assumed for γ, i.e. piecewise constant or piecewise linear. For more details see Chapter 3 or Chapter 22 of [48].

4.3 THE GENERAL PRICING FORMULA FOR UNILATERAL COUNTERPARTY RISK

Let us call T the final maturity of the payoff we are going to evaluate. Consider the two parties in the deal as the investor and the counterparty. We present the calculations from the point of view of the investor, typically an investment bank "B". We consider the unilateral counterparty risk case, in that we assume that the investor "B" can consider itself to be default free, and that the defaultable counterparty "C" agrees.

A quick analysis of the cash flows with respect to default of the counterparty is as follows:

- If $\tau > T$ there is no default by the counterparty during the life of the product and the counterparty has no problems in repaying the investors.
- To the contrary, if $\tau \leq T$ the counterparty cannot fulfil its obligations and the following happens.
- At τ the Net Present Value (NPV) of the residual payoff until maturity is computed:
  - If this NPV is negative (respectively positive) for the investor (defaulted counterparty), it is completely paid (received) by the investor (counterparty) itself.
  - If the NPV is positive (negative) for the investor (counterparty), only a recovery fraction REC of the NPV is received (paid) by the investor (liquidators of the defaulted counterparty).

We will follow this structure in deriving the credit valuation adjustment.

Here all the expectations $\mathbb{E}_t$ are taken under the risk-neutral measure $\mathbb{Q}$ and with respect to the filtration $\mathcal{G}_t$.

Let us define $\Pi(u, s)$ as the net cash flows of the claim under examination as seen from the investor "B" but traded with a hypothetical default-free counterparty, between time u and time s, discounted back at u and added up. In other words, this is the default-free contract that is exchanged between the two parties "B" and "C" before including any counterparty default risk analysis. Then we define the default-free Net Present Value at time t as $\text{NPV}(t) = \mathbb{E}_t[\Pi(t, T)]$. Recall that in Chapter 2 the quantity $(\text{NPV}(t))^+$ has been defined as $\text{Ex}(t)$.

Let us call $\bar{\Pi}(t, T)$ the same payoff but traded with the defaultable counterparty. We have

$$\begin{aligned}\bar{\Pi}(t, T) &= \mathbf{1}_{\{\tau > T\}} \Pi(t, T) \\ &\quad + \mathbf{1}_{\{t < \tau \leq T\}} \left[\Pi(t, \tau) + D(t, \tau) \left(\text{REC}\, (\text{NPV}(\tau))^+ - (-\text{NPV}(\tau))^+ \right) \right]. \end{aligned} \tag{4.3}$$

This last expression is the general payoff under counterparty risk.

- Indeed, if there is no early default this expression reduces to risk-neutral valuation of the payoff (first term in the right-hand side)

$$\mathbf{1}_{\{\tau > T\}} \Pi(t, T).$$

- in case of early default,
  - the payments due before default occurs are exchanged regularly (second term),

$$\Pi(t, \tau)$$

  and then
  - if the residual net present value is positive only a recovery of it is received by the investor "B" (third term),

$$\text{REC}\, (\text{NPV}(\tau))^+$$

– whereas if it is negative it is paid in full (fourth term)

$$-(-\mathrm{NPV}(\tau))^+$$

Here REC is the recovery fraction of "C", and we recall that τ is the default time of "C". It is possible to prove the following:

Proposition 4.3.1 ***(General Unilateral Counterparty Risk Pricing Formula)****. At valuation time t, and provided the counterparty has not defaulted before t, i.e. on $\{\tau > t\}$, the price of our payoff with maturity T under counterparty risk is*

$$\begin{aligned}\mathbb{E}_t[\bar{\Pi}(t,T)] &= \mathbb{E}_t[\Pi(t,T)] - \underbrace{\mathbb{E}_t[\mathrm{L{\small GD}}\,\mathbf{1}_{\{t<\tau\le T\}}D(t,\tau)(\mathrm{NPV}(\tau))^+]}_{\text{positive counterparty-risk adjustment}} \\ &= \mathbb{E}_t[\Pi(t,T)] - \mathrm{U{\small CVA}}(t,T) \end{aligned} \tag{4.4}$$

with

$$\begin{aligned}\mathrm{U{\small CVA}}(t,T) &:= \mathbb{E}_t\left[\mathrm{L{\small GD}}\,\mathbf{1}_{\{t<\tau\le T\}}D(t,\tau)(\mathrm{NPV}(\tau))^+\right] \\ &= \mathbb{E}_t\left[\mathrm{L{\small GD}}\,\mathbf{1}_{\{t<\tau\le T\}}D(t,\tau)\mathrm{Ex}(\tau)\right] \\ &= \mathbb{E}_t\left[\mathrm{L{\small GD}}\,\mathbf{1}_{\{t<\tau\le T\}}D(t,\tau)\mathrm{EAD}\right]\end{aligned}$$

where $\mathrm{L{\small GD}} := 1 - \mathrm{R{\small EC}}$ is the loss given default, and the recovery fraction $\mathrm{R{\small EC}}$, unless differently specified, is assumed to be deterministic. It is clear that the value of a defaultable claim is the sum of the value of the corresponding default-free claim minus a positive adjustment. The positive adjustment to be subtracted is called (Unilateral) Credit Valuation Adjustment ((U)CVA), and it is given by a call option (with zero strike) on the residual NPV at default, giving nonzero contribution only in scenarios where $\tau \le T$. Counterparty risk thus adds an optionality level to the original payoff. This renders the counterparty risky payoff model dependent even when the original payoff is model independent. This implies, for example, that while the valuation of swaps without counterparty risk is model independent, requiring no dynamical model for the term structure (no volatility and correlations in particular), the valuation of swaps under counterparty risk will require an interest rate model. This implies that quick fixes of existing pricing routines to include counterparty risk are difficult to obtain.

We now prove the proposition. The reader that is not interested in technicalities may go directly to the next section, where we start to apply this formula to particular financial contracts, in the specific to single interest rate swaps and to a portfolio of IRS's with netting coefficients.

Proof. Since

$$\Pi(t,T) = \mathbf{1}_{\{\tau>T\}}\Pi(t,T) + \mathbf{1}_{\{\tau\le T\}}\Pi(t,T)$$

we can rewrite the terms inside the expectation in the right-hand side of (4.4) as

$$\begin{aligned}&\Pi(t,T) - \mathrm{L{\small GD}}\,\mathbf{1}_{\{\tau\le T\}}D(t,\tau)(\mathrm{NPV}(\tau))^+ \\ &\quad= \mathbf{1}_{\{\tau>T\}}\Pi(t,T) + \mathbf{1}_{\{\tau\le T\}}\Pi(t,T) + (\mathrm{R{\small EC}} - 1)\mathbf{1}_{\{\tau\le T\}}D(t,\tau)(\mathrm{NPV}(\tau))^+ \\ &\quad= \mathbf{1}_{\{\tau>T\}}\Pi(t,T) + \mathbf{1}_{\{\tau\le T\}}\Pi(t,T) + \mathrm{R{\small EC}}\,\mathbf{1}_{\{\tau\le T\}}D(t,\tau)(\mathrm{NPV}(\tau))^+ \\ &\qquad -\mathbf{1}_{\{\tau\le T\}}D(t,\tau)(\mathrm{NPV}(\tau))^+\end{aligned} \tag{4.5}$$

Conditional on the information at τ the second and the fourth terms are equal to

$$\begin{aligned}
&\mathbb{E}_\tau[\mathbf{1}_{\{\tau\le T\}}\Pi(t,T) - \mathbf{1}_{\{\tau\le T\}}D(t,\tau)(\mathrm{NPV}(\tau))^+] \\
&= \mathbb{E}_\tau[\mathbf{1}_{\{\tau\le T\}}[\Pi(t,\tau) + D(t,\tau)\Pi(\tau,T) - D(t,\tau)(\mathbb{E}_\tau[\Pi(\tau,T)])^+]] \\
&= \mathbf{1}_{\{\tau\le T\}}[\Pi(t,\tau) + D(t,\tau)\mathbb{E}_\tau[\Pi(\tau,T)] - D(t,\tau)(\mathbb{E}_\tau[\Pi(\tau,T)])^+] \\
&= \mathbf{1}_{\{\tau\le T\}}[\Pi(t,\tau) - D(t,\tau)(\mathbb{E}_\tau[\Pi(\tau,T)])^-] \\
&= \mathbf{1}_{\{\tau\le T\}}[\Pi(t,\tau) - D(t,\tau)(\mathbb{E}_\tau[-\Pi(\tau,T)])^+] \\
&= \mathbf{1}_{\{\tau\le T\}}[\Pi(t,\tau) - D(t,\tau)(-\mathrm{NPV}(\tau))^+] \qquad (4.6)
\end{aligned}$$

since trivially

$$\mathbf{1}_{\{\tau\le T\}}\Pi(t,T) = \mathbf{1}_{\{\tau\le T\}}(\Pi(t,\tau) + D(t,\tau)\Pi(\tau,T))$$

and $f = f^+ - f^- = f^+ - (-f)^+$. Then we can see that after conditioning on the information at time τ (4.5) and substituting the second and the fourth terms for (4.6), the expected value of (4.3) with respect to $\mathcal{F}_t$ coincides exactly with (4.4) by the properties of iterated expectations.

Notice finally that the previous formula can be approximated as follows. Take $t = 0$ for simplicity and write, on a discretization time grid $T_0, T_1, \ldots, T_b = T$,

$$\begin{aligned}
\mathbb{E}[\bar{\Pi}(0,T_b)] &= \mathbb{E}[\Pi(0,T_b)] - \mathrm{L{\scriptstyle GD}}\sum_{j=1}^{b}\mathbb{E}[\mathbf{1}_{\{T_{j-1}<\tau\le T_j\}}D(0,\tau)(\mathbb{E}_\tau[\Pi(\tau,T_b)])^+] \\
&\approx \mathbb{E}[\Pi(0,T_b)] - \underbrace{\mathrm{L{\scriptstyle GD}}\sum_{j=1}^{b}\mathbb{E}[\mathbf{1}_{\{T_{j-1}<\tau\le T_j\}}D(0,T_j)(\mathbb{E}_{T_j}[\Pi(T_j,T_b)])^+]}_{\text{approximated (positive) adjustment}} \qquad (4.7)
\end{aligned}$$

where the approximation consists in postponing the default time to the first T_i following τ in each bucket. From this last expression, under independence between Π and τ, one can factor the outer expectation inside the summation in products of default probabilities times option prices. Under independence between Π and τ:

$$\begin{aligned}
&\mathbb{E}[\bar{\Pi}(0,T_b)] \approx \mathbb{E}[\Pi(0,T_b)] \\
&\qquad -\mathrm{L{\scriptstyle GD}}\sum_{j=1}^{b}\underbrace{\mathbb{Q}\{T_{j-1}<\tau\le T_j\}}_{\text{default probability}}\underbrace{\mathbb{E}_{T_j}[D(0,T_j)(\mathbb{E}_{T_j}\Pi(T_j,T_b))^+]}_{\substack{\text{option on residual NPV}\\ \text{with maturity } T_j}}. \qquad (4.8)
\end{aligned}$$

This way we would not need a default model but only survival probabilities and an option model for the underling market of Π. This is only possible, in our case, if the default process and interest rates are independent, and as a consequence have zero correlation. This is what led to earlier results on swaps with counterparty risk in [47], which we are going to see below. In later chapters we do not assume independence, so that in general we need to compute the counterparty risk without factoring the expectations. To do so we will need a default model, to be correlated with the basic interest rate market.

4.4 INTEREST RATE SWAP (IRS) PORTFOLIOS

In this first part devoted to specific products we deal with counterparty risk in interest rate swaps (IRS) portfolios. The results can easily be transferred to single IRS with nonstandard features such as zero coupon IRS, amortizing IRS, bullet IRS etc. It suffices to suitably define the α and χ portfolio coefficients below.

The remaining sections of this chapter are structured as follows: in Section 4.4.1 we apply the general formula to a single IRS. We find the already known result (see also [186], [7], Chapter 6, [18], Chapter 14, [79], or [47], among other references) that the component of the IRS price due to counterparty risk is the sum of swaption prices with different maturities, each weighted with the probability of defaulting around that maturity.

Things become more interesting in Section 4.4.2 when we consider a portfolio of IRSs towards a single counterparty in the presence of a netting agreement. When default occurs, we need to consider the option on the residual present value of the whole portfolio. This option cannot be valued as a standard swaption, and we need either to resort to Monte Carlo simulation (under the LIBOR model, or alternatively the swap model) or to derive analytical approximations. We derive an analytical approximation based on the standard "drift freezing" technique for swaptions pricing in the LIBOR model [30], see also Chapter 6 of [48], presenting a standard derivation of the formula and numerical tests.

We find a formula that we can expect to work in a case where all IRS in the portfolio have the same direction: if we have a portfolio of IRS that are all long or short towards the same counterparty, the pricing problems become similar to that of a swap with different multiples of LIBOR and strikes at each payment date. The problem is then reduced to pricing an option on an IRS with non-standard flows. We do so by means of the abovementioned drift freezing technique and derive an analytical approximation. We test this approximation in Section 4.5 by using a Monte Carlo simulation under different stylized compositions of the netting portfolio. Consistently, with well-known results for standard swaptions under the LIBOR model with drift freezing, we find the approximation to work well within reasonable limits.

The more interesting part, however, is allowing for IRS's towards a given counterparty but going in both directions, long and short. This time the situation becomes more complicated: we can see the residual present value at the early default time as an option on the difference of two swap rates, each approximately lognormal. We study the drift freezing procedure and also an alternative three moments matching procedure. We test both approximations in Section 4.5 against Monte Carlo simulation under different portfolio configurations. We obtain a good approximation in most situations.

The approximated formula is well suited to risk management, where the computational time under each risk factors scenario is crucial and an analytical approximation may be needed to contain it.

4.4.1 Counterparty Risk in Single IRS

For the theory relative to the Interest Rate Swap we refer, for example, to [48]. Let us suppose that we are a default-free counterparty "B" entering a payer swap with a defaultable counterparty "C", exchanging fixed for floating payments at times $T_{a+1}, \ldots, T_b$.

Denote by β_i the year fraction between T_{i-1} and T_i, and by $P(t, T_i)$ the default-free zero coupon bond price at time t for maturity T_i. We take a unit notional on the swap. The contract requires us to pay a fixed rate K and to receive the floating rate L resetting one period earlier until the default time τ of "B" or until final maturity T if $\tau > T$. The fair (forward-swap) rate K at a given time t in a default-free market is the one which renders the swap zero-valued in t.

In the risk-free case the discounted payoff for a payer IRS is

$$\sum_{i=a+1}^{b} D(t, T_i)\, \beta_i\, (L(T_{i-1}, T_i) - K) \tag{4.9}$$

and the forward swap rate rendering the contract fair is

$$K = S(t; T_a, T_b) = S_{a,b}(t) = \frac{P(t, T_a) - P(t, T_b)}{\sum_{i=a+1}^{b} \beta_i P(t, T_i)}. \tag{4.10}$$

Of course, if we consider the possibility that "C" may default, the correct spread to be paid in the fixed leg is lower, as we are willing to be rewarded for bearing this default risk. In particular, using the previous Formula (4.4) we find

$$\bar{\Pi}_{\mathrm{IRS}}(t, T_b) = \Pi_{\mathrm{IRS}}(t, T_b) - \mathrm{UCVA}(t, T_b) \tag{4.11}$$

where $\mathrm{UCVA}(\cdot)$ is the unilateral credit valuation adjustment (UCVA) due to default

$$\begin{aligned} \mathrm{UCVA}(t, T_b) &= \mathrm{LGD}\, \mathbb{E}_t \left[\mathbf{1}_{\{\tau \le T_b\}} D(t, \tau)\, (\mathrm{NPV}(\tau))^+ \right] \\ &= \mathrm{LGD} \int_{T_a}^{T_b} \mathrm{PS}(t; s, T_b, K, S(t; s, T_b), \sigma_{s,T_b})\, d_s \mathbb{Q}\{\tau \le s\} \end{aligned} \tag{4.12}$$

being $\mathrm{PS}(t; s, T_b, K, S(t; s, T_b), \sigma_{s,T_b})$ the price in t of a swaption with maturity s, strike K, underlying forward swap rate $S(t; s, T_b)$, volatility σ_{s,T_b} and underlying swap with final maturity T_b. When $s = T_j$ for some j we replace the arguments s, T_b by indices j, b.

The proof is easy: given independence between τ and interest rates, and given that the residual NPV is a forward start IRS starting at the default time, the option on the residual NPV is a sum of swaptions with maturities ranging the possible values of the default time, each weighted (thanks to independence) by the probabilities of defaulting around each time value.

We can simplify Equation (4.12) through some assumptions: we allow the default to happen only at points T_i of the fixed leg payments grid. In particular two different specifications could be applied: one for which the default is anticipated to the last T_i preceding τ and one for which it is postponed to the first T_i following τ. In this way the expected loss part in expression (4.12) is simplified. Indeed, in the case of the postponed (P) payoff we obtain:

$$\begin{aligned} \mathrm{UCVA}^P(t, T_b) &:= \mathrm{LGD} \sum_{i=a+1}^{b-1} \mathbb{Q}\{\tau \in (T_{i-1}, T_i]\}\ \mathrm{PS}_{i,b}(t; K, S_{i,b}(t), \sigma_{i,b}) \\ &= \mathrm{LGD} \sum_{i=a+1}^{b-1} (\mathbb{Q}\{\tau > T_{i-1}\} - \mathbb{Q}\{\tau > T_i\})\ \mathrm{PS}_{i,b}(t; K, S_{i,b}(t), \sigma_{i,b}) \end{aligned} \tag{4.13}$$

and this can be easily computed summing across the T_i's and using the default probabilities implicitly given in market CDS prices by means of the intensity function γ.

A similar result can be obtained considering the anticipated (A) default:

$$\begin{aligned}\text{UCVA}^A(t, T_b) &:= \text{LGD} \sum_{i=a}^{b-1} \mathbb{Q}\{\tau \in (T_i, T_{i+1}]\} \ \text{PS}_{i,b}(t; K, S_{i,b}(t), \sigma_{i,b}) \\ &= \text{LGD} \sum_{i=a}^{b-1} (\mathbb{Q}\{\tau > T_i\} - \mathbb{Q}\{\tau > T_{i+1}\}) \ \text{PS}_{i,b}(t; K, S_{i,b}(t), \sigma_{i,b}). \quad (4.14)\end{aligned}$$

We carried out some numerical experiments to analyze the impact of counterparty risk on the fair rate of the swap. For the discounts and the swap rates we used the data of 10 March 2004. The volatility matrix of the swaptions has been chosen arbitrarily and in particular we kept a flat swaption volatility matrix of 15% across all tenors and maturities. We also considered different default-risk profiles for the counterparty, studying stylized cases of high, medium and low default risk. Also, we choose a piecewise constant intensity γ.

The choice of the shape of γ poses some problems. Mainly, one might face the problem of evaluating a 30-year swap when the market quotes CDS's up to only a 10-years maturity. In this case we need to strip the intensities from the available CDS's and then we have to extrapolate the intensity values for the longer maturities, or perhaps use bond information if available, while paying attention to the difference between intensities stripped by CDSs and by bonds, leading to the so-called CDS Bond basis. If we use piecewise linear intensity then, when extrapolating up to 20 years, we could find strange results (in principle also with negative probabilities). The use of a piecewise constant intensity has the drawback of not being continuous but generally it provides less dramatic distorsions when extrapolating (at least granting positive default probabilities after 10 years).

In Table 4.1 we report the survival probabilities and the intensities in the three cases with different credit quality for the counterparty while in Table 4.2 we report the risk-free swap rates for different maturities together with the spread that has to be subtracted to make the swap fair when including counterparty risk.

We see that, as expected, the spread adjustment (to be subtracted from the implied risk-free swap rate) grows together with the riskiness of the counterparty, and also with the increasing maturity of the underlying swap. We also see that the difference between the two

Table 4.1 Intensities nodes and related survival probabilities $\mathbb{Q}\{\tau > T\}$ in three different cases for the credit quality of the counterparty

	Low Risk		Medium Risk		High Risk	
Date	Intensity	Survival	Intensity	Survival	Intensity	Survival
10-mar-04	0.0036	100.00%	0.0202	100.00%	0.0534	100.00%
12-mar-05	0.0036	99.64%	0.0202	97.96%	0.0534	94.70%
12-mar-07	0.0065	98.34%	0.0231	93.48%	0.0564	84.47%
12-mar-09	0.0099	96.38%	0.0266	88.57%	0.0600	74.78%
12-mar-11	0.0111	94.24%	0.0278	83.71%	0.0614	66.03%
12-mar-14	0.0177	89.31%	0.0349	75.27%	0.0696	53.42%
12-mar-19	0.0177	81.64%	0.0349	63.05%	0.0696	37.53%
12-mar-24	0.0177	74.63%	0.0349	52.80%	0.0696	26.36%
12-mar-29	0.0177	68.22%	0.0349	44.23%	0.0696	18.51%
12-mar-34	0.0177	62.36%	0.0349	37.05%	0.0696	13.01%

Table 4.2 Risk-free implied swap rate and related counterparty risk spread negative adjustment. We report the spread to be subtracted (in basis points) for both anticipated and postponed default approximations

Maturity (yrs)	Risk-free swap rate	Low Risk		Medium Risk		High Risk	
		Antic.	Postp.	Antic.	Postp.	Antic.	Postp.
5	3.248%	0.64	0.50	1.91	1.80	4.27	4.25
10	4.075%	2.52	2.16	6.09	5.8	12.28	12.26
15	4.462%	4.92	4.47	10.52	10.2	19.55	19.68
20	4.676%	7.24	6.78	14.51	14.22	25.44	25.77
25	4.775%	9.1	8.63	17.53	17.28	29.46	29.93
30	4.810%	10.51	10.07	19.66	19.45	31.97	32.54

approximations is very low (most of the time it is smaller than 0.5 basis points). One could decide to use an average of the two values, just to reach a better proxy for the exact correction in expression (4.12), but in any case the error would be negligible for most practical purposes.

As a further remark, we mention the fact that in case we enter a *receiver* IRS and still consider that only our counterparty can default, a similar procedure can be applied, but in that case there is a higher value for the swap rate K than in the default-free case (this is intuitive since if we are "B" we are receiving fixed and we want a premium to bear the default risk of "C").

4.4.2 Counterparty Risk in an IRS Portfolio with Netting

In case we are dealing with an IRS portfolio towards a single counterparty under a netting agreement, we need to take into account the netting possibilities. This complicates matters considerably, as we are going to see shortly. We will derive an analytical approximation that we will test under different netting coefficients.

Remark 4.4.1 *(IRS Portfolios) In an IRS portfolio consisting of several single IRSs towards the same counterparty with different tenors and maturities put together, some long and some short, we may think of assembling the cash flows at each resetting date. Floating rates add and subtract into multiples (positive or negative) of LIBOR rates at each reset and the fixed rates (strikes) of the basic IRSs behave similarly.*

Suppose that we have a portfolio of N IRSs with homogeneous resetting dates but different maturities and inception dates. Let

$$\alpha_i := \beta_i \left| \sum_{j=1}^{N} A_i^j \phi_j \right| , \quad K_i := \beta_i \left| \sum_{j=1}^{N} A_i^j K_j \phi_j \right|$$

$$\chi_i := \text{sign}\left(\sum_{j=1}^{N} A_i^j \phi_j \right) , \quad \psi_i := \text{sign}\left(\sum_{j=1}^{N} A_i^j K_j \phi_j \right)$$

for all $i \in [a+1, b]$, where: $A_i^j \geq 0$ is the notional amount relative to the IRS j on the resetting date T_i (this allows the inclusion of any amortizing plan); ϕ_j is the payer/receiver fixed rate flag which takes values $\{-1, 1\}$ (e.g. 1 for payer, -1 for receiver); $K_j > 0$ is the fixed rate.

Example 4.4.2 *Basically χ_i may not be equal to ψ_i. Consider a portfolio with three bullet IRSs, having the same maturities, same notional (suppose $A_i^j = 1$ for all $\{i, j\} \in [a+1, b] \cup [1, N]$) and common resetting periods. Suppose that we are facing the following structure:*

- *IRS1(Payer fixed rate): $K_1 = 1\%$;*
- *IRS2(Payer fixed rate): $K_2 = 2\%$;*
- *IRS3(Receiver fixed rate): $K_3 = 4\%$.*

It follows that $\chi_i = 1$ whereas $\psi_i = -1$.

We indicate by $L(T_{i-1}, T_i)$ the LIBOR rate on the resetting period T_{i-1} and T_i (where T_i is expressed in terms of year-fraction).

The total portfolio discounted payoff at time $t \leq T_a$ may be written as

$$\begin{aligned}\Pi_{\text{PIRS}}(t, T_b) &= \sum_{i=a+1}^{b} D(t, T_i)(\chi_i \alpha_i L(T_{i-1}, T_i) - \psi_i K_i) \\ &= \sum_{i=a+1}^{b} D(t, T_i)\chi_i \left(\alpha_i L(T_{i-1}, T_i) - \widetilde{K}_i\right)\end{aligned}$$

where $\widetilde{K}_i := (\frac{\psi_i}{\chi_i})K_i$. The α_i is the positive total year fraction (also called netting coefficient) in front of the LIBOR rates in the total portfolio of IRS towards a given counterparty.

This framework can also be used for single non-standard IRS (zero coupon, bullet, amortizing...) by suitably defining the α's and K's. The $\widetilde{K}_i$ represents the cumulated fixed rate of the total portfolio to be exchanged at time T_i, when the valuation is made at time t.

The expected value at time t for a default-free portfolio is known to be

$$\mathbb{E}_t[\Pi_{\text{PIRS}}(t, T_b)] = \sum_{i=a+1}^{b} P(t, T_i)\chi_i \left(\alpha_i F_i(t) - \widetilde{K}_i\right)$$

where each expectation in the sum has been easily computed by resorting for example to the related forward measure, and $F_i(t)$ is the forward LIBOR rate at time t for expiry at T_{i-1} and maturity T_i. This expected value represents the swap price without counterparty risk, and we see that this price is model independent. One only needs the initial time-t interest rate curve to compute forward rates $F_i(t)$ and discounts $P(t, T_i)$, with no need to postulate a dynamics for the term structure. Using Formula (4.4) we can compute the expected value for the IRS portfolio under counterparty risk by

$$\mathbb{E}_t\left[\bar{\Pi}_{\text{PIRS}}(t, T_b)\right] = \mathbb{E}_t\left[\Pi_{\text{PIRS}}(t, T_b)\right] - \text{LGD}\,\mathbb{E}_t\left[\mathbf{1}_{\{t<\tau\leq T_b\}} D(t, \tau)(\text{NPV}(\tau))^+\right] \quad (4.15)$$

where $\text{NPV}(\tau) = \mathbb{E}_\tau\left[\Pi_{\text{PIRS}}(\tau, T_b)\right]$.

The UCVA part of (4.15) can be rewritten as

$$\begin{aligned}\text{UCVA}(t, T_b) &= \text{LGD}\,\mathbb{E}_t\left[\mathbf{1}_{\{\tau\leq T_b\}} D(t, \tau)(\text{NPV}(\tau))^+\right] \\ &= \text{LGD} \sum_{i=a+1}^{b} \mathbb{E}_t\left[\mathbf{1}_{\{\tau\in(T_{i-1}, T_i]\}} D(t, \tau)(\text{NPV}(\tau))^+\right]\end{aligned}$$

Since we are assuming a deterministic intensity, if we postpone the default event up to the first T_i following τ, i.e.:

$$\inf\{T_i : i \in \mathbb{Z},\ T_i \geq \tau\}$$

we finally have that

$$\text{UCVA}(t, T_b) = \text{LGD} \sum_{i=a+1}^{b} \mathbb{Q}\{\tau \in (T_{i-1}, T_i]\}\, \mathbb{E}_t\left[D(t, T_i)(\text{NPV}(T_i))^+\right]. \tag{4.16}$$

Recall that in this case

$$\text{NPV}(T_i) = \sum_{k=i+1}^{b} P(T_i, T_k)\chi_k[\alpha_k F_k(T_i) - \widetilde{K}_k]$$

Since the counterparty-risky portfolio is decomposed into a swap (with non-standard coefficients) and a weighted sum of expectations on NPV(τ)'s, the only issue we are facing now is to get an evaluation of $\mathbb{E}_t[D(t, T_i)(\text{NPV}(T_i))^+]$. After multiplying and dividing by $\widehat{C}_{i,b}(T_i) := \sum_{h=i+1}^{b} \alpha_h P(T_i, T_h)$, this expectation can be rewritten as

$$\mathbb{E}_t\left[D(t, T_i)(\text{NPV}(T_i))^+\right] = \mathbb{E}_t\left[D(t, T_i)\widehat{C}_{i,b}(T_i)\left(\widehat{S}_{i,b}(T_i) - \widehat{K}(T_i)\right)^+\right]$$

where, if we set for all T, $\widehat{w}_k(T) := \alpha_k P(T, T_k)/\widehat{C}_{i,b}(T)$ we have

$$\widehat{S}_{i,b}(T) := \sum_{k=i+1}^{b} \widehat{w}_k(T)\chi_k F_k(T), \quad \widehat{K}(T) := \sum_{k=i+1}^{b} \widehat{w}_k(T)\chi_k \frac{\widetilde{K}_k}{\alpha_k}$$

4.4.3 The Drift Freezing Approximation

Now consider the following approximation:

$$\widehat{S}_{i,b}(T_i) \approx \sum_{k=i+1}^{b} \widehat{w}_k(t)\chi_k F_k(T_i)$$

so that $d\widehat{S}_{i,b}(t') \approx \sum_{k=i+1}^{b} \widehat{w}_k(t)\chi_k dF_k(t')$, for $t' \in [t, T_i]$.

It follows by arguments completely analogous to those used for the approximated swaption pricing formula (Brace, Gatarek and Musiela (1997) [30], and Brigo and Mercurio (2001) [48], Proposition 6.13.1) that the variance of $\widehat{S}_{i,b}(T_i)$ at time t can be easily approximated by

$$\begin{aligned} v_{i,b}^2 &= v_{i,b}^2(t, T_i) \\ &\approx \widehat{S}_{i,b}(t)^{-2} \sum_{h,k=i+1}^{b} \widehat{w}_h(t)\widehat{w}_k(t)\chi_h\chi_k F_h(t)F_k(t)\rho_{h,k} \int_t^{T_i} \sigma_h(s)\sigma_k(s)ds \end{aligned}$$

where σ_h and σ_k are the instantaneous volatilities of the forward rates F_h and F_k whereas $\rho_{h,k}$ is the instantaneous correlation between the Brownian motions of F_h and F_k. Notice that this procedure is very close to a two-moment matching technique. We investigate a three-moment matching technique in the next section.

Finally, changing numeraire and using the approximated dynamics, if $\widehat{S}_{i,b}(t)$ and $\widehat{K}$ have the same sign

$$\begin{aligned}\mathbb{E}_t[D(t,T_i)(\mathrm{NPV}(T_i))^+] &= \mathbb{E}_t^B[B(t)(\mathrm{NPV}(T_i))^+/B(T_i)]\\ &= \widehat{\mathbb{E}}_t^{i,b}[\widehat{C}_{i,b}(t)(\mathrm{NPV}(T_i))^+/\widehat{C}_{i,b}(T_i)]\\ &= \widehat{C}_{i,b}(t)\widehat{\mathbb{E}}_t^{i,b}[(\widehat{S}_{i,b}(T_i)-\widehat{K}(T_i))^+]\\ &\approx \widehat{C}_{i,b}(t)\phi\mathrm{Bl}(\widehat{K},\widehat{S}_{i,b}(t),v_{i,b}^2,\phi)\end{aligned}\tag{4.17}$$

where Bl(K,S,Q,f) denotes the core of Black's formula, namely

$$fK\Phi(fd_1)-fS\Phi(fd_2),$$

for a standard swaption with strike K, spot S, squared volatility Q, $f=1$ for a call and $f=-1$ for a put. Furthermore, we have

$$\phi := \begin{cases} +1, & \text{if } \widehat{S}_{i,b}(t) > 0 \text{ and } \widehat{K} > 0;\\ -1, & \text{if } \widehat{S}_{i,b}(t) < 0 \text{ and } \widehat{K} < 0;\end{cases}$$

If instead $\widehat{S}_{i,b}(t) > 0$ and $\widehat{K} < 0$, the price is simply reduced to a forward on $\widehat{S}_{i,b}(t)$ whereas for $\widehat{S}_{i,b}(t) < 0$ and $\widehat{K} > 0$ the price is zero.

Notice that $\widehat{S}_{i,b}$ is a martingale under the measure associated with the numeraire $\widehat{C}_{i,b}$ since it can be written as a portfolio of zero coupon bonds divided by the numeraire itself. Indeed, by definition of $\widehat{S}$ we can write:

$$\begin{aligned}\widehat{S}_{i,b}(t') &= \sum_{k=i+1}^{b}\widehat{w}_k(t')\chi_k F_k(t')\\ &= \sum_{k=i+1}^{b}\frac{\alpha_k P(t',T_k)}{\widehat{C}_{i,b}(t')}\chi_k F_k(t')\\ &= \sum_{k=i+1}^{b}\frac{\alpha_k P(t',T_k)}{\widehat{C}_{i,b}(t')}\chi_k\frac{1}{\beta_k}\left(\frac{P(t',T_{k-1})}{P(t',T_k)}-1\right)\\ &= \sum_{k=i+1}^{b}\frac{\alpha_k}{\widehat{C}_{i,b}(t')}\chi_k\frac{1}{\beta_k}(P(t',T_{k-1})-P(t',T_k)).\end{aligned}\tag{4.18}$$

The above pricing formula has to be handled carefully. Notice in particular that the initial condition of the approximated dynamics, i.e. $\widehat{S}_{i,b}(t)$, could be negative. In this case $\widehat{S}_{i,b}$ follows approximately a geometric Brownian motion with negative initial condition, which is just minus a geometric Brownian motion with the opposite (positive) initial condition and the same volatility. The call option becomes then a put on the opposite geometric Brownian motion and has to be valued as such.

We may expect these formulas to work in all cases where the swaps in the portfolio all have the same direction, i.e. when all χ are equal to each other. In this case the underlying $\widehat{S}_{i,b}$ has always the same sign in all scenarios, and the approximation by a geometric Brownian motion is in principle reasonable.

In the other cases with mixed χ's (i.e. a portfolio with IRS both long and short), the underlying $\widehat{S}_{i,b}$ can be both positive and negative in different scenarios and at different times (even if it is still a martingale). In this case we approximate it with a geometric Brownian motion maintaining a constant sign equal to the sign of the initial condition, and with the usual approximated volatility. We will see that results are not as bad as one can expect, provided some tricks are used. In particular, using put-call parity one has to set oneself into the correct tail of the lognormal approximated density.

Indeed, consider for example as initial time $t = 0$ a case where $\widehat{S}_{i,b}(0)$ is positive but where the netting coefficients generate some negative future scenarios of $\widehat{S}_{i,b}(T_i)$. This way, the density of $\widehat{S}_{i,b}(T_i)$ will have both a positive and a negative tail. If we fit a lognormal distribution associated with a geometric Brownian motion with positive initial condition $\widehat{S}_{i,b}(0)$, when we price a call option on $\widehat{S}_{i,b}(T_i)$ both the true density and the approximated lognormal have the (right) tail, whereas if we price a put option we have the true underlying $\widehat{S}_{i,b}(T_i)$ with a left tail and the lognormal approximated process with no left tail. This means that the call will be priced in the presence of tails both in the true underlying and in the approximated process, whereas the approximated process in the put case is missing the tail. Hence, from this point of view, it is best to price a call rather than a put. If we do have to price a put, we can still price a call and apply the parity to get the put. This will result in a better approximation than integrating directly the put payoff against an approximated density that is missing the tail. We apply this method in Section 4.5.3, Case C, by computing the put prices with the call price and the parity. The relative error we had obtained when integrating directly the put payoff in the money at $2y - 10y$ is -3.929% whereas by applying the parity we obtained -2.156%.

Even so, at times precision will not be sufficient. We resort then to a method that takes into account also an approximated estimate of the third moment of the underlying $\widehat{S}_{i,b}$.

4.4.4 The Three-Moments Matching Technique

As explained above a lognormal approximation may not be the right choice in the case of mixed (i.e. positive and negative) netting coefficients. In particular, linear combinations of lognormal variables with unit-weights (positive or negative) are no longer a lognormal.

In this case we have used the three-moments matching technique, by the shifting of a parameter X an auxiliary martingale lognormal process Y with a flag $\phi \in \{-1, +1\}$ (to consider the correct side of the distribution), leading to a dynamics of the form:

$$
\begin{aligned}
A_{T_i} &= X + \phi\, Y(T_i) \\
&= X + \phi\, Y(t) \exp\left(\int_t^{T_i} \eta(s) dW_s - 1/2 \int_t^{T_i} \eta(s)^2 ds \right)
\end{aligned}
$$

with W a Brownian motion under the $\widehat{C}_{i,b}$-measure and where η is the volatility of the process Y. In particular we have:

$$
\begin{aligned}
\widehat{\mathbb{E}}_t^{i,b}[A_{T_i}] &= X + \phi\, Y(t)\,, \\
\widehat{\mathbb{E}}_t^{i,b}[(A_{T_i})^2] &= X^2 + Y(t)^2 \exp\left(\int_t^{T_i} \eta(s)^2 ds \right) + 2\phi\, XY(t)\,, \\
\widehat{\mathbb{E}}_t^{i,b}[(A_{T_i})^3] &= X^3 + \phi\, Y(t)^3 \exp\left(3 \int_t^{T_i} \eta(s)^2 ds \right) + 3\phi\, X^2 Y(t) \\
&\quad + 3XY(t)^2 \exp\left(\int_t^{T_i} \eta(s)^2 ds \right).
\end{aligned}
$$

These non-central moments have to be matched against the first three moments of $\widehat{S}_{i,b}(T_i)$:

$$\widehat{\mathbb{E}}_t^{i,b}[(\widehat{S}_{i,b}(T_i))^m] = \sum_{j_1=i+1}^{b} \cdots \sum_{j_m=i+1}^{b} \prod_{\ell=j_1}^{j_m} \widehat{w}_\ell(t)\chi_\ell F_\ell(t) \cdot \exp\left\{ \sum_{k=i+1}^{m+i-1} \sum_{h=k+1}^{m+i} \rho_{j_k,j_h} \int_t^{T_i} \sigma_{j_k}(s)\sigma_{j_h}(s)ds \right\} \tag{4.19}$$

for $m = 1, 2, 3$.

Assuming η constant and taking $t = 0$ for simplicity, and solving analytically the system

$$\begin{aligned} \widehat{\mathbb{E}}_t^{i,b}[\widehat{S}_{i,b}(T_i)] &= \widehat{\mathbb{E}}_t^{i,b}[A_{T_i}] \\ \widehat{\mathbb{E}}_t^{i,b}[(\widehat{S}_{i,b}(T_i))^2] &= \widehat{\mathbb{E}}_t^{i,b}[(A_{T_i})^2] \\ \widehat{\mathbb{E}}_t^{i,b}[(\widehat{S}_{i,b}(T_i))^3] &= \widehat{\mathbb{E}}_t^{i,b}[(A_{T_i})^3] \end{aligned}$$

for $X, Y(0), \eta$, we can exploit the auxiliary process to approximate the price (4.17) by

$$\widehat{C}_{i,b}(0)\phi \mathrm{Bl}((\widehat{K} - X), Y(0), \eta^2(T_i), \phi) \tag{4.20}$$

where the triplet $(Y(0), \eta^2(T_i), X)$ is the solution of the following system of equations:

$$Y(0) = \sqrt{\frac{m_2 - m_1^2}{\exp(\eta^2(T_i)) - 1}}, \qquad X = m_1 + \phi Y(0)$$

and

$$\sqrt{\exp(\eta^2(T_i)) - 1} = \frac{(-4\beta + 4\sqrt{4 + \beta^2})^{1/3}}{2} - \frac{2}{(-4\beta + 4\sqrt{4 + \beta^2})^{1/3}}$$

for

$$\beta = \phi \frac{m_1(3m_2 - 2m_1^2) - m_3}{(m_2 - m_1^2)^{3/2}},$$

and with (m_1, m_2, m_3) being the moments achieved by formula

$$m_n(T_i) = \sum_{j_1=i+1}^{b} \cdots \sum_{j_n=i+1}^{b} \prod_{\ell=j_1}^{j_n} \widehat{w}_\ell(0)\chi_\ell F_\ell(0) \cdot \exp\left\{ \sum_{k=i+1}^{n+i-1} \sum_{h=k+1}^{n+i} \rho_{j_k,j_h} \int_0^{T_i} \sigma_{j_k}(s)\sigma_{j_h}(s)ds \right\}$$

for $n = 1, 2, 3$.

This holds provided that $Y(0)$ and $(\widehat{K} - X)$ have the same sign. Otherwise, depending on the sign of the pair $(Y(0), \widehat{K} - X)$ we will have a forward on $Y(0)$ or a claim with zero present value (as illustrated in the previous discussion following Equation (4.17)).

The role of ϕ is to switch the distribution on the correct side of the mass-points which, once again, depend on sign of netting coefficients. Therefore, the ϕ is the switch-factor and the X is the shift-factor of our auxiliary process.

4.5 NUMERICAL TESTS

Here, we report the results we have achieved by testing our approximation versus Monte Carlo simulation (MC). We set $t = T_a = 0$, $T_b = 10$ and $\beta_i = 0.25$ for each $i \in (a, b] = (0, 40]$. Then, for a fixed T_i, we have compared the expectation $\mathbb{E}_t[D(t, T_i)(\text{NPV}(T_i))^+]$ computed via MC and via a Black-like approximation for sets of tests with different volatilities, instantaneous correlations, forward rates curve and for several schemes of netting coefficients α_i.

We have assumed $\chi_i = \psi_i$ for all $i \in (a, b]$.

In the following tables, **B** denotes the Black-like approximation formula (**3MM** the Black three-moment matching approximation), MC the Monte Carlo simulation, CI the confidence interval 1.96*(MC Standard Error), B-MC (3MM-MC) the difference between **B** (**3MM**) and MC, %BM the relative difference $(\mathbf{B}/MC - 1) * 100$ $((\mathbf{3MM}/MC - 1) * 100)$. Notice that once the forward rate curve is changed (steepened upwards or parallel shifted by +200bp) then the swap rates and hence the $\widetilde{K}_i$'s have to change as well. The check point T_i is fixed along the life of our portfolio. Finally, for each test, in the first column we used the following notations:

σ,ρ,F: to indicate a test under initial market inputs;
$2\sigma,\rho,F$: to indicate a test with double volatilities with respect to the initial market inputs;
$\sigma,\rho,\vec{F}$: to indicate a test with the initial forward curve steepened upwards w.r.t. the initial market inputs;
$\sigma,\rho,\widetilde{F}$: to indicate a test with the initial forward curve shifted by +200bp w.r.t. the initial market inputs;
$\sigma,\rho \approx 1,F$: to indicate a test with instantaneous correlations close to 1.

In Sections 4.5.1, and 4.5.2 we consider only positive netting coefficients, while in Sections 4.5.3, 4.5.4, and 4.5.5 we allow our portfolio to be long or short along its tenor. With the former choice we have two cases: increasing (A) and decreasing (B) cash flows. With the latter choice we have two symmetric cases (C, D) and one asymmetric case (E) where we assume a less conservative portfolio strategy; further, here, we include at-, in- and out-of-the-money tests as well, by setting:

ATM at the money test: strike at $\widetilde{K}_i$, $i \in (a, b]$;
ITM in the money test: strike at $0.75\widetilde{K}_i$, $i \in (a, b]$;
OTM out-of-the-money test: strike at $1.25\widetilde{K}_i$, $i \in (a, b]$.

As pointed out before, given the current structure of the netting coefficients, we have to test the MC simulation both versus the Black approximation and versus the Black three-moment matching approximation (derived in Section 4.4.4).

4.5.1 Case A: IRS with Co-Terminal Payment Dates

In this case we proceed with the following schemes of netting coefficients and strikes:

I: $\alpha_i = (T_i - T_a)$ for each $i \in (a, b]$ (where $T_\cdot$ is expressed in terms of year-fraction whereas all the $i's$ are integers), i.e. we are considering IRS's with increasing start date and with common maturities T_b, as shown in Figure 4.1;

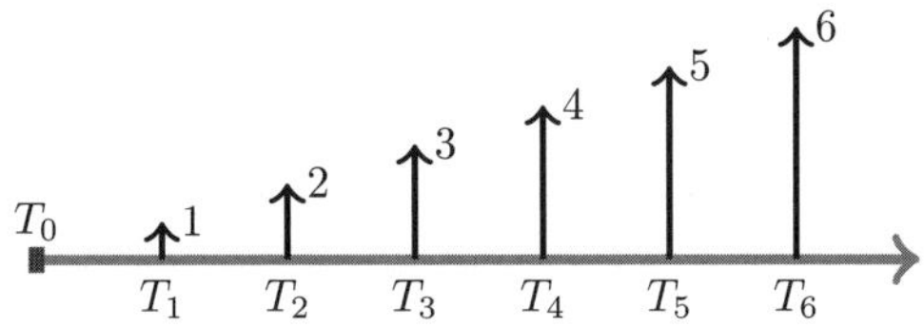

Figure 4.1 Case A: co-terminal IRS portfolio with positive cash flows: at the first reset we only have one flow, at the second reset two flows and so on

II: $\widetilde{K}_i = \beta_i \sum_{j=a}^{i-1} S_{j,b}(t)$ for each $i \in (a, b]$;

III: $$S_{i,b}(t) = \frac{\sum_{j=i+1}^{b} \beta_j P(t, T_j) F_j(t)}{\sum_{j=i+1}^{b} \beta_j P(t, T_j)}$$

We list the numerical results for different tests in Table 4.3.

Table 4.3 Tests for IRS with co-terminal payment dates

Test A1	T_i	MC (400K paths)	CI	**B**	B-MC	%BM
$[\sigma,\rho,F]$	2y10y	0.564613	0.002746	0.56672	0.002107	0.373176
$[\sigma,\rho,F]$	5y10y	0.680602	0.003811	0.68034	−0.00026	−0.0385
$[\sigma,\rho,F]$	8y10y	0.393573	0.00278	0.39438	0.000807	0.205045

(a) Test A1: standard market inputs

Test A2	T_i	MC (4M paths)	CI	**B**	B-MC	%BM
$[2\sigma,\rho,F]$	2y10y	1.07034	0.001755	1.0799	0.00956	0.893174
$[2\sigma,\rho,F]$	5y10y	1.2291	0.002506	1.2377	0.0086	0.699699
$[2\sigma,\rho,F]$	8y10y	0.713387	0.001975	0.71503	0.001643	0.23031

(b) Test A2: doubled volatilities

Test A3	T_i	MC (400K paths)	CI	**B**	B-MC	%BM
$[\sigma,\rho,\vec{F}]$	5y10y	0.870294	0.004875	0.87496	4.67E-03	0.536141

(c) Test A3: forward rates curve tilted upwards with $\vec{F}_{a+1}(0) = F_{a+1}(0)$

Test A4	T_i	MC (400K paths)	CI	**B**	B-MC	%BM
$[\sigma,\rho,\widetilde{F}]$	5y10y	0.773326	0.004813	0.7753	1.97E-03	0.255261

(d) Test A4: forward rates curve shifted by +200bp

Test A5	T_i	MC (4M paths)	CI	**B**	B-MC	%BM
$[\sigma,\rho \approx 1,F]$	5y10y	0.726936	0.001313	0.72829	1.35E-03	0.186261

(e) Test A5: perfect correlations

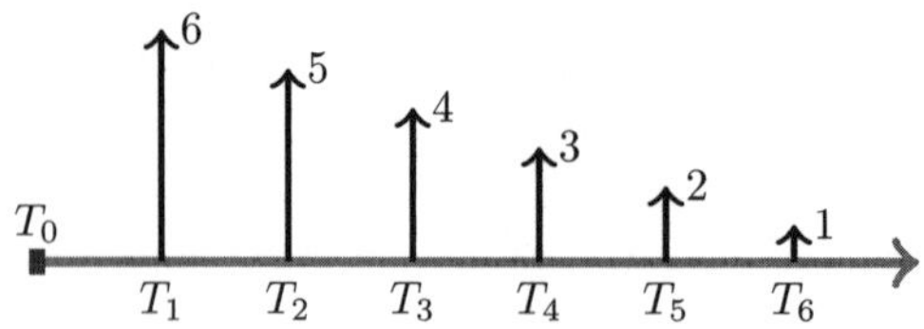

Figure 4.2 Case B: co-starting IRS portfolio with positive cash flows: at the last reset we only have one flow, at the second-last reset two flows and so on

4.5.2 Case B: IRS with Co-Starting Resetting Date

In this case we proceed with the following schemes of netting coefficients and strikes:

I: $\alpha_i = (T_b + \beta_i - T_i)$ for each $i \in (a, b]$, i.e. for a portfolio of IRS's with decreasing tenor and same start date, as shown in Figure 4.2.

II: $\widetilde{K}_i = \beta_i \sum_{j=i}^{b} S_{a,j}(t)$ for each $i \in (a, b]$;

III: $$S_{a,i}(t) = \frac{\sum_{j=a+1}^{i} \beta_j P(t, T_j) F_j(t)}{\sum_{j=a+1}^{i} \beta_j P(t, T_j)}$$

We list the numerical results for different tests in Table 4.4.

4.5.3 Case C: IRS with First Positive, Then Negative Flow

In this case we proceed with the following schemes of netting coefficients and strikes:

I: $\alpha_i = (T_{b/2} + \beta_i - T_i)\mathbf{1}_{\{T_i \le T_{b/2}\}} - (T_i - T_{b/2} - T_a)\mathbf{1}_{\{T_i > T_{b/2}\}}$ for each $i \in (a, b]$, which leads to the cash flow structures shown in Figure 4.3;

II: $\chi_i \widetilde{K}_i = \beta_i \sum_{j=i}^{b/2} S_{a,j}(t)\mathbf{1}_{\{T_i \le T_{b/2}\}} - \beta_i \sum_{j=b/2+1}^{i} S_{j,b}(t)\mathbf{1}_{\{T_i > T_{b/2}\}}$ for each $i \in (a, b]$;

III: $$S_{i,b}(t) = \frac{\sum_{j=i+1}^{b} \beta_j P(t, T_j) F_j(t)}{\sum_{j=i+1}^{b} \beta_j P(t, T_j)};$$

IV: $$S_{a,i}(t) = \frac{\sum_{j=a+1}^{i} \beta_j P(t, T_j) F_j(t)}{\sum_{j=a+1}^{i} \beta_j P(t, T_j)};$$

V: $\chi_i = \mathbf{1}_{\{T_i \le T_{b/2}\}} - \mathbf{1}_{\{T_i > T_{b/2}\}}$.

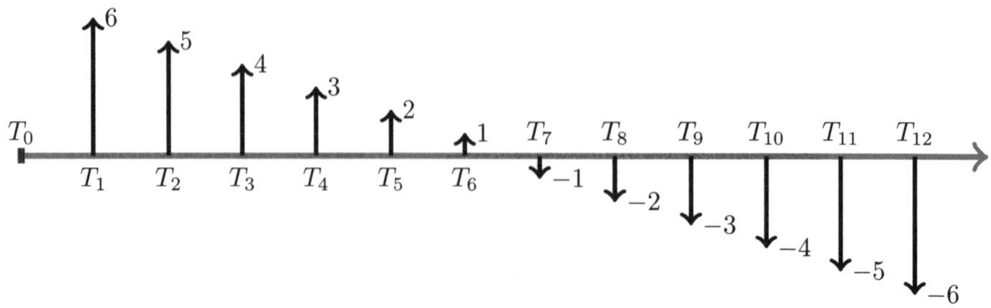

Figure 4.3 Case C: IRS portfolio with decreasing cash flows: first positive flows, then negative flows

Table 4.4 Tests for IRS with co-starting resetting date

Test B1	T_i	MC (400K paths)	CI	**B**	B-MC	%BM
$[\sigma,\rho,F]$	2y10y	0.673734	0.002688	0.67721	0.003476	0.515931
$[\sigma,\rho,F]$	5y10y	0.386824	0.001781	0.38792	0.001096	0.283333
$[\sigma,\rho,F]$	8y10y	0.069669	0.000408	0.069615	−5.4E-05	−0.07737

(a) Test B1: standard market inputs

Test B2	T_i	MC (4M paths)	CI	**B**	B-MC	%BM
$[2\sigma,\rho,F]$	2y10y	1.04435	0.001664	1.0532	0.00885	0.847417
$[2\sigma,\rho,F]$	5y10y	0.577499	0.001138	0.58102	0.003521	0.609698
$[2\sigma,\rho,F]$	8y10y	0.106133	0.000277	0.10643	0.000297	0.279838

(b) Test B2: doubled volatilities

Test B3	T_i	MC (400K paths)	CI	**B**	B-MC	%BM
$[\sigma,\rho,\vec{F}]$	5y10y	0.560052	0.0024	0.56053	0.000478	0.085349

(c) Test B3: forward rates curve tilted upwards with $\vec{F}_{a+1}(0) = F_{a+1}(0)$

Test B4	T_i	MC (400K paths)	CI	**B**	B-MC	%BM
$[\sigma,\rho,\widetilde{F}]$	5y10y	0.415113	0.002266	0.41611	0.000997	0.240176

(d) Test B4: forward rates curve shifted by +200bp

Test B5	T_i	MC (4M paths)	CI	**B**	B-MC	%BM
$[\sigma,\rho \approx 1,F]$	5y10y	0.399305	0.000598	0.40002	0.000715	0.179061

(e) Test B5: perfect correlations

Case C has been obtained by exploiting the put-call parity.[1] We list the numerical results for different tests for ATM, ITM, and OTM cases respectively in Tables 4.5, 4.6, and 4.7.

4.5.4 Case D: IRS with First Negative, Then Positive Flows

In this case we proceed with the following schemes of netting coefficients and strikes:

I: $\alpha_i = -(T_{b/2} + \beta_i - T_i)\mathbf{1}_{\{T_i \le T_{b/2}\}} + (T_i - T_{b/2} - T_a)\mathbf{1}_{\{T_i > T_{b/2}\}}$ for each $i \in (a, b]$, which leads to the cash flow structures shown in Figure 4.4;

II: $\chi_i \widetilde{K}_i = -\beta_i \sum_{j=i}^{b/2} S_{a,j}(t)\mathbf{1}_{\{T_i \le T_{b/2}\}} + \beta_i \sum_{j=b/2+1}^{i} S_{j,b}(t)\mathbf{1}_{\{T_i > T_{b/2}\}}$ for each $i \in (a, b]$;

III: $S_{i,b}(t) = \dfrac{\sum_{j=i+1}^{b} \beta_j P(t, T_j) F_j(t)}{\sum_{j=i+1}^{b} \beta_j P(t, T_j)}$;

[1] By the symmetry between Case C and Case D we used MC Case D and the forward values on $\widehat{S}_{i,b}$ to get MC Case C.

Table 4.5 ATM tests for an IRS portfolio with decreasing cash flows: first positive flows, then negative flows

Test C1	T_i	MC (4M paths)	CI	**B**	B-MC	%BM
$[\sigma,\rho,F]$	2y10y	0.1501014	0.000393	0.15149	0.001389	0.925108
$[\sigma,\rho,F]$	5y10y	0.189583	0.001151	0.18967	8.7E-05	0.04589
$[\sigma,\rho,F]$	8y10y	0.1481094	0.001186	0.14812	1.06E-05	0.007157
Test C1	T_i	MC (4M paths)	CI	**3MM**	3MM-MC	%BM
$[\sigma,\rho,F]$	2y10y	0.1501014	0.000393	0.15122	0.001119	0.74523
$[\sigma,\rho,F]$	5y10y	0.189583	0.001151	0.1897	0.000117	0.061714
$[\sigma,\rho,F]$	8y10y	0.1481094	0.001186	0.14812	1.06E-05	0.007157

(a) Test C1/ATM: standard market inputs

Test C2	T_i	MC (4M paths)	CI	**B**	B-MC	%BM
$[2\sigma,\rho,F]$	2y10y	0.247454	0.000299	0.24694	−0.00051	−0.20772
$[2\sigma,\rho,F]$	5y10y	0.37552	0.000773	0.3765	0.00098	0.260971
$[2\sigma,\rho,F]$	8y10y	0.2954154	0.000868	0.2961	0.000685	0.231741
Test C2	T_i	MC (4M paths)	CI	**3MM**	3MM-MC	%BM
$[2\sigma,\rho,F]$	2y10y	0.247454	0.000299	0.25069	0.003236	1.307718
$[2\sigma,\rho,F]$	5y10y	0.37552	0.000773	0.37663	0.00111	0.29559
$[2\sigma,\rho,F]$	8y10y	0.2954154	0.000868	0.29606	0.000645	0.218201

(b) Test C2/ATM: doubled volatilities

Test C3	T_i	MC (400K paths)	CI	**B**	B-MC	%BM
$[\sigma,\rho,\vec{F}]$	5y10y	0.228914	0.00143	0.22984	0.000926	0.404519
Test C3	T_i	MC (400K paths)	CI	**3MM**	3MM-MC	%BM
$[\sigma,\rho,\vec{F}]$	5y10y	0.228914	0.00143	0.22987	0.000956	0.417624

(c) Test C3/ATM: forward rates curve tilted upwards with $\vec{F}_{a+1}(0) = F_{a+1}(0)$

Test C4	T_i	MC (400K paths)	CI	**B**	B-MC	%BM
$[\sigma,\rho,\widetilde{F}]$	5y10y	0.220466	0.001444	0.2208	0.000334	0.151497
Test C4	T_i	MC (400K paths)	CI	**3MM**	3MM-MC	%BM
$[\sigma,\rho,\widetilde{F}]$	5y10y	0.220466	0.001444	0.22082	0.000354	0.160569

(d) Test C4/ATM: forward rates curve shifted by +200bp

Test C5	T_i	MC (4M paths)	CI	**B**	B-MC	%BM
$[\sigma,\rho \approx 1,F]$	5y10y	0.203206	0.000392	0.20363	0.000424	0.208655
Test C5	T_i	MC (4M paths)	CI	**3MM**	3MM-MC	%BM
$[\sigma,\rho \approx 1,F]$	5y10y	0.203206	0.000392	0.20362	0.000414	0.203734

(e) Test C5/ATM: perfect correlations

Table 4.6 ITM tests for IRS portfolio with decreasing cash-flows: first positive flows, then negative flows

Test C1	T_i	MC (400K paths)	CI	**B**	B-MC	%BM
$[\sigma,\rho,F]$	2y10y	0.017351	0.000676	0.016977	−0.00037	−2.1555
$[\sigma,\rho,F]$	5y10y	0.024322	0.00159	0.024541	0.000219	0.900419
$[\sigma,\rho,F]$	8y10y	0.032865	0.001535	0.032859	−6E-06	−0.01826
Test C1	T_i	MC (400K paths)	CI	**3MM**	3MM-MC	%BM
$[\sigma,\rho,F]$	2y10y	0.017351	0.000676	0.018907	0.001556	8.967783
$[\sigma,\rho,F]$	5y10y	0.024322	0.00159	0.02449	0.000168	0.690733
$[\sigma,\rho,F]$	8y10y	0.032865	0.001535	0.03281	−5.5E-05	−0.16735

(a) Test C1/ITM: standard market inputs

Test C2	T_i	MC (4M paths)	CI	**B**	B-MC	%BM
$[2\sigma,\rho,F]$	2y10y	0.089582	0.000388	0.08282	−0.00676	−7.54839
$[2\sigma,\rho,F]$	5y10y	0.139803	0.000915	0.1405	0.000697	0.498559
$[2\sigma,\rho,F]$	8y10y	0.137311	0.000975	0.13767	0.000359	0.26145
Test C2	T_i	MC (4M paths)	CI	**3MM**	3MM-MC	%BM
$[2\sigma,\rho,F]$	2y10y	0.089582	0.000388	0.092842	0.00326	3.639124
$[2\sigma,\rho,F]$	5y10y	0.139803	0.000915	0.14033	0.000527	0.376959
$[2\sigma,\rho,F]$	8y10y	0.137311	0.000975	0.13745	0.000139	0.10123

(b) Test C2/ITM: doubled volatilities

Test C3	T_i	MC (400K paths)	CI	**B**	B-MC	%BM
$[\sigma,\rho,\vec{F}]$	5y10y	0.029607	0.001972	0.029813	0.000206	0.695781
Test C3	T_i	MC (400K paths)	CI	**3MM**	3MM-MC	%BM
$[\sigma,\rho,\vec{F}]$	5y10y	0.029607	0.001972	0.029748	0.000141	0.476239

(c) Test C3/ITM: forward rates curve tilted upwards with $\vec{F}_{a+1}(0) = F_{a+1}(0)$

Test C4	T_i	MC (400K paths)	CI	**B**	B-MC	%BM
$[\sigma,\rho,\widetilde{F}]$	5y10y	0.029094	0.001991	0.02869	−0.0004	−1.3886
TestC4	T_i	MC (400K paths)	CI	**3MM**	3MM-MC	%BM
$[\sigma,\rho,\widetilde{F}]$	5y10y	0.029094	0.001991	0.028625	−0.00047	−1.61202

(d) Test C4/ITM: forward rates curve shifted by +200bp

Test C5	T_i	MC (4M paths)	CI	**B**	B-MC	%BM
$[\sigma,\rho \approx 1,F]$	5y10y	0.030852	0.000533	0.030943	9.1E-05	0.294957
Test C5	T_i	MC (4M paths)	CI	**3MM**	3MM-MC	%BM
$[\sigma,\rho \approx 1,F]$	5y10y	0.030852	0.000533	0.030794	−5.8E-05	−0.18799

(e) Test C5/ITM: perfect correlations

Table 4.7 OTM tests for an IRS portfolio with decreasing cash-flows: first positive flows, then negative flows

Test C1	T_i	MC (400K paths)	CI	**B**	B-MC	%BM
$[\sigma,\rho,F]$	2y10y	0.413263	0.000144	0.41434	0.001077	0.260674
$[\sigma,\rho,F]$	5y10y	0.536445	0.000626	0.53685	0.000405	0.075497
$[\sigma,\rho,F]$	8y10y	0.348977	0.000805	0.34906	8.32E-05	0.023841
Test C1	T_i	MC (400K paths)	CI	**3MM**	3MM-MC	%BM
$[\sigma,\rho,F]$	2y10y	0.413263	0.000144	0.41321	−5.3E-05	−0.01276
$[\sigma,\rho,F]$	5y10y	0.536445	0.000626	0.53694	0.000495	0.092274
$[\sigma,\rho,F]$	8y10y	0.348977	0.000805	0.34912	0.000143	0.041034

(a) Test C1/OTM: standard market inputs

Test C2	T_i	MC (4M paths)	CI	**B**	B-MC	%BM
$[2\sigma,\rho,F]$	2y10y	0.479013	0.000212	0.48127	0.002257	0.471156
$[2\sigma,\rho,F]$	5y10y	0.706206	0.00062	0.70742	0.001214	0.171905
$[2\sigma,\rho,F]$	8y10y	0.496787	0.000761	0.49733	0.000543	0.109302
Test C2	T_i	MC (4M paths)	CI	**3MM**	3MM-MC	%BM
$[2\sigma,\rho,F]$	2y10y	0.479013	0.000212	0.47918	0.000167	0.034842
$[2\sigma,\rho,F]$	5y10y	0.706206	0.00062	0.70778	0.001574	0.222881
$[2\sigma,\rho,F]$	8y10y	0.496787	0.000761	0.49745	0.000663	0.133458

(b) Test C2/OTM: doubled volatilities

Test C3	T_i	MC (400K paths)	CI	**B**	B-MC	%BM
$[\sigma,\rho,\vec{F}]$	5y10y	0.650079	0.000782	0.65003	−4.9E-05	−0.0076
Test C3	T_i	MC (400K paths)	CI	**3MM**	3MM-MC	%BM
$[\sigma,\rho,\vec{F}]$	5y10y	0.650079	0.000782	0.65014	6.06E-05	0.009322

(c) Test C3/OTM: forward rates curve tilted upwards with $\vec{F}_{a+1}(0) = F_{a+1}(0)$

Test C4	T_i	MC (400K paths)	CI	**B**	B-MC	%BM
$[\sigma,\rho,\widetilde{F}]$	5y10y	0.623693	0.000788	0.62412	0.000427	0.068495
Test C4	T_i	MC (400K paths)	CI	**3MM**	3MM-MC	%BM
$[\sigma,\rho,\widetilde{F}]$	5y10y	0.623693	0.000788	0.62422	0.000527	0.084529

(d) Test C4/OTM: forward rates curve shifted by +200bp

Test C5	T_i	MC (4M paths)	CI	**B**	B-MC	%BM
$[\sigma,\rho \approx 1,F]$	5y10y	0.547512	0.000228	0.5475	−1.2E-05	−0.00217
Test C5	T_i	MC (4M paths)	CI	**3MM**	3MM-MC	%BM
$[\sigma,\rho \approx 1,F]$	5y10y	0.547512	0.000228	0.54764	0.000128	0.023397

(e) Test C5/OTM: perfect correlations

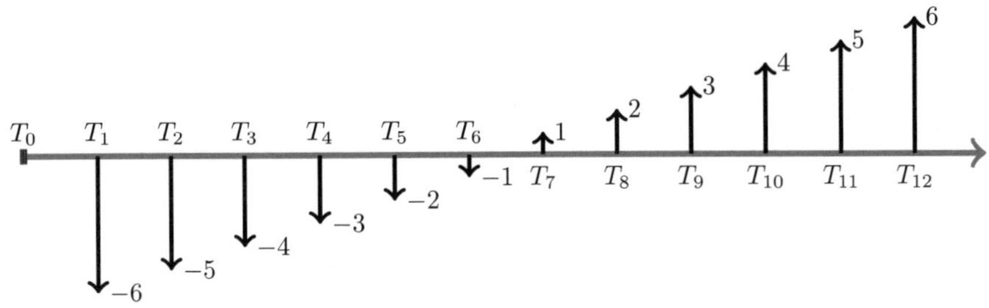

Figure 4.4 Case D: IRS portfolio with increasing cash flows: first negative flows, then positive flows

IV: $S_{a,i}(t) = \dfrac{\sum_{j=a+1}^{i} \beta_j P(t, T_j) F_j(t)}{\sum_{j=a+1}^{i} \beta_j P(t, T_j)}$;

V: $\chi_i = -\mathbf{1}_{\{T_i \le T_{b/2}\}} + \mathbf{1}_{\{T_i > T_{b/2}\}}$.

Case D is symmetric compared to Case C. We list the numerical results for different tests for ATM, ITM, and OTM cases respectively in Tables 4.8, 4.9 and 4.10.

4.5.5 Case E: IRS with First Alternate Flows

In this case we proceed with the following schemes of netting coefficients and strikes:

I: $\alpha_i = (-1)^{i+1}(T_b + \beta_i - T_i)$ for each $i \in (a, b]$,
which leads to the cash flow structures shown in Figure 4.5;

II: $\chi_i \widetilde{K}_i = (-1)^{i+1} \beta_i \sum_{j=i}^{b} S_{a,j}(t)$ for each $i \in (a, b]$;

III: $S_{a,i}(t) = \dfrac{\sum_{j=a+1}^{i} \beta_j P(t, T_j) F_j(t)}{\sum_{j=a+1}^{i} \beta_j P(t, T_j)}$;

IV: $\chi_i = (-1)^{i+1}$.

Case E is completely asymmetric hence put-call parity is no longer applied. Actually Case E is a special case of Case D with common first resetting date (described in Section 4.5.2) but with long and short position which switch along the tenor of our portfolio. We list the numerical results for different tests for ATM, ITM, and OTM cases respectively in Tables 4.11, 4.12 and 4.13.

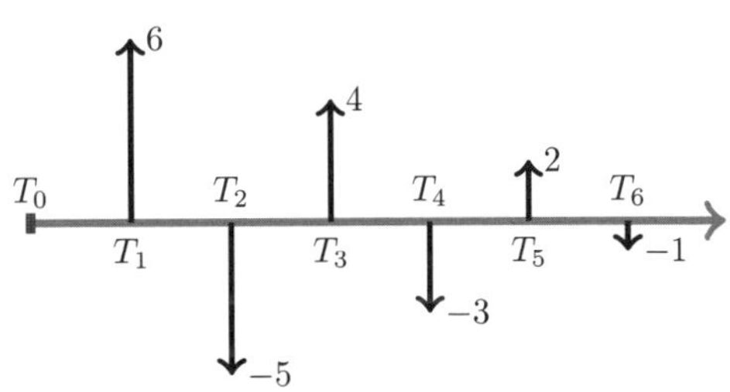

Figure 4.5 Case E: IRS portfolio with alternate cash flows

Table 4.8 ATM tests for an IRS portfolio with increasing cash-flows: first negative flows, then positive flows

Test D1	T_i	MC (4M paths)	CI	**B**	B-MC	%BM
$[\sigma,\rho,F]$	2y10y	0.059502	0.000393	0.06089	0.001388	2.332007
$[\sigma,\rho,F]$	5y10y	0.189583	0.001151	0.18967	8.7E-05	0.04589
$[\sigma,\rho,F]$	8y10y	0.155868	0.001186	0.15588	1.2E-05	0.007699
Test D1	T_i	MC (4M paths)	CI	**3MM**	3MM-MC	%BM
$[\sigma,\rho,F]$	2y10y	0.059502	0.000393	0.060626	0.001124	1.888327
$[\sigma,\rho,F]$	5y10y	0.189583	0.001151	0.1897	0.000117	0.061714
$[\sigma,\rho,F]$	8y10y	0.155868	0.001186	0.15588	1.2E-05	0.007699

(a) Test D1/ATM: standard market inputs

Test D2	T_i	MC (4M paths)	CI	**B**	B-MC	%BM
$[2\sigma,\rho,F]$	2y10y	0.156855	0.000299	0.15635	−0.00051	−0.32195
$[2\sigma,\rho,F]$	5y10y	0.37552	0.000773	0.3765	0.00098	0.260971
$[2\sigma,\rho,F]$	8y10y	0.303174	0.000868	0.30386	0.000686	0.226273
Test D2	T_i	MC (4M paths)	CI	**3MM**	3MM-MC	%BM
$[2\sigma,\rho,F]$	2y10y	0.156855	0.000299	0.16009	0.003235	2.062414
$[2\sigma,\rho,F]$	5y10y	0.37552	0.000773	0.37663	0.00111	0.29559
$[2\sigma,\rho,F]$	8y10y	0.303174	0.000868	0.30381	0.000636	0.209781

(b) Test D2/ATM: doubled volatilities

Test D3	T_i	MC (400K paths)	CI	**B**	B-MC	%BM
$[\sigma,\rho,\vec{F}]$	5y10y	0.228914	0.001428	0.22984	0.000926	0.404519
Test D3	T_i	MC (400K paths)	CI	**3MM**	3MM-MC	%BM
$[\sigma,\rho,\vec{F}]$	5y10y	0.228914	0.001428	0.22987	0.000956	0.417624

(c) Test D3/ATM: forward rates curve tilted upwards with $\vec{F}_{a+1}(0) = F_{a+1}(0)$

Test D4	T_i	MC (400K paths)	CI	**B**	B-MC	%BM
$[\sigma,\rho,\tilde{F}]$	5y10y	0.220466	0.001444	0.2208	0.000334	0.151497
Test D4	T_i	MC (400K paths)	CI	**3MM**	3MM-MC	%BM
$[\sigma,\rho,\tilde{F}]$	5y10y	0.220466	0.001444	0.22082	0.000354	0.160569

(d) Test D4/ATM: forward rates curve shifted by +200bp

Test D5	T_i	MC (4M paths)	CI	**B**	B-MC	%BM
$[\sigma,\rho \approx 1,F]$	5y10y	0.203206	0.000392	0.20363	0.000424	0.208655
Test D5	T_i	MC (4M paths)	CI	**3MM**	3MM-MC	%BM
$[\sigma,\rho \approx 1,F]$	5y10y	0.203206	0.000392	0.20362	0.000414	0.203734

(e) Test D5/ATM: perfect correlations

Table 4.9 ITM tests for IRS portfolio with increasing cash-flows: first negative flows, then positive flows

Test D1	T_i	MC (4M paths)	CI	**B**	B-MC	%BM
$[\sigma,\rho,F]$	2y10y	0.241171	0.000676	0.2408	−0.00037	−0.15383
$[\sigma,\rho,F]$	5y10y	0.508562	0.00159	0.50878	0.000218	0.042866
$[\sigma,\rho,F]$	8y10y	0.332985	0.001535	0.33298	−5E-06	−0.0015
Test D1	T_i	MC (4M paths)	CI	**3MM**	3MM-MC	%BM
$[\sigma,\rho,F]$	2y10y	0.241171	0.000676	0.24273	0.001559	0.646429
$[\sigma,\rho,F]$	5y10y	0.508562	0.00159	0.50873	0.000168	0.033034
$[\sigma,\rho,F]$	8y10y	0.332985	0.001535	0.33293	−5.5E-05	−0.01652

(a) Test D1/ITM: standard market inputs

Test D2	T_i	MC (4M paths)	CI	**B**	B-MC	%BM
$[2\sigma,\rho,F]$	2y10y	0.313402	0.000388	0.30665	−0.00675	−2.15442
$[2\sigma,\rho,F]$	5y10y	0.624043	0.000915	0.62474	0.000697	0.111691
$[2\sigma,\rho,F]$	8y10y	0.437431	0.000975	0.4378	0.000369	0.084356
Test D2	T_i	MC (4M paths)	CI	**3MM**	3MM-MC	%BM
$[2\sigma,\rho,F]$	2y10y	0.313402	0.000388	0.31667	0.003268	1.04275
$[2\sigma,\rho,F]$	5y10y	0.624043	0.000915	0.62457	0.000527	0.084449
$[2\sigma,\rho,F]$	8y10y	0.437431	0.000975	0.43757	0.000139	0.031776

(b) Test D2/ITM: doubled volatilities

Test D3	T_i	MC (400K paths)	CI	**B**	B-MC	%BM
$[\sigma,\rho,\vec{F}]$	5y10y	0.615777	0.001972	0.61598	0.000203	0.032966
Test D3	T_i	MC (400K paths)	CI	**3MM**	3MM-MC	%BM
$[\sigma,\rho,\vec{F}]$	5y10y	0.615777	0.001972	0.61591	0.000133	0.021599

(c) Test D3/ITM: forward rates curve tilted upwards with $\vec{F}_{a+1}(0) = F_{a+1}(0)$

Test D4	T_i	MC (400K paths)	CI	**B**	B-MC	%BM
$[\sigma,\rho,\tilde{F}]$	5y10y	0.591784	0.001991	0.59138	−0.0004	−0.06827
Test D4	T_i	MC (400K paths)	CI	**3MM**	3MM-MC	%BM
$[\sigma,\rho,\tilde{F}]$	5y10y	0.591784	0.001991	0.59131	−0.00047	−0.0801

(d) Test D4/ITM: forward rates curve shifted by +200bp

Test D5	T_i	MC (4M paths)	CI	**B**	B-MC	%BM
$[\sigma,\rho \approx 1,F]$	5y10y	0.515092	0.000533	0.51518	8.8E-05	0.017084
Test D5	T_i	MC (4M paths)	CI	**3MM**	3MM-MC	%BM
$[\sigma,\rho \approx 1,F]$	5y10y	0.515092	0.000533	0.51504	−5.2E-05	−0.0101

(e) Test D5/ITM: perfect correlations

Table 4.10 OTM tests for IRS portfolio with increasing cash-flows: first negative flows, then positive flows

Test D1	T_i	MC (400K paths)	CI	**B**	B-MC	%BM
$[\sigma,\rho,F]$	2y10y	0.008243	0.000144	0.009317	0.001074	13.02687
$[\sigma,\rho,F]$	5y10y	0.052205	0.000626	0.05261	0.000405	0.775788
$[\sigma,\rho,F]$	8y10y	0.064367	0.000805	0.064456	8.92E-05	0.138581
Test D1	T_i	MC (400K paths)	CI	**3MM**	3MM-MC	%BM
$[\sigma,\rho,F]$	2y10y	0.008243	0.000144	0.008185	−5.8E-05	−0.70644
$[\sigma,\rho,F]$	5y10y	0.052205	0.000626	0.052694	0.000489	0.936692
$[\sigma,\rho,F]$	8y10y	0.064367	0.000805	0.064509	0.000142	0.220921

(a) Test D1/OTM: standard market inputs

Test D2	T_i	MC (4M paths)	CI	**B**	B-MC	%BM
$[2\sigma,\rho,F]$	2y10y	0.073993	0.000212	0.076245	0.002252	3.043392
$[2\sigma,\rho,F]$	5y10y	0.221966	0.00062	0.22318	0.001214	0.546931
$[2\sigma,\rho,F]$	8y10y	0.212177	0.000761	0.21272	0.000543	0.255918
Test D2	T_i	MC (4M paths)	CI	**3MM**	3MM-MC	%BM
$[2\sigma,\rho,F]$	2y10y	0.073993	0.000212	0.074158	0.000165	0.222859
$[2\sigma,\rho,F]$	5y10y	0.221966	0.00062	0.22354	0.001574	0.709118
$[2\sigma,\rho,F]$	8y10y	0.212177	0.000761	0.21285	0.000673	0.317188

(b) Test D2/OTM: doubled volatilities

Test D3	T_i	MC (400K paths)	CI	**B**	B-MC	%BM
$[\sigma,\rho,\vec{F}]$	5y10y	0.063909	0.000782	0.063864	−4.5E-05	−0.07104
Test D3	T_i	MC (400K paths)	CI	**3MM**	3MM-MC	%BM
$[\sigma,\rho,\vec{F}]$	5y10y	0.063909	0.000782	0.063971	6.16E-05	0.096386

(c) Test D3/OTM: forward rates curve tilted upwards with $\vec{F}_{a+1}(0) = F_{a+1}(0)$

Test D4	T_i	MC (400K paths)	CI	**B**	B-MC	%BM
$[\sigma,\rho,\widetilde{F}]$	5y10y	0.061003	0.000788	0.061427	0.000424	0.695378
Test D4	T_i	MC (400K paths)	CI	**3MM**	3MM-MC	%BM
$[\sigma,\rho,\widetilde{F}]$	5y10y	0.061003	0.000788	0.061532	0.000529	0.867501

(d) Test D4/OTM: forward rates curve shifted by +200bp

Test D5	T_i	MC (4M paths)	CI	**B**	B-MC	%BM
$[\sigma,\rho\approx 1,F]$	5y10y	0.063272	0.000228	0.063256	−1.6E-05	−0.02513
Test D5	T_i	MC (4M paths)	CI	**3MM**	3MM-MC	%BM
$[\sigma,\rho\approx 1,F]$	5y10y	0.063272	0.000228	0.063397	0.000125	0.197718

(e) Test D5/OTM: perfect correlations

Table 4.11 ATM tests for IRS portfolio with alternate cash flows

Test E1	T_i	MC (4M paths)	CI	**B**	B-MC	%BM
$[\sigma,\rho,F]$	2y10y	0.017589	0.000101	0.017398	−0.00019	−1.08422
$[\sigma,\rho,F]$	5y10y	0.016347	0.000101	0.016079	−0.00027	−1.64005
$[\sigma,\rho,F]$	8y10y	0.007337	4.94E-05	0.007325	−1.2E-05	−0.16573
Test E1	T_i	MC (4M paths)	CI	**3MM**	3MM-MC	%BM
$[\sigma,\rho,F]$	2y10y	0.017589	0.000101	0.017545	−4.4E-05	−0.24845
$[\sigma,\rho,F]$	5y10y	0.016347	0.000101	0.016255	−9.2E-05	−0.5634
$[\sigma,\rho,F]$	8y10y	0.007337	4.94E-05	0.007348	1.05E-05	0.143648

(a) Test E1/ATM: standard market inputs

Test E2	T_i	MC (4M paths)	CI	**B**	B-MC	%BM
$[2\sigma,\rho,F]$	2y10y	0.036143	7.59E-05	0.035204	−0.00094	−2.59855
$[2\sigma,\rho,F]$	5y10y	0.029971	7.70E-05	0.028942	−0.00103	−3.433
$[2\sigma,\rho,F]$	8y10y	0.012224	3.71E-05	0.012083	−0.00014	−1.15509
Test E2	T_i	MC (4M paths)	CI	**3MM**	3MM-MC	%BM
$[2\sigma,\rho,F]$	2y10y	0.036143	7.59E-05	0.036503	0.00036	0.995485
$[2\sigma,\rho,F]$	5y10y	0.029971	7.70E-05	0.030137	0.000166	0.554204
$[2\sigma,\rho,F]$	8y10y	0.012224	3.71E-05	0.012231	6.8E-06	0.055627

(b) Test E2/ATM: doubled volatilities

Test E3	T_i	MC (400K paths)	CI	**B**	B-MC	%BM
$[\sigma,\rho,\vec{F}]$	5y10y	0.021802	0.000135	0.021471	−0.00033	−1.51595
Test E3	T_i	MC (400K paths)	CI	**3MM**	3MM-MC	%BM
$[\sigma,\rho,\vec{F}]$	5y10y	0.021802	0.000135	0.021717	−8.5E-05	−0.38759

(c) Test E3/ATM: forward rates curve tilted upwards with $\vec{F}_{a+1}(0) = F_{a+1}(0)$

Test E4	T_i	MC (400K paths)	CI	**B**	B-MC	%BM
$[\sigma,\rho,\widetilde{F}]$	5y10y	0.020228	0.00014	0.020002	−0.00023	−1.1158
Test E4	T_i	MC (400K paths)	CI	**3MM**	3MM-MC	%BM
$[\sigma,\rho,\widetilde{F}]$	5y10y	0.020228	0.00014	0.020182	−4.6E-05	−0.22593

(d) Test E4/ATM: forward rates curve shifted by +200bp

Test E5	T_i	MC (4M paths)	CI	**B**	B-MC	%BM
$[\sigma,\rho \approx 1,F]$	5y10y	0.013206	2.48E-05	0.013109	−9.7E-05	−0.73451
Test E5	T_i	MC (4M paths)	CI	**3MM**	3MM-MC	%BM
$[\sigma,\rho \approx 1,F]$	5y10y	0.013206	2.48E-05	0.013103	−0.0001	−0.77995

(e) Test E5/ATM: perfect correlations

Table 4.12 ITM tests for IRS portfolio with alternate cash flows

Test E1	T_i	MC (4M paths)	CI	**B**	B-MC	%BM
$[\sigma,\rho,F]$	2y10y	0.041527	0.000137	0.041063	−0.00046	−1.11758
$[\sigma,\rho,F]$	5y10y	0.030593	0.000124	0.030207	−0.00039	−1.26205
$[\sigma,\rho,F]$	8y10y	0.012757	5.80E-05	0.012744	−1.3E-05	−0.09956

Test E1	T_i	MC (4M paths)	CI	**3MM**	3MM-MC	%BM
$[\sigma,\rho,F]$	2y10y	0.041527	0.000137	0.041482	−4.5E-05	−0.1086
$[\sigma,\rho,F]$	5y10y	0.030593	0.000124	0.030454	−0.00014	−0.45468
$[\sigma,\rho,F]$	8y10y	0.012757	5.80E-05	0.012769	1.23E-05	0.09642

(a) Test E1/ITM: standard market inputs

Test E2	T_i	MC (4M paths)	CI	**B**	B-MC	%BM
$[2\sigma,\rho,F]$	2y10y	0.055429	8.76E-05	0.053473	−0.00196	−3.52849
$[2\sigma,\rho,F]$	5y10y	0.0407	8.46E-05	0.039227	−0.00147	−3.61964
$[2\sigma,\rho,F]$	8y10y	0.016122	4.02E-05	0.015923	−0.0002	−1.23679

Test E2	T_i	MC (4M paths)	CI	**3MM**	3MM-MC	%BM
$[2\sigma,\rho,F]$	2y10y	0.055429	8.76E-05	0.055487	5.82E-05	0.105
$[2\sigma,\rho,F]$	5y10y	0.0407	8.46E-05	0.040647	−5.3E-05	−0.13071
$[2\sigma,\rho,F]$	8y10y	0.016122	4.02E-05	0.01609	−3.2E-05	−0.20096

(b) Test E2/ITM: doubled volatilities

Test E3	T_i	MC (400K paths)	CI	**B**	B-MC	%BM
$[\sigma,\rho,\vec{F}]$	5y10y	0.03946	0.000163	0.039052	−0.00041	−1.0327

Test E3	T_i	MC (400K paths)	CI	**3MM**	3MM-MC	%BM
$[\sigma,\rho,\vec{F}]$	5y10y	0.03946	0.000163	0.039364	−9.5E-05	−0.24202

(c) Test E3/ITM: forward rates curve tilted upwards with $\vec{F}_{a+1}(0) = F_{a+1}(0)$

Test E4	T_i	MC (400K paths)	CI	**B**	B-MC	%BM
$[\sigma,\rho,\widetilde{F}]$	5y10y	0.038709	0.000174	0.038346	−0.00036	−0.93649

Test E4	T_i	MC (400K paths)	CI	**3MM**	3MM-MC	%BM
$[\sigma,\rho,\widetilde{F}]$	5y10y	0.038709	0.000174	0.038597	−0.00011	−0.28805

(d) Test E4/ITM: forward rates curve shifted by +200bp

Test E5	T_i	MC (4M paths)	CI	**B**	B-MC	%BM
$[\sigma,\rho \approx 1,F]$	5y10y	0.028727	3.15E-05	0.028723	−4.3E-06	−0.01497

Test E5	T_i	MC (4M paths)	CI	**3MM**	3MM-MC	%BM
$[\sigma,\rho \approx 1,F]$	5y10y	0.028727	3.15E-05	0.028708	−1.9E-05	−0.06718

(e) Test E5/ITM: perfect correlations

Table 4.13 OTM tests for IRS portfolio with alternate cash flows

Test E1	T_i	MC (400K paths)	CI	**B**	B-MC	%BM
$[\sigma,\rho,F]$	2y10y	0.005991	6.12E-05	0.006199	0.000208	3.474119
$[\sigma,\rho,F]$	5y10y	0.007945	7.48E-05	0.007883	−6.2E-05	−0.77584
$[\sigma,\rho,F]$	8y10y	0.003923	3.86E-05	0.003916	−6.7E-06	−0.17182
Test E1	T_i	MC (400K paths)	CI	**3MM**	3MM-MC	%BM
$[\sigma,\rho,F]$	2y10y	0.005991	6.12E-05	0.005998	7.14E-06	0.119176
$[\sigma,\rho,F]$	5y10y	0.007945	7.48E-05	0.00789	−5.5E-05	−0.69654
$[\sigma,\rho,F]$	8y10y	0.003923	3.86E-05	0.003922	−2.4E-07	−0.00612

(a) Test E1/OTM: standard market inputs

Test E2	T_i	MC (4M paths)	CI	**B**	B-MC	%BM
$[2\sigma,\rho,F]$	2y10y	0.023315	6.42E-05	0.023247	−6.8E-05	−0.29337
$[2\sigma,\rho,F]$	5y10y	0.022213	6.98E-05	0.021605	−0.00061	−2.73626
$[2\sigma,\rho,F]$	8y10y	0.009391	3.41E-05	0.009268	−0.00012	−1.30774
Test E2	T_i	MC (4M paths)	CI	**3MM**	3MM-MC	%BM
$[2\sigma,\rho,F]$	2y10y	0.023315	6.42E-05	0.023708	0.000393	1.683866
$[2\sigma,\rho,F]$	5y10y	0.022213	6.98E-05	0.022465	0.000252	1.135381
$[2\sigma,\rho,F]$	8y10y	0.009391	3.41E-05	0.009382	−8.8E-06	−0.09381

(b) Test E2/OTM: doubled volatilities

Test E3	T_i	MC (400K paths)	CI	**B**	B-MC	%BM
$[\sigma,\rho,\vec{F}]$	5y10y	0.010923	0.000101	0.010896	−2.7E-05	−0.24992
Test E3	T_i	MC (400K paths)	CI	**3MM**	3MM-MC	%BM
$[\sigma,\rho,\vec{F}]$	5y10y	0.010923	0.000101	0.010929	5.7E-06	0.052182

(c) Test E3/OTM: forward rates curve tilted upwards with $\vec{F}_{a+1}(0) = F_{a+1}(0)$

Test E4	T_i	MC (400K paths)	CI	**B**	B-MC	%BM
$[\sigma,\rho,\widetilde{F}]$	5y10y	0.009574	0.000102	0.009557	−1.7E-05	−0.17912
Test E4	T_i	MC (400K paths)	CI	**3MM**	3MM-MC	%BM
$[\sigma,\rho,\widetilde{F}]$	5y10y	0.009574	0.000102	0.009568	−6.6E-06	−0.06841

(d) Test E4/OTM: forward rates curve shifted by +200bp

Test E5	T_i	MC (4M paths)	CI	**B**	B-MC	%BM
$[\sigma,\rho \approx 1,F]$	5y10y	0.005087	1.65E-05	0.004942	−0.00015	−2.86004
Test E5	T_i	MC (4M paths)	CI	**3MM**	3MM-MC	%BM
$[\sigma,\rho \approx 1,F]$	5y10y	0.005087	1.65E-05	0.004954	−0.00013	−2.61825

(e) Test E5/OTM: perfect correlations

4.6 CONCLUSIONS

In this chapter we introduced counterparty risk formulas in general for unilateral default risk, and then applied them to Interest Rate Swaps (IRS), also under netting agreements. For swap portfolios under netting we derived two approximated formulas and tested both of them against Monte Carlo simulation, finding a good agreement under most market configurations.

More in detail, as expected, the Black-like approximation works well for netting coefficients going into a single direction. However, when we consider a portfolio with both positive and negative coefficients, results are not as good, particularly for "in-the-money" and "out-of-the-money" strikes. In general the more refined formula (Black three moment matching approximation, shifted lognormal distribution) outperforms the standard Black approximation (lognormal distribution). This result does not hold for the particular C/ITM case of Section 4.5.3, where the three moment matching formula does not outperform the simpler Black approximation. We note however that both results are still within the Monte Carlo standard error.

There are several cases where the moment matching brings in a considerable improvement with respect to the basic Black formula. For example, Case D in Section 4.5.4, OTM Test B1, and Case C (characterized by asymmetric coefficients) both for ATM, ITM and OTM Tests.

In general, the possibility to include netting agreements lowers considerably the size of the price adjustment due to counterparty risk. In fact, in the absence of netting we would obtain just the sum of counterparty risk pricing in each single IRS, meaning that we are counting multiple times the default impact of flows that are more than in a single IRS. In a way it is like pricing a payoff given by a sum of positive parts by doing the pricing of each positive part and then adding up. Since

$$(\Pi_{\mathrm{IRS}_1} + \Pi_{\mathrm{IRS}_2} + \ldots + \Pi_{\mathrm{IRS}_n})^+ \leq \Pi^+_{\mathrm{IRS}_1} + \Pi^+_{\mathrm{IRS}_2} + \ldots + \Pi^+_{\mathrm{IRS}_n}$$

(the left hand side corresponding to a netted portfolio of residual NPVs) we see that the price under netting agreements is always smaller than the price with no netting agreement. Since this option component (times LGD) is subtracted from the default-free value to determine the counterparty risk price, we end up subtracting more in absence of netting agreements; netting agreements produce a smaller "option" counterparty price component in general, so that the total value of the claim is larger. The interested reader can use our approximated Formula (4.16, 4.17) or the more refined (4.16, 4.20) to check cases with different given curves of default probabilities to assess the typical impact of netting agreements in different default probability configurations, all the needed tools have been given in this part.

Notice that in this chapter we considered a first approach to counterparty risk pricing when no collateral is given as a guarantee. The price for this risk is charged upfront and is computed in a risk-neutral valuation framework. For some first considerations involving collateral we refer to [79] and to our later Chapter 13. Also, in Chapter 5 we plan to analyze the impact of credit spread volatility (stochastic intensity) and of intensity/interest-rate correlation (wrong way risk) on the swaption-counterparty risk.

5 Wrong Way Risk (WWR) for Interest Rates

This chapter re-elaborates and expands material originally presented in Brigo and Pallavicini (2006, 2007, 2008) [56], [57] and [58].

In this chapter we consider counterparty risk pricing for interest rate payoffs in presence of correlation between the default event and interest rates.

In particular we analyze in detail counterparty-risky (or default-risky) Interest-Rate Swaps (IRS), continuing the work of Sorensen and Bollier (1994) [186] and of Brigo and Masetti (2005) [47] summarized in Chapter 4, where correlation is not taken into account. We also analyze option payoffs under counterparty risk.

As before we have two parties in the deal, an investor or Bank ("B") and a counterparty "C" that could be a corporate, another bank or a different entity. We look at the valuation from the point of view of "B". As in the previous chapter, we assume here the following:

Assumption 5.0.1 ***Unilateral Default Assumption (UDA): Assuming one party (B) to be default free.*** *In this chapter we assume that calculations are done considering "B" to be default free. Valuation of the contract is done usually from "B"'s point of view.*

As in Chapter 4 above, we are looking at the problem from the viewpoint of a default-free counterparty "B" entering a financial contract with another counterparty "C" having a positive probability of defaulting before the final maturity. We formalize the general and reasonable fact that the value of a generic claim, subject to counterparty risk, is always smaller than the value of a similar claim having a null default probability, expressing the discrepancy in precise quantitative terms through a credit valuation adjustment (CVA).

As we have seen before in previous chapters, when evaluating default-risky assets one has to introduce the default time and the default probabilities in the pricing models. We consider Credit Default Swaps (CDS) as liquid sources of market default probabilities. Different models can be used to calibrate CDS data and obtain default probabilities, as we have seen in Chapter 3. In this chapter we adopt the second framework, namely intensity models, since this lends itself more naturally to interact with interest rate modelling and allows for a very natural way to correlate the default event to interest rates. Here we have the first important difference with Chapter 4, here we will allow the default intensity of "C" to be stochastic, so that the credit volatility of "C", and more importantly the correlation between the credit quality of "C" and interest rates will be in the picture.

This chapter will illustrate how counterparty risk has a relevant impact on the product prices and then, in turn, how correlation between interest rates and default has a relevant impact on the adjustment due to counterparty risk on an otherwise default-free interest rate payout. We analyze the pattern of such impacts as product characteristics and tenor structures change through some fundamental numerical examples and find stable and financially reasonable patterns for the CVA adjustment.

In particular, we find the (positive) CVA counterparty risk adjustment to be subtracted from the default-free price (computed by "B"), to decrease with correlation for receiver payoffs. The analogous adjustment for payer payoffs increases with correlation. We analyze products such as standard swaps, swap portfolios, European and Bermudan swaptions, mostly of the receiver type. We also consider Constant Maturity Swap (CMS) spread options, which being based on interest rate spreads are out of our "payer/receiver" classification.

In general our results confirm the counterparty risk adjustment and the impact of correlation on counterparty risk to be relevant. We comment our findings in more detail in the conclusions.

Finally, we recall that credit hybrid products such as Contingent Credit Default Swaps (Contingent CDS) with interest rate underlying, assume exactly the same form as the CVA term, or optional part in the counterparty risk valuation problem for the interest rate payoff. This renders our approach useful also for Contingent CDS valuation.

Before reading the chapter in detail, we invite the reader who is not yet familiar with Chapter 4 to familiarize themselves with Formula 4.4.

5.1 MODELLING ASSUMPTIONS

In this section we consider a model that is stochastic both in the interest rates (underlying market) and in the default intensity (counterparty). Joint stochasticity is needed to introduce correlation. The interest rate sector is modelled according to a shifted two-factor Gaussian short-rate process (hereafter G2++) while the default intensity sector is modelled according to a square-root process (hereafter CIR++). Details for both models can be found in Brigo and Mercurio (2001, 2006). The two models are coupled by correlating their Brownian shocks.

5.1.1 G2++ Interest Rate Model

We assume that the dynamics of the instantaneous short-rate process under the risk-neutral measure is given by

$$r_t := x_t + z_t + \varphi(t;\alpha). \tag{5.1}$$

where α is a set of parameters and the processes x and z are $\mathcal{F}_t$ adapted and satisfy

$$\begin{aligned} dx_t &= -ax_t dt + \sigma\, dZ_t^1, \quad x(0) = 0 \\ dz_t &= -bz_t dt + \eta\, dZ_t^2, \quad z(0) = 0, \end{aligned} \tag{5.2}$$

where (Z^1, Z^2) is a two-dimensional Brownian motion with instantaneous correlation $\rho_{1,2}$ as from

$$dZ_t^1 dZ_t^2 = \rho_{1,2}\, dt,$$

where r_0, a, b, σ, η are positive constants, and where $-1 \le \rho_{1,2} \le 1$. These are the parameters entering φ, in that $\alpha = [r_0, a, b, \sigma, \eta, \rho_{1,2}]$. The function $\varphi(\cdot;\alpha)$ is deterministic and well defined in the time interval $[0, T^*]$, with T^* a given time horizon, typically 10, 30 or 50 (years). In particular, $\varphi(0;\alpha) = r_0$. This function can be set to a value automatically calibrating the

Table 5.1 EUR zero-coupon continuously compounded spot rates (ACT/360) observed on 23 June 2006

Date	Rate	Date	Rate	Date	Rate	Date	Rate
26-Jun-06	2.83%	20-Sep-07	3.46%	27-Jun-16	4.19%	27-Jun-28	4.51%
27-Jun-06	2.83%	19-Dec-07	3.52%	27-Jun-17	4.23%	27-Jun-29	4.51%
28-Jun-06	2.83%	19-Mar-08	3.57%	27-Jun-18	4.27%	27-Jun-30	4.52%
04-Jul-06	2.87%	19-Jun-08	3.61%	27-Jun-19	4.31%	27-Jun-31	4.52%
11-Jul-06	2.87%	18-Sep-08	3.65%	29-Jun-20	4.35%	28-Jun-32	4.52%
18-Jul-06	2.87%	29-Jun-09	3.75%	28-Jun-21	4.38%	27-Jun-33	4.52%
27-Jul-06	2.88%	28-Jun-10	3.84%	27-Jun-22	4.41%	27-Jun-34	4.52%
28-Aug-06	2.92%	27-Jun-11	3.91%	27-Jun-23	4.43%	27-Jun-35	4.52%
20-Sep-06	2.96%	27-Jun-12	3.98%	27-Jun-24	4.45%	27-Jun-36	4.52%
20-Dec-06	3.14%	27-Jun-13	4.03%	27-Jun-25	4.47%	27-Jun-46	4.49%
20-Mar-07	3.27%	27-Jun-14	4.09%	29-Jun-26	4.48%	27-Jun-56	4.46%
21-Jun-07	3.38%	29-Jun-15	4.14%	28-Jun-27	4.50%		

initial zero coupon curve observed in the market. In our numerical tests we use the market inputs listed in Tables 5.1 and 5.2 corresponding to parameters α given by

$$a = 0.0558, \quad b = 0.5493, \quad \sigma = 0.0093, \quad \eta = 0.0138, \quad \rho_{1,2} = -0.7.$$

In Section 12.2.1 we consider again the G2++ model and we try to calibrate it to more recent data. We will discuss also the issues occurring with post-crisis data sets.

5.1.2 CIR++ Stochastic Intensity Model

For the stochastic intensity model we set

$$\lambda_t := y_t + \psi(t;\beta), \quad t \geq 0, \tag{5.3}$$

Table 5.2 Market at-the-money swaption volatilities, with expiry date t and tenor b, observed on 23 June 2006

$t \downarrow / b \rightarrow$	1y	2y	5y	7y	10y	15y	20y
1y	17.51%	15.86%	14.63%	14.20%	13.41%	12.14%	11.16%
2y	16.05%	15.26%	14.55%	14.09%	13.29%	12.03%	11.09%
3y	15.58%	15.06%	14.43%	13.92%	13.10%	11.87%	10.96%
4y	15.29%	14.90%	14.20%	13.67%	12.85%	11.66%	10.79%
5y	15.05%	14.67%	13.90%	13.36%	12.55%	11.42%	10.60%
7y	14.39%	14.00%	13.22%	12.70%	11.96%	10.95%	10.20%
10y	13.25%	12.94%	12.23%	11.79%	11.17%	10.31%	9.65%
15y	11.87%	11.64%	11.11%	10.76%	10.26%	9.52%	8.89%
20y	11.09%	10.92%	10.45%	10.14%	9.67%	8.91%	8.27%

where ψ is a deterministic function, depending on the parameter vector β (which includes y_0), that is integrable on closed intervals. The initial condition y_0 is one more parameter at our disposal: we are free to select its value as long as

$$\psi(0; \beta) = \lambda_0 - y_0.$$

We take y to be a Cox-Ingersoll-Ross process (see Brigo and Mercurio (2001) or (2006) [50]):

$$dy_t = \kappa(\mu - y_t)\,dt + \nu\sqrt{y_t}\,dZ_t^3,$$

where the parameter vector is $\beta = (\kappa, \mu, \nu, y_0)$, with κ, μ, ν, y_0 positive deterministic constants. As usual, Z^3 is a standard Brownian motion process under the risk-neutral measure, representing the stochastic shock in our dynamics. We assume the origin to be inaccessible, that is

$$2\kappa\mu > \nu^2.$$

We will often use the integrated quantities

$$\Lambda(t) := \int_0^t \lambda_s\,ds, \quad Y(t) := \int_0^t y_s\,ds, \quad \Psi(t, \beta) := \int_0^t \psi(s, \beta)\,ds.$$

5.1.3 CIR++ Model: CDS Calibration

Assume that the intensity λ, and the cumulated intensity Λ, are independent of the short rate r, and of interest rates in general. Since in our Cox process setting $\tau = \Lambda^{-1}(\xi)$ with ξ exponential and independent of interest rates, in this zero correlation case the default time τ and interest rate quantities r, $D(s, t)$, ... are independent. It follows that the (receiver) CDS valuation becomes model independent and is given by the formula

$$\begin{aligned} \text{CDS}_0(T_a, T_b; S, \text{L}\textsc{gd}) := {} & S \sum_{i=a+1}^{b} D(0, T_i)\alpha_i \mathbb{Q}\{\tau > T_i\} \\ & - S \int_{T_a}^{T_b} D(0, u)(u - T_{\beta(u)})\,d\mathbb{Q}\{\tau > u\} \\ & + \text{L}\textsc{gd} \int_{T_a}^{T_b} D(t, u)\,d\mathbb{Q}\{\tau > u\} \end{aligned} \tag{5.4}$$

where α_i is the coupon's accrual period, $\beta(u)$ is the last coupon date before time u (see, for example, the Credit chapters in Brigo and Mercurio (2006) [48] for the details). Here S is the periodic premium rate (or "spread") received by the protection seller from the premium leg, until final maturity or until the first T_i following default, whereas $\text{L}\textsc{gd} = 1 - \text{R}\textsc{ec}$ is the loss given default protection payment to be paid to the protection buyer in the default (or protection) leg in case of early default, at the first T_i following default.

This formula implies that if we strip survival probabilities from CDS in a model independent way, to calibrate the market CDS quotes we just need to make sure that the survival probabilities we strip from CDS are correctly reproduced by the CIR++ model. Since the survival probabilities in the CIR++ model are given by

$$\mathbb{Q}\{\tau > t\}_{model} = \mathbb{E}_0\left[e^{-\Lambda(t)}\right] = \mathbb{E}_0\left[e^{-\Psi(t,\beta)-Y(t)}\right] \tag{5.5}$$

we just need to make sure

$$\mathbb{E}_0\left[e^{-\Psi(t,\beta)-Y(t)}\right] = \mathbb{Q}\{\tau > t\}_{market}$$

from which

$$\Psi(t,\beta) = \ln\left(\frac{\mathbb{E}_0\left[e^{-Y(t)}\right]}{\mathbb{Q}\{\tau > t\}_{market}}\right) = \ln\left(\frac{P^{\text{CIR}}(0,t,y_0;\beta)}{\mathbb{Q}\{\tau > t\}_{market}}\right) \tag{5.6}$$

where we choose the parameters β in order to have a positive function ψ (i.e. an increasing Ψ) and P^{CIR} is the closed-form expression for bond prices in the time-homogeneous CIR model with initial condition y_0 and parameters β (see for example Brigo and Mercurio (2001, 2006) [48]). Thus, if ψ is selected according to this last formula, as we will assume from now on, the model is easily and automatically calibrated to the market survival probabilities (possibly stripped from CDS data).

This CDS calibration procedure assumes zero correlation between default and interest rates, so in principle when taking non-zero correlation we cannot adopt it. However, we have seen in [35] and further in Brigo and Mercurio (2006) that the impact of interest rate/default correlation is typically negligible on CDSs, so that we may retain this calibration procedure even under nonzero correlation, and we will do so in this chapter.

Once we have done this and calibrated CDS data through $\psi(\cdot,\beta)$, we are left with the parameters β, which can be used to calibrate further products. However, this will be interesting when single-name option data on the credit derivatives market will become more liquid. Currently the bid-ask spreads for single-name CDS options are large and suggest to consider these quotes with caution. At the moment we content ourselves with calibrating only CDSs for the credit part. To help specifying β without further data we set some values of the parameters implying possibly reasonable values for the implied volatility of hypothetical CDS options on the counterparty.

In our tests we take stylized flat CDS curves for the counterparty, assuming they imply initial survival probabilities at time 0 consistent with the following hazard-function formulation:

$$\mathbb{Q}\{\tau > t\}_{market} = e^{-\gamma t}, \tag{5.7}$$

for a constant deterministic value of γ. This is to be interpreted as a quoting mechanism for survival probabilities and not as a model. Assuming our counterparty CDSs are at time 0 for different maturities to imply a given value of γ, we will value counterparty risk under different values of γ. This assumption on CDS spreads is stylized but our aim is checking impacts rather than having an extremely precise valuation.

In our numerical examples we take as values of the intensity volatility parameters y_0, κ, μ, ν the following values:

$$y_0 = 0.0165, \quad \kappa = 0.4, \quad \mu = 0.026, \quad \nu = 0.14.$$

Paired with stylized CDS data consistent with survivals (5.7) for several possible values of γ, these parameters imply the CDS volatilities[1] listed in Table 5.3.

[1] See [31] and [32] for a precise notion of CDS implied volatility.

Table 5.3 Black volatilities for CDS options implied by CIR++ model (with parameters $y_0 = 0.0165$, $\kappa = 0.4$, $\mu = 0.026$, $\nu = 0.14$) for different choices of the default probability parameter γ. Interest rates are modelled according to section 5.1.1 and $\bar{\rho} = 0$

	σ_{impl}			
γ	1×1	1×4	4×1	1×9
3%	42%	25%	26%	15%
5%	25%	15%	15%	9%
7%	18%	11%	11%	7%

5.1.4 Interest Rate/Credit Spread Correlation

We take the short interest rate factors x and z and the intensity process y to be correlated, by assuming the driving Brownian motions Z_1, Z_2 and Z_3 to be instantaneously correlated according to

$$dZ_t^i \, dZ_t^3 = \rho_{i,3} \, dt, \quad i \in \{1, 2\}.$$

Notice that the instantaneous correlation between the resulting short rate and the intensity, i.e. the instantaneous interest rate/credit spread correlation is

$$\bar{\rho} := \text{Corr}(dr_t, d\lambda_t) = \frac{\sigma\rho_{1,3} + \eta\rho_{2,3}}{\sqrt{\sigma^2 + \eta^2 + 2\sigma\eta\rho_{1,2}}}. \tag{5.8}$$

We find the limit values of -1, 0 and 1 according to Table 5.4.

5.1.5 Adding Jumps to the Credit Spread

CDS volatilities quoted on the market are not liquid, but they are usually higher than the CDS implied volatilities obtained with the CIR++ model. Adding jumps to the intensity model is one means to enhance the implied volatility (see [31]), and it agrees to the historical time series of credit spread too. Thus, by following [58], we consider also a square-root process with exponential jumps (hereafter JCIR++) for the default intensity sector of our model

$$dy_t = \kappa(\mu - y_t)\, dt + \nu\sqrt{y_t}\, dZ_t^3 + dJ_t(\zeta_1, \zeta_2),$$

Table 5.4 Values of model instantaneous correlations $\rho_{1,3}$ and $\rho_{2,3}$ ensuring special interest rate/credit-spread instantaneous correlations $\bar{\rho}$ for the chosen interest rate and intensity dynamics parameters. Notice that the instantaneous correlations are state dependent in presence of jumps, i.e. when $\zeta_1 > 0$ and $\zeta_2 > 0$, so that the last two rows of the table are only indicative values obtained in the limit $y_t \longrightarrow \mu$

$\rho_{1,3}$		4.05%	0.00%	−4.05%
$\rho_{2,3}$		−74.19%	0.00%	74.19%
ζ_1	ζ_2		$\bar{\rho}$	
0	0	−100.00%	0.00%	100.00%
0.1	0.1	−45.06%	0.00%	45.06%
0.15	0.15	−26.49%	0.00%	26.49%

Table 5.5 Black volatilities for CDS options implied by JCIR++ model (with parameters $y_0 = 0.035$, $\kappa = 0.35$, $\mu = 0.045$, $\nu = 0.15$) for different choices of the jump parameters. Interest rates are modelled according to Section 5.1.1 and $\bar{\rho} = 0$

			R			
ζ_1	ζ_2	σ_{impl} 1 × 5	1	3	5	10
0	0	28%	2.59%	2.71%	2.77%	2.84%
0.1	0.1	40%	2.89%	3.37%	3.64%	3.93%
0.15	0.15	57%	3.25%	4.12%	4.58%	5.07%

where the parameter vector β is now augmented to include the jump parameters, and each parameter is a positive deterministic constant. As before, Z_3 is a standard Brownian motion process under the risk-neutral measure, while the jump part $J_t(\zeta_1, \zeta_2)$ is defined as

$$J_t(\zeta_1, \zeta_2) := \sum_{i=i}^{M_t(\zeta_1)} X_i(\zeta_2)$$

where M is a time-homogeneous Poisson process with intensity ζ_1 (independent of Z), the Xs being exponentially distributed with positive finite mean ζ_2 independent of M (and Z).

Notice that the instantaneous correlation between the resulting short rate and the intensity is now reduced due to the jumps, as shown in Table 5.4, and it is given by

$$\bar{\rho} := \text{Corr}(dr_t, d\lambda_t) = \frac{\sigma\rho_{1,3} + \eta\rho_{2,3}}{\sqrt{\sigma^2 + \eta^2 + 2\sigma\eta\rho_{1,2}}\sqrt{1 + \frac{2\zeta_1\zeta_2^2}{\nu^2 y_t}}}.$$

As in the CIR++ case we assume the independence of the default intensity and interest rates while calibrating, so that, given market-implied default probabilities, extracted from CDS quotes, it is always possible to get a close form formula for $\psi(\cdot, \beta)$ such that the JCIR++ model fits exactly the market default probabilities, see, for example, [46], reported also in Brigo and Mercurio (2006) [48].

We set the diffusion part intensity parameters for the JCIR++ model to

$$y_0 = 0.035, \quad \kappa = 0.35, \quad \mu = 0.045, \quad \nu = 0.15$$

Then, we consider different possibilities for the values of the jump parameters ζ_1 and ζ_2 for three different choices of the CDS curves to reproduce different realistic market situations, as shown in Table 5.5.

5.2 NUMERICAL METHODS

A Monte Carlo simulation is used to value all the payoffs considered in the present chapter. We adopt the following prescriptions to implement effectively the algorithm. The standard error of each Monte Carlo run is within the last digit of numbers reported in tables.

5.2.1 Discretization Scheme

Payoff present values can be calculated with the joint interest rate and credit model by means of a Monte Carlo simulation of the three underlying variables x, z and y, whose joint transition density is needed. The transition density for the G2++ model is known in closed form, while the CIR++ model requires a discretization scheme, leading to a three-dimensional Gaussian local discretization. For CIR++ we adopt a discretization with a weekly step and we find similar convergence results both with the *full-truncation scheme* introduced by [144] and with the *implied scheme* by [35]. In the following we adopt the former scheme.

5.2.2 Simulating Intensity Jumps

In order to add the jumps on the intensity process, we first simulate the diffusive part of the process at a fixed set of dates $0 = t_0 < t_1 < \ldots < t_n$, according to the discretization scheme (we adopt the same discretization scheme from the CIR++ model). Then, we compute on each path the number of jumps occuring per time interval and their amplitudes. Finally, the jumps are added by considering all the contribution as occuring at the end of each discretization period.

5.2.3 "American Monte Carlo" (Pallavicini 2006)

Here we look at an approximate way to compute forward expectations. The simulation algorithm allows the counterparty to default on the contract payment dates, unless the time interval between two payment dates is longer than two months. In such case additional checks on counterparty default are added in order to ensure that the gap between allowed default times is at most two months. The calculation of the forward expectation, required by counterparty risk evaluation, as given in Equation (4.7) (inner expectation $\mathbb{E}_{T_j}$) is taken by approximating the expectation at the effective default time T_j with a polynomial series in the interest rate model underlying assets, x and z, valued at the first allowed default time after τ, i.e. at T_j. The coefficients of the series expansion are calculated by means of a least squares regression, as usually done to price Bermudan options, by means of the least squares simulation algorithm introduced progressively in [188], [72], and [143].

To the best of our knowledge, this technique, when applied to CVA and named "American Monte Carlo" elsewhere, first appeared in [57].

It is worth noticing that while the suboptimality of the approximate exercise ensures that the bias is unidirectional in the early exercise option pricing cases in [188], [72], and [143], here with CVA we do not know the direction of the bias involved in the least squares approximation, and therefore it is less safe to apply this technique to CVA than it is to early exercise options.

5.2.4 Callable Payoffs

Counterparty risk for callable payoffs is calculated in two steps. First, given a riskless version of the payoff, the payoff exercise boundary is calculated by a Monte Carlo simulation with the Longstaff and Schwartz algorithm. Since the default time is unpredictable from the point of view of the interest rate sector of the model, the same exercise boundary, as a function of the underlying at exercise date, is assumed to hold also for the default-risky payoff. Then the risky payoff along with the exercise boundary is treated as a standard European default-risky option, given that the continuation value at any relevant time is now a function of the underlying processes.

5.3 RESULTS AND DISCUSSION

We consider the pricing of different payoffs in the presence of counterparty risk for three different default probability scenarios (as expressed by hazard rates $\gamma = 3\%, 5\%$ and 7%) and for three different correlation scenarios ($\bar{\rho} = -1$, 0 and 1). For a detailed description of the payoffs the reader is referred to [48].

5.3.1 WWR in Single IRS

In the following we consider payoffs depending on at-the-money fix-receiver forward interest rate swap (IRS) paying on the EUR market. These contracts reset a given number of years from trade date and start accruing two business days later. The IRS's fixed leg pays a 30E/360 annual strike rate, while the floating leg pays LIBOR twice per year. The first products we analyze are simple IRS of this kind. We list in Table 5.6 the counterparty risk adjustment for the 10y IRS and the impact of correlation, for different levels of default probabilities.

We price the counterparty risk for the single IRS also in the case that the default intensity can jump. We list the results in Table 5.7. Notice that, in presence of jumps on the default intensity, the correlation impact may be enhanced.

5.3.2 WWR in an IRS Portfolio with Netting

After a single IRS, we consider portfolios of at-the-money IRSs either with different starting dates or with different maturities. In particular we focus on the following two portfolios:

1. ($\Pi 1$) given a set of annually spaced dates $\{T_i : i = 0 \ldots N\}$, with T_0 at two business days from trade date, consider the portfolio of swaps maturing at each T_i, with $i > 0$, and all starting at T_0. The netting of the portfolio is equal to an ammortizing swap with decreasing outstanding, which is shown in Figure 5.1.

Table 5.6 Counterparty risk price for the receiver IRS portfolio defined in section 5.3.2 for a maturity of ten years, along with the counterparty risk price for a ten year swap. Every IRS constituting the portfolio has unitary notional. Prices are in basis points

γ	$\bar{\rho}$	$\Pi 1$	$\Pi 2$	IRS
3%	−1	−140	−294	−36
	0	−84	−190	−22
	1	−47	−115	−13
5%	−1	−181	−377	−46
	0	−132	−290	−34
	1	−99	−227	−26
7%	−1	−218	−447	−54
	0	−173	−369	−44
	1	−143	−316	−37

Table 5.7 Counterparty risk price for ten year receiver IRS defined in Section 5.3.1, for three different calibrations of the JCIR++ model with jumps as given in Table 5.5. Prices are in basis points and are followed by the bracketed Monte Carlo statistical error

ζ_1	ζ_2	$\bar{\rho}$	10y
0	0	−100%	−56(0)
		0	−45(0)
		100%	−37(0)
0.1	0.1	−45%	−69(1)
		0	−58(0)
		45%	−50(1)
0.15	0.15	−26%	−93(4)
		0	−71(3)
		26%	−57(3)

2. ($\Pi 2$) given the same set of annually spaced dates, consider the portfolio of swaps starting at each T_i, with $i < N$, and all maturing at T_N. The netting of the portfolio is equal to an amortizing swap with increasing outstanding, which is shown in Figure 5.2.

We list in Table 5.6 the counterparty risk adjustment for both portfolios.

5.3.3 WWR in European Swaptions

We consider contracts giving the opportunity to enter a receiver IRS at an IRS's reset date. The strike rate in the swap to be entered is fixed at the at-the-money forward swap level observed at option inception, i.e. at trade date. We list in Table 5.8 the price of both the riskless and the risky contract. In Table 5.10 the same data are cast in terms of Black implied swaption volatility, i.e. we compute the Black swaption volatility that would match the counterparty risk-adjusted swaption price when put in a default-free Black formula for swaptions. In Table 5.9 we show an example with payer swaptions instead.

5.3.4 WWR in Bermudan Swaptions

We consider contracts giving the opportunity to enter a portfolio of IRSs, as defined in Section 5.3.2, every two business days before the starting of each accruing period of the swap's fix

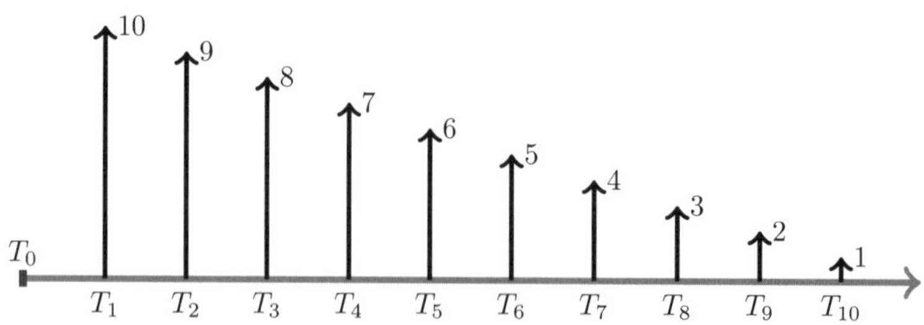

Figure 5.1 Portfolio $\Pi 1$: co-starting the IRS portfolio with positive cash flows: at the last reset we only have one flow, at the second-last reset two flows and so on

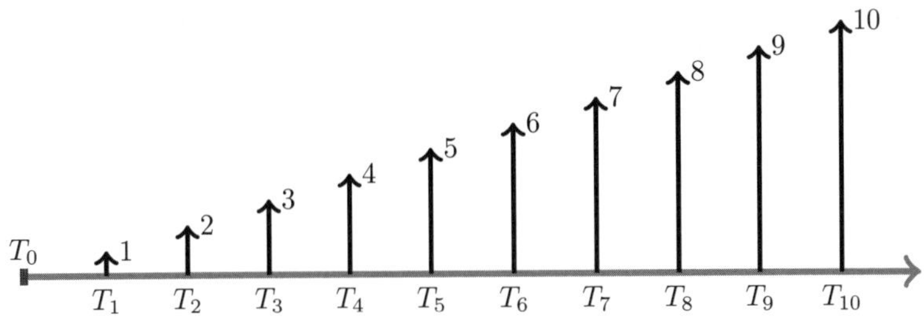

Figure 5.2 Case Π2: co-terminal IRS portfolio with positive cash flows: at the first reset we only have one flow, at the second reset two flows and so on

Table 5.8 Counterparty risk price for European receiver swaptions defined in Section 5.3.3 for different expiries and tenors. Riskless prices are listed too. Contracts have a unit notional. Prices are in basis points

γ	$\bar{\rho}$	1×5	5×5	10×5	20×5
3%	−1	−14	−37	−53	−56
	0	−9	−27	−42	−48
	1	−6	−19	−34	−41
5%	−1	−19	−50	−71	−70
	0	−14	−41	−61	−65
	1	−11	−35	−55	−61
7%	−1	−23	−61	−84	−79
	0	−19	−53	−77	−75
	1	−16	−47	−72	−73
riskless		106	205	215	157
γ	$\bar{\rho}$	1×10	5×10	10×10	20×10
3%	−1	−38	−78	−98	−98
	0	−25	−56	−78	−83
	1	−16	−43	−64	−72
riskless		184	342	353	256
γ	$\bar{\rho}$	1×20	5×20	10×20	20×20
3%	−1	−87	−140	−160	−150
	0	−61	−107	−129	−131
	1	−45	−83	−107	−114
riskless		261	474	486	354

Table 5.9 Counterparty risk price for European payer swaptions defined in Section 5.3.3 for different expiries and tenors. Riskless prices are listed too. Contracts have a unit notional. Prices are in basis points

γ	$\bar{\rho}$	1×5	5×5	10×5	20×5
3%	−1	−6	−20	−33	−40
	0	−10	−28	−44	−50
	1	−16	−39	−56	−58
riskless		106	205	215	157

Table 5.10 Counterparty risk implied volatilities for European receiver swaptions defined in Section 5.3.3 for different expiries and tenors. Riskless implied volatilities are listed too. Contracts have a unit notional

γ	$\bar{\rho}$	1×5	5×5	10×5	20×5
3%	−1	−1.96%	−2.52%	−3.06%	−3.74%
	0	−1.26%	−1.82%	−2.38%	−3.20%
	1	−0.77%	−1.32%	−1.93%	−2.78%
5%	−1	−2.60%	−3.40%	−4.06%	−4.71%
	0	−1.96%	−2.78%	−3.51%	−4.37%
	1	−1.54%	−2.35%	−3.16%	−4.09%
7%	−1	−3.19%	−4.14%	−4.81%	−5.32%
	0	−2.62%	−3.60%	−4.39%	−5.06%
	1	−2.22%	−3.23%	−4.11%	−4.89%
riskless		14.63%	13.90%	12.23%	10.45%
γ	$\bar{\rho}$	1×10	5×10	10×10	20×10
3%	−1	−2.74%	−2.86%	−3.14%	−3.72%
	0	−1.84%	−2.08%	−2.50%	−3.17%
	1	−1.19%	−1.59%	−2.03%	−2.75%
riskless		13.41%	12.55%	11.17%	9.67%
γ	$\bar{\rho}$	1×20	5×20	10×20	20×20
3%	−1	−3.71%	−3.14%	−3.19%	−3.53%
	0	−2.63%	−2.40%	−2.57%	−3.09%
	1	−1.95%	−1.87%	−2.14%	−2.68%
riskless		11.16%	10.60%	9.65%	8.27%

leg. We list in Table 5.11 the price of entering each portfolio, risky and riskless, along with the price of entering at the same exercise dates, the contained IRS of longest tenor.

5.3.5 WWR in CMS Spread Options

We consider a contract on the EUR market starting within two business days which pays, quarterly on an ACT/360 basis and up to maturity t_M, the following exotic index:

$$(L(S_a(t_i) - S_b(t_i)) - K)^+$$

where L and K are positive constants and $S_k(t_i)$, with $k \in \{a, b\}$ and $i = 0 \dots M$, is the constant maturity swap rate (hereafter CMS) fixing two business days before each accruing period start date t_i, i.e. the at-the-money rate for an IRS with tenor of k years fixing at t_i. We list in Table 5.12 the option prices, default-risky and riskless.

5.4 CONTINGENT CDS (CCDS)

A Contingent Credit Default Swap (CCDS) is a CDS that, upon the default of the reference credit, pays the loss given default on the residual net present value of a given portfolio if this is positive. The standard CDS instead pays the loss given default on a pre-specified notional amount, which we assumed to be 1 in our earlier CDS Formula (5.4).

Table 5.11 Counterparty risk price for callable receiver IRS portfolio defined in Section 5.3.4 for a maturity of ten years, along with the counterparty risk price for a spot-starting ten year Bermuda swaption. Riskless prices are listed too. Every IRS, constituting the portfolio, has a unit notional. Prices are in basis points

γ	$\bar{\rho}$	$\Pi1$	$\Pi2$	IRS
3%	−1	−197	−387	−47
	0	−140	−289	−34
	1	−101	−219	−25
5%	−1	−272	−528	−65
	0	−223	−446	−54
	1	−188	−387	−46
7%	−1	−340	−652	−80
	0	−295	−578	−70
	1	−266	−529	−63
riskless		1083	1917	240

It is immediate then that the default leg CCDS valuation, when the CCDS underlying portfolio constituting the protection notional is Π, is simply the counterparty risk adjustment in Formula (4.4). Our adjustments calculations above can then be interpreted also as examples of contingent CDS pricing.[2]

5.5 RESULTS INTERPRETATION AND CONCLUSIONS

In this chapter we have found that counterparty risk has a relevant impact on interest rate payoffs prices and that, in turn, correlation between interest rates and default (intensity) has a relevant impact on the adjustment due to counterparty risk. The same applies to Contingent Credit Default Swap pricing, given the strong analogies with counterparty risk valuation. We

Table 5.12 Counterparty risk price for CMS spread options defined in Section 5.3.5 with $L = 15$, $K = 15\%$, $a = 10y$, $b = 2y$ and three different maturities $t_M \in \{5y, 10y, 15y\}$. Riskless prices are listed too. Prices are in basis points

γ	$\bar{\rho}$	5y	10y	20y
3%	−1	−5	−16	−34
	0	−4	−11	−24
	1	−2	−8	−18
5%	−1	−7	−22	−44
	0	−6	−17	−37
	1	−5	−15	−31
7%	−1	−9	−26	−52
	0	−7	−23	−46
	1	−6	−20	−42
riskless		58	122	182

[2] We are grateful to Gloria Ikosi of the Federal Deposit Insurance Corporation in Washington DC for helpful correspondence on this subject.

have analyzed the pattern of such impacts as product characteristics and tenor structures change through some fundamental numerical examples and we have found stable and reasonable patterns. In particular, the (positive) CVA counterparty risk adjustment to be subtracted from the default-free price decreases with correlation for receiver payoffs (IRS, IRS portfolios, European and Bermudan swaptions). This is to be expected. If default intensities increase, with high positive correlation their correlated interest rates will increase more than with low correlation; since when interest rates increase a receiver swaption value decreases, we see that all things being equal a higher correlation implies a lower value for the swaptions impacting the adjustment, so that with higher correlation the adjustment absolute value decreases. The analogous adjustment for payer payoffs increases with correlation instead, as is to be expected.

In general our results, including the CMS spread options, confirm the counterparty risk adjustment to be relevant and the impact of correlation on counterparty risk to be relevant in turn, expecially in presence of jumps on default intensity, as can be required in order to achieve higher implied volatilites for CDS options. We have found the following further stylized facts, holding throughout all payoffs. As the default probability implied by the counterparty CDS increases, the size of the adjustment due to counterparty risk increases as well, but the impact of correlation on it tends to decrease. This is partly expected: given large default probabilities for the counterparty, fine details on the dynamics, such as the correlation with interest rates, become less relevant as everything is being wiped out by massive defaults anyway. To the contrary, with smaller default probabilities, the fine structure of the dynamics and correlation in particular is more important.

The conclusion is that we should take into account interest-rate/credit-spread correlation in valuing counteparty-risky interest rate payoffs, especially when the default probabilities are not extremely high. Although when we were first writing this in 2006 [56] there was not much focus on wrong way risk, today this aspect of the CVA modelling problem is considered to be paramount.

6

Unilateral CVA for Commodities with WWR

This chapter re-elaborates and expands material originally presented in Brigo and Bakkar (2009) [36].

The inclusion of counterparty risk pricing into commodities valuation is important. The issue has long been debated and is related to the difference between commodities forward and futures contracts. Indeed, due to margining, futures often have very small or negligible counterparty risk (leaving aside Gap risk for the time being, as we will explore Gap risk between margin calls later in the book). Forward contracts, instead, may bear the full risk of default for the counterparty when traded with brokers or outside clearing houses, or when embedded in other contracts such as swaps. It is commonly accepted that commodity futures and forward prices, in principle, agree under absence of counterparty risk. However, the assumption of absence of counterparty risk is proving more and more difficult to accept, and as a consequence the inclusion of CVA is now required in more and more commodities transactions.

In this chapter we focus on energy commodities and on oil in particular. We use a hybrid commodities-credit model to assess the impact of unilateral counterparty risk in pricing formulas, both in the gross effect of default probabilities and on the subtler effects of credit-spread volatility, commodities volatility and credit-commodities correlation (and wrong way risk). We illustrate our general approach with a case study based on an oil swap, showing that, similarly to other asset classes, an accurate valuation of counterparty risk depends on volatilities and correlation and cannot be accounted for precisely through a pre-defined multiplier. Our finding is the same as we have seen earlier for other asset classes: a precise valuation of CVA requires explicit modelling choices. In this chapter we neglect collateral modelling, bilateral counterparty risk (Debit Valuation Adjustment, DVA), and close-out amount evaluation, since we will approach such matters in later chapters. This is just as well, since even the simple case of unilateral CVA is sufficient to highlight the complexity of the CVA pricing problem for commodities, showing that quick fixes to default-free valuation frameworks are not available.

As in previous chapters, we enforce here the following:

Assumption 6.0.1 ***Unilateral Default Assumption (UDA): Assuming one party to be default free.*** *In this chapter we assume that calculations are done considering one of the two parties to be default free, although we will exchange the parties' roles occasionally.*

6.1 OIL SWAPS AND COUNTERPARTY RISK

Going a little more into detail, in this chapter we consider counterparty risk for commodities payoffs in the presence of correlation between the default event and the underlying commodity, while taking into account volatilities for both credit and commodities. In this chapter we focus on oil, but much of our reasoning can be adapted to other commodities with similar characteristics (storability, liquidity, and similar seasonality).

Past work on pricing counterparty risk for different asset classes is in [186], [47] and [56], [57] and [58], for interest rate swaps and exotic underlyings, as seen also in Chapters 4 and 5. Counterparty risk for credit (CDS) underlyings was worked on by [140] and [43], and will be discussed in Chapter 7.

Here we analyze in detail counterparty-risky (or default-risky) oil forward and swaps contracts.

In general, the reason to introduce counterparty risk when evaluating a contract is linked to the fact that many financial contracts are traded over the counter, so that the credit quality of the counterparty can be relevant. This is particularly appropriate when thinking of the different defaults experienced by some important companies during the past years, especially in the energy and financial sectors.

Earlier works in counterparty risk for commodities include, for example, [70], who analyze this notion more from a capital adequacy/risk management point of view. In particular, their approach is not dynamical and does not consider explicitly credit spread volatility and especially correlation between the underlying commodity and credit spread. In our approach wrong way risk is modelled through said correlation. Mostly, however, the difference is in the purpose. We are valuing counterparty risk more from a pricing than a risk management perspective, resorting to a fully arbitrage- free and finely-tuned risk-neutral approach. This is why all our processes are calibrated to liquid market information both on forward curves and volatilities. Correlations are harder to estimate but we analyze their impact by letting them range across a set of possible values.

In general we are looking at the problem from the viewpoint of a safe (default-free) institution entering a financial contract with another counterparty having a positive probability of defaulting before the final maturity, so that we are looking at unilateral counterparty risk. We formalize the general and reasonable fact that the value of a generic claim subject to counterparty risk is always smaller than the value of a similar claim having a null default probability, expressing the discrepancy between the two (the Credit Valuation Adjustment, CVA) in precise quantitative terms.

We consider Credit Default Swaps (CDS) for the counterparty as liquid sources of market default probabilities. We could use bonds issued by the counterparty, alternatively, while paying attention to possible CDS-Bond basis. Different models can be used to calibrate CDS or corporate's bond data and obtain default probabilities: here we resort to stochastic intensity models as studied in [35], whose jump extension with analytical formulas for CDS options is illustrated in [46]. This is the model we have seen in Sections 3.3.5 and 3.3.6.

As a model for oil we adopt a two-factor model shaping both the short-term deviation in prices and the equilibrium price level, as in [182]. This model can be shown to be equivalent to a more classical convenience yield model like in [114], and a stochastic volatility extension of a similar approach is considered in [112]. What is modelled is the oil spot price, under the implicit assumption that such a spot price process exists. This is not true for electricity, for example, and even for markets like crude oil where spot prices are quoted daily, the exact meaning of the spot is difficult to single out. Nonetheless, we assume, along with most of the industry, that there is a traded spot asset.

In the chapter we find that counterparty risk has a relevant impact on the product prices and that, in turn, correlation between oil and credit spreads of the counterparty has a relevant impact on the adjustment due to counterparty risk. Similarly, oil and credit spread volatilities have relevant impact on the adjustment. We illustrate this with a case study based on an oil swap.

The chapter is organized as follows. In Section 6.2 we summarize again the CIR++ specification which serves as the credit model, and in Section 6.2.1 we outline the two-factor Schwartz and Smith commodity model. Sections 6.3 and 6.4 illustrate the counterparty adjustments for forwards and swaps respectively. An example, based on a swap contract between a bank and an airline company is presented in Section 6.5, where we assume that we have a airline company buying a swap contract on oil from a bank with a very high credit quality. Thus we assume first the bank to be default free. The bank wants to charge counterparty risk to the airline in defining the forward price, as there is no collateral posted and no margining is occurring. We will consider also the case where, although initially the credit risk of the bank is very low, it grows later, due to a crisis, and surpasses the credit risk of the airline, which then becomes free with respect to the bank. As example of this is the case of an oil swap started by Lehman brothers in 2006 and revalued in September 2008.

Before reading the chapter in detail, we invite the reader who is not yet familiar with Chapter 4 to familiarize themself with Formula 4.4.

6.2 MODELLING ASSUMPTIONS

In this section we consider a reduced form model that is stochastic in the default intensity for the counterparty. We will later correlate the credit spread of this model with the underlying commodity model, which will allow us to consider wrong way risk (WWR).

We assume deterministic default-free instantaneous interest rate $t \mapsto r_t$ (and hence deterministic discount factors $D(s,t), \ldots$), although our analysis would work well even with stochastic rates independent of oil and credit spreads.

6.2.1 Commodity Model

We consider crude oil. As a model for oil we adopt a two-factor model shaping both the short-term deviation in prices and the equilibrium price level, as in [182]. This model can be shown to be equivalent to a more classical convenience-yield model like in [114], and a stochastic-volatility extension of a similar approach is considered in [112]. What is modelled is the oil spot price, under the implicit assumption that such a spot price process exists. This is not true for electricity, for example, and even for markets like crude oil where spot prices are quoted daily, the exact meaning of the spot is difficult to single out. Nonetheless, we assume, along with most of the industry, that there is a traded spot asset.

If we denote by S_t the oil spot price at time t, the log-price process is written as

$$\log S_t = \varphi(t) + x_t + L_t,$$

where, under the risk-neutral measure,

$$\begin{aligned} dx_t &= -\kappa_x x_t \, dt + \sigma_x \, dZ_t^x \\ dL_t &= \mu_L \, dt + \sigma_L \, dZ_t^L \end{aligned} \tag{6.1}$$

where Z_t^x and Z_t^L are two correlated Brownian motions with

$$dZ_t^x dZ_t^L = \rho_{xL} \, dt$$

with φ a deterministic shift, which we use to calibrate quoted oil futures prices, and with κ_x,σ_x,μ_L,σ_L positive constants. The process x_t represents the short-term deviation, whereas L_t represents the backbone of the equilibrium price level in the long run.

For applications it can be important to derive the transition density of the spot commodity in this model. For the two factors we have a joint Gaussian transition, whose mean and variance are given as

$$\mathbb{E}_s[x_t] = x_s e^{-\kappa_x(t-s)}, \quad \mathbb{E}_s[L_t] = L_s + \mu_L(t-s)$$

$$\mathrm{Var}_s[x_t] = \frac{\sigma_x^2}{2\kappa_x}\left(1 - e^{-2\kappa_x(t-s)}\right), \quad \mathrm{Var}_s[L_t] = \sigma_L^2(t-s)$$

$$\mathrm{Cov}_s[x_t, L_t] = \frac{\sigma_x \sigma_L \rho_{xL}}{\kappa_x}\left(1 - e^{-\kappa_x(t-s)}\right).$$

This can be used for exact simulation between times s and u. As we know that the sum of two jointly Gaussian random variables is Gaussian, we have

$$\log S_t|_{x_s, L_s} \sim \mathcal{N}(m(s,t), V(s,t))$$

where

$$m(s,t) := \varphi(t) + x_s e^{-\kappa_x(t-s)} + L_s + \mu_L(t-s)$$

$$v(s,t) := \frac{\sigma_x^2}{2\kappa_x}\left(1 - e^{-2\kappa_x(t-s)}\right) + \sigma_L^2(t-s) + 2\mathrm{Cov}_s[x_t, L_t]$$

from which, in particular, we see that

$$\mathbb{E}_s[S_t] = \exp\left\{\varphi(t) + x_s e^{-\kappa_x(t-s)} + L_s + \mu_L(t-s) + \frac{1}{2}v(s,t)\right\}.$$

Hence we can compute the forward price $\mathbb{E}_t[S_T]$ at time t of the commodity at maturity T when counterparty risk is negligible and under deterministic interest rates, as

$$F_t(T) = \exp\left\{\varphi(T) + x(t)e^{-\kappa_x(T-t)} + L(t) + \mu_L(T-t) + \frac{1}{2}v(t,T)\right\}. \tag{6.2}$$

In particular, given the forward curve $T \mapsto F_0^M(T)$ from the market, the expression for the shift $\varphi^M(T)$ that makes the model consistent with said curve is

$$\varphi^M(T) = \log F_0^M(T) - x_0 e^{-\kappa_x T} - L_0 - \mu_L T - \frac{1}{2}v(0,T).$$

In the following we set $x_0 = L_0 = 0$, since we can achieve a perfect calibration to market forward prices by using only φ.

The short term/equilibrium price model (x, L), when $\varphi = 0$, is equivalent to the more classical Gibson and Schwartz (1990) model, formulated as

$$\begin{aligned} d\log S_t &= \left(r(t) - q_t - \frac{1}{2}\sigma_x^2\right) dt + \sigma_S\, dZ_t^S \\ dq_t &= \kappa_q(\mu_q - q_t)\, dt + \sigma_q dZ_t^q \end{aligned} \tag{6.3}$$

with

$$dZ_t^S dZ_t^q = \rho_{qS}\, dt$$

where the relationships are (we promote μ_L to be a deterministic function of time)

$$x_t = \frac{1}{\kappa_q}(q_t - \mu_q), \quad L_t = \log S_t - \frac{1}{\kappa_q}(q_t - \mu_q)$$

$$\kappa_x = \kappa_q, \quad \mu_L(t) = r(t) - \mu_q - \frac{1}{2}\sigma_S^2$$

$$\sigma_x = \frac{\sigma_q}{\kappa_q}, \quad \sigma_L = \sqrt{\sigma_S^2 + \frac{\sigma_q^2}{\kappa_q^2} - 2\frac{\sigma_S\sigma_q\rho_{qS}}{\kappa_q}}$$

$$dZ_t^x = dZ_t^q, \quad dZ_t^L = \frac{\sigma_S}{\sigma_L}\, dZ_t^S - \frac{\sigma_q}{\kappa_x\sigma_L}\, dZ_t^q, \quad \rho_{xL} = \frac{\sigma_S\rho_{qS}}{\sigma_L} - \frac{\sigma_q}{\kappa_x\sigma_L}.$$

6.2.2 CIR++ Stochastic-Intensity Model

For the stochastic intensity model we follow Section 3.3.5, or more specifically Section 3.3.6 without jumps. We implement the same model also in Section 5.1.2, when dealing with interest rate derivatives. For the stochastic intensity model we set

$$\lambda_t := y_t + \psi(t), \quad t \geq 0, \tag{6.4}$$

where ψ is a deterministic function, and we take y to be a Cox-Ingersoll-Ross process (see [48]):

$$dy_t = \kappa(\mu - y_t)\, dt + \nu\sqrt{y_t}\, dZ_t^3,$$

where the parameters are positive deterministic constants, and we call β the vector with their values. As usual, Z^3 is a standard Brownian motion process under the risk-neutral measure, representing the stochastic shock in our dynamics. We will often use the integrated quantities

$$\Lambda(t) := \int_0^t \lambda_s\, ds, \quad Y(t) := \int_0^t y_s\, ds \text{ and } \quad \Psi(t, \beta) := \int_0^t \psi(s, \beta)\, ds.$$

More in detail, we assume intensity paths to be strictly positive almost everywhere, so that $t \mapsto \Lambda(t)$ are invertible functions. The default event is modelled as in a Cox-Ingersoll-Ross process by setting

$$\tau = \Lambda^{-1}(\xi),$$

with ξ a standard (unit-mean) exponential random variable independent of interest rates.

The default-intensity process of each name can be calibrated as in Section 5.1.3 to CDS quoted spreads. Yet, not all model parameters can be fixed in this way. Once we have done this and calibrated CDS or corporate bond data we are left with volatility parameters which can be used to calibrate further products. However, this will be interesting when single-name option data on the credit derivatives market will become more liquid. Currently the bid-ask spreads for single name CDS options are large and suggest to either consider these quotes with caution, or to try and deduce volatility parameters from more liquid index options through some ad-hoc single name re-scaling. At the moment we content ourselves of calibrating only CDS's and no options. To help specifying β without further data we set some values of the parameters implying possibly reasonable values for the implied volatility of hypothetical CDS options on the counterparty, that are in line with possible historical volatilities of credit spreads. Another possibility is to use the much more liquid implied volatility of options on CDS indices (iTraxx or CDX) with corrections accounting for the single name idiosyncrasies.

6.3 FORWARD VERSUS FUTURES PRICES

The inclusion of counterparty risk is related to the difference between commodities forward and futures contracts. Owing to margining, futures often have very small or negligible counterparty risk. Instead forward contracts may bear the full risk of default for the counterparty. Consider now a forward contract. The prototypical forward contract agrees on the following:

Let t be the valuation time. At the future time T a party agrees to buy from a second party a commodity at the price K fixed today. This is expressed by saying that the first party has entered a payer Forward Rate Agreement (FRA). The second party has agreed to enter a receiver Forward Rate Agreement. The value of this contract to the first and second party respectively, at maturity, will be

$$S_T - K, \quad K - S_T$$

i.e. the actual price of the commodity at maturity minus the pre-agreed price in the payer case, and the opposite of this in the receiver case. Let us focus on the payer case. When this is discounted back at t with deterministic interest rates, and risk-neutral expectation is taken, this leads to the price being given by

$$\mathbb{E}_t[D(t,T)(S_T - K)] = D(t,T)(\mathbb{E}_t[S_T] - K) = D(t,T)(F(t,T) - K). \qquad (6.5)$$

Note that the forward price is exactly the value of the pre-agreed rate K that sets the contract price to zero, i.e. $K = F(t,T)$. Let us maintain a general K in the forward contract under examination.

In the oil model above, the forward contract price is given by plugging Formula (6.2) into (6.5). Let us denote by $\text{Fwdp}(t,T;K)$ such price ("p" is for payer),

$$\text{Fwdp}(t,T;K) = D(t,T)\left(\exp\left\{\varphi(T) + x_t e^{-\kappa_x(T-t)} + L(t) + \mu_L(T-t) + \tfrac{1}{2}v(t,T)\right\} - K\right) \qquad (6.6)$$

whereas the opposite of this quantity is denoted by $\text{Fwdr}(t,T;K)$ ("r" is for receiver).

We may apply our counterparty risk framework to the forward contract, where now $\Pi(t,T) = D(t,T)(S_T - K)$, and NPV$(t)$ =Fwdp$(t,T;K)$. We obtain the price of the payer forward contract, under counterparty risk, from Equation (4.4):

$$\overline{\text{Fwdp}}(t,T;K) = \text{Fwdp}(t,T;K) \\ \underbrace{-\,\text{LGD}\,\mathbb{E}_t\left[\mathbf{1}_{\{t<\tau\le T\}} D(t,\tau)\,(\text{Fwdp}(\tau,T;K))^+\right]}_{\text{Positive counterparty-risk adjustment}}. \tag{6.7}$$

Under the bucketing approximation given by Equation (4.7), we obtain

$$\overline{\text{Fwdp}}(t,T;K) = \text{Fwdp}(t,T;K) \\ -\text{LGD}\sum_{j=1}^{b} D(t,T_j)\mathbb{E}_t\left[\mathbf{1}_{\{T_{j-1}<\tau\le T_j\}}(\text{Fwdp}(T_j,T;K))^+\right].$$

6.3.1 CVA for Commodity Forwards without WWR

If one assumes independence between the underlying commodity and the counterparty default, one may factor the above expectation obtaining:

$$\overline{\text{Fwdp}_0}(t,T;K) = \text{Fwdp}(t,T;K) \\ -\text{LGD}\sum_{j=1}^{b}\mathbb{Q}(T_{j-1} < \tau \le T_j)\mathbb{E}_t\left[D(t,T_j)(\text{Fwdp}(T_j,T;K))^+\right]$$

where we use the index zero in risky price to recall the independence assumption. The last term is the price of an option on a forward price that is known in closed form in the Schwartz and Smith model, although we have to incorporate the shift in our formulation. We have:

$$\mathbb{E}_t\left[D(t,T_j)(\text{Fwdp}(T_j,T;K))^+\right] = D(t,T)\exp\left\{M(t,T,T_j;x_t,L_t) + \frac{1}{2}V(t,T,T_j)\right\} \\ \cdot\Phi\left(\frac{M(t,T,T_j;x_t,L_t) + V(t,T,T_j) - \log K}{\sqrt{V(t,T,T_j)}}\right) \\ -D(t,T)K\,\Phi\left(\frac{M(t,T,T_j;x_t,L_t) - \log K}{\sqrt{V(t,T,T_j)}}\right)$$

where

$$M(t,T,T_j;x_t,L_t) := \varphi(T) + x_t e^{-\kappa_x(T-t)} + L_t + \frac{1}{2}v(T_j,T)$$

and

$$V(t,T,T_j) := \sigma_L^2(T_j - t) \\ +\frac{\sigma_x^2}{2\kappa_x}e^{-2\kappa_x(T-T_j)}(1 - e^{-2\kappa_x(T_j-t)}) \\ +2\frac{\sigma_x\sigma_L\rho_{xL}}{\kappa_x}e^{-\kappa_x(T-T_j)}(1 - e^{-\kappa_x(T_j-t)})$$

where Φ is the cumulative distribution function of the standard Gaussian.

Thus, we have the adjustment as a stream of options on forwards weighted by default probabilities.

6.3.2 CVA for Commodity Forwards with WWR

If we do not assume independence then we need to substitute for the intensity model. Through iterated conditioning we obtain easily

$$\overline{\mathrm{Fwdp}}_0(t,T;K) = \mathrm{Fwdp}(t,T;K)$$
$$-\mathrm{LGD}\sum_{j=1}^{b} D(t,T_j)\mathbb{E}_t\left[\left(e^{-\Lambda(T_{j-1})} - e^{-\Lambda(T_j)}\right)(\mathrm{Fwdp}(T_j,T;K))^+\right].$$

If in particular we select $K = F(t,T)$ then $\mathrm{Fwdp}(t,T;K)$ will be zero.

This price can be computed by joint simulation of default intensity λ, and the commodity's driving factors x and L. We may correlate the credit spread to the commodity by correlating the shock Z^3 in the default intensity to the shocks Z^x, Z^L in the commodity. If we assume

$$dZ_t^x dZ_t^3 = \rho_x\,dt, \quad dZ_t^L dZ_t^3 = \rho_L\,dt$$

then the instantaneous correlation between the default intensity and the commodity's price is given by

$$\mathrm{Corr}(d\lambda_t,\ dS_t) = \frac{\sigma_x\rho_x + \sigma_L\rho_L}{\sqrt{\sigma_x^2 + \sigma_L^2 + 2\sigma_x\sigma_L\rho_{xL}}}.$$

This is the correlation one may try to infer from the market, through historical estimation or implying it from liquid market quotes. In general, the only parameters that have not been calibrated previously are ρ_x and ρ_L. If we make, for example, the assumption that the two are the same,

$$\bar{\rho} := \rho_x = \rho_L$$

then we get the model correlation parameters as a function of the already calibrated parameters, and of the market correlation as

$$\bar{\rho} = \frac{\sqrt{\sigma_x^2 + \sigma_L^2 + 2x\sigma_x\sigma_L\rho_{xL}}}{\sigma_x + \sigma_L}\mathrm{Corr}(d\lambda_t,\ dS_t).$$

6.4 SWAPS AND COUNTERPARTY RISK

Consider now a swap contract. The prototypical swap contract is actually a portfolio of forward contracts with different maturities, and is formulated as follows:

Let t be the valuation time. At the future times T_i in $\mathcal{T} := \{T_{a+1}, T_{a+2}, \ldots, T_b\}$, a party agrees to buy from a second party a commodity at the price K fixed today, on a notional α_i. This is expressed by saying that the first party has entered a payer swap agreement. The second party has agreed to enter a receiver swap. We consider deterministic interest rates. The value of the payer commodity swap contract to the first party, at time t, will be:

$$\begin{aligned}\text{Swapp}(t, \mathcal{T}; K) &= \mathbb{E}_t\left[\sum_{i=a+1}^{b} D(t, T_i)\alpha_i(S_{T_i} - K)\right]\\ &= \sum_{i=a+1}^{b} \alpha_i D(t, T_i)(F(t, T_i) - K)\\ &= \sum_{i=a+1}^{b} \alpha_i \text{Fwdp}(t, T_i; K).\end{aligned}$$

Since the last formula is known in our oil model, in terms of the processes x_t and L_t, we easily obtain a formula for the commodity swap by summation.

If we look for the value of K that sets the contract price to zero, i.e. the so-called forward swap commodity price $S_{a,b}(t)$, we have:

$$S_{a,b}(t) := \frac{\sum_{i=a+1}^{b} \alpha_i D(t, T_i)F(t, T_i)}{\sum_{i=a+1}^{b} \alpha_i D(t, T_i)}.$$

By using such rate we can also express the payer commodity swap price at a general strike level K as

$$\text{Swapp}(t, \mathcal{T}; K) = (S_{a,b}(t) - K) \sum_{i=a+1}^{b} \alpha_i D(t, T_i)$$

whereas the receiver commodity swap would be

$$\text{Swapr}(t, \mathcal{T}; K) = (K - S_{a,b}(t)) \sum_{i=a+1}^{b} \alpha_i D(t, T_i).$$

These formulas provide the value of these contracts when a clearing house or margining agreements are in place, and when we neglect Gap risk and extreme contagion. However, swaps are often traded outside such contexts and as such they embed counterparty risk.

Our general Formula (4.4), for a payer commodity swap, when including counterparty risk, would read in the swap case:

$$\begin{aligned}\overline{\text{Swapp}}(t, \mathcal{T}; K) &= \text{Swapp}(t, \mathcal{T}; K) - \underbrace{\mathbb{E}_t\left[\text{LGD}\, \mathbf{1}_{\{t<\tau\le T_b\}} D(t, \tau)\, (\text{Swapp}(\tau, \mathcal{T}; K))^+\right]}_{\text{Positive counterparty-risk adjustment}}\\ &= \text{Swapp}(t, \mathcal{T}; K) - \mathbb{E}_t\left[\text{LGD}\, \mathbf{1}_{\{t<\tau\le T_b\}} D(t, \tau)\left(\sum_{i=a+1}^{b} \alpha_i \text{Fwdp}(\tau, T_i; K)\right)^+\right]. \quad (6.8)\end{aligned}$$

Since the forward formula is known in closed form in our model, we can proceed similarly to the forward case to value the counterparty risk adjustment for the swap case through simulation. The receiver case is completely analogous.

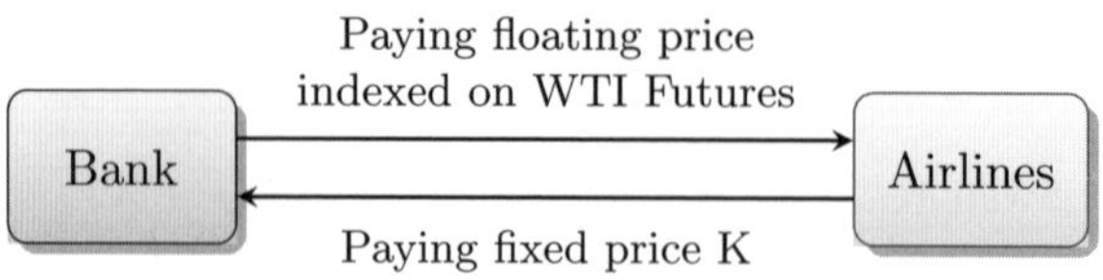

Figure 6.1 The contract between the airline and the bank

6.5 UCVA FOR COMMODITY SWAPS

As a case study we consider an oil swap. An airline needs to buy oil in the future and is concerned about possible changes in the oil price. To hedge this price movement the airline asks a bank to enter a swap where the bank pays periodically to the airline a (floating) amount indexed at a relevant oil futures price at the coupon date. In exchange for this, the airline pays periodically an amount K that is fixed in the beginning.

We assume that, in the past, the credit risk of the bank was low. At that point in time, if one had to assume the unilateral UDA formulation as in Assumption 6.0.1, it makes sense for the bank to be considered as default free and to compute the unilateral CVA to be charged to the airline. However, due to the global financial crisis, the credit risk of the bank has subsequently increased above the credit risk of the airline. In that respect, at this later date, if again one is to enforce Assumption 6.0.1, it makes sense to assume that the airline is default free and the airline computes the counterparty risk adjustment to be charged to the bank. We will thus look at the unilateral counterparty risk adjustment from the point of view of each of the two parties separately, by calibrating the credit model adequately in each case.

The oil model has been calibrated to exactly fit the forward curve extracted from West Texas Intermediate (WTI) futures, shown in shown in Figure 6.2, and to best-fit the implied volatilities of at-the-money options on futures, shown in Figure 6.3. The model parameter μ_L is set to zero, as it can be substituted by the deterministic shift φ. The resulting oil model parameters are shown in Table 6.1.

The oil swap we consider has a final maturity of 5 years, monthly payments and strike K given by $K = 126$ USD, that is the strike setting to zero the value of the 5 years default-free oil swap. α_i is equal to one (barrel).

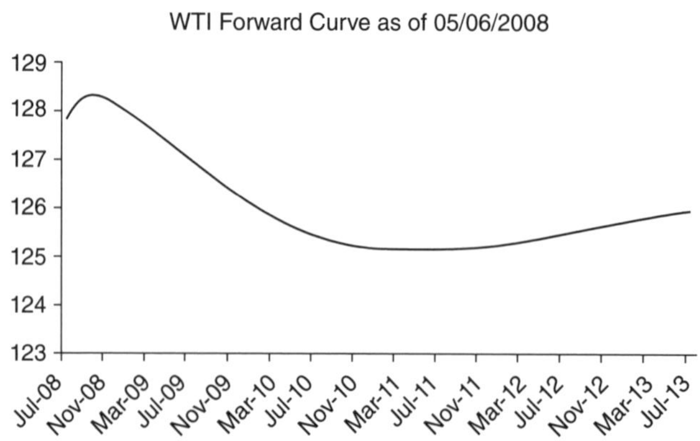

Figure 6.2 Calibration: forward curve

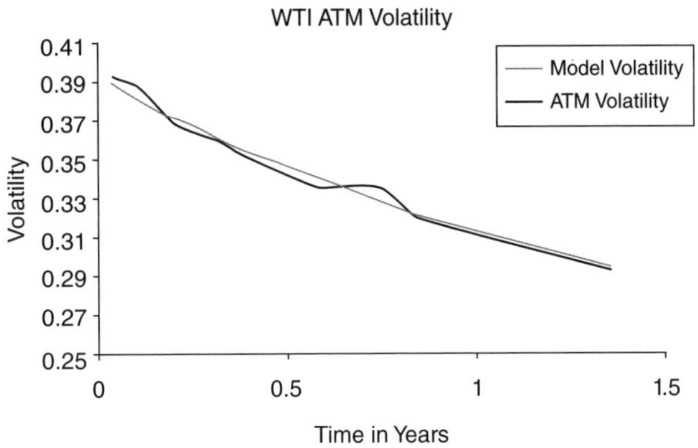

Figure 6.3 Calibration: ATM volatility curve

6.5.1 Counterparty Risk from the Payer's Perspective: The Airline Computes Counterparty Risk

Here we are now at the hypothetical later date, and the credit risk of the bank has become higher than the credit risk of the airline, due to the financial crisis. We use the CDS spreads for the bank, which are given in Table 6.2. The yield curve is given in Table 6.3.

In the following we assume the bank credit quality to be characterized by a CIR++ stochastic intensity model that, at spread levels, is consistent with Table 6.2 through the shift ψ, while allowing for credit spread volatility through the CIR dynamics. We use the base CIR parameter set given in Table 6.4. Later, we change the spread volatility parameter ν by reducing it through multiplicative factors smaller than one, and re-calibrate the model shift to maintain consistency with Table 6.2. This way we investigate the impact of the spread volatility on the counterparty adjustment.

The graphs in Figure 6.4 and Figure 6.6 illustrate some of our results for CVA. The counterparty risk is expressed as a percentage of a 5y maturing swap fixed leg value, which is 6852.35 USD. First we observe the effect of varying the commodity volatility while keeping the credit intensity volatility fixed at $\nu_{Bank} = 59\%$.[1] The commodity volatility was varied by applying multiplicative factors to the two factors instantaneous volatilities σ_x and σ_L. As an indication of implied volatility levels, the term structure of the commodity implied volatility when we apply the multiplicative factor 2 is given in Figure 6.5.

Then, we observe the effect of varying the intensity volatility while keeping the commodity spot volatility fixed at $\sigma_S = 32.82\%$ as implied by Table 6.1. The same results are presented in a different way in Tables 6.5 and 6.6. In these tables, we give the absolute value of the adjustment in US dollars. We also express it as an adjusted strike price that the payer might choose to pay to its counterparty by taking into account the estimated adjustment.

[1] The CDS implied vol associated to these parameters is 26%. Brigo (2005, 2006), under the CDS market model, shows that implied volatilities for CDS options can easily exceed 50%.

Table 6.1 Calibration parameters

κ_x	σ_x	σ_L	ρ_{xL}
0.7170	0.3522	0.19	−0.0392

Table 6.2 CDS spreads term structure for the bank

maturity (years)	0.5	1	2	3	4	5
spread (bps)	345	332	287	256	232	217

Table 6.3 Zero-coupon continuously compound spot interest rates

maturity (years)	3/12	6/12	2	5	10	30
yield (percent)	2.68	2.92	3.40	4.27	4.87	5.376

Table 6.4 CIR parameters for the base case for the bank credit spread volatility

y_0	κ	μ	ν
0.0560	0.6331	0.0293	0.5945

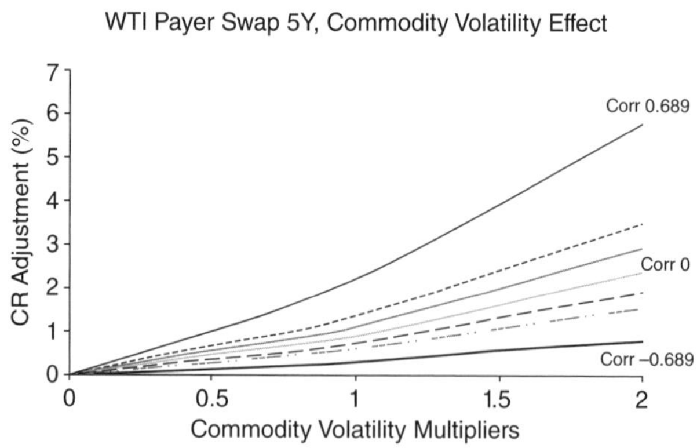

Figure 6.4 Commodity swap CVA: commodity volatility effect. Fixed leg price maturity 5Y: USD6852.35 for a notional of 1 barrel per month, CVA as a (%) of the fixed leg price

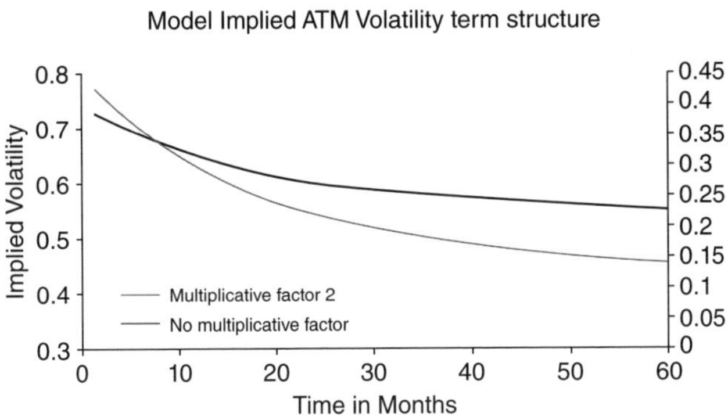

Figure 6.5 Model Implied Volatility without (right scale) and with (left scale) multiplicative factors

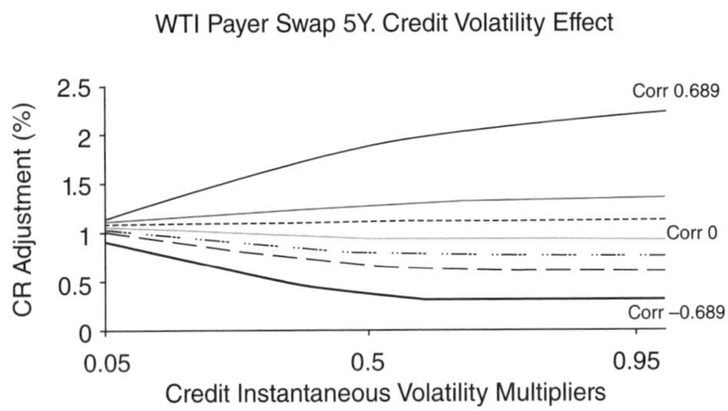

Figure 6.6 Commodity swap CVA: credit volatility effect. Fixed leg Price maturity 5Y: USD6852.35 for a notional of 1 barrel per month, CVA as a (%) of the fixed leg price

Table 6.5 Effect of credit spread volatility on the CVA. Fixed leg price maturity 5Y: USD6852.35 for a notional of 1 barrel per month, fair strike without counterparty risk USD126

$\bar{\rho}$	intensity vol. ν	0.0295	0.295	0.59
−68.9%	Adjustement in USD	63.49	25.17	21.58
	Adjusted Strike	124.84	125.54	125.60
−27.6%	CVA (USD)	69.99	45.89	41.50
	Adjusted Strike	124.71	125.16	125.24
−13.8%	CVA (USD)	71.83	55.02	51.48
	Adjusted Strike	124.68	124.99	125.05
0%	CVA (USD)	73.30	65.23	63.42
	Adjusted Strike	124.66	124.80	124.84
13.8%	CVA (USD)	74.62	76.63	77.36
	Adjusted Strike	124.63	124.59	124.58
27.6%	CVA (USD)	75.88	88.93	93.08
	Adjusted Strike	124.61	124.37	124.29
68.9%	CVA (USD)	79.32	130.39	152.05
	Adjusted Strike	124.54	123.61	123.21

Table 6.6 Effect of oil volatility on the CVA. Fixed leg price maturity 5Y: USD6852.35 for a notional of 1 barrel per month, fair strike without counterparty risk USD126

$\bar{\rho}$	comdty spot vol. σ_S	0.033	0.1642	0.3285	0.657
−68.9%	CVA (USD)	1.17	11.05	21.58	57.11
	Adjusted Strike	125.98	125.79	125.60	124.95
−27.6%	CVA (USD)	1.63	21.75	41.50	107.48
	Adjusted Strike	125.97	125.60	125.24	124.03
−13.8%	CVA (USD)	1.80	26.71	51.48	133.49
	Adjusted Strike	125.96	125.51	125.05	123.55
0%	CVA (USD)	1.98	32.40	63.42	164.27
	Adjusted Strike	125.96	125.41	124.84	122.98
13.8%	CVA (USD)	2.15	38.85	77.36	200.08
	Adjusted Strike	125.96	125.28	124.58	122.33
27.6%	CVA (USD)	2.34	46.05	93.08	240.41
	Adjusted Strike	125.96	125.15	124.29	121.59
68.9%	CVA (USD)	2.92	72.47	152.05	397.87
	Adjusted Strike	125.95	124.67	123.21	118.70

6.5.2 Counterparty Risk from the Receiver's Perspective: The Bank Computes Counterparty Risk

Now we place ourselves in the position of the bank, and we use the CDS spreads for the airline, which are given in Table 6.7. We use the same discount curve as in Table 6.3.

Here, the airline credit quality is represented by a CIR++ stochastic intensity model that, as spreads level, is consistent with Table 6.7 through the shift ψ, while allowing for credit spread volatility through the CIR dynamics. We use the base CIR parameter set given in Table 6.8. Later, we reduce the spread volatility parameter ν via multiplicative factors smaller than one, and recalibrate the shift to maintain each time the model consistent with Table 6.7. This way we investigate again the impact of the spread volatility on the counterparty adjustment.

As before, we observe the effect of varying the commodity volatility and of the airline credit intensity volatility, starting from $\sigma_S = 32.82\%$ as from Table 6.1 and $\nu_{Airline} = 21\%$. We apply the same multiplicative factors as before and the results are summarized in the graphs in Figure 6.8 and Figure 6.7. The same results are presented in more detail in Tables 6.9 and 6.10.

6.6 INADEQUACY OF BASEL'S WWR MULTIPLIERS

We may recall here that the Basel II agreement, under the "Internal Model Method", models wrong way risk by means of a 1.4 multiplying factor to be applied to the zero-correlation case,

Table 6.7 CDS spreads term structure for the airline

maturity (years)	0.5	1	2	3	4	5
spread (bps)	76	82	104	122	139	154

Table 6.8 CIR parameters for the base case for the airline credit spread volatility

y_0	κ	μ	ν
0.0000	0.5341	0.0328	0.2105

Table 6.9 Effect of credit spread volatility on the CVA. Fixed leg price maturity 5Y: USD6852.35 for a notional of 1 barrel per month, fair strike without counterparty risk USD126

$\bar{\rho}$	intensity vol. ν	0.0295	0.295	0.59
−68.9%	CVA (USD)	29.62	38.95	46.62
	Adjusted Strike	126.54	126.71	126.85
−27.6%	CVA (USD)	28.41	32.58	35.82
	Adjusted Strike	126.52	126.59	126.66
−13.8%	CVA (USD)	28.21	31.02	32.40
	Adjusted Strike	126.52	126.57	126.59
0%	CVA (USD)	27.99	29.37	29.16
	Adjusted Strike	126.51	126.54	126.53
13.8%	CVA (USD)	27.78	27.72	26.09
	Adjusted Strike	126.51	126.51	126.48
27.6%	CVA (USD)	27.49	26.15	23.42
	Adjusted Strike	126.50	126.48	126.43
68.9%	CVA (USD)	26.48	22.23	16.31
	Adjusted Strike	126.48	126.41	126.30

Table 6.10 Effect of oil volatility on the CVA. Fixed leg price maturity 5Y: USD6852.35 for a notional of 1 barrel per month, fair strike without counterparty risk USD126

$\bar{\rho}$	Comdty spot vol. σ_S	0.033	0.1642	0.3285	0.657
−68.9%	CVA (USD)	0.12	26.33	46.62	80.26
	Adjusted Strike	126.00	126.48	126.85	127.47
−27.6%	CVA (USD)	0.09	19.33	35.82	59.23
	Adjusted Strike	126.00	126.35	126.65	127.08
−13.8%	CVA (USD)	0.08	17.35	32.40	53.64
	Adjusted Strike	126.00	126.32	126.59	126.98
0%	CR-CVA (USD)	0.07	15.42	29.16	48.59
	Adjusted Strike	126.00	126.28	126.53	126.89
13.8%	CVA (USD)	0.06	13.58	26.09	43.88
	Adjusted Strike	126.00	126.25	126.48	126.80
27.6%	CVA (USD)	0.05	11.86	23.42	39.09
	Adjusted Strike	126.00	126.22	126.43	126.72
68.9%	CVA (USD)	0.03	7.40	16.31	27.16
	Adjusted Strike	126.00	126.13	126.30	126.50

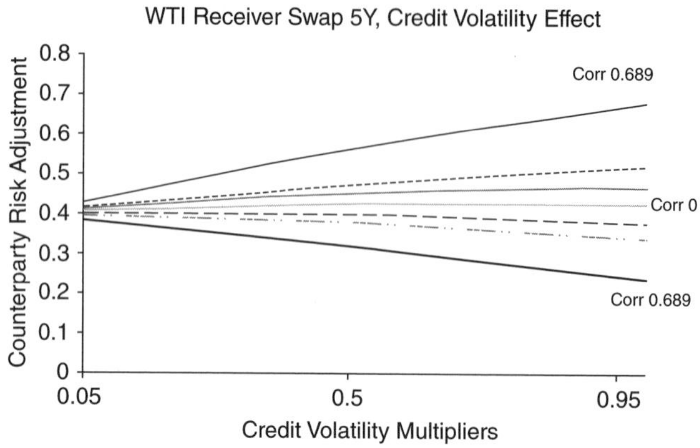

Figure 6.7 Commodity Swap CVA: credit volatility effect. Fixed leg price maturity 5Y: USD6852.35 for a notional of 1 barrel per month, CVA as a (%) of the fixed leg price

even if banks have the option to compute their own estimate of the multiplier, which can never go below 1.2 anyway. This multiplier is used to convert the credit-risk measurement under the zero-correlation assumption into a credit-risk measurement taking into account wrong way risk. We should specify that this methodology is meant to be applied to risk measurement and risk measures such as Credit VaR (see Chapters 1, 2), and not to pricing, and only to large and diversified portfolios. However, in the past the industry also applied this multipliers method to price CVA.

If we do this with our oil swap, in our tables we have the following two cases of wrong way risk adjustment, among many others, from Tables 6.6 and 6.9:

$$(397.87 - 124.67)/124.67 = 219\% \gg 40\%$$

$$(29.62 - 27.99)/27.99 = 5.82\% \ll 20\%$$

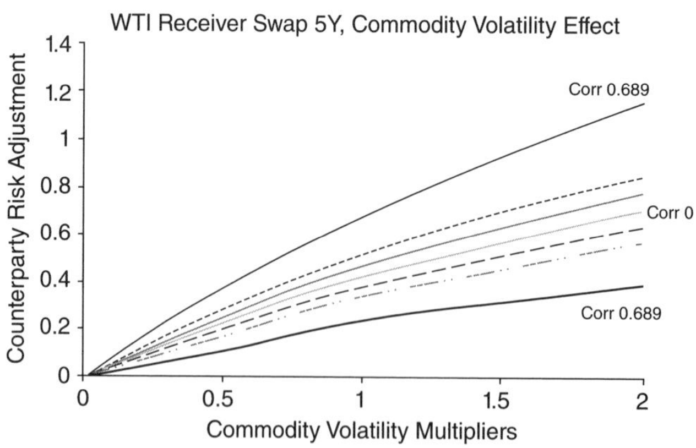

Figure 6.8 Commodity Swap CVA: commodity volatility effect. Fixed leg price maturity 5Y: USD6852.35 for a notional of 1 barrel per month, CVA as a (%) of the fixed leg price

The size of the CVA depends on the precise value of the volatility and correlation dynamic parameters that cannot be explained only through the zero correlation case via a rough one-size-fits-it-all multiplier in the range between 1.2 and 1.4. Indeed, in our examples, with correlations well below one, the multiplier takes easily values such as 1.06 or 3.19.

6.7 CONCLUSIONS

The patterns we observe in the counterparty risk credit valuation adjustment (CVA) are natural. Starting with the receiver case, for a fixed credit spread volatility, the receiver CVA increases in oil volatility and decreases in correlation. Given the embedded oil option, the increase with respect to oil volatility is natural (as in the payer case). As regards correlation, as this increases, the oil tends to move in line with credit spreads. This means that higher credit spreads will lead to higher oil values, and the option will end up less in the money as the oil spot goes up. The opposite appears in the payer case. Patterns in credit spread volatility are similarly explained.

This concludes our chapter on CVA for commodities, and oil swaps in particular. We next move to a different asset class that is particularly relevant in terms of wrong way risk: credit itself.

7 Unilateral CVA for Credit with WWR

This chapter is based on Brigo and Chourdakis (2009) [43] and is actually a particular case of Brigo, Capponi and Pallavicini (2012) [40], which will be illustrated in Chapter 15.

Counterparty risk is a particularly cogent aspect of Credit Default Swaps (CDS) management, since it may diminish considerably the effectiveness of protection bought through a credit default swap. In this chapter we will discuss the Unilateral Credit Valuation Adjustment (UCVA) for CDS.

7.1 INTRODUCTION TO CDSs WITH COUNTERPARTY RISK

In this chapter we consider counterparty risk pricing for Credit Default Swaps (CDS) held by an assumed default-free investor or bank (name "I") in the presence of correlation between default of the counterparty (name "C") and default of the CDS underlying reference credit (name "U"). Our approach in [43] has been innovative in that, besides default correlation, which used to be taken into account in earlier approaches, we also modelled credit spread volatility. We will re-elaborate those findings here and show credit volatility to play a fundamental role in determining the credit valuation adjustment (CVA) on a CDS to be charged to "C" from "I". This is particularly important when the underlying reference contract itself is a CDS, as the counterparty credit valuation adjustment involves CDS options, and modelling options without volatility in the underlying asset is quite undesirable. We investigate the impact of the reference volatility on the counterparty adjustment as a fundamental feature that is ignored or not studied explicitly in other approaches.

An important point on notation:

Here the previous notation "B" for the Investor or Bank is replaced by "I". This is because in the case of a CDS it is not obvious that the protection buyer is a bank, and it may happen in several cases that the UCVA is computed by other types of entities. While even the notation with "B" is fully general, we prefer to denote the Investor by "I" in the present chapter, since this is more explicit.

As in earlier chapters, in this chapter we enforce the unilateral default assumption:

Assumption 7.1.1 ***Unilateral Default Assumption (UDA): Assuming one party ("I") to be default free.*** *In this chapter we assume that calculations are done considering "I" to be default free. Valuation of the CDS contract is usually done from "I"'s point of view.*

This assumption in practice is a possible approximation to situations where "I" has a much higher credit quality than the counterparty "C". We will consider both cases where "I" holds a CDS contract selling (receiver CDS) or buying (payer CDS) protection, the second one being more interesting for wrong way risk issues. Since we are not considering default of "I", we will need to model jointly only two default times: τ_U (CDS reference credit) and τ_C. Without the unilateral Assumption 7.1.1, we would need to model a third default time, namely τ_I, which we will be doing later in the book. Even without τ_I, this is the first explicit case where we need a model for default dependency or "correlation". We use the term "correlation" in its broadest sense of dependency.

Going a little more into detail on the modelling framework of the chapter, stochastic intensity models are adopted for the default events, and defaults are connected through a copula function. To assess the relevant impact of both default correlation and credit spread volatility on the positive counterparty risk credit valuation adjustment (CVA), to be subtracted from the counterparty risk-free price, we vary correlation and volatility in some fundamental numerical examples, analyzing wrong way risk in particular. Given the theoretical equivalence of the unilateral credit valuation adjustment with a contingent CDS, we are also proposing a methodology for valuation of contingent CDS on CDS.

Our analysis can be particularly relevant for a financial institution that has bought protection or insurance on CDS from other institutions whose credit quality is deteriorating. The case of monoline insurers after the sub-prime crisis is just a possible example.

In terms of earlier literature on CDS CVA, [123] address the counterparty risk problem for CDS by resorting to default barrier correlated models, without considering explicitly credit spread volatility in the reference CDS. While [140], building on [81] model default intensities as deterministic constants with default indicators of other names as feeds. The exponential triggers of the default times are taken to be independent and default correlation results from the cross feeds, although again there is no explicit modelling of credit spread volatility. Furthermore, most models in the industry, especially when applied to Collateralized Debt Obligations (CDO) or k-th to default baskets, model default correlation but ignore credit spread volatility. As shown earlier in the book, and in particular in Section 3.4, in credit correlation models for multiname payoffs credit spreads are typically assumed to be deterministic and a copula is postulated on the exponential triggers of the default times to model default correlation, see also [60]. This is done despite evidence for very high credit volatility, see, for example, [31]. This is the opposite of what used to happen with counterparty risk for interest-rate derivatives, for example in [187] or [47], see Chapter 4, where correlation was ignored and volatility was modelled instead.

Here we rectify this, with a model that takes into account credit spread volatility besides the still very important underlying/counterparty correlation. We find that results under extreme default correlation (wrong way risk) are very sensitive to credit spread volatility. This points out that credit spread volatility should not be ignored in these cases. Ignoring correlation among underlying and counterparty can also be dangerous, especially when the underlying instrument is a credit-sensitive instrument such as a CDS. This credit underlying case involves default correlation, which is perceived in the market as more relevant than the dubious interest-rate/credit-spread correlation of the interest rate underlying case we have seen in Chapter 5. It is not so much that the latter is less relevant because it would have no impact on counterparty risk credit valuation adjustments. We have seen in [56], [57] and [58] and in Chapter 5 that changing this correlation parameter has a relevant impact for interest rate derivatives. The point is that the value of said correlation is difficult to estimate historically or imply from market quotes, and the historical estimation often produces a very low or even slightly negative correlation parameter. So even if this parameter has an impact, it is difficult to assign a value to it and often this value would be practically null. On the contrary, default correlation is more clearly perceived as measured also by the (however dubious) implied correlation in the quoted indices tranches markets (iTraxx and CDX), see again [60].

7.1.1 The Structure of the Chapter

In order to get the most benefit from this chapter we have set out a guide to its structure below, from the point of view of readers with different requirements.

The essential results are described in the case study in Section 7.4, so the reader aiming to get the main message of the chapter with minimal technical implications can go directly to this section, that has been written to be as self-contained as possible.

Otherwise, the reader may start by going momentarily back to Section 4.3, describing the counterparty risk valuation problem in quite general terms and then continue by reading Section 7.2. This section describes the reduced-form model setup of the chapter with stochastic intensities and a copula on the exponential triggers (but see also Chapter 3). A detailed presentation of the shifted squared root jump-diffusion model (JCIR++) and of its calibration to CDS, previously analyzed in [35], [45] and [46], is given, but again, this is also available in Chapter 3. Section 7.3 details how the general formula for the counterparty credit valuation adjustment (CVA), given in Section 4.3, can be written under the specific CDS payoff and modelling assumptions of the chapter, although formulas derived here will not be used, as we will proceed through a more direct numerical approach based on results to be found later in the book. This section can, however, give a feeling for the complexity of the problem and for the kind of issues one has to face in these situations, and is presented for this reason. Finally, Section 7.4 briefly recaps the modelling assumptions and illustrates the chapter conclusions with the case study itself.

Before reading the chapter in detail, we invite the reader who is not yet familiar with Chapter 4 to familiarize themselves with Formula 4.4.

In this chapter we do not assume we have collateral in place, yet. We will address collateral and Gap risk for CDS further on in the book, as well as the case of bilateral CVA and DVA.

Finally, we mention that in order to keep this chapter as self-contained as possible, the modelling part will overlap somewhat with previous chapters.

7.2 MODELLING ASSUMPTIONS

In this section we consider a reduced form model that is stochastic in the default intensity both for the counterparty and for the CDS reference credit. We will not correlate the spreads with each other, as typically spread correlation has a much lower impact on dependence of default times than default correlation, see [134]. The latter is rigorously defined as a dependence structure on the exponential random variables characterizing the default times of the two names. This dependence structure is typically modelled with a copula function.

In terms of probabilistic framework, we place ourselves in a probability space $(\Omega, \mathcal{G}, \mathcal{G}_t, \mathbb{Q})$, see also Section 4.2 for an interpretation of this space. The set Ω represents the set of all possible outcomes of the random experiment, and the σ-field $\mathcal{G}$ represents the set of events $A \subset \Omega$ with which we shall work. The σ-field $\mathcal{G}_t$ represents the information available up to time t. The (non-decreasing) family of σ-fields $(\mathcal{G}_t)_{t\geq 0}$ is called filtration. The probability measure $\mathbb{Q}$ is the risk-neutral measure or pricing measure. We use the symbol $\mathbb{E}$ to denote expectation with respect to the probability measure $\mathbb{Q}$. The default times τ will be defined on this probability space. This space is endowed with a right-continuous and complete sub-filtration $\mathcal{F}_t$ representing all the observable market quantities but the default event (hence $\mathcal{F}_t \subseteq \mathcal{G}_t := \mathcal{F}_t \vee \mathcal{H}_t$ where $\mathcal{H}_t = \sigma(\{\tau \leq u\} : u \leq t)$ is the right-continuous filtration generated by the default event). We set $\mathbb{E}_t[\cdot] := \mathbb{E}[\cdot|\mathcal{G}_t]$.

In more colloquial terms, throughout the chapter $\mathcal{G}_t$ is the filtration modelling the market information up to time t, including explicit default monitoring up to t, whereas $\mathcal{F}_t$ is the default-free market information up to t (FX, interest rates, pre-default credit spreads λ, etc), without default monitoring.

In terms of the specific model for this chapter, we assume that the counterparty default intensity λ^C, and the cumulated intensity $\Lambda^C(t) = \int_0^t \lambda^C(s)ds$, are independent of the default intensity for the reference CDS λ^U, whose cumulated intensity we denote by Λ^U. We assume intensities to be strictly positive, so that $t \mapsto \Lambda(t)$ are invertible functions.

We assume deterministic default-free instantaneous interest rate r (and hence deterministic discount factors $D(s,t), \ldots$), but all our conclusions hold also under stochastic rates that are independent of default times.

We are in a Cox process setting, where

$$\tau_U = (\Lambda^U)^{-1}(\xi_U), \quad \tau_C = (\Lambda^C)^{-1}(\xi_C)$$

with ξ_U and ξ_C standard (unit-mean) exponential random variables whose associated uniforms Υ are correlated through a copula function C_ρ. We assume

$$\Upsilon_j = 1 - \exp(-\xi_j), j \in \{C, U\}, \quad C_\rho(\upsilon_U, \upsilon_C) := \mathbb{Q}(\Upsilon_U < \upsilon_U, \Upsilon_C < \upsilon_C).$$

In the case study below we assume the copula to be Gaussian and with correlation parameter ρ, although the choice can be easily changed, as the framework is general. The Gaussian copula is not a bad choice in this particular case. Despite its lack of upper-tail dependence, when varying ρ from 0 to 1, the Gaussian copula attains the whole possible range of finite dependency, since it leads to a Kendall tau (a good general measure of dependency) going from 0 (independence) to 1 (co-monotonicity), see Section 3.4. This can be helpful for stress-testing purposes, since we will be able to range from independence to co-monotonicity.

7.2.1 CIR++ Stochastic-Intensity Model

For the stochastic intensity model we set

$$\lambda_t^j = y_t^j + \psi^j(t; \beta^j), \quad t \geq 0, \ j \in \{U, C\} \tag{7.1}$$

where ψ^j is a deterministic function, depending on the parameter vector β^j (which includes y_0^j), that is integrable on closed intervals. The initial condition y_0^j is one more parameter at our disposal: we are free to select its value as long as

$$\psi^j(0; \beta^j) = \lambda_0^j - y_0^j,$$

we take each y^j to be a Cox-Ingersoll-Ross (CIR) process (see [48]):

$$dy_t^j = \kappa^j(\mu^j - y_t^j)\,dt + \nu^j\sqrt{y_t^j}\,dZ_{3,t}^j, \quad j \in \{U, C\}$$

where the parameter vectors $\beta^j = \{\kappa^j, \mu^j, \nu^j, y_0^j\}$, are constituted by positive deterministic constants. As usual, the Z's are standard Brownian motion processes under the risk-neutral measure, representing the stochastic shock in our dynamics.

Usually, for the CIR model one assumes a condition ensuring the origin to be inaccessible, the condition being $2\kappa^j\mu^j > (\nu^j)^2$. However, this limits the CDS implied volatility generated by the model when imposing also positivity of the shift ψ^j, a condition we will always impose in the following to avoid negative intensities. This is why we do not enforce such conditions and in our case study below it will be violated.

Correlation in the spreads is a minor driver with respect to default correlation, so we assume that the two Brownian motions Z's are independent. We will often use the integrated quantities for each $j \in \{U, C\}$

$$\Lambda^j(t) = \int_0^t \lambda_s^j ds, \quad Y^j(t) = \int_0^t y_s^j ds, \quad \Psi^j(t, \beta^j) = \int_0^t \psi^j(s, \beta^j) ds.$$

This kind of model and the related calibration to CDS has been investigated in detail in [35], and here in Chapter 3, while [45] examine the CDS implied volatility patterns associated with the model.

Notice that we can easily introduce jumps in the diffusion process. [46] consider a formulation where

$$dy_t^j = \kappa^j(\mu^j - y_t^j)dt + \nu^j \sqrt{y_t^j}\, dZ_{3,t}^j + dJ_t^j(\zeta_1^j, \zeta_2^j), \quad j \in \{U, C\}$$

where the parameter vectors β^j are now augmented to include the jump parameters, and each parameter is a positive deterministic constant. As before, Z's are standard Brownian motion processes under the risk-neutral measure, while the jump part $J_t^j(\zeta_1^j, \zeta_2^j)$ is defined as

$$J_t^j(\zeta_1^j, \zeta_2^j) := \sum_{i=i}^{M_t^j(\zeta_1^j)} X_i^j(\zeta_2^j)$$

where each M^j is a time-homogeneous Poisson process with intensity ζ_1^j and independent of all the other processes, the X^j's being exponentially distributed with positive finite mean ζ_2^j also independent of all other processes.

Besides deriving log-affine survival probability formulas re-shaped exactly in the same form as in the CIR model without jumps, [46] also derive a closed-form solution for CDS options, see again Chapter 3. In the sequel we assume no jumps. However, all calculations and also the fractional Fourier (FRFT) transform method, are exactly applicable to the extended model with jumps.

7.2.2 CIR++ Model: CDS Calibration

We calibrate the default-intensity models as in Section 5.1.3. We recall here the pricing formula for a (payer) CDS buying protection at time 0 for defaults between times T_a and T_b on name j in exchange of a periodic premium rate S in case of deterministic interest rates.

$$\begin{aligned}
\text{CDS}_0(T_a, T_b; S_j, \text{LGD}_j) := &-S_j \sum_{i=a+1}^{b} D(0, T_i)\alpha_i \mathbb{Q}\left\{\tau_j > T_i\right\} \\
&- S_j \int_{T_a}^{T_b} D(0, u)(u - T_{\beta(u)})\, d\mathbb{Q}\left\{\tau_j < u\right\} \\
&+ \text{LGD}_j \int_{T_a}^{T_b} D(0, u)\, d\mathbb{Q}\left\{\tau_j < u\right\} \qquad (7.2)
\end{aligned}$$

Table 7.1 Intensity parameters for the reference credit "U" and the counterparty "C"

Name	y_0	κ	μ	ν
"U"	0.03	0.50	0.05	0.50
"C"	0.01	0.80	0.02	0.20

where in general $T_{\beta(t)}$ is is the last T_i preceding t. Recall that we could replace all default probabilities differentials $d\mathbb{Q}\left\{\tau_j < u\right\}$ with the opposite of survival probabilities differentials $-d\mathbb{Q}\left\{\tau_j \geq u\right\}$.

Formula 7.2 is model independent. This means that if we strip survival (or default) probabilities from the CDS market in a model independent way at time 0, to calibrate the market CDS quotes we just need to make sure that the survival probabilities we strip from CDS are correctly reproduced by the CIR++ model. See Section 5.1.3 for details.

Once we have done this and calibrated the CDS data through $\psi^j(\cdot, \beta^j)$, we are left with the parameters β^j, which can be used to calibrate further products. However, this will be interesting when single-name option data on the credit derivatives market will become more liquid. Currently the bid-ask spreads for single-name CDS options are large and suggest to either consider these quotes with caution, or to try and deduce volatility parameters from more liquid index options, with ad hoc adjustments for idiosyncrasies of single names. At the moment we content ourselves by calibrating only CDSs, while to help specifying β^j without further data we set some values for the parameters implying possibly reasonable values for the implied volatility of the hypothetical CDS options on the counterparty and reference credit.

We assume that the base-case intensities parameter values that we will use for numerical examples are given in Table 7.1. We work with a counterparty that is of higher credit quality than the reference credit, on which the traded CDS is issued, with default intensities which are between two and three times smaller (y_0 and μ are smaller) and significantly less volatile (higher κ and lower ν). This is a natural case to examine at the inception of a CDS contract, since it is rather unusual for a firm to buy protection from a protection seller that is riskier than the underlying reference risk. To benchmark our results we use the case with no counterparty risk. The spread for a five-year CDS, assuming a flat risk-free interest rate curve at 3% and recovery rates of 30%, is equal to 252bp. The curve of spot CDS spreads across maturities corresponding to the two parameter sets is in Table 7.2.

7.3 CDS OPTIONS EMBEDDED IN CVA PRICING

We now move to computing the counterparty risk adjustment, using Formula 4.4:

$$\text{UCVA}(0, T) = \mathbb{E}_0\left[\text{LGD}\,\mathbf{1}_{\{\tau_C \leq T\}} D(0, \tau_C)\left(\mathbb{E}_{\tau_C}[\Pi(\tau_C, T)]\right)^+\right]. \tag{7.3}$$

We now compute the adjustment UCVA$(0, T)$. The only non-trivial term to compute (interest rates are assumed to be deterministic) is

$$\mathbb{E}_0[\mathbf{1}_{\{\tau_C \leq T\}}(\mathbb{E}[\Pi(\tau_C, T_b)|\mathcal{G}_{\tau_C}])^+].$$

Here we follow a heuristic approach, but a rigorous derivation of the formula in a more general context with bilateral credit risk, DVA and with collateral, will be presented later in Chapter 15, Section 15.2.2.

Table 7.2 CDS spreads for different maturities corresponding to the intensity parameters given in Table 7.1 with shifts ψ to zero. LGD for both CDS is 0.7

	Spread (in bp)	
Maturity	"U"	"C"
1y	234	92
2y	244	104
3y	248	112
4y	251	117
5y	252	120
6y	253	123
7y	253	125
8y	254	126
9y	254	127
10y	254	128

We write (again we take deterministic interest rates and assume deterministic recovery and LGD)

$$\begin{aligned}\text{UCVA}(0,T) &= \text{LGD}\int_{T_a}^{T_b} D(0,t)\mathbb{E}_0\left[(\mathbb{E}_t[\Pi(t,T)])^+\,1_{\{\tau_C\in[t,t+dt)\}}\right]\\ &= \text{LGD}\int_{T_a}^{T_b} D(0,t)\mathbb{E}_0\left[(\mathbb{E}_t[\Pi(t,T)])^+\,\mathbb{Q}(\tau_C\in[t,t+dt)|\mathcal{G}_t)\right].\end{aligned} \tag{7.4}$$

Let us assume we are the investor "I" and we are dealing with a counterparty "C" from which we are buying protection at a given spread S_U through a CDS on the relevant reference credit "U". This is where we would be in the most critical situation upon counterparty default. We are holding a payer CDS (we are buying protection and *paying* the periodic premium) on the reference credit "U". Therefore $\mathbb{E}_t\Pi(t,T_b)$ is the residual Net Present Value (NPV) of a payer CDS between t and T_b at time t, with $T_a < t \leq T_b$. The NPV of a payer CDS at time t can be written similarly to 7.2, except that now valuation occurs at t and has to be conditional on the information available in the market at t, i.e. $\mathcal{G}_t$.

By simply looking at the relevant CDS payout definition, we can see that such future time-t CDS prices will be completely determined by survival probabilities of the type

$$\mathbb{Q}(\tau_U > u|\mathcal{G}_t)$$

for $u > t$. In computing such probabilities we have to pay attention to a very subtle point.

This calculation, leading to an easy formula for CDS_t, would be simple if we were to compute the above probabilities under the filtration $\mathcal{G}_t^U := \mathcal{F}_t \vee \mathcal{H}_t^U$ of the default time τ_U alone, rather than $\mathcal{G}_t$ incorporating information on τ_C as well. Indeed, in the first case we could write

$$\begin{aligned}\mathbb{Q}\left\{\tau_U \geq u\,|\mathcal{G}_t^U\right\} &= \mathbf{1}_{\{\tau_U>t\}}\mathbb{E}\left[\exp\left(-\int_t^u \lambda_s^U ds\right)\Big|\mathcal{F}_t\right]\\ &= \mathbf{1}_{\{\tau_U>t\}}P^{CIR++}(t,u;y^U(t))\\ &= \mathbf{1}_{\{\tau_U>t\}}\exp\left(-(\Psi^U(u)-\Psi^U(t))\right)P^{CIR}(t,u;y^U(t))\end{aligned} \tag{7.5}$$

namely the bond price in the CIR++ model for λ^U, $P^{CIR}(t, u; y^U(t))$ being the non-shifted time homogeneous CIR bond price formula for y^U. Substitution in the CDS price formula in terms of survival probabilities at t would give us the NPV at time t, since CDS_t would be computed using 7.5. Hence, we would have all the needed components to compute our counterparty risk adjustment through mere simulation of the λ's up to T_b.

Yet, there is a fatal drawback in this approach. The survival probabilities contributing to the valuation of CDS_t have to be calculated conditional also on the information on the counterparty default τ_C available at time t.

This leads to a much more complicated expression for the conditional probability, involving quite complex copula terms. Again, the full calculation is presented in a more general context in Section 15.2.2, Chapter 15. We implement such a formula here in this special case, without collateral and without investor "I" default risk.

7.4 UCVA FOR CREDIT DEFAULT SWAPS: A CASE STUDY

We consider a default free institution trading a CDS on a reference name "U" with counterparty "C", where the counterparty "C" is subject to default risk. The default-free assumption can also be an approximation for situations where the credit quality of the first institution is much higher than the credit quality of the counterparty. The CDS on the reference credit "U", on which we compute counterparty risk, is a five-year maturity CDS with recovery rate 0.3. The CDS spreads for both the underlying name "U" and the counterparty name "C" for the basic set of parameters we will consider are given in Table 7.2.

We aim at checking the separated and combined impact of two important quantities on the counterparty risk credit valuation adjustment (CVA): Default correlation and credit spread volatility. In order to do this, we devise a modelling apparatus accounting for both features. What is especially novel in our analysis is the second feature, as earlier attempts focused mostly on the first.

In order to model "default correlation", or more precisely the dependence of the two named defaults, we postulate a Gaussian copula on the exponential triggers of the default times, although we could use any other tractable copula. By "default correlation" parameter we mean the Gaussian copula parameter ρ.

In this context, if we define the cumulated intensities $\Lambda^j(t) := \int_0^t \lambda_u^j du$, $j = 1, C$, the default times τ_U and τ_C of the reference credit and the counterparty, respectively, are given by $\tau_j = (\Lambda^j)^{-1}(\xi_j)$, with ξ_U and ξ_C unit-mean exponential random variables connected through the Gaussian copula with correlation parameter ρ.

When we say "credit spread volatility" parameters, we mean ν^U for the reference credit and ν^C for the counterparty. As the focus is mostly on credit spread volatility for the reference credit, we also check what implied CDS volatilities are produced by our choice of ν^U and other parameters for hypothetical reference credit CDS options, maturing in one year and, in case the option is exercised, entering a CDS that is four years long at option maturity. This way we have a more direct market quantity linked to our parameter for credit spread volatility.

7.4.1 Changing the Copula Parameters

We begin with a case where the credit spread for the counterparty, as driven by λ^C, is almost deterministic. We assume here that $\nu^C = 0.01$.

Table 7.3 CVA in basis points for the case $\nu^C = 0.01$ including the LGD = 0.7 factor; numbers within round brackets represent the Monte Carlo standard error; the reference credit CDS also has LGD = 0.7 and a five year maturity

ρ	Vol parameter ν^U CDS Implied vol	0.01 1.5%	0.10 15%	0.20 28%	0.30 37%	0.40 42%	0.50 42%
−99%	Payer adj	0(0)	0(0)	0(0)	0(0)	0(0)	0(0)
	Receiver adj	39(2)	38(2)	42(2)	38(2)	40(2)	41(2)
−90%	Payer adj	0(0)	0(0)	0(0)	0(0)	0(0)	0(0)
	Receiver adj	39(2)	38(2)	41(2)	39(2)	40(2)	41(2)
−60%	Payer adj	0(0)	0(0)	0(0)	0(0)	0(0)	1(0)
	Receiver adj	37(2)	36(1)	38(1)	35(1)	38(1)	37(1)
−20%	Payer adj	0(0)	0(0)	1(0)	3(0)	3(0)	4(1)
	Receiver adj	18(1)	16(1)	18(1)	18(1)	20(1)	21(1)
0%	Payer adj	3(0)	4(0)	6(0)	7(1)	6(1)	6(1)
	Receiver adj	0(0)	2(0)	5(0)	7(0)	10(0)	12(1)
20%	Payer adj	28(1)	27(1)	23(1)	21(1)	17(2)	15(1)
	Receiver adj	0(0)	0(0)	1(0)	1(0)	2(0)	3(0)
60%	Payer adj	87(4)	78(4)	73(4)	66(4)	55(3)	52(3)
	Receiver adj	0(0)	0(0)	0(0)	0(0)	0(0)	0(0)
90%	Payer adj	80(6)	81(6)	77(5)	82(5)	78(5)	73(5)
	Receiver adj	0(0)	0(0)	0(0)	0(0)	0(0)	0(0)
99%	Payer adj	2(1)	7(2)	30(3)	66(5)	61(5)	84(5)
	Receiver adj	0(0)	0(0)	0(0)	0(0)	0(0)	0(0)

Table 7.3 reports our results. We notice a number of interesting patterns. First, one can examine the table columns. Let us start from the first five columns. We see that as the correlation increases, the CVA for the payer CDS increases, except on the very end of the correlation spectrum. Indeed, when increasing correlation in the final step from 0.9 to 0.99, the CVA goes down.

At first sight one does not like the fact that an extreme correlation (dependency, since this is in one-to-one correspondence with a Kendall's tau) parameter corresponds to a diminished wrong way risk after an initially increasing pattern. Unfortunately, this is somehow natural given the way default times are modelled when using copulas and intensity models, and we may explain it as follows. Let us take the case of the first column. Here the volatility parameter of the reference credit ν^U is also very small. So essentially the intensities λ^U and λ^C are almost deterministic. Suppose for simplicity they are also constant in time. Then under default correlation 0.99 also the exponential triggers ξ_U and ξ_C are almost perfectly correlated, say $\xi_U \approx \xi_C =: \xi$. Then we have $\tau_U = \xi/\lambda^U$, $\tau_C = \xi/\lambda^C$. As $\lambda^U > \lambda^C$, we get $\xi/\lambda^U < \xi/\lambda^C$ in all scenarios, so that $\tau_U < \tau_C$ in all scenarios. But if this happens, then the residual NPV of the CDS on reference credit "U" at counterparty default time τ_C is zero, since the reference credit always defaults before the counterparty does. This explains why we find almost zero CVA when λ^U's volatility is very small. Notice that this is not just a drawback of the Gaussian copula but of any copula.

If we increase λ^U's volatility, and, in our idealized example, we still keep λ^U constant in time but increase its variance as a static random variable, then $\xi/\lambda^U < \xi/\lambda^C$ is no longer going

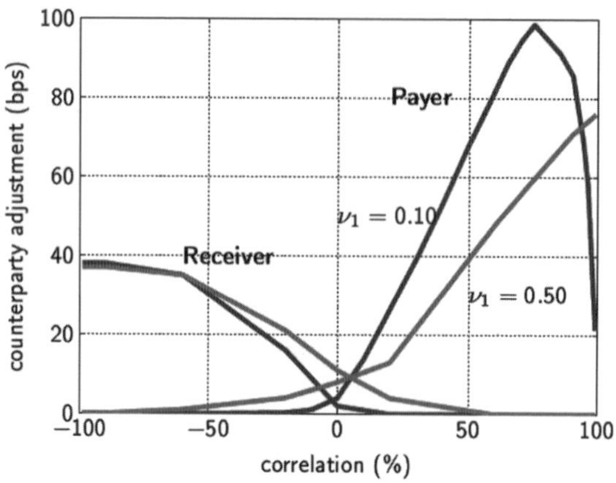

Figure 7.1 CVA patterns in correlations for payer and receiver CDS and for low (0.1) and high (0.5) reference credit volatility ν^U, when counterparty volatility ν^C is 0.1

to happen in all scenarios, since randomness in λ^U can produce some paths where actually λ^U is now smaller than λ^C, and hence $\tau_U > \tau_C$. As we increase the volatility, following the last row of the table we see that the payer adjustment gets away from zero and increases in value, as the increased randomness in λ^U produces more and more paths where λ^U is smaller than λ^C. We reach an extreme case for correlation equal to 0.99: in this case the CVA for correlation 0.99 does not even go back and keeps on increasing with respect to the case with correlation 0.9. In this sense the last column of the table is qualitatively different from all others, in that it is the only one where CVA keeps on increasing until the end of the considered correlation spectrum.

We zoom on these patterns for the later case with $\nu^C = 0.1$ in Figure 7.1, as exemplified by the "payer" graph for the case with low volatility $\nu^U = 0.1$ and the "payer" one for the case with high volatility $\nu^U = 0.5$. The former graph reverts towards zero in the end, whereas the latter graph keeps increasing.

Notice also that typically the payer CDS CVA vanishes for very negative correlations. This happens because, in that region, when the counterparty defaults the underlying CDS does not. In such a case, we have a CDS option at the counterparty default time where the underlying CDS spread had a negative large jump due to the copula contagion coming from default by the counterparty. This negative jump causes the option to become worthless as the underlying goes below the strike in almost all scenarios.

We may also analyze the receiver adjustment, which evolves in a more stylized pattern. The adjustment remains substantially decreasing as default correlation increases, and goes to zero for high correlations. This happens because in this case, in the few scenarios where $\tau_U > \tau_C$ and the reference CDS still has value at the counterparty default, the positive correlation induces a contagion copula-related term on the intensity of the survived reference name "U". This causes in turn the option to go far out of the money and hence to be negligible, leading to a null CVA.

As the counterparty volatility ν^C increases first to 0.1 and then to 0.2 all qualitative features we described above are maintained, although somehow smoothed by the larger counterparty volatility. Detailed results are given in Tables 7.4 and 7.5.

Table 7.4 CVA for the case $\nu^C = 0.1$ including the LGD = 0.7 factor; numbers within round brackets represent the Monte Carlo standard error; the reference credit CDS also has LGD = 0.7 and a five year maturity

ρ	Vol parameter ν^U CDS Implied vol	0.01 1.5%	0.10 15%	0.20 28%	0.30 37%	0.40 42%	0.50 42%
−99%	Payer adj	0(0)	0(0)	0(0)	0(0)	0(0)	0(0)
	Receiver adj	40(2)	38(2)	39(2)	38(2)	36(1)	37(1)
−90%	Payer adj	0(0)	0(0)	0(0)	0(0)	0(0)	0(0)
	Receiver adj	39(2)	38(2)	38(2)	38(2)	35(1)	37(2)
−60%	Payer adj	0(0)	0(0)	0(0)	0(0)	0(0)	1(0)
	Receiver adj	36(1)	35(1)	36(1)	36(1)	32(1)	35(1)
−20%	Payer adj	0(0)	0(0)	1(0)	2(0)	3(0)	4(1)
	Receiver adj	16(1)	16(1)	17(1)	19(1)	18(1)	21(1)
0%	Payer adj	3(0)	4(0)	5(0)	7(1)	7(1)	8(1)
	Receiver adj	0(0)	2(0)	5(0)	8(0)	10(0)	11(1)
20%	Payer adj	27(1)	25(1)	23(1)	20(1)	16(2)	13(1)
	Receiver adj	0(0)	0(0)	1(0)	2(0)	2(0)	4(0)
60%	Payer adj	80(4)	82(4)	67(4)	64(4)	55(3)	48(3)
	Receiver adj	0(0)	0(0)	0(0)	0(0)	0(0)	0(0)
90%	Payer adj	87(6)	86(6)	88(6)	78(5)	80(5)	71(4)
	Receiver adj	0(0)	0(0)	0(0)	0(0)	0(0)	0(0)
99%	Payer adj	10(2)	21(3)	52(5)	68(5)	73(5)	76(5)
	Receiver adj	0(0)	0(0)	0(0)	0(0)	0(0)	0(0)

Table 7.5 CVA for the case $\nu^C = 0.2$ including the LGD = 0.7 factor; numbers within round brackets represent the Monte Carlo standard error; the reference credit CDS also has LGD = 0.7 and a five year maturity

ρ	Vol parameter ν^U CDS Implied vol	0.01 1.5%	0.10 15%	0.20 28%	0.30 37%	0.40 42%	0.50 42%
−99%	Payer adj	0(0)	0(0)	0(0)	0(0)	0(0)	0(0)
	Receiver adj	41(2)	40(2)	39(2)	40(2)	40(2)	40(2)
−90%	Payer adj	0(0)	0(0)	0(0)	0(0)	0(0)	0(0)
	Receiver adj	41(2)	39(2)	39(2)	41(2)	40(2)	40(2)
−60%	Payer adj	0(0)	0(0)	0(0)	0(0)	1(0)	1(0)
	Receiver adj	39(1)	37(1)	37(1)	37(1)	36(1)	35(1)
−20%	Payer adj	0(0)	0(0)	2(0)	3(0)	3(0)	4(1)
	Receiver adj	17(1)	17(1)	17(1)	19(1)	21(1)	20(1)
0%	Payer adj	3(0)	5(0)	6(0)	7(1)	6(1)	6(1)
	Receiver adj	0(0)	2(0)	4(0)	7(0)	10(0)	12(1)
20%	Payer adj	25(1)	24(1)	23(1)	20(1)	17(1)	15(1)
	Receiver adj	0(0)	0(0)	1(0)	2(0)	2(0)	4(0)
60%	Payer adj	74(4)	74(4)	69(4)	59(3)	54(3)	52(3)
	Receiver adj	0(0)	0(0)	0(0)	0(0)	0(0)	1(0)
90%	Payer adj	91(6)	90(6)	88(5)	80(5)	81(5)	81(5)
	Receiver adj	0(0)	0(0)	0(0)	0(0)	0(0)	0(0)
99%	Payer adj	43(4)	56(5)	57(5)	72(5)	74(5)	78(5)
	Receiver adj	0(0)	0(0)	0(0)	0(0)	0(0)	0(0)

Table 7.6 CVA for three cases: (i) the first column tabulates the example given in Figure 7.1 for the payer case with $\nu^U = 0.1$ (and $\nu^C = 0.1$); (ii) the second column shows the same adjustments in case we swap the parameters in Table 7.1, so that now the counterparty "C" is riskier than the reference credit of the CDS "U"; (iii) the third case shows what happens if, under the original parameters again, we increase the reference credit initial level and long term mean to $\lambda^U(0) = 0.05$ and $\mu^U = 0.07$

ρ	base	risky counterparty	high intensity
10%	14	12	15
20%	25	29	28
30%	39	46	40
40%	53	66	53
50%	68	88	65
60%	82	115	75
65%	89	131	79
70%	94	148	81
75%	99	168	81
80%	95	191	74
85%	91	220	65
90%	86	254	48
99%	21	359	2

7.4.2 Changing the Market Parameters

We also check what happens if we swap the reference credit and the counterparty CIR parameters, now having the counterparty to be riskier. Results are in Table 7.6. We see that λ^C now tends to be larger than λ^U. As a consequence, in the case with correlation .99 and almost deterministic intensities, we would this time have $\tau_U = \xi/\lambda^U > \xi/\lambda^C = \tau_C$ in most scenarios, so that we do not expect any more the CVA to be killed or reduced for extreme correlations. And indeed we see that in the "risky counterparty" column of Table 7.6 the adjustment keeps on increasing even for very high correlation.

Finally, we check what happens if we increase the levels (rather than volatilities) of intensities for the reference credit. If we do this, the inversion of the CVA pattern (for the payer case) as correlation increases towards extreme values arrives earlier, as expected.

7.5 CONCLUSIONS

We see from the above case study that both credit spread volatility and default correlation matter considerably in valuing counterparty risk. And we see that the patterns of the adjustments in credit spread volatility depend qualitatively on correlation, in that they can be either flat, decreasing or increasing according to the particular default correlation value one fixes. As to the pattern in correlation, this too depends qualitatively on the credit spread volatility that is chosen. For payer CDS, extreme correlation (sometimes referred to as "wrong way risk") may result in counterparty risk getting smaller with respect to more moderated correlation values, *unless the credit spread volatility is large enough.*

Indeed, to have a relevant impact of wrong way risk for counterparty risk on payer CDS we need also credit spread volatility to go up. This is a feature of the copula model of which we need to be aware. In a copula model with deterministic credit spreads (a standard assumption in the industry), by ignoring credit spread volatility we would have wrong way risk causing counterparty risk almost to vanish with respect to cases with lower correlation. To get a relevant impact of wrong way risk we need to put credit spread volatility back into the picture, if we are willing to use a reduced form copula based model. While this may be appropriate given the high levels of credit volatilities in the market, see for example [31], it raises concerns on the use of copulas and credit-intensity models in representing wrong way risk.

8 Unilateral CVA for Equity with WWR

This chapter is based on Brigo and Tarenghi (2004, 2005) [61], [62], Brigo and Morini (2006) [49], Brigo, Morini and Tarenghi (2011) [55] and Brigo and Morini (2009) [51]. In this chapter we deal with counterparty risk pricing in the equity market.

The models we use first are the AT1P and SBTV models already introduced in Chapter 3. As a first illustrative case we consider an example of counterparty risk pricing for an Equity Return Swap (ERS) in Section 8.1 and related subsections. Here, we do not consider the equity dynamics of a company as an endogenous output of our structural model, but as an exogenous process to be added to our modelling framework. In other words while for the counterparty default we adopt a firm value model, for the underlying equity we assume directly an equity model that is not stemming from a credit model. A fully consistent approach would have required us to assume the same type of credit model we postulated for the counterparty also for the underlying equity, and then deduce the underlying equity process from the underlying credit model. This second approach is pursued later in the chapter.

The ERS example in 8.1.2 is an interesting choice since the value of this contract is all due to counterparty risk: as we shall see, without counterparty risk, the fair spread for this contract is null. We show the ERS valuation under the different families of models considered.

From Section 8.2 on, we commit to the ambitious task of computing the endogenous process for the equity price of the underlying company implied by a credit model that is analogous to the one we adopted for the counterparty. This is the most consistent approach to pricing credit-equity hybrids and the credit counterparty risk of an equity derivative. In fact, in this case, the model is calibrated jointly to credit and equity data, including equity implied volatility and smile. After presenting various examples of model calibration in Section 8.3, we show an application for the Credit Valuation Adjustment (CVA) of equity options in Section 8.4, where we also debate our findings, summarize our results and conclude the chapter.

A final note on notation: by $f[t, T]$ in general we denote the set of the values of the function f in the interval $[t, T]$, so for example $\sigma[0, T] = \{\sigma(s) : s \in [0, T]\}$.

8.1 COUNTERPARTY RISK FOR EQUITY WITHOUT A FULL HYBRID MODEL

As we have seen earlier in Chapter 3, classical structural models [148] and [24] postulate a Geometric Brownian Motion (GBM, Black and Scholes) lognormal dynamics for the value of the firm V. In these models the value of the firm V is the sum of the firm equity value E (or S) and of the firm debt value D. The firm equity value S, in particular, can be seen as a type of (vanilla or barrier-like) option on the value of the firm V. This link is important also when in need of pricing hybrid equity/credit products. This is the reason why in this chapter we use the structural models introduced in Chapter 3. However, in this first section we do not model fully consistently equity and credit. We will assume that the counterparty firm value follows a classical firm value model, which we calibrate to the CDS of the counterparty, and then assume that the underlying equity for the ERS follows a GBM as well. This means that the

Table 8.1 Vodafone CDS quotes on 10 March 2004

	CDS maturity T_b	$R_{0,b}^{\text{BID}}(0)$ (bps)	$R_{0,b}^{\text{ASK}}(0)$	$R_{0,b}^{\text{MID}}(0)$
1y	20-Mar-05	19	24	21.5
3y	20-Mar-07	32	34	33
5y	20-Mar-09	42	44	43
7y	20-Mar-11	45	53	49
10y	20-Mar-14	56	66	61

underlying equity cannot default, since equity in a GBM never hits zero. In this setup wrong way correlation is artificially introduced as an instantaneous (Brownian) correlation between the counterparty firm value and the underlying equity. A fully consistent approach would require us to model the firm value of the underlying equity with a model of the same type as the firm value for the counterparty; then deduce the underlying (defaultable) equity from the underlying firm value, while correlating the underlying firm value with the counterparty firm value. We tackle this in Section 8.2. First we illustrate the simpler approach where the underlying equity is not derived by a firm value model.

8.1.1 Calibrating AT1P to the Counterparty's CDS Data

We first calibrate the AT1P to the following data for Vodafone on 10 March 2004. We have set the payout ratio $q(t)$ identically equal to zero. We present the calibration performed with the AT1P structural model to CDS contracts having Vodafone as underlying with recovery rate $\text{Rec} = 40\%$ ($\text{Lgd} = 0.6$). In Table 8.1 we report the maturities T_b of the contracts and the corresponding "mid" CDS rates $R_{0,b}^{\text{MID}}(0)$ (quarterly paid) in basis points ($1bp = 10^{-4}$). We take $T_a = 0$ in all cases.

In Table 8.2 we report the values (in basis points) of the CDSs computed inserting the bid-offer premium rate R quotes into the payoff, and valuing the CDSs with deterministic intensities stripped by mid quotes. This way we transfer the bid-offer spread on rates R to a bid-offer spread on the CDS present value. In Table 8.3 we present the results of the calibration performed with the structural model and, as a comparison, the calibration performed with a deterministic intensity (credit spread) model (using piecewise linear intensity). In this first example the parameters used for the structural model have been selected on qualitative considerations, and are $q = 0$, $\beta = 0.5$ and $H/V_0 = 0.4$ (this is a significant choice since this value is in line

Table 8.2 CDS values computed with deterministic default intensities stripped from mid R Vodafone quotes but with bid and ask rates R in the premium legs. These can be taken as proxies of bid-offer CDS NPVs rather than spreads

CDS mat T_b	$\text{CDS}_{0,b}$ value bid (bps)	$\text{CDS}_{0,b}$ value ask (bps)
1y	2.56	−2.56
3y	2.93	−2.93
5y	4.67	−4.67
7y	24.94	−24.94
10y	41.14	−41.14

Table 8.3 Results of the calibrations performed with both models

T_i	$\sigma(T_{i-1}, T_i)$	$\mathbb{Q}(\tau > T_i)$ AT1P	Intensity	$\mathbb{Q}(\tau > T_i)$ int model
0	32.625%	100.000%	0.357%	100.000%
1y	32.625%	99.625%	0.357%	99.627%
3y	17.311%	98.315%	0.952%	98.316%
5y	17.683%	96.353%	1.033%	96.355%
7y	17.763%	94.206%	1.189%	94.206%
10y	21.861%	89.650%	2.104%	89.604%

with the expected value of the random H, completely determined by market quotes, in the scenario-based model presented later on).

We report the values of the calibrated parameters (volatilities and intensities) in the two models and the survival probabilities that appear to be very close under the two different models. This is not surprising, since in the deterministic interest rates framework default probabilities can be extracted from the CDS in a model-independent way.

Further comments on the realism of short-term credit spreads and on the robustness of default probabilities with respect to CDSs are in [61], and here in Chapter 3.

8.1.2 Counterparty Risk in Equity Return Swaps (ERS)

This section summarizes the results on counterparty risk pricing in Equity Return Swaps under AT1P in [61, 62]. This is an example of counterparty risk pricing with the calibrated structural model in the equity market. This method can be easily generalized to different equity payoffs.

Let us consider the payoff of an ERS. Assume we are a company "B" entering a contract with company "C", our counterparty. The reference underlying equity is company "U". The contract, in its prototypical form, is built as follows. Companies "B" and "C" agree on a certain amount K of stocks from reference entity "U" (with price $S = S^U$) to be taken as nominal ($N = K\, S_0$). The contract starts in $T_a = 0$ and has final maturity $T_b = T$. At $t = 0$ there is no exchange of cash (alternatively, we can think that "C" delivers to "B" an amount K of "U" stock and receives a cash amount equal to $K S_0$). At intermediate times "B" pays to "C" the dividend flows of the stocks (if any) in exchange for periodic interest rates (for example, a semi-annual LIBOR rate L, or possibly the overnight rate) plus a spread X. At final maturity $T = T_b$, "B" pays $K S_T$ to "C" (or gives back the amount K of stocks) and receives a payment $K S_0$. This can be summarized as follows:

Initial Time 0: no flows, or
B $\longrightarrow K S_0^U$ cash $\longrightarrow$ C
B $\longleftarrow K$ equity of "U" $\longleftarrow$ C

....

Time T_i :
B $\longrightarrow$ equity dividends of "U" $\longrightarrow$ C
B $\longleftarrow$ Floating Risk-Free Rate + Spread $\longleftarrow$ C

....

Final Time T_b :
B $\longrightarrow$ K equity of "U" $\longrightarrow$ C
B $\longleftarrow K S_0^U$ cash $\longleftarrow$ C.

The price of this product can be derived using risk-neutral valuation, and the (fair) spread is chosen in order to obtain a contract with value at inception of zero. We ignore default of underlying "U", thus assuming it has a much stronger credit quality than counterparty "C", which remains our main interest. It can be proved that if we do not consider default risk for the counterparty "C" either, the fair spread is identically equal to zero. This renders the ERS an interesting contract since all its value is due to counterparty risk. Indeed, when taking into account counterparty default risk in the valuation the fair spread is no longer zero. In case an early default of the counterparty "C" occurs, the following happens. Let us call $\tau = \tau_C$ the default instant. Before τ everything is as before, but if $\tau \leq T$, the net present value (NPV) of the position at time τ is computed. If this NPV is negative for us, i.e. for "B", then its opposite is completely paid to "C" by us at time τ. To the contrary, if the NPV is positive for "B" then it is not received completely, only a recovery fraction, R_{EC}, of that NPV is received by us. It is clear that to us ("B") counterparty risk is a problem when the NPV is large and positive, since if "C" defaults we receive only a fraction of it.

The risk-neutral expectation of the discounted payoff is given in the following proposition (see [61], $L(S, T)$ is the simply compounded rate at time S for maturity T):

Proposition 8.1.1 ***(Equity Return Swap price under Counterparty Risk).*** *The fair price of the Equity Return Swap defined above can be simplified as follows:*

$$ERS(0) = K S_0 X \sum_{i=1}^{b} \alpha_i P(0, T_i) - \mathrm{LGD}\, \mathbb{E}_0 \left[\mathbf{1}_{\{\tau \leq T_b\}} D(0, \tau)(NPV(\tau))^+ \right]$$

where

$$\begin{aligned} NPV(\tau) := {} & \mathbb{E}_\tau \left[\left(K S_0 - K S_{T_b} \right) D(\tau, T_b) \right] - K\, NPV_{dividends}^{[\tau, T_b]}(\tau) \\ & + \mathbb{E}_\tau \left[K S_0 \sum_{i=\beta(\tau)}^{b} D(\tau, T_i) \alpha_i \left(L(T_{i-1}, T_i) + X \right) \right] \end{aligned} \tag{8.1}$$

and where we denote by $NPV_{dividends}^{[s,t]}(u)$ the net present value of the dividend flows between s and t computed in u.

The first term in ERS(0) is the equity swap price in a default-free world, whereas the second one is the optional price component due to counterparty risk, see the general Formula 12.3 derived in the first part.

If we try to find the above price by computing the expectation through a Monte Carlo simulation, we have to simulate both the behavior of S_t for the equity "U" underlying the swap, and the default for counterparty "C". In particular we need to know exactly $\tau = \tau_C$. Obviously the correlation between "C" and "U" could have a relevant impact on the contract value. Here the structural model can be helpful: suppose we were to calibrate the underlying process V to CDSs for name "C", finding the appropriate default barrier and volatilities according to the procedure outlined in Chapter 3, with the AT1P model. We could set a correlation between the processes V_t^C (firm value for "C") and S_t^U (equity for "U"), derived, for example, through historical estimation directly based on equity returns, and simulate the joint evolution of $[V_t^C, S_t^U]$. As a proxy of the correlation between these two quantities we may consider a correlation deduced from the correlation between S_t^C and S_t^U, i.e. between equities. This may work well when the names are distressed, but in general one has to be careful in identifying credit correlation with equity correlation, since the two asset classes can be rather different.

For the underlying equity we assume simply a geometric Brownian motion. Summarizing:

$$\begin{aligned} dV_t^C &= rV_t^C dt + \sigma_V^C(t) V_t^C dW_t^C, \quad V_0^C = 1 \\ dS_t^U &= (r - q^U) S_t^U dt + \sigma_S^U(t) S_t^U dW_t^U, \quad S_0^U \\ dW_t^C dW_t^U &= \rho\, dt \end{aligned}$$

where r is the risk-free short-term rate (supposed constant).

As we explained earlier, this is not a fully consistent approach. To be fully consistent, we should assume a firm value model

$$dV_t^U = rV_t^U dt + \sigma_V^U(t) V_t^U \, dW_t^U,$$

for the underlying name, possibly correlated with the firm value for the counterparty, and then deduce the underlying equity from V^U rather than postulating directly a dynamics for S^U as we did above. This will be tackled with a more consistent and comprehensive approach in Section 8.2 and to distinguish the approach we will call the equity process E rather than S there.

Going back to our equity swap, now it is possible to run the Monte Carlo simulation, looking for spread X that makes the contract fair.

- We performed some simulations under different assumptions on the correlation between the firm value of "C" and the equity of "U". We considered five cases:

  $$\rho = -1, \rho = -0.2, \rho = 0, \rho = 0.5 \text{ and } \rho = 1.$$

- In Table 8.4 we present the results of the simulation, together with the error given by one standard deviation (Monte Carlo standard error).
- For counterparty "C" we used the Vodafone CDS rates seen earlier.
- For the reference stock "U" we used a hypothetical stock with initial price $S_0 = 20$, volatility $\sigma = 20\%$ and constant dividend yield $q = 0.80\%$.
- The contract has maturity $T = 5y$ and the settlement of the Floating Risk-Free rate has a semi-annual frequency.
- We included a recovery rate $\text{REC} = 0.4$ in $\text{LGD} = 1 - \text{REC}$.
- The starting date is the same used for the calibration, i.e. 10 March 2004.
- Since the reference number of stocks K is just a constant multiplying the whole payoff, without losing generality we set it equal to one.

Table 8.4 Spread X (in bps) under five correlation values, $S_0 = 20$, basic AT1P model. We also report the value of the simulated payoff average (times 10,000) across the 2,000,000 scenarios and its standard error, thus showing that X is fair (leading to an almost zero NPV)

ρ	X	ERS Payoff (bps)	MC Error (bps)
−1	0	0	0
−0.2	2.45	−0.02	1.71
0	4.87	−0.90	2.32
0.5	14.2	−0.53	2.71
1	24.4	−0.34	0.72

In order to reduce the errors of the simulations, we have adopted a variance reduction technique using the default indicator (whose expected value is the known default probability) as a control variate. In particular we have used the default indicator $1_{\{\tau \leq T\}}$ at the maturity T of the contract, which has a large correlation with the final payoff. Even so, a large number of scenarios is needed to obtain errors with a lower order of magnitude than X. In our simulations we have used $N = 2{,}000{,}000$.

We notice that X increases together with ρ. This is because given the same firm value and barrier levels, the correlation controls the moneyness of the equity swap option embedded in the CVA adjustment, so as to move along the table patterns. A positive correlation that is large in absolute value will imply that now when the firm value of the counterparty falls down to some level, the underlying equity will go down more than in the case with lower correlation. A low equity means that the option embedded in the CVA adjustment will be more in the money, so that the CVA will be larger, and will require a larger spread X to compensate it.

To check the impact of the barrier assumptions [62] has re-priced with the same X's found in Table 8.4 for AT1P under a model with stochastic barriers like the SBTV model introduced in Chapter 3 (3.1.9). The different dynamics assumptions in the AT1P and SBTV models lead to different counterparty risk valuations in the equity return swap, but the difference is not large when compared to bid-offer spreads CDSs, so that in this instance model risk seems to be partly under control.

We will analyze random barriers in connection with the present chapter in Section 8.3.2.

8.2 COUNTERPARTY RISK WITH A HYBRID CREDIT-EQUITY STRUCTURAL MODEL

In the following we describe a joint model for equity and credit based on a structural first passage model with time-dependent parameters and a realistic default barrier. We start from the credit models AT1P and SBTV, partly introduced in Chapter 3 and then we follow [51] to see how simple but reasonable economic assumptions can lead from this representation of credit risk to a model that can produce endogenously also the value of equity and equity options. The model is particularly suitable for the evaluation of counterparty risk in equity derivatives, since equity derivatives with counterparty risk require a hybrid credit-equity model. A remark on notation: the equity value will be denoted by E here, to distinguish this approach from that adopted earlier of directly assuming a dynamic S for equity.

8.2.1 The Credit Model

The starting model is AT1P with the parameter B set to 0, since we do not need the additional flexibility given by keeping it as a general parameter. We will also resort to the random barrier extension of AT1P, namely SBTV. It is worth re-stating Proposition 3.1.2 and the SBTV case as well for this specific case where $B = 0$, since we will be using this model a lot here.

Proposition 8.2.1 *(AT1P Model with B = 0) Assume the risk-neutral dynamics for the value of the firm V is characterized by a risk-free rate $r(t)$, a payout ratio $q(t)$ and an instantaneous volatility $\sigma(t)$, according to equation*

$$dV_t = V_t\,(r(t) - q(t))\,dt + V_t\,\sigma(t)\,dW_t \tag{8.2}$$

and assume a default barrier $H(t)$ (depending on the parameter H) of the form

$$H(t) = H \exp\left(\int_0^t (r(u) - q(u))du\right) = \boxed{\frac{H}{V_0} E^{\mathbb{Q}}[V_t]} \tag{8.3}$$

and let τ be defined as the first time where $V(t)$ hits $H(t)$ from above, starting from $V_0 > H$,

$$\tau = \inf\{t \geq 0 : V_t \leq H(t)\}.$$

Then the survival probability is given analytically by

$$\mathbb{Q}\{\tau > T\} = \Phi\left(\frac{\log \frac{V_0}{H} - \frac{1}{2}\int_0^T \sigma(t)^2 dt}{\sqrt{\int_0^T \sigma(t)^2 dt}}\right) - \frac{V_0}{H}\Phi\left(\frac{\log \frac{H}{V_0} - \frac{1}{2}\int_0^T \sigma(t)^2 dt}{\sqrt{\int_0^T \sigma(t)^2 dt}}\right). \tag{8.4}$$

If instead the default barrier is assumed to take random scenarios, namely is given by

$$H^I(t) = H^I \exp\left(\int_0^t (r(u) - q(u))du\right) = \frac{H^I}{V_0}\mathbb{E}[V_t] \tag{8.5}$$

where H^I assumes scenarios H^1 and H^2 with $\mathbb{Q}$ probabilities p^1, p^2, then we have a random barrier version of AT1P, called SBTV. Both probabilities p are in $[0, 1]$ and add up to one, and H^I is independent of W. The default time τ is still defined as the first time where V hits the barrier from above. If we are to price a default-sensitive discounted payoff Π, by iterated expectation we have

$$\mathbb{E}[\Pi] = \mathbb{E}\left[\mathbb{E}\left[\Pi | H^I\right]\right] = \sum_{i=1}^{2} p^i\, \mathbb{E}\left[\Pi | H^I = H^i\right]$$

so that the price of a security is a weighted average of the prices for the security in the different scenarios, with weights equal to the probabilities of the different scenarios.

As we hinted in Chapter 3 (Section 3.1.6), the behaviour of $H(t)$ has a simple economic interpretation. The backbone of the default barrier at t is a proportion, controlled by the parameter H, of the expected value of the company assets at t. H may depend on the value of liabilities, on safety covenants, and in general on the characteristics of the capital structure of the company. This barrier is in line with observations in [116], pointing out that first passage models with flat barriers lead to an unrealistic decrease of credit spreads as maturity increases. In fact the firm value is expected to grow at a rate $r(t) - q(t)$, and so credit spreads will decrease with maturity if the default barrier is instead flat. As pointed out in [80], firms aim at maintaining a stable leverage rather than a stable level of debt, so that the debt will also increase when the value of the assets increases, and the default barrier should follow the behaviour of the debt. Consistently, in the model above the default barrier remains a proportion $\frac{H}{V(0)}$ of the expected value of the firm. [61] shows for the first time how in a structural model of this kind we can have analytic formulas for default probabilities even with time-dependent parameters. Here we write Formula (8.4) more briefly as

$$\mathbb{Q}\{\tau > T\} = Q(T, V_0, H, \sigma[0; T]).$$

where by $\sigma[0; T]$ we indicate the function $\sigma(t)$ for $0 \leq t \leq T$. A similar notation will be applied also in the following, if possible, when the input of a formula is a function of time.

In Chapter 3 (3.1.7), we saw that the model is able to calibrate Lehman's CDS market quotes until the very day of Lehman's default. In this model, however, calibration is usually obtained by very high values in the short term for the volatility $\sigma(t)$ that then decrease in the long term. An analogous study, with similar findings, is conducted in [61] and in [49] for Parmalat's default.

This behaviour could depend on a feature typical of first passage models based on diffusion processes with a deterministic barrier. In such models the default arrival within a short time horizon is quite unlikely due to the firm value having continuous paths that take time to cross the default boundary. This is related to our discussion in Section 3.1.2 of the hazard rate in the Merton model approaching zero for short maturities.

Thus, when the barrier is deterministic, it is hard for classical firm value models to calibrate a non-vanishing probability of default in a very short horizon, without supposing particularly high short-term volatility.

The model assumption that the default barrier is a deterministic and known function of time corresponds to assuming that accounting data are fully reliable. This was not the case for Parmalat because of an accounting fraud, neither it was for Lehman, in the latter case due mainly to lack of transparency in the accounting of credit derivatives and deep uncertainty on the correct valuation of such products. It seems that in many of the most critical actual defaults there has been uncertainty about the financial situation of a company, so that the assumption of the deterministic default barrier appears to be unrealistic.

As we saw in Chapter 3, in order to take market uncertainty into account in a simple but reasonable manner, in the above model H can be replaced by a random variable assuming different values in different scenarios, each scenario with a different probability, leading to the model we called SBTV. With this different model, assuming $N = 2$, which means two possible scenarios, in [49] the credit data are calibrated with no need of a discontinuity in volatility between short- and long term, and the obtained distribution of the barrier represents the unfolding of the Parmalat crisis in a very reasonable and economically meaningful way. In fact in the [49] calibration exercise, the probability of the most pessimistic scenario increases as evidence of the accounting fraud emerges, and the associated default barrier comes closer and closer to the firm's value as breaking news shows the real situation of Parmalat is much worse than that revealed by official accounting.

In the following, we will extend to equity pricing the model with deterministic barrier given by (8.2) and (8.3); we will resort to the model with uncertain barrier (8.5) only when this is required by the market situation we are analyzing.

8.2.2 The Equity Model

A model for the Equity value and the price of equity options is derived from the above credit model in [51]. In Chapter 3 (3.1.2) in the standard Merton model it is shown that for implying an expression for the value of equity $E(t)$ from the credit model, one needs to assume that there exists a terminal time T for the company, when the value of the firm $V(T)$ is distributed to bondholders and stockholders. Equity at T is then just what remains of firm value (if positive) when all debt has been paid

$$E(T) = (V(T) - D(T))^+,$$

where $D(T)$ is the value of debt at time T. In Merton's model T is the only possible terminal time for the life of a company, since default cannot happen earlier, thus the equity value corresponds to the value of a European call option

$$E(t) = \mathbb{E}_t \left[e^{-\int_t^T (r(s)-q(s))ds} (V(T) - D(T))^+ \right].$$

We briefly comment on discounting at rate $r - q$. In short, discounting at rate $r(s)$ is correct when the interest rate to pay for financing the equity asset is $r(s)$, for example, see [25]. A discounting rate $r(s)$ is correct only if the asset pays no dividends. If the asset pays a continuous dividend yield $q(s)$, the actual cost of financing is $r(s) - q(s)$ and this is the rate we have to use for discounting if we want to have an arbitrage-free model. This argument is the simplified representation, under a number of simplifying assumptions, of a general approach to funding costs that will be analyzed in Chapter 17.

Going back to our derivation, in a Merton model one can consider $D(T)$ as a default threshold or barrier $H(T)$ where default happens at T when $V(T) < H(T)$, so with a change of notation we write

$$E(t) = \mathbb{E}_t \left[e^{-\int_t^T (r(s)-q(s))ds} (V(T) - H(T))^+ \right].$$

This is valid under the assumption of a single zero-coupon debt maturity T. Now we move to a first passage model, where default can happen also before T, and we want to keep a model that implies an expression for the equity value $E(t)$. We still have to assume, at least at the beginning, that there exists a terminal time T for the company when the firm value $V(T)$ is distributed to bondholders and stockholders if default did not happen earlier. Additionally now we have to consider the possibility that default happens before T, due to $V(t)$ falling lower than $H(t)$, in which case there will be nothing left for stockholders. Thus in the structural model Equity at T is

$$E(T) = 1_{\{V(s)>H(s), 0 \le s < T\}} (V(T) - H(T))^+$$

and its value at a generic time $0 \le t \le T$ is

$$E(t) = 1_{\{V(s)>H(s), 0 \le s \le t\}} \mathbb{E}_t \left[1_{\{V(s)>H(s), t<s<T\}} e^{-\int_t^T (r(s)-q(s))ds} (V(T) - H(T))^+ \right]$$

thus the equity value corresponds to the value of a Down-and-Out Call barrier option. We write

$$E(t) = 1_{\{\tau>t\}} \mathbb{E}_t \left[1_{\{V(s)>H(s), t<s<T\}} e^{-\int_t^T (r(s)-q(s))ds} (V(T) - H(T))^+ \right]$$

where we have indicated by $1_{\{\tau>t\}}$ the indicator $1_{\{V(s)>H(s), 0 \le s \le t\}}$, since the latter simply corresponds to a survival indicator guaranteeing that the company is alive at the valuation time t.

Remark 8.2.2 *(**T does not need to be the debt maturity**) In Merton-style models, usually T is interpreted as the unique maturity of the company debt. It follows that $H(T) = D(T)$, which must be equal to the value of the debt at T, also equals the notional of the debt. This simplifying assumption is not strictly necessary here. In fact, for the above model setting to be realistic, we just need $D(T) = H(T)$ to be the market value of the debt at T. Indeed, if T is not the debt maturity, a company whose firm value is higher than the market value of this debt can close down its operations at T, just buying back its own debt at market value, without defaulting, and giving the rest to equity holders. This way it is possible to have a value for $H(T)$ that is lower than the debt notional, for example. If T happens to be a moment of crisis, then $H(T)$ can be even closer to the expected recovery level than the debt notional level. We* *point this out because in all first passage models the barrier must be close to the recovery debtors receive at default τ, since $H(\tau) = V(\tau)$ and*

$$V(\tau) = H(\tau) \approx \textsc{Rec} \cdot \textit{DebtNotional}(\tau) \quad vs \quad \textit{DebtNotional}(T),$$

where REC *is the recovery rate. If T were treated as the debt maturity and therefore $H(T)$ were associated to the notional of the debt, this would imply a recovery close to the entire notional, at least at T, unrealistically and inconsistently with subsequent tests where we assume lower recovery. This is avoided since we avoid associating T with the maturity of the debt.*

Remark 8.2.3 ***(A framework that does not depend on** T**)*** *We have highlighted the above remark to help the reader thinking about the meaning of a structural model, but in practice the assumptions made on the fictive terminal date T will not influence the results since T will disappear completely from the model in the subsequent computations. This is an important point in favour of the reasonableness of the approach taken in [51].*

8.2.3 From Barrier Options to Equity Pricing

Since the above equity model has a structure similar to a barrier option [51] look for an analytic formula for this barrier option when parameters are time-dependent. They look at the results from [174] and [142] that were used in [61] to derive Formula (8.4) and which consider barriers that, after some adjustments, can be adapted to the shape of our default barrier. We recall these computations in the following.

8.2.3.1 Pricing Formulas for a Barrier Option

According to [174] and [142], when the underlying is $X(s)$ and the barrier is $H_X(s)$, with the following dynamics

$$dX(s) = X(s)\,(r(s) - q_X(s))\,dt + X(s)\,\sigma_X(s)\,dW(s), \tag{8.6}$$

$$H_X(s) = H_X \exp\left(-\int_s^T (r(u) - q_X(u))\,du\right), \tag{8.7}$$

the price of a down-and-out call option with strike K and maturity T,

$$\mathbb{E}_t\left[1_{\{X(s)>H_X(s),t\le s\le T\}} e^{-\int_t^T r(s)ds}(X(T)-K)^+\right],$$

can be computed analytically as

$$DO_t\,(T, X(t), H_X, K, r[t,T], q_X[t,T], \sigma_X[t,T]) = e^{-\int_t^T r(s)ds} \tag{8.8}$$

$$\cdot\left\{X(t)e^{\int_t^T\left(v(s)+\frac{\sigma_X(s)^2}{2}\right)ds}\,\Phi\left(\frac{\ln\left(\frac{X(t)}{H_X}\right)-\ln\left(\frac{K}{H_X}\right)+\int_t^T(v(s)+\sigma_X(s)^2)ds}{\Sigma}\right)\right.$$

$$-KN\left(\frac{\ln\left(\frac{X(t)}{H_X}\right)-\ln\left(\frac{K}{H_X}\right)+\int_t^T v(s)ds}{\Sigma}\right)+$$

$$-H_X(t)e^{\int_t^T\left(v(s)+\frac{\sigma_X(s)^2}{2}\right)ds}\Phi\left(\frac{\ln\left(\frac{H_X(t)^2}{X(t)H_X}\right)-\ln\left(\frac{K}{H_X}\right)+\int_t^T(v(s)+\sigma_X(s)^2)ds}{\Sigma}\right)$$

$$+K\left(\frac{X(t)}{H_X(t)}\right)\Phi\left(\frac{\ln\left(\frac{H_X(t)^2}{X(t)H_X}\right)-\ln\left(\frac{K}{H_X}\right)+\int_t^T v(s)ds}{\Sigma}\right)\Bigg\}.$$

having indicated $v(s)=r(s)-q_X(s)-\frac{\sigma_X(s)^2}{2}$ and $\Sigma=\sqrt{\int_t^T\sigma_X(s)^2ds}$.

8.2.3.2 *Adapting the Barrier Option to the First Passage Model*

The main difference between the assumptions (8.2) and (8.3) for the credit model and the assumptions (8.6) and (8.7) underlying the option pricing formula relate to the barrier dynamics. The barrier depends on time-to-maturity in the option formula, while it depends on time in the model. For closing this gap we can set

$$q_X(s)=r(s), \tag{8.9}$$

so that the barrier $H_X(s)$ is flat at the level H_X. Now for pricing equity at a generic time t we additionally set

$$\begin{aligned} X(t)&=V(t), \\ \sigma_X(s)&=\sigma(s),\ s>t \\ H_X&=H(t). \end{aligned} \tag{8.10}$$

We have a process very similar to $V(t)$ (apart from $q(t)\neq q_X(t)$) and associated to the flat barrier $H_X=H(t)$. We can price with the analytic formula (8.8) the barrier option problem (with strike equal to the flat barrier, $K=H_X$)

$$1_{\{X(t)>H_X\}}\mathbb{E}_t\left[1_{\{X(s)>H_X,t<s<T\}}e^{-\int_t^T r(s)ds}(X(T)-H_X)^+\right].$$

For computing the equity value, we need instead to compute

$$E(t)=1_{\{\tau>t\}}e^{\int_t^T q(s)ds}\mathbb{E}_t\left[1_{\{V(s)>H(s),t<s<T\}}e^{-\int_t^T r(s)ds}(V(T)-H(T))^+\right].$$

We notice that, for $s\geq t$

$$\begin{aligned} V(s)&=X(s)\exp\left(\int_t^s(-q(u)+r(u))du\right), \\ H(s)&=H_X\exp\left(\int_t^s(-q(u)+r(u))du\right) \end{aligned}$$

therefore, for $t<s<T$,

$$\begin{aligned} X(s)>H_X&\iff V(s)>H(s), \\ 1_{\{X(s)>H_X,t<s\leq<T\}}&=1_{\{V(s)>H(s),t<s<T\}} \end{aligned}$$

and we can write

$$\mathbb{E}_t\left[1_{\{V(s)>H(s),t<s<T\}}e^{-\int_t^T r(s)ds}(V(T)-H(T))^+\right]$$
$$=\exp\left(\int_t^T(-q(u)+r(u))du\right)\mathbb{E}_t\left[1_{\{X(s)>H_X,t<s<T\}}e^{-\int_t^T r(s)ds}(X(T)-H_X)^+\right].$$

We have (8.8) for the latter expectations, so that

$$\begin{aligned}E(t)&=1_{\{\tau>t\}}e^{\int_t^T q(s)ds}\mathbb{E}_t\left[1_{\{V(s)>H(s),t<s<T\}}e^{-\int_t^T r(s)ds}(V(T)-H(T))^+\right]\\&=1_{\{\tau>t\}}e^{\int_t^T q(s)ds}\exp\left(\int_t^T -q(u)+r(u)du\right)\qquad(8.11)\\&\cdot DO_t\left(T,V(t),H(t),H(t),r[t,T],\left[r(s)-(1+2\beta)\frac{\sigma(s)^2}{2}\right]_{t\le s\le T},\sigma[t,T]\right)\\&=1_{\{\tau>t\}}\exp\left(\int_t^T r(u)du\right)\cdot DO_t(\ldots).\end{aligned}$$

Now we compute explicitly the formula starting from the general one (8.8) and recalling (8.9) and (8.10). We obtain:

$$\begin{aligned}&DO_t(T,V(t),H(t),H(t),r[t,T],r[t,T],\sigma[t,T])=\qquad(8.12)\\&=e^{-\int_t^T r(s)ds}\left\{V(t)\Phi\left(\left(\ln\left(\frac{V(t)}{H(t)}\right)+\frac{1}{2}\int_t^T\sigma(s)^2ds\right)\Big/\Sigma\right)\right.\\&-H(t)\Phi\left(\left(\ln\left(\frac{V(t)}{H(t)}\right)-\frac{1}{2}\int_t^T\sigma(s)^2ds\right)\Big/\Sigma\right)\\&-H(t)\Phi\left(\left(\ln\left(\frac{H(t)}{V(t)}\right)+\frac{1}{2}\int_t^T\sigma^2(s)ds\right)\Big/\Sigma\right)\\&\left.+V(t)\Phi\left(\left(\ln\left(\frac{H(t)}{V(t)}\right)-\frac{1}{2}\int_t^T\sigma(s)^2ds\right)\Big/\Sigma\right)\right\}\\&=e^{-\int_t^T r(s)ds}(V(t)-H(t))\end{aligned}$$

This gives a surprising analytic expression for equity in the model:

Theorem 8.2.4 ***(Equity in AT1P: An option formula that reduces to a forward contract on the firm value.)*** *In the AT1P firm value model, the price of equity is given by:*

$$E(t)=1_{\{V(s)>H(s),0\le s<t\}}(V(t)-H(t))$$

and reduces to the price of a forward contract.

We have reached a surprising result according to which, under the hypotheses of this work, the value of the Down-and-Out Call barrier option is the same as a forward contract on the underlying. [51] further illustrates and verifies this result in three ways, using three different model specifications:

- When $V(t)$ is just a driftless arithmetic Brownian motion, [51] intuitively use the method of images.
- In the restriction of the model where parameters are flat, [51] use standard barrier options formulas, for example [122].

- For the general case, [51] use the results of [71].

The interested reader is referred to [51]. We now provide the expression for equity and equity options endogenous to our credit model.

8.2.4 Equity and Equity Options

Adapting (8.11) to the case of a barrier not depending on volatility, namely with $B = 0$ as in Proposition 8.2.1, we have again:

$$
\begin{aligned}
E(t) &= 1_{\{\tau>t\}}\mathbb{E}_t\left[1_{\{V(s)>H(s),t<s<T\}}e^{-\int_t^T (r(s)-q(s))ds}(V(T)-H(T))^+\right] \\
&= 1_{\{\tau>t\}}\exp\left(\int_t^T r(u)du\right)\cdot \\
&\quad \cdot DO_t\left(T, V(t), H(t), H(t), r[t,T], r[t,T], \sigma[t,T]\right) \\
&= 1_{\{\tau>t\}}e^{\int_t^T r(u)du}e^{-\int_t^T r(u)du}\left(V(t)-H(t)\right) \\
&= 1_{\{V(s)>H(s),0\le s<t\}}(V(t)-H(t)).
\end{aligned} \tag{8.13}
$$

Thus we have an expression for equity in terms of firm value and default barrier which is simple and relatively tractable.

Remark 8.2.5 ***(The formula does not depend on the final maturity*** T*) Notice that the equity value does not depend anymore on the arbitrary expiry date of the company debt that we introduced in order to represent equity as an option on the firm's value. Although this value was based on this assumption, whatever arbitrary expiry date one assumes the result does not change.*

The equity has dynamics similar to a shifted lognormal process with time-dependent drift and, more importantly, time-dependent shift. These dynamics, however, allows us to price equity options with an analytic formula. An equity option with maturity $\hat{T}$ has price

$$
\begin{aligned}
Call_t(\hat{T}, K, E(t)) &= \mathbb{E}_t\left[e^{-\int_t^{\hat{T}} r(u)du}(E(\hat{T})-K)^+\right] \\
&= \mathbb{E}_t\left[e^{-\int_t^{\hat{T}} r(u)du}\left(1_{\{V(s)>H(s),0\le s<\hat{T}\}}[V(\hat{T})-H(\hat{T})]-K\right)^+\right] \\
&= 1_{\{\tau>t\}}\mathbb{E}_t\left[e^{-\int_t^{\hat{T}} r(u)du}1_{\{V(s)>H(s),t<s<\hat{T}\}}([V(\hat{T})-H(\hat{T})]-K)^+\right].
\end{aligned}
$$

Indicating

$$
\hat{K} = H(t) + e^{-\int_t^{\hat{T}}(r(u)-q(u))du}K
$$

we have

$$
\begin{aligned}
Call_t(\hat{T}, K, E(t)) &= 1_{\{\tau>t\}}e^{\int_t^{\hat{T}} -q(u)+r(u)du}\mathbb{E}_t\left[e^{-\int_t^{\hat{T}} r(u)du}1_{\{X(s)>H(t),t\le s<\hat{T}\}}(X(\hat{T})-\hat{K})^+\right] \\
&= 1_{\{\tau>t\}}e^{-\int_t^{\hat{T}} q(u)-r(u)du}\mathbb{E}_t\left[e^{-\int_t^{\hat{T}} r(u)du}1_{\{X(s)>H(t),t\le s<\hat{T}\}}(X(\hat{T})-\hat{K})^+\right] \\
&= 1_{\{\tau>t\}}e^{-\int_t^{\hat{T}} q(u)-r(u)du} \times DO_t(\hat{T}, V(t), H(t), \hat{K}, r[t,\hat{T}], r[t,\hat{T}], \sigma[t,\hat{T}]),
\end{aligned} \tag{8.14}
$$

where

$$DO_t\left(\hat{T}, V(t), H(t), \hat{K}, r[t,\hat{T}], r[t,\hat{T}], \sigma[t,\hat{T}], -\frac{1}{2}\right)$$
$$= e^{-\int_t^{\hat{T}} r(s)ds}\left\{V(t)N\left(\left(\ln\left(\frac{V(t)}{\hat{K}}\right)+\int_t^{\hat{T}}\frac{\sigma_X(s)^2}{2}ds\right)\Big/\Sigma\right)\right.$$
$$-\hat{K}N\left(\left(\ln\left(\frac{V(t)}{\hat{K}}\right)-\int_t^{\hat{T}}\frac{\sigma_X(s)^2}{2}ds\right)\Big/\Sigma\right)$$
$$-H(t)N\left(\left(\ln\left(\frac{H(t)^2}{V(t)\hat{K}}\right)+\int_t^{\hat{T}}\frac{\sigma_X(s)^2}{2}ds\right)\Big/\Sigma\right)$$
$$\left.+\hat{K}\left(\frac{V(t)}{H(t)}\right)N\left(\left(\ln\left(\frac{H(t)^2}{V(t)\hat{K}}\right)-\int_t^{\hat{T}}\frac{\sigma_X(s)^2}{2}ds\right)\Big/\Sigma\right)\right\}.$$

This provides an analytic pricing also for equity options. In the next section we are going to test if this system of expressions is consistent with the real prices of equity, equity options, and credit default swaps. Before that we remind the reader that in [51], the authors provide instruction on why equity (normally a barrier option on the firm value) reduces to a forward firm value price. In [51] the result of Theorem 8.2.4 is explained in three different ways.

8.3 MODEL CALIBRATION AND EMPIRICAL RESULTS

Now we see how we can calibrate our model. In the dynamics of firm value (8.2),

$$dV(s) = V(s)(r(s)-q(s))\,dt + V(s)\sigma(s)\,dW_s,$$

the market provides directly $r[t,T], q[t,T]$ while the remaining parameters are $V(0), \sigma[t,T]$. In the barrier dynamics

$$H(s) = H\exp\left(-\int_0^s q(u)-r(u)du\right)$$

the only remaining parameter is H. These parameters need to be calibrated to credit and equity quotes. If we assume the volatility to be a piecewise constant structure that can take M different values,

$t\in[T_0,T_1]$	$t\in[T_1,T_2]$	...	$t\in[T_{M-1},T_M=T]$
$\sigma(t)=\sigma_1$	$\sigma(t)=\sigma_2$	...	$\sigma(t)=\sigma_M$

(8.15)

then we have $M+2$ unknown parameters to calibrate. If volatility is flat, there are only three parameters:

$$V(0) \quad H \quad \sigma.$$

One may remember that the default probabilities in the AT1P model depend on V_0/H rather than on V_0 and H separately, so one may argue that as far as Credit Default Swaps are concerned the model only has two parameters. This is true as long as we do not extend the model to equity; when pricing equity and equity options V_0 and H separately become important, as we show below when explaining how the parameters are used.

How many parameters should we be comfortable with? A related question is the following. Consider liquid market products whose prices depend on the above three parameters in our model and at the same time can be priced with analytic formulas, so that it is reasonable to use them in calibration. How many such products can we observe?

We have CDSs (or alternatively corporate bonds) for different maturities, we have the equity price, and we have European options for different maturities and different strikes on equity. The approach we will follow is to calibrate $V(0)$, H and σ as follows:

1. $Q(T, V_0/H, \sigma[0;T])$, the model default probability, is used to calibrate the market CDSs.
2. $E(0) = (V(0) - H)$, the model value for market equity, is used as a constraint to write $V(0)$ as a function of H: $V(0) = E(0) + H$.
3. $Call(0, K_i, T; V(0), H, \sigma)$, the model option price, is used to calibrate a set of equity call options with different strikes K_i, $i = 1, 2, \ldots, n$.

We want to test how the model can be calibrated jointly to equity and credit. The most liquid equity options usually have a short maturity, so we will test the model behaviour when fitted to credit and equity using a set of European options with maturity around 1y, and the 1y CDS. Further liquid data, for example the entire CDS term structure, can be fitted through the time dependency (8.15) of the asset volatility. Credit and equity data jointly can fix all model parameters, replacing the approximated preliminary calibration to only credit data which was used in [49] to determine the value of $H/V(0)$. For this test we keep volatility flat at σ. If we are interested in calibrating different maturities, we can make volatility time-dependent as in (8.15) to increase our degrees of freedom.

We have selected two companies with different characteristics:

BP: The first company is British Petroleum (BP), an example of a company that went through the credit crunch remaining financially solid and with good growth perspectives. This company was impacted after the beginning of the crunch by an unexpected and deep crisis owing to an oil spill in 2010.

FIAT: The other company is FIAT Spa, the Italian automotive company that expanded during the years of the credit crunch, most notably by the acquisition of Chrysler. The market sentiment about FIAT appeared to change dramatically after Lehman's default, when market investors appeared to think that the crisis of the auto sector was going to take a heavy toll on the Italian car maker, considering also that the group had increased its leverage in the recent expansions.

8.3.1 BP and FIAT in 2009

We show calibration results for different days.

8.3.1.1 BP on 6 April 2009

We start from 6 April 2009. For BP we have the market data listed in Table 8.5.

Both equity and credit data are those of a healthy company, compared to the general market situation in spring 2009. We use the equity price to write $V(0) = E^{Mkt}(0) - H$, so that we are left with two parameters H and σ. These two parameters are used to calibrate the above set of six market data (CDS spread and five equity options) obtaining the calibration results listed in Table 8.6 and Figure 8.1.

Table 8.5 Market data for BP on 6 April 2009

BP, 6 April 2009					
Equity:					
Equity price: 458.25					
Dividend yield=6%					
9m expiry option:					
Strike	420	440	460	480	500
Implied Vol	42.7%	40.6%	39%	38.7%	37.5%
Credit:					
Recovery: 40%					
1y CDS spread: 64.7 bps					

Table 8.6 Calibration results for BP on 6 April 2009. CDS Spread Error (Market spread minus Model spread) is 0 bp

Errors (Market Vol minus Model Vol) on 9m expiry option:					
Strike	420	440	460	480	500
Implied Vol	0.48%	0.18%	−0.1%	0.17%	−0.23%

Considering that the credit spread is fitted exactly and the implied volatility error is within the bid-ask spread, this calibration is satisfactory and would suggest that the consistency relationship between equity and credit that we derived is reasonable and consistent with market data. Taking this point of view we can consider it safe to use the model for assessing counterparty risk when the relationship between credit and equity is involved.

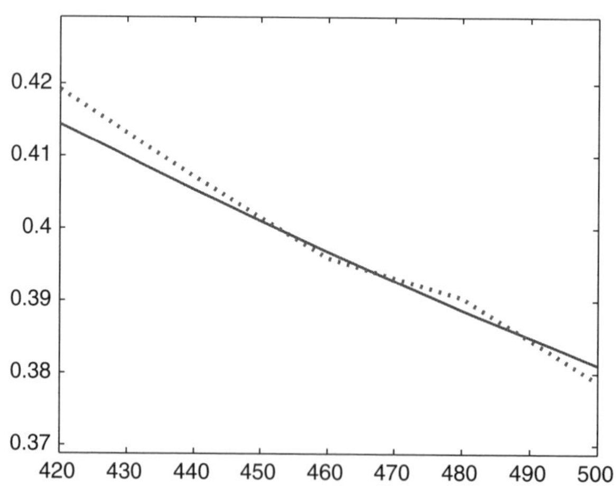

Figure 8.1 Model implied volatility for BP on 6 April 2009. Dots are market data. Continuous line is model-implied volatilities

Table 8.7 Market data for FIAT on 6 April 2009

FIAT, 6 April 2009

Equity:
Equity price: 7.215
Dividend yield=0%

9m expiry option:

Strike	6.8	7	7.2	7.4	7.6
Implied Vol	72.9%	71.5%	70.5%	69.5%	68.6%

Credit:
Recovery: 40%
1y CDS spread: 1211 bps

Table 8.8 Calibration results for FIAT on 6 April 2009. CDS Spread Error (Market spread minus Model spread) is 305 bp

Errors (Market-Model) on 9m expiry option:

Strike	6.8	7	7.2	7.4	7.6
Implied Vol	−7.7%	−7.6%	−37.2%	−6.8%	−6.5%

8.3.1.2 FIAT on 6 April 2009

We move now to consider FIAT on the same day. The market data are listed in Table 8.7.

Both markets clearly reveal a more stressed situation, particularly the credit market. One can see when this dramatic worsening of the FIAT credit spread started by looking at Figure 8.2.

Results of the calibration are listed in Table 8.8

The errors are now not negligible for the equity option market as one can see in Figure 8.3.

In particular, the model underestimates credit spreads and overestimates implied volatility. It is then interesting to see which level of implied volatility the model predicts if we force good fit to the CDS spread leaving equity volatilities to be determined by credit calibration. The results are shown in Table 8.9 and Figure 8.4.

It is confirmed that credit data seem to imply an equity volatility much higher, and a steeper skew, than we have in the equity market. Now we see what happens if we force a good fit to

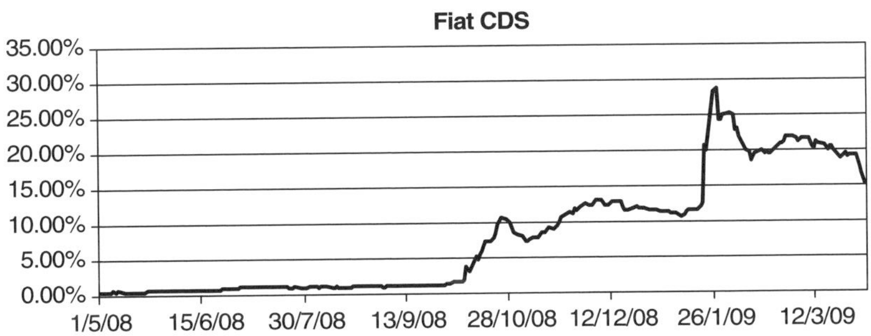

Figure 8.2 FIAT historical data for CDS

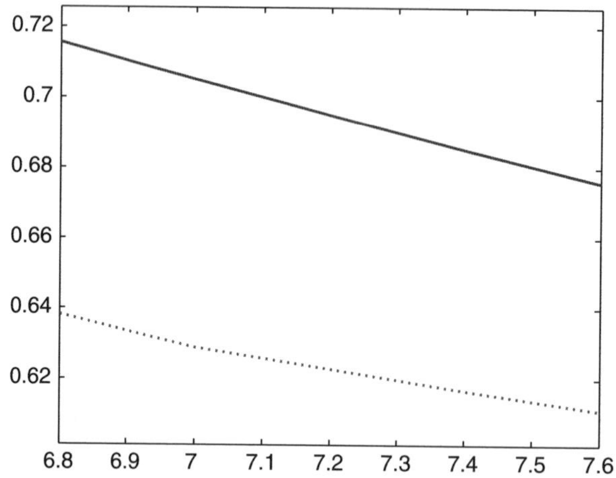

Figure 8.3 Model-implied volatility for FIAT on 6 April 2009. Dots are market data. Continuous line is model implied volatilities

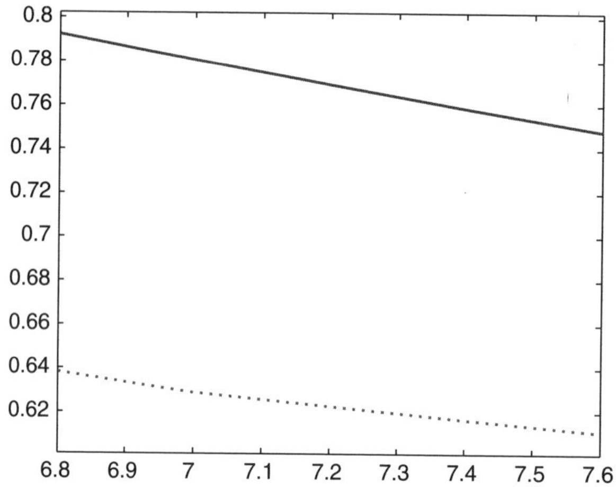

Figure 8.4 Model implied volatility for FIAT on 6 April 2009 when calibration error on credit spreads is forced within 5 bp. Dots are market data. Continuous line is model-implied volatilities

Table 8.9 Calibration results for FIAT on 6 April 2009 when calibration error on credit spreads is forced within 5 bp

Errors (Market-Model) on 9m expiry option:					
Strike	6.8	7	7.2	7.4	7.6
Implied Vol	−15.4%	−15%	−14.6%	−14.2%	−13.7%

Table 8.10 Calibration results for FIAT on 6 April 2009 when credit spreads are not calibrated. CDS Spread Error (Market spread minus Model spread) is 567 bp

Errors (Market-Model) on 9m expiry option:					
Strike	6.8	7	7.2	7.4	7.6
Implied Vol	−0.5%	−0.5%	−0.2%	−0.04%	−0.3%

equity options, leaving the credit spread to be determined by equity calibration. The results are shown in Table 8.10 and Figure 8.5.

Consistent with the results of the previous calibration, but now reversing the approach, we see that a good fit to equity options implies a CDS which is 567 bp lower than the actual market CDS spread.

8.3.1.3 The Impact of Recovery Rates

What can we deduce from these results? A player with strong faith in all the assumptions of the model being used will think that this is a typical case of "capital structure arbitrage". This means that there is an inconsistency between what the credit market and the equity market say about this company. This inconsistency is revealed by the very same model that for BP explained both markets with negligible errors. We may think that this inconsistency cannot last; as soon as the market realizes this inconsistency, it will go back to a situation where the model can calibrate well the two markets. This means that either CDS spreads are going to decrease, or the equity volatility skew is going to get higher and steeper. In fact it is well known that a number of banks were involved in FIAT CDS-Equity arbitrage trading, by betting exactly on such a market move.

However, there are different ways to explain the situation. First, notice that our pricing assumes a recovery of 40%. Although this was the quote by Markit CDS data, both for FIAT and BP, one may think that an implied recovery of 40% was too high for FIAT in a time of

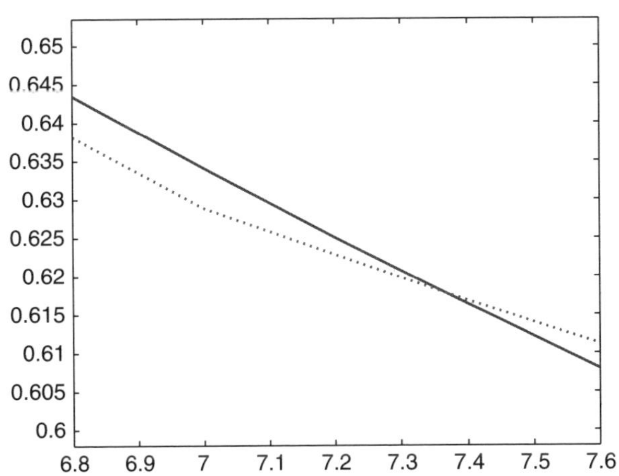

Figure 8.5 Model implied volatility for FIAT on 6 April 2009 when credit spreads are not calibrated. Dots are market data. Continuous line is model-implied volatilities

Table 8.11 Calibration results for FIAT on 6 April 2009. Recovery rate set to 0%. CDS Spread Error (Market spread minus Model spread) is 45 bp

Errors (Market-Model) on 9m expiry option:

Strike	6.8	7	7.2	7.4	7.6
Implied Vol	−2.1%	−2%	−1.8%	−1.5%	−1.2%

crisis. This is reasonable. However, even if we set the recovery rate equal to 0%, we are not able to fit the market with the precision we saw for BP. See the results listed in Table 8.11.

Lowering the recovery seems a step in the right direction, but even with the minimum possible recovery of 0%, which is certainly a conservative underestimation, we do not obtain the good fit we got for BP, on equity and even more on CDS. There are still noticeable errors on both credit and equity options. And if we use a value of recovery lower than 40% but more realistic than 0%, such as 20%, the errors are even bigger. Should we now conclude that to some extent we are really in front of a capital structure arbitrage? Before accepting and adopting this explanation, there is an important objection to consider.

8.3.2 Uncertainty in Market Expectations

Recall that, as we explained in Section 3.1.9 and Section 8.2.1 (see also [49] and [55]), calibration results may be improved by adopting first passage models with an uncertain default barrier. In models such as SBTV, one takes into account that the default barrier is not perfectly known to market players, since actual liabilities are not perfectly known and it is over-simplistic to take the barrier as a deterministic parameter like in the simple AT1P model. The uncertainty on the barrier can be due to the risk of an accounting fraud as in the Parmalat or Enron cases, or to accounting opacity and illiquidity in the market of CDOs as in the case of Lehman. Market investors may have been in a situation of similar uncertainty towards FIAT in April 2009, since compared to its size the company was increasing its leverage for very big investments, and the outcome of such investments was still unclear, particularly after Lehman's default. The issue can be addressed in our modelling framework by assuming that the barrier is uncertain. In particular we assume that the barrier can take two different values, one higher (higher default risk) and one lower (lower default risk), so that the deterministic barrier (8.3) is replaced by (8.5) with

$$H^I = \begin{cases} H^1 & \text{with probability } p_1 \\ H^2 & \text{with probability } p_2 \end{cases}.$$

8.3.2.1 *BP on 6 April 2009*

We applied this model to the first company we tested. Are we able to improve the already good results we obtained for BP by introducing uncertainty in the default barrier, which appears in any case a realistic feature? The results of the application of this new model to the BP data on 6 April that we have already used is listed in Table 8.12.

Compared to the results we obtained with the model having a deterministic barrier, the addition of two parameters (one level of the barrier H^2 and its probability p_2) does not improve the situation at all. In fact, looking at the details of the calibration results, we have obtained $H^1 \cong H^2$. Uncertainty in the company liabilities does not appear to be necessary to fit

Table 8.12 Calibration results for BP on 6 April 2009. CDS Spread Error (Market spread minus Model spread) is 0 bp

Errors (Market Vol minus Model Vol) on 9m expiry option:

Strike	420	440	460	480	500
Implied Vol	0.48%	0.18%	−0.1%	0.17%	−0.23%

Table 8.13 Barrier scenarios and scenario probabilities resulting from calibration for FIAT on 6 April 2009

$H^1/V_1 = 0.98$	$p_1 = 0.35$
$H^2/V_2 = 0.0001$	$p_2 = 0.65$

jointly BP equity and credit data, since this is done easily also in the more parsimonious model where the default barrier is deterministic. The calibration returns two barrier values which are the same. This confirms that we do not need any uncertainty in the balance sheet to explain BP market data: this is done very well by the deterministic model. The model, for the little it can say, says that the market was not uncertain on BP's financial situation – on 6 April 2009.

8.3.2.2 *FIAT on 6 April 2009*

Now we test this new model with barrier uncertainty on FIAT market data, again on 6 April 2009, keeping the initial recovery of 40%. The results for the barrier scenarios and the scenario probabilities are listed in Figure 8.13.

We no longer have $H^1 \cong H^2$. On the contrary the barriers under the two scenarios are different, (1) giving a very pessimistic scenario, less likely, and (2) a more likely optimistic scenario. With this model, the calibration results are listed in Table 8.14 and Figure 8.6.

8.3.2.3 *Results Discussion*

It is a dramatic improvement compared to the previous results we obtained with the deterministic barrier. Although due to uncertainty on the default barrier, this model has 4 rather than 2 parameters, the model is still parsimonious since we are fitting 6 market quotes (CDS spread and 5 equity options). But the fit is now perfect from a financial point of view. Since perfect fit has been obtained by introducing an element of realism in the model, which does not make the model overly complex, we do not think there is any ground to claim we are in front of a capital structure arbitrage. One simpler answer is available: additional uncertainty on the financial situation of the company.

Table 8.14 Calibration results for FIAT on 6 April 2009. CDS Spread Error (Market spread minus Model spread) is 0.2 bp

Errors (Market-Model) on 9m expiry option:

Strike	6.8	7	7.2	7.4	7.6
Implied Vol	−0.18%	−0.36%	−0.17%	−0.07%	0.4%

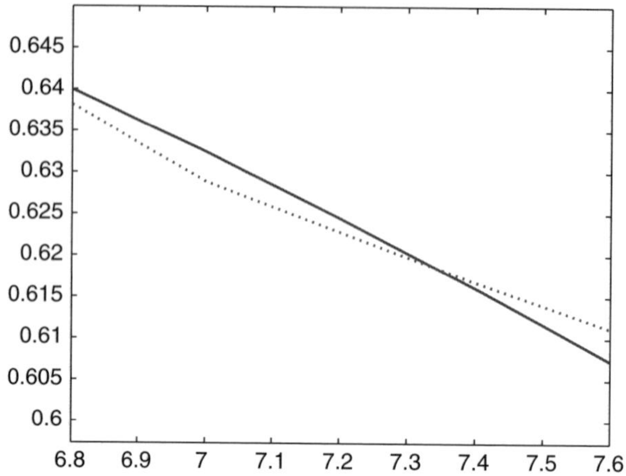

Figure 8.6 Model implied volatility for FIAT on 6 April 2009 with uncertain barrier. Dots are market data. Continuous line is model-implied volatilities

This answer is not necessarily less attractive for a trader than the idea of a "capital structure arbitrage". When the arbitrageur sees an arbitrage, he bets the market will go back to a no-arbitrage situation as soon as the market itself realizes the presence of arbitrage. In our case, this means a lower CDS or a higher and steeper equity volatility skew, namely a situation where the deterministic barrier model can calibrate well equity and credit jointly. If the trader, instead, accepts the indications of the model that the market is just pricing an uncertainty about the financial situation of FIAT, in this case then can also see a trading opportunity. The trader can find it reasonable to suppose that uncertainty will be resolved sooner or later; this also means a lower CDS or a higher and steeper equity volatility skew, because in this case lower uncertainty means the possibility to calibrate the deterministic barrier model. The same directional trade can be justified by saying "there is an arbitrage, the market will eliminate it *as soon as* it realizes it, and I want to bet on it" or by saying "there is uncertainty about the market situation of this company; *sooner or later* this uncertainty can be resolved, and I want to bet on it".

From the point of view of a financial modeller, the results we obtained above with the quantitative models justify the second but not the first approach. The first can be justified only by an operator who has an external belief that market uncertainty on company books in impossible, even for a short period of time. Notice also that the two approaches can justify the same trade, but pay attention that some not irrelevant details are different in the two cases. One fact is that the uncertainty factor for the barrier influences market completeness and clearly hedging techniques. Secondly, and more importantly, the mechanisms and the timing that can lead the trade to be a success or a failure are different. In the first case you claim you have found an "inconsistency" and you expect the market to eliminate it. In the second case you claim you are giving a description of the market and then you take a view on what will happen in the future.

8.3.3 Further Results: FIAT in 2008 and BP in 2010

In the following we further investigate this model. We aim to confirm that this model can actually provide a simplified but reasonable interpretation of reality. For example, the results so far suggest that uncertainty on the default barrier is important when some event suddenly

Table 8.15 Market data for FIAT on 11 March 2008

FIAT, 11 March 2008

Equity:
Equity price: 12.588
Dividend yield=0%

6m expiry option:				
Strike	11.33	12.27	12.9	13.85
Implied Vol	44.6%	43.2%	42.8%	41.8%

Credit:
Recovery: 40%
1y CDS spread: 173 bps

disarranges market expectations about a company. For example, Lehman's default event may have generated worries about a company involved in a risky expansion such as FIAT. Otherwise uncertainty in the barrier seems less important – or not important at all, as in the case of BP in April 2009.

8.3.3.1 FIAT on 11 March 2008 – Before Lehman's Default Event

To see if this interpretation is reasonable, we try to calibrate the simpler model without uncertainty to FIAT data from before Lehman's default. We see below market data for 11 March 2008 listed in Table 8.15.

The market views on the credit quality of the company appear much better. Calibrating the model with deterministic barrier we obtain the results listed in Table 8.16 and Figure 8.7.

Differing from what happened after Lehman's default, on these earlier data the simpler model with deterministic barrier can fit exactly the credit spread while implying errors around the bid-ask spread on equity options, similar to the results obtained for BP, the healthy company. This confirms the initial interpretation.

8.3.3.2 BP on 17 June 2010 – after Deepwater Horizon's accident

There is an additional test of our conclusion that we can perform. The other company we considered, BP, was hit by an unexpected crisis when on 20 April 2010, the BP's Deepwater Horizon drilling rig exploded, killing 11 employees and starting an oil spill that became one of the worst environmental disasters of the past decades. This created real disarray in the market

Table 8.16 Calibration results for FIAT on 11 March 2008 with uncertain barrier. CDS Spread Error (Market spread minus Model spread) is 0 bp

Errors (Market-Model) on 6m expiry options:

6m expiry option:				
Strike	11.33	12.27	12.9	13.85
Implied Vol	−1.1%	−0.7%	−0.05%	0.4%

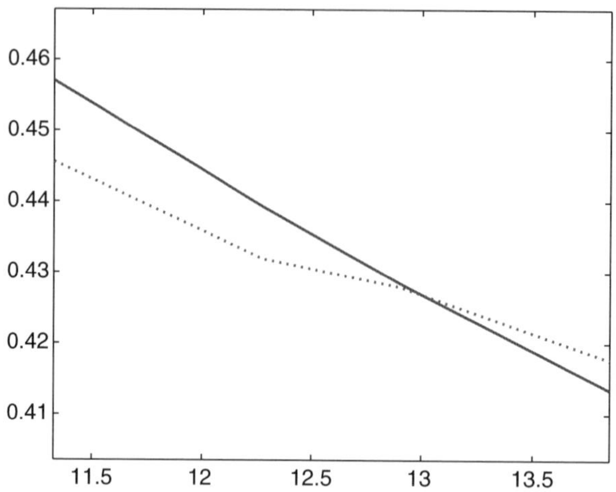

Figure 8.7 Model implied volatility for FIAT on 11 March 2008 with uncertain barrier. Dots are market data. Continuous line is model-implied volatilities

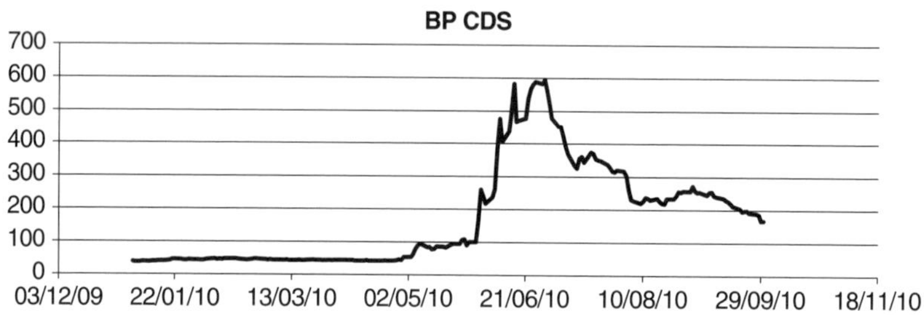

Figure 8.8 BP historical data for CDS

views on BP's perspectives. BP could be considered responsible for tens of billions of damage to the environment; but it may also prove to have followed best practice and due diligence, reducing its responsibilities. From being one of the most solid international companies in the world it turned into one with a troubled future. The value of its assets was certainly high and probably not so difficult to evaluate for market investors, but the value of its liabilities had become very difficult to assess, making BP a typical example of a company affected by high uncertainty.[1] The crisis that hit BP is clearly visible from the chart of its CDS spread shown in Figure 8.8 and from the market data of CDS and equity options that we report in Table 8.17 for 17 June 2010, just after BP agreed to pay a initial $20 billion dollar to the US government to repay the damages created by the oil spill.

If the interpretation we gave above is correct, after this event it should be very difficult to calibrate jointly to BP CDS and equity option with the basic model that assumes a deterministic default barrier. In fact, the results are listed in Table 8.18.

[1] We point out that we chose BP as a benchmark for our tests at the beginning of 2009, well before the rig explosion in 2010. Thus the possibility to test our hypotheses given by this subsequent event had not been planned in advance. In spite of the confirmation of the initial hypothesis that we got from the test, we strongly regret having been given the possibility to perform this test. We would have very much preferred clearer waters in the Gulf of Mexico rather than clearer ideas on any financial problem.

Table 8.17 Market data for BP on 17 June 2010

BP, 17 June 2010

Equity:
Equity price: 337
Dividend yield=0%

9m expiry option:

Strike	280	320	360	400	440
Implied Vol	53%	49.7%	46.8%	45.7%	44%

Credit:
Recovery: 40%
1y CDS spread: 635 bps

Table 8.18 Calibration results for BP on 17 June 2010. CDS Spread Error (Market spread minus Model spread) is 244 bp

Errors (Market Vol minus Model Vol) on 9m expiry option:

Strike	280	320	360	400	440
Implied Vol	−7.2%	−6.6%	−6.3%	−5.2%	−3.7%

In such a situation, a model with explicit uncertainty on the level of liabilities (default barrier) should work better. We have tried this, obtaining the results listed in Table 8.19.

This has been obtained with the parameters listed in Table 8.20 for the uncertain barrier. It shows uncertainty between a higher level of BP's liabilities and a lower one, with almost the same probability. In confirmation of the above interpretation, with only these two scenarios we are able to calibrate market data for BP at the peak of the Deepwater Horizon's oil spill crisis.

8.4 COUNTERPARTY RISK AND WRONG WAY RISK

The good results obtained in joint calibration of credit default swaps and equity options, and the easy financial interpretation of these results, suggest that the model may be suitable for pricing counterparty risk in equity derivatives. The model introduces a structural relationship between credit and equity. If the relationship is reasonable, as the above results seem to confirm, this approach is preferable to the use of intensity or copula models where a relationship between these two asset classes can only be superimposed from the outside. The same considerations also affect structural models where the relationship between equity and credit is introduced just by simplified assumptions, as in the first part of this chapter, in Section 8.1 (and in [49] or [55]), rather than being analytically derived as here.

Table 8.19 Calibration results for BP on 17 June 2010 with an uncertain barrier. CDS Spread Error (Market spread minus Model spread) is 3 bp

Errors (Market Vol minus Model Vol) on 9m expiry option:

Strike	280	320	360	400	440
Implied Vol	−0.4%	−0.9%	−1.3%	−0.6%	0.8%

Table 8.20 Barrier scenarios and scenario probabilities resulting from calibration for FIAT on 6 April 2009

$H^1/V_1 = 0.92$	$p_1 = 0.52$
$H^2/V_2 = 0.6$	$p_2 = 0.48$

We consider counterparty risk in derivatives where the underlying is the equity (stocks) of some reference company or institution or index, and the counterparty has a non-negligible risk of default. If one assumes independence between the underlying equity and the credit risk of the counterparty, we do not have the so-called *wrong way risk* and pricing is not difficult even in the absence of a true credit-equity hybrid model. However, this independence assumption, in case of equity derivatives, cannot be considered to be realistic.

In fact the equity value of the counterparty and the equity value of the underlying reference are very likely to be correlated: stock prices are all strongly dependent on the trend of the global economy, so that a positive correlation is almost guaranteed. In this case the only way to have independence between reference equity and credit risk of the counterparty is to assume that the counterparty equity value and credit risk are independent. And this is definitely impossible, so much so that when default risk becomes actual default the value of equity must be zero. We have also seen in the examples of the last section that not only market credit- and equity-derivative prices change due to the same events, but they can even be explained jointly by one single model with few parameters. It is this feature of our model that we exploit in the following to give a picture of the effect of wrong way risk. This is obtained by using a market based correlation between the reference equity and the counterparty equity, and then using the model built-in link between equity and credit.

First we consider the model with deterministic barrier that seems good enough to fit the market data for stable companies; here the only dependence we can introduce is through correlation of the value of the firms. Notice that in this model, thanks to (8.13), the instantaneous correlation between the two firm's values equals the instantaneous correlation of the equity prices conditional on the two firms to be alive. Thus this parameter can be estimated, for example, historically or via basket derivatives, in the equity market.

Then we consider the more general model with a stochastic barrier, required in particular for moments of instability; in this second case we have another possible default dependence between two counterparties given by the joint distribution of the barriers, as we will see in detail.

We will explore in particular the counterparty risk adjustment of equity options, considering both calls and puts, and different strikes; considering different strikes is particularly interesting in our framework, since our model is naturally consistent with the smile that can be observed in the equity derivatives market, as we have shown in the calibration examples. It is not unlikely that banks are worried about the counterparty risk of equity options. For example, in 2008 and 2009 many banks were worried about the counterparty risk they bore towards Berkshire Hathaway, the financial company managed by the legendary investor Warren Buffett, that in previous years had financed itself by writing put options on stocks and stock indices on a notional value of \$35 billion. These puts had original terms of either 15 or 20 years and were struck at the market, resulting in a total premium of \$4.5 billion. They were not collateralized. Namely, the banks bore a huge counterparty risk when these put options, following the credit crunch of 2007 and 2008, went strongly in-the-money. Although Warren Buffet had to mark a huge loss on these options in those years, from the counterparty risk viewpoint he was happy to be on the 'right' side of the deal: in the 2007 Berkshire Hathaway annual report, he wrote "Two aspects of our derivative contracts are particularly important. First, in all cases we hold the money, which means that we have no counterparty risk. . . . "

For call options, we have provided all the details for pricing them in the previous sections. For put options, we can use the put-call parity as follows (recall that we assume deterministic risk-free short-term interest rates r). We know

$$Call\,(0, K, T) - Put\,(0, K, T) = Forw\,(0, K, T),$$

where

$$Forw\,(0, K, T) = \mathbb{E}\left[e^{-\int_0^T r(u)du} E(T)\right] - e^{-\int_t^T r(u)du} K.$$

One of the possible ways to compute the first expectation, by modification of the previous results, is as follows:

$$\begin{aligned}\mathbb{E}\left[e^{-\int_0^T r(u)du} E(T)\right] &= \mathbb{E}\left[e^{-\int_0^T r(u)du} 1_{\{V(s)>H(s),0\le s<T\}}[V(T) - H(T)]\right]\\ &= \mathbb{E}\left[e^{-\int_0^T r(u)du} 1_{\{V(s)>H(s),t<s<T\}}([V(T) - H(T)])^+\right]\end{aligned}$$

where the last passage comes from the presence of the default indicator and the continuity of $V(t)$ and $H(t)$. Now we have:

$$\begin{aligned}\mathbb{E}\left[e^{-\int_0^T r(u)du} E(T)\right] &= e^{-\int_0^T q(u)du}\mathbb{E}\left[e^{-\int_0^T (r(u)-q(u))du} 1_{\{V(s)>H(s),t<s<T\}}([V(T) - H(T)])^+\right]\\ &= e^{-\int_0^T q(u)du} E(0)\end{aligned}$$

where we have just used (8.13). This leads to the unsurprising result

$$Put\,(0, K, T) = Call\,(0, K, T) - e^{-\int_0^T q(u)du} E(0) + e^{-\int_0^T r(u)du} K$$

8.4.1 Deterministic Default Barrier

We have seen that the model with a deterministic barrier is sufficient to fit the market data of companies in moments of stability; here the only dependence we can produce between the counterparty default and the underlying equity is through correlation of the values of the firms. In this example we use as underlying equity a company with flat $\sigma(t) = 10\%$, and a barrier with $H = 0.7$. There are no expected dividends and the market interest rates are as of 9 April 2009. We take the value of the firm $V(0)$ as our unit, so that the equity price is $E(0) = 0.3$. The 1.5-year-maturity equity call options of such a company, if priced risk-free, have the prices and implied volatilities listed in Table 8.21, where the strikes

Table 8.21 Market data for a company used as an example. We list 1.5-year-maturity equity call options on 9 April 2009

Strike	0.8	0.9	1	1.1	1.2
Implied Vol	37.3%	35.7%	34.35%	33.16%	32.13%
Price	0.089	0.070	0.054	0.040	0.030

Table 8.22 Credit value adjustment of equity call options

$\rho\backslash K$	0.8	0.9	1	1.1	1.2
−1	0.01346	0.01221	0.01096	0.00971	0.00846
−0.75	0.01081	0.00957	0.00835	0.00716	0.00602
−0.5	0.00828	0.00712	0.00602	0.00499	0.00406
−0.25	0.00601	0.00500	0.00408	0.00327	0.00257
0	0.00408	0.00321	0.00247	0.00186	0.00136
0.25	0.00246	0.00185	0.00136	0.00098	0.00070
0.5	0.00121	0.00084	0.00057	0.00038	0.00026
0.75	0.00040	0.00026	0.00017	0.00013	0.00010
1	0.00013	0.00011	0.00010	0.00010	0.00009

Table 8.23 Monte Carlo uncertainty for the CVA of equity call options

$\rho\backslash K$	0.8	0.9	1	1.1	1.2
−1	0.00051	0.00046	0.00042	0.00037	0.00033
−0.75	0.00043	0.00039	0.00035	0.00031	0.00027
−0.5	0.00036	0.00032	0.00028	0.00025	0.00021
−0.25	0.00029	0.00025	0.00022	0.00019	0.00016
0	0	0	0	0	0
0.25	0.00016	0.00013	0.00011	0.00010	0.00008
0.5	0.00010	0.00009	0.00008	0.00007	0.00006
0.75	0.00007	0.00006	0.00006	0.00005	0.00005
1	0.00002	0.00002	0.00002	0.00002	0.00002

are expressed as percentages of the equity price. The prices of the equity options are computed analytically by (8.14).

The counterparty is a company with similar features but more risky, since it has $H = 0.8$ (still assuming $V(0) = 1$). For such a company the 1.5-year default probability is 7.6%, computed analytically by (8.4). We take the recovery to be $R = 40\%$. In this simple setting, we compute counterparty risk of calls and puts with 1.5 year maturity, under different assumptions about asset correlation, from -1 to $+1$.

In Table 8.22 we report the value of the credit valuation adjustment (CVA) for the above options with different strikes on the columns and different correlations on the rows. In Table 8.23 we report the corresponding Monte Carlo half-error window at 98% confidence. In case of $\rho = 0$ the analytic CVA is given by the product of the analytic option price and the analytic default probability, all multiplied by $(1 - R)$. Therefore the Monte Carlo error is 0. When the CVA is particularly low instead (see in particular the bottom of the table) and the Monte Carlo window risks including zero, we have increased the number of scenarios in simulation, so that the Monte Carlo window is reduced.[2]

[2] We recall that Monte Carlo simulation can be lengthy in the context of structural models, since monitoring when a continuous process crosses a barrier requires a very short Monte Carlo step (we used 300 steps per year). A solution to this computational burden would be Brownian Bridge methods.

We see immediately in Table 8.22 that the CVA decreases when the correlation increases, with no exceptions. The reason is simple. In a call option, the option buyer expects to receive the equity price at maturity if the option ends in-the-money. When the equity price of the underlying entity is high, we know that, by (8.13), also its firm value is high. If there is a positive correlation we expect that in these scenarios also the firm value of the counterparty is high and the probability of default is low. Since in the scenarios when the net present value of the option is high the risk of default is low, counterparty risk is reduced.

Since in the equity market correlation tends to be positive, and gets particularly high in times of crisis, a call option tends to be not very exposed to counterparty risk.

There is another feature to notice in Table 8.22. It is the behaviour of counterparty risk for different options with different strikes. We can summarize it as follows: the effect of correlation is stronger when the option is in-the-money, and weaker when it is out-of-the-money. In fact the growth of CVA when correlation decreases, and the decrease of CVA when correlation goes up, are strongest in the first column on the left and weakest in the last one. The reason for this is rather simple. CVA is the price of a payoff which is non-zero only conditional on default. The correlation modifies the expectation of the equity price conditional on default. Higher correlation means a lower conditional expected equity price, lower correlation means a higher conditional expected equity price. Therefore the sensitivity of an option to wrong way risk is similar to its sensitivity to the underlying equity price, namely it is similar to its *delta*, $\frac{\partial \, Call}{\partial E}$. The delta grows with moneyness. In Table 8.22 we are not seeing precisely the behaviour of a sensitivity since we consider discrete changes in correlation, but the patterns are approximately what we can expect knowing the behaviour of the delta sensitivity.

The above corrections may appear low, but they are not if we present them as percentages of the option price, as in Table 8.24.

Table 8.24 shows also that, for a fixed strike, when the correlation decreases and the CVA is higher in absolute terms, it is higher also as a percentage of the risk-free option price. To the contrary, the behaviour of CVA with strike appears almost reversed! Now the relevance of correlation or wrong way risk decreases with moneyness, with the exception of the highest correlation values. We can start from the above explanation of the *absolute* variations of the CVA to understand the patterns we see in Table 8.24, where we consider variations of the CVA *relative to the option price*. The delta, $\frac{\partial \, Call}{\partial E}$, increases with moneyness. But here we should not look at the delta – that measures absolute variations of the option price – but at the elasticity,

Table 8.24 CVA of equity call options as a percentage of the call price

$\rho \backslash K$	0.8	0.9	1	1.1	1.2
−1	15.17%	17.49%	20.45%	24.16%	28.80%
−0.75	12.19%	13.72%	15.59%	17.83%	20.48%
−0.5	9.33%	10.20%	11.23%	12.43%	13.83%
−0.25	6.77%	7.16%	7.62%	8.14%	8.75%
0	4.59%	4.59%	4.59%	4.59%	4.59%
0.25	2.77%	2.65%	2.54%	2.44%	2.37%
0.5	1.36%	1.20%	1.06%	0.96%	0.90%
0.75	0.45%	0.37%	0.32%	0.32%	0.35%
1	0.15%	0.16%	0.19%	0.24%	0.30%

Table 8.25 Market data for a company used as an example. We list 1.5-year-maturity equity put options on 9 April 2009

Strike	0.8	0.9	1	1.1	1.2
Implied Vol	37.3%	35.7%	34.35%	33.16%	32.13%
Price	0.021	0.031	0.044	0.059	0.077

that measures variations in the option price relative to the value of the option itself. Actually we have here a special case of elasticity

$$\left(\frac{\partial\, Call^1\left(E^1\right)}{\partial E^1}\right)/Call^2\left(E^2\right), \tag{8.16}$$

where the option $Call^1$ at numerator and the option $Call^2$ at denominator are evaluated with potentially different expectations of the underlying, E^1 and E^2. In fact the option $Call^2$ is a standard option where $E^2 = \mathbb{E}\left[E^{ref}(T)\right]$, the standard expectation of the equity price $E^{ref}(T)$ of the reference entity at maturity under the pricing measure, while $Call^1$ is the CVA of the option and therefore it is evaluated conditional to default by the counterparty, so that $E^1 = \mathbb{E}\left[E^{ref}(\tau)|E^{cr}(\tau)=0\right]$, where $E^{cr}(\tau)$ is the value of the equity of the counterparty at its own default time τ. The conditional expectation E^1 depends on correlation between counterparty and reference entity, in particular positive correlation means $E^1 < E^2$ while negative correlation means $E^1 > E^2$. The elasticity (8.16) decreases with moneyness (it increases with strike in the call case) except when $E^1 \ll E^2$. This is analogous to the behaviour we see in Table 8.24, where the effect of correlation decreases with moneyness except for the highest values of correlation.

We now consider put options with the same strikes as the call options considered above. The prices are listed in Table 8.25.

In Table 8.26 we present the CVA, in Table 8.27 the corresponding Monte Carlo half-window, and then in Table 8.28 the CVA expressed as a percentage of the option price.

Here we see that the relation between CVA and correlation is reversed. In a put option, the option buyer will see its payoff reduced by the equity value of the reference entity. His return will be higher when the equity value is lower. However, in a structural model lower

Table 8.26 Credit value adjustment of equity put options

$\rho\backslash K$	0.8	0.9	1	1.1	1.2
−1	0.00013	0.00013	0.00013	0.00013	0.00014
−0.75	0.00014	0.00015	0.00019	0.00025	0.00036
−0.5	0.00022	0.00031	0.00046	0.00069	0.00101
−0.25	0.00049	0.00073	0.00106	0.00150	0.00205
0	0.00099	0.00142	0.00196	0.00262	0.0038
0.25	0.00173	0.00237	0.00313	0.00400	0.00497
0.5	0.00274	0.00361	0.00460	0.00567	0.00680
0.75	0.00409	0.00520	0.00637	0.00758	0.00880
1	0.00593	0.00717	0.00841	0.00966	0.01090

Table 8.27 Monte Carlo uncertainty for the CVA of equity put options

$\rho\backslash K$	0.8	0.9	1	1.1	1.2
−1	0.00003	0.00003	0.00003	0.00003	0.00003
−0.75	0.00003	0.00003	0.00003	0.00003	0.00003
−0.5	0.00008	0.00008	0.00008	0.00009	0.00010
−0.25	0.00008	0.00009	0.00010	0.00012	0.00014
0	0	0	0	0	0
0.25	0.00012	0.00014	0.00017	0.00020	0.00023
0.5	0.00015	0.00018	0.00021	0.00025	0.00029
0.75	0.00019	0.00022	0.00026	0.00030	0.00035
1	0.00023	0.00027	0.00032	0.00036	0.00041

equity means lower firm value, corresponding to higher default probability. If there is positive correlation between the reference entity and the counterparty, for example for a common trend in the stock market, the option buyer expects higher credit risk exactly when he expects to receive more money from the option. The counterparty risk grows with correlation. Since correlation is usually positive in the equity market, an uncollateralized put option is particularly risky since it is negatively affected by wrong way risk. According to structural models, if the economy enters a crisis – when equity prices go down while risk of default and correlations go up – the puts buyer has a very high counterparty risk. This has recently been confirmed by the example of Warren Buffet and Berkshire Hathaway. For increasing correlation the counterparty risk is increasing, both in absolute terms, as one can see in Table 8.26, and as a percentage of the risk-free option price, as one can see in Table 8.28.

Also the relation between the effect of wrong way risk and the strike is reversed. We have that the absolute effect of correlation on CVA is stronger for higher strikes, while the relative effect appears stronger for lower strikes, apart from cases when correlation is negative. However a call is in-the-money for low strikes, while the put is in-the-money for high strikes, thus we are not surprised that the put options tables have patterns almost symmetric to the ones for the call options. Notice that for correlations equal to zero the CVA is always a constant proportion of the option price: when expressed in terms of the option value, it does not depend on the strike.

Table 8.28 CVA of equity put options as a percentage of the put price

$\rho\backslash K$	0.8	0.9	1	1.1	1.2
−1	0.62%	0.41%	0.29%	0.22%	0.18%
−0.75	0.67%	0.50%	0.43%	0.42%	0.47%
−0.5	1.05%	1.00%	1.05%	1.16%	1.31%
−0.25	2.36%	2.36%	2.43%	2.54%	2.65%
0	4.59%	4.59%	4.59%	4.59%	4.59%
0.25	8.34%	7.69%	7.17%	6.76%	6.42%
0.5	13.22%	11.72%	10.53%	9.56%	8.77%
0.75	19.77%	16.88%	14.59%	12.79%	11.36%
1	28.66%	23.27%	19.27%	16.30%	14.07%

8.4.2 Uncertainty on the Default Barrier

We introduced earlier a more general model with stochastic barrier, SBTV that appears particularly useful for explaining market quotes in moments of instability. Compared to the previous model with deterministic barrier, here we have another possible dependence between two counterparties, given by the joint distribution of the (now random) barriers. Also in this case, the model for one company requires no ad hoc extension to be applied to a multiname context like counterparty risk, since the two risk factors (the driving value of the firm and the random barrier) have a natural way to be put in relation to the corresponding factor of the model for another company. Additionally the two stochastic factors are each related to one of the two main kinds of credit interdependency analyzed in the literature.

As shown by [98], [116] points out that credit spreads are smoothly correlated due to the common dependence on smoothly varying macroeconomic factors. This is often called "cyclical default correlation". Additionally, as pointed out in [6] and confirmed by the recent crisis, there are also common sudden large changes in spreads, and at times the sudden default of a company is accompanied by very high spreads for related companies, and even by other defaults that follow closely. For example, in 2008 after the Lehman default, there were a number of other default events in one single month, including the joint default of three Icelandic banks. In particular, there was a joint default of eight financials in one month. This cannot be explained as a common dependence on smoothly varying macroeconomic factors, but rather as the consequence of business or financial or legal links between companies, or as the common dependence on unexpected and dramatic macroeconomic or sector scenarios. This phenomenon is often called "default contagion", and for a discussion of this in the different context of CDOs and multiname credit derivatives see [60].

The cyclical default correlation can be introduced in our model naturally by the instantaneous correlation in the dynamics of the asset value, as we have done for the model with deterministic barrier. Furthermore the randomness of the barrier introduced in the extended model allows us to introduce the non-smooth risk factors that lead to default contagion.

8.4.2.1 The Model

For simplicity we consider two companies, 1 and 2, for which the distribution of the barrier level allows for two scenarios:

$$\mathbf{H}_i = \begin{cases} H_i^h & \text{with prob } p_i^h \\ H_i^l & \text{with prob } p_i^l \end{cases}, \quad H_i^h > H_i^l, \quad i = 1, 2.$$

Considering that there are also two values of the firm V^1 and V^2 driven by two stochastic Brownian shocks W^1 and W^2, the elements in the model that control the default dependency are:

- The correlation of the diffusion shocks driving the values of the asset

$$\rho = corr\left(dW_t^1, dW_t^2\right) = \frac{d}{dt}\langle W^1, W^2\rangle_t.$$

  This naturally represents the amount of default dependency coming from smoothly varying common variables, related to equity correlation in non-stressed times.

- The multivariate joint distribution of $(\mathbf{H}_1, \mathbf{H}_2)$

$$(\mathbf{H}_1, \mathbf{H}_2) = \begin{cases} H_1^h, H_2^h & \text{with prob } p^{hh} \\ H_1^h, H_2^l & \text{with prob } p^{hl} \\ H_1^l, H_2^h & \text{with prob } p^{lh} \\ H_1^l, H_2^l & \text{with prob } p^{ll} \end{cases}.$$

This naturally represents the amount of default dependency coming from more abrupt contagion effects.

Two companies can have strong equity correlation, due to the general trend of common dependence on the global or national economy, while not experiencing contagion in case of default, and also the other way around: they can belong to two different countries or sectors and appear little correlated in normal times, but show strong links when approaching default. Maybe because, like Lehman and AIG in the credit crunch, the latter has sold protection on the former. It becomes interesting to see which level of flexibility the model gives us in representing the different cases, and what is the effect of the different assumptions.

There are three interesting extreme scenarios on the barriers:

1. Strong links: $p^{hh}, p^{ll} \gg p^{hl}, p^{lh}$ (positive dependence)
2. Scarcely related firms: $p^{ab} \approx p_1^a p_2^b$ (independence)
3. Competitors: $p^{hh}, p^{ll} \ll p^{hl}, p^{lh}$ (negative dependence).

The cases 1), 2) and 3) parallel, respectively, the gaussian copula default correlation cases $\rho \approx 1, \rho \approx 0, \rho \approx -1$. As in the Gaussian correlation case, the third case is quite unlikely and applies only to very special situations.

We get the marginal (individual) distributions from calibration of single-name data, and we aim at constructing a joint distribution both consistent with marginals and allowing for maximum positive dependence, maximum negative dependence, independence, and all intermediate situations. It is not difficult to verify that, once we know the marginals, the cumulative probability distribution

$$F_{\mathbf{H}_1,\mathbf{H}_2}(h_1, h_2) = \mathbb{Q}(\mathbf{H}_1 \leq h_1, \mathbf{H}_2 \leq h_2),$$

can be defined just by choosing for example p^{ll}. The following constraints must be respected:

- Joint probabilities need to be lower than marginal probabilities

$$p^{ll} \leq \min\left(p_1^l, p_2^l\right) \tag{8.17}$$

- All resulting probabilities must be non-negative, which means

$$\begin{aligned} p^{hl} &= p_2^l - p^{ll} \geq 0, \\ p^{lh} &= p_2^h - p^{hh} \geq 0, \\ p^{hh} &= 1 - p_2^l - p_1^l + p^{ll} \geq 0. \end{aligned} \tag{8.18}$$

The first two conditions of (8.18) are already guaranteed by (8.17), so the constraints summarize into:

$$\max\left(p_2^l + p_1^l - 1, 0\right) \leq p^{ll} \leq \min\left(p_1^l, p_2^l\right), \tag{8.19}$$

that clearly parallel the Fréchet-Hoeffding bounds of copula modelling. This shows how to obtain the three pivot stylized cases for the barrier dependence:

1. Maximum dependence $\longrightarrow p^{ll} = \min(p_1^l, p_2^l)$
2. Independence $\longrightarrow p^{ll} = p_1^l \cdot p_2^l$
3. Maximum negative dependence $\longrightarrow p^{ll} = \max(p_2^l + p_1^l - 1, 0)$.

8.4.2.2 Counterparty Risk in Equity Options under Uncertainty

As in the previous example we consider two firms, one is the underlying of an equity option and the other one is the option seller. The CVA is computed by the option buyer. The contract is not collateralized. The two firms have the same marginal distribution for default probabilities. They both have flat $\sigma(t) = 10\%$, and the following barrier distribution:

$$\mathbf{H} = \begin{cases} H^h = 0.95 & \text{with prob } 0.11 \\ H^l = 0.4 & \text{with prob } 0.89 \end{cases}.$$

This is the representation of a company for which there is a limited uncertainty about its real financial conditions. With high probability the company is solid. But with a small and yet non-negligible probability its financial conditions may turn out to be worse than expected, so much so that the company will be on the verge of default. This is not so different from FIAT when the speculators' run started on it, or from Parmalat before its crisis or Vodafone in the examples of [49].

For a company with the above parameters the 1.5-year default probability is 7.6%, as it was in the previous example with the deterministic barrier. There are no expected dividends and the market interest rates are as of 9 April 2009. We take the value of the firm $V(0)$ as our unit, so that the equity price is now $E(0) = 0.54$. The 1.5-year-maturity equity call options of such a company, if priced risk-free, have the prices and implied volatilities listed in Table 8.29.

The skew is steeper in this model with an uncertain barrier. We give the CVA of the above three options in Table 8.30, considering the pivot cases for wrong way risk given by $\rho = \{-1; 0, 1\}$ and by maximum negative dependence, independence and maximum positive dependence.

The first evidence is that different levels of barrier dependence have an effect with the same sign as the effect of correlation. For a call, whose payoff is higher the higher the equity price, the CVA is higher for higher antidependence, corresponding to the case with negative ρ. In fact the maximum CVA is obtained for $\rho = -1$ and maximum negative dependence of the barrier. The effect of the different strikes is the same as above: options in-the-money are more affected by wrong way risk, be it wrong way risk by barrier dependence or by Brownian asset correlations. Table 8.31 shows the CVA expressed as a fraction of the call option. The analogy between correlation and barrier dependence is confirmed also in relative terms; while the effect of strike is slightly less clear due to the presence of stochastic barriers, it is still similar to the one we found for deterministic barriers. This evidence will be confirmed by put options.

Table 8.29 Market data for a company used as example. We list 1.5-year-maturity equity call options on 9 April 2009

Strike	0.8	1	1.2
Implied Vol	40.02%	30.03%	24.35%
Price	0.165	0.086	0.034

Table 8.30 Credit value adjustment of equity call options

Max Neg Dep Barriers			
$\rho\backslash K$	0.8	1	1.2
−1	0.0104	0.0060	0.0025
0	0.0082	0.0043	0.0017
1	0.0059	0.0023	0.0006
Indep Barriers			
$\rho\backslash K$	0.8	1	1.2
−1	0.0093	0.0053	0.0022
0	0.0075	0.0039	0.0015
1	0.0053	0.0020	0.0005
Max Dep Barriers			
$\rho\backslash K$	0.8	1	1.2
−1	2.58E-05	1.04E-05	6.81E-06
0	1.89E-05	8.62E-06	5.78E-06
1	8.24E-06	6.73E-06	5.10E-06

Indeed, the results for put options confirm the observations made in the case of deterministic barriers, and the analogy between the role of correlations on the firm's value and the role of the barrier dependency. The prices of puts when priced risk-free are listed in Table 8.32.

Tables 8.33 and 8.34 show that for put options the highest CVA is when $\rho = 1$ and the barriers are perfectly dependent, while it is zero for negative dependence both on the barriers and on the firm's value.

Table 8.31 CVA of equity call options as a percentage of the call price

Max Neg Dep Barriers			
$\rho\backslash K$	0.8	1	1.2
−1	6.30%	6.98%	7.44%
0	4.97%	5.01%	5.06%
1	3.58%	2.68%	1.79%
Indep Barriers			
$\rho\backslash K$	0.8	1	1.2
−1	5.64%	6.17%	6.55%
0	4.55%	4.54%	4.46%
1	3.21%	2.33%	1.49%
Max Dep Barriers			
$\rho\backslash K$	0.8	1	1.2
−1	0.02%	0.01%	0.02%
0	0.01%	0.01%	0.02%
1	0.00%	0.01%	0.02%

Table 8.32 Market data for a company used as example. We list 1.5-year-maturity equity put options on 9 April 2009

Strike	0.8	1	1.2
Implied Vol	40.02%	30.03%	24.35%
Price	0.042	0.068	0.120

Table 8.33 Credit value adjustment of equity put options

Max Neg Dep Barriers

$\rho\backslash K$	0.8	1	1.2
−1	0	0.0002	0.0013
0	0.0001	0.0008	0.0028
1	0.0001	0.0012	0.0041

Indep Barriers

$\rho\backslash K$	0.8	1	1.2
−1	0.0015	0.0022	0.0037
0	0.0019	0.0031	0.0055
1	0.0022	0.0036	0.0067

Max Dep Barriers

$\rho\backslash K$	0.8	1	1.2
−1	0.0141	0.0187	0.0233
0	0.0163	0.0209	0.0256
1	0.0187	0.0233	0.0279

Table 8.34 CVA of equity put options as a percentage of the put price

Max Neg Dep Barriers

$\rho\backslash K$	0.8	1	1.2
−1	0.00%	0.30%	1.09%
0	0.24%	1.19%	2.34%
1	0.24%	1.78%	3.43%

Indep Barriers

$\rho\backslash K$	0.8	1	1.2
−1	3.54%	3.26%	3.10%
0	4.48%	4.59%	4.60%
1	5.19%	5.33%	5.61%

Max Dep Barriers

$\rho\backslash K$	0.8	1	1.2
−1	33.02%	27.70%	19.50%
0	38.44%	30.96%	21.42%
1	44.10%	34.52%	23.35%

Above we have pointed out the analogies between the effect of firm value correlation and the effect of Barrier Dependency. Now that we have seen all the results, we can also analyze the differences in the two effects. First, look at the effect of correlation when the barriers are assumed stochastic, different from the previous section, but kept independent. The effect of ρ is now much smaller compared to what we have seen with deterministic barriers in the previous sections. This makes sense: when the barriers are stochastic, default time and equity value depend on two sources of randomness. Now playing with ρ just affects one of the two, and does not create as much dependence as ρ did when the firm value was the only stochastic driver.

Looking at the put results, it appears quite clear that the barrier distribution is more relevant than the Brownian asset (Gaussian) correlation. This is an expected consequence of the companies we have chosen, which have low firm value volatility $\sigma(t) = 10\%$ and instead a barrier distribution that creates a dramatic difference in default probability between the optimistic and the pessimistic scenario (a bit more than zero in the optimistic scenario, almost 70% in the pessimistic scenario). When two companies are in such a situation, default contagion is the main worry. Other tests we made show that when we consider different companies, with higher volatility and less diverging H^l and H^u – a bit like BP during its crisis – the relevance of the two sources of correlation can reverse, and the correlation of the volatile firm values can be more important.

One final striking evidence is that in this example the CVA of Call options can be almost zero under some dependency assumptions and never grows above a single-digit percentage of the Call price. The CVA of Put options can never become negligible and in turn under the most unfavourable dependency assumptions can be almost 50% of the Put value. Can we explain these patterns? We have to look again at the distribution of the barriers. The case of two companies with a low probability of finding themselves in a very risky condition and a high probability of being instead in a more optimistic condition does not allow us to set much negative dependence between the two barriers. Look at the lower “Fréchet bound” of (8.19): it takes a value of 0.78, while in principle it can be as low as 0. In all Tables above, the case of maximum negative dependence is not so different from the independence case, due to the constraints set by the marginals, while the maximum positive dependence case is very different. In a market condition where the possibility of setting antidependence between the two default times is limited, clearly the benefit goes to the Call, for which antidependence is the most dangerous case, while the Put has no benefit.

We have found out a feature of this modelling framework: here the assumptions on the distribution of the individual companies affect how you can link them together. It is the lack of flexibility of this framework compared to reduced-form frameworks, but it may also be one of its added values. It makes financial sense that the individual situation of two companies affects in which way and in which measure their defaults can be related; and additionally in this example, the limit on how much negative correlation there can be in the equity market, and how countermonotonic two default times can be, corresponds to the analogous limits that one can observe in market reality.

Indeed, reduced-form models often have no such safeguards. We have seen in Section 7.4.1 that, when pushing the copula default correlation to its maximum value while having very low credit spread volatility, one obtains totally unrealistic results where the default of one name triggers the default of the other name at a future time that becomes known at the first default. This is a form of co-monotonicity that may lead to the misunderstanding of wrong way risk profiles, as we pointed out for the case of CVA for CDS again in Section 7.4.1. In this sense it is good news that the firm value models we analyzed here seem to avoid this problem.

9

Unilateral CVA for FX

In this chapter, based largely on Facchinetti and Morini (2008) [107], we evaluate the CVA of different kinds of Cross Currency Swap (CCS), an evaluation involving risk from interest rates, currency and credit. The issue has been particularly relevant during the credit crunch. In fact cross currency deals are a very popular hedging instrument against currency risk, and the large variations in exchange rates seen during the global financial crisis have meant many CCSs are deeply in-the-money for one party, which therefore bears a huge counterparty default risk when the counterparty has lower credit quality.

This chapter also deals with the concept of Novation, which is importantly related to Counterparty Risk and Contingent Credit Default Swaps. Although we will not be defining Novation explicitly in any chapter, clearly, much of what we say can be applied to Novation modelling.

In what follows we will focus on the simplified setting where, similarly to what was shown in Chapter 4, we assume independence of the underlying forward exchange rates and the credit risk of the counterparty. When it is acceptable to make this assumption, we can reduce the evaluation to easy and intuitive closed-form formulas. The closed-form formulas will be based on drift freezing techniques which are the same as those used in the literature on the LIBOR market model (or BGM models) when pricing plain-vanilla interest rate products such as swaptions: see, for example, [48]. Notice that the independence assumption is a relatively standard and usual choice when the CCS is written on the rate of exchange between widespread currencies such as the Dollar or Euro, or when the deal has large international companies as counterparties. However, this assumption must be handled carefully when the CCS involves the currency of an emerging market country, which is also the centre of the business of the risky counterparty. In this case the presence of wrong way risk or right way risk is very likely. Since it can be very difficult to estimate the correct correlation between the underlying rate of exchange and the risk of default of the counterparty, the zero-correlation framework below may remain an easy benchmark, but one must be aware that choosing a zero correlation can lead to an underestimation or overestimation of the CVA and is by no means a neutral assumption. It is also an assumption that neglects the impact of systemic risk.

Even in case of independence between counterparty credit risk and the market risk of the underlying FX rates, the problem keeps some complexity because one has to take into account correctly the correlations among forward rates of exchange, market quantities that involve a spot rate of exchange and bonds coming from the term structures of two different currencies. In fact, we will devote some room to the parameterization of such correlations. This whole chapter, similarly to Chapter 4 , is an illustration of how – even when assuming zero dependence between underlying and counterparty default – calculating CVA can still be a very complex option pricing problem.

The reader will notice that in our treatment of CCS we do not consider an element of complexity which is well known to CCS traders: the presence of the so-called cross currency basis. The two most liquid cross currency derivatives, FX forwards and CCS, have payoffs that appear very easy to replicate. The FX forwards, in fact, correspond to the exchange of two zero coupon bonds, one in domestic currency and one in foreign currency, while the standard CCS appears to be the combination of two positions, one long and one short, in a domestic floating rate bond and in a foreign one. However, the prices of market FX forwards and CCS deviate from the price of the replications, and this deviation is the basis. The existence of the CCS basis is documented even before the credit crisis that started in 2007. It was pointed out by [29] that since CCS are exchanges of floating rate bonds and floating rate bonds are always worth par at inception, once the notional of the domestic currency leg is equal to the notional of the foreign leg converted in domestic currency, the CCS should be fair. "But in practice" as people say, the CCS is quoted at par only if "there is a certain spread, called cross currency basis spread, on the top of the floating rate of one leg of the basis swap". Even earlier [191] say that cross currency swaps are "normally quoted as USD LIBOR versus the foreign currency plus or minus a spread".

The reason why we assume in the following that CCS is at par with no need for a basis, is that the most up-to-date theory explaining the cross currency basis makes it depend on the collateralization of CCS quoted in the market. Since when we speak about CVA we are implicitly assuming non- or partial collateralization of the underlying derivative, we will see that according to this theory the market-quoted basis should not affect the valuation of the CVA of non-collateralized CCS.

The chapter is organized as follows: in Section 9.1 we look at foundations for multicurrency products pricing. We recall the main no-arbitrage results in such context, with a treatment that is similar to the analysis in Chapter 2 of [48]. In Section 9.2 we start analyzing unilateral CVA for CCS with fixed legs, resorting to a formula based on a stream of cross currency swaptions. In particular, in Section 9.2.1 we deal with a volatility approximation for CCS swap rates that becomes very important for calculating UCVA for CCS, and in Section 9.2.2 we focus on correlations between different forward FX rates, which are needed to compute the CCS swap volatility formula, leading to a simple formula for CVA of the CCS. Section 9.3 analyzes CVA when the CCS has a floating leg. Section 9.4 discusses the basis, which we ignore in the rest of the chapter, and explains why a basis is now present in the CCS market, mostly because LIBOR is not risk free and several discount curves are now present in the market. In Section 9.5 we summarize our findings and show some important examples of CVA for CCS. Section 9.6 analyzes an instrument that can be used to cover counterparty risk and is similar to a synthetic contingent credit default swap: Novation. In particular, Section 9.6.2 explains how to extend the framework by including liquidity, so as to be able to price Novations properly.

In order to understand the following results, we need first to revise the foundations of cross currency modelling, to which we now turn.

9.1 PRICING WITH TWO CURRENCIES: FOUNDATIONS

Since we need to model simultaneously two markets, we have to understand how the standard concept of no-arbitrage is translated in this context (see [48] for a more extended treatment). We start by considering prices of securities before introducing interest rates. We indicate foreign prices or foreign rates (in foreign currency) by superscript ^{f}.

Consider the foreign tradable asset X^f paying X_T^f at T. For the foreign investor, standard single-currency no-arbitrage pricing for the foreign market implies that its price is the discounted expectation of the payoff under the foreign risk-neutral measure, associated with the foreign bank account.

$$X_0^f = B_0^f \mathbb{E}_0^f \left[\frac{X_T^f}{B_T^f} \right]$$

where B_t^f is the foreign bank account at time t and $\mathbb{Q}^f$ is the associated risk-neutral measure.

What is the price of this security for a domestic investor? We need to define φ_t, the rate of exchange:

$$\varphi_t = \text{amount of domestic currency for a unit of foreign currency}$$

and, in particular,

$$X_0 = \varphi_0 X_0^f, \quad X_T = \varphi_T X_T^f.$$

Because of the definition of exchange rate, for the domestic investor, the above investment is an asset with price

$$X_0 = \varphi_0 X_0^f = \varphi_0 B_0^f \mathbb{E}_0^f \left[\frac{X_T^f}{B_T^f} \right]. \tag{9.1}$$

Moreover a domestic investor has another way of looking at this product. For a domestic investor this product has a payoff $\varphi_T X_T^f$ at T . Therefore standard single-currency no-arbitrage pricing for the domestic market implies that its price is the discounted expectation of this payoff under the domestic risk-neutral measure, associated with the domestic bank account.

$$X_0 = B_0 \mathbb{E}_0 \left[\frac{\varphi_T X_T^f}{B_T} \right]. \tag{9.2}$$

The required no-arbitrage consistency between these two prices of the same asset, (9.1) and (9.2), gives the following relationship

$$\mathbb{E}_0^f \left[\frac{\varphi_0 B_0^f}{\varphi_T B_T^f} X_T \right] = \mathbb{E}_0 \left[\frac{B_0}{B_T} X_T \right] \tag{9.3}$$

or equivalently

$$\mathbb{E}_0^f \left[\frac{B_0^f}{B_T^f} X_T^f \right] = \mathbb{E}_0 \left[\frac{B_0/\varphi_0}{B_T/\varphi_T} X_T^f \right]. \tag{9.4}$$

There are two points worth noticing here. The first one is that the above equations constrain the stochastic behaviour of at least one variable among foreign interest rates, domestic interest rates and the rate of exchange. In fact we can assume that the strategy with payoff X_T^f is simply what one foreign investor gets investing B_0^f at 0 in the foreign bank account, namely $X_T^f = B_T^f$. By recalling that we typically assume

$$dB_t = r^d(t) B_t dt, \quad dB_t^f = r^f(t) B_t^f dt,$$

with r^d and r^f adapted processes for the short-term interest rates of the two currencies (domestic and foreign respectively), we have from (9.4) with $X_T^f = B_T^f$,

$$\mathbb{E}_0\left[\frac{e^{\int_0^T r^f(s)ds}}{e^{\int_0^T r^d(s)ds}}\frac{\varphi_T}{\varphi_0}\right] = 1, \tag{9.5}$$

where r^d and r^f are the short rates used for discounting that in this classic context coincide with the risk-free rates of the two currencies. We see that the growth of the rate of exchange must match, in expectation, the ratio between the foreign and the domestic bank accounts. One can derive similarly the equation:

$$\mathbb{E}_t\left[\frac{e^{\int_t^T r^f(s)ds}}{e^{\int_t^T r^d(s)ds}}\frac{\varphi_T}{\varphi_t}\right] = 1, \quad \text{for all } 0 \leq t \leq T. \tag{9.6}$$

This makes sense. For the market to be arbitrage free, if one expects to gain much more from a risk-free investment in the foreign currency compared to an analogous investment in the domestic currency, this must be matched by an expected decrease in the value of the domestic currency.

By using the fact that t and T are completely arbitrary, one may deduce that if we assume a dynamics of the rate of exchange given by

$$d\varphi_t = \mu_t \varphi_t dt + \sigma_t \varphi_t dW_t,$$

with μ_t and σ_t adapted processes and W a Brownian motion under the domestic risk-neutral measure with numeraire B^d, then (9.6) considered over all possible t and T implies

$$\mu_t = r^d(t) - r^f(t),$$

saying that the drift of the rate to exchange the foreign currency with the domestic one under the risk-neutral measure of the domestic currency is the difference between the risk-free rate of the domestic currency and that of the foreign one, a well-known result, for example, see [48]. An immediate informal proof may be obtained by taking $T = t + dt$ for vanishingly small dt. This no-arbitrage relation, that applies to a world of risk-free discount rates, will be useful later when it comes to understanding the presence of the basis in collateralized CCS.

The second point to make on (9.3) and (9.4) is that these relations look like a change of numeraire, and they are telling us which numeraires we have to consider if we want to treat this change of measure exactly as a change of numeraire. As shown in [48], we are moving between numeraire B_t^f, the foreign bank account, and numeraire B_t/φ_t, the domestic bank account expressed in foreign currency, or equivalently between numeraire $\varphi_t B_t^f$, the foreign bank account expressed in domestic currency, and numeraire B_t, the domestic bank account. The latter expression has the advantage of not altering our definition of the domestic risk-neutral measure, and we will follow this. Obviously, we need to express quantities in the same currency for finding no-arbitrage relationships.

The above relationships can be summarized saying that X_t^f *is a foreign tradable asset IFF* $\varphi_t X_t^f$ *is a domestic tradable asset.*

For forward measures, a chain of measure changes leads to

$$P^f(0,T)\,\mathbb{E}_0^{\mathbb{Q}^{fT}}\left[X_T^f\right] = P(0,T)\,\mathbb{E}_0^{\mathbb{Q}^T}\left[\frac{\varphi_T}{\varphi_0}X_T^f\right].$$

The above relationship shows that to change from $\mathbb{Q}^{N1} = \mathbb{Q}^{fT}$ (*foreign*) to $\mathbb{Q}^{N2} = \mathbb{Q}^T$ (*domestic*) we have:

$$\frac{N1_T N2_0}{N1_0 N2_T} = \frac{P(0,T)}{P(T,T)}\frac{\varphi_T P^f(T,T)}{\varphi_0 P^f(0,T)},$$

so that $N1_t = P^f(t,T)$, $N2_t = P(t,T)/\varphi_t$, or equivalently $N1_t = P^f(t,T)\varphi_t$, $N2_t = P(t,T)$.

In introducing foreign forward measures we have used a new symbol $P^f(0,T)$; the price of a foreign bond. Using foreign numeraire and measure, it is obviously defined as

$$P^f(0,T) = \mathbb{E}_0^f\left[\frac{B_0^f}{B_T^f}\right] = \mathbb{E}_0^f\left[D^f(0,T)\right]$$

but now that we have a relationship between foreign and domestic pricing it is useful to see it also from a domestic point of view:

$$P^f(0,T) = \frac{\mathbb{E}_0\left[D(0,T)\varphi_T\right]}{\varphi_0}. \tag{9.7}$$

The domestic price is $P^f(0,T)\varphi_0$. We can now define both *domestic forward rates*

$$F_i^d(t) = \frac{1}{(T_i - T_{i-1})}\left[\frac{P(t,T_{i-1})}{P(t,T_i)} - 1\right],$$

foreign forward rates

$$F_i^f(t) = \frac{1}{(T_i - T_{i-1})}\left[\frac{P^f(t,T_{i-1})}{P^f(t,T_i)} - 1\right],$$

and the *forward exchange rate*

$$\Phi_i(t) = \frac{P^f(t,T_i)}{P(t,T_i)/\varphi_t} = \frac{\varphi_t P^f(t,T_i)}{P(t,T_i)}. \tag{9.8}$$

The latter definition can be derived from a contract entered at t to buy at T_i one unit of foreign currency for $\Phi_i(0)$ domestic units of currency, and imposing the contract to be fair at inception

$$\mathbb{E}_0\left[D(0,T_i)\left(\varphi_{T_i} - \Phi_i(0)\right)\right] = 0,$$

leading to

$$\mathbb{E}_0\left[D(0,T_i)\varphi_{T_i}\right] = P(0,T_i)\,\Phi_i(0),$$

$$\Phi_i(0) = \frac{\mathbb{E}_0\left[D(0,T_i)\varphi_{T_i}\right]}{P(0,T_i)} \overset{\text{by (9.7)}}{=} \frac{\varphi_0 P^f(0,T_i)}{P(0,T_i)}.$$

The foreign forward rates are martingales under their natural foreign forward measures $\mathbb{Q}^{if}$. The quotation standard market model assumes they are log-normal

$$\boxed{dF_i^f(t) = \sigma_i^f F_i^f(t)\, dV_i^{if}(t)}$$

where V^{if} is a Brownian motion under $\mathbb{Q}^{if}$. We can see their dynamics under the domestic measure $\mathbb{Q}^i$. We need the diffusion coefficient of the numeraire ratio which is now $\frac{N1}{N2} = \frac{P^f(t,T)\varphi_t}{P(t,T)}$. Notice that this is $\Phi_i(t)$, the forward exchange rate. This variable is a martingale under $\mathbb{Q}^i$, since it is given by the price of an asset tradable in the domestic market divided by the domestic numeraire of $\mathbb{Q}^i$. In the market there are options on the foreign exchange rate, and their quotation standard implies a lognormal dynamic for the forward exchange rate,

$$d\Phi_i(t) = \sigma_i \Phi_i(t)\, dW_i^i(t)$$

where W^i is a Brownian motion under $\mathbb{Q}^i$. This implies that, under the domestic measure $\mathbb{Q}^i$, the foreign forward rates have dynamics

$$dF_i^f(t) = -F_i^f(t)\sigma_i^f \sigma_i \rho_i^f + \sigma_i^f F_i^f(t)\, dV_i^i(t),$$

where V^i is a Brownian motion under $\mathbb{Q}^i$ and $\rho_i^f dt = dV_i^i(t) dW_i^i(t)$.

9.2 UNILATERAL CVA FOR A FIXED-FIXED CCS

A cross currency swap (CCS) may involve the payment of fixed legs in different currencies and floating interest rate legs indexed to different currencies. Differing from quanto derivatives, however, there is no mismatch between indexation and currency of payments. What makes it difficult to evaluate the unilateral counterparty risk in CCS is that in the presence of counterparty default risk we need to compute the expectation of the positive part of the CCS net present value at the default time τ of the counterparty,

$$\mathbb{E}_t\left[1_{\{\tau<T\}} D(t,\tau) \left(NPV_\tau^{CCS}\right)^+\right],$$

introducing an optionality (and a dependency on volatilities and correlations) that was not present in a default-free CCS. If we use the bucketing assumption and the independence assumptions (the latter is always adopted in this chapter), leading to the ICVAA definition we have seen in Section 2.3, then we end up pricing a stream of Cross Currency Swaptions, which are not liquid products in the market.

A typical fixed-fixed cross currency swap between two counterparties A and B involves the following payments, on a grid $[T_0, \ldots, T_M]$ with $T_i - T_{i-1} =: \alpha_i$:

Initial exchange:

- At T_0 Party A pays N^f in foreign currency to Party B.
- At T_0 Party B pays N in domestic currency to Party A. Consistently with market practice we assume $N = \varphi_0 N^f$ so there is no real exchange.

Running Legs:

- Domestic fixed leg: at T_i $(i = 1, \ldots, M)$ Party A pays the deterministic quantity $N\alpha_i K(T_i)$ in domestic currency.
- Foreign fixed leg: at T_i $(i = 1, \ldots, M)$ Party B pays the deterministic quantity $N^f \alpha_i K^f(T_i)$ in foreign currency.

Final exchange:

- At T_M Party A pays N in domestic currency to Party B.
- At T_M Party B pays N^f in foreign currency to Party A.

In the following we show how to evaluate in closed-form the Net Present Value or Exposure of the residual CCS at any fixing date $T_i \geq T_0$ included in the swap tenor structure. This Exposure (with sign) is, to the receiver of the domestic leg, i.e. B,

$$\begin{aligned}\mathrm{Exs}(T_i, T_M) := \mathbb{E}_{T_i} \Bigg[& N \sum_{j=i+1}^{M} \alpha_j D(T_i, T_j) K(T_j) + \\ & -N^f \sum_{j=i+1}^{M} \alpha_j \varphi_j D(T_i, T_j) K^f(T_j) + \left(N - \varphi_M N^f\right) D(T_i, T_M) \Bigg]\end{aligned}$$

where $\varphi_j = \varphi_{T_j}$ and the expectation is taken under the domestic risk-neutral measure. In the following the second argument T_M is omitted when clear from the context. We also show how, under the assumption of credit risk independent of the underlying, one can compute in closed-form formula the value of an option on the above NPV,

$$\mathbb{E}_t \left[D(t, T_i)(\mathrm{Exs}(T_i))^+ \right].$$

This is all we need to compute the unilateral CVA since

$$\begin{aligned} NPV^D(0) &= NPV(0) - CVA(0), \\ CVA(0) &= \mathrm{L{\scriptsize GD}}\, \mathbb{E}_0 \left[1_{\{0 \leq \tau \leq T_M\}} D(0, \tau)(\mathrm{Exs}(\tau))^+ \right] \end{aligned}$$

and, as in Chapter 4 for an IRS, when default risk is independent of the underlying, we can simplify the computation by assuming that default can happen only at point T_i of the grid of payments for the two legs. Thus, assuming postponed default, we have:

$$ICVAA^P(0) = \mathrm{L{\scriptsize GD}} \sum_{i=1}^{M} \mathbb{Q}\{\tau \in (T_{i-1}, T_i]\} \mathbb{E}_0 \left[D(0, T_i)(\mathrm{Exs}(T_i))^+ \right], \quad (9.9)$$

while in the case of anticipated payoff we obtain

$$ICVAA^A(0) = \mathrm{L{\scriptsize GD}} \sum_{i=0}^{M-1} \mathbb{Q}\{\tau \in (T_i, T_{i+1}]\} \mathbb{E}_0 \left[D(0, T_i)(\mathrm{Exs}(T_i))^+ \right]. \quad (9.10)$$

We see in the following that, while $\mathrm{Exs}(T_i)$ can be computed following standard techniques, computing $\mathbb{E}_0 \left[D(0, T_i)(\mathrm{Exs}(T_i))^+ \right]$ requires some more effort, also because options on CCS are not a liquid product like options on IRS (swaptions), so that one does not have ready made market quotes and needs to devise a pricing methodology consistent with market standards.

We now rewrite $\mathrm{Exs}(T_i)$ in a way that makes it as comfortable as possible to compute the CCS option price. Switching to *domestic T_i-forward measure*:

$$\mathrm{Exs}(T_i) = N \sum_{j=i+1}^{M} \alpha_j P(T_i, T_j) K(T_j) - N^f \sum_{j=i+1}^{M} \alpha_j \mathbb{E}_{T_i}^{j}[\varphi_j] P(T_i, T_j) K^f(T_j)$$
$$+ \left(N - \mathbb{E}_{T_i}^{M}[\varphi_M] N^f\right) P(T_i, T_M).$$

Notice that $\mathbb{E}_{T_i}^{j}[\varphi_j] = \mathbb{E}_{T_i}^{j}[\Phi_j(T_j)]$ and $\Phi_j(t) = \varphi_t \frac{P^f(t,T_j)}{P(t,T_j)}$ is a martingale under the measure T_j-forward, so

$$\mathrm{Exs}(T_i) = N \sum_{j=i+1}^{M} \alpha_j P(T_i, T_j) K(T_j) - N^f \sum_{j=i+1}^{M} \alpha_j P(T_i, T_j) \Phi_j(T_i) K^f(T_j)$$
$$+ \left(N - \Phi_j(T_i) N^f\right) P(T_i, T_M). \tag{9.11}$$

First, we define for the foreign leg

$$K_j^f \equiv \begin{cases} \dfrac{K^f(T_j)}{\varphi_0} & j = i+1, \ldots, M-1 \\ \dfrac{K^f(T_j) + 1/\alpha_M}{\varphi_0} & j = M \end{cases}$$

so that we have:

$$\mathrm{Exs}(T_i) = N \left[\sum_{j=i+1}^{M} \alpha_j P(T_i, T_j) K(T_j) - \frac{N^f}{N} \sum_{j=i+1}^{M} \alpha_j P(T_i, T_j) \Phi_j(T_i) K^f(T_j) \right.$$
$$\left. + \left(1 - \frac{\Phi_M(T_i) N^f}{N}\right) P(T_i, T_M) \right]$$
$$= N \left[\sum_{j=i+1}^{M} \alpha_j P(T_i, T_j) K(T_j) - \frac{1}{\varphi_0} \sum_{j=i+1}^{M} \alpha_j P(T_i, T_j) \Phi_j(T_i) K^f(T_j) \right.$$
$$\left. + \left(1 - \frac{\Phi_M(T_i)}{\varphi_0}\right) P(T_i, T_M) \right]$$
$$= N \left[\sum_{j=i+1}^{M} \alpha_j P(T_i, T_j) K(T_j) - \sum_{j=i+1}^{M} \alpha_j K_j^f P(T_i, T_j) \Phi_j(T_i) + P(T_i, T_M) \right].$$

Then we look at the domestic leg and we define

$$K_j \equiv \begin{cases} K(T_j) & j = i+1, \ldots, M-1 \\ K(T_j) + 1/\alpha_M & j = M \end{cases}$$

that is:

$$\mathrm{Exs}(T_i) = N \left[\sum_{j=i+1}^{M} \alpha_j K_j P(T_i, T_j) - \sum_{j=i+1}^{M} \alpha_j K_j^f P(T_i, T_j) \Phi_j(T_i) \right]$$

Just like a standard swap, we look for the common *fair domestic fixed rate*, namely the rate $K_{i,M}^{eq}(T_i)$ setting the NPV to zero at inception when

$$K_{i+1} = K_{i+2} = \ldots = K_M = K_{i,M}^{eq}(T_i).$$

We obtain

$$K_{i,M}^{eq}(T_i) = \frac{\sum_{j=i+1}^{M} \alpha_j K_j^f P(T_i, T_j)\, \Phi_j(T_i)}{\sum_{j=i+1}^{M} \alpha_j P(T_i, T_j)}$$

and

$$\mathrm{Exs}(T_i) = N \left[\sum_{j=i+1}^{M} \alpha_j K_j P(T_i, T_j) - K_{i,M}^{eq}(T_i) \sum_{j=i+1}^{M} \alpha_j P(T_i, T_j) \right].$$

Like a standard swap, we find that the equilibrium rate is a weighted average of the underlying variables. Here, however, the variables are forward exchange rates rather than forward interest rates, and, unlike a standard swap, the weights do not sum up to 1.

To understand the reason for this difference, we compute the *effective foreign rate*, namely the flat rate that leaves unchanged the NPV of the foreign leg,

$$\widetilde{K^f}_{i,M}(T_i) \sum_{j=i+1}^{M} \alpha_j P(T_i, T_j)\, \Phi_j(T_i) = \sum_{j=i+1}^{M} \alpha_j K_j^f P(T_i, T_j)\, \Phi_j(T_i),$$

that is:

$$\begin{aligned}\widetilde{K^f}_{i,M}(T_i) &= \frac{\sum_{j=i+1}^{M} \alpha_j K_j^f P(T_i, T_j)\, \Phi_j(T_i)}{\sum_{j=i+1}^{M} \alpha_j P(T_i, T_j)\, \Phi_j(T_i)} = \frac{\sum_{j=i+1}^{M} \alpha_j K_j^f P(T_i, T_j)\, \varphi_{T_i} \frac{P^f(T_i, T_j)}{P(T_i, T_j)}}{\sum_{j=i+1}^{M} \alpha_j P(T_i, T_j)\, \varphi_{T_i} \frac{P^f(T_i, T_j)}{P(T_i, T_j)}} \\ &= \sum_{j=i+1}^{M} \frac{\alpha_j P^f(T_i, T_j)}{\sum_{k=i+1}^{M} \alpha_k P^f(T_i, T_k)} K_j^f = \sum_{j=i+1}^{M} \varpi_j^f(T_i)\, K_j^f \end{aligned} \tag{9.12}$$

where the weights

$$\varpi_j^f(T_i) := \frac{\alpha_j P^f(T_i, T_j)}{\sum_{k=i+1}^{M} \alpha_k P^f(T_i, T_k)}$$

are the same as those that appear when expressing the foreign swap rate in terms of foreign forward rates, and sum up to 1.

We go back to the fair domestic rate, which can now be written as

$$\begin{aligned} K^{eq}_{i,M}(T_i) &= \widetilde{K^f}_{i,M}(T_i) \frac{\sum_{j=i+1}^{M} \alpha_j P(T_i, T_j)\, \Phi_j(T_i)}{\sum_{k=i+1}^{M} \alpha_k P(T_i, T_k)} \\ &= \widetilde{K^f}_{i,M}(T_i) \sum_{j=i+1}^{M} \frac{\alpha_j P(T_i, T_j)}{\sum_{k=i+1}^{M} \alpha_k P(T_i, T_k)} \Phi_j(T_i) \\ &= \widetilde{K^f}_{i,M}(T_i) \sum_{j=i+1}^{M} \varpi_j(T_i)\, \Phi_j(T_i). \end{aligned}$$

Here too the weights

$$\varpi_j(T_i) := \frac{\alpha_j P(T_i, T_j)}{\sum_{k=i+1}^{M} \alpha_k P(T_i, T_k)}$$

are the same as those that appear when expressing the domestic swap rate in terms of domestic forward rates, and sum up to 1.

In order to obtain a more convenient way to write down the (unaltered) NPV

$$\mathrm{Exs}(T_i) = N \left[\sum_{j=i+1}^{M} \alpha_j K_j P(T_i, T_j) - K^{eq}_{i,M}(T_i) \sum_{j=i+1}^{M} \alpha_j P(T_i, T_j) \right]$$

we introduce also the *effective domestic rate* $\widetilde{K}_{i,M}(T_i)$:

$$\widetilde{K}_{i,M}(T_i) \sum_{j=i+1}^{M} \alpha_j P(T_i, T_j) = \sum_{j=i+1}^{M} \alpha_j P(T_i, T_j) K_j$$

that is:

$$\widetilde{K}_{i,M}(T_i) = \sum_{j=i+1}^{M} \frac{\alpha_j P(T_i, T_j)}{\sum_{j=i+1}^{M} \alpha_j P(T_i, T_j)} K_j = \sum_{j=i+1}^{M} \varpi_j(T_i) K_j,$$

and the usual considerations on the weights apply. We have reached a convenient expression for the net present value of the CCS

$$\mathrm{Exs}(T_i) = N \sum_{j=i+1}^{M} \alpha_j P(T_i, T_j) \left(\widetilde{K}_{i,M}(T_i) - K^{eq}_{i,M}(T_i) \right). \tag{9.13}$$

We have to calculate the expected value of the *positive part* of residual NPV:

$$Ex(T_i) = (\mathrm{Exs}(T_i))^+ = N \sum_{j=i+1}^{M} \alpha_j P(T_i, T_j) \left(\widetilde{K}_{i,M}(T_i) - K^{eq}_{i,M}(T_i) \right)^+.$$

The expectations of the CCS payoff did not involve volatilities and correlations (or marginal distributions and dependency evolutions), but now we have moved to an option, therefore we have to perform an assessment based on the volatilities and correlations of the relevant variables involved.

There are three crucial variables in the valuation of this payoff: the foreign and domestic effective rates, and the fair CCS rate, given by:

$$\widetilde{K^f}_{i,M}(t) = \sum_{j=i+1}^{M} \varpi_j^f(t)\, K_j^f$$

$$\widetilde{K}_{i,M}(t) = \sum_{j=i+1}^{M} \varpi_j(t)\, K_j$$

$$K_{i,M}^{eq}(t) = \widetilde{K^f}_{i,M}(t) \sum_{j=i+1}^{M} \varpi_j(t)\, \Phi_j(t).$$

They are all weighted sums of more elementary variables, as the standard swap rate $S_{i,M}(t)$ is a weighted sum of standard forward rates $F_j(t)$, and additionally *weights* $\varpi_j(t)$ *are exactly the same as in the case of the swap rate*. For the effective foreign rate, obviously, we have to consider the foreign swap rate.

Therefore we follow the approach which is typical of the application of the LIBOR and Swap market models to interest rate derivatives. The variability of the weights $\varpi_j(t)$ is shown by [30], [175] and [48] to be very low. This is shown both by Monte Carlo simulation and by historical analysis, and has led to the standard market approximation for the swap rate volatility in the LIBOR market model, when one assumes for $t > 0$

$$\varpi_j(t) \approx \varpi_j(0) = \varpi_j \quad \text{(weights freezing)}.$$

According to this approximation, $\widetilde{K}_{i,M}(t)$ and $\widetilde{K^f}_{i,M}(t)$ can be treated as deterministic quantities $\widetilde{K}_{i,M} = \widetilde{K}_{i,M}(0)$ and $\widetilde{K^f}_{i,M} = \widetilde{K^f}_{i,M}(0)$, while the crucial stochastic quantity $K_{i,M}^{eq}(t)$ can be written as a linear combination of forward exchange rates. This corresponds to the approach in Chapter 4 (see also [47]) for interest rate swaps with maturity-dependent or tenor-dependent strikes, and allows us to compute the CCS credit risk adjustment in closed form. The low variability of the weights is usually intuitively motivated by recalling that

$$\varpi_j(t) = \frac{\alpha_j P(t, T_j)}{\sum_{k=i+1}^{M} \alpha_k P(t, T_k)} = \frac{\frac{P(t,T_j)}{P(t,T_i)}\alpha_j}{\sum_{k=i+1}^{M} \frac{P(t,T_k)}{P(t,T_i)}\alpha_k}$$

$$= \frac{\alpha_j \prod_{h=i+1}^{j} \frac{1}{1+\alpha_h F_h(t)}}{\sum_{k=i+1}^{M} \alpha_k \prod_{h=i+1}^{k} \frac{1}{1+\alpha_h F_h(t)}}$$

and we have a specific functional form with forward rates both at the denominator and at the numerator, which causes their volatility to cancel out. As a warning, we remind you that this is essentially true for parallel movements of the term structure for rates; but it can be a less good approximation for movements of principal components of a higher order.

In our application we need to evaluate:

$$\mathbb{E}_t\left[D(t,T_i)(\text{Exs}(T_i))^+\right] = N\mathbb{E}_t\left[D(t,T_i)\left(\widetilde{K}_{i,M} - K^{eq}_{i,M}(T_i)\right)^+ \sum_{j=i+1}^{M} \alpha_j P(T_i,T_j)\right]$$
$$= N\sum_{j=i+1}^{M} \alpha_j P(t,T_j)\,\mathbb{E}_t^{i,M}\left[\left(\widetilde{K}_{i,M} - K^{eq}_{i,M}(T_i)\right)^+\right]$$

where in the last passage we switched to the domestic swap measure with numeraire $C_{i,M}$ whose expression at time t is given by:

$$C_{i,M}(t) = \sum_{j=i+1}^{M} \alpha_j P(t,T_j)$$

(see, for example, the change of numeraire toolkit in [48]). What are the drift and the volatility of the underlying $K^{eq}_{i,M}(t)$ under this swap pricing measure?

9.2.1 Approximating the Volatility of Cross Currency Swap Rates

We already know that again, similar analogously to the standard swap rate $S_{i,M}(t)$, $K^{eq}_{i,M}(t)$ is a martingale under the pricing swap measure, since

$$K^{eq}_{i,M}(t) \approx \widetilde{Kf}_{i,M} \frac{\sum_{j=i+1}^{M} \alpha_j P(t,T_j)\,\Phi_j(t)}{\sum_{j=i+1}^{M} \alpha_j P(t,T_j)}. \tag{9.14}$$

Thus there will be no drift in the dynamics. As for the volatility, we have to start from the dynamics of the forward exchange rates $\Phi_j(t)$. If we want to be consistent with the standard market model for foreign exchange options, we have to assume that $\Phi_j(t)$ are lognormal martingales under their natural measures. We know from the literature on the LIBOR market model that a linear combination of lognormal variables, such as $K^{eq}_{i,M}(t)$, will not be exactly lognormal, but that it can be approximated by a lognormal process with an appropriate volatility, computed in the following:

By standard stochastic calculus, when

$$dK^{eq}_{i,M}(t) = \sigma_{i,M}(t)\,K^{eq}_{i,M}(t)\,dW_t^{i,M},$$

one isolates the volatility as

$$\frac{dK^{eq}_{i,M}(t)\,dK^{eq}_{i,M}(t)}{\left(K^{eq}_{i,M}(t)\right)^2} = \frac{\sigma^2_{i,M}(t)\left(K^{eq}_{i,M}(t)\right)^2 dt}{\left(K^{eq}_{i,M}(t)\right)^2} = \sigma^2_{i,M}(t)\,dt.$$

We perform now the same passage starting from the market dynamics of forward exchange rates, where we freeze time to 0 in $\widetilde{K^f}_{i,M}(t)$ and in the weights $\varpi(t)$

$$K_{i,M}^{eq}(t) \approx \widetilde{K^f}_{i,M} \sum_{j=i+1}^{M} \varpi_j \Phi_j(t)$$

$$\frac{dK_{i,M}^{eq}(t)\, dK_{i,M}^{eq}(t)}{\left(K_{i,M}^{eq}(t)\right)^2} \approx \frac{\left(\widetilde{K^f}_{i,M}\right)^2 \sum_{j=i+1}^{M} \varpi_j d\Phi\left(t, T_j\right) \sum_{k=i+1}^{M} \varpi_k d\Phi\left(t, T_k\right)}{\left(\widetilde{K^f}_{i,M} \sum_{j=i+1}^{M} \varpi_j \Phi_j(t)\right)^2}.$$

The forward exchange rate $\Phi_j(t)$ has dynamics:

$$d\Phi_j(t) = \sigma_j(t)\, \Phi_j(t)\, dW_t^j$$

leading to

$$\frac{dK_{i,M}^{eq}(t)\, dK_{i,M}^{eq}(t)}{\left(K_{i,M}^{eq}(t)\right)^2} \approx \frac{\sum_{j,k=i+1}^{M} \varpi_j \varpi_k\, \Phi_j(t)\, \Phi_k(t)\, \rho_{jk}\, \sigma_j(t)\, \sigma_k(t)}{\left(\sum_{m=i+1}^{M} \varpi_m\, \Phi_m(t)\right)^2} dt$$

where ρ_{jk} is the instantaneous correlation between the Brownian motions dW_t^j and dW_t^k of Φ_j and Φ_k. It follows by arguments similar to those used for the approximated swaption pricing formula ([30], [175] and [48]) that an approximation of the CCS rate volatility is given by:

$$\hat{\sigma}_{i,M}^2(t) = \sum_{j,k=i+1}^{M} \frac{\varpi_j \varpi_k\, \Phi_j(0)\, \Phi_k(0)\, \rho_{jk}\, \sigma_j(t)\, \sigma_k(t)}{\left(\sum_{j=i+1}^{M} \varpi_j \Phi_j(0)\right)^2} \tag{9.15}$$

where the proposed approximation amounts to freezing, at their current level, all quantities deemed to be of low volatilty. In the form of a matrix product, $\hat{\sigma}_{i,M}^2(t)$ is given by:

$$\frac{\left(\varpi_{i+1}\Phi_{i+1}(0)\,\sigma_{i+1}(t), \ldots, \varpi_M \Phi_M(0)\,\sigma_M(t)\right) \begin{pmatrix} \rho_{11} & \cdots & \rho_{M1} \\ \cdots & \cdots & \cdots \\ \rho_{1M} & \cdots & \rho_{MM} \end{pmatrix} \begin{pmatrix} \varpi_{i+1}\Phi_{i+1}(0)\,\sigma_{i+1}(t) \\ \cdots \\ \varpi_M \Phi_M(0)\,\sigma_M(t) \end{pmatrix}}{\left(\sum_{j=i+1}^{M} \varpi_j \Phi_j(0)\right)^2}.$$

This allows us to use a standard Black-formula based pricing methodology, obtaining

$$\text{ICVAA}^P(0) = \text{LGD} \sum_{i=1}^{M} \mathbb{Q}\{\tau \in (T_{i-1}, T_i]\}\, \mathbb{E}_0\left[D(0, T_i)\,(\text{Exs}(T_i))^+\right],$$

with

$$\mathbb{E}_0\left[D(0,T_i)(\mathrm{Exs}(T_i))^+\right] = NC_{i,M}(0)\,\mathbb{E}_0^{i,M}\left[\left(\widetilde{K}_{i,M} - K_{i,M}^{eq}(T_i)\right)^+\right]$$
$$= NC_{i,M}(0)\,Bl\left(\widetilde{K}_{i,M}, K_{i,M}^{eq}(0), \sqrt{\int_0^{T_i} \hat{\sigma}_{i,M}^2(s)\,ds}, \omega = -1\right).$$

where

$$Bl(K,F,v,\omega) = F\omega\mathbb{N}(\omega d_1(K,F,v)) - K\omega\mathbb{N}(\omega d_2(K,F,v))$$
$$d_1(K,F,v) = \frac{\ln(\frac{F}{K}) + \frac{1}{2}v^2}{v}, \qquad d_2(K,F,v) = \frac{\ln(\frac{F}{K}) - \frac{1}{2}v^2}{v}$$

9.2.2 Parameterization of the FX Correlation

We pointed out that the above formula for pricing the CVA of a CCS reduces to the price of a cross currency swap options portfolio weighted by default probabilities, as the CVA for IRSs reduces to a portfolio of swaptions (see again Chapter 4 for IRS results). However, an important difference is that while interest rate swaptions are quoted in the market, and therefore the implied volatility to use for each option is available, this is not true for cross currency swap options, that are not quoted. Only options on exchange rates are quoted. Therefore we are forced to compute a formula for obtaining the volatility of a cross currency option underlying starting from the volatility of forward exchange rates quoted by the market, and the correlations $[\rho]_{jk}$ among forward exchange rates $\Phi_j(t)$ and $\Phi_k(t)$. The latter input can be obtained by market information only through historical estimation, as is done at times in the pricing of multiname interest rate derivatives with the LIBOR market model, see [48].

In interest rate applications, usually the historically estimated correlations are not plugged directly into the calculations. This is because they can be irregular, unstable and incomplete, in the sense that the time series can be missing for some intermediate maturity of interest, and are often missing for the longest maturities in long-dated deals. For completing the matrix for illiquid maturities, it is common to fit onto the historical estimations one of the typical parameterizations for forward interest rate correlations, in particular the two-parameter [176] form:

$$\rho_{ij} = \gamma + (1-\gamma)\exp\{-\beta\,|i-j|\}$$

or the three-parameter version:

$$\rho_{ij} = \gamma + (1-\gamma)\exp\{-|i-j|\,[\beta - \alpha(\max(i,j)-1)]\}$$

(which is not guaranteed to be positive-semidefinite). These parameterizations are known to fit very well the behaviour of the forward interest rates correlation matrix, which in fact is characterized by an exponential decline in the columns starting from the unit entry on the main diagonal, $i \geq j$. We can observe this in the correlation matrix of Table 9.1, whose columns are plotted in Figure 9.1. The correlation matrix is estimated on Euribor interest rate data using one year of data from beginning to end of 2008.

Correlations decrease rapidly as $|i-j|$ increases at the beginning of the column, allowing the exponential forms to fit this behaviour very well. Unfortunately, these features of interest

Table 9.1 Interest Rate Correlation. Historical estimation for year 2008

$d\langle F_i^d, F_j^d\rangle$	1	2	3	4	5	6	7	8	9	10
1	1.00	0.79	0.46	0.50	0.48	0.39	0.37	0.42	0.38	0.38
2	0.79	1.00	0.63	0.67	0.68	0.57	0.54	0.64	0.62	0.60
3	0.46	0.63	1.00	0.85	0.71	0.65	0.57	0.67	0.64	0.62
4	0.50	0.67	0.85	1.00	0.77	0.66	0.62	0.74	0.72	0.69
5	0.48	0.68	0.71	0.77	1.00	0.93	0.91	0.89	0.77	0.76
6	0.39	0.57	0.65	0.66	0.93	1.00	0.96	0.86	0.71	0.70
7	0.37	0.54	0.57	0.62	0.91	0.96	1.00	0.84	0.69	0.68
8	0.42	0.64	0.67	0.74	0.89	0.86	0.84	1.00	0.93	0.92
9	0.38	0.62	0.64	0.72	0.77	0.71	0.69	0.93	1.00	0.99
10	0.38	0.60	0.62	0.69	0.76	0.70	0.68	0.92	0.99	1.00

rate correlation matrices cannot be found in correlations among the forward rates of exchange, which are shown in Table 9.2 and Figure 9.2.

We see that forward exchange rate correlations do not decrease rapidly at the beginning of the columns. On the contrary, the decrease in correlation is slower at the beginning, and then gets steeper. Towards the end of the column, the steepness reduces again. Alternatively, we could say that correlation, seen as a function of the distance between the maturities of the forward exchange rates, is a concave function at the short end, and a convex function at the long end of the range considered.

How can we get a parameterization that allows for such a behaviour? One possibility is shown in [107], through a modification of the framework of [180].

Proposition 9.2.1 *We know that parameterizations for correlation must guarantee the following properties:*

- *unit diagonal:* $\rho_{ii} = 1, i = 1, \ldots, n$
- *symmetry:* $\rho_{ij} = \rho_{ji},\ i, j = 1, \ldots, n$
- *positive semidefinite matrix:* $x^T \rho x \geq 0\ \forall x \in R^n$

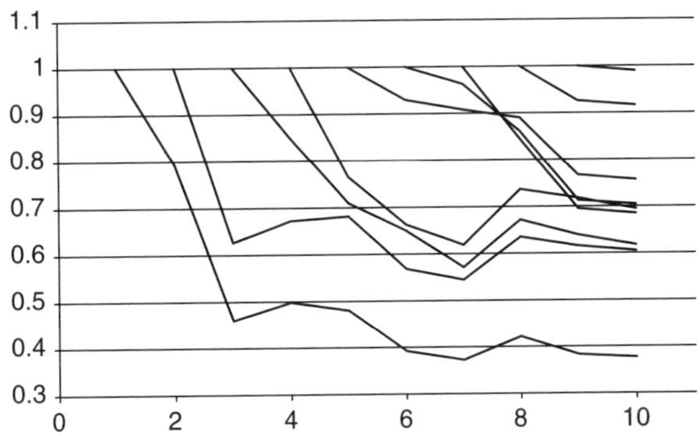

Figure 9.1 Interest rate correlation matrix (columns). Historical estimation, 2008

Table 9.2 FX (forward exchange rates) correlation. EUR/USD historical estimation, 2008

$d\langle\Phi_i, \Phi_j\rangle$	1	2	3	4	5	6	7	8	9	10
1	1.00	0.99	0.93	0.91	0.86	0.74	0.71	0.64	0.61	0.59
2	0.99	1.00	0.97	0.92	0.88	0.75	0.73	0.66	0.63	0.61
3	0.93	0.97	1.00	0.89	0.86	0.75	0.72	0.66	0.62	0.60
4	0.91	0.92	0.89	1.00	0.99	0.80	0.79	0.73	0.70	0.68
5	0.86	0.88	0.86	0.99	1.00	0.81	0.79	0.74	0.71	0.69
6	0.74	0.75	0.75	0.80	0.81	1.00	0.98	0.96	0.93	0.92
7	0.71	0.73	0.72	0.79	0.79	0.98	1.00	0.97	0.94	0.95
8	0.64	0.66	0.66	0.73	0.74	0.96	0.97	1.00	0.96	0.96
9	0.61	0.63	0.62	0.70	0.71	0.93	0.94	0.96	1.00	0.96
10	0.59	0.61	0.60	0.68	0.69	0.92	0.95	0.96	0.96	1.00

[180] show that by setting

$$\rho(i, j) = \frac{b(i)}{b(j)}, \quad j \geq i$$

where $b(j) > 0$ and $b(j)$ is strictly increasing in j on $[1, n]$, then all above properties are guaranteed.

Proof. Let $b_i, i = 1, \ldots, n$ be positive increasing numbers. Then set

$$c_i := \begin{cases} \sqrt{b_i^2 - b_{i-1}^2} \text{ when } i = 2, \ldots, n \\ b_1 \text{ when } i = 1 \end{cases}$$

Let $Z_i, i = 1, \ldots, n$ be independent standard gaussian and set $Y_i = \sum_{k=1}^{i} c_k Z_k$. Then, for $i \leq j$,

$$Cov\left(Y_i, Y_j\right) = \mathbb{E}\left[\sum_{k=1}^{i} c_k Z_k \sum_{h=1}^{j} c_h Z_h\right]$$

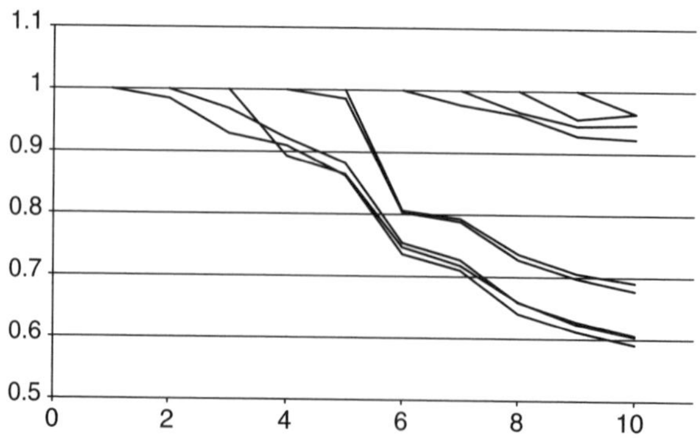

Figure 9.2 FX correlation matrix (columns). EUR/USD historical estimation, 2008

$$Cov\left(Y_i, Y_j\right) = \mathbb{E}\left[\sum_{k=1}^{i} c_k Z_k \left(\sum_{k=1}^{i} c_k Z_k + \sum_{h=i+1}^{j} c_h Z_h\right)\right]$$

$$= \mathbb{E}\left[\left(\sum_{k=1}^{i} c_k Z_k\right)^2\right] = Var\left(\sum_{k=1}^{i} c_k Z_k\right)$$

$$= Var\left(Z_1 b_1 + \sum_{k=2}^{i} \sqrt{b_k^2 - b_{k-1}^2} Z_k\right) = b_1^2 + \sum_{k=2}^{i} \left(b_k^2 - b_{k-1}^2\right) = b_i^2$$

$$Corr\left(Y_i, Y_j\right) = \frac{Cov\left(Y_i, Y_j\right)}{\sqrt{Var\left(Y_i\right)}\sqrt{Var\left(Y_j\right)}} = \frac{b_i^2}{b_i b_j} = \frac{b_i}{b_j}.$$

As long as we follow this framework, the matrix we build is guaranteed to be a correlation matrix. Additionally, [180] also require the function $h\left(j\right) = \frac{b(j)}{b(j+1)}$ to be strictly increasing in j. They show that if this condition is guaranteed, not only we have all the necessary and sufficient conditions for the matrix to be a correlation matrix, but also we have two properties that are desirable for forward interest rate correlation matrices:

1. Decreasing columns: $\rho_{i,i+k}$ is decreasing in k for $k > 0$.
2. Increasing sub-diagonals: $\rho_{i,i+k}$ is increasing in i.

Looking at the above matrix, we see that the first property is relevant to us, while the second property is not consistent with our empirical evidence (such a property is also not observed in interest rate correlation matrices, see [50]).

On the other hand, there are other properties we are interested in, in particular we would like to be able to control the convexity of the columns. We show below that in the [180] framework we can control the behaviour of the correlation matrix columns by controlling the behaviour of the function $b\left(j\right)$. For understanding this point it is convenient to rewrite the condition as

$$\rho\left(i, j\right) = \frac{b\left(j\right)}{b\left(i\right)}, \; i \geq j$$

and define $a\left(j\right) = \frac{1}{b(j)}$ so that

$$\rho\left(i, j\right) = \frac{b\left(j\right)}{b\left(i\right)} = \frac{a\left(i\right)}{a\left(j\right)}, \; i \geq j$$

so that now controlling the behaviour of the matrix columns corresponds to controlling the behaviour of $\rho\left(i, j\right)$ as a function of i for j fixed, and in particular, since for each column j is a positive constant, the behaviour of each column replicates the one of $a\left(i\right)$.

In order to remain in the framework that guarantees that the matrix is well defined we have to choose a decreasing function $a\left(j\right)$ (corresponding to an increasing $b\left(j\right)$). This translates into decreasing columns (Property 1) by [180], and this is desirable since it corresponds to our empirical evidence. Additionally we would like the function to be concave on the short end, turning convex for longer maturities. A decreasing function with such behaviour of the second derivative is, for example, the cosine in the range $[0, \pi]$.

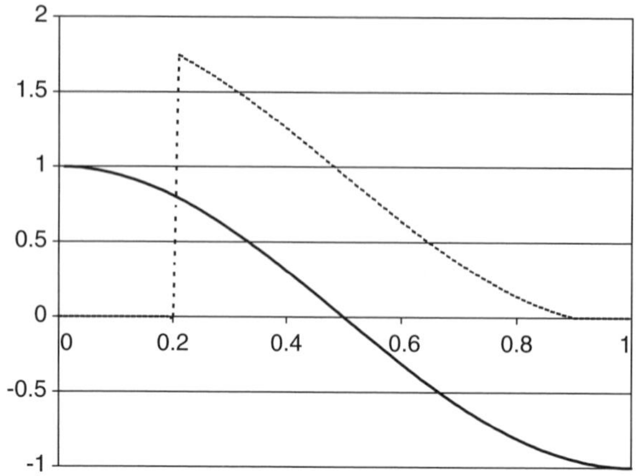

Figure 9.3 A cosine parameterization for FX correlations

Obviously, we will need to turn it into a positive function and be flexible about the inflection point where the convexity reverts. Such a goal can be obtained by the following parameterization:

$$a(j) = \cos\left(\pi\alpha + \pi(\beta - \alpha)\frac{j}{n}\right) - \cos(\beta\pi) + \gamma, \quad 0 \le \alpha \le \beta \le 1, \gamma > 0. \tag{9.16}$$

where the addition of $-\cos(\beta\pi)$ moves the minimum of the function to zero, and γ gives some more flexibility in recovering market patterns by shifting the function in the positive semiplan (the condition $\gamma > 0$ guarantees that $a(j) > 0$, required for $\rho(i, j)$ to be well defined). The coefficients α and β allow us to choose the "convexity area" of the cosine which best corresponds to market patterns. In Figure 9.3 we plot $\cos(x\pi)$ for $x \in (0, 1]$ and $\cos(\pi\alpha + \pi(\beta - \alpha)x) - \cos(\beta\pi)$ for $x \in (0, 1]$, having set $\alpha = 0.2$ and $\beta = 0.9$.

Notice that if we write $x = \frac{j}{n}$, we have

$$a(j) = y(x) = \cos(\pi\alpha + \pi(\beta - \alpha)x) - \cos(\beta\pi) + \gamma, \quad x \in (0, 1]. \tag{9.17}$$

The argument $\pi\alpha + \pi(\beta - \alpha)x$ of the cosine function can take values in the set $[0, \pi]$ since $0 \le \alpha \le \beta \le 1$. We have

$$y'(x) = -\sin(\pi\alpha + \pi(\beta - \alpha)x)\pi(\beta - \alpha)$$
$$y''(x) = -\cos(\pi\alpha + \pi(\beta - \alpha)x)\pi^2(\beta - \alpha)^2$$

thus

$$y'(x) > 0 \Longrightarrow x > \frac{1 - \alpha}{\beta - \alpha},$$

$$y''(x) \ge 0 \Longrightarrow \frac{1/2 - \alpha}{\beta - \alpha} \le x \le \frac{3/2 - \alpha}{\beta - \alpha},$$

Since $\frac{1-\alpha}{\beta-\alpha} \ge 1$, the condition on the first derivative is never satisfied, thus correlation cannot be increasing consistently with the typical market patterns. Since $\frac{3/2-\alpha}{\beta-\alpha} > 1$, the condition on

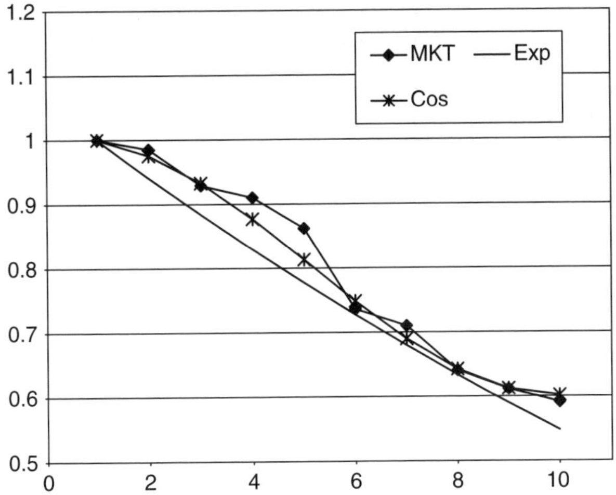

Figure 9.4 Fit to historical FX correlations by different parameterizations

the second derivative reduces to the fact that for $\alpha \geq 1/2$ the convexity is always non-negative, otherwise we can have a change of convexity from negative to positive at $x = \frac{1/2-\alpha}{\beta-\alpha}$.

We fit this form onto our historical estimation and we find a percentage mean square error $\left(\sqrt{\sum_{i,j}\left(\frac{\rho_{ij}-\hat{\rho}_{ij}}{\rho_{ij}}\right)^2}\right)$ of 5% versus an equivalent error of 7% with an exponential form with three parameters. The difference is small but it is reassuring, observing the plot of the first column, to see that while the best the exponential form can do to fit the market patterns is to become a straight line, our parameterization can reproduce the actual behaviour of correlations.

One can find it annoying that the above parameterization depends on n, which means that one should know in advance the maximum possible size of the correlation matrix when estimating the parameters. This can be avoided with a slight variation of the above parameterization, where we do not refer to the size of the correlation matrix but we obtain an analogous behaviour,

$$a(j) = \cos\left(\pi\alpha + \pi(1-\alpha)\left(1 - e^{-\varepsilon(j-1)}\right)\right) + 1 + \gamma, \quad 0 \leq \alpha \leq 1, \varepsilon \geq 0, \gamma > 0.$$

This parameterization can be extended to a matrix of any size while always remaining well-defined.

When we apply the cosine parameterizations to cross currency correlation, the optimal value for the parameter α is $\alpha^* = 0$, thus the two parameterizations have effectively only two parameters. This appears to be a very specific feature of this market condition. Keeping α as a free parameter allows the parameterization to also fit different configurations, including exponential configurations like the Table 9.1, from the interest rate market (in this case the optimal value for the parameter α tends to be $\alpha^* > 0.5$, so that the parameterization turns out to be always convex).

Apart from the reduced impact that this parameterization can have on the solution of this problem, we find it useful as an example of how we can construct well-defined parameterizations with features that allow us to capture a market shift or to fit a specific market, being more general than an exponential parameterization.

9.3 UNILATERAL CVA FOR CROSS CURRENCY SWAPS WITH FLOATING LEGS

Now we see how to modify the above framework when the deal also involves the payment of floating legs indexed to domestic and foreign LIBOR rates $L_j^d(T_{j-1})$ and $L_j^f(T_{j-1})$,

$$L_j^d(T_{j-1}) = \frac{1}{(T_j - T_{j-1})}\left[\frac{1}{P(T_{j-1}, T_j)} - 1\right],$$
$$L_j^f(T_{j-1}) = \frac{1}{(T_j - T_{j-1})}\left[\frac{1}{P^f(T_{j-1}, T_j)} - 1\right].$$

In a generic CCS we can have:

Initial exchange:

- at T_0 Party A pays N^f in foreign currency and Party B pays N in domestic currency, again with $N = \varphi_0 N^f$.

Legs:

- Domestic leg: at T_j ($j = 1, \ldots, M$) Party A pays $N\alpha_j\left(K + L_j^d(T_{j-1})\right)$ in domestic currency to Party B.
- Foreign leg: at T_j ($j = 1, \ldots, M$) Party B pays $N^f\alpha_j\left(K^f + L_j^f(T_{j-1})\right)$ in foreign currency to Party A.

Final exchange:

- At T_M Party A pays N in domestic currency and Party B pays N^f in foreign currency.

Under the domestic risk-neutral measure, the value of the domestic leg to party B is:

$$\begin{aligned}
\text{Exs}(T_i, T_M) &= NPV_{T_i}^d \\
&= \mathbb{E}_{T_i}\left[NK\sum_{j=i+1}^{M}\alpha_j D(T_i, T_j) + N\sum_{j=i+1}^{M}\alpha_j L_j^d(T_{j-1}) D(T_i, T_j) + ND(T_i, T_M)\right].
\end{aligned}$$

Switching to the domestic T_j-forward measures:

$$\begin{aligned}
NPV_{T_i}^d &= N\left[K\sum_{j=i+1}^{M}\alpha_j P(T_i, T_j) + \sum_{j=i+1}^{M}\alpha_j P(T_i, T_j)\mathbb{E}_{T_i}^j\left[L_j^d(T_{j-1})\right] + P(T_i, T_M)\right] \\
&= N\left[K\sum_{j=i+1}^{M}\alpha_j P(T_i, T_j) + \sum_{j=i+1}^{M}\alpha_j P(T_i, T_j)\mathbb{E}_{T_i}^j\left[F_j^d(T_{j-1})\right] + P(T_i, T_M)\right] \\
&= N\left[K\sum_{j=i+1}^{M}\alpha_j P(T_i, T_j) + \sum_{j=i+1}^{M} P(T_i, T_j)\left[\frac{P(T_i, T_{j-1})}{P(T_i, T_j)} - 1\right] + P(T_i, T_M)\right]
\end{aligned}$$

where F is the forward LIBOR rates associated with LIBOR rates L, namely $F_j^f(t)$ is the forward LIBOR rate for the foreign market

$$F_j^f(t) = \frac{1}{T_j - T_{j-1}} \left(\frac{P^f(t, T_{j-1})}{P^f(t, T_j)} - 1 \right)$$

at time t for the LIBOR rate $L_j^f(T_{j-1})$ see, for example [48]. We have the same for the domestic currency. In the above we have used the fact that F_j^d is a martingale under the T_j domestic forward measure (see later in the book for the impact of multicurves with basis). This easily simplifies to

$$NPV_{T_i}^d = NK \sum_{j=i+1}^{M} \alpha_j P\left(T_i, T_j\right) + N\ P\left(T_i, T_i\right) - N\ P\left(T_i, T_M\right) + NP\left(T_i, T_M\right)$$

$$NPV_{T_i}^d = NK \sum_{j=i+1}^{M} \alpha_j P\left(T_i, T_j\right) + N.$$

The same holds for the foreign payer, under the foreign measure

$$NPV_{T_i}^f = N^f\ K \sum_{j=i+1}^{M} \alpha_j P^f\left(T_i, T_j\right) + N^f.$$

Turning the value into domestic currency

$$\begin{aligned}\varphi\left(T_i\right) NPV_{T_i}^f &= N^f\ K^f \sum_{j=i+1}^{M} \varphi\left(T_i\right) P^f\left(T_i, T_j\right) \alpha_j + N^f \varphi\left(T_i\right) \\ &= N^f\ K^f \sum_{j=i+1}^{M} P\left(T_i, T_j\right) \Phi_j\left(T_i\right) \alpha_j + N^f \Phi_i\left(T_i\right).\end{aligned}$$

So we have moved from an NPV of the CCS without floating legs given in (9.11) by

$$\begin{aligned}NPV_{T_i} = {} & NK \sum_{j=i+1}^{M} \alpha_j P\left(T_i, T_j\right) + NP\left(T_i, T_M\right) \\ & - N^f K^f \sum_{j=i+1}^{M} \alpha_j P\left(T_i, T_j\right) \Phi_j\left(T_i\right) - N^f P\left(T_i, T_M\right) \Phi_M\left(T_i\right)\end{aligned}$$

to an NPV of the CCS also involving floating legs which is

$$\begin{aligned}NPV_{T_i} = {} & NK \sum_{j=i+1}^{M} \alpha_j P\left(T_i, T_j\right) + N \\ & - N^f\ K^f \sum_{j=i+1}^{M} P\left(T_i, T_j\right) \Phi_j\left(T_i\right) \alpha_j - N^f \Phi_i\left(T_i\right)\end{aligned}$$

We have moved the notional payment from the end to the beginning of the forward starting deal. Through a simple redefinition of K_j and K_j^f we can still use the approach of the previous section to compute the credit value adjustment of the CCS.

9.4 WHY A CROSS CURRENCY BASIS?

Let $x \in \{f, d\}$ be an index denoting whether we are in foreign or domestic currency, and denote notionals, discount factors, zero coupon bonds, and interest rates in currency x with N^x,D^x, P^x, L^x respectively. Let expectations under measures associated with currency x be denoted by $\mathbb{E}^{(x)}$. We can write, for the standard market CCS that exchanges two purely floating legs:

$$
\begin{aligned}
\mathrm{NPV}^x_{T_i} &= N^x \mathbb{E}^{(x)}_{T_i}\left[\sum_{j=i+1}^{M} \alpha_j L^x_j\left(T_{j-1}\right) D^x\left(T_i, T_j\right) + D^x\left(T_i, T_M\right)\right] \\
&= N^x\left[\sum_{j=i+1}^{M} \alpha_j P^x\left(T_i, T_j\right) \mathbb{E}^{(x)j}_{T_i}\left[L^x_j\left(T_{j-1}\right)\right] + P^x\left(T_i, T_M\right)\right] \\
&= N^x\left[\sum_{j=i+1}^{M} P^x\left(T_i, T_j\right)\left[\frac{P^x\left(T_i, T_{j-1}\right)}{P^x\left(T_i, T_j\right)} - 1\right] + P^x\left(T_i, T_M\right)\right] \\
&= N^x.
\end{aligned} \tag{9.18}
$$

This implies that the CCS is fair when valued at a fixing date T_i whenever we set

$$
N = N^f \Phi_i\left(T_i\right).
$$

If we assume such conditions to hold then there should be no basis spread to be added to one of the two legs to set the CCS at equilibrium. What can be different from the above setup in the reality of market quoted CCS, so as to justify the presence of a basis? It is clear that, if the discount factor did not belong to the same curve as the rate in the payoff, we would not have the simplification performed in the last passage of (9.18). It is well known that after the summer of 2007 a large basis opened between the LIBOR rates paid in payoffs, like CCS, and the OIS (overnight indexed swaps) that must be used for discounting collateralized payoffs. See [155] for an analysis of the basis spreads that opened in the quotes of collateralized interest rate derivatives at the start of the global financial crisis. Since market quoted CCS refer to collateralized products, it is not surprising that the two legs of the CCS are not valued at par, thus leading to a CCS basis. The fact that LIBOR-indexed floaters are no longer valued at par is visible also in the single currency swap market, and it is natural to expect that CCS will inherit the single currency basis spreads. In particular, if the single currency LIBOR-OIS spreads are different in the two currencies (for example, for a EUR-USD CCS, we see that the basis between Euribor and Eonia-based OIS is different from the basis between USD LIBOR and Fed-Funds-based OIS) this difference emerges in the CCS valuation.

However, this does not explain why the CCS basis existed well before summer 2007. Before summer 2007 the single currency basis was negligible (and often neglected by traders) while the CCS basis often reached 10 basis points or more even for maturities of only a few years. Today, a theory is emerging that can explain this basis. The starting point is that the above description of (9.18) is wrong for collateralized CCS because it does not take into account the consequences of *collateralization*. As we mentioned earlier, discounting should be based on the rate paid for collateralizing a deal – this will be discussed in more detail in Chapter 16. In the above description, each of the two legs is discounted using the short rate of the corresponding currency, but this is impossible in a CCS because collateral is in *one single currency*, therefore there must be at least one leg, paying a rate of currency y, but to be discounted with the short rate of currency x chosen for collateralization. This leg may not be valued at par, and this explains why to bring the CCS into equilibrium a positive or negative spread should be added to the leg.

9.4.1 The Approach of Fujii, Shimada and Takahashi (2010)

This intuition is developed more in detail in some recent papers, in particular [109], [110] and [111]. They assume for CCS a so-called "perfect collateralization", where the collateral is cash, collateral update and interest payments are continuous, and there are no thresholds or minimum transfer amounts under which collateralization is suspended. We analyze, as a particular case of a general framework, the conditions of perfect collateralization in Section 16.2.1 and we reiterate the results of Takahashi and co-authors in Section 16.3.

The fundamental variables we have are:

- $r^x(t)$: the risk-free short rates of the currency x, at which the domestic risk-free bank account $D^x(t,T) = B_t^x/B_T^x$ grows;
- $c^x(t)$: the short rate at which the collateral account C_t^x in currency x grows. $C^x(t,T) = C_t^x/C_T^x$.

What happens in a CCS is that there are two legs associated to two currencies x and y, while collateral for both legs will be in one single currency. It can even be in a third currency z, but for simplicity, and yet without losing the core of the issue, we will consider the case of the leg in currency x when collateral is in currency y. We denote by $P_X^{x,C,y}(t)$ the price at time t of the originally uncollateralized simple claim $X^x(T)$ (in currency x) payable at T and without earlier cash flows, adjusted for collateralization in currency y, and still expressed in currency x. The currency x is typically the domestic currency.

$$P_X^{x,C,y}(t) = \mathbb{E}_t^x\left[D^x(t,T)X^x(T)\right] + \varphi^{x,y}(t)\,\mathbb{E}_t^y\left[\int_t^T D^y(t,u)\left(r^y(u) - c^y(u)\right)\left(\frac{P_X^{x,C,y}(u)}{\varphi^{x,y}(u)}\right)du\right] \tag{9.19}$$

where $\varphi(t)^{x,y}$ is the number of x units required to get a unit of y. How do we explain such a pricing formula?

1. The first expectation is standard pricing, but then we add a second expectation: the net return from the collateral expressed as a discounted flow of spread payments, indexed to the net present value of the deal.
2. Indexation to the deal's NPV arises from the fact that, by definition, and under the stylized "perfect collateralization" assumptions of this chapter – that we will relax in the following chapters – collateral must always match the potential loss one party would have if the other party defaults. In particular, when the NPV is positive the investor is receiving collateral, when it is negative the investor is paying collateral, so the sign of the NPV determines the sign of the collateral payments.
3. The presence of rates of exchange comes from the fact that if the collateral is in y the indexation to the NPV is in y; all rates involved in collateral flows refer to y; finally the net present value of these flows is converted in the accounting currency x.

4. The net collateral payment is given by the spread between the collateral rate and the risk-free rate of the collateral currency, because of the assumption that collateral cash is reinvested at the risk-free rate when received and borrowed risk-free when it must be posted. (Notice that rehypothecation is implicitly allowed. We will see more about this assumption in the chapters that follow.) For example, when we hold collateral, the assumption is that we invest it and we are remunerated at the foreign risk-free rate r^y, while we remunerate the collateral provider at the rate c^y, singling out a net return of $r^y - c^y$.

While the rest of the formula is almost self-evident, the last assumption requires some comments. Collateral may be invested at a risky rate, namely a rate remunerating some risk of default. This, however, does not invalidate the above formula because in such a case the higher rate of return should, in an arbitrage-free market, be matched by the higher risk of default, bringing the net return back to risk-free. Under a simple model, where recovery of this alternative investment is zero, the intensity of the investment default is $\lambda(t)$, and the investment payout is paid at maturity T in case of no default, lack of arbitrage requires this risk of default be compensated by a return $z(t)$ equal to $r(s) + \lambda(s)$, so that the expected payout is

$$\mathbb{E}\left[e^{\int_0^T z(t)ds} 1_{(\tau>T)}\right] = \mathbb{E}\left[e^{\int_0^T (r(s)+\lambda(s))ds} 1_{(\tau>T)}\right]$$
$$= \mathbb{E}\left[e^{\int_0^T (r(s)+\lambda(s))ds} e^{\int_0^T -\lambda(s)ds}\right] = \mathbb{E}\left[e^{\int_0^T r(s)ds}\right] \tag{9.20}$$

as in a risk-free investment. An analogous reasoning can apply to the cost of funding the collateral. Funding is usually not risk free since it is affected by the risk of default by the investor in need of liquidity; but this probability of not paying back the funding due to default will be compensated by a higher funding spread, which will leave the expected cost of funding equal to that of risk-free funding. This reasoning, first introduced in [157], is presented later in Section 11.3, and is discussed as a component of a particular liquidity policy in Section 17.3. Obviously for this probability to be true an investor must take its own risk of default into account in the valuation of its funding cost. This is disturbing, similar to DVA, and for analogous reasons it may not be fully applied by banks in practice. But from the general point of view of the economy it is the correct representation of the deal flows even if it is not the point of view of the investor. For a debate see [155].

9.4.2 Collateral Rates versus Risk-Free Rates

There is one aspect of Formula (9.20) that generates more perplexity. It is quite clear that (9.20) implies that the collateral account is a risk-free (default-free) account. There are no default indicators in the formula. In fact, collateralizing the deal with what we called "perfect collateral" makes both the collateral and the deal risk free if we assume that there can be no instantaneous jump in the underlying instrument value at counterparty default. (We will see a case with underlying CDS where this assumption is violated in Chapter 15.) Under these assumptions collateral and the underlying deal guarantee each other. However, we are assuming that the collateral rate c^y does not coincide with the risk-free rate r^y, and you will see in the following that the explanation of CCS basis is based on assuming $c^y > r^y$ due to riskiness of c^y. This means that the risk-free collateral account accrues at a risky rate. Shouldn't this be an arbitrage? Is this not quite disturbing in a context where all conclusions are reached based on the hypothesis of lack of arbitrage opportunities?

Only a treatment including default in imperfectly collateralized deals or instantaneous contagion and an explicit representation of what makes the collateral rate risky could clarify this issue. We partially tackle this in Part III where we assume that, consistent with reality, collateralized deals are not risk free, since collateral is updated, at best, daily not continuously. On the other hand, such collaterals have an indexation to overnight rates, which are not completely risk free, a topic tackled in [155], where they are affected by the probability that a counterparty admitted today to the overnight market defaults overnight. This is the minimum riskiness available in the market, but it is not an absence of default risk. So do we really have a risky rate applied to a riskless account, or is it that the overnight riskiness of collateral rates matches the overnight margin period of risk for the collateral account? Lacking such an analysis, we can treat the case of risky rates applied to risk-free collateral as a market segmentation: when involved in a collateral agreement, an investor accesses a special money market where risk-free amounts of money are lent at a special rate that may not be consistent with the actual risk-free rate of the market.

9.4.3 Consequences of Perfect Collateralization

Now that we have discussed Formula (9.20), we can follow [111] to see that it is equivalent to

$$P_X^{x,C,y}(t) = \mathbb{E}_t^x\left[e^{-\int_0^T (r^x(s)+c^y(s)-r^y(s))ds} X_T^x\right]. \tag{9.21}$$

This formula says that the correct discount rate is the "domestic" risk-free rate plus the spread of the collateral over the risk-free rate of the same collateral currency. This has some crucial corollaries.

First, when the domestic and collateral currency coincide ($x = y$) we get the notorious result mentioned a few times earlier, according to which collateralized deals should be discounted at the collateral rate

$$P_X^{x,C,y}(t) = \mathbb{E}_t^x\left[e^{-\int_0^T c^x(s)ds} X_T^x\right]. \tag{9.22}$$

Such a result is derived later from a general framework in Section 16.2.1. Moreover, when the collateral rate is the risk-free rate ($x = y$, $c^x = r^x$), this is simply standard Black and Scholes pricing.

$$P_X^{x,C,y}(t) = \mathbb{E}_t^x\left[e^{-\int_0^T r^x(s)ds} X_T^x\right]. \tag{9.23}$$

The second interesting aspect of Formula (9.21) is that when the collateral rate coincides with the risk-free rate of its own currency ($c^y = r^y$), even if it is different from the risk-free rate of the domestic currency r^x, the collateral currency is irrelevant, because we have Formula (9.23) so it is as if we were collateralizing in domestic risk-free collateral. This is consistent with the standard no-arbitrage relations of a multi-currency market. In fact, we have seen in (9.5) that the rate of exchange is expected to compensate differences in return from risk-free investments in two different currencies. Thus, even if collateralization in y means funding in y and therefore discounting in y, we have to consider that the collateral is indexed to the deal's NPV *expressed in* y, and the joint effect of y risk-free discounting, together with a rate of exchange $\frac{1}{\varphi^{x,y}(u)} = \varphi^{y,x}(u)$ in the quantity to be discounted, is therefore equivalent to x risk-free discounting, as in (9.4).

Thus, under risk-free collateral, an x leg collateralized in y has the same price as an x leg collateralized in x, and we should expect no basis. When, however, the collateral is not risk free, $(c^y > r^y)$, as it may well be with real world overnight collateral rates, things are different. For the global market to be arbitrage free we need to know that if we invest in y currency an amount corresponding to a unit in x currency, the expected net present value is, as in (9.5),

$$\mathbb{E}_0^x\left[D^x(0,T)\,\varphi(T)^{x,y}\left(\frac{B_0^x}{B_0^y}\frac{1}{\varphi(0)^{x,y}}\right)B_T^y\right]$$

$$= \mathbb{E}_0^x\left[e^{-\int_0^T r^x(s)ds}\varphi(T)^{x,y}\left(\frac{1}{\varphi(0)^{x,y}}e^{\int_0^T r^y(s)ds}\right)\right] = 1,$$

making the foreign risk-free investment equivalent to the unit domestic risk-free investment,

$$\mathbb{E}_0^x\left[D^x(0,T)\,B_T^x\right] = 1.$$

But if we are discounting at a risky collateral rate c^y higher than the risk-free rate, which is higher since it is affected by a possible default event at τ, the rate of exchange $\varphi(t)^{y,x}$ will not be driven to adjust the difference between this rate and the risk-free rate r^x of x, since for the part of c^y that exceeds r^y absence of arbitrage is already guaranteed by risk of default like in (9.20),

$$\mathbb{E}_0^y\left[D^y(0,T)\,e^{\int_0^T c^y(s)ds}1_{(\tau>T)}\right] = \mathbb{E}_0^y\left[D^y(0,T)\,e^{\int_0^T (r^y(s)+\underbrace{c^y(s)-r^y(s)}_{\textit{default intensity}})ds}1_{(\tau>T)}\right]$$

$$= \mathbb{E}_0^y\left[D^y(0,T)\,e^{\int_0^T r^y(s)ds}\right] = 1.$$

It is only to differences between $r^y(t)$ and $r^x(t)$ that the rate of exchange will adapt. Thus, when collateral is risky, a leg paying x rates but collateralized in y is actually discounted with rate $r^x(s) + c^y(s) - r^y(s)$. This is not consistent with the rates paid which are indexed to $r^x(s)$. The leg will not be valued at par and a basis can emerge.

The market-quoted CCS basis, according to the most up-to-date theory, is therefore related to specific collateralized deals (in particular, [111] refer to the practice of collateralizing CCS in dollars). Such a basis does not enter into the valuation of non-collateralized CCS – the focus of this chapter – which are priced with standard discounting and CVA. Thus we resume our analysis of CCS CVA, with no market basis in the computation.

9.5 CVA FOR CCS IN PRACTICE

First we summarize the main results from previous sections in this chapter.

$$\text{ICVAA}^P(0) = \text{LGD}\sum_{i=0}^{M-1}\mathbb{Q}\{\tau \in (T_i, T_{i+1}]\}\,\mathbb{E}_0\left[D(0,T_i)(\text{Exs}(T_i))^+\right],$$

$$\mathbb{E}_0\left[D(0,T_i)(\text{Exs}(T_i))^+\right] = N\sum_{j=i+1}^{M}\alpha_j P(0,T_j)\,\mathbb{E}_0^{i,M}\left[\left(\widetilde{K}_{i,M} - K_{i,M}^{eq}(T_i)\right)^+\right],$$

$$\mathbb{E}_0^{i,M}\left[\left(\widetilde{K}_{i,M} - K_{i,M}^{eq}(T_i)\right)^+\right] = Bl\left(\widetilde{K}_{i,M}, K_{i,M}^{eq}(0), \sqrt{\int_0^{T_i} \hat{\sigma}_{i,M}^2(s)\,ds}, \omega = -1\right)$$

$$\hat{\sigma}_{i,M}^2(t) = \sum_{j,k=i+1}^{M} \frac{\varpi_j \varpi_k\ \Phi_j(0)\ \Phi_k(0)\ \rho_{jk}\ \sigma_j(t)\sigma_k(t)}{\left(\sum_{m=i+1}^{M} \varpi_m \Phi_m(0)\right)^2}$$

where

$$K_{i,M}^{eq}(0) = \widetilde{K^f}_{i,M} \sum_{j=i+1}^{M} \varpi_j(0)\,\Phi_j(0),$$

$$\widetilde{K^f}_{i,M} = \sum_{j=i+1}^{M} \varpi_j^f(0)\,K_j^f,$$

$$\widetilde{K}_{i,M} = \sum_{j=i+1}^{M} \varpi_j(0)\,K_j.$$

As for the correlation entries, we have shown the advantages of parameterizing them as

$$\rho(i,j) = \frac{b(j)}{b(i)} = \frac{a(i)}{a(j)}, i \geq j,$$

with

$$a(j) = \cos\left(\pi\alpha + \pi(\beta - \alpha)\frac{j}{n}\right) - \cos(\beta\pi) + \gamma, \quad 0 \leq \alpha \leq \beta \leq 1, \gamma > 0.$$

or, if one looks for a parameterization independent of the deal maturity,

$$a(j) = \cos\left(\pi\alpha + \pi(1-\alpha)\left(1 - e^{-\varepsilon(j-1)}\right)\right) + 1 + \gamma, \quad 0 \leq \alpha \leq 1, \varepsilon \geq 0, \gamma > 0.$$

Now we will see the above formulas applied in practice. We consider, as an example, a very simple EUR-USD CCS. The CCS has been set up at a time when the rate of exchange was 0.833 so that the foreign nominal is the domestic nominal divided by 0.833, because $N = \varphi_0 N^f$. The CCS is evaluated at a subsequent time, when the spot rate of exchange has moved to 0.803. The CCS has the features listed in Table 9.3, including the expected recovery rate for the counterparty and the initial FX rate that determines the foreign nominal.

We consider "domestic" as the leg paying EUR, and "foreign" as the leg paying USD, and compute the bucketed anticipated CVA for the payer of the domestic leg. In Table 9.4 we see an example of the fundamental market inputs required for computing the price of a cross currency swap. In the first two columns we have the payment dates of the CCS, both

Table 9.3 Features of CCS analyzed as example

Initial FX rate	0.83300	Domestic Fixed	4.39%
Spot FX rate	0.80300	Foreign Fixed	4.56%
Domestic Nom	1bn	Recovery	40%

Table 9.4 Fundamental market inputs required for computing the price of a cross currency swap

i	Dates T_i	Fwd FX Rate $\Phi_i(0)$	Dom. Bond $P(0, T_i)$
0	22/9/08	0.682	1
1	15/7/09	0.692	0.959761
2	15/7/10	0.696	0.920115
3	15/7/11	0.694	0.881873
4	15/7/12	0.691	0.844823
5	17/7/13	0.688	0.808879
6	16/7/14	0.685	0.774026
7	15/7/15	0.681	0.73982
8	15/7/16	0.678	0.706354
9	15/7/17	0.675	0.673447
10	15/7/18	0.673	0.641121
11	17/7/19	0.672	0.60966
12	15/7/20	0.671	0.579588
13	15/7/21	0.671	0.55082
14	15/7/22	0.670	0.523415
15	15/7/23	0.669	0.497557
16	17/7/24	0.668	0.473089
17	16/7/25	0.667	0.450273
18	15/7/26	0.665	0.428842
19	15/7/27	0.663	0.408648
20	15/7/28	0.660	0.389695
21	15/7/29	0.657	0.371996
22	17/7/30	0.654	0.3553
23	16/7/31	0.650	0.33968
24	15/7/32	0.646	0.324927
25	15/7/33	0.641	0.310889

as calendar dates and as T_i in the model. The time is partitioned according to these payment dates, so the fundamental quantities will be computed to correspond with each of these dates, starting from T_0 as here we show the anticipated CVA. We need the spot rate of exchange, and the foreign and domestic term structures for the maturities associated to dates T_i. These quantities together give the forward rates of exchange through Formula (9.8). In Table 9.4 one has all the inputs necessary to price the CCS. If the goal is pricing not only the CCS but also the CVA of the CCS, one needs information about volatilities and also forward exchange rate correlations. We use a flat volatility of 20.7% and a correlation matrix where all terms are equal to 1, to keep the inputs as simple and replicable as possible.

In Table 9.5 we show the main calculations required to reach a value for the CVA. We compute the effective domestic and foreign rates, and the equilibrium cross currency swap rate. Since we have chosen a simple Fixed vs Fixed CCS with flat domestic and foreign fixed rates, the growth of these quantities with respect to time is mainly due to the presence of the notional exchange at the end of the deal. With these inputs we can compute the exposure at any future time, but for obtaining the positive exposures we need to compute the volatility of the cross currency swap rate, which is computed through Formula (9.15) and given in the 'Vol' column. By adding period default probabilities, we can compute the period CVAs associated to the possibility of defaulting in the different intervals $T_i - T_{i+1}$. Summing them together we have the CCS CVA. This table serves the purpose of showing in this approximated approach

Table 9.5 Main calculation outputs required to compute the CVA. In particular we list effective domestic and foreign rates, and the equilibrium cross currency swap rate

i	Eff. Dom $\widetilde{K}_{i,M}(T_i)$	Eff. For $\widetilde{K^f}_{i,M}(T_i)$	CCS Rate $K^{eq}_{i,M}(T_i)$	Exp. Sign $\mathbb{E}_0[D(0,T_i)\mathrm{Exs}(T_i)]$	Vol $\hat{\sigma}^2_{i,M}$	Pos. Exp $\mathbb{E}_0[D(0,T_i)\mathrm{Ex}(T_i)]$	Def Prob $\{\tau \in T_{i-1}, T_i\}$	CVA $\mathrm{ICVAA}^P(t)$
0	6.50%	7.87%	6.26%	34,563,289	20.69%	89,043,843	4.7%	2,499,422
1	6.64%	8.05%	6.39%	35,220,428	20.69%	118,842,891	5.5%	3,901,217
2	6.81%	8.24%	6.53%	36,082,386	20.69%	137,843,757	5.2%	4,266,766
3	6.99%	8.45%	6.68%	36,823,733	20.69%	151,119,838	4.9%	4,420,421
4	7.19%	8.69%	6.85%	37,377,855	20.69%	160,595,630	4.6%	4,438,595
5	7.41%	8.95%	7.05%	37,738,705	20.69%	167,174,388	4.3%	4,318,642
6	7.66%	9.25%	7.26%	37,904,451	20.69%	171,719,569	4.1%	4,181,692
7	7.94%	9.58%	7.51%	37,886,845	20.69%	174,679,892	3.8%	4,031,047
8	8.26%	9.95%	7.79%	37,720,201	20.69%	176,264,048	3.6%	3,822,937
9	8.62%	10.37%	8.11%	37,451,397	20.69%	176,830,384	3.4%	3,615,164
10	9.02%	10.85%	8.47%	37,116,713	20.69%	176,608,622	3.2%	3,421,728
11	9.50%	11.41%	8.89%	36,746,979	20.69%	175,628,080	3.0%	3,181,112
12	10.04%	12.05%	9.38%	36,351,551	20.69%	174,192,997	2.9%	2,982,484
13	10.68%	12.80%	9.95%	35,957,447	20.69%	172,314,161	2.7%	2,781,019
14	11.43%	13.70%	10.63%	35,565,199	20.69%	170,092,263	2.5%	2,587,635
15	12.34%	14.77%	11.44%	35,155,061	20.69%	167,620,455	2.4%	2,422,877
16	13.46%	16.11%	12.45%	34,736,738	20.69%	164,812,926	2.2%	2,220,818
17	14.85%	17.77%	13.70%	34,311,889	20.69%	161,894,672	2.1%	2,056,649
18	16.64%	19.90%	15.31%	33,859,858	20.69%	158,829,625	2.0%	1,907,311
19	19.03%	22.77%	17.46%	33,365,432	20.69%	155,623,649	1.9%	1,766,259
20	22.39%	26.79%	20.49%	32,813,063	20.69%	152,278,825	1.8%	1,624,539
21	27.42%	32.83%	25.03%	32,216,772	20.69%	148,879,109	1.7%	1,505,093
22	35.86%	42.98%	32.66%	31,566,789	20.69%	145,351,991	1.6%	1,373,679
23	52.62%	63.17%	47.83%	30,867,810	20.69%	141,825,606	1.5%	1,267,014
24	103.02%	123.88%	93.47%	30,107,240	20.69%	138,238,288	1.4%	1,164,101
								71,758,224

that the computation can be easily implemented in a worksheet, where all fundamental CVA spot and forward elements can be easily read and interpreted.

The crucial ingredient for the computation of the counterparty risk adjustment are the positive exposures on the different discrete dates, represented in Figure 9.5, together with the expected exposure. The growth of both exposures in time is a fundamental feature of

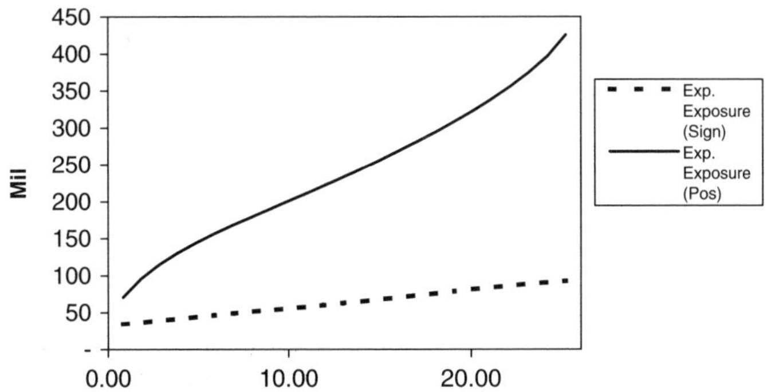

Figure 9.5 CCS with notional exchange. Expected Exposure with Sign $\mathbb{E}_0[D(0,T_i)(\mathrm{Exs}(T_i))]$ and Expected Exposure (Positive) $\mathbb{E}_0\left[D(0,T_i)(\mathrm{Exs}(T_i))^+\right]$ plotted against T_i

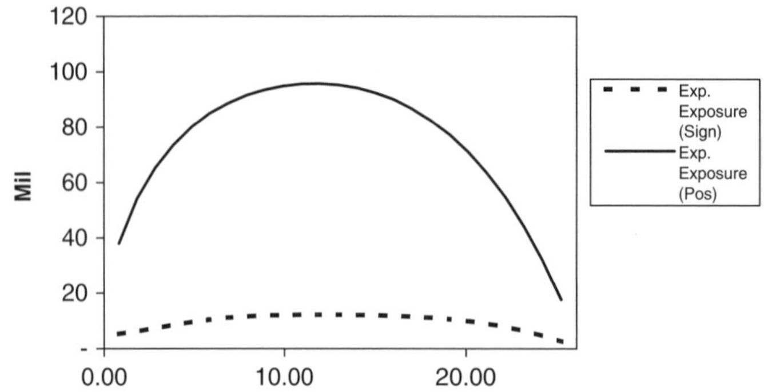

Figure 9.6 CCS without notional exchange. Expected Exposure with Sign and Expected Exposure (Positive) plotted against T_i

counterparty risk for a CCS, due mainly to the exchange of the notional at the end of the deal. This can be very well assessed in the simple approach presented here that makes the exposures different from the pattern we have in the counterparty risk for a standard IRS. If we consider a contract exchanging the same running flows of the CCS above, but without a final exchange of notionals (as it happens for an IRS) we would find an exposure that starts to decrease after reaching a maximum, as in Figure 9.6.

9.5.1 Changing the CCS Moneyness

Another crucial element that determines the size of the CCS counterparty risk is the moneyness of the underlying CCS, here intended as the difference between the initial rate of exchange φ_0 (that determines the ratio between domestic and foreign notional) and the current rate of exchange φ_t. It is interesting to observe what would happen to the counterparty risk of the above CCS if evaluated with different exchange rates. For example, supposing (i) it was entered into in September 2005 and evaluated after the beginning of the credit crunch, at the spot exchange rate for February 2008, as in Table 9.6, then (ii) evaluated in February 2008 as if it were reset to be ATM, as in Table 9.7, and then (iii) re-evaluated at the spot exchange rate for 7 months later, in September 2008, as in Table 9.8. In the three cases we consider the same CCS as previously, with the same inputs as Table 9.4, expect for the dates which are always shifted forward to keep the CCS the same length. Thus we compare exactly the same product changing only the rates of exchange φ_0. We use a flat exchange rate volatility of 10%, since a relatively low level of volatility allows us to see more precisely the effect of the moneyness. We consider first a re-evaluation in February 2008.

The CCS has gone strongly in-the-money for one counterparty (the one that suffers the risk of default), due to the decline in the value of the USD vs EUR. The CVA is high, due to high

Table 9.6 Features of a CCS entered into in September 2005 and evaluated after the beginning of the credit crunch at the spot exchange rate of February 2008

Initial FX Rate (September 2005)	0.833
Spot FX Rate (February 2008)	0.682
CCS CVA	69,605,911

Table 9.7 Features of a CCS entered into in February 2008 as if it was reset to be ATM

Initial FX Rate (February 2008)	0.682
Spot FX Rate (February 2008)	0.682
CCS CVA	35,577,156

Positive Exposure. Also the Expected Exposure with Sign is high and not so far away from Positive Exposure, as one can see in Figure 9.7, showing that the level of the CVA does not depend so much on the volatility.

In February 2008 it may be reasonable to repackage the deal and enter a new CCS at-the-money, like the one described in Table 9.8.

The CVA has been cut by a half. It remains quite high, despite the fact that the Expected Exposure starts at zero. The Positive Exposure, the really relevant quantity for CVA, is now much higher than the Expected Exposure with Sign, showing here the volatility of the underlying forward exchange rates (which depends on the volatility of the spot exchange rate and on the forward rates of the two term structures, as one can see in (9.8)), plays a more important role.

If we evaluate an analogous CCS at the spot EUR/USD just 7 months later, the CCS has gone out-of-the-money, since the EUR-USD exchange rate has increased again, going back to the values it had in 2005.

The CVA is around a half of what it was in February, and the Expected Exposure is negative on all future dates, showing that the positive level of the Positive Expected Exposure is driven by the volatility. See Figure 9.9.

9.5.2 Changing the Volatility

We have understood that the interplay between moneyness and volatility is an important driver of the CVA for a CCS. Now we investigate another aspect of this interplay. How would the CVA change in the case of an increase in the volatility from a flat 10% to a flat 20%, for the three CCSs (ITM, ATM, OTM) just analyzed? We see Table 9.9 and Figure 9.10, showing the CVA under the different assumptions, and also how such changes depend strongly on the moneyness.

For the OTM CCS the effect of doubling the volatility is to increase almost three times the CVA. For the ATM CCS the CVA is less than doubled. For the ITM CCS the effect amounts to around one third of the CVA.

9.5.3 Changing the FX Correlations

The last aspect we analyze is the effect of correlation. As we have seen in Section 9.2.1, the volatility that enters the final formula for the CVA is the volatility of the cross currency swap

Table 9.8 Features of a CCS entered into in February 2008 at the spot exchange rate of 7 months later

Initial FX Rate (February 2008)	0.682
Spot FX Rate (October 2008)	0.803
CCS CVA	18,132,494

Table 9.9 Moneyness and volatility of CCSs analyzed as examples

	Low vol	High vol	Low/High
OTM	19,129,036	51,710,552	37%
ATM	36,322,172	68,484,453	53%
ITM	67,502,482	92,590,984	73%

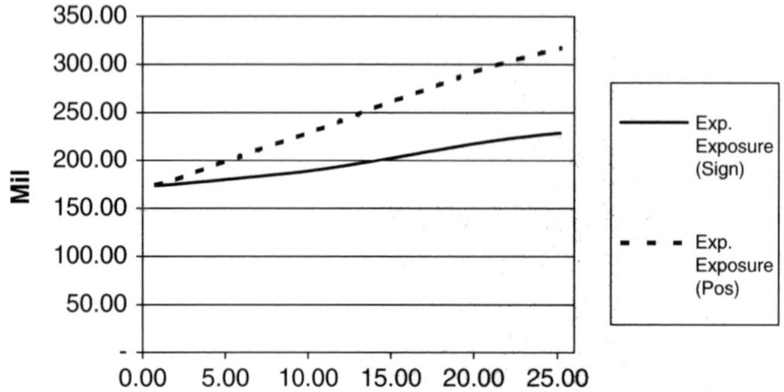

Figure 9.7 ITM CCS. Expected Exposure with Sign and Expected Exposure (Positive) plotted against T_i

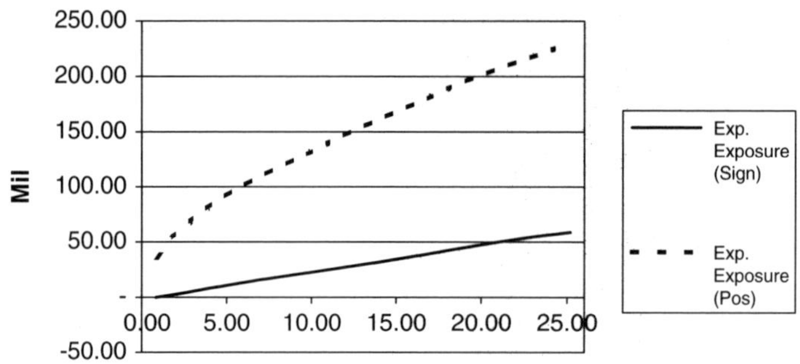

Figure 9.8 ATM CCS. Expected Exposure with Sign and Expected Exposure (Positive) plotted against T_i

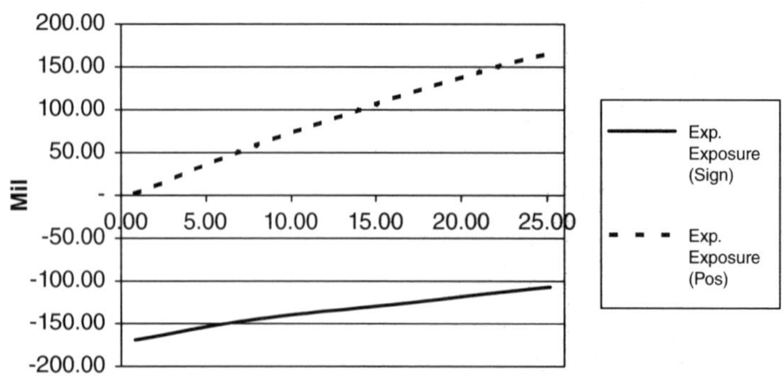

Figure 9.9 OTM CCS. Expected Exposure with Sign and Expected Exposure (Positive) plotted against T_i

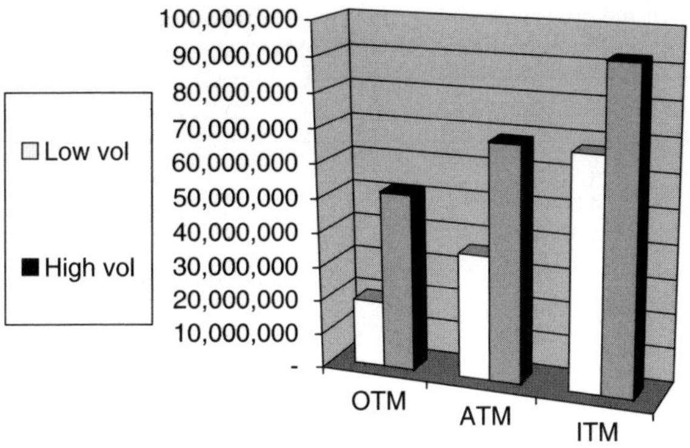

Figure 9.10 The CCS CVA for three different levels of moneyness and two levels of volatility (10% and 20%)

rate, and this volatility is a combination of the volatilities of the forward exchange rates modulo and a transformation through the correlation matrix of the forward exchange rates. Starting from a flat volatility of the forward exchange rates at 20.69%, keeping a correlation matrix where all terms are equal to 1, implies that the volatility of the cross currency swap rate is flat at the same level. Decreasing the correlations introduces "diversification" and reduces the resulting volatilities. We see that moving it to 0 can have a relevant effect on the CVA, reducing it to little more than one third. Also moving to a realistic historically estimated correlation matrix, where most entries are relatively close to one, we can have a non-negligible effect, as see in Table 9.10.

9.6 NOVATIONS AND THE COST OF LIQUIDITY

In this section we consider a type of deal, the Novation, that had years of popularity after the start of the global financial crisis. The deal is related to CVA, since it is a form of protection against counterparty risk, and it is related to FX since the underlying risk has often been cross currency risk, so the end of this chapter is a convenient place to discuss it. Like a CDS, a Novation protects from default risk and involves three parties: a protection buyer, a protection seller, and a reference entity. The Novation is related to Contingent CDS (CCDS). Contingent CDS was introduced briefly in Chapter 1 in the "Hedging Counterparty Risk: CCDS" section, and then in Section 5.4. The Novation has financial effects similar to a Contingent CDS, but with two important differences. First, the Novation does not require a specific term-sheet like the Contingent CDS, but is obtained synthetically from elementary deals and a standard Collateral Agreement. Second, the Novation involves a funding liquidity exchange that is not provided for in a Contingent CDS. The Novation is one of the first contexts that showed funding liquidity had become so relevant after the start of the credit crunch, it became a crucial ingredient in the pricing of many deals. In the following we analyze a simple approach to evaluate this provision. It is similar in spirit to the approach shown above for the valuation of the CVA in swaps or cross currency swaps with independence between counterparty credit risk and the value of the underlying deal.

Table 9.10 Volatility of the cross currency swap rate at different times, depending on correlation. The volatility of the forward rates of exchange is flat at 20.69%

	$\rho = [0]$	$\rho = Hist$	$\rho = 1$
1	4.40%	15.13%	20.69%
2	4.47%	15.06%	20.69%
3	4.55%	15.00%	20.69%
4	4.64%	14.95%	20.69%
5	4.73%	14.92%	20.69%
6	4.82%	14.91%	20.69%
7	4.93%	14.91%	20.69%
8	5.05%	14.93%	20.69%
9	5.17%	14.96%	20.69%
10	5.31%	15.01%	20.69%
11	5.47%	15.08%	20.69%
12	5.64%	15.16%	20.69%
13	5.84%	15.27%	20.69%
14	6.06%	15.41%	20.69%
15	6.32%	15.57%	20.69%
16	6.61%	15.76%	20.69%
17	6.95%	15.99%	20.69%
18	7.36%	16.26%	20.69%
19	7.86%	16.57%	20.69%
20	8.48%	16.94%	20.69%
21	9.28%	17.39%	20.69%
22	10.36%	17.92%	20.69%
23	11.95%	18.57%	20.69%
24	14.63%	19.40%	20.69%
25	20.69%	20.69%	20.69%
CVA	28,846,834.70	56,644,007	71,758,224

9.6.1 A Synthetic Contingent CDS: The Novation

Consider a situation where there exists a deal, that we will refer to as "The Original Deal", between a bank, that we will call "The Bank", and a counterparty which does not have a collateral agreement with the Bank. When a bank does not have a collateral agreement with a counterparty, usually this counterparty is a company from some industry other than finance. Thus we call this counterparty "The Corporate". The Original Deal is usually a swap, either on interest rates, cross currency or commodities, and it has a strongly positive Net Present Value, or Exposure with Sign, for the Bank. In principle both the Bank and the Corporate are exposed to the risk of counterparty default, but we neglect the Bank's default risk for the following considerations:

1. For the deal to be financially convenient, the Bank must have a lower probability of default than the Corporate. This was typical at the start of the credit crunch, although not in some subsequent phases of the crisis.
2. More importantly, since the NPV of the deal is strongly positive for the Bank, only the Bank has an actual exposure to counterparty default, while the Corporate has an exposure which is only potential. In other words the Bank expects to receive in the future from the Corporate much more than it expects to pay to it, hence only the Bank worries about the risk of default of the counterparty.

The situation is explained in the chart below, where we represent all the cash flows that the Bank (or the Corporate) should pay in the future to the Corporate (or the Bank). The "default" label over the arrow representing the payments from the Corporate indicates that, as there is no collateral, these cash flows are subject to default risk. The arrow for the payments due from the Corporate is thicker to indicate that they are larger, in expected value, than those due from the Bank, consistent with the sign for the exposures of the two counterparties: the Bank exposure Exs is positive, while the Corporate exposure $\overline{\text{Exs}} = -\text{Exs}$ is obviously negative.

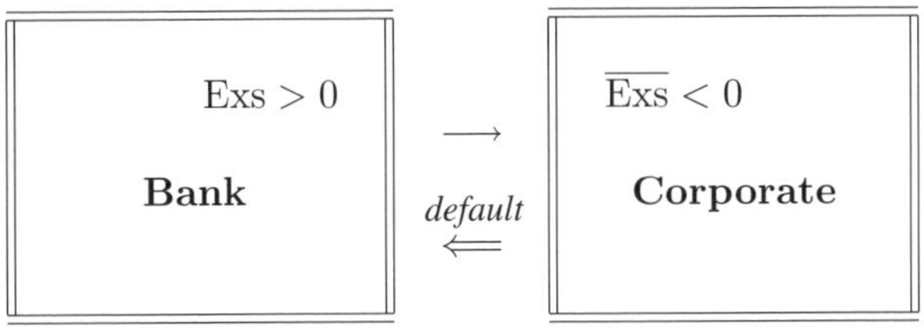

This situation materialized quite often during the credit crunch. The rather extreme movements in currencies, interest rate term structures and commodity prices between the end of 2007 and the beginning of 2008 led many deals to have a very strong NPV in favour of one counterparty.

In the situation above the Bank can protect itself from default risk by entering as a protection buyer in a Contingent CDS with another bank, that we will call "The Guarantor", having the Corporate as the reference entity and the Original Deal as the underlying transaction. In case of Corporate default at time τ, the Guarantor would pay to the Bank the default loss, computed as usual as

$$\text{LGD}\,(\text{Exs}\,(\tau))^{+}\,.$$

There is, however, a simple alternative to provide the Bank with default protection. This alternative is the Novation, where the Original Deal is replaced by two contracts stipulated by the Guarantor. The Guarantor must be chosen among the banks that have a collateral agreement with the Bank. We consider in the following the most standard collateral agreement, where:

- the collateral exchanged is pure cash;
- the amount $C\,(t)$ of collateral provided at t by the Guarantor is given by the simple rule

$$C\,(t) = \text{Exs}\,(t)\,;$$

- the collateral is regulated daily and so is the interest generated by it. The interest paid on this collateral by the Bank at t_i is given by

$$C\,(t_i)\,R_O\,(t_i)\,(t_i - t_{i-1})$$

  where $C\,(t_i)$ is the amount of collateral at time t_i, $(t_i - t_{i-1})$ is the length of a one day period and $R_O\,(t_i)$ is the interest rate for the day that starts at time t_i (let us say t_i is midnight on day i). We take $R_O\,(t_i)$ to be the quoted overnight rate, as is the case in most collateral agreements.

The Guarantor must enter into two contracts that replicate the residual Original Deal. One contract will be stipulated with the Bank, and here the Guarantor takes the same position as the Corporate in the Original Deal. This contract is covered by the collateral agreement between the Bank and the Guarantor and therefore it is virtually risk free. The second contract is between the Guarantor and the Corporate, with the Guarantor taking the same position as the Bank in the Original Deal. The resulting situation is shown in the chart below.

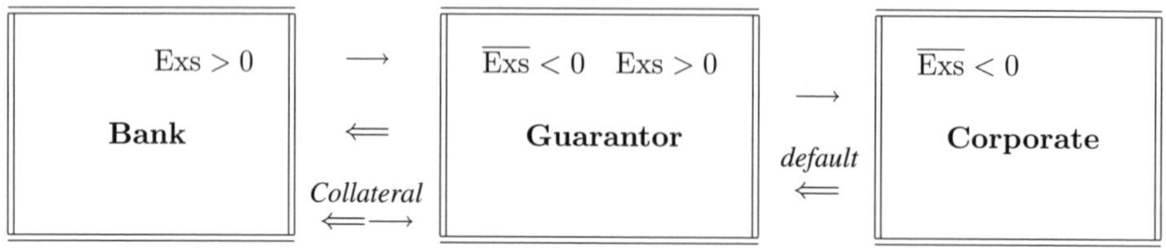

What has changed compared to the Original Deal? For the Corporate, nothing at all. For the Bank, the cash flows involved are the same as in the Original Contracts, so that the exposure to market risk has remained, but there are two differences:

1. The Bank receives collateral from the Guarantor. If the collateral is cash, the Bank is now funding the deal via a liquidity facility provided by the Guarantor.
2. Due to collateralization, the cashflows for the deal between Bank and Guarantor are no longer subject to default risk. The Bank is protected from risk of default.

As for the Guarantor, we have symmetrically:

1. The Guarantor posts collateral, which means a liquidity outflow.
2. If there is no default, the Guarantor has no net outflows or inflows other than collateral (it is not exposed to market risk). In case of default of the Corporate, the Guarantor will suffer the following loss:

$$\text{LGD}\,(\text{Exs}\,(\tau))^{+}\,.$$

It is clear that in this Novation the Guarantor is providing the Bank with default protection and an amount of funding, as shown in the chart below, therefore the Guarantor requires a compensation from the Bank, which is usually regulated upfront.

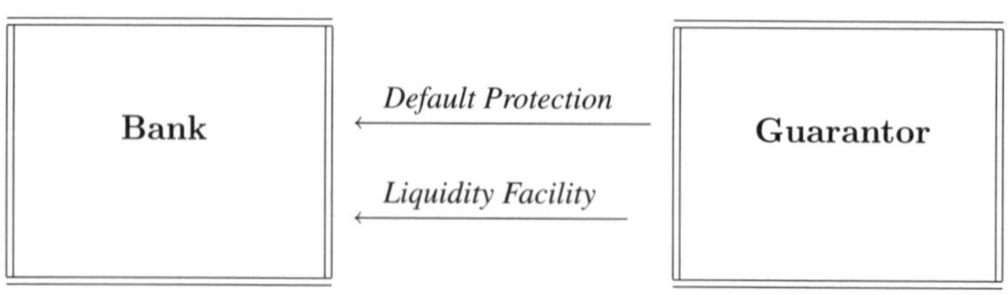

The value of the default protection can be computed as usual. If the deal has maturity T_M, the risk-neutral discounted expected value of this protection is

$$\text{LGD}\,\mathbb{E}_0\left[1_{\{0\leq\tau\leq T_M\}}D\,(0,\tau)\,(\text{Exs}\,(\tau))^{+}\right],$$

which is equal both to the CVA of the Original Deal and to the upfront price of a Contingent CDS written on the Original Deal with the Corporate as a Reference entity. The difference compared to the Contingent CDS is that the Novation is probably easier and faster to implement, since it does not require any specific term sheet. The evaluation of this credit part of the Guarantor compensation follows the methodology detailed above. The evaluation of the liquidity facility in a simplified, practical manner is instead approached as shown below.

9.6.2 Extending the Approach to the Valuation of Liquidity

The collateral agreement requires the Bank to pay to the Guarantor an interest $R_O(t_i)$ on the liquidity posted as collateral, thus one may think that this liquidity facility does not need to be compensated by any upfront amount. This is true whenever in the market the *term premium* is negligible, but this is rarely the case, and it was certainly not the case during the credit crunch. When a different rate $R(0, T_M)$ exists that includes a term premium associated to the fact that liquidity is guaranteed from now to T_M, the liquidity provision implicit in a Novation must be evaluated at such rate. The value of this liquidity provision can be tackled in two diverse but equivalent ways: either by computing the difference in pricing of the two deals involved in a Novation, the collateralized and the non-collateralized (which differ because of CVA and FVA, the so-called Funding Value Adjustment), and paying this positive difference to the guarantor, or by evaluating the money received in the collateral account at the spread between $R(0, T_M)$ and $R_O(t_i)$ and making this an upfront payment to the Guarantor. The former approach is theoretically sounder and will be considered in Chapter 11 and in Chapter 17 where the impact of funding liquidity will be addressed in a rigorous framework. Here we are adopting an informal analysis based on a number of practical, and somehow "traditional", assumptions. Notice also that although here we are neglecting the results of [157], we will review them later in Chapter 11.

Going back to our analysis, if the amount of liquidity provided by the Guarantor was a constant and deterministic quantity C, the fair compensation that the Bank should pay at T_M would be

$$R(0, T_M)\, C T_M.$$

If this compensation is paid upfront, we have by risk-free discounting

$$R(0, T_M)\, C T_M P(0, T_M).$$

Instead we know that

$$C(t) = \text{Exs}(t),$$

so it is stochastic and it can even change sign: when $\text{Exs}(t) < 0$ the Bank will provide liquidity to the Guarantor. It is customary in the market to compute the value of this liquidity provision using a deterministic *equivalent amount* $\overline{C}$ of money such that

$$\mathbb{E}_0\left[\int_0^{T_M} D(0, t)\, \text{Exs}(t)\, dt\right] = \overline{C} T_M P(0, T_M),$$

leading to

$$\overline{C} = \frac{\mathbb{E}_0\left[\int_0^{T_M} D(0, t)\, \text{Exs}(t)\, dt\right]}{T_M P(0, T_M)}.$$

This is an average of the expected liquidity provided from 0 to T_M. As done with the discretized CVA of (9.9), we can discretize the computation of the integral on the dates

$$[T_0, T_1, \ldots, T_M].$$

We obtain

$$\begin{aligned} \overline{IC}^P &= \mathbb{E}_0\left[\sum_{i=1}^M \frac{D(0,T_i)(T_i - T_{i-1})}{P(0,T_M)\,T_M}\mathrm{Exs}(T_i)\right] \\ &= \sum_{i=1}^M \mathbb{E}[\mathrm{Exs}(T_i)]\frac{P(0,T_i)}{P(0,T_M)}\frac{T_i - T_{i-1}}{T_M}. \end{aligned} \tag{9.24}$$

The above formula holds under independence between the underlying exposure $\mathrm{Exs}(T_i)$ and the discount factor. In case the underlying depends on interest rates or, in general, whenever such independence is not appropriate, the formula holds by replacing risk-neutral expectation with expectation under the T_i-forward measure.

The fair interest, paid at T_M, on the deterministic amount of liquidity $\overline{IC}^P$ provided from 0 to T_M has a value today which is given by

$$\overline{IC}^P R(0,T_M)\,T_M P(0,T_M) \tag{9.25}$$

If instead the same amount of liquidity is compensated overnight, as provided by the Collateral Agreement, the today value of this compensation is

$$\overline{IC}^P \mathbb{E}_0^M\left[\prod_{i=1}^M [1 + R_O(t_i)(t_i - t_{i-1})] - 1\right] P(0,T_M) = \overline{IC}^P OIS(0,T_M)\,T_M P(0,T_M), \tag{9.26}$$

where $OIS(0,T_M)$ denotes the Overnight Indexed Swap (OIS) rate for maturity $T_M = t_M$. In an OIS contract with notional 1 and maturity t_M one party pays a fixed amount Kt_M while the other party pays an amount which is computed at t_M as the compounding of the overnight rates fixed in the period from 0 to t_M. The OIS rate is the level of K that makes the current values of the two legs equal, namely:

$$\mathbb{E}_0\left[D(0,t_M)\prod_{i=1}^M [1 + R_O(t_i)(t_i - t_{i-1})]\right] = P(0,t_M)(1 + OIS(0,t_M)\,t_M),$$

and this explains (9.26).

The Guarantor receives a compensation for collateral liquidity given by (9.26) while he should receive (9.25). This difference is settled upfront and is trivially given by the independence-based liquidity valuation approximated adjustment

$$\begin{aligned} \mathrm{ILVAA}^P(0) &= P(0,T_M)\,\overline{IC}^P R(0,T_M)\,T_M - P(0,T_M)\,\overline{IC}^P OIS(0,T_M)\,T_M \\ &= P(0,T_M)\,\overline{IC}^P S(0,T_M)\,T_M \end{aligned}$$

where

$$S(0,T_M) := R(0,T_M) - OIS(0,T_M)$$

is the market spread over OIS capturing the term premium for lending until the term T_M.

We have, by (9.24):

$$\mathrm{ILVAA}^P(0) = \sum_{i=1}^M P(0,T_i)\,\mathbb{E}_0[\mathrm{Exs}(T_i)]\,S(0,T_M)(T_i - T_{i-1}) \tag{9.27}$$

which reminds us of (9.9):

$$\mathrm{ICVAA}^P(0) = \sum_{i=1}^{M} P(0, T_i)\,\mathbb{E}_0\left[(\mathrm{Exs}(T_i))^+\right]\mathbb{Q}\{\tau \in (T_{i-1}, T_i]\}\,\mathrm{LGD}.$$

In the term $\mathrm{ILVAA}^P(0)$ the L stands for 'liquidity' and replaces the C ('credit') of $\mathrm{ICVAA}^P(0)$.

There are two differences between (9.27) and (9.9). First $\mathbb{E}_0[\mathrm{Exs}(T_i)]$ replaces $\mathbb{E}_0\left[(\mathrm{Exs}(T_i))^+\right]$, and this makes sense since unilateral counterparty risk affects the deal only proportionally to the (positive) exposure: when at default the net present value is negative for the surviving party, the deal is unaffected by counterparty default. On the other hand, the cost of liquidity applies to the exposure with sign, since in case the net present value turns negative to the Guarantor there will be an exchange of roles (the Guarantor is no longer a lender but a borrower) but there will still be a liquidity provision that must be accounted for.

The second difference is that

$$S(0, T_M)(T_i - T_{i-1})$$

replaces

$$\mathbb{Q}\{\tau \in (T_{i-1}, T_i]\}\, Lgd.$$

We note that these two quantities are less different than appears at first sight. In fact with flat deterministic default intensity λ we obtain by first order Maclaurin Taylor expansion:

$$\begin{aligned}\mathbb{Q}\{\tau \in (T_{i-1}, T_i]\} &= e^{-\lambda T_{i-1}} - e^{-\lambda T_i}\\ &\approx \lambda(T_i - T_{i-1}).\end{aligned}$$

Another common market approximation, based first on flat intensity and secondly on approximating a market CDS with a CDS paying a continuous premium, yields (see Formula 3.13)

$$\lambda \approx \frac{S^{CDS}(0, T_M)}{\mathrm{LGD}}$$

where $S^{CDS}(0, T_M)$ is the CDS spread of the counterparty at time 0 for maturity T_M. Finally we get

$$\mathbb{Q}\{\tau \in (T_{i-1}, T_i]\}\,\mathrm{LGD} \approx S^{CDS}(0, T_M)(T_i - T_{i-1}),$$

which is formally analogous to

$$S(0, T_M)(T_i - T_{i-1}).$$

9.7 CONCLUSIONS

In this chapter we have evaluated unilateral CVA for different kinds of Cross Currency Swaps (CCS), thus covering FX as an asset class through some of its more representative products. Actually, CCS involve risk from interest rates, currency and credit.

This chapter also dealt with the concept of Novation, which is importantly related to Counterparty Risk and Contingent Credit Default Swaps. This also prompted us to analyze an early and simplified approach to the valuation of funding liquidity, that will be generalized and perfected in Chapters 11 and 17.

Overall this chapter illustrates in detail the fact that even if one gives away the need to adopt a credit model through the independence assumption of default and underlying contract (no wrong way risk), one still needs to develop advanced dynamical models for the underlying portfolio option markets.

Part III

ADVANCED CREDIT AND FUNDING RISK PRICING

10

New Generation Counterparty and Funding Risk Pricing

This chapter is the beginning of Part III, namely the most advanced part of the book. In a way, by summarizing the earlier chapters, discussing the following chapters and by introducing further analysis, it illustrates the areas covered by this book that are not covered by earlier counterparty risk books such as Pykthin (2005) [173], Cesari et al. (2010) [76], Gregory (2010) [119], Kenyon and Stamm (2012) [136] (although this last book deals with some of the key issues we illustrate here), thus making this a unique advanced counterparty risk pricing book.

This chapter can be read independently as a guided tour to advanced issues on CVA, since, apart from explicit references to other chapters, it is relatively self-contained. However, the chapter may be best appreciated after reading the introductory dialogue in Chapter 1.

10.1 INTRODUCING THE ADVANCED PART OF THE BOOK

The advanced part of the book will deal with the following key areas:

- Own credit risk (Debit Valuation Adjustment, DVA).
- Close-out modelling: risk-free close-out vs. replacement close-out.
- The importance of properly including the first-to-default time in close-out and a common (and inappropriate) approximation used in the industry.
- Collateral modelling and re-hypothecation.
- Gap risk and cases where even continuous collateralization is not effective in reducing CVA and DVA.
- Consistent inclusion of funding costs modelling.
- Counterparty risk restructuring.
- From contingent CDS and CDO-type structures to floating rate CVA/DVA and margin lending.
- Modelling is becoming holistic, and we need consistent global valuation techniques. "Divide and analyze separately" does not work well anymore.

We start the chapter by introducing DVA. So far we have looked at counterparty risk and credit valuation adjustments (CVA) mostly from the point of view of an entity (say B, the Bank) that considers itself as default free and who looks at the other entity, the counterparty (say C, a Corporate) as defaultable. We have termed the resulting CVA as Unilateral, since it is computed by embedding only the default risk of side C and not of side B.

If both parties agree to this and there is no collateral posted as a guarantee, as is often the case with deals occurring with corporate entities [192], what happens with counterparty risk valuation is what we have seen in the earlier part of the book. In particular, we have seen how the related Unilateral CVA (UCVA) can be computed, with and without wrong way risk (WWR).

Even without collateral and with a default-free bank, the calculation of UCVA can be model intensive and quite complex. We have seen this in the chapters that dealt with UCVA for different asset classes.

UCVA has been introduced informally in Chapter 1, a little more formally in Chapter 2 and formally in Chapter 4. In those and in the following chapters we adopted the UDA Assumption 4.1.3 that we report here:

Assumption 10.1.1 ***Unilateral Default Assumption (UDA): Assuming one party (B) to be default-free.*** *Calculations are done considering B to be default free. Valuation of the contract is done usually from B's point of view.*

As explained in Chapter 4, we are interested in distinguishing symmetry from asymmetry in valuation. We are in the symmetric case if the price of the deal to B is just minus the price of the deal to C, as in a swap. Under Assumption 10.1.1, we have symmetry if B is recognized by C to be default free. Whereas if C does not recognize B as default free, we have asymmetry. Indeed, if C does not recognize B as default free, it will charge a counterparty risk adjustment to B that B does not recognize, leading to asymmetry in the valuation.

One situation where the asymmetric case can work, in practice, is when it is an approximation for the symmetric case. If B has a much higher credit quality than C, then C may agree that B assumes itself to be default free when valuing counterparty risk to C for practical purposes. This way C also assumes that, if C itself were to compute the counterparty risk valuation adjustment of the position towards B, this would be zero since B is considered as having null default probability for practical purposes.

The Unilateral Default Assumption was an acceptable approximation of reality before the start of the global financial crisis in 2007. At that time banks had very low credit spreads, much lower than those of corporates. At the same time, corporates did not have the technology to take into account the bank's credit risk, so neglecting such risk was convenient for both parties in the deal. As already mentioned in Chapter 4, this Assumption is no longer acceptable. Since 2008, it is very difficult to accept the notion that any market party can be default free. Even sovereign debts have faced considerable credit problems during the global crisis started in 2007. Moreover, the eight credit events on financial institutions that occurred in one month of 2008 (Fannie Mae, Freddie Mac, Lehman Brothers, Washington Mutual, Landsbanki, Glitnir, Kaupthing, and in a way also Merrill Lynch) clearly show that the assumption that important financial institutions are default-free is not realistic. We should therefore accept the fact that B may default, and we should include this in the valuation, even if we are B itself.

On the other hand, the idea that counterparty risk is bilateral goes way back. Bilateral risk is mentioned in the credit risk measurement space by the Basel II documentation, Annex IV, 2/A:

> Unlike a firm's exposure to credit risk through a loan, where the exposure to credit risk is unilateral and only the lending bank faces the risk of loss, the counterparty credit risk creates a bilateral risk of loss: the market value of the transaction can be positive or negative to either counterparty to the transaction.

We will now remove the Unilateral Default Assumption and allow both parties to default in valuing the contract. This, however, will open a Pandora's box called

DVA – Debit Valuation Adjustment–

on which the industry and regulators are quite divided, beyond the usual opportunistic/political moves. We may roughly identify the modern CVA calculation as the case where DVA enters the picture and is being discussed (whether one decides to keep it or not).

10.2 WHAT WE HAVE SEEN BEFORE: UNILATERAL CVA

We start by giving a summary, with a few new twists, of what we have seen in earlier chapters, mostly on unilateral CVA.

Let us consider the bank B and corporate C and assume the UDA assumption above is in force. Consider a market product whose cash flows between times t and T, added up and discounted back at t, but without counterparty default risk, and denoted by $\Pi_B(t,T)$. The same cash flows in the presence of C's default risk are denoted by $\Pi_B^D(t,T)$.

Earlier in the book and in Chapter 4 in particular, the payout under C's counterparty default risk, seen by B is written as

$$\begin{aligned}\Pi_B^D(t,T) = {} & \mathbf{1}_{\tau_C>T}\Pi_B(t,T) \\ & + \mathbf{1}_{t<\tau_C\le T}\left[\Pi_B(t,\tau_C) + D(t,\tau_C)\left(\text{Rec}_C\,(\text{NPV}_B(\tau_C))^+ - (-\text{NPV}_B(\tau_C))^+\right)\right],\end{aligned} \tag{10.1}$$

where as usual

$$\text{NPV}_B(u) = \mathbb{E}_u[\Pi_B(u,T)]$$

is the risk-neutral expectation or price (Net Present Value (NPV)) of the residual position at time u for Π. This last expression $\Pi_B^D(t,T)$ is the general payoff seen from the point of view of B under C's unilateral counterparty default risk. Indeed, looking at Formula (10.1):

1. If there is no early default, this expression reduces to the first term on the right-hand side, which is the payoff of a default-free claim.
2. In the case of early default by the counterparty, the payments due before default occurs are received (the second term).
3. If the residual net present value is positive, only the recovery value of the counterparty Rec_C is received (the third term).
4. If the residual net present value is negative it is paid in full by the bank B (the fourth term).

As we have seen in Chapter 4, if one simplifies the cash flows and takes the risk-neutral expectation, one obtains the fundamental formula for the valuation of counterparty risk when the calculating bank B is default free:

$$\mathbb{E}_t\left[\Pi_B^D(t,T)\right] = 1_{\{\tau_C>t\}}\mathbb{E}_t\left[\Pi_B(t,T)\right] - \mathbb{E}_t\left[\text{Lgd}_C 1_{\{t<\tau_C\le T\}} D(t,\tau_C)\left[\text{NPV}_B(\tau_C)\right]^+\right] \tag{10.2}$$

This formula is composed of the following parts:

- First term: Value without counterparty risk.
- Second term: Unilateral Counterparty Valuation Adjustment.
- $\text{NPV}(\tau_C) = \mathbb{E}_{\tau_C}[\Pi(\tau_C,T)]$ is the value of the transaction on the counterparty default date. $\text{Lgd} := 1 - \text{Rec}$.

We define the unilateral CVA (computed including C's default risk but not B's) as computed by B as

$$\text{UCVA}_B(t) = \mathbb{E}_t\left[\text{Lgd}_C 1_{\{t<\tau_C\le T\}} D(t,\tau_C)\left[\text{NPV}_B(\tau_C)\right]^+\right] \tag{10.3}$$

We observe immediately that:

- The value of the same deal under counterparty default risk is smaller, since we subtract the positive UCVA adjustment. This is to be expected. If B is given the choice to trade Π with a default-free counterparty or with a defaultable counterparty, B will always choose the default-free, unless the defaultable counterparty compensates B with a discount on the deal price. This discount is the UCVA term.
- Including counterparty risk in the valuation of an otherwise default-free derivative leads to a credit-hybrid derivative.
- The inclusion of counterparty risk adds a level of optionality to the payoff. If the original Π is a portfolio of plain vanilla swaps, then CVA becomes an option on a swap portfolio with a random maturity given by the counterparty default. Therefore, differing from a swap with no counterparty risk, a swap with CVA depends on opinions about the underlying market dynamics and volatility, as well as an opinion on statistical dependence (or "correlation") between the underlying market risk and the counterparty default.

10.2.1 Approximation: Default Bucketing and Independence

If we bucket defaults in a set of time intervals $(T_{j-1}, T_j]$ spanning the whole $(0, T]$, we may approximate UCVA as follows:

$$\text{UCVAB}_B(0) = \text{LGD} \sum_{j=1}^{b} \mathbb{E}_0[1\{\tau \in (T_{j-1}, T_j]\}\ D(0, T_j)(\mathbb{E}_{T_j}\Pi(T_j, T))^+].$$

In this formulation defaults are bucketed and postponed to the final point of each bucket, but we still need a joint model for τ and the underlying Π, including their statistical dependency ("correlation"). An option model is also needed for Π in τ scenarios.

If we further assume independence between Π and default by C we obtain:

$$\text{UCVABI}_B(0) = \text{LGD} \sum_{j=1}^{b} \mathbb{Q}\{\tau \in (T_{j-1}, T_j]\}\mathbb{E}_0[D(0, T_j)(\mathbb{E}_{T_j}\Pi(T_j, T))^+].$$

In this formulation defaults are bucketed and postponed to the final point of each bucket, and only survival probabilities are needed (no default model). However, an option model is STILL needed for the underlying of Π.

In the previous chapters we saw how UCVA can be calculated both under the Bucketing plus Independence assumptions (Chapters 4 and 9) and without such assumptions, in presence of wrong way risk (Chapters 5, 6, 7 and 8).

10.3 UNILATERAL DEBIT VALUATION ADJUSTMENT (UDVA)

We now carry out a useful exercise that is rarely done explicitly, but that can be quite illuminating. Consider the same situation as in the previous section but from the point of view of the counterparty C. Namely, consider the deal from the point of view of C, while still staying in a world where only C may default. We have:

$$\begin{aligned}\Pi^D_C(t, T) &= \mathbf{1}_{\tau_C > T}\Pi_C(t, T) \\ &\quad + \mathbf{1}_{t<\tau_C \le T}\left[\Pi_C(t, \tau_C) + D(t, \tau_C)\left((\text{NPV}_C(\tau_C))^+ - \text{REC}_C\,(-\text{NPV}_C(\tau_C))^+\right)\right].\end{aligned}$$

This last expression is the general payoff seen from the point of view of C (Π_C, NPV_C) under unilateral counterparty default risk. Indeed:

1. If there is no early default, this expression reduces to the first term on the right-hand side, which is the payoff of a default-free claim.
2. In the case of early default of C, the payments due before default occurs go through (the second term).
3. If the residual net present value is positive to the defaulted C, it is received in full from B (the third term).
4. If it is negative, only the recovery fraction REC_C is paid to B (the fourth term).

The above formula simplifies to

$$\mathbb{E}_t\left[\Pi_C^D(t,T)\right] = 1_{\tau_C>t}\mathbb{E}_t\left[\Pi_C(t,T)\right] + \mathbb{E}_t\left[\text{LGD}_C 1_{t<\tau_C\leq T} D(t,\tau_C)(-\text{NPV}_C(\tau_C))^+\right] \quad (10.4)$$

and the adjustment term with respect to the risk-free price $\mathbb{E}_t\left[\Pi_C(t,T)\right]$ is called Unilateral Debit Valuation Adjustment (UDVA):

$$\text{UDVA}_C(t) = \mathbb{E}_t\left[\text{LGD}_C 1_{\{t<\tau_C\leq T\}} D(t,\tau_C)(-\text{NPV}_C(\tau_C))^+\right]. \quad (10.5)$$

In this case the price of the deal to C is increased by a positive term call UDVA. This makes sense. Here C expects to be charged more by B to enter into the deal Π than another default-free counterparty. The increase in the deal price occurs because C may default and is called the UDVA.

We note the important fact that

$$\text{UDVA}_C = \text{UCVA}_B.$$

Notice also that in this universe under Assumption UDA 10.1.1,

$$0 = \text{UDVA}_B = \text{UCVA}_C.$$

This is expected: if we are making calculations by assuming that B is default free, then the CVA term that C computes on B will be zero, since B cannot default, and there is no counterparty risk C sees coming from B. Similarly, if B computes the DVA, i.e. the change in price because B may default, this is zero if we make the calculations by assuming that B cannot default.

10.4 BILATERAL RISK AND DVA

Suppose for a minute that we are bank B. An important question at this stage, which we listed at the beginning of the chapter, is:

Should we (bank B) include our own default in the valuation, besides C's?

Often the bank, when computing a counterparty risk adjustment, considers itself to be default free. This can be either an unrealistic assumption, or an approximation for the case when the counterparty has a much higher default probability than the bank. If this assumption is made when no party is actually default free, the unilateral valuation adjustment is asymmetric: if C were to consider itself as default free in dealing now with counterparty B, and if C computed its counterparty risk adjustment towards B, this adjustment would not be the opposite of the one computed by B in the original case.

The total NPV including counterparty risk is similarly also asymmetric, in that the total value of the position to B is not the opposite of the total value of the position to C. There is no *total cash conservation.*

We get back symmetry if we allow for default by bank B too in computing counterparty risk. This also results in an adjustment that is cheaper to counterparty C. Counterparty C may then be willing to ask bank B to include B's default event in the model, when the counterparty risk adjustment is computed by B.

Suppose now that we allow for both parties to default in our model. What is the total adjustment allowing for default by B, and C, when computed by B?

We denote by τ_B, τ_C the default times of B and C respectively. T is the final maturity in the deal.

We consider the following events, forming a partition of the whole sample space:

$$\begin{aligned}
\mathcal{A} &= \{\tau_B \le \tau_C \le T\} \quad & E &= \{T \le \tau_B \le \tau_C\}\\
\mathcal{B} &= \{\tau_B \le T \le \tau_C\} \quad & F &= \{T \le \tau_C \le \tau_B\}\\
\mathcal{C} &= \{\tau_C \le \tau_B \le T\} & &\\
\mathcal{D} &= \{\tau_C \le T \le \tau_B\}. & &
\end{aligned}$$

Define $\mathrm{NPV}_{\{B,C\}}(t) := \mathbb{E}_t[\Pi_{\{B,C\}}(t,T)]$, and recall $\Pi_B = -\Pi_C$. We may write the cash flows of the deal Π adjusted for the default risk of both B and C, as seen by B, namely Π_B^D, as

$$\begin{aligned}
\Pi_B^D(t,T) = {} & \mathbf{1}_{E\cup F}\Pi_B(t,T) \\
& + \mathbf{1}_{\mathcal{C}\cup\mathcal{D}}\left[\Pi_B(t,\tau_C) + D(t,\tau_C)\left(\mathrm{REC}_C\,(\mathrm{NPV}_B(\tau_C))^+ - (-\mathrm{NPV}_B(\tau_C))^+\right)\right]\\
& + \mathbf{1}_{\mathcal{A}\cup\mathcal{B}}\left[\Pi_B(t,\tau_B) + D(t,\tau_B)\left((\mathrm{NPV}_B(\tau_B))^+ - \mathrm{REC}_B\,(-\mathrm{NPV}_B(\tau_B))^+\right)\right].
\end{aligned} \tag{10.6}$$

The explanation for these cash flows is as follows:

1. If no early default ⇒ payoff of a default-free claim (first term);
2. In case of early default by the counterparty, the payments due before default occurs are received (second term);
3. And then if the residual net present value is positive only the recovery value of the counterparty REC_C is received (third term);
4. Whereas if negative, it is paid in full by the investor/bank (fourth term);
5. In case of early default of the investor, the payments due before default occurs are received (fifth term);
6. And then if the residual net present value is positive it is paid in full by the counterparty to the investor/bank (sixth term);
7. Whereas if it is negative only the recovery value of the investor/bank REC_B is paid to the counterparty (seventh term).

The valuation of the payout, adjusted for bilateral default risk of B and C, is obtained by taking the risk-neutral expectation of the above cash flows. In [39] we proved rigorously the following result:

$$\begin{aligned}
&\mathbb{E}_t\left[\Pi_B^D(t,T)\right] = \mathbb{E}_t\left[\Pi_B(t,T)\right] + \mathrm{DVA}_B(t) - \mathrm{CVA}_B(t)\\
&\mathrm{DVA}_B(t) = \mathbb{E}_t\left[\mathrm{LGD_B}\cdot 1(t < \tau^{1st} = \tau_B < T)\cdot D(t,\tau_B)\cdot(-\mathrm{NPV_B}(\tau_B))^+\right]\\
&\mathrm{CVA}_B(t) = \mathbb{E}_t\left[\mathrm{LGD_C}\cdot 1(t < \tau^{1st} = \tau_C < T)\cdot D(t,\tau_C)\cdot(\mathrm{NPV_B}(\tau_C))^+\right]\\
&1(\mathcal{A}\cup\mathcal{B}) = 1(t < \tau^{1st} = \tau_B < T),\quad 1(\mathcal{C}\cup\mathcal{D}) = 1(t < \tau^{1st} = \tau_C < T).
\end{aligned} \tag{10.7}$$

Highlights:

- This formula is obtained in two steps: firstly we simplify the previous formula, and secondly we take expectation on the simplified expression.
- The second term is the adjustment due to scenarios where $\tau_B < \tau_C$. This is positive to the bank B and is called (bilateral) "Debit Valuation Adjustment" (DVA).
- The third term: Counterparty CVA adjustment *due to scenarios* $\tau_C < \tau_B$. Notice that this is not the same as the unilateral CVA we have seen so far, and we call this "bilateral CVA".
- Total Bilateral Valuation Adjustment (BVA) as seen from B:

$$\text{BVA}_B(t) = \text{DVA}_B(t) - \text{CVA}_B(t).$$

  This is to be added to the default-free price of the instrument to adjust for default risk of B and C, as priced from B.
- If computed from the opposite point of view of C having counterparty B, $\text{BVA}_C = -\text{BVA}_B$. We have symmetry.

10.5 UNDESIRABLE FEATURES OF DVA

DVA is a quite controversial quantity. Among the points that fuel debate, we have the following:

10.5.1 Profiting From Own Deteriorating Credit Quality

When the credit quality of bank B worsens, B books a positive mark-to-market. Indeed, all things being equal, an increase on the default probability of B would make the indicator:

$$1(t < \tau^{1st} = \tau_B < T)$$

in the DVA_B term more likely, and therefore make the DVA term larger. This corresponds to reducing the probability that a bank will pay back its debts, so reducing the value of its liabilities while leaving the assets unaltered. Similarly, if the credit quality of the bank improves, then the bank books a negative mark-to-market.

This is not just an academic case: this calculation does happen. Citigroup in its press release on the first quarter revenues of 2009 reported a *positive* mark-to-market due to its *worsened* credit quality:

> Revenues also included [...] a net $2.5 billion positive CVA on derivative positions, excluding monolines, mainly due to the widening of Citi's CDS spreads.

Another example is the news article that appeared on 18 October 2011, 3:59 pm ET, *Wall Street Journal* "Goldman Sachs Hedges Its Way to Less Volatile Earnings".

> Goldman's DVA gains in the third quarter totaled $450 million [...] That amount is comparatively smaller than the $1.9 billion in DVA gains that J.P. Morgan Chase and Citigroup each recorded for the third quarter. Bank of America reported $1.7 billion of DVA gains in its investment bank. Analysts estimated that Morgan Stanley will record $1.5 billion of net DVA gains when it reports earnings on Wednesday [...]

10.5.2 DVA Hedging?

We computed DVA through a risk-neutral expectation, because we assumed it is a price that can be computed through standard no-arbitrage theory. However, is this correct? Is DVA real?

For DVA to be real and possibly to be implemented as a price, we may need a hedging strategy. Can one hedge DVA? One should sell protection on oneself, a quite difficult feat. . . . In the CDS market no counterparty would accept such protection because the day when the protection seller should pay is the very day it defaults. An alternative could be buying back bonds one has issued (funded sale of protection), but such bonds may become illiquid in difficult situations, or there may be no issued bonds left. Most often, DVA is hedged by proxying. Instead of selling protection on oneself, one sells protection on a number of names that one thinks are highly correlated to oneself.

Again from the same *Wall Street Journal* article:

> [. . .] Goldman Sachs CFO David Viniar said Tuesday that the company attempts to hedge [DVA] using a basket of different financials. A Goldman spokesman confirmed that the company did this by selling CDS on a range of financial firms. [. . .] Goldman wouldn't say what specific financials were in the basket, but Viniar confirmed [. . .] that the basket contained 'a peer group.' Most would consider peers to Goldman to be other large banks with big investment-banking divisions, including Morgan Stanley, J.P. Morgan Chase, Bank of America, Citigroup and others. The performance of these companies' bonds would be highly correlated to Goldman's.

This can approximately hedge the spread risk of DVA, but not the jump to default risk. A top investment bank hedging DVA risk by selling protection on Lehman would not have been a good idea back in 2008: at default of Lehman, the other top investment banks did not default, so there was no material DVA hedging. At the same time the other bank was going through a difficult period that would have been exacerbated if it had had to pay CDS protection on Lehman in addition to direct losses from Lehman default. In fact this hedging technique may worsen systemic risk and is quite unlikely to be appreciated by regulators.

10.5.3 DVA: Accounting versus Capital Requirements

Capital requirements regulation and accounting regulation are at odds on whether DVA should be introduced or not. We have:

10.5.3.1 Yes DVA: FAS 157

In Financial Accounting Standard (FAS) 157 we find (see also International Accounting Standards (IAS) 39)

> Because nonperformance risk (the risk that the obligation will not be fulfilled) includes the reporting entity's credit risk, the reporting entity should consider the effect of its credit risk (credit standing) on the fair value of the liability in all periods in which the liability is measured at fair value under other accounting pronouncements.

This is a natural consequence of a basic principle of accounting: financial assets and liabilities should be accounted at *fair value,* defined as follows: "Fair value is the price that would be received to sell an asset or paid to transfer a liability in an orderly transaction" (FAS 157). Since DVA of a party enters into the market price as the CVA computed by the counterparty, it is naturally included in this definition of fair value.

10.5.3.2 No DVA: Basel III

In the Basel III, page 37, July 2011 release, we find

> This CVA loss is calculated without taking into account any offsetting debit valuation adjustments which have been deducted from capital under paragraph 75.

Stefan Walter, former secretary of the Basel Committee, declared:

> The potential for perverse incentives resulting from profit being linked to decreasing creditworthiness means capital requirements cannot recognise it [. . .] The main reason for not recognising DVA as an offset is that it would be inconsistent with the overarching supervisory prudence principle under which we do not give credit for increases in regulatory capital arising from a deterioration in the firm's own credit quality.

10.5.4 DVA: Summary and Debate on Realism

We will introduce DVA rigorously from Chapter 12 based on papers by Brigo and Capponi (2008) [39], Brigo, Pallavicini and Papatheodorou (2011) [59], Brigo, Capponi, Pallavicini and Papatheodorou (2011) [41] and Brigo, Capponi and Pallavicini (2011) [40].

Here we analyzed DVA in a more informal way and we observed that:

- DVA: we have one more term with respect to the unilateral case.
- depending on credit spreads and correlations, the total adjustment to be subtracted (CVA-DVA) can now be either positive or negative. In the unilateral case it can only be positive.
- Ignoring the symmetry is clearly more expensive for the counterparty and cheaper for the bank.
- Hedging DVA is difficult. Proxy hedging "by peers" ignores jump to default risk and systemic risk

The following is an important remark:

DVA is a strange object because when used in our mark-to-market formulae, as we saw above, it goes up when our credit quality worsens. In a way we receive a discount on our debt because all of a sudden it is less likely that we may have to pay it back. But this is a profit that we can only realize as a cash flow by defaulting. And once we have defaulted, perhaps our liquidators will be interested in this but we will not be there to realize this profit.

This is used by DVA detractors to say that DVA is unreal and should not be booked. While this is understandable, these critics should also consider the following two facts:

- Without DVA, the price cannot be symmetric and two default-risky parties cannot agree on the price of a deal.
- DVA seen from B's side is CVA seen from C's side. Since there is no debate that CVA is real, we have that realism of a price would become a matter of perspective. The price can be hedged and is real if seen by C, but is not if seen by B.

These further considerations on DVA criticisms are not conclusive, but show that the case against DVA is all but final. There are pros and cons in the notion of DVA, as is illustrated by the fact that even regulators cannot make up their minds on whether they want it to stay or go.

10.6 CLOSE-OUT: RISK-FREE OR REPLACEMENT?

When we computed the bilateral adjustment formula from

$$\begin{aligned}\Pi_B^D(t,T) &= \mathbf{1}_{E\cup F}\Pi_B(t,T)\\ &\quad+\mathbf{1}_{C\cup D}\left[\Pi_B(t,\tau_C)+D(t,\tau_C)\left(\mathrm{Rec}_C\,(\mathrm{NPV}_B(\tau_C))^+-(-\mathrm{NPV}_B(\tau_C))^+\right)\right]\\ &\quad+\mathbf{1}_{A\cup B}\left[\Pi_B(t,\tau_B)+D(t,\tau_B)\left((-\mathrm{NPV}_C(\tau_B))^+-\mathrm{Rec}_B\,(\mathrm{NPV}_C(\tau_B))^+\right)\right]\end{aligned}$$

(where we now substituted $\mathrm{NPV}_B = -\mathrm{NPV}_C$ in the last two terms) we used the risk-free NPV upon the first default, to close the deal. But what if upon default of the first entity, the deal needs to be valued by taking into account the credit quality of the surviving party? What if we make the substitutions:

$$\begin{aligned}\mathrm{NPV}_B(\tau_C) &\rightarrow \mathrm{NPV}_B(\tau_C)+\mathrm{UDVA}_B(\tau_C)\\ \mathrm{NPV}_C(\tau_B) &\rightarrow \mathrm{NPV}_C(\tau_B)+\mathrm{UDVA}_C(\tau_B).\end{aligned} \tag{10.8}$$

This is what would happen if the surviving party (for example B) tried to replace the deal with a new one, done with a new default-free party, an Exchange, for example. The surviving party B would be charged its unilateral CVA as seen by the Exchange, and this CVA, when seen by the surviving party B, is surviving party B's unilateral DVA in the deal, UDVA_B. Hence the above substitutions.

These substitutions are partly granted by ISDA documentation: ISDA (2009) Close-out Amount Protocol.

> In determining a Close-out Amount, the Determining Party may consider any relevant information, including, [. . .] quotations (either firm or indicative) for replacement transactions supplied by one or more third parties that may take into account the creditworthiness of the Determining Party at the time the quotation is provided.

This makes valuation more continuous: upon default we still price including our DVA, as we were doing before default. This has now become a unilateral DVA, given that the other party has defaulted.

The final formula with replacement close-out is then obtained by implementing the substitutions (10.8) into the standard bilateral adjusted payout (10.6) leading to the new adjusted payout

$$\begin{aligned}\Pi_B^D(t,T) &= \mathbf{1}_{E\cup F}\Pi_B(t,T)+\mathbf{1}_{C\cup D}\Big[\Pi_B(t,\tau_C)+D(t,\tau_C)\\ &\quad\cdot\left(\mathrm{Rec}_C\,(\mathrm{NPV}_B(\tau_C)+\mathrm{UDVA}_B(\tau_C))^+-(-\mathrm{NPV}_B(\tau_C)-\mathrm{UDVA}_B(\tau_C))^+\right)\Big]\\ &\quad+\mathbf{1}_{A\cup B}\Big[\Pi_B(t,\tau_B)+D(t,\tau_B)\\ &\quad\cdot\left((-\mathrm{NPV}_C(\tau_B)-\mathrm{UDVA}_C(\tau_B))^+-\mathrm{Rec}_B\,(\mathrm{NPV}_C(\tau_B)+\mathrm{UDVA}_C(\tau_B))^+\right)\Big].\end{aligned} \tag{10.9}$$

We refer to bilateral CVA and DVA calculated without substitutions (10.8), leading to the adjusted payout (10.6) as to the "Risk-Free Close-Out" case. This is because, at close-out, we value the deal as a risk-free, without including any residual credit risk (for the surviving party). When the substitutions are adopted, we refer instead to the "Replacement" or "Substitution

Close-Out", leading to the adjusted payout (10.9). Indeed, as we have explained, the price at close-out is now the price one would pay to replace the deal with a new one.

We will describe the two types of close-out in Chapter 12, and we will look at their subtleties and differences in Chapter 14. Differences can be rather material and can penalize either creditor or debtors, see also Brigo and Morini (2010) [52] and Brigo and Morini (2011) [54]. What is more, convenience of a close-out with respect to the other one will be a function of default dependency between B and C. This is quite an important choice on which regulators have given little guidance so far.

Furthermore, when we introduce margining costs in Chapter 16 and funding costs in Chapter 17, we see that a sensitive definition for close-out amounts should include also such costs as explicitly stated also in the ISDA "Market Review of OTC Derivative Bilateral Collateralization Practices" (2010).

10.7 CAN WE NEGLECT THE FIRST-TO-DEFAULT TIME?

In this section we illustrate a simplified formula without first-to-default time for bilateral valuation adjustments.

- The simplified formula is only a simplified representation of bilateral risk and ignores that, upon the first default, close-out proceedings are started. This simplification then involves a degree of double counting.
- It is attractive because it allows for the construction of a bilateral counterparty risk pricing system based only on unilateral counterparty risk pricing analytics.
- The correct formula involves default dependence between the two parties through τ^{1st} and allows no such incremental construction.
- We analyze the impact of default dependence between investor "B" and counterparty "C" on the difference between the two formulas by looking at a zero-coupon bond and at an equity forward.

We have seen in Formula (10.7) that the bilateral valuation adjustment to B,

$$\mathrm{BVA}_B(t) = \mathrm{DVA}_B(t) - \mathrm{CVA}_B(t)$$

to be added to the risk-free payout to obtain the adjusted price, is obtained as a difference of bilateral DVA and CVA terms, both containing first-to-default indicators. However, the industry often advocates a similar but simpler formula consisting of the adjustment

$$\mathrm{BVAS}_B(t) = \mathrm{UDVA}_B(t) - \mathrm{UCVA}_B(t)$$

which is basically the same but where the first-to-default time check has been removed from the payout. Such a formula is advocated in part of the CVA literature, for example, see [167].

We now analyze the difference between the correct BVA formula and the approximated formula BVAS. We refer to [37] for the full details.

One can show easily that the difference between the full correct bilateral formula and the simplified formula is

$$\begin{aligned} D^{BC} &= \mathrm{BVA}_B(t) - \mathrm{BVAS}_B(t) \\ &= (\mathrm{DVA}_B(t) - \mathrm{CVA}_B(t)) - (\mathrm{UDVA}_B(t) - \mathrm{UCVA}_B(t)) \\ &= \mathbb{E}_0\left[1_{\{\tau_B<\tau_C<T\}}\mathrm{LGD}_C D(0,\tau_C)(\mathbb{E}_{\tau_C}[\Pi(\tau_C,T)])^+\right] \\ &\quad - \mathbb{E}_0\left[1_{\{\tau_C<\tau_B<T\}}\mathrm{LGD}_B D(0,\tau_B)(-\mathbb{E}_{\tau_B}[\Pi(\tau_B,T)])^+\right]. \end{aligned} \tag{10.10}$$

We work under deterministic interest rates. We consider $P(t, T)$ held by B (the lender) who will receive the notional 1 from C (the borrower) at final maturity T if there has been no default by C.

The difference between the correct bilateral formula and the simplified one is, under risk-free close-out,

$$D^{BC}_{\text{BOND}} = \text{LGD}_C P(0, T)\mathbb{Q}(\tau_B < \tau_C < T).$$

The case with substitution close-out is instead trivial and the difference is null. For a bond, the simplified formula coincides with the full substitution close-out formula. Therefore the difference above is the same as the difference between risk-free close-out and substitution close-out formulas, and has been examined in [52], also in terms of contagion. For more on this see also Chapter 14.

10.7.1 A Simplified Formula without First-to-Default: The Case of an Equity Forward

In this case the payoff at maturity time T is given by $S_T - K$ where S_T is the price of the underlying equity at time T and K the strike price of the forward contract (typically $K = S_0$, 'at-the-money', or $K = S_0/P(0, T)$, 'at-the-money forward'). We compute the difference D^{BC} between the correct bilateral risk-free close-out formula and the simplified one. We obtain $D^{BC} := A_1 - A_2$, where

$$A_1 = E_0 \left[1_{\{\tau_B<\tau_C<T\}} \text{LGD}_C D(0, \tau_C)(S_{\tau_C} - P(\tau_C, T)K)^+\right]$$
$$A_2 = E_0 \left[1_{\{\tau_C<\tau_B<T\}} \text{LGD}_B D(0, \tau_B)(P(\tau_B, T)K - S_{\tau_B})^+\right]$$

The worst cases will be the ones where the terms A_1 and A_2 do not compensate. For example, assume there is a high probability that $\tau_B < \tau_C$ and that the forward contract is deep in-the-money. In such a case A_1 will be large and A_2 will be small.

Similarly, a case where $\tau_C < \tau_B$ is very likely and where the forward is deep out-of-the money will lead to a large A_2 and to a small A_1.

However, we show with a numerical example in Figure 10.1 that even when the forward is at-the-money the difference can be relevant. For more details see Brigo, Buescu and Morini (2011) [37].

10.8 PAYOFF RISK

As we have seen so far in this chapter, the exact payout corresponding with the Credit and Debit valuation adjustment is not clear. This originates a new kind of risk that we could term "Payout Risk" or "Payoff Risk". Divergences come from:

- Whether to include DVA or not?
- The type of close-out?
- A first-to-default check or not?
- How are collateral and funding accounted for exactly? (we look at this later)

At a recent industry panel on CVA chaired by one of the authors, it was agreed among a number of industry representatives that "five banks might compute CVA in 15 different ways". This was not a joke. Different banks can use different CVA models because they

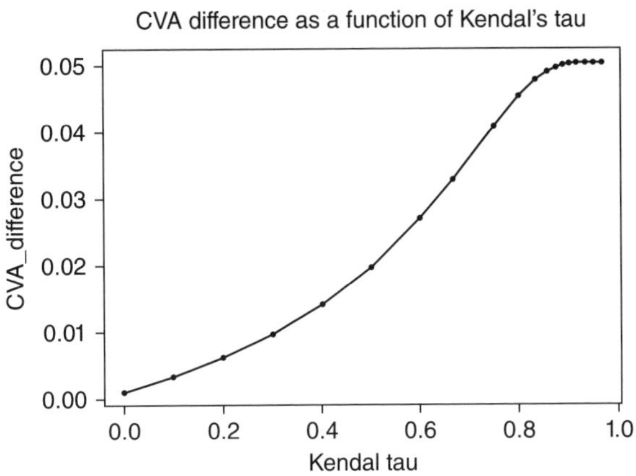

Figure 10.1 D^{BC} for the equity forward plotted against Kendall's tau between τ_B and τ_C, all other quantities being equal: Spot equity $S_0 = 1$, maturity $T = 5$, Equity volatility in Black-Scholes $\sigma = 0.4$, Strike $K = 1$, Constant default intensity of B $\lambda_B = 0.1$, $\lambda_C = 0.05$. Recoveries are at zero

have different pricing models. They can make different close-out assumptions. Even a single bank can internally calculate CVA in other ways. Its CVA management group can use a full portfolio bilateral CVA modelling framework, but use a simple UCVA approach with a less sophisticated counterparty, and certainly a different CVA model, based on maybe historical calculations, is used for regulatory capital purposes.

Payoff risk precedes model risk. From the chapters on UCVA we have seen so far one can understand that CVA involves a lot of model risk. Now we have seen that one not only has model risk, before that one has payout risk, since two banks trading CVA may not even be sure about what type of payout is being priced.

10.9 COLLATERALIZATION, GAP RISK AND RE-HYPOTHECATION

The next modern aspect of CVA that became paramount after the start of "the crisis" was properly accounting for collateral. Collateral (as regulated by the Credit Support Annex (CSA)), is considered to be the solution to counterparty risk. Roughly speaking, the position is re-valued (marked-to-market) periodically, and a quantity related to the change in value is posted on the collateral account by the party being penalized by the change in value.

This way, the collateral account at the periodic dates contains an amount that is close to the actual value of the portfolio, and if one counterparty were to default, the amount would be used by the surviving party as a guarantee (and vice versa).

Gap risk is the residual risk left because the realignment is only periodical. If the market were to move a lot between two realigning (margining) dates, a significant loss would still be faced.

Folklore: Collateral completely kills CVA, and Gap risk is negligible.

We are going to show that while this is often the case, there are also occasions where this is not the case at all (see Chapter 15 and also Brigo, Capponi and Pallavicini (2011) [40]).

- Risk-neutral evaluation of counterparty risk in the presence of collateral management can be a difficult task due to the complexity of clauses.

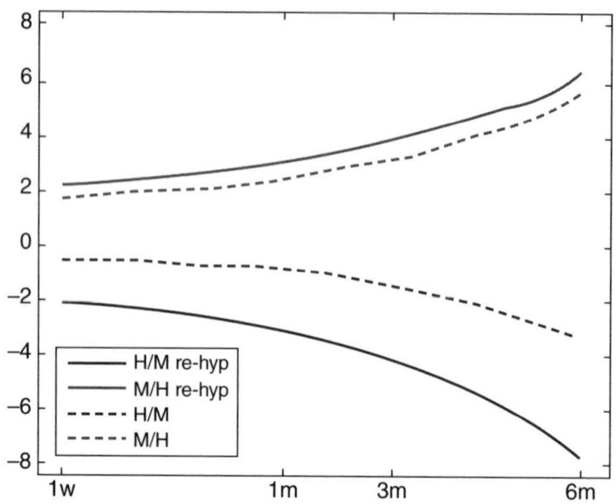

Figure 10.2 CVA and DVA for IRS: Effective collateralization

- Only a few papers in the literature deal with this. Among them we cite [79], [1], [196], [8], [41] and citations therein.
- Example: In Figure 10.2 we show the collateralized bilateral CVA for a netted portfolio of IRS with a 10 year maturity and a 1 year coupon tenor for different margining frequencies with (and without) collateral re-hypothecation. See Brigo, Capponi, Pallavicini and Papatheodorou (2011) [41].

Figure 10.2 shows the Bilateral Valuation Adjustment (DVA-CVA) for a ten-year IRS under collateralization through margining as a function of the update frequency δ with zero correlation between rates and counterparty spread, zero correlation between rates and investor spread, and zero correlation between the counterparty and the investor defaults. The model also allows for non-zero correlations.

Continuous lines represent the re-hypothecation, namely cases where collateral posted or received can be re-used by the receiving party as a further guarantee for other deals. Dotted lines represent the opposite case. The top line represents an investor riskier than the counterparty, while the bottom line represents an investor less risky than the counterparty. All values are in basis points.

From Figure 10.2, we see that where an investor is riskier than the counterparty (M/H) this leads to a positive value for the difference of the DVA-CVA, but when an investor is less risky than the counterparty this has the opposite effect. If we inspect the DVA and CVA terms (see also Chapter 15) we see that when the investor is riskier the DVA part of the correction dominates; but when the investor is less risky, the counterparty has the opposite behaviour.

Re-hypothecation enhances the absolute size of the correction, a reasonable behaviour, since in such cases, each party has a greater risk because of being unsecured on the collateral amount posted to the other party in case of default.

This is a case where collateral is quite effective in killing CVA and DVA, even under re-hypothecation. The residual adjustment is just a few basis points. See [41] for the details, and also Chapter 15.

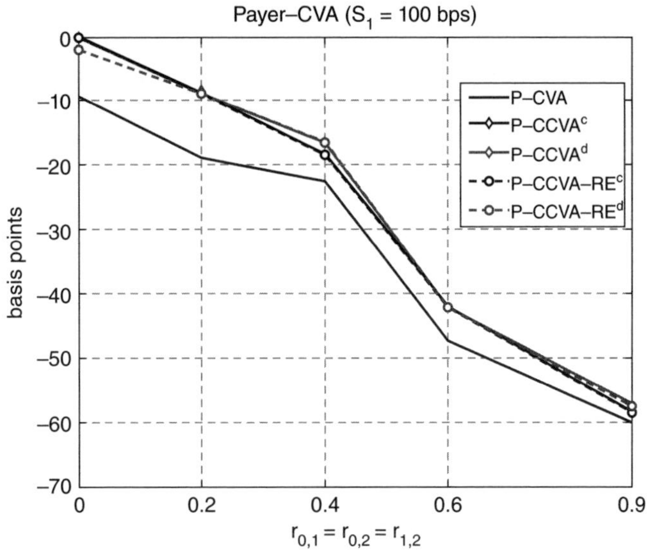

Figure 10.3 CVA and DVA for a CDS: collateralization is ineffective

Let us now look at a case with more contagion and where Gap risk is relevant: a CDS as an underlying trade. This is illustrated in Figure 10.3.

The figure refers to a payer CDS contract as underlying. See the full paper Brigo, Capponi and Pallavicini (2011) [40] for more cases.

If the investor holds a payer CDS, he is buying protection from the counterparty, i.e. he is a protection buyer. We assume that the spread in the fixed leg of the CDS is 100 basis points while the initial equilibrium spread is about 250 basis points. Given that the payer CDS will be positive in most scenarios, when the investor defaults it is quite unlikely that the net present value will be in favour of the counterparty. We then expect the CVA term to be relevant, given that the related option will be mostly in-the-money. This is confirmed by our outputs. We see in Figure 10.3 a relevant CVA component (part of the bilateral DVA–CVA) starting at 10 basis points and ending up at 60 basis points when under high correlation. We also see that, for zero correlation, the collateralization succeeds in completely removing CVA, which drops from 10 to 0 basis points. However, collateralization seems to become less effective as default dependence grows, in that collateralized and uncollateralized CVA come closer and closer; for high correlations we still get 60 basis points for CVA, even under continuous collateralization.

The reason for this is the instantaneous default contagion that, under positive dependency, pushes up the intensity of the survived entities, as soon as there is a default of the counterparty.

Indeed, the term structure of the on-default survival probabilities lies significantly below that for the pre-default survival probabilities conditioned on $\mathcal{G}_{\tau-}$, especially for large default correlations. The result is that the default leg of the CDS will increase in value due to contagion, and instantaneously the payer CDS will be worth more. This will instantly increase the loss to the investor, and most of the CVA value will come from this jump.

Given the instantaneous nature of the jump, the value at default will be quite different from the value at the last date of collateral posting, before the jump, and this explains the limited effectiveness of collateral under significantly positive default dependence.

See [40] for the details, and also Chapters 13 and 15 to see how CVA and DVA are formulated precisely in the presence of collateral and re-hypothecation, leading to the above figures.

10.10 FUNDING COSTS

Counterparty risk pricing also requires, especially after the start of the 2007 global financial crisis, an analysis of funding costs. In fact, the growth of credit risk has implied that banks and companies have more difficulty obtaining funding liquidity, making the issue more crucial. At the same time, the spreads they have to pay for funding are now high, and diversified across banks, requiring a precision that could be by-passed before 2007 by the use of a single "risk-free" funding/interest rate curve. The crisis acted like a microscope, allowing a more precise analysis by giving more visibility to previously minor details, and at the same time forcing banks to be much more precise.

Margining and funding costs cannot simply be switched off to price a "bare" derivative product, pretending that the resulting price has a meaning on the market. Any market quote should be evaluated taking into account collateralization clauses and funding costs, so that financial models calibrated to the market must include such corrections, and discard built-in non-arbitrage relationships which are now violated. As an example, we cite the rise of basis swap spreads in interest rate markets after the 2007 crisis, leading to multiple yield-curve models to price interest rate swaps on a single currency. Standard financial models should be re-thought from the basis, see [151] and [152].

We looked at funding costs in Chapter 2, and we will be looking at them again in Chapters 11 and 17. There we will see two crucial aspects of funding costs computation that although already mentioned are worth repeating:

1. The funding costs computation is not independent of the DVA and CVA computation, there can be a partial overlap between DVA and the funding charge (see in particular Chapter 11), while generally, identifying DVA with funding is not appropriate (see in particular Chapter 17).
2. Proper inclusion of funding costs leads to a recursive pricing problem. The recursive problem may be formulated as a backwards stochastic differential equation (BSDE, as in [85]), or to a discrete time backward induction equation, as in [165], see Chapter 17.

While the industry is often advocating a theory of funding costs based on simple tools such as discounting or additive adjustments, this is simply not possible if one tries to build a theory that is consistent with CVA, DVA and collateral. The problem is inherently recursive because the value of the cash and collateral processes may depend on the price of the derivative, which, in turn, depends on such processes, transforming the credit-funding adjustment pricing equation into a recursive equation. Thus, funding costs cannot be considered as a simple additive term (FVA) to a price obtained by disregarding them.

10.11 RESTRUCTURING COUNTERPARTY RISK

So far we have addressed the question, "What is counterparty risk and how do we price it, possibly in a way that is consistent with other risks and arbitrage free?"

- Early attempts to price it have shown considerable CVA volatility, resulting in important mark-to-market losses during the crisis, as we have seen in the dialogue in Chapter 1. Let us recall the relevant quote here.
  When the valuation of a risk is more dangerous than the risk itself:

  > Under Basel II, the risk of counterparty default and credit migration risk were addressed but mark-to-market losses due to credit valuation adjustments (CVA) were not. During the financial crisis, however, roughly two-thirds of losses attributed to counterparty credit risk were due to CVA losses and only about one-third were due to actual defaults.

  Basel Committee on Banking Supervision, BIS (2011). Press release available at http://www.bis.org/press/p110601.pdf.
- This volatility is related to the high volatility of credit spreads (see for instance [31]), high volatility of exposure and wrong way risk. This has been addressed in the previous chapters.
- To deal with CVA mark-to-market risk, according to regulators, there are mainly two choices: collateral/CSA and margins posting or CVA VaR and related capital requirements. Both ways are likely to worsen the liquidity landscape. Collateral will be looked at in more detail in the following chapters, and CVA and VaR were coverered briefly in the dialogue in Chapter 1 and in more detail in Chapter 2.
- Starting from this, we now look at the question: "What do we do with counterparty risk?"
- The industry has been looking at possible ways to deal with CVA risks and requirements. Here we will analyze ways to restructure or outsource CVA.
- Historically, contingent CDS (seen in Chapters 1 and 5) would be a good hedge for counterparty risk. However, such products are opaque, they are not liquid, can be expensive, and are themselves subject to counterparty risk. As such, their effectiveness has been quite limited. Most of these problems still stand even after the partial standardization of the underlying for such contracts suggested by the ISDA.
- A subsequent more recent attempt in the industry has been based on securitization of CVA through traditional cash CDO-type structures (e.g. "Papillon" and "Score" deals).
- Here a bank pools together CVA for a large portfolio across several counterparties and tranches it, trading protection on such tranches. We have seen an informal account of these (mostly failed) attempts in Chapter 1.
- These traditional structures would offer a fixed periodic premium or an upfront as compensation for the protection being traded. However, as we shall see below, this implies a high volatility of CVA mark-to-market.
- We will therefore explore an innovative proposal to restructure CVA, namely a form of securitization based both on margin lending and on a floating rate notion of CVA.

10.11.1 CVA Volatility: The Wrong Way

The problem with the traditional upfront charge or fixed periodic fee for unilateral CVA is that it leaves CVA volatility with the investor/bank and not with the risky counterparty that generated it. This also affects current attempts to restructure counterparty risk (Papillon and Score).

In the unilateral case, the bank charges an upfront for CVA to the counterparty and then implements a hedging strategy. Thus the bank is exposed to CVA mark-to-market volatility in the future. Alternatively the bank may request collateral from the counterparty, but not all counterparties are able to regularly post collateral [192], and this can be rather punitive for some corporate counterparties.

Floating margin lending, based on a floating CVA, is a proposal to solve this problem with volatility going the "right way".

10.11.2 Floating Margin Lending

Traditionally, the CVA is typically charged by the structuring bank B (investor) either on an upfront basis or it is built into the structure as a fixed coupon stream. Floating margin lending is predicated instead on the notion of floating rate CVA. Then, in six months, the bank will require a CVA payment for protection for a further six months, prevailing at that time on what the exposure will be at that time, and so on, up to the final maturity.

Floating margin lending is designed in such a way to transfer the conditional credit spread volatility risk and the mark-to-market volatility risk, or in other words CVA volatility, from the bank to the counterparties.

Pure floating CVA can be combined with margin lending. This is explained in detail by the arrows in Figure 10.4.

To avoid posting collateral, C enters into a floating margin lending transaction. Periodically C pays (say semi-annually) a floating rate CVA to margin lender A ("premium" arrow connecting C to A), which A pays to investors ("premium arrow" connecting A to Investors). This latest payment can have a seniority structure similar to that of a cash CDO. In exchange, for six months the investors provide A with daily collateral posting ("collateral" arrow connecting investors to A) and A passes the collateral to a custodian ("collateral" arrow connecting A to the custodian). This collateral need not be cash, it can be in the form of hypothecs. This simplifies a number of operational risk issues. If C defaults within the semi-annual period, the collateral is paid to B to provide protection ("protection" arrow connecting the custodian to B)

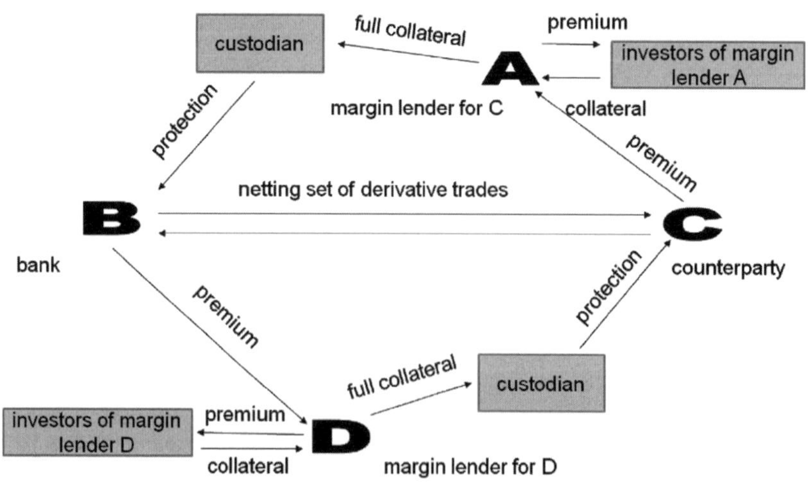

Figure 10.4 Margin lending via a floating CVA

and the loss in taken by the investors who provided the collateral. At the end of the six-month period, the margin lender may decide whether to continue with the deal or to back off. With this mechanism C is bearing the CVA volatility risk, whereas B is not exposed to CVA volatility risk, which is the opposite of what happens with traditional upfront CVA charges.

In traditional CVA, Albanese, Brigo and Oertel (2011) [3] argue that whenever an entity's credit worsens, it receives a subsidy from its counterparties in the form of a DVA positive mark-to-market which can be monetized by the entity's bond holders only upon their own default. Whenever an entity's credit improves it is effectively taxed as its DVA depreciates. Wealth is thus transferred from firms with improving credit quality to firms with deteriorating credit quality, the transfer being mediated by the traditional CVA/DVA mechanics. Again, [3] submit that floating margin lending structures may help reversing this macroeconomic effect.

In spite of these positive features, there are a number of possible problems with the above floating margin lending scheme. Corporate counterparties may find a floating credit spread payment as punitive as other solutions, since it increases their payments just when they start experiencing credit problems, with a pro-cyclical effect. Second, proper valuation and hedging of this to the investors who are providing collateral to the lender is going to be tough. There is no satisfactory standard for even simple synthetic CDOs, see, for example, [60]. Admittedly this requires an effective global valuation framework, see the discussion in [2]. Another problem is: what if all margin lenders pull out at some point due to a systemic crisis? One may argue that the market is less likely to arrive in such a situation in the first place if the wrong incentives to defaulting firms are stopped and an opposite structure, such as floating margin lending, is implemented.

There is also a pentapartite version including a clearing house, which is illustrated in Figure 10.5.

10.11.3 Global Valuation

A fair valuation, and risk management of CVA restructuring, through floating margin lending requires a global model, in order to have consistency and sensible greeks. But even when staying with traditional upfront CVA and DVA in large portfolios, as our examples above pointed out, different models are used in different asset classes. This can lead to models that are inconsistent with each other. For instance, our equity example in Chapter 8 used a firm value model, whereas in the other asset classes we used reduced form models. What if one has

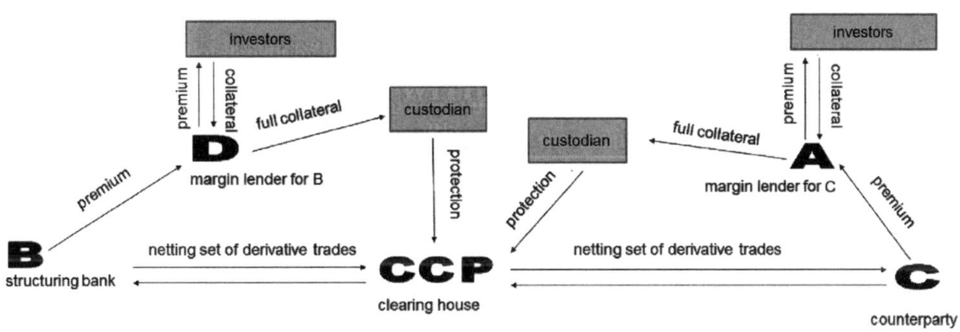

Figure 10.5 Margin lending with a pentapartite structure

a portfolio with all asset classes together? More generally, how does one ensure a consistent modelling framework to get meaningful prices and especially cross correlation sensitivities? The problem is rather difficult and involves important computational resources and intelligent systems architecture. Few papers have appeared attempting a global valuation framework, but see [2].

Delicate points include: modelling and calibrating dependencies across defaults; modelling and calibrating dependencies between defaults and each other asset class; modelling and calibrating dependencies between different asset classes; properly including credit volatility with positive credit spreads.

10.12 CONCLUSIONS

We may summarize our conclusions as a series of points that we have investigated or will investigate in the chapters and that remain quite debated in the industry. We have the following points:

- Counterparty risk adds one level of optionality (Chapters 1, 2, and 4 in particular but virtually every chapter in the book). Even portfolios whose valuation is model independent become model dependent by adding CVA. This makes updating pricing libraries quite a cumbersome task.
- Analysis including underlying asset/counterparty default correlation requires a credit model to be correlated with the underlying assets of the traded portfolio (see Chapter 3; we use intensity credit models in Chapters 5, 6, 7, 12, 15, and firm value credit models in Chapter 8).
- This leads to a highly specialized hybrid modelling framework (Chapters 5, 6, 7, 8, 12, 15).
- Only this allows for accurate scenarios for wrong way risk (Chapters 5, 6, 7, 8, 12, 15).
- Outputs vary and can be very different from Basel's transposed multipliers or tables (Chapters 5, 6, 7, 8).
- Outputs are strongly model dependent and involve payout risk, model risk and model choices (Chapters 5, 6, 7, 8, 12, 15, and the present chapter).
- Bilateral CVA and DVA brings in symmetry but also paradoxical statements (this chapter and Chapter 12).
- Bilateral CVA requires a choice of close-out (risk-free or substitution), and this is relevant (this chapter, Chapter 13, and Chapter 14).
- The DVA term in bilateral CVA is hard to hedge, especially in the jump-to-default risk component (this chapter).
- Approximations ignoring first-to-default risk (sometimes used in the industry) do not work well (this chapter).
- Inclusion of collateral and netting rules is possible (Chapters 2, 4 and 5 deal with netting, while Chapters 13, 15, 16, and 17 deal with collateral and possible netting).
- Gap risk in collateralization remains relevant in the presence of strong contagion (Chapter 15). Furthermore, Gap risk may arise from a deal's collaterals (Chapter 16).
- Margining procedure enforced by the CSA contract may require collateral accruing at a pre-fixed rate leading to relevant modifications of funding requirements in pricing equations (Chapter 16).
- Funding costs open a new dimension in derivative pricing. Now, pricing depends on funding liquidity policies and hedging strategies. A single price cannot be any more defined: prices

depend on who is pricing, which is its counterparty, and on market conditions. Also close-out amount evaluation may change (Chapter 17).

- Basel III will make capital requirements rather severe (Chapter 1 and this one).
- Contingent CDS as hedging instruments have limited effectiveness (Chapter 1).
- CVA restructuring through floating margin lending and hypothecs is a possible alternative (Chapter 1 and this chapter).
- Proper valuation and management of CVA and especially CVA restructuring requires a consistent global valuation approach (Chapter 1 and this chapter).
- This also holds for other possible forms of CVA securitization.

It is possibly misleading to condense the whole book in a single message, but if the reader asked for a single paragraph summarizing our understanding of CVA-DVA-FVA etc it would be this:

Counterparty and funding risk pricing is a very complex, model-dependent task and requires a holistic approach to modelling that challenges the ingrained culture in most investment banks and in most of the financial industry. Regulators are desperately trying to standardize the related calculation in the simplest ways possible but our conclusion is that such calculations are complex and need to remain so to be accurate. The attempt to standardize every risk to simple formulas is misleading and may result in the relevant risks not being addressed at all. This approach fuels the so-called regulatory arbitrage, where banks exploit the weaknesses and the rigidities of regulations; it favours procyclicality, making all banks herd together during bubbles and crises. And, most dangerously, it prompts many institutions to commit to following the simple standardized rules given by regulators and then to use this formal compliance as a justification for being particularly lax in terms of substantial risk management. Rather, the industry and regulators should acknowledge the complexity of this problem and work to attain the necessary methodological and technological prowess rather than bypass it, with help from academia and private research.

There is no easy way out.

11

A First Attack on Funding Cost Modelling

This chapter is based on Morini and Prampolini (2010) [158] and Morini and Prampolini (2011) [157].

In this chapter we deal first with an attack to Funding Costs modelling and calculations. The funding problem, as we have seen in Section 2.6, is a fundamental problem banks are facing at this point in history.

As we observed in the introductory dialogue in Chapter 1 and then in Section 2.6, when one manages a trading position, one needs to obtain cash in order to do a number of operations: hedging the position, posting collateral, paying coupons or notionals or other cash flows, setting liquidity reserves in place, paying interest on collateral received, managing Novation costs, and so on. Cash may be obtained from one's Treasury department or in the market. Cash may also be received as a consequence of being in the position: a coupon, a cash flow, a notional reimbursement, a positive mark-to-market move, collateral adjustments, etc. In short, if one is borrowing, this will have a cost, and if one is lending, this will provide revenues. So, again roughly speaking, including the cost of funding means to properly account for such features.

We have seen an initial history of the funding problem with a few references in Section 2.6, to which we refer for a general introduction.

Here we repeat briefly that in Chapter 17 we follow [165] that, with [85], it is the first attempt at a really comprehensive framework. But before that, we present the main results of the seminal paper by [157], because it is the first step in the fundamental challenge of accounting for funding costs consistently with counterparty default risk.

A note: this funding chapter depends on basic intensity/reduced form models and on the CDS market. The reader who is not familiar with such notions should go back to Section 3.1.4 and Section 3.3 (especially Subsection 3.3.2). This may help to fully appreciate the funding results [158] and [157] summarized here. This part also relies on the basic definition of DVA. This was introduced informally in Chapter 1 and in the previous chapter and will be tackled in detail in the next part of the book. The reader may wish to come back to this part after reading about DVA in detail, although the informal introduction already given should be enough for a first reading of this part.

11.1 THE PROBLEM

In following [158], [157], we consider a deal in which one entity, that we call B (borrower), commits to pay a fixed amount K at time T to a party L (lender). This is a very simple payoff that allows us to focus on liquidity and credit costs without unnecessary complications. The simple payoff limits the scope of the analysis but is the derivative equivalent of a zero-coupon bond issued by B or a loan from L to B, so it allows comparison of the results with the well-established market practice for such products. For the general framework, and for more elaborated examples, derived within such a framework, see Chapter 17, based on [165].

Let us assume that party X, with $X \in \{B, L\}$, has a recovery rate R_X and that the risk-free interest rate that applies to maturity T has a deterministic value r. A party X makes funding in the market, that we shall call for simplicity *the bond market*. Party X is also the reference entity in the CDS market. We have therefore the following information:

1. The CDS spread π_X. We take this spread to be deterministic and paid continuously (rather than quarterly) in the premium leg of the CDS. Following the standard market model for credit risk in the CDS market, the reduced-form or intensity model we saw in Section 3.3.2. In such a setup, we have:

$$\pi_X = \lambda_X \, \mathsf{LGD}_X \tag{11.1}$$

   where λ_X is the deterministic default intensity and $\mathsf{LGD}_X = 1 - \mathsf{R}_X$ is the loss given default of entity X. If recovery is null, as we will assume for simplicity, we have $\mathsf{LGD}_X = 1$ and the CDS spread coincides with λ_X, so that $\mathbb{Q}(\tau_X > T) = e^{-\pi_X T}$. This formula follows from the exponential distribution assumption for τ that is typical of intensity models, and that we saw in detail in Section 3.3.
2. The cost of funding s_X. For most issuers this is measured in the secondary bond market and represents the best estimate of the spread over a risk-free rate that a party pays on his funding. We take s_X to be short-term/instantaneous and deterministic too, so that we can compute by difference a liquidity basis γ_X with the same properties, such that

$$s_X = \pi_X + \gamma_X$$

The liquidity basis is an approximation for the difference between bond spread and CDS spread of an entity.

In a simple credit setting, the above deal has total value for the lender L given by

$$V_L = e^{-rT} K - \mathsf{CVA}_L - P, \tag{11.2}$$

where P is the premium paid by the lender L at inception, and CVA takes into account the probability that the borrower B defaults before maturity, thus

$$\begin{aligned} \mathsf{CVA}_L &= \mathbb{E}[e^{-rT} K 1_{\{\tau_B \le T\}}] = e^{-rT} K \, \mathbb{Q}[\tau_B \le T] \\ &= e^{-rT} K \left[1 - e^{-\pi_B T}\right]. \end{aligned}$$

We have that

$$V_L = 0 \quad \Rightarrow \quad P = e^{-rT} K - \mathsf{CVA}_L.$$

At the same time party B (the borrower) sees a value

$$\begin{aligned} V_B &= -e^{-rT} K + \mathsf{DVA}_B + P \\ V_B &= 0 \Rightarrow P = e^{-rT} K - \mathsf{DVA}_B \end{aligned} \tag{11.3}$$

with $\mathsf{CVA}_L = \mathsf{DVA}_B$.

This guarantees the symmetry $V_B = V_L = 0$ and the possibility for the parties to agree on the premium of the deal,

$$P = e^{-rT} e^{-\pi_B T} K. \tag{11.4}$$

This approach does not consider explicitly the value of liquidity. In fact, in exchange for the claim, at time 0 party B receives a cash flow from party L equal to P, so while party L has to finance the amount until the maturity of the deal at its funding spread s_L, party B can reduce its funding by P. So party B should see a funding benefit, and party L should see the fair value of its claim reduced by the financing costs. How come these funding components do not appear in the above valuation? Can we justify this by assuming that the two companies have negligible funding costs? Not completely. In fact the absence of the funding term for L can indeed be justified by assuming $s_L = 0$. This implies $\pi_L = 0$. However, the same assumption cannot be made for B without changing completely the nature of the deal. In fact assuming $s_B = 0$ would imply $\pi_B = 0$, which would cancel the DVA and CVA term. Thus when B is a party with non-negligible risk of default he must have a funding cost given at least by $s_B = \pi_B > 0$. The effect of this funding cost seems to be missing in the above formula. In the next sections we analyze if it is really missing.

11.2 A CLOSER LOOK AT FUNDING AND DISCOUNTING

Let us see what happens if we introduce liquidity costs by adjusting the discounting term, along the lines of [168], but introducing also defaultability of the payoff. One gets for the lender

$$\begin{aligned} V_L &= \mathbb{E}\left[e^{-(r+s_L)T} K 1_{\{\tau_B > T\}}\right] - P \\ &= \mathbb{E}\left[e^{-rT} e^{-\gamma_L T} e^{-\pi_L T} K 1_{\{\tau_B > T\}}\right] - P \\ &= e^{-(r+\gamma_L+\pi_L+\pi_B)T} K - P, \end{aligned} \tag{11.5}$$

and analogously for the borrower

$$\begin{aligned} V_B &= -\mathbb{E}\left[e^{-(r+s_B)T} K 1_{\{\tau_B > T\}}\right] + P \\ &= -\mathbb{E}\left[e^{-rT} e^{-\pi_B T} e^{-\gamma_B T} K 1_{\{\tau_B > T\}}\right] + P \\ &= -e^{-rT} e^{-\pi_B T} e^{-\gamma_B T} K e^{-\pi_B T} + P \\ &= -e^{-(r+\gamma_B+2\pi_B)T} K + P. \end{aligned} \tag{11.6}$$

To compare this result, including CVA, DVA and liquidity from discounting, with results on DVA obtained previously and resulting in Formula (11.4), it is convenient to reduce the situation to the simplest case where: L is default free and with no liquidity spread, while B is defaultable and has the minimum liquidity spread allowed in this case. We obtain

$$s_L = 0, \quad s_B = \pi_B > 0.$$

Imposing $V_L = V_B = 0$, we have that the "fair" P is different for L and for B:

$$\begin{aligned} P_L &= e^{-rT} e^{-\pi_B T} K \\ P_B &= e^{-rT} e^{-2\pi_B T} K = e^{-rT} e^{-\pi_B T} \boxed{e^{-\pi_B T}} K. \end{aligned}$$

There are two bizarre aspects in this representation.

- First, even in a situation where we have assumed no liquidity spread, two counterparties do not agree on the simplest transaction with default risk, since P_L and P_B are now different, unlike in our previous case leading to Formula (11.4). The formulas we just found imply that a *day-one profit* should be accounted by borrowers in all transactions with CVA. This belies years of market reality.
- Secondly, the explicit inclusion of the DVA term results in the duplication of the funding benefit for the party that assumes the liability. The formula implies, against all evidence, that the funding benefit is remunerated twice. If this were correct then a consistent accounting of liabilities at fair value would require pricing zero-coupon bonds by multiplying *twice* their risk-free present value by their survival probabilities. This also belies years of market reality.

11.3 THE APPROACH PROPOSED BY MORINI AND PRAMPOLINI (2010)

In order to solve the puzzle, [158] do not compute liquidity by the adjusted discounting of (11.5) and (11.6), but generate liquidity costs and benefits by modelling explicitly the funding strategy. The approach they take is that companies capitalize and discount money with the risk-free rate r, and then they add or subtract the actual credit and funding costs that arise in the management of the deal. Following this approach, we see that the above deal has two legs. If we consider, for example, the lender L,

- One leg is the "deal leg", with net present value

$$\mathbb{E}\left[-P + e^{-rT}\,\Pi\right]$$

where Π is the payoff at T, including a potential default indicator. This leg accounts for the positive amount P that the lender transfers (hence the minus sign) to the borrower initially, and for the re-payment of the loan at maturity T the lender will receive (if the borrower is solvent), namely Π.
- The other leg is the "funding leg" with net present value

$$\mathbb{E}\left[+P - e^{-rT}\,F\right]$$

where F is the funding payback at T, including a potential default indicator. This leg features a positive amount P the lender is obtaining to finance the payment $-P$ at the previous point, and this financing will have to be paid back at future time T with a cash flow F.

When there is no default risk or liquidity cost involved, this funding leg can be overlooked because it has a value

$$\mathbb{E}\left[+P - e^{-rT}\,e^{rT}\,P\right] = 0.$$

Instead, in the general case the total net present value is

$$\begin{aligned}V_L &= \mathbb{E}\left[-P + e^{-rT}\,\Pi + P - e^{-rT}\,F\right]\\ &= \mathbb{E}\left[e^{-rT}\,\Pi - e^{-rT}\,F\right].\end{aligned}$$

Thus the premium at time 0 cancels out with its funding, and we are left with the discounting of a total payoff including the deal's payoff Π and the liquidity payback $-F$.

11.3.1 The Borrower's Case

Now we detail the above scheme for the simple payoff we are considering, starting from the borrower's case. The borrower B has a liquidity advantage from receiving the premium P at time zero, as it allows him to reduce its funding requirement by an equivalent amount P. The amount P of funding would have generated a negative cash flow at T, when funding must be paid back, equal to

$$- P\, e^{rT}\, e^{s_B T}\, 1_{\{\tau_B > T\}} \tag{11.7}$$

The outflow equals P capitalized at the cost of funding, times a default indicator $1_{\{\tau_B>T\}}$. Why do we need to include a default indicator $1_{\{\tau_B>T\}}$? Because in case of default, under the assumption of zero recovery, the borrower does not pay back the borrowed funding and there is no outflow. Thus reducing the funding by P corresponds to receiving at T a positive amount equal to (11.7) in absolute value,

$$P\, e^{rT}\, e^{s_B T}\, 1_{\{\tau_B > T\}} = P\, e^{rT}\, e^{\pi_B T}\, e^{\gamma_B T}\, 1_{\{\tau_B > T\}} \tag{11.8}$$

to be added to what B has to pay in the deal: $-K\, 1_{\{\tau_B>T\}}$.

Thus the total payoff at T is

$$1_{\{\tau_B > T\}} P\, e^{rT}\, e^{\pi_B T}\, e^{\gamma_B T} - 1_{\{\tau_B > T\}} K. \tag{11.9}$$

Taking discounted expectation,

$$V_B = e^{-\pi_B T}\, P\, e^{\pi_B T}\, e^{\gamma_B T} - K\, e^{-\pi_B T}\, e^{-rT} = P\, e^{\gamma_B T} - K\, e^{-\pi_B T}\, e^{-rT}. \tag{11.10}$$

Compare with (11.6). Now we have no unrealistic double accounting of default probability. Notice that

$$V_B = 0 \quad \Rightarrow \quad P_B = K\, e^{-\pi_B T} e^{-\gamma_B T}\, e^{-rT} \tag{11.11}$$

where P_B is the breakeven premium for the borrower, in the sense that the borrower will find this deal convenient as long as

$$V_B \geq 0 \quad \Rightarrow \quad P \geq P_B.$$

Assume, as in (11.3), that $\gamma_B = 0$ so that in this case

$$P_B = K\, e^{-\pi_B T}\, e^{\ rT}. \tag{11.12}$$

and compare with (11.4). We can conclude that in this case the standard computation leading to (11.4) is correct, as taking into account the probability of default in the valuation of the funding benefit removes any liquidity advantage for the borrower. Our formula shows what happens when there is also a "pure liquidity basis" component in the funding cost, $\gamma_B > 0$. On the other hand, charging liquidity costs by an adjusted funding spread as in Section 11.2 cannot be naturally extended to the case where we want to observe explicitly the possibility of default events in our derivatives; for it to be consistent we need, as in [168], to take the default events out of the picture.

Remark 11.3.1 ***(Spread filtration and full default-monitoring filtration).*** *An interesting interpretation of this result is noticing that the idea of discounting at a spread π_B already corresponds to taking an expectation of a survival indicator object such as $1_{\{\tau_B>T\}}$ in that*

$$\mathbb{E}_0[1_{\{\tau_B > T\}}] = \mathbb{E}[1_{\{\tau_B > T\}} | \mathcal{F}_T] = \exp(-\pi_B T), \quad \mathbb{E}[1_{\{\tau_B > T\}} | \mathcal{G}_T] = 1_{\{\tau_B > T\}}$$

where $\mathcal{G}_T$ is the whole filtration including default monitoring up to T whereas $\mathcal{F}_T$ is the pre-default filtration, including credit spread information up to T but not default. This distinction, leading to

$$1_{\{\tau_B>T\}} \text{ under } \mathcal{G}_T \quad \longrightarrow \quad \exp(-\pi_B T) \text{ under } \mathcal{F}_T$$

is important in intensity models (introduced in Section 3.3). In this sense, when we include terms such as $\exp(-\pi_B T)$ *we are already including default risk but under the filtration $\mathcal{F}$, and this is usually called credit risk. This distinction between credit risk and default risk, which underlies, for example, the treatment in [168], is as we saw quite artificial and misleading in a number of ways. The original term* $\exp(-\pi_B T)$ *already embedded default risk, if under a partial filtration.*

11.3.2 The Lender's Case

Now we consider the lender's case. If the lender pays P at time 0, he incurs a liquidity cost. In fact he needs to finance (borrow) P until T. At T, L will give back the borrowed money with interest, but only if he has not defaulted. Otherwise he gives back nothing, so the outflow is

$$P\, e^{rT}\, e^{s_L T}\, 1_{\{\tau_L>T\}} = P\, e^{rT}\, e^{\gamma_L T}\, e^{\pi_L T}\, 1_{\{\tau_L>T\}} \tag{11.13}$$

while he receives in the deal: $K\; 1_{\{\tau_B>T\}}$. The total payoff at T is therefore

$$-\,P\, e^{rT}\, e^{\gamma_L T}\, e^{\pi_L T}\, 1_{\{\tau_L>T\}} + K\; 1_{\{\tau_B>T\}}. \tag{11.14}$$

Taking discounted expectation

$$V_L = -P\, e^{\gamma_L T}\, e^{-\pi_L T}\, e^{\pi_L T} + K\, e^{-rT}\, e^{-\pi_B T} = -P\, e^{\gamma_L T} + K\, e^{-rT}\, e^{-\pi_B T}. \tag{11.15}$$

The condition that makes the deal convenient for the lender is

$$\begin{aligned} &V_L \geq 0 \quad \Rightarrow \quad P \leq P_L, \\ &P_L = K\, e^{-rT}\, e^{-\gamma_L T}\, e^{-\pi_B T} \end{aligned} \tag{11.16}$$

where P_L is the break-even premium for the lender. It is interesting to note that the lender, when he computes the value of the deal, taking into account all future cash flows as they are seen from the counterparties, does not include a charge to the borrower for that component π_L of the cost of funding which is associated with his own risk of default. This is cancelled by the fact that funding is not given back in case of default. In terms of relative valuation of a deal this fact about the lender is exactly symmetric to the fact that for the borrower the inclusion of the DVA eliminates the liquidity advantage associated with π_B. In terms of managing cash flows, instead, there is an important difference between borrower and lender, which is discussed in Section 11.3.4. For reaching an agreement in the market we need

$$V_L \geq 0, \;\; V_B \geq 0$$

which, recalling (11.11) and (11.16), implies

$$\begin{aligned} P_L &\geq P \geq P_B \\ K\, e^{-rT}\, e^{-\gamma_L T}\, e^{-\pi_B T} &\geq P \geq K e^{-rT} e^{-\gamma_B T} e^{-\pi_B T}. \end{aligned} \tag{11.17}$$

Thus an agreement can be found whenever

$$\gamma_B \geq \gamma_L$$

This shows that, if we only want to guarantee a positive *expected* return from the deal, the liquidity cost that needs to be charged to the counterparty of an uncollateralized derivative transaction is just the liquidity basis, rather than the bond spread or the CDS spread. This is in line with what happened during the liquidity crisis in 2007–2009, when the bond-CDS basis exploded. The results of the last two sections go beyond [168] in showing that only the bond-CDS basis is a proper liquidity spread, while the CDS spread associated with the default intensity is a component of the funding cost offset by the probability of defaulting in the funding strategy. For extension to positive recovery see [157].

11.3.3 The Controversial Role of DVA: The Borrower

Clearly, in this context one is taking into account the DVA of the funding strategy. One of the most controversial aspects of DVA is that DVA allows a borrower to condition future liabilities on survival, and this may create a distorted perspective in which our default is our lucky day. Therefore, let us see what happens if the borrower does not condition its liabilities upon survival, namely it pretends to be default free thereby ignoring DVA and avoiding a possibly distorted view where default is a positive event.

Let a party B pretend, for accounting purposes, to be default free. The premium P paid by the lender gives B a reduction of the funding payback at T corresponding to a cash flow at T

$$P e^{rT} e^{s_B T},$$

where there is no default indicator because B is treating itself as default free. This cash flow must be compared with the payout of the deal at T, which is

$$-K$$

again without indicator, i.e. without DVA. Thus the total payoff at T is

$$e^{rT} e^{s_B T} - K \tag{11.18}$$

By discounting to zero we obtain an accounting value V_B such that

$$V_B = P\, e^{s_B T} - K\, e^{-rT}$$

which yields an accounting break-even premium P_B for the borrower equal to the break-even of (11.11),

$$P_B = K\, e^{-rT} e^{-\pi_B T} e^{-\gamma_B T}. \tag{11.19}$$

So, once again the borrower B recognizes on its liability a funding benefit that actually takes into account its own market risk of default π_B, plus additional liquidity basis γ_B, thereby matching the premium computed by a borrower that includes the CVA/ DVA term. But now this term is accounted for as a funding benefit and not as a benefit coming from the reduction of future expected liabilities thanks to default. Keep in mind Remark 11.3.1.

11.3.4 The Controversial Role of DVA: The Lender

The above results show that the borrower's valuation does not change if he considers himself default free, and it does not depend on how the funding spread in the market is divided into credit spread and liquidity basis. Do we have a similar property also for the lender? Not at all. Since, following Section 11.3.2, we have

$$P_L = K\, e^{-rT}\, e^{-\gamma_L T}\, e^{-\pi_B T},$$

the break-even premium and the agreement that will be reached in the market depend crucially on γ_L. This is not the only difference between the situation of the borrower and the lender. Notice that the borrower's net payout at maturity T is given in (11.9) and is non-negative in all states of the world if we keep $P \geq P_B$, although the latter condition was designed only to guarantee that the *expected* payout is non-negative. For the lender, instead, the payout at maturity is given by (11.14). The condition (11.16) for the non-negativity of the expected payout for the lender does not imply the non-negativity of (11.14), in particular we can have a negative carry even if we assume that both counterparties will survive until maturity. If we want to guarantee a non-negative carry, at least when nobody defaults, in addition to (11.16) we need the following condition to be satisfied

$$\pi_L \leq \pi_B. \tag{11.20}$$

Otherwise the lender, unlike the borrower, is exposed to liquidity shortage and negative carry even if the deal is, on average, convenient to him. Liquidity shortages, when no one defaults, can be excluded by imposing for each deal (11.20), or, with a solution working for whatever deal with whatever counterparty, by working as if the lender was default free. Only if the lender pretends for accounting purposes to be default free the condition for the convenience of the deal based on expected cash flows becomes

$$P \leq K\, e^{-rT}\, e^{-s_L T}\, e^{-\pi_B T} = K\, e^{-rT}\, e^{-\gamma_L T}\, e^{-\pi_L T} e^{-\pi_B T}$$

that clearly implies the non-negativity of (11.14).

Assuming ourselves to be default free leads to results equivalent to [168]. In fact, under this assumption, uncollateralized payoffs should be discounted at the full funding also in our simple setting. Let's consider a bank X that pretends to be default free. When the bank is in the borrower position we have

$$P_B = P_X = e^{-s_X T} e^{-rT} K$$

while when it is in a lender position with respect to a *risk-free* counterparty (as in the example of [168]) the break-even premium will be given by

$$P_L = e^{-s_X T} e^{-rT} K = P_B = P_X.$$

and the discounting at the funding rate $r + s_X$ is recovered for both positive and negative exposures.

But on the other hand, for general counterparties with non-null credit risk and liquidity costs, the lender's assumption to be default free makes a market agreement very difficult, since in this case the agreement

$$K\, e^{-rT}\, e^{-\gamma_B T}\, e^{-\pi_B T} \leq P \leq K\, e^{-rT}\, e^{-\gamma_L T}\, e^{-\pi_L T} e^{-\pi_B T}$$

implies

$$\boxed{\gamma_B \geq \gamma_L + \pi_L}$$

rather than

$$\boxed{\gamma_B \geq \gamma_L}$$

In a market where everyone treats himself as default free and counterparties as defaultable, a party wants to fund itself at a spread that includes only its own CDS

$$(\gamma_B + \pi_B)$$

but when it finances other parties it charges them a spread including two CDS spreads

$$(\gamma_L + \pi_L + \pi_B).$$

11.3.5 Discussion

Which one is the right solution? Both have their own pros and cons. In the first case a bank looks at itself like counterparties do, takes into account its own default and thus reduces the discounting rate for assets enough to avoid to charge two credit spreads to counterparties that borrow money from the bank. This is good because one of the two credit spreads is just what the bank must pay due to its own risk of not paying its obligations, and there is no financial rationale to charge it to borrowers. This way the bank charges to borrowers a total cost which is consistent with the way the bank computes its own funding costs, the bank will remain competitive and an agreement in the market will not be impossible.

On the other hand, in this way the bank bases its decisions on treating its own default as a financial advantage: a strategy may look convenient only because the bank is pricing in the fact that, in case it defaults, it will not pay back its own funding. But if the bank does not default, this will appear an absurdity! Where is it going to find the money to finance deals that could lead to negative carry when both parties survive?

In the second case the bank avoids this problem, it assumes it cannot default and in this way it risks no moral hazard and no funding losses in case it does not default: all its funding costs are fully charged to counterparties. However, this is a viewpoint that is in contrast with how counterparties look at the bank: they know the bank can default, they know that part of the funding costs of the bank are only due to this, and may not accept to be charged these costs when they are borrowing money from the bank. Think of yourself: if you asked a bank for a mortgage, would you find it fair if the bank told you: you have a credit spread of 3% because this one is your default probability, but I have a spread of 4% because this is my probability of default, so I will charge you 7%. Would you accept?

Today, it seems that banks are taking an approach which is in-between the two alternatives. Credit spread for the lender is not fully charged to the borrower. This is based on taking into account that the funding cost measured in the bond market is only part of the funding costs of a bank, that also involve much cheaper funding, like central bank lending or deposits, where a bank is not charged its full credit risk. At the same time, the bank's credit spread enters partially into the charging of liquidity costs. For further discussion on the implications of different choices, see [155].

11.4 WHAT NEXT ON FUNDING?

The above analysis is a fundamental development on funding-cost analysis, but it is only a first step towards a general pricing framework. Indeed, in terms of further generalization, we may note that relevant points are not addressed.

- One may not always rely on a clear distinction between borrower and lender. There are products such as swaps and exotics that go beyond such distinction.
- One may want to include an assumption on the funding policy of the bank and on its Treasury (e.g. micro vs. macro funding, at different levels of homogeneity), and to view the funding benefit as one of the elements of such policies.
- One may want to model the collateralization process and its interaction with CVA/DVA in full generality from a cash flow point of view.
- One may want to re-think close-out amount evaluation by taking into account funding costs.
- One may want to investigate the effects of funding on the definition of underlying risk factor dynamics.
- One may want to size the impact of funding on the choice of hedging strategies.
- One may want to introduce credit-spread volatility and default correlation.
- One may want to include wrong way risk.
- One may want to derive a master equation that is consistent with arbitrage-free theory while being as general as possible.

This is a long and non-exhaustive list of topics, that we have to approach, if we wish to include funding costs within our pricing framework. These points have been addressed in [85] and [165], who try to build the first general theory of funding valuation adjustments.

We will look at this in Chapters 16 and 17, after having extended our pricing framework to include collateralization,

12

Bilateral CVA–DVA and Interest Rate Products

This chapter is based on Brigo and Capponi (2008) [39] and Brigo, Pallavicini and Papatheodorou (2011) [59].

As we observed in the opening of Chapter 10, the bilateral nature of counterparty credit risk is mentioned already in the credit risk measurement space by the Basel II documentation, Annex IV, 2/A:

> Unlike a firm's exposure to credit risk through a loan, where the exposure to credit risk is unilateral and only the lending bank faces the risk of loss, the counterparty credit risk creates a bilateral risk of loss: the market value of the transaction can be positive or negative to either counterparty to the transaction.

In the present chapter, by following [41], we focus on interest rate products, generalizing to the bilateral case on unilateral CVA mentioned earlier in Chapter 5, and then we present some numerical results for rate products. The first general arbitrage-free formula for interest rate swaps under bilateral default risk is in [18]. Here, we go into more detail on model selection, numerical examples and the impact of dynamic parameters and wrong way risk, in the spirit of earlier work on CVA with unilateral features. Indeed, previous research on accurate arbitrage-free valuation of unilateral CVA with dynamical models on commodities [36] in Chapter 6, on rates [57] in Chapter 5 and on credit [43] in Chapter 7, assumed the party computing the valuation adjustment to be default free. We present here the general arbitrage-free valuation framework for counterparty risk adjustments in the presence of bilateral default risk, as introduced in [39] and sketched in the introductory Chapter 10, including default of by the investor. We illustrate the symmetry in the valuation and show that the adjustment involves a long position in a put option plus a short position in a call option, both with zero strike and written on the residual net value of the contract at the relevant default times. We allow for statistical dependence ("correlation") between the default times of the investor, counterparty and underlying portfolio risk factors. We use arbitrage-free stochastic dynamical models.

We then specialize our analysis to interest rate payouts as underlying portfolio. In comparing with the CDS case as underlying instrument, an important point is that most credit models in the industry, especially when applied to Collateralized Debt Obligations or k-th to default baskets, consider default correlation but ignore credit-spread volatility. Credit spreads are typically assumed to be deterministic and a copula is postulated on the exponential triggers of the default times to model default correlation. This is the opposite of what used to happen with counterparty risk for interest rate products, for example, in [186] or [47] in Chapter 4, where correlation was ignored and volatility was modelled instead. The authors of [43], see Chapter 7, rectify this in the CDS context, but only deal with unilateral and asymmetric counterparty risk. Then, [39] generalize this approach for CDS, including credit spread volatility as well as default correlation into the bilateral case, and [40] add the impact of collateral margining.

For interest rate products, previous literature dealing with both underlying assets' volatility and correlation with counterparty credit-spread is in [57], see Chapter 5, who address both plain vanilla interest rate swaps and exotics under unilateral counterparty risk. In that work, a stochastic intensity model along the lines of [35] and [46] is assumed, see Chapter 3, and this model is correlated with the multi-factor short rate process driving the interest rate dynamics. Netting is also examined in some basic examples. The present chapter aims at generalizing this approach to the bilateral case. In such a case one needs to model the following correlations, or better dependencies:

- Dependence between default by the counterparty C and default by the Bank B. Incidentally, we mention that we call the "Bank" (B) also "Investor" (I) in this chapter, since B may be a different corporate or another entity rather than a real bank; hence, in this chapter "B" = "I".
- Correlation between the underlying asset (interest rates) and the counterparty credit spread.
- Correlation between the underlying asset (interest rates) and the investor "I" credit spread.
- Besides default correlation between the counterparty and the investor, we might wish to model also credit spread correlation.

In the following, we will model all such dependencies except the last one, since default correlation is dominant over spread correlation in the cases we will investigate. Notice that if we extended our model to include collateral, depending on the credit quality of the counterparty, we should also model the last dependency, which would be relevant in such a case. A feature that is usually ignored is credit spread volatility for the investor and the counterparty, in that credit spreads are usually taken as deterministic. We improve this by assuming stochastic spreads for both investor and counterparty. The dangers of neglecting credit spread volatility in CVA of CDS have been highlighted in Chapter 7, as in [43].

We specify that we do not consider specific collateral clauses or guarantees in the present work, although we deal with some stylized cases of netting. We assume we are dealing with counterparty risk for an over-the-counter interest rate portfolio transaction where there is no periodic margining or collateral posting. This may be the case when the counterparty is a corporate, for example, see [192]. Past works where netting has been addressed in the interest rate context are [57] and [47], see Chapters 4 and 5. The impact of credit triggers for the counterparty on CVA is analyzed in [194]. The works [8] and [41] analyze the modelling of collateralization and margining in CVA calculations, and we will deal with this in later chapters.

Finally, given the theoretical equivalence of the credit valuation adjustment with a contingent CDS, we are also proposing a methodology for valuation of contingent CDS on interest rates. See [57] for more details on contingent CDS and also the discussion in Chapters 1 and 5.

The chapter is structured as follows: Section 12.1 summarizes the bilateral counterparty risk valuation formula from [39], establishing also the appropriate notations. A discussion on the specific features of bilateral risk and of some seemingly paradoxical aspects of the same, also in connection with real banking reports, is presented. Section 12.2 provides the details of the application of the methodology to interest rate swaps. A two-factor Gaussian interest rate model is proposed to deal with the option features of the bilateral counterparty risk adjustment. The model is calibrated to the zero-coupon curve of interest rates and to swaptions. Then, shifted square root diffusion credit spread models for both the counterparty "C" and the investor "I" are introduced. The defaults of the counterparty and of the investor are linked by a Gaussian copula. The correlation structures originating dependence between interest rates and defaults are explained in detail, and finally the numerical Monte Carlo techniques used to value the adjustment are illustrated. Section 12.4 presents a case study based on a single interest rate swap as well as on three possible interest rate swaps portfolios, some embedding netting clauses. We analyze the impact of credit spread levels and volatilities, of correlations between the underlying interest rates and defaults, the future moneyness of the swaps or the portfolios, and of dependence between default of the counterparty and of the investor. Section 12.5 concludes the chapter.

12.1 ARBITRAGE-FREE VALUATION OF BILATERAL COUNTERPARTY RISK

As we observed in the introduction, the bilateral counterparty risk is mentioned in the Basel II documentation. However, Basel II is more concerned with Risk Measurement than pricing. For an analysis of counterparty risk in the risk-measurement space we refer, for example, to [93], who consider modelling of stochastic credit exposures for derivatives portfolios. In the valuation space, however, bilateral features are also quite relevant and can often be responsible for seemingly paradoxical statements, as pointed out in [39] and as we have seen in Chapter 10. For example, let us recall again that Citigroup, in its press release on the first quarter revenues of 2009 reported a *positive* mark-to-market due to its *worsened* credit quality: "Revenues also included [. . .] a net $2.5 billion positive CVA on derivative positions, excluding monolines, mainly due to the widening of Citigroup's CDS spread". In this chapter we explain precisely how such a situation may originate.

We refer to the two names involved in the transaction and subject to default risk as:

$$\text{investor} \rightarrow I$$
$$\text{counterparty} \rightarrow C$$

In general, we will address valuation as seen from the point of view of the investor (I), so that cash flows received by I will be positive whereas cash flows paid by I (and received by C) will be negative.

We denote by τ_I and τ_C respectively the default times of the investor and counterparty. We place ourselves in a probability space $(\Omega, \mathcal{G}, \mathcal{G}_t, \mathbb{Q})$. The filtration $\mathcal{G}_t$ models the flow of information of the whole market, including credit, and $\mathbb{Q}$ is the risk-neutral measure. This space is endowed also with a right-continuous and complete sub-filtration $\mathcal{F}_t$ representing all the observable market quantities except the default events, thus $\mathcal{F}_t \subseteq \mathcal{G}_t := \mathcal{F}_t \vee \mathcal{H}_t$. Here, $\mathcal{H}_t = \sigma(\{\tau_I \leq u\} \vee \{\tau_C \leq u\} : u \leq t)$ is the right-continuous filtration generated by the default events, either of the investor or of his counterparty.

We assume that there is no possibility to have completely simultaneous defaults, therefore we assume that

$$\mathbb{Q}(\tau_I = \tau_C) = 0.$$

This assumption is verified by most models, with a few notable exceptions (such as, for example, the multivariate Marshall-Olkin exponential distribution [146], featuring a discrete component).

Let us call T the final maturity of the payoff which we need to evaluate and let us define the stopping time

$$\tau = \min\{\tau_I, \tau_C\}. \tag{12.1}$$

If $\tau > T$, there is neither default of the investor, nor of his counterparty during the life of the contract and they both can fulfil the agreements of the contract. On the contrary, if $\tau \leq T$ then either the investor or his counterparty (or both) default within the maturity of the contract. At τ, the Net Present Value (NPV) of the residual payoff until maturity is computed.[1] We then distinguish two cases:

- $\tau = \tau_C$. If the NPV at default time is negative (respectively positive) for the investor (defaulted counterparty), it is completely paid (received) by the investor (defaulted counterparty) itself. If the NPV at default time is positive (negative) for the investor (counterparty), only a recovery fraction REC_C of the NPV is exchanged.
- $\tau = \tau_I$. If the NPV at default time is positive (respectively negative) for the defaulted investor (counterparty), it is completely received (paid) by the defaulted investor (counterparty) itself. If the NPV at default time is negative (positive) for the defaulted investor (counterparty), only a recovery fraction REC_I of the NPV is exchanged.

Let us define the following (mutually exclusive and exhaustive) events ordering the default times:

$$\begin{aligned} \mathcal{I}_1 &= \{\tau_I < \tau_C < T\}, \quad \mathcal{I}_2 = \{\tau_I < T \leq \tau_C\}, \quad \mathcal{I}_3 = \{\tau_C \leq \tau_I < T\} \\ \mathcal{I}_4 &= \{\tau_C < T \leq \tau_I\}, \quad \mathcal{I}_5 = \{T \leq \tau_I < \tau_C\}, \quad \mathcal{I}_6 = \{T \leq \tau_C \leq \tau_I\}. \end{aligned} \tag{12.2}$$

Let us call $\bar{\Pi}(t, T)$ the discounted payoff of a generic defaultable claim at t and $\Pi(t, T)$ the discounted payoff for an equivalent claim with a default-free counterparty. Notice that in earlier chapters we also used the notation Π^D, so that

$$\bar{\Pi}(t, T) = \Pi^D(t, T).$$

We then have the following Proposition, proven in [39] and sketched less formally here in Chapter 10.

Proposition 12.1.1 ***(General bilateral counterparty risk pricing formula)*** *At valuation time t, and on the event $\{\tau > t\}$, the price of the payoff under bilateral counterparty risk is*

$$\begin{aligned} \mathbb{E}_t\left[\bar{\Pi}(t, T)\right] = \mathbb{E}_t\left[\Pi(t, T)\right] &+ \mathbb{E}_t\left[\text{LGD}_I \mathbf{1}_{\{\mathcal{I}_1 \cup \mathcal{I}_2\}} D(t, \tau_I)(-NPV(\tau_I))^+\right] \\ &- \mathbb{E}_t\left[\text{LGD}_C \mathbf{1}_{\{\mathcal{I}_3 \cup \mathcal{I}_4\}} D(t, \tau_C)(NPV(\tau_C))^+\right] \end{aligned} \tag{12.3}$$

where $\text{LGD}_i := 1 - \text{REC}_i$ *is the* Loss Given Default *and* REC_i *is the recovery fraction, with $i \in \{I, C\}$. We also define*

$$NPV(u) := \mathbb{E}_u[\Pi(u, T)].$$

It is clear that the value of a defaultable claim is the value of the corresponding default-free claim plus a long position in a put option (with zero strike) on the residual NPV giving non-zero contributions only in scenarios where the investor is the earliest to default (and does so before final maturity) plus a short position in a call option (with zero strike) on the residual NPV giving non-zero contribution in scenarios where the counterparty is the earliest to default (and does so before final maturity). Finally, we define the Bilateral Debit Valuation Adjustment (DVA) and the Bilateral Credit Valuation Adjustment (CVA) as seen by the investor "I" as

$$\begin{aligned} \text{DVA}(t, T) &= \mathbb{E}_t\left[\text{LGD}_I \mathbf{1}_{\{\mathcal{I}_1 \cup \mathcal{I}_5\}} \cdot D(t, \tau_I) \cdot (-NPV(\tau_I))^+\right] \\ \text{CVA}(t, T) &= \mathbb{E}_t\left[\text{LGD}_C \mathbf{1}_{\{\mathcal{I}_3 \cup \mathcal{I}_4\}} \cdot D(t, \tau_C) \cdot (NPV(\tau_C))^+\right]. \end{aligned}$$

[1] In the present chapter we evaluate close-out amounts as the mid market mark-to-market value of the transaction. In Chapter 13 we discuss how to evaluate close-out amounts. We refer to [127] for different strategies. See also [41], [52] as summarized in Chapter 14 for specific examples of the effects of adopting a replacement close-out rather than a mid market one.

The DVA *and* CVA *terms depend on T through the events $\mathcal{I}_1, \ldots, \mathcal{I}_4$ and* LGD_i*, with $i \in \{I, C\}$, it is a shorthand notation to denote the dependence on the loss given defaults of each name.*

Proof We have that

$$\Pi(t,T) = \mathbf{1}_{\mathcal{I}_1 \cup \mathcal{I}_2} \Pi(t,T) + \mathbf{1}_{\mathcal{I}_3 \cup \mathcal{I}_4} \Pi(t,T) + \mathbf{1}_{\mathcal{I}_5 \cup \mathcal{I}_6} \Pi(t,T) \tag{12.4}$$

since the events in Equation (12.2) form a complete set. We can rewrite the right-hand side of the Equation (12.3) using Equation (12.4) as

$$\begin{aligned} \mathbb{E}_t\left[\bar{\Pi}(t,T)\right] = {} & \mathbb{E}_t\left[\mathbf{1}_{\mathcal{I}_1 \cup \mathcal{I}_2} \Pi(t,T) + (1 - \text{REC}_I) \mathbf{1}_{\mathcal{I}_1 \cup \mathcal{I}_2} D(t, \tau_I)[-NPV(\tau_I)]^+\right] \\ & + \mathbb{E}_t\left[\mathbf{1}_{\mathcal{I}_3 \cup \mathcal{I}_4} \Pi(t,T) + (\text{REC}_C - 1) \mathbf{1}_{\mathcal{I}_3 \cup \mathcal{I}_4} D(t, \tau_C)[NPV(\tau_C)]^+\right] \\ & + \mathbb{E}_t[\mathbf{1}_{\mathcal{I}_5 \cup \mathcal{I}_6} \Pi(t,T)]. \end{aligned} \tag{12.5}$$

We next develop each of the three expectations in the equality of Equation (12.5).

The expression inside the first expectation can be rewritten as

$$\begin{aligned} & \mathbf{1}_{\mathcal{I}_1 \cup \mathcal{I}_2} \Pi(t,T) + (1 - \text{REC}_I) \mathbf{1}_{\mathcal{I}_1 \cup \mathcal{I}_2} D(t,\tau_I)[-NPV(\tau_I)]^+ \\ & = \mathbf{1}_{\mathcal{I}_1 \cup \mathcal{I}_2} \Pi(t,T) + \mathbf{1}_{\mathcal{I}_1 \cup \mathcal{I}_2} D(t,\tau_I)[-NPV(\tau_I)]^+ - \text{REC}_I \mathbf{1}_{\mathcal{I}_1 \cup \mathcal{I}_2} D(t,\tau_I)[-NPV(\tau_I)]^+. \end{aligned} \tag{12.6}$$

Conditional on the information at τ_I, the expectation of the expression in Equation (12.6) is equal to:

$$\begin{aligned} & \mathbb{E}_{\tau_I}\left[\mathbf{1}_{\mathcal{I}_1 \cup \mathcal{I}_2} \Pi(t,T) + \mathbf{1}_{\mathcal{I}_1 \cup \mathcal{I}_2} D(t,\tau_I)(-NPV(\tau_I))^+ - \text{REC}_I \mathbf{1}_{\mathcal{I}_1 \cup \mathcal{I}_2} D(t,\tau_I)[-NPV(\tau_I)]^+\right] \\ & = \mathbb{E}_{\tau_I}[\mathbf{1}_{\mathcal{I}_1 \cup \mathcal{I}_2}[\Pi(t,\tau_I) + D(t,\tau_I)\Pi(\tau_I,T) + D(t,\tau_I)\left(-\mathbb{E}_{\tau_I}[\Pi(\tau_I,T)]\right)^+ \\ & \quad - \text{REC}_I D(t,\tau_I)[-NPV(\tau_I)]^+]] \\ & = \mathbf{1}_{\mathcal{I}_1 \cup \mathcal{I}_2}[\Pi(t,\tau_I) + D(t,\tau_I)\mathbb{E}_{\tau_I}[\Pi(\tau_I,T)] + D(t,\tau_I)\left(-\mathbb{E}_{\tau_I}[\Pi(\tau_I,T)]\right)^+ \\ & \quad - \text{REC}_I D(t,\tau_I)[-NPV(\tau_I)]^+] \\ & = \mathbf{1}_{\mathcal{I}_1 \cup \mathcal{I}_2}[\Pi(t,\tau_I) + D(t,\tau_I)\left(\mathbb{E}_{\tau_I}[\Pi(\tau_I,T)]\right)^+ - \text{REC}_I D(t,\tau_I)[-NPV(\tau_I)]^+] \\ & = \mathbf{1}_{\mathcal{I}_1 \cup \mathcal{I}_2}[\Pi(t,\tau_I) + D(t,\tau_I)(NPV(\tau_I))^+ - \text{REC}_I D(t,\tau_I)[-NPV(\tau_I)]^+] \end{aligned}$$

where the first equality in Equation (12.7) follows bccausc:

$$\mathbf{1}_{\mathcal{I}_1 \cup \mathcal{I}_2} \Pi(t,T) = \mathbf{1}_{\mathcal{I}_1 \cup \mathcal{I}_2}[\Pi(t,\tau_I) + D(t,\tau_I)\Pi(\tau_I,T)] \tag{12.7}$$

being the default time τ_I always smaller than T under the event $\mathcal{I}_1 \cup \mathcal{I}_2$. Conditioning the obtain result on the information available at t, and using the fact that $\mathbb{E}_t[\mathbb{E}_{\tau_I}[.]] = \mathbb{E}_t[.]$ due to that $t < \tau_I$, we obtain that the first term in Equation (12.5) is given by

$$\mathbb{E}_t\left[\mathbf{1}_{\mathcal{I}_1 \cup \mathcal{I}_2}\left[\Pi(t,\tau_I) + D(t,\tau_I)(NPV(\tau_I))^+ - \text{REC}_I D(t,\tau_I)(-NPV(\tau_I))^+\right]\right] \tag{12.8}$$

which coincides with the expectation of the third term in Equation (12.3).

We next repeat a similar argument for the second expectation in Equation (12.5). We have:

$$\begin{aligned} & \mathbf{1}_{\mathcal{I}_3 \cup \mathcal{I}_4} \Pi(t,T) + (\text{REC}_C - 1) \mathbf{1}_{\mathcal{I}_3 \cup \mathcal{I}_4} D(t,\tau_C)[NPV(\tau_C)]^+ \\ & = \mathbf{1}_{\mathcal{I}_3 \cup \mathcal{I}_4} \Pi(t,T) - \mathbf{1}_{\mathcal{I}_3 \cup \mathcal{I}_4} D(t,\tau_C)[NPV(\tau_C)]^+ + \text{REC}_C \mathbf{1}_{\mathcal{I}_3 \cup \mathcal{I}_4} D(t,\tau_C)[NPV(\tau_C)]^+. \end{aligned} \tag{12.9}$$

Conditional on the information available at time τ_C, we have:

$$
\begin{aligned}
&\mathbb{E}_{\tau_C}\left[\mathbf{1}_{\mathcal{I}_3\cup\mathcal{I}_4}\Pi(t,T) - \mathbf{1}_{\mathcal{I}_3\cup\mathcal{I}_4}D(t,\tau_C)(NPV(\tau_C))^+\,\mathrm{Rec}_C\mathbf{1}_{\mathcal{I}_3\cup\mathcal{I}_4}D(t,\tau_C)[NPV(\tau_C)]^+\right]\\
&= \mathbb{E}_{\tau_C}[\mathbf{1}_{\mathcal{I}_3\cup\mathcal{I}_4}[\Pi(t,\tau_C) + D(t,\tau_C)\Pi(\tau_C,T) - D(t,\tau_C)\left(\mathbb{E}_{\tau_C}[\Pi(\tau_C,T)]\right)^+\\
&\quad +\mathrm{Rec}_C D(t,\tau_C)[NPV(\tau_C)]^+]]\\
&= \mathbf{1}_{\mathcal{I}_3\cup\mathcal{I}_4}[\Pi(t,\tau_C) + D(t,\tau_C)\mathbb{E}_{\tau_C}[\Pi(\tau_C,T)] - D(t,\tau_C)\left(\mathbb{E}_{\tau_C}[\Pi(\tau_C,T)]\right)^+\\
&\quad +\mathrm{Rec}_C D(t,\tau_C)[NPV(\tau_C)]^+]\\
&= \mathbf{1}_{\mathcal{I}_3\cup\mathcal{I}_4}\left[\Pi(t,\tau_C) - D(t,\tau_C)\left(\mathbb{E}_{\tau_C}[-\Pi(\tau_C,T)]\right)^+ + \mathrm{Rec}_C D(t,\tau_C)[NPV(\tau_C)]^+\right]\\
&= \mathbf{1}_{\mathcal{I}_3\cup\mathcal{I}_4}\left[\Pi(t,\tau_C) - D(t,\tau_C)(-NPV(\tau_C))^+ + \mathrm{Rec}_C D(t,\tau_C)[NPV(\tau_C)]^+\right] \qquad (12.10)
\end{aligned}
$$

where the first equality follows because:

$$\mathbf{1}_{\mathcal{I}_3\cup\mathcal{I}_4}\Pi(t,T) = \mathbf{1}_{\mathcal{I}_3\cup\mathcal{I}_4}[\Pi(t,\tau_C) + D(t,\tau_C)\Pi(\tau_C,T)] \qquad (12.11)$$

being the default time τ_C is always smaller than T under the event $\mathcal{I}_3 \cup \mathcal{I}_4$. Conditioning the obtain result on the information available at $t < \tau_C$, we obtain that the second term in Equation (12.5) is given by

$$\mathbb{E}_t\left[\mathbf{1}_{\mathcal{I}_3\cup\mathcal{I}_4}\left[\Pi(t,\tau_C) + D(t,\tau_C)\mathrm{Rec}_C(NPV(\tau_C))^+ - D(t,\tau_C)(-NPV(\tau_C))^+\right]\right] \qquad (12.12)$$

which coincides exactly with the expectation of the second term in Equation (12.3).

The third expectation in Equation (12.5) coincides with the first term in Equation (12.3), therefore their expectations ought to be the same. Since we have proven that the expectation of each term in Equation (12.3) equals the expectation of the corresponding term in Equation (12.5), the desired result is obtained.

Definition 12.1.2 ***(Bilateral VA, Bilateral DVA, Bilateral CVA)*** *We called "BVA" (Bilateral Valuation Adjustment, or Bilateral VA) the positive additive adjustment*

$$\mathrm{Bva}(t,T) = \mathrm{Dva}(t,T) - \mathrm{Cva}(t,T) \qquad (12.13)$$

to the risk-free price in Chapter 10. With this definition, we have

$$\mathbb{E}_t\left[\bar{\Pi}(t,T)\right] = \mathbb{E}_t[\Pi(t,T)] + \mathrm{Bva}(t,T). \qquad (12.14)$$

It is important to point out that the industry is using several different names for the bilateral adjustment and this is creating confusion.

The main source of confusion is that, in the industry, by the term "Bilateral Credit Valuation Adjustment", or "Bilateral CVA", usually one means −BVA = CVA − DVA, namely the adjustment to be subtracted from the default risk-free price to obtain the default risk-adjusted price. Strictly speaking, with this terminology it is difficult to distinguish between Cva, *namely the CVA component of the bilateral adjustment, and the total adjustment −*Bva. *When one says "Bilateral Credit Valuation Adjustment", is one referring to −*Bva *or to* Cva*?*

To avoid this ambiguity, we refer to the total bilateral valuation adjustment DVA − CVA simply as to the Bilateral Valuation Adjustment, Bva. *We also point out that we define* Bva *as the adjustment to be added, rather than subtracted, to the default risk-free price, but this is clearly a matter of convention. If one wants to stay with an adjustment to be subtracted, it is obviously enough to take* $-\text{BVA}$.[2]

The BVA adjustment may be either negative or positive depending on whether the counterparty is more or less likely to default than the investor and on the volatilities and dependencies ("correlations").

Again, as in the unilateral case, the pricing formula for CVA often requires a numerical integration. Let us consider the simple case of a zero-coupon bond with deterministic recovery rate. Even in this case we must resort to a numerical algorithm to calculate the CVA due to right and wrong way risk. Indeed, we get

$$\text{BVA}(t, T) = -\text{LGD}_C \mathbb{E}_t \left[\mathbf{1}_{\{\mathcal{I}_3 \cup \mathcal{I}_4\}} D(t, T) \right] ,$$

which cannot be calculated in closed form due to the dependency between the default indicators and the discount factor.

Notice that in this chapter we assume the recovery fractions (and hence loss given defaults) to be deterministic.

12.1.1 Symmetry versus Asymmetry

As we predicted in Chapter 10, for the earlier results on counterparty risk valuation, Equation (12.13) has the great advantage of being symmetric. This is to say if C were to compute counterparty risk for its position towards I, i.e. the term to be added to the default-free price to include counterparty risk, C would find exactly $-\text{BVA}(t, T)$. However, if each party computed the adjustment to be added by assuming itself to be default free, and considering only the default of the other party, then the adjustment calculated by I would be

$$-UCVA_I(t) = -\mathbb{E}_t \left[LGD_C \mathbf{1}_{\{\tau_C < T\}} \cdot D(t, \tau_C) \cdot (NPV(\tau_C))^+ \right]$$

whereas the adjustment calculated by name C would be

$$-UCVA_C(t) = -\mathbb{E}_t \left[LGD_I \mathbf{1}_{\{\tau_I < T\}} \cdot D(t, \tau_I) \cdot (-NPV(\tau_I))^+ \right]$$

and they would not be the opposite of each other. This means that only in the first case resorting to the full bilateral adjustment BVA the two parties would agree on the value of the counterparty risk adjustment to be added to the default-free price.

12.1.2 Worsening of Credit Quality and Positive Mark-to-Market

As we anticipated in Chapter 10 (to which we refer for more information and examples), earlier results on asymmetric counterparty risk valuation, concerned with a default-free investor, would find an adjustment to be added that is always negative. However, in our symmetric case even if the initial adjustment is negative due to $\text{CVA}(t, T) > \text{DVA}(t, T)$, namely:

$$\mathbb{E}_t \left[LGD_C \mathbf{1}_{\{\mathcal{I}_3 \cup \mathcal{I}_4\}} D(t, \tau_C) (\text{NPV}(\tau_C))^+ \right] > \mathbb{E}_t \left[LGD_I \mathbf{1}_{\{\mathcal{I}_1 \cup \mathcal{I}_2\}} D(t, \tau_I) (-\text{NPV}(\tau_I))^+ \right]$$

[2] In [39] tables report the opposite quantity, namely $-\text{BVA}$. While this definition is more consistent with the idea of subtracting the adjustment term from the risk-free price, which is what we find in the unilateral CVA case, we felt that once it is understood that the adjustment can go in both directions then it is more natural to express that the adjustment be added to the risk-free price, rather than subtracted. However this can be converted easily to the adjustment to be subtracted by simply changing the sign.

the situation may change in time, to the point that the two terms may cancel or the adjustment may change sign as the credit quality of I deteriorates and that of C improves, so that the inequality changes direction.

In particular, if the investor marks-to-market its position at a later time using Equation (12.3), we can see that the term in LGD_I increases, all things being equal, if the credit quality of I worsens. If, for example, we increase the credit spreads of the investor, now $\tau_I < \tau_C$ will happen more often, giving more weight to the term in LGD_I. This is at the basis of statements like the Citigroup one above.

12.2 MODELLING ASSUMPTIONS

In this section, the modelling setup is quite similar to the one adopted in Chapter 5, to which we refer the reader for more details. Here we go bilateral and add the default of the investor "I". The investor (the bank "B") was assumed to be default free in Chapter 5.

In this section we consider a model that is stochastic both in the interest rates (underlying market) and in the default intensity (counterparty). Joint stochasticity is needed to introduce correlation between these two quantities. The interest rates are modelled according to a short-rate Gaussian shifted two-factor process (hereafter G2++), while each of the two default intensities is modelled according to a square-root process (hereafter CIR++). Details for both models can be found in, for example, [48]. The two models are coupled by correlating their Brownian shocks.

12.2.1 G2++ Interest Rate Model

For interest rates, we assume a G2++ model as in Section 5.1.1 which we calibrate to the ATM swaption volatilities quoted by the market on 26 May 2009. Market data are listed in Tables 12.1 and 12.2, while more details on the methodology can be found in [57].

In Figure 12.1 we report the calibrated model parameters and absolute calibration errors in basis points (expiries on the left axis, tenors on the right axis).

Table 12.1 EUR zero-coupon continuously compounded spot rates (ACT/360) observed on 26 May 2009

Date	Rate	Date	Rate	Date	Rate
27-May-09	1.15%	28-Dec-09	1.49%	29-May-17	3.40%
28-May-09	1.02%	28-Jan-10	1.53%	28-May-18	3.54%
29-May-09	0.98%	26-Feb-10	1.56%	28-May-19	3.66%
04-Jun-09	0.93%	29-Mar-10	1.59%	28-May-21	3.87%
11-Jun-09	0.92%	28-Apr-10	1.61%	28-May-24	4.09%
18-Jun-09	0.91%	28-May-10	1.63%	28-May-29	4.19%
29-Jun-09	0.91%	30-May-11	1.72%	29-May-34	4.07%
28-Jul-09	1.05%	28-May-12	2.13%	30-May-39	3.92%
28-Aug-09	1.26%	28-May-13	2.48%		
28-Sep-09	1.34%	28-May-14	2.78%		
28-Oct-09	1.41%	28-May-15	3.02%		
30-Nov-09	1.46%	30-May-16	3.23%		

Table 12.2 Market at-the-money swaption volatilities, with expiry date t and tenor b, observed on 26 May 2009

$t \downarrow / b \rightarrow$	1y	2y	3y	4y	5y
1y	42.8%	34.3%	31.0%	28.8%	27.7%
2y	28.7%	25.6%	24.1%	23.1%	22.4%
3y	23.5%	21.1%	20.4%	20.0%	19.7%
4y	19.9%	18.5%	18.2%	18.1%	18.0%
5y	17.6%	16.8%	16.9%	16.9%	17.0%
7y	15.4%	15.3%	15.3%	15.3%	15.3%
10y	14.2%	14.2%	14.2%	14.3%	14.4%

$t \downarrow / b \rightarrow$	6y	7y	8y	9y	10y
1y	26.9%	26.5%	26.3%	26.2%	26.2%
2y	22.3%	22.2%	22.3%	22.4%	22.4%
3y	19.7%	19.7%	19.8%	19.9%	20.1%
4y	18.1%	18.1%	18.2%	18.2%	18.4%
5y	16.9%	17.0%	17.0%	17.0%	17.1%
7y	15.3%	15.3%	15.4%	15.5%	15.6%
10y	14.5%	14.6%	14.7%	14.8%	15.0%

The G2++ model links the dependence on tenors of swaption volatilities to the form of an initial yield curve. Before the crisis period such constraint of the G2++ model seems not so relevant, but the situation changed from spring 2008, when the yield curve steepened in conjunction with a movement in the market volatility surface which could not be reproduced by the model. Yet, versions of the model with time-dependent volatilities can calibrate ATM swaption volatilities in a satisfactory way. For instance, if we introduce a time grid $t_0 = 0, t_1, \ldots, t_m$, we can consider the following time-dependent volatilities:

$$\sigma(t) := \bar{\sigma} f(\ell(t)) , \quad \eta(t) := \bar{\eta} f(\ell(t))$$

a	0.0002
b	7.6630
σ	0.0080
η	0.0182
ρ_{12}	0.9734

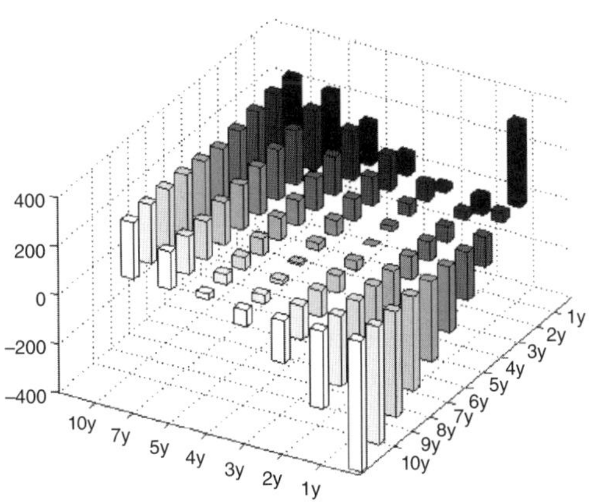

Figure 12.1 Calibrated model parameters for time-homogeneous G2++ model and absolute calibration errors in basis points (expiries on the left axis, tenors on the right axis)

a	0.0001
b	1.9478
σ	0.0062
η	0.0299
ρ_{12}	-0.7661
β_0	1.6241
β_1	9.0793
β_2	1.7074

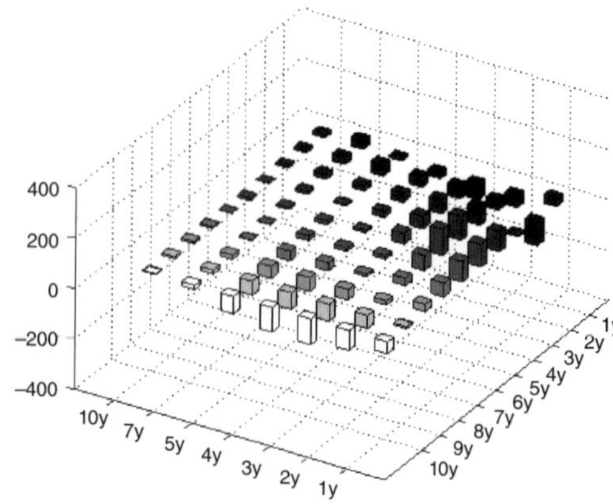

Figure 12.2 Calibrated model parameters for time-dependent G2++ model and absolute calibration errors in basis points (expiries on the left axis, tenors on the right axis)

where the $\ell(t) := \max\{t^* \in \{t_0, \ldots, t_m\} : t^* \leq t\}$ function selects the left extremum of each interval and

$$f(t) := 1 - e^{-\beta_1 t} + \beta_0 e^{-\beta_2 t}$$

Notice that in this way we do not alter the analytical tractability of the G2++ model, since all integrals involving model piece-wise-constant parameters can be performed as finite summations.

However, in this chapter on counterparty risk we consider the simpler constant parameter version of the G2++ model. Nonetheless, we report in Figure 12.2 model parameters and absolute calibration errors in basis points for the time-dependent version of the G2++ model (expiries on the left axis, tenors on the right axis).

12.2.2 CIR++ Stochastic Intensity Model

For credit spreads, we assume a copy of the CIR++ model from Section 5.1.2 for each name, one for the investor and one for the counterparty. All the related quantities gain a superscript to identify them: I means the investor and C the counterparty.

The two intensity processes λ^I and λ^C are assumed to be independent, so that the Brownian motion driving the investor's intensity (Z_3^I) is independent of the one driving the counterparty's intensity (Z_3^C). This is assumed to simplify the parameterization of the model and focus on default correlation rather than spread correlation, but the assumption can be removed if one is willing to complicate the parameterization of the model. In general, when stochastic intensities follow diffusion processes, spread correlation is of second order with respect to default correlation. However, spread correlation would become relevant in case collateralization is introduced. In our Cox process setting the default times are modelled as

$$\tau_i = (\Lambda^i)^{-1}(\xi_i)\,, \quad i \in \{I, C\}$$

where $\Lambda^i(t)$ is the cumulated default intensity up to time t for name i, and ξ is an exponential unit-mean random variable independent of interest rates. The two ξ's are assumed to be connected via a bivariate Gaussian copula function with correlation parameter ρ_G. This is a

Table 12.3 Mid risk initial CDS term structure

T	1y	2y	3y	4y	5y	6y	7y	8y	9y	10y
CDS Spread	92	104	112	117	120	122	124	125	126	127

default correlation, and the two default times are connected via default correlation, even if their spreads are independent. In general, high default correlation creates more dependence between the default times than a high correlation in their spreads for diffusion intensity models.

12.2.3 Realistic Market Data Set for CDS Options

The default-intensity process of each name can be calibrated, as in Section 12.2.2, to CDS quoted spreads. Yet, not all model parameters can be fixed in this way. The remaining free parameters can be used to fit the price of further products, such as single name option data. However, single-name options on the credit derivatives market are not liquid. Indeed, currently the bid-ask spreads for single name CDS options are large and suggest that one should consider these quotes with caution, see Section 12.2.2, so that we set free model parameters to imply possibly reasonable values for the volatilities of hypothetical at-the-money CDS options on the counterparty and investor names.

Such CDS options would typically be options to enter in t years into a CDS selling protection up to a future time T. These options are at-the-money, in that if the option is exercised the future CDS is entered at time t at a spread given by the initial CDS spread at time 0 for maturity $t + T$. Also, the CDS to be entered is a receiver CDS and we do not consider front-end protection for defaults up to t. For details on the market formula that we use to extract implied volatility from CDS option prices see, for example [31].

We focus on two different sets of CDS quotes, that we name hereafter *Mid* and *High* risk settings. Then, we introduce a different set of model parameters for each CDS setting. In the following tables we show them along with the implied volatilities for CDSs starting at t and maturing at T. The implied volatilities are calculated via a Jamshidian decomposition as described in [35] or [48].

The interest-rate curve is bootstrapped from the market on 26 May 2009 (see 12.1). Notice that the zero-curve is increasing in time. Further, we always consider that recovery rates are at 40% level.

We introduce two realistic market settings for the credit quality and volatility of names I and C: a mid-risk setting and a high-risk setting. The parameters for the two risk settings are given in Table 12.5, and the associated CDS term structure and implied volatilities are reported in Tables 12.3 and 12.4.

In Tables 12.6 and 12.7 we show the CDS volatilities implied by the our model in the two market settings.

Table 12.4 High risk initial CDS term structure

T	1y	2y	3y	4y	5y	6y	7y	8y	9y	10y
CDS Spread	234	244	248	250	252	252	254	253	254	254

Table 12.5 Mid and high-risk credit spread parameters

	y_0	κ	μ	ν
Mid	0.01	0.80	0.02	0.20
High	0.03	0.50	0.05	0.50

Table 12.6 Mid-risk CDS implied volatility associated to the parameters in Table 12.5. Each column contains volatilities of CDS options of a given maturity T for different expiries t

$t \downarrow / T \rightarrow$	2y	3y	4y	5y	6y	7y	8y	9y	10y
1y	52%	36%	27%	21%	17%	15%	13%	12%	11%
2y		39%	28%	21%	17%	14%	12%	11%	10%
3y			33%	24%	18%	15%	12%	11%	9%
4y				29%	21%	16%	13%	11%	9%
5y					26%	19%	15%	12%	10%
6y						24%	17%	13%	11%
7y							23%	16%	12%
8y								21%	15%
9y									19%

Table 12.7 High-risk CDS implied volatility associated to the parameters in Table 12.5. Each column contains volatilities of CDS options of a given maturity T for different expiries t

$t \downarrow / T \rightarrow$	2y	3y	4y	5y	6y	7y	8y	9y	10y
1y	96%	69%	53%	43%	36%	31%	28%	26%	24%
2y		71%	52%	40%	32%	27%	24%	21%	19%
3y			59%	43%	33%	26%	22%	20%	18%
4y				51%	37%	28%	23%	20%	17%
5y					45%	33%	26%	21%	18%
6y						40%	30%	24%	19%
7y							40%	29%	22%
8y								36%	26%
9y									34%

12.3 NUMERICAL METHODS

A Monte Carlo simulation is used to value all the payoffs.

The transition density for the G2++ model is known in closed form, while the CIR++ model, when correlated with G2++, requires a discretization scheme for the joint evolution. We find similar convergence results both with the full truncation scheme introduced by [144] and with the implied scheme by [35]. In the following we adopt the former scheme. For alternative approaches to the joint simulation of market relevant quantities with a Monte Carlo algorithm see [63].

Further, we bucket default times by assuming that the default events can occur only on a time grid $\{T_i : 0 \leq i \leq b\}$, with $T_0 = t$ and $T_b = T$, by anticipating each default event to the last T_i preceding it. In the following calculations we choose a weekly interval and we check a posteriori that the time-grid spacing is small enough to have a stable value for the BVA price.

The calculation of the future time expectation, required by counterparty risk evaluation, is taken by approximating the expectation at the actual (bucketed) default time T_i with a finite series in the interest rate model underlying assets, x and z, on a polynomial basis $\{\psi_j\}$ valued at the allowed default times within the interval $[t, T_i[$.

$$\mathrm{NPV}(T_i) := \mathbb{E}_{T_i}\left[\Pi(T_i, T)\right] = \sum_{j=0}^{\infty} \alpha_{ij}\psi_j(x_{t:T_i}, z_{t:T_i}) \simeq \sum_{j=0}^{N} \alpha_{ij}\psi_j(x_{t:T_i}, z_{t:T_i})$$

Notice that if the payoff is not time-dependent, the functions ψs needs to be valued only at T_i. The coefficients α_{ij} of the series expansion are calculated by means of a least-squares regression, as usually done to price Bermudan options with the Least-Squares Monte Carlo method.

Thus, the credit valuation adjustment is calculated as follows:

$$\begin{aligned}\mathrm{BVA}(t, T) \simeq & -\mathrm{LGD}_C \sum_{i=0}^{b-1} \mathbb{E}_t\left[\mathbf{1}_{\{\tau_I \geq \tau_C\}}\mathbf{1}_{\{T_i \leq \tau_C < T_{i+1}\}} D(t, T_i)\left(\mathbb{E}_{T_i}\left[\Pi(T_i, T)\right]\right)^+\right] \\ & +\mathrm{LGD}_I \sum_{i=0}^{b-1} \mathbb{E}_t\left[\mathbf{1}_{\{\tau_I \leq \tau_C\}}\mathbf{1}_{\{T_i \leq \tau_I < T_{i+1}\}} D(t, T_i)\left(-\mathbb{E}_{T_i}\left[\Pi(T_i, T)\right]\right)^+\right]\end{aligned}$$

where the forward expectations are approximated as

$$\mathbb{E}_{T_i}\left[\Pi(T_i, T)\right] \simeq \sum_{j=0}^{N} \alpha_{ij}\psi_j(x_{t:T_i}, z_{t:T_i})$$

$$\{\alpha_{ij}\} = \underset{\alpha_{i0}, \ldots, \alpha_{iN}}{\arg\min}\ \mathbb{E}_t\left[\left(\Pi(T_i, T) - \sum_{j=0}^{N} \alpha_{ij}\psi_j(x_{t:T_i}, z_{t:T_i})\right)^2\right]$$

In the following numerical examples we consider non-path-dependent payoffs, and we empirically find stable prices by using a polynomial basis up to the second degree in the function parameters, namely

$$\begin{aligned}&\psi_0(x, z) := 1\,, \quad \psi_1(x, z) := x\,, \quad \psi_2(x, z) := z \\ &\psi_3(x, z) := x^2\,, \quad \psi_4(x, z) := z^2\,, \quad \psi_5(x, z) := xz\end{aligned}$$

Notice also that since the payoff evaluation depends on the projection coefficients which, in turn, depend on the simulated path, we are introducing a correlation between our Monte Carlo samples which, in principle, makes the standard deviation a biased estimator of the statistical error. However, in our experience the bias introduced by using a single Monte Carlo for both evaluating the αs and the BVA price is negligible.

12.4 RESULTS AND DISCUSSION

In the following numerical examples we use as free correlation parameters:

$$\bar{\rho}_C\,, \quad \bar{\rho}_I\,, \quad \rho_G\,.$$

The first two parameters are defined by Equation (5.8), and they represent the correlation between the short rate and the default intensity of each name. The third term is the Gaussian copula parameter between default times. We recover the other correlations from them. In particular, we consider the following cases:

- Varying $\bar{\rho}_C$, keeping fixed $\bar{\rho}_I = 0$.
- Varying both $\bar{\rho}_C$ and $\bar{\rho}_I$, keeping them equal, i.e. $\bar{\rho}_C = \bar{\rho}_I$.
- For each choice of $\bar{\rho}_C$ and $\bar{\rho}_I$, we consider $\rho_G \in \{-80\%, 0\%, 80\%\}$.
- Varying ρ_G and keeping $\bar{\rho}_C = \bar{\rho}_I = 0$.

We consider payoffs depending on at-the-money forward interest rate swap (IRS) paying on the EUR market. These contracts reset a given number of years from trade date and start accruing two business days later. The IRS's fixed legs pay annually a 30E/360 strike rate, while the floating legs pay LIBOR twice per year.

In general our results confirm, both in the mid- and in the high-risk settings, the bilateral valuation adjustment (BVA) to be relevant and structured. We notice in particular that the impact of correlations between the investor's and counterparty's default risks is relevant. We also find a relevant impact of credit spread volatilities for the credit qualities of both names, and correlation between defaults and interest rates, as was earlier found for unilateral CVA calculations in [57].

In several scenarios the value of the BVA price may change sign according to the investor's and the counterparty's credit risk level and volatilities and depending on the correlation of these risks with the interest rates. This change of sign feature is a further convincing reason of the impact of dynamics on rigorous CVA valuation. The possible change of sign is also unique to the bilateral case, the unilateral adjustment always having the same sign.

We are going to detail our findings in a number of illustrative examples from our extensive set of results, by focusing on single IRS and IRS portfolios.

12.4.1 Bilateral VA in Single IRS

In this section, we show the impact of correlations, interest rate curve and credit spreads level, and volatility scenarios on the bilateral VA calculations for both receiver and payer

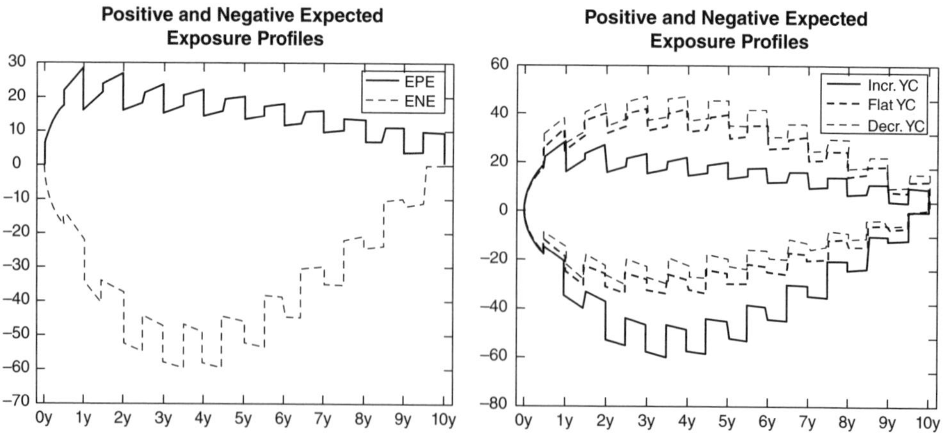

Figure 12.3 Expected positive (EPE) and negative (ENE) exposure profiles of a single receiver IRS with ten years' maturity and unitary notional. Profiles have been generated using: (left panel) the EUR yield curve bootstrapped from the market on 26 May 2009; (right panel) the increasing, flat at 3% and decreasing yield curves. Exposures are in basis points

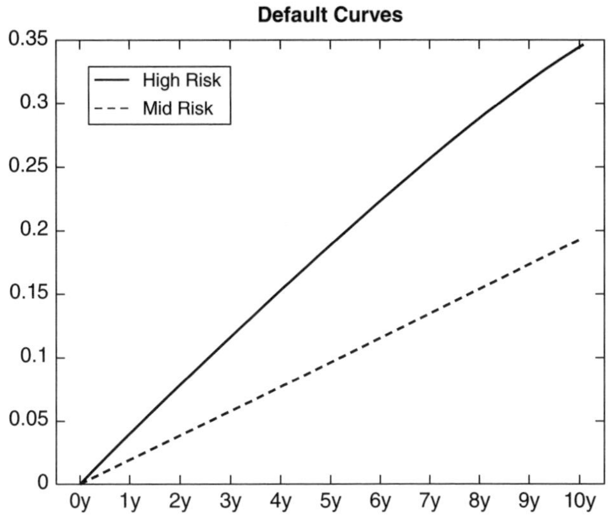

Figure 12.4 Default probability curves for the high and mid-credit risk scenarios

at-the-money swaps. We show in Figure 12.3 the expected positive and negative exposures (respectively EPE and ENE) for the single IRS case for both the EUR yield curve bootstrapped from market quotes on 26 May 2009, and for three stylized yield curves. Figure 12.4 shows the default probability curves for the high and mid-credit risk scenarios.

Table 12.8 shows a strong dependency of bilateral VA on correlation between the credit spread and the interest rates. Notice the opposite pattern between a receiver and a payer IRS due to the sign of cash flows: for receiver IRS increasing the correlation leads to a greater adjustment; the opposite is true for the payer case.

Table 12.9 investigates the dependency of bilateral VA on the parameter set of the CIR++ model, whereas Tables 12.10 and 12.11 investigate the dependency of bilateral VA on the Gaussian copula parameter for varying and zero correlation parameters between the rates and the credit spread processes of the two parties. We refer to the next section on IRS portfolios for a complete discussion of the numerical patterns.

Table 12.8 Bilateral valuation adjustment for a single receiver and payer swap with ten years' maturity and unitary notional, using a high-risk parameter set for the counterparty and mid-risk parameter set for the investor ("H/M") with uncorrelated default times. Prices are in basis points. Monte Carlo standard errors are small and thus are omitted

		H/M				H/M	
$\bar{\rho}_C$	$\bar{\rho}_I$	Rec	Pay	$\bar{\rho}_C$	$\bar{\rho}_I$	Rec	Pay
−60%	0%	−22	−27	−60%	−60%	−31	−20
−40%	0%	−12	−34	−40%	−40%	−18	−30
−20%	0%	−3	−43	−20%	−20%	−6	−41
0%	0%	4	−51	0%	0%	4	−51
20%	0%	10	−62	20%	20%	13	−64
40%	0%	14	−75	40%	40%	21	−78
60%	0%	17	−87	60%	60%	28	−91

Table 12.9 Bilateral valuation adjustment, by changing the parameter set, for a receiver and a payer swap with ten years maturity and unitary notional, with uncorrelated default times. The column title "H/M" means a high-risk parameter set for the counterparty and a mid-risk parameter set for the investor, "M/H" means the opposite situation, and "H/H" means both the parties have a high-risk parameter set. Prices are in basis points. Monte Carlo standard errors are small and thus are omitted

		Receiver			Payer		
$\bar{\rho}_C$	$\bar{\rho}_I$	H/M	H/H	M/H	H/M	H/H	M/H
−60%	−60%	−31	−11	19	−20	−9	30
−40%	−40%	−18	5	29	−30	−6	18
−20%	−20%	−6	20	41	−41	−21	6
0%	0%	4	33	51	−51	−34	−4
20%	20%	13	48	64	−64	−48	−13
40%	40%	21	61	77	−78	−63	−21
60%	60%	28	75	90	−91	−77	−29

Table 12.10 Bilateral valuation adjustment, by changing the Gaussian copula parameter ρ_G for a receiver and a payer swap with ten years maturity and unitary notional, using a high-risk parameter set for the counterparty and a mid-risk parameter set for the investor ("H/M"). Prices are in basis points. Monte Carlo standard errors are small and thus are omitted

		H/M					
		Receiver			Payer		
$\bar{\rho}_C$	$\bar{\rho}_I$	−80%	0%	80%	−80%	0%	80%
−60%	−60%	−31	−31	−38	−18	−20	−23
−40%	−40%	−17	−18	−26	−30	−30	−32
−20%	−20%	−3	−6	−14	−42	−41	−42
0%	0%	8	4	−5	−54	−51	−52
20%	20%	19	13	3	−68	−64	−64
40%	40%	29	21	10	−83	−78	−77
60%	60%	38	28	15	−98	−91	−90

Table 12.11 Bilateral valuation adjustment, by changing the Gaussian copula parameter ρ_G with all other correlations set to zero, for a receiver and a payer swap with ten years maturity and unitary notional. The column title "H/M" means a high-risk parameter set for the counterparty and a mid-risk parameter set for the investor, "M/H" means the opposite situation. Prices are in basis points. Monte Carlo standard errors are small and thus are omitted

	Receiver		Payer	
ρ_G	H/M	M/H	H/M	M/H
−60%	7.3	53	−55	−7.2
−40%	6.4	53	−54	−6.4
−20%	4.4	52	−54	−5.0
0%	3.9	51	−53	−3.9
20%	2.2	51	−53	−2.4
40%	−0.3	50	−53	−0.3
60%	−2.9	51	−53	2.6

Table 12.12 Bilateral valuation adjustment, by changing the volatility ν^2 of counterparty's credit spreads for a receiver and a payer swap with ten years maturity and unitary notional, using a high-risk parameter set for the counterparty and a mid-risk parameter set for the investor ("H/M"). Prices are in basis points. Monte Carlo standard errors are small and thus are omitted

		H/M					
		Receiver			Payer		
$\bar{\rho}_C$	$\bar{\rho}_I$	0%	30%	40%	0%	30%	40%
−60%	−60%	−5	−26	−30	−45	−20	−20
−40%	−40%	−2	−15	−17	−48	−31	−30
−20%	−20%	1	−5	−6	−50	−42	−41
0%	0%	4	4	4	−52	−53	−53
20%	20%	8	13	14	−54	−64	−63
40%	40%	12	21	22	−56	−75	−78
60%	60%	15	29	29	−57	−88	−91

Table 12.12 shows the impact of changing the volatility of the counterparty's credit spread. We can see the impact is small.

Finally Table 12.13 shows the impact of the yield curve on the bilateral VA. We can see in the left graph in Figure 12.3 how different yield curve shapes impact the EPE and ENE profiles of the receiver swap. The impact is opposite on the EPE and ENE profiles of the payer swap. We can see that a decreasing yield curve results in higher EPE profiles for the receiver swap than for the flat and the increasing yield curves. We consider the case where the counterparty has higher credit spreads than the investor, i.e. it is more likely that the counterparty will default first. This means that the CVA term has greater impact on the bilateral VA than the DVA term. The previous observations explain why the bilateral VA (left panel) of the receiver swap is smaller (more negative) for a decreasing yield curve than that for flat and increasing curves. The opposite is true for the payer swap.

Table 12.13 Bilateral valuation adjustment, by changing the yield curve (increasing, flat at 3% and decreasing curves) for a receiver and a payer swap with ten years maturity and unitary notional, using a high-risk parameter set for the counterparty and a mid-risk parameter set for the investor ("H/M"). We also assume uncorrelated default times. Prices are in basis points. Monte Carlo standard errors are small and thus are omitted

		H/M					
		Receiver			Payer		
$\bar{\rho}_C$	$\bar{\rho}_I$	Incr.	Flat	Decr.	Incr.	Flat	Decr.
−60%	−60%	−31	−77	−87	−20	14	24
−40%	−40%	−18	−60	−71	−30	5	15
−20%	−20%	−6	−45	−57	−41	−4	6
0%	0%	4	−32	−43	−51	−13	−1
20%	20%	13	−20	−31	−64	−25	−12
40%	40%	21	−10	−21	−78	−37	−24
60%	60%	28	−1	−11	−91	−50	−36

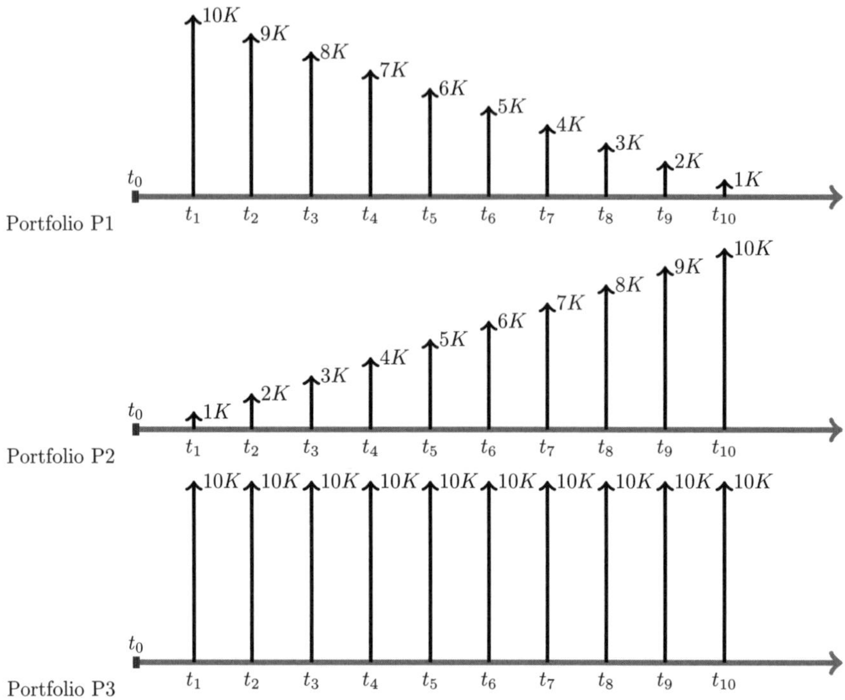

Figure 12.5 Graphical representation of the amortizing plan for the three interest rate portfolio swaps: P1, P2, and P3

12.4.2 Bilateral VA in an IRS Portfolio with Netting

In order to account for possible netting agreements, we consider three portfolios of swaps (see also Figure 12.5):

- (P1) A portfolio of 10 swaps, where all the swaps start at date T_0 and the i-th swap matures i years after the starting date. The netting of the portfolio is equal to an amortizing swap with decreasing outstanding.
- (P2) A portfolio of 10 swaps, where all the swaps mature in 10 years from date T_0, but they start at different dates, namely the i-th swap starts $i - 1$ years from date T_0. The netting of the portfolio is equal to an amortizing swap with increasing outstanding.
- (P3) A portfolio of 10 swaps, where all the swaps start at date T_0 and mature in 10 years. The netting of the portfolio is equal to a swap similar to the ones in the portfolio but with 10 times larger notional.

We show in Figure 12.6 the expected positive and negative exposures (respectively EPE and ENE) for the three IRS portfolio cases for the EUR yield curve bootstrapped from market quotes on 26 May 2009.

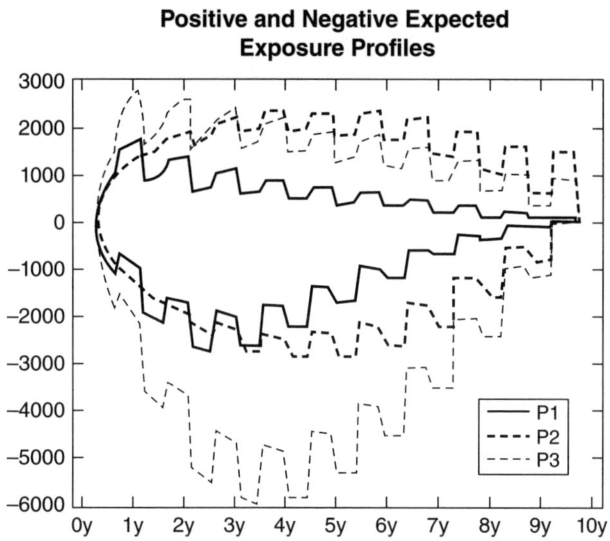

Figure 12.6 Expected positive (EPE) and negative (ENE) exposure profiles of the three different portfolios under consideration. Profiles have been generated using the EUR yield curve as of 26 May 2009. Exposures are in basis points

12.4.2.1 WWR in an IRS Portfolio with Netting

Tables 12.14 and 12.15 report a first panel of results. It is the bilateral valuation adjustment for three different receiver IRS portfolios with ten years maturity, using the high-risk parameter set for the counterparty credit spread and the mid-risk parameter set for the investor credit spread. The two default times are assumed uncorrelated, $\rho_G = 0$. This first set considers the bilateral VA calculation for the three different portfolios for a number of possible behaviours of wrong way correlations.

When $\bar{\rho}_0$ is kept to zero, we notice the same pattern in $\bar{\rho}_2$ we saw in the unilateral case in [57]. Increasing correlation $\bar{\rho}_2$ means that, all things being equal, higher interest rates will

Table 12.14 Bilateral valuation adjustment for three different receiver IRS portfolios for a maturity of ten years, using a high-risk parameter set for the counterparty and a mid-risk parameter set for the investor ("H/M") with uncorrelated default times. Every IRS has unitary notional. Prices are in basis points

		H/M		
$\bar{\rho}_C$	$\bar{\rho}_I$	P1	P2	P3
−60%	0%	−117(7)	−382(12)	−237(16)
−40%	0%	−74(6)	−297(11)	−138(15)
−20%	0%	−32(6)	−210(10)	−40(14)
0%	0%	−1(5)	−148(9)	31(13)
20%	0%	24(5)	−96(9)	87(12)
40%	0%	44(4)	−50(8)	131(11)
60%	0%	57(4)	−22(7)	159(11)

Table 12.15 Bilateral valuation adjustment for three different receiver IRS portfolios for a maturity of ten years, using a high-risk parameter set for the counterparty and a mid-risk parameter set for the investor ("H/M") with uncorrelated default times. Every IRS has unitary notional. Prices are in basis points

		H/M		
$\bar{\rho}_C$	$\bar{\rho}_I$	P1	P2	P3
−60%	−60%	−150(6)	−422(12)	−319(15)
−40%	−40%	−98(6)	−329(11)	−197(14)
−20%	−20%	−46(5)	−230(10)	−74(13)
0%	0%	−1(5)	−148(9)	31(13)
20%	20%	38(5)	−77(9)	121(12)
40%	40%	75(5)	−6(8)	208(12)
60%	60%	106(5)	49(8)	280(12)

correspond to high credit spreads, putting the receiver swaptions embedded in the LGD_C term of the adjustment more out-of-the-money. This will cause the LGD_C term of the adjustment to diminish in absolute value, so that the final value of the bilateral VA will be larger for high correlation. This is clearly seen in Table 12.14, where the bilateral VA is seen to increase as $\bar{\rho}_2$ increases, given that the table columns increase.

When, in Table 12.15, $\bar{\rho}_0$ is taken to follow $\bar{\rho}_2$, the behaviour is the same but more marked. This is reasonable: when $\bar{\rho}_2$ is large, also $\bar{\rho}_0$ is now large. This means that, all things being equal, higher interest rates will correspond to high credit spreads, putting the payer swaptions embedded in the LGD_I term of the adjustment more in-the-money, so that this term is larger. This makes the bilateral VA increase further. Not surprisingly, the numbers in Table 12.15 corresponding to positive correlation (bottom part of the table) are all larger than the corresponding numbers in Table 12.14.

It is worth finally checking the impact of correlation on the bilateral VA, comparing it with the typical [1.2, 1.4] interval adjustment factor postulated by Basel II for the credit risk measurement correction due to wrong way risk. Depending on whether we look at the deal from the investor's or counterparty's point of view, we find the following ratios between non-zero correlation bilateral VA and zero correlation bilateral VA. For example, we find:

$$382/148 \approx 2.58, \quad 159/31 \approx 5.13$$

which are both much larger than 1.4. This means that mimicking the Basel II rules in the valuation space is not going to work, since the impact of correlations and volatilities is much more complex than what can be achieved with a simple multiplier.

Finally, we notice that depending on the correlations $\bar{\rho}_0, \bar{\rho}_2$ the bilateral VA does change sign, and in particular for portfolios P1 and P3 the sign of the adjustment follows the sign of the correlations. P2 is an exception because of the massive presence of cash flows in the future.

12.4.2.2 Varying the Credit Spread of Counterparties

In Table 12.16 we report our second example of relevant results. We analyze the bilateral valuation adjustment for the two portfolios P1 and P2, again with uncorrelated default times, $\rho_G = 0$.

Table 12.16 Bilateral valuation adjustment, by changing the parameter set, for a decreasing (P1) and an increasing (P2) IRS portfolio for a maturity of ten years, with uncorrelated default times. Every IRS has unitary notional. The column title "H/M" means a high-risk parameter set for the counterparty and a mid-risk parameter set for the investor, "M/H" means the opposite situation, and "H/H" means both the parties have a high-risk parameter set. Prices are in basis points

		P1			P2		
$\bar{\rho}_C$	$\bar{\rho}_I$	H/M	H/H	M/H	H/M	H/H	M/H
−60%	−60%	−150(6)	−76(7)	47(5)	−422(12)	−284(12)	−40(9)
−40%	−40%	−98(6)	−12(6)	97(5)	−329(11)	−179(12)	36(9)
−20%	−20%	−46(5)	48(6)	135(5)	−230(10)	−77(10)	102(9)
0%	0%	−1(5)	110(6)	187(6)	−148(10)	16(10)	179(9)
20%	20%	38(5)	173(6)	241(6)	−77(9)	112(10)	262(10)
40%	40%	75(5)	239(7)	297(6)	−6(9)	218(10)	351(10)
60%	60%	106(5)	304(7)	361(7)	49(9)	315(11)	450(11)

Here too, depending on the correlations $\bar{\rho}_0$, $\bar{\rho}_2$, we see that the bilateral VA may change sign. Also, we notice from Table 12.16 for P2 portfolio that two examples of wrong way risk we would get, as ratios of high (positive or negative) correlation bilateral VA over zero correlation bilateral VA, are:

$$422/148 \approx 2.85, \quad 315/16 \approx 19.7$$

which are dramatically larger than 1.4.

We also notice, in the table, as we move left to right along one row, that the bilateral VA always grows. This is expected, since we are looking at the bilateral VA adjustment to be added by the investor. This way the configuration where the counterparty has high spread risk and the investor medium spread risk will produce smaller bilateral VA's with respect to the case where both investor and counterparty have high spread risk. This is because in the case where the investor has medium spread risk default times of the investor will tend to be later than in the case where the investor has high spread risk. Therefore, investor default probabilities will be larger in the latter case of high investor spread risk, and as a consequence the $\text{L}{\small\text{GD}}_I$ term in the adjustment will be larger in the latter case. Since this term is positive in the adjustment to be added by the investor, this will produce a larger bilateral VA.

12.4.2.3 Varying the Default-Time Correlation

In Table 12.17 we focus on the impact of ρ_G on the adjustment. This is rich in structure and complex. Indeed, we see for example that, depending on the particular values of $\bar{\rho}_0$ and $\bar{\rho}_2$, an increase of ρ_G can imply either an increase or a decrease of the adjustment. Even when staying with just negative $\bar{\rho}_0$ and $\bar{\rho}_2$'s this happens, as one can see by comparing the first and third row of the "M/H" setting.

Then, we show in Table 12.18 the impact of varying the copula parameter in different portfolios.

Table 12.17 Bilateral valuation adjustment, by changing the Gaussian copula parameter ρ_G for a decreasing IRS portfolio (P1) for a maturity of ten years. The column title "H/M" means a high-risk parameter set for the counterparty and a mid-risk parameter set for the investor, "M/H" means the opposite situation. Every IRS has unitary notional. Prices are in basis points

		P1					
		H/M			M/H		
$\bar{\rho}_C$	$\bar{\rho}_I$	−80%	0%	80%	−80%	0%	80%
−60%	−60%	−150(7)	−150(6)	−169(6)	32(5)	47(5)	61(5)
−40%	−40%	−91(6)	−98(6)	−122(6)	86(5)	97(5)	103(5)
−20%	−20%	−33(6)	−46(5)	−72(5)	146(6)	135(5)	137(5)
0%	0%	18(6)	−1(5)	−34(5)	194(6)	187(6)	183(5)
20%	20%	61(5)	38(5)	−3(4)	256(6)	241(6)	232(6)
40%	40%	102(5)	75(5)	29(4)	320(7)	297(6)	287(6)
60%	60%	140(5)	106(5)	53(4)	384(7)	361(7)	344(7)

12.4.2.4 Impact of the Credit-Spread Volatility

Tables 12.19 illustrates the impact of the counterparty's credit spreads volatility on the adjustment. We use high-risk credit spreads for the counterparty and mid-risk credit spreads and parameters set for the investor. Every time we change the main volatility parameter ν^2 in the counterparty credit spread model, we apply a shift $\psi^2(t, \beta^2)$ to fit the credit spread curve of the high-risk scenario, so that the credit spread model for the counterparty fits the same initial high-risk CDS spread curve even if altering the credit spread volatility.

Our results highlight once again the importance of credit spread volatilities, often neglected in the literature. The adjustment can increase by several multiples because of spread volatility. Assuming zero volatility is quite a strong tacit assumption that is certainly not granted by CDS volatilities, either implied or historical (see for example [31]).

Table 12.18 Bilateral valuation adjustment, by changing the Gaussian copula parameter ρ_G and all other correlations equal to zero. The column titled "H/M" means a high-risk parameter set for the counterparty and a mid-risk parameter set for the investor, "M/H" means the opposite situation. Every IRS has unitary notional. Prices are in basis points

	H/M			M/H		
ρ_G	P1	P2	P3	P1	P2	P3
−60%	21(5)	−121(10)	95(14)	198(6)	187(10)	539(14)
−40%	15(5)	−131(10)	76(13)	197(5)	186(10)	535(14)
−20%	7(5)	−138(9)	56(13)	193(5)	184(9)	523(14)
0%	−1(5)	−148(9)	31(12)	190(5)	186(9)	515(13)
20%	−7(5)	−157(9)	11(11)	185(5)	186(9)	502(13)
40%	−14(5)	−166(8)	−11(11)	186(5)	190(9)	501(13)
60%	−22(5)	−172(8)	−31(11)	181(5)	206(8)	506(13)

Table 12.19 Bilateral valuation adjustment, by changing the volatility ν^2 of counterparty's credit spreads for a decreasing (P1) and increasing (P2) IRS portfolio for a maturity of ten years. We use high-risk credit spreads for the counterparty and mid-risk credit spreads and parameter set for the investor ("H/M"). Every IRS has unitary notional. Prices are in basis points

		H/M					
		P1			P2		
$\bar{\rho}_C$	$\bar{\rho}_I$	0%	30%	40%	0%	30%	40%
−60%	−60%	−36 (5)	−128(6)	−152(6)	−196 (9)	−396(11)	−423(12)
−40%	−40%	−23 (5)	−84(6)	−94(6)	−182 (9)	−313(11)	−317(11)
−20%	−20%	−13 (5)	−43(5)	−48(5)	−168 (9)	−235(10)	−237(10)
0%	0%	1 (5)	−2(5)	−2(5)	−151 (10)	−155(10)	−151(10)
20%	20%	14 (5)	35(5)	35(5)	−133 (10)	−82(9)	−79(9)
40%	40%	31 (6)	71(5)	73(5)	−108 (10)	−12(9)	−11(9)
60%	60%	46 (6)	106(5)	105(5)	−85 (10)	58(8)	49(9)

12.4.2.5 Changing the Shape of the Interest Rate Curve

Table 12.20 illustrates the impact of the shape of the initial interest rate curve across maturity on the adjustment. We compare three possible shapes: increasing, flat, and decreasing curves. We run this for the flat portfolio P3, but results will be possibly more dramatic for P2. As we see from the numbers in the table, the adjustment is quite sensitive to the shape of the initial curve. Figure 12.6 shows how the initial curve affects the future moneyness/exposure of each of the three porfolios.

12.4.3 Bilateral VA in Exotic Interest Rate Products

In Table 12.21 we show the adjustment for exotic options on interest rates. In particular we focus on options whose payoff may change sign depending on future fixing of quoted rates.

Table 12.20 Bilateral valuation adjustment, by changing the yield curve (increasing, flat at 3% and decreasing curves) for a flat IRS portfolio (P3) for a maturity of ten years. The column title "H/M" means high-risk parameter set for the counterparty and mid-risk parameter set for the investor, "M/H" means the opposite situation. We also assume uncorrelated default times. Every IRS has unitary notional. Prices are in basis points

		P3					
		H/M			M/H		
$\bar{\rho}_C$	$\bar{\rho}_I$	Incr.	Flat	Decr.	Incr.	Flat	Decr.
−60%	−60%	−319(15)	−777(18)	−1193(21)	169(13)	−140(13)	−410(15)
−40%	−40%	−197(14)	−630(17)	−1032(20)	288(13)	−46(13)	−325(14)
−20%	−20%	−74(13)	−472(15)	−852(18)	384(13)	40(12)	−247(13)
0%	0%	31(13)	−344(14)	−709(17)	507(14)	142(13)	−159(13)
20%	20%	121(12)	−228(13)	−571(15)	637(15)	251(13)	−66(13)
40%	40%	208(12)	−115(12)	−436(14)	773(16)	374(14)	42(14)
60%	60%	280(12)	−25(12)	−328(13)	925(17)	511(15)	166(14)

Table 12.21 Bilateral valuation adjustment, by changing the Gaussian copula parameter ρ_G, for an auto-callable IRS portfolio (P3) for a maturity of ten years, using a high-risk parameter set for the counterparty and mid-risk parameter set for the investor ("H/M"). The contract has unitary notional. Prices are in basis points. Intrinsic price is 608, with an auto-callable strike level of $A = 3\%$

		H/M		
$\bar{\rho}_C$	$\bar{\rho}_I$	−99%	0%	99%
−70%	−70%	−71	−64	−55
0%	0%	−47	−43	−34
70%	70%	−28	−26	−20

The calculation of unilateral CVA for exotic interest rate options is covered in [57]. Here we address the bilateral case.

For instance, we consider IRS portfolio P3, and we add an auto-callable feature triggered by the LIBOR rate, namely we exit from the IRS contract when on a fixed-leg payment date the fixing of the LIBOR rate is greater than a strike level A. We can appreciate that once again the correlations have quite an impact on the value of the adjustment.

12.5 CONCLUSIONS

In general our results confirm the bilateral valuation adjustment to be quite sensitive to finely tuned dynamics parameters such as volatilities and correlations, similar to what was found in the unilateral case in Chapter 5, but with more complex patterns, because now we have also the default of the investor/bank in the picture.

The impact of the dynamics and dependency parameters is both relevant and structured.

We noticed in particular the impact of correlations between the investor's and the counterparty's default risks, of credit spread volatilities for the credit qualities of both names, of credit spread levels and of correlations between defaults and interest rates. Variations in these parameters can produce an excursion in the adjustment of several multiples, or even have the adjustment changing in sign.

In particular, there seems to be no single multiplier that can provide the adjustment for high correlations starting from the adjustment with zero correlations. Hence if one aims at capturing right way risk and wrong way risk properly, one needs to include such correlations in the modelling apparatus in a rigorous way. This leads us to reiterate the closing message of Chapter 10:

> Counterparty and funding risk pricing is a very complex, model-dependent task. Regulators are trying to standardize the related calculation in the simplest possible ways but our conclusion is that such calculations are complex and need to remain so to be accurate. The attempt to standardize counterparty risk to simple formulas is misleading and may result in the relevant risks not being addressed properly. Rather, the industry and regulators should acknowledge the complexity of this problem and work to attain the necessary methodological and technological prowess instead of trying to bypass it.

Indeed, there is no easy way out.

We proposed a possible modelling choice for addressing this problem in the interest rate products context, with a two-factor Gaussian model (G2++) for interest rates and a shifted square root process (CIR++) for the credit spreads of investor and counterparty. Defaults of the two names are linked by a Gaussian copula function. Jumps can be added easily to make the dynamics more realistic, similar to what was hinted at in Chapter 5.

The reason why we use such simple models is because they are benchmarks in risk management in the respective asset classes. G2++ is not very suited to the current markets, since calibration of large volatility with relatively low short-term rates would imply a large probability of negative rates. Despite this, we illustrated how G2++ can be used (or extended) in concert with a stochastic credit spread model to have wrong way risk, but the reader is clearly encouraged to consider different interest rate models that are more realistic, for example, see the book on interest rate modelling [48].

We detailed our findings in a number of illustrative examples from an extensive set of results.

In our examples we found that when the correlation between investor credit spreads and interest rates is kept to zero, we had the same CVA pattern in the correlation between counterparty spread and rates we had seen in the unilateral case in [57], as seen in Chapter 5. Increasing the latter correlation implies that, all things being equal, higher interest rates will correspond to higher credit spreads, causing the receiver swaptions embedded in the adjustment to go more out-of-the-money. This causes the counterparty term of the adjustment to diminish in absolute value, so that the final value of the bilateral VA will be larger for high correlation. When the correlation between investor credit spread and rates is taken to follow the value of the correlation between the counterparty and rates, the above effect is amplified. This is to be expected: when the correlation counterparty/rates are large, the correlation investor/rates will also be large. This implies that, all things being equal, higher interest rates will correspond to higher credit spreads, putting the payer swaptions embedded in the investor (DVA) term of the adjustment more in-the-money, so that this term is larger. This makes the bilateral VA increase further.

The estimation of correlations between interest rates and counterparty and investor credit spreads is most likely to be obtained historically. Indeed, implying such correlation from market products could be quite difficult.

We finally noticed that the bilateral VA term has a tendency to change dramatically if we include non-zero investor and counterparty credit spread volatilities. This is to be expected: with zero volatilities, the credit spreads would be deterministic and credit spread/interest rate correlation would have no way to act.

13

Collateral, Netting, Close-Out and Re-Hypothecation

This chapter is based on Brigo, Capponi, Pallavicini and Papatheodorou (2011) [41].

In this chapter, we study how counterparty risk exposure can be reduced through the use of collateralization. The idea of collateralization of counterparty risk is very similar to the way collateral is used to mitigate lending risk, with collateral used to reduce credit exposure. However, because of the uncertainty of counterparty credit exposure and the bilateral nature of counterparty credit risk, collateral management is much more complex in the case of counterparty risk. Exposure of one counterparty to another changes every day, and to keep the current exposure under control, it is necessary to post collateral frequently, ideally on a daily basis. The collateral should be used to hedge the exposure that one party has to the other on the default event. The collateral can be in the form of risk-free cash flow or of a (defaultable) asset. In the latter case, it should not be correlated to the value of the transaction, and be liquid, i.e. sold quickly and easily if the need arises.

We develop an arbitrage-free valuation framework for bilateral counterparty risk adjustments, inclusive of collateralization. We provide model independent formulas that give the bilateral collateralized credit and debit valuation adjustment. We abbreviate this adjustment as CBVA, standing for Collateral-inclusive Bilateral Valuation Adjustment. We thus consider portfolios exchanged between a default-risky investor and a default-risky counterparty. Such CBVA formulas are given by the sum of option payoff terms, where each term depends on the netted exposure, i.e. the difference between the on-default exposure and the on-default collateral account. We consider the case when collateral is a risk-free asset kept in a segregated account and only used upon default occurrence to net exposure, and also the case when collateral can be lent or re-hypothecated before default occurrence, thus making the party who posted collateral an unsecured creditor.

For the moment, we leave aside some issues linked to counterparty risk evaluation, which may be relevant in particular settings; among them we cite collateral dispute resolutions and independent amounts. Funding costs, in the general setup of this chapter, will be treated in Chapter 17. Since these problems are currently under active investigation by the International Swaps and Derivatives Association (ISDA) to tune the Master Agreement and Credit Support Annexes in an ongoing crisis scenario, we prefer to address them in a further development of our work awaiting ISDA recommendation on definitions and relative market practice. We also leave aside the inclusion of features such as goodwill, for which we refer to [137], see also [136].

Risk-neutral evaluation of counterparty risk in the presence of collateral management can be difficult, due to the complexity of clauses. There are only a few papers in the literature dealing with this, among them [79], [8], and [1]. [8] consider a highly stylized model for the collateral process without accounting for minimum transfer amounts, collateral thresholds, and assume that the collateral account is risk free and cannot be re-hypothecated. Features discussed by [1] include minimum transfer amount and collateral thresholds and give model independent formulas for the counterparty exposure, netted from collateralization, but again assuming the collateral is a risk-free asset.

In this chapter we follow [41] and we generalize the framework for risk-neutral valuation of bilateral counterparty risk introduced in Chapter 12, which does not model the impact of collateralization. We then specialize our analysis to interest rate payouts as underlying portfolio, and allow for correlation between the default times of the investor, counterparty and underlying portfolio risk factors. By following [59] we use arbitrage-free stochastic dynamical models and consider the following dependencies (or "correlations"):

- Dependence between default of the counterparty and default of the investor;
- Correlation between the underlying (interest rates) and the counterparty credit spread;
- Correlation between the underlying (interest rates) and the investor credit spread.

The rest of the chapter is organized as follows: Section 13.1 introduces the framework of trading under a master agreement, looking at documentation and at its reflection on delay and disputes, on close-out netting rules between exposure and collateral, and on re-hypothecation of collateral.

Section 13.2 provides general payoff-based model-independent formulas for adjusting cash flows for credit and debit default risk and for collateralization, which follow naturally from the written standards and contractual rules described in the earlier sections. This is where CBVA is defined formally and derived in precise mathematical terms. Section 13.3 discusses the issues of calculating on-default exposures. Section 13.4 looks at particular cases of CBVA, showing that CBVA is a generalization of earlier BVA, CVA and DVA definitions. Section 13.5 presents some examples of collateralization mechanisms, while Section 13.6 concludes the chapter.

13.1 TRADING UNDER THE ISDA MASTER AGREEMENT

Risk-neutral evaluation of counterparty risk in presence of collateral management can be difficult, due to the complexity of clauses.

This section introduces the framework of trading under a Master Agreement, referring explicitly to the ISDA documentation such as [127].

Subsection 13.1.1 introduces the mathematical setup. Subsection 13.1.2 hints at collateral delay and disputes. Subsection 13.1.3 discusses the close-out netting rules and introduces the concept of counterparty and investor on-default exposure. Subsection 13.1.4 discusses how the collateral account can be used throughout the life of the transaction, for example, it can be re-hypothecated.

13.1.1 Mathematical Setup and CBVA Definition

We refer to the two names involved in the financial contract and subject to default risk as

$$\text{investor} \rightarrow I$$
$$\text{counterparty} \rightarrow C$$

The Investor "I" used to be called Bank or "B" in earlier chapters.

We denote by τ_I and τ_C respectively the default times of the investor and counterparty. We place ourselves in a probability space $(\Omega, \mathcal{G}, \mathcal{G}_t, \mathbb{Q})$. The filtration $\mathcal{G}_t$ models the flow of information of the whole market, including defaults and $\mathbb{Q}$ is the risk-neutral measure. This space is endowed also with a right-continuous and complete sub-filtration $\mathcal{F}_t$ representing all the observable market quantities except the default event, thus $\mathcal{F}_t \subseteq \mathcal{G}_t := \mathcal{F}_t \vee \mathcal{H}_t$. Here, $\mathcal{H}_t = \sigma(\{\tau_I \leq u\} \vee \{\tau_C \leq u\} : u \leq t)$ is the right-continuous filtration generated by the default events, either of the investor or of his counterparty (and of the reference credits if the underlying portfolio is credit sensitive).

Let us call T the final maturity of the payoff which we need to evaluate and define the stopping time

$$\tau = \tau_I \wedge \tau_C. \tag{13.1}$$

We define the *collateral account* C_t to be a stochastic process adapted to the filtration $\mathcal{G}_t$. Intuitively, this means that the collateral account at time t is known to the information set $\mathcal{G}_t$ constituted by all the market observables up to time t, including which entities have defaulted by t.

We assume that the collateral account is held by the *collateral taker*, with both investor and counterparty posting or withdrawing collateral during the life of a deal, to or from the collateral account. The other party is the *collateral provider*. We see all payoffs from the point of view of the investor. Therefore, when $C_t > 0$, this means that by time t the overall collateral account is in favour of the investor and the net posting has been done by the counterparty, meaning that what is in the account at t is the excess of posting done by the counterparty with respect to the investor posting. In this case the collateral account $C_t > 0$ can be used by the investor to reduce his on-default exposure in case of early default by "C". On the contrary, when $C_t < 0$, this means that the overall collateral account by time t is in favour of the counterparty, and has been net posted by the investor. In this case collateral can be used by the counterparty to reduce his on-default exposure in case of early default by "I".

Thus when $C_t > 0$ this means that, at time t, the collateral taker is the investor and the collateral provider is the counterparty, whereas in the second case the collateral taker is the counterparty and the collateral provider is the investor.

We assume the collateral account to be a risk-free cash account, although in general it can be any other (defaultable) asset, which can be liquidated at the default time. Further, we assume that the collateral account is opened anew for each new deal and it is closed upon a default event or when maturity is reached. If the account is closed, then any collateral held by the collateral taker would have to be returned to the originating party. We assume $C_t = 0$ for all $t \leq 0$, and $C_t = 0$, if $t \geq T$.

As in earlier chapters, we call $\Pi(u, s)$ the sum of the net cash flows of the claim under consideration (not including the collateral account) without investor or counterparty default risk between time u and time s, discounted back at u, as seen from the point of view of the investor. We denote by $\bar{\Pi}(u, s; C)$ the analogous net cash flows of the claim under counterparty and investor default risk, and inclusive of collateral netting. The *Collateral-inclusive Bilateral credit and debit Valuation Adjustment* (CBVA) is given by:

$$\text{CBVA}(t, T; C) := \mathbb{E}_t\left[\bar{\Pi}(t, T; C)\right] - \mathbb{E}_t\left[\Pi(t, T)\right]$$

so that, as with BVA in Chapter 12, CBVA is to be added to the risk-free price to obtain the default-risk and collateral adjusted price:

$$\mathbb{E}_t\left[\bar{\Pi}(t, T; C)\right] = \mathbb{E}_t\left[\Pi(t, T)\right] + \text{CBVA}(t, T; C).$$

In order to evaluate BVA inclusive of collateralization, we need to express $\bar{\Pi}(t, T; C)$ in terms of risk-free quantities, default indicators and collateral. In particular we should describe which operations the investor and the counterparty perform to monitor and mitigate counterparty credit risk, and which operations, on a default event, the surviving party performs to recover from potential losses. We need to do so while keeping in mind documentation such as [127]. This documentation provides guidelines on, for example, collateral delay and disputes.

13.1.2 Collateral Delay and Dispute Resolutions

In practice there is a delay between the time when collateral is requested and the time when it gets posted. This is due to collateral settlement rules or to one party (or both parties) disputing on portfolio or collateral pricing.

Typically, the delay is limited to one day, but it may be longer. According to the ISDA Collateral Dispute Resolution Protocol (2009) the parties may agree either on a standard timing schedule (disputes end within three days), or on an extended one (disputes end within nine days). Exceptionally, further delay may take place due to mutual consent by both parties or due to specific market concerns (total delay cannot exceed thirty days). We do not consider collateral posting delay here, leaving this issue for future research.

13.1.3 Close-Out Netting Rules

The ISDA Market Review of OTC Derivative Bilateral Collateralization Practices (2010), section 2.1.1 states the following:

> The effect of close-out netting is to provide for a single net payment requirement in respect of all the transactions that are being terminated, rather than multiple payments between the parties. Under the applicable accounting rules and capital requirements of many jurisdictions, the availability of close-out netting allows parties to an ISDA Master Agreement to account for transactions thereunder on a net basis

This means that, upon the occurrence of a default event, the parties should terminate all transactions and do a netting of due cash flows. Moreover, the ISDA Credit Support Annex, subject to New York Law, on paragraph 8 states:

> The Secured Party will transfer to the Pledgor any proceeds and posted credit support remaining after liquidation, and/or set-off after satisfaction in full of all amounts payable by the Pledgor with respect to any obligations; the Pledgor in all events will remain liable for any amounts remaining unpaid after any liquidation and/or set-off.

This means that the surviving party should evaluate the transactions just terminated, due to the default event occurrence, and claim for a reimbursement only after the application of netting rules, inclusive of collateral accounts. We can find similar clauses also in the CSA, subject to different laws.

The ISDA Master Agreement defines the term *close-out amount* to be the amount of losses or costs the surviving party would incur in replacing or in providing for an economic equivalent at the time when the counterparty defaults. Notice that the close-out amount is not a symmetric quantity with respect to the exchange of the role of two parties, since it is valued by one party after default by the other.

The replacing counterparty may ask the surviving party to post more than the exposure to the old defaulted counterparty to compensate for liquidity, or the deteriorated credit quality of the surviving party. For the close-out amount we stay with the *on-default exposure*, namely the price of the replacing transaction or its economic equivalent. We distinguish between on-default exposure of investor to counterparty and of counterparty to investor at time t, and denote it as follows:

- $\varepsilon_{I,t}$ denotes the on-default exposure of the investor to the counterparty at time t. A positive value for $\varepsilon_{I,t}$ means that the investor is a creditor of the counterparty.
- $\varepsilon_{C,t}$ denotes the on-default exposure of the counterparty to the investor at time t. A negative value for $\varepsilon_{C,t}$ means that the counterparty is a creditor to the investor.

In other words while I and C may measure exposure differently, we always assume the sign of the cash flows to be those seen by "I".

13.1.4 Collateral Re-Hypothecation

In the case of no-default happening, at final maturity the collateral provider expects to get back from the collateral taker the outstanding collateral. Similarly, in the case of default happening earlier (and assuming the collateral taker before default to be the surviving party), after netting the collateral with the cash flows of the transaction, the collateral provider expects to get back, if anything, the remaining collateral on the account, if any. However, it is often considered to be important, commercially, for the collateral taker to have relatively unrestricted use of the collateral until it must be returned to the collateral provider. This unrestricted use includes the ability to sell collateral to a third party in the market, free and clear of any interest of the collateral provider. Other uses would include lending the collateral or selling it under a "repo" agreement or *re-hypothecating* it. Although under the English Deed the taker is not permitted to re-hypothecate the collateral, the taker is allowed to do so under the New York Annex, the English Annex or the Japanese Annex. When the collateral taker re-hypothecates the collateral, he leaves the collateral provider as an unsecured creditor with respect to collateral reimbursement.

In case of re-hypothecation, the collateral provider must therefore consider the possibility of recovering only a fraction of his collateral. If the investor is the collateral taker, we denote the recovery fraction on collateral re-hypothecated by the defaulted investor by REC'_I, while if the counterparty is the collateral taker, then we denote the recovery fraction on collateral re-hypothecated by the counterparty by REC'_C. Accordingly, we define the collateral loss incurred by the counterparty upon investor default by $\text{LGD}'_I = 1 - \text{REC}'_I$ and the collateral loss incurred by the investor upon counterparty default by $\text{LGD}'_C = 1 - \text{REC}'_C$. Typically, the surviving party has precedence on other creditors to get back his collateral, thus $\text{REC}_I \leq \text{REC}'_I \leq 1$, and $\text{REC}_C \leq \text{REC}'_C \leq 1$. Here, REC_I (REC_C) denote the recovery fraction of the market value of the transaction that the counterparty (investor) gets when the investor (counterparty) defaults.

Notice that in the case where collateral cannot be re-hypothecated and has to be kept in a segregated account it is obtained by setting $\text{REC}'_I = \text{REC}'_C = 1$.

We need to mention that collateral re-hypothecation has been heavily criticized and is currently being debated. See, for example, the [183] report, that observes the following:

> Custody of assets and re-hypothecation practices were dominant drivers of contagion, transmitting liquidity risks to other firms. In the United Kingdom, there was no provision of central bank liquidity to the main broker-dealer entity, Lehman Brothers International (Europe), and no agreement was struck to transfer client business to a third-party purchaser. As a result, LBIE filed for bankruptcy while holding significant custody assets that would not be returned to clients

for a long time, and therefore could not be traded or easily hedged by clients. In addition, the failure of LBIE exposed the significant risks run by hedge funds in allowing their prime broker to exercise re-hypothecation rights over their securities. Under U.K. law, clients stand as general creditor for the return of such assets. The loss of re-hypothecated assets and the "freezing" of custody assets created alarm in the hedge fund community and led to an outflow of positions from similar accounts at other firms. Some firms' use of liquidity from re-hypothecated assets to finance proprietary positions also exacerbated funding stresses.

13.2 BILATERAL CVA FORMULA UNDER COLLATERALIZATION

We start by listing all the situations that may arise on counterparty default and investor default events. Our goal is to calculate the present value of all cash flows involved by the contract by taking into account (i) collateral margining operations, and (ii) close-out netting rules in case of default. Notice that we can safely aggregate the cash flows of the contract with those of the collateral account, since on contract termination all the posted collateral is returned to the originating party.

13.2.1 Collecting CVA Contributions

We start by considering all possible situations which may arise at the counterparty's default time, which is assumed to default before the investor. In our notation

$$X^+ = \max(X, 0), \quad X^- = \min(X, 0).$$

Important: Notice that our notation for the negative part X^- is not standard.
We have:

1. The investor measures a positive (on-default) exposure on counterparty default ($\varepsilon_{I,\tau_C} > 0$), and some collateral posted by the counterparty is available ($C_{\tau_C} > 0$). Then, the investor exposure is reduced by netting, and the remaining collateral (if any) is returned to the counterparty. If the collateral is not enough, the investor suffers a loss for the remaining exposure. Thus we have

$$\mathbf{1}_{\{\tau=\tau_C<T\}}\mathbf{1}_{\{\varepsilon_{I,\tau}>0\}}\mathbf{1}_{\{C_\tau>0\}}(\mathrm{REC}_C(\varepsilon_{I,\tau} - C_\tau)^+ + (\varepsilon_{I,\tau} - C_\tau)^-)$$

2. The investor measures a positive (on-default) exposure on counterparty default ($\varepsilon_{I,\tau_C} > 0$), and some collateral posted by the investor is available ($C_{\tau_C} < 0$). Then, the investor suffers a loss for the whole exposure. All the collateral (if any) is returned to the investor if it is not re-hypothecated, otherwise only a recovery fraction of it is returned. Thus, we have

$$\mathbf{1}_{\{\tau=\tau_C<T\}}\mathbf{1}_{\{\varepsilon_{I,\tau}>0\}}\mathbf{1}_{\{C_\tau<0\}}(\mathrm{REC}_C\varepsilon_{I,\tau} - \mathrm{REC}'_C C_\tau)$$

3. The investor measures a negative (on-default) exposure on counterparty default ($\varepsilon_{I,\tau_C} < 0$), and some collateral posted by the counterparty is available ($C_{\tau_C} > 0$). Then, the exposure is paid to the counterparty, and the counterparty gets back its collateral in full.

$$\mathbf{1}_{\{\tau=\tau_C<T\}}\mathbf{1}_{\{\varepsilon_{I,\tau}<0\}}\mathbf{1}_{\{C_\tau>0\}}(\varepsilon_{I,\tau} - C_\tau)$$

4. The investor measures a negative (on-default) exposure on counterparty default ($\varepsilon_{I,\tau_C} < 0$), and some collateral posted by the investor is available ($C_{\tau_C} < 0$). Then, the exposure is reduced by netting and paid to the counterparty. The investor gets back its remaining

collateral (if any) in full if it is not re-hypothecated, otherwise he gets back only the recovery fraction of that part of the collateral exceeding the exposure.

$$\mathbf{1}_{\{\tau=\tau_C<T\}}\mathbf{1}_{\{\varepsilon_{I,\tau}<0\}}\mathbf{1}_{\{C_\tau<0\}}((\varepsilon_{I,\tau}-C_\tau)^- + \mathrm{REC}'_C(\varepsilon_{I,\tau}-C_\tau)^+)$$

Symmetrically, we consider all possible situations which can arise at the default time of the investor, which is the earliest to default. We have

1. The counterparty measures a positive (on-default) exposure on investor default ($\varepsilon_{C,\tau_I}<0$), and some collateral posted by the investor is available ($C_{\tau_I}<0$). Then, the counterparty exposure is reduced by netting, and the remaining collateral (if any) is returned to the investor. If the collateral is not enough, the investor suffers a loss for the remaining exposure. Thus, we have

$$\mathbf{1}_{\{\tau=\tau_I<T\}}\mathbf{1}_{\{\varepsilon_{C,\tau}<0\}}\mathbf{1}_{\{C_\tau<0\}}(\mathrm{REC}_I(\varepsilon_{C,\tau}-C_\tau)^- + (\varepsilon_{C,\tau}-C_\tau)^+)$$

2. The counterparty measures a positive (on-default) exposure on investor default ($\varepsilon_{C,\tau_I}<0$), and some collateral posted by the counterparty is available ($C_{\tau_I}>0$). Then, the counterparty suffers a loss for the whole exposure. All the collateral (if any) is returned to the counterparty if it is not re-hypothecated, otherwise only a recovery fraction of it is returned. Thus, we have

$$\mathbf{1}_{\{\tau=\tau_I<T\}}\mathbf{1}_{\{\varepsilon_{C,\tau}<0\}}\mathbf{1}_{\{C_\tau>0\}}(\mathrm{REC}_I\varepsilon_{C,\tau} - \mathrm{REC}'_I C_\tau)$$

3. The counterparty measures a negative (on-default) exposure on investor default ($\varepsilon_{C,\tau_I}>0$), and some collateral posted by the investor is available ($C_{\tau_I}<0$). Then, the exposure is paid to the investor, and the investor gets back its collateral in full.

$$\mathbf{1}_{\{\tau=\tau_I<T\}}\mathbf{1}_{\{\varepsilon_{C,\tau}>0\}}\mathbf{1}_{\{C_\tau<0\}}(\varepsilon_{C,\tau}-C_\tau)$$

4. The counterparty measures a negative (on-default) exposure on investor default ($\varepsilon_{C,\tau_I}>0$), and some collateral posted by the counterparty is available ($C_{\tau_I}>0$). Then, the exposure is reduced by netting and paid to the investor. The counterparty gets back its remaining collateral (if any) in full if it is not re-hypothecated, otherwise it only gets the recovery fraction of the part of the collateral exceeding the exposure.

$$\mathbf{1}_{\{\tau=\tau_I<T\}}\mathbf{1}_{\{\varepsilon_{C,\tau}>0\}}\mathbf{1}_{\{C_\tau>0\}}((\varepsilon_{C,\tau}-C_\tau)^+ + \mathrm{REC}'_I(\varepsilon_{C,\tau}-C_\tau)^-)$$

Now, we can aggregate all these cash flows, along with cash flows coming from the default by the investor and those due in case of non-default, inclusive of the cash-flows of the collateral account. Let $D(t,T)$ denote the risk-free discount factor. By summing all contributions, we obtain:

$$\begin{aligned}
\bar{\Pi}(t,T;C) = {} & \mathbf{1}_{\{\tau>T\}}\Pi(t,T) + \mathbf{1}_{\{\tau<T\}}(\Pi(t,\tau)+D(t,\tau)C_\tau) \\
& + \mathbf{1}_{\{\tau=\tau_C<T\}}D(t,\tau)\mathbf{1}_{\{\varepsilon_{I,\tau}<0\}}\mathbf{1}_{\{C_\tau>0\}}(\varepsilon_{I,\tau}-C_\tau) \\
& + \mathbf{1}_{\{\tau=\tau_C<T\}}D(t,\tau)\mathbf{1}_{\{\varepsilon_{I,\tau}<0\}}\mathbf{1}_{\{C_\tau<0\}}((\varepsilon_{I,\tau}-C_\tau)^- + \mathrm{REC}'_C(\varepsilon_{I,\tau}-C_\tau)^+) \\
& + \mathbf{1}_{\{\tau=\tau_C<T\}}D(t,\tau)\mathbf{1}_{\{\varepsilon_{I,\tau}>0\}}\mathbf{1}_{\{C_\tau>0\}}((\varepsilon_{I,\tau}-C_\tau)^- + \mathrm{REC}_C(\varepsilon_{I,\tau}-C_\tau)^+) \\
& + \mathbf{1}_{\{\tau=\tau_C<T\}}D(t,\tau)\mathbf{1}_{\{\varepsilon_{I,\tau}>0\}}\mathbf{1}_{\{C_\tau<0\}}(\mathrm{REC}_C\varepsilon_{I,\tau} - \mathrm{REC}'_C C_\tau) \\
& + \mathbf{1}_{\{\tau=\tau_I<T\}}D(t,\tau)\mathbf{1}_{\{\varepsilon_{C,\tau}>0\}}\mathbf{1}_{\{C_\tau<0\}}(\varepsilon_{C,\tau}-C_\tau) \\
& + \mathbf{1}_{\{\tau=\tau_I<T\}}D(t,\tau)\mathbf{1}_{\{\varepsilon_{C,\tau}>0\}}\mathbf{1}_{\{C_\tau>0\}}((\varepsilon_{C,\tau}-C_\tau)^+ + \mathrm{REC}'_I(\varepsilon_{C,\tau}-C_\tau)^-) \\
& + \mathbf{1}_{\{\tau=\tau_I<T\}}D(t,\tau)\mathbf{1}_{\{\varepsilon_{C,\tau}<0\}}\mathbf{1}_{\{C_\tau<0\}}((\varepsilon_{C,\tau}-C_\tau)^+ + \mathrm{REC}_I(\varepsilon_{C,\tau}-C_\tau)^-) \\
& + \mathbf{1}_{\{\tau=\tau_I<T\}}D(t,\tau)\mathbf{1}_{\{\varepsilon_{C,\tau}<0\}}\mathbf{1}_{\{C_\tau>0\}}(\mathrm{REC}_I\varepsilon_{C,\tau} - \mathrm{REC}'_I C_\tau).
\end{aligned}$$

By a straightforward calculation we get:

$$\begin{aligned}\bar{\Pi}(t,T;C) = \Pi(t,T) &- \mathbf{1}_{\{\tau<T\}} D(t,\tau)\left(\Pi(\tau,T) - \mathbf{1}_{\{\tau=\tau_C\}}\varepsilon_{I,\tau} - \mathbf{1}_{\{\tau=\tau_I\}}\varepsilon_{C,\tau}\right)\\ &- \mathbf{1}_{\{\tau=\tau_C<T\}} D(t,\tau)(1-\text{R}\textsc{ec}_C)(\varepsilon^+_{I,\tau} - C^+_\tau)^+\\ &- \mathbf{1}_{\{\tau=\tau_C<T\}} D(t,\tau)(1-\text{R}\textsc{ec}'_C)(\varepsilon^-_{I,\tau} - C^-_\tau)^+\\ &- \mathbf{1}_{\{\tau=\tau_I<T\}} D(t,\tau)(1-\text{R}\textsc{ec}_I)(\varepsilon^-_{C,\tau} - C^-_\tau)^-\\ &- \mathbf{1}_{\{\tau=\tau_I<T\}} D(t,\tau)(1-\text{R}\textsc{ec}'_I)(\varepsilon^+_{C,\tau} - C^+_\tau)^-\end{aligned}$$

Notice that the collateral account enters only as a term reducing the exposure of each party upon default of the other one, taking into account which party posted the collateral.

13.2.2 CBVA General Formula

As a last step we introduce the risk-free price of the contract V_u with $t \le u \le T$ as given by

$$V_u := \mathbb{E}_u \Pi(u,T), \quad t \le u \le T$$

which represents the risk-free price of all cash flows remaining after time u up to maturity T. Hence, by taking risk-neutral expectation of both sides of the equation expressing BCVA, and by plugging in the definition of mid-market exposure, we obtain the general expression for collateral-inclusive bilateral (CVA and DVA) valuation adjustment.

$$\begin{aligned}\text{C}\textsc{bva}(t,T;C) = &-\mathbb{E}_t\left[\mathbf{1}_{\{\tau<T\}} D(t,\tau)\left(V_\tau - \mathbf{1}_{\{\tau=\tau_C\}}\varepsilon_{I,\tau} - \mathbf{1}_{\{\tau=\tau_I\}}\varepsilon_{C,\tau}\right)\right]\\ &- \mathbb{E}_t\left[\mathbf{1}_{\{\tau=\tau_C<T\}} D(t,\tau)\text{L}\textsc{gd}_C(\varepsilon^+_{I,\tau} - C^+_\tau)^+\right]\\ &- \mathbb{E}_t\left[\mathbf{1}_{\{\tau=\tau_C<T\}} D(t,\tau)\text{L}\textsc{gd}'_C(\varepsilon^-_{I,\tau} - C^-_\tau)^+\right]\\ &- \mathbb{E}_t\left[\mathbf{1}_{\{\tau=\tau_I<T\}} D(t,\tau)\text{L}\textsc{gd}_I(\varepsilon^-_{C,\tau} - C^-_\tau)^-\right]\\ &- \mathbb{E}_t\left[\mathbf{1}_{\{\tau=\tau_I<T\}} D(t,\tau)\text{L}\textsc{gd}'_I(\varepsilon^+_{C,\tau} - C^+_\tau)^-\right]\end{aligned} \tag{13.2}$$

The first term on the right-hand side of the above equation represents the mismatch in calculating risk-free exposure and on-default exposures. The second and third terms are the counterparty risk due to the counterparty's default (also known as the counterparty valuation adjustment or CVA), and come with a negative sign (always from the point of view of the investor). The fourth and fifth terms represent the counterparty risk due to investor's default (also known as debit valuation adjustment or DVA) and come with a positive sign (again from the point of view of the investor).

13.2.3 CCVA and CDVA Definitions

We may introduce Collateral-inclusive Credit Valuation Adjustment (CCVA) and Collateral-inclusive Debit Valuation Adjustment (CDVA), and rewrite the general expression for collateralized bilateral CVA as

$$\begin{aligned}\text{C}\textsc{bva}(t,T;C) = &-\mathbb{E}_t\left[\mathbf{1}_{\{\tau<T\}} D(t,\tau)\left(V_\tau - \mathbf{1}_{\{\tau=\tau_C\}}\varepsilon_{I,\tau} - \mathbf{1}_{\{\tau=\tau_I\}}\varepsilon_{C,\tau}\right)\right]\\ &- \text{C}\textsc{cva}(t,T;C) + \text{C}\textsc{dva}(t,T;C)\end{aligned}$$

where

$$\begin{aligned}\text{C}\textsc{cva}(t,T;C) := \;&\mathbb{E}_t\left[\mathbf{1}_{\{\tau=\tau_C<T\}} D(t,\tau)\text{L}\textsc{gd}_C(\varepsilon^+_{I,\tau} - C^+_\tau)^+\right]\\ &\mathbb{E}_t\left[\mathbf{1}_{\{\tau=\tau_C<T\}} D(t,\tau)\text{L}\textsc{gd}'_C(\varepsilon^-_{I,\tau} - C^-_\tau)^+\right]\end{aligned}$$

and

$$\begin{aligned}\text{CDVA}(t, T; C) := &-\mathbb{E}_t\left[\mathbf{1}_{\{\tau=\tau_I<T\}} D(t,\tau)\text{LGD}_I(\varepsilon_{C,\tau}^- - C_\tau^-)^-\right] \\ &-\mathbb{E}_t\left[\mathbf{1}_{\{\tau=\tau_I<T\}} D(t,\tau)\text{LGD}'_I(\varepsilon_{C,\tau}^+ - C_\tau^+)^-\right].\end{aligned}$$

Remark 13.2.1 ***(CCVA/CDVA vs. Collateral Adjusted UCVA and UDVA)*** *Notice that CCVA is not the unilateral CVA inclusive of collateral as seen from the investor "I" when assuming only counterparty C may default. Indeed, such a quantity would not depend on the default time of investor I, whereas CCVA does. Similarly, CDVA is not simply the collateral-inclusive unilateral DVA seen from the investor when assuming that only the investor may default, since CDVA also contains the counterparty default time.*

13.3 CLOSE-OUT AMOUNT EVALUATION

The ISDA Market Review of OTC Derivative Bilateral Collateralization Practices (2010), section 2.1.5. states the following:

> Upon default close-out, valuations will in many circumstances reflect the replacement cost of transactions calculated at the terminating party's bid or offer side of the market, and will often take into account the creditworthiness of the terminating party. However, it should be noted that exposure is calculated at mid-market levels so as not to penalize one party or the other. As a result of this, the amount of collateral held to secure exposure may be more or less than the termination payment determined upon a close-out.

The close-out amount is defined by the ISDA Master Agreement either as a replacement cost or as an economic equivalent of the terminated transaction, by acting in "good faith" and by using "commercially reasonable" procedures. See Chapter 14 for a detailed treatment of the topic. Notice that the choice on how to compute the on-default exposure is left to the surviving party and there is not a clear statement on the evaluation timing schedule. Indeed, the surviving party may require several days to complete the close-out procedure. We refer to [166] for a detailed description of failings and issues related to the close-out amount evaluation procedure.

Remark 13.3.1 ***(Margin Period of Risk)*** *The time elapsed between the default event and the completion of the close-out procedure is named the* margin period of risk. *The warning from [13] is to increase the margin period of risk to capture the illiquidity of collateral and trades, the length of margin call disputes, as well as the costs of trade replacement and operations, in order to avoid exposure underestimates. For instance [13] say that, if the trade involves illiquid collateral, or derivative that cannot be easily replaced, the margin period of risk should be equal to the collateral margining update interval plus 20 days.*

The ISDA Market Review continues with:

> Other differences in the valuation methodologies applied to the determination of any payment on early termination also contribute to the potential for discrepancy between these two amounts. A party may take into account the costs of terminating, liquidating or re-establishing any hedge or related trading position. Further, it will also be reasonable to consider the cost of funding.

The on-default exposure depends on many other factors besides the credit worthiness of the surviving party. If we start considering such effects, we should add also the funding costs for our trading and collateral positions. In particular while determining a close-out amount, the determining party may consider any relevant information, including:

1. Quotations (either firm or indicative) for replacement transactions supplied by one or more third parties that may take into account the credit worthiness of the determining party;
2. Informations consisting of relevant market data; or
3. Informations from internal sources if used by the determining party in the regular course of its business for the valuation of similar transactions.

Such a broad framework prevents achieving a tight definition of close-out amount or on-default exposure, and it can clearly produce a wide range of results. See Chapter 14, where the most likely simple choices about close-out are singled out and analyzed, or [193] where the authors show various examples for evaluating the close-out amount.

In the following we approximate on-default exposures ε_{I,τ_C} and ε_{C,τ_I} with the value of a replacement operation with a risk-free counterparty (with the same collateralization rule). See Chapter 14 for an explanation of this choice, and a detailed discussion on the effects of employing such approximation. Hence, if we apply our collateral-inclusive bilateral VA formula to the risk-free payoff to include the creditworthiness of the surviving party, we get:

$$\begin{aligned}\varepsilon_{I,\tau_C} \doteq \varepsilon_{\tau_C} &- \mathbb{E}_t\left[\mathbf{1}_{\{\tau_C<\tau_I<T\}} D(\tau_C,\tau_I)\text{L}\textsc{gd}_I(\varepsilon^-_{\tau_I} - C^-_{\tau_I})^-\right] \\ &- \mathbb{E}_t\left[\mathbf{1}_{\{\tau_C<\tau_I<T\}} D(\tau_C,\tau_I)\text{L}\textsc{gd}'_I(\varepsilon^+_{\tau_I} - C^+_{\tau_I})^-\right]\end{aligned}$$

and

$$\begin{aligned}\varepsilon_{C,\tau_I} \doteq \varepsilon_{\tau_I} &- \mathbb{E}_t\left[\mathbf{1}_{\{\tau_I<\tau_C<T\}} D(\tau_I,\tau_C)\text{L}\textsc{gd}_C(\varepsilon^+_{\tau_C} - C^+_{\tau_C})^+\right] \\ &- \mathbb{E}_t\left[\mathbf{1}_{\{\tau_I<\tau_C<T\}} D(\tau_I,\tau_C)\text{L}\textsc{gd}'_C(\varepsilon^-_{\tau_C} - C^-_{\tau_C})^+\right].\end{aligned}$$

13.4 SPECIAL CASES OF COLLATERAL-INCLUSIVE BILATERAL CREDIT VALUATION ADJUSTMENT

In this section, we specialize the general CVA formula given in Equation 13.2. We start showing the formula in the case where all exposures are evaluated at mid-market, i.e. we consider:

$$\varepsilon_{I,t} \doteq \varepsilon_{C,t} \doteq V_t$$

We then obtain the collateralized bilateral VA (CDVA–CCVA) equal to:

$$\begin{aligned}\text{C}\textsc{bva}(t,T;C) = &-\mathbb{E}_t\left[\mathbf{1}_{\{\tau=\tau_C<T\}} D(t,\tau)\text{L}\textsc{gd}_C(\varepsilon^+_\tau - C^+_\tau)^+\right] \\ &- \mathbb{E}_t\left[\mathbf{1}_{\{\tau=\tau_C<T\}} D(t,\tau)\text{L}\textsc{gd}'_C(\varepsilon^-_\tau - C^-_\tau)^+\right] \\ &- \mathbb{E}_t\left[\mathbf{1}_{\{\tau=\tau_I<T\}} D(t,\tau)\text{L}\textsc{gd}_I(\varepsilon^-_\tau - C^-_\tau)^-\right] \\ &- \mathbb{E}_t\left[\mathbf{1}_{\{\tau=\tau_I<T\}} D(t,\tau)\text{L}\textsc{gd}'_I(\varepsilon^+_\tau - C^+_\tau)^-\right]\end{aligned} \tag{13.3}$$

If collateral re-hypothecation is not allowed ($\text{L}\textsc{gd}'_C = \text{L}\textsc{gd}'_I = 0$), then the above formula simplifies to:

$$\begin{aligned}\text{C}\textsc{bva}(t,T;C) = &-\mathbb{E}_t\left[\mathbf{1}_{\{\tau=\tau_C<T\}} D(t,\tau)\text{L}\textsc{gd}_C(\varepsilon^+_\tau - C^+_\tau)^+\right] \\ &- \mathbb{E}_t\left[\mathbf{1}_{\{\tau=\tau_I<T\}} D(t,\tau)\text{L}\textsc{gd}_I(\varepsilon^-_\tau - C^-_\tau)^-\right]\end{aligned} \tag{13.4}$$

On the other hand, if re-hypothecation is allowed and the surviving party always faces the worst case ($\text{LGD}'_C = \text{LGD}_C$ and $\text{LGD}'_I = \text{LGD}_I$), then we get:

$$\begin{aligned}\text{CBVA}(t, T; C) = &-\mathbb{E}_t\left[\mathbf{1}_{\{\tau=\tau_C<T\}}D(t,\tau)\text{LGD}_C(\varepsilon_\tau - C_\tau)^+\right]\\ &- \mathbb{E}_t\left[\mathbf{1}_{\{\tau=\tau_I<T\}}D(t,\tau)\text{LGD}_I(\varepsilon_\tau - C_\tau)^-\right].\end{aligned} \tag{13.5}$$

Finally, if we remove collateralization, i.e. $C_t = 0$, then we recover the result of Chapter 12. See also [39] and [59].

$$\begin{aligned}\text{BVA}(t, T) = &-\mathbb{E}_t\left[\mathbf{1}_{\{\tau=\tau_C<T\}}D(t,\tau)\text{LGD}_C\varepsilon_\tau^+\right]\\ &- \mathbb{E}_t\left[\mathbf{1}_{\{\tau=\tau_I<T\}}D(t,\tau)\text{LGD}_I\varepsilon_\tau^-\right].\end{aligned} \tag{13.6}$$

If we remove collateralization ($C_t = 0$) and we consider a risk-free investor ($\tau_I \to \infty$), we recover the result of the UCVA presented in previous chapters, starting from Chapter 2. See also [57] and [69].

$$\text{CVA}(t, T) = -\mathbb{E}_t\left[\mathbf{1}_{\{\tau_C<T\}}D(t,\tau_C)\text{LGD}_C\varepsilon_{\tau_C}^+\right]. \tag{13.7}$$

13.5 EXAMPLE OF COLLATERALIZATION SCHEMES

We consider a setting where investor and counterparty exposures equal the mid-market mark-to-market exposure, where there are no funding costs for either party, and where re-hypothecation is not allowed. Therefore, the resulting CVA and DVA formula is given by Equation (13.4). We consider two collateralization mechanisms.

The first mechanism removes all the exposure risk from the parties and is therefore called *perfect collateralization*.

The second mechanism is the most realistic and follows instead the margining practice where during the life of the deal both parties post or withdraw collateral on a fixed set of dates, according to their current exposure, to or from an account held by the collateral taker. In general, the collateral taker may be a third party or the party in the transaction who is not posting collateral. We call the second mechanism *collateralization through margining*.

13.5.1 Perfect Collateralization

In case of contracts with a continuous mark-to-market at default events, we can achieve perfect collateralization by updating the collateral account continuously, thereby obtaining the following collateralization rule:

$$C_t^{\text{perfect}} := V_t,$$

and by assuming a risk-free close-out amount

$$\varepsilon_{I,t} \doteq \varepsilon_{C,t} \doteq V_t.$$

Thus, if we plug it into the collateralized bilateral CVA equation, we get that all terms drop, as expected, leading to:

$$\text{CBVA}(t, T; C^{\text{perfect}}) = 0.$$

We will see in Chapter 17 that, under this collateralization rule, the proper discount curve for pricing the deal is the collateral accrual curve. See also [109] and [168].

13.5.2 Collateralization Through Margining

We assume that collateral posting only occurs at discrete times on a fixed grid ($t_0 = t, \ldots, t_N = T$), and we allow for the presence of minimum transfer amounts ($M > 0$), and thresholds (K), with $K \geq M$. Thresholds represent the amount of permitted unsecured risk, so that they may depend on the credit quality[1] of the counterparties.

A realistic margining practice also includes independent amounts, which represent a further insurance on the transaction and are often posted as an upfront protection, but these amounts may be updated according to exposure changes. We do not consider independent amounts in the following.

At each collateral posting date t_i, the collateral account is updated according to changes in exposure. We denote by $C_{t_i^-}$ the collateral account right before the collateral update for time t_i takes place. We first consider how much collateral the investor should post to, or withdraw from, the collateral account. This is given by:

$$\mathbf{1}_{\{|(V_{t_i}+K_I)^- - C^-_{t_i^-}| > M\}}((V_{t_i} + K_I)^- - C^-_{t_i^-}). \tag{13.8}$$

Then, we consider how much collateral the counterparty should post to, or withdraw from, the collateral account. This is given by:

$$\mathbf{1}_{\{|(V_{t_i}-K_C)^+ - C^+_{t_i^-}| > M\}}((V_{t_i} - K_C)^+ - C^+_{t_i^-}). \tag{13.9}$$

We have

$$C_{t_0} := 0, \quad C_{t_n} := 0, \quad C_{u^-} := \frac{C_{\beta(u)}}{D(\beta(u), u)}$$

and

$$\begin{aligned} C_{t_i} := C_{t_i^-} &+ \mathbf{1}_{\{|(V_{t_i}+K_I)^- - C^-_{t_i^-}| > M\}}((V_{t_i} + K_I)^- - C^-_{t_i^-}) \\ &+ \mathbf{1}_{\{|(V_{t_i}-K_C)^+ - C^+_{t_i^-}| > M\}}((V_{t_i} - K_C)^+ - C^+_{t_i^-}) \end{aligned} \tag{13.10}$$

where $\beta(u)$ is the last update time before u, and $t_0 < u \leq t_n$.

We are also implicitly assuming that, on default occurrence at time t_i, all collateral requests initiated, but not yet completed, are neglected.

In case of no thresholds ($K_I = K_C = 0$) and no minimum transfer amount ($M = 0$), we obtain a simpler rule

$$C_{t_0} = C_{t_n} = 0, \quad C_{t^-} = \frac{V_{\beta(u)}}{D(\beta(u), u)}, \quad C_{t_i} = V_{t_i}.$$

13.6 CONCLUSIONS

In this chapter we described a complete framework for bilateral CVA risk-neutral pricing inclusive of close-out netting rules and collateral margining, considering also the case when

[1] Moving thresholds depending on a deterioration of the credit quality of the counterparties (downgrade triggers) have been a source of liquidity strain during the market crisis. See BIS white paper: The role of margin requirements and haircuts in pro-cyclicality (2010).

collateral can be re-hypothecated. In Chapter 15 we will consider interest rate and credit-default swap contracts, and show the impact of collateralization frequency on the collateral inclusive bilateral CVA and DVA via numerical simulations.

Finally, the complexity, the multiple optionalities and the random maturities implicit in the CBVA formula (13.2), and on the definitions given in Section 13.2.3, even before we populate the processes with models, dynamics and dependencies, prompt us to reiterate the closing message of Chapters 10 and 12:

> Counterparty credit and debit adjustment pricing is a very complex, model dependent task. Properly accounting for collateral makes the relevant formulas even more complex. Regulators, and occasionally banks, are trying to standardize the related calculations in the simplest possible ways, often for different purposes. Our conclusion is that such calculations are complex, even more so in the presence of collateral, and need to remain so to be accurate. The attempt to standardize every risk to simple formulas is misleading and may result in the relevant risks not being addressed at all. Rather, the industry and regulators should acknowledge the complexity of this problem and work to attain the necessary methodological and technological prowess rather than trying to elude it.

There is no easy way out.

In the next chapter we are going to address close-out modelling in more detail, illustrating the subtleties that already show up with simple products. We will continue this chapter's themes in Chapter 15, where we will apply the apparatus we developed in this chapter directly to interest rates and CDS, illustrating extreme cases of Gap risk. The reader who aims at continuity in the development of the theory and examples may jump straight to Chapter 15 and return to read the relatively self-contained Chapter 14 later.

14

Close-Out and Contagion with Examples of a Simple Payoff

This chapter is based on Brigo and Morini (2010) [52] and Brigo and Morini (2011) [54].

14.1 INTRODUCTION TO CLOSE-OUT MODELLING AND EARLIER WORK

As already discussed in Chapter 13, when a default event happens to one of the counterparties in a deal, the deal is stopped and marked-to-market: the net present value of the residual part of the deal is computed. This net present value is called the close-out amount, it is used to determine the default payments. When we consider the payments of the defaulting party, they will amount to the recovery fraction of the close-out amount. While modelling the recovery is known to be a difficult task, the computation of the close-out amount has never been the focus of extensive research. Before the credit crunch, and actually up to the time of the Lehman default, the close-out amount was usually computed as the expectation of future payments, discounted back to the default day by a LIBOR-based curve of discount factors.

Today, however, things are not so trivial. LIBOR is not considered to be risk free anymore. We are aware that discounting a deal that is default free and backed by liquid collateral should be performed using a default-free curve of discount factors, based on overnight quotations. Whereas a deal which is not collateralized, and is thus subject to default risk, should be discounted taking liquidity and credit costs into account. Credit costs take the form of a Credit Valuation Adjustment. Therefore, when we speak of the net present value, we are now aware that this must be computed in different ways even for equal payoffs, depending on the liquidity and credit conditions of the deal parties. This is actually one of the themes we have been covering so far in the book.

Some features of close-out modelling had been hinted at in the dialogue in Chapter 1 and in the introduction to Part III in Chapter 10. Chapter 13 introduced close-out modelling in the most general setting of bilateral CVA and DVA with consistent collateral cash flows. Now we go more into detail on simple payoffs and see what a different definition of close-out would imply on counterparty risk pricing of simple deals, such as bonds or loans. Even for simple payoffs, results may be quite surprising.

Before doing so, we summarize earlier developments and literature.

14.1.1 Close-Out Modelling: Context

Historically, literature on counterparty risk assumes that, when default happens, the net present value of the residual deal is computed treating the deal as if it were risk free. We call this assumption the "risk-free close-out", and it is basically the "mid-market mark-to-market exposure" assumption of Chapter 13.

In the first approach called "unilateral counterparty risk" (UCVA and UDVA) which we explored in Part II one of the two parties, usually the bank, was treated as default-free, based generally on its very superior credit standing. In this case the net present value after a default can only be risk free: in fact the only party that can default has just defaulted, while the surviving party was assumed to be risk free from the start, and hence there is no credit or debit risk left in the deal.

Nowadays no counterparty can be considered to be risk free. If default happens, the surviving party can still default before the maturity of the deal. In spite of this, even recent literature that assumes such a "bilateral counterparty risk" still adopts a risk-free close-out amount at default, for example, see [39] or [118].

The basic idea of the replacement close-out that we are proposing as an alternative to the risk-free one, is that upon default of an entity (say, for example "C", the corporate counterparty), the surviving Bank/Investor "I" tries to replace the defaulted deal with a new one, by entering a new equivalent trade with a default-free party (e.g. an exchange or a very high credit quality institution). However, this new institution will recognize that the investor is default risky and charge a unilateral CVA to the investor on the restarted deal. As explained in Chapter 10, the UCVA calculated by the new default-free party is the same as the UDVA computed by the "I", who is charged this additional cost to enter into the deal. In other words, because "I" is not default free, "I" is charged an additional cost by the new default-free party, an additional cost due to the surviving party ("I") credit risk. Hence the replacement close-out considers as a price for the deal seen by "I" upon default of "C" the risk-free price at the time of default of "C" plus $\text{UDVA}_I(\tau_C)$, namely the unilateral DVA of "I" on the deal.

14.1.2 Legal Documentation on Close-Out

The legal (ISDA) documentation on the settlement of a default does not confirm the risk-free close-out assumption. The Market Review of OTC Derivative Bilateral Collateralization Practices, published by the ISDA on 1 March, 2010, says:

> Upon default close-out, valuations will in many circumstances reflect the replacement cost of transactions calculated at the terminating party's bid or offer side of the market, *and will often take into account the creditworthiness of the terminating party* (emphasis added).

Similarly, the ISDA Close-out Amount Protocol, published in 2009, says that in determining a close-out amount the information used includes

> quotations (either firm or indicative) for replacement transactions supplied by one or more third parties that *may take into account the creditworthiness of the Determining Party at the time the quotation is provided* (emphasis added).

Thus documentation admits that a 'replacement close-out' may apply, and points out explicitly that such a replacement close-out may take into account the creditworthiness of the surviving party. In fact, a real market counterparty replacing the defaulted one would not neglect it. On the other hand, there is no binding prescription – the documentation speaks of creditworthiness which is taken into account *often*, not always, and that *may*, not must, be included. This leaves room for a risk-free close-out, which is probably easier to compute since it is independent of the features of the surviving party.

14.1.3 Literature

Since the publication of the ISDA Close-out Amount Protocol a debate on close-out evaluation has started in specialized literature. See for instance the paper [166], where the authors discuss the weakness of the ISDA's close-out evaluation along with possible suggestions for changing it, the similar analysis of [154] focused on contagion effects, and also [193]. Such a debate soon moved on to CVA pricing workshops, where the authors of this book presented work on close-out, see, for instance, the presentation [161] and the many presentations based on [52]. In the dedicated literature close-out was discussed in a more articulated way. In particular, we refer the readers again to the technical articles [52] and [54]. We suggest also recent papers on replacement close-out (now more often called "risky close-out"), and we refer to the informal account [73], to [120], and to [92], where further considerations on close-out amount are introduced.

14.1.4 Risk-Free versus Replacement Close-Out: Practical Consequences

The counterparty risk adjustments change strongly depending on which close-out amount is considered. The effects at the moment of a company default are very different under the two close-out conventions, with some dramatic consequences on default contagion, which we show in what follows. Lest there are unpleasant surprises at the moment of the next default, these results should be considered carefully by the financial community, and in particular by the ISDA, which has the possiblity to give more clarity on this issue.

We show first that a risk-free close-out has implications that are very different from what we usually expect in a case of default in standardized markets such as the bond or loan markets. If the owner of a bond defaults, or if the lender in a loan defaults, this means no losses to the bond issuer or to the loan borrower. Instead, if the risk-free default close-out applies, when there is default by the party that is a net creditor in a derivative (thus in a position similar to a bond owner or loan lender), the liability value for the net debtor will suddenly jump up. In fact, before default, the liability for the net debtor had a mark-to-market that took into account the risk of default for the debtor itself. After the creditor's default, if a risk-free close-out applies, this mark-to-market transforms into a risk-free one, surely larger in absolute value than the pre-default mark-to-market.

The larger the credit spread of the debtor, the larger will be the increase. This is a dramatic surprise for the debtor that will soon have to pay this increased amount of money to the liquidators of the defaulted party. There is true contagion of a default event towards the debtors of a defaulted entity, which does not exist in the bond or loan market. Net debtors at default will not like a risk-free close-out. They will prefer a replacement close-out that does not imply a necessary increase of the liabilities because it continues taking into account the creditworthiness of the debtor also after the creditor's default. As a consequence, the replacement close-out inherits one property typical of fundamental markets: if one of the two parties in the deal has no future obligations, like a bond or option holder, its default probability does not influence the value of the deal at inception.

On the other hand, the replacement close-out has shortcomings opposite to those of the risk-free close-out. While the replacement close-out is preferred by debtors of a defaulting company, symmetrically a risk-free close-out will be preferred by the creditors. The more money debtors pay, the higher the recovered amount will be. The replacement close-out, while protecting the debtor, can, in some situations, worryingly penalize the creditors by reducing the recovered amount. Consider the case where the defaulted entity is a company with high systemic impact, so that when it defaults the credit spreads of its counterparties are expected to jump high. Lehman's default would be a good example of such a situation. If the credit spreads of the counterparties increase at default, under a replacement close-out the market value of their liabilities will be strongly reduced, since it will take into account the reduced creditworthiness of the debtors themselves. All the claims of the liquidators towards the debtors of the defaulted company will be deflated, and the low level of the recoverable amount may again be a dramatic surprise, but this time for the creditors of the defaulting company.

We will now proceed to formalize the above analysis rigorously and mathematically. In doing so a little overlap with earlier chapters will occur, in order to keep the analysis here relatively self-contained.

14.2 CLASSICAL UNILATERAL AND BILATERAL VALUATION ADJUSTMENTS

Consider two parties entering a deal with final maturity T, an investor "I" and a counterparty "C". Assume the deal discounted total cash flows at time t when defaults by "I" or "C" are not considered and seen by "I" to be $\Pi_I(t, T)$. The analogous cash flows seen from "C" are denoted with $\Pi_C(t, T) = -\Pi_I(t, T)$. In a "unilateral" situation where only the counterparty risk of "C" is considered, one can write the value of the deal to "I" including counterparty risk as

$$\begin{aligned} NPV_I^C(t) &= \mathbb{E}_t\left\{\mathbf{1}_{\tau_C>T}\Pi_I(t,T)\right\} \\ &+\mathbb{E}_t\left\{\mathbf{1}_{t<\tau_C\le T}\left[\Pi_I(t,\tau_C)+D(t,\tau_C)\left(REC_C\,(NPV_I(\tau_C))^+-(-NPV_I(\tau_C))^+\right)\right]\right\} \end{aligned}$$

where REC and LGD = 1-REC will denote recoveries and loss given defaults, where $D(t, T)$ will be the discount factor between times t and T, and $NPV_I(t) = \mathbb{E}_t\left[\Pi_I(t, T)\right]$ is the default risk-free value of the residual deal at time t, seen by "I".

Notice our notation here:

$$\text{NPV}^{\text{Default risky parties}}_{\text{Calculating party}},$$

so that, for example, NPV_I^C is the NPV of the deal computed by "I" when assuming "C" (and only "C") may default.

The above formula simplifies the more usual formula expressing the price as the price without counterparty risk *minus* the familiar positive unilateral CVA adjustment, for example, see [47] as in Chapter 4.

We can do the same calculation again from the point of view of "C", and again in a context where only "C" can default. This leads to:

$$\begin{aligned} NPV_C^C(t) &= \mathbb{E}_t\left\{\mathbf{1}_{\tau_C>T}\Pi_C(t,T)\right\} \\ &+\mathbb{E}_t\left\{\mathbf{1}_{t<\tau_C\le T}\left[\Pi_C(t,\tau_C)+D(t,\tau_C)\left((NPV_C(\tau_C))^+-REC_C\,(-NPV_C(\tau_C))^+\right)\right]\right\} \end{aligned}$$

This formula too can be simplified into a formula featuring the price without credit risk *plus* a positive adjustment that could be termed unilateral debit valuation adjustment, which is equal to the unilateral CVA adjustment in the previous formula. We have actually done this in Chapter 10. We now move to the situation where "I" is not default free anymore, and where both "I" and "C" may default. This leads to a bilateral valuation adjustment, see [39] (Chapter 12) or [118]. Notice that our setting does not allow for simultaneous defaults. In general this is not a problem, as simultaneous defaults are extremely unlikely also in practice, with the exception of companies with very strong links with each other. Even in these cases defaults are not really "simultaneous" in the mathematical sense; what happens in practice is that after one of the company's defaults the second company defaults a short time after, so that at the default settlement of the first company the second company is also in a default state. The standard formulas cannot capture this because they make the simplification that default is settled exactly at default time. In the following, we take this explicitly into account when making examples that can be impacted by this simplification. We define τ^1 to be the first to default time, $\tau^1 = \min(\tau_I, \tau_C)$.

Inclusion of bilateral default risk leads to the price:

$$\begin{aligned}
NPV_I^{Free,I,C}(t,T) &= \mathbb{E}_t\left\{\mathbf{1}_{\{\tau^1>T\}}\Pi_I(t,T)\right\}\\
&+\mathbb{E}_t\left\{\mathbf{1}_{\{\tau^1=\tau_C<T\}}\left[\Pi_I(t,\tau_C)+D(t,\tau_C)\left(REC_C\,(NPV_I(\tau_C))^+ - (-NPV_I(\tau_C))^+\right)\right]\right\}\\
&+\mathbb{E}_t\left\{\mathbf{1}_{\{\tau^1=\tau_I<T\}}\left[\Pi_I(t,\tau_I)+D(t,\tau_I)\left((NPV_I(\tau_I))^+ - REC_I\,(-NPV_I(\tau_I))^+\right)\right]\right\}
\end{aligned}$$

that could be simplified along the lines seen in Chapter 12. The superscript "Free" indicates we are using a risk-free close-out, whereas the superscripts "I" and "C" will be omitted when it is clear from the context that both "I" and "C" may default.

14.3 BILATERAL ADJUSTMENT AND CLOSE-OUT: RISK-FREE OR REPLACEMENT?

When we computed the bilateral adjustment formula we used the risk-free net present value NPV_I on the first default, to close the deal. But, as we discussed earlier, this choice is not obvious in a bilateral setting since the surviving party is not default free, and even ISDA documentation considers a replacement close-out taking into account the credit quality of the surviving party. What if we make the substitutions

$$NPV_I(\tau_C) \to NPV_I^I(\tau_C),$$
$$NPV_I(\tau_I) = -NPV_C(\tau_I) \to NPV_I^C(\tau_I) = -NPV_C^C(\tau_I)?$$

The final formula with replacement close-out is

$$\begin{aligned}
NPV_I^{Repl}(t,T) &= \mathbb{E}_t\left\{\mathbf{1}_{\{\iota^1>T\}}\Pi_I(t,T)\right\}\\
&+\mathbb{E}_t\left\{\mathbf{1}_{\{t\le\tau^1=\tau_C<T\}}\left[\Pi_I(t,\tau_C)+D(t,\tau_C)\left(REC_C\left(NPV_I^I(\tau_C)\right)^+ - \left(-NPV_I^I(\tau_C)\right)^+\right)\right]\right\}\\
&+\mathbb{E}_t\left\{\mathbf{1}_{\{t\le\tau^1=\tau_I<T\}}\left[\Pi_I(t,\tau_I)+D(t,\tau_I)\left(\left(-NPV_C^C(\tau_I)\right)^+ - REC_I\left(NPV_C^C(\tau_I)\right)^+\right)\right]\right\},
\end{aligned}$$

as in [52] and as anticipated more informally in Chapter 10.

14.4 A QUANTITATIVE ANALYSIS AND A NUMERICAL EXAMPLE

Here we choose quite simple payoffs and modelling assumptions. This is done to show the effects of the close-out conventions by dinsentangling them from complex modelling and payout assumptions that would obscure patterns. We consider a simple T-maturity call option on stock S, with risk-free price for I, the option holder, given by:

$$NPV_I(0,K,T) = P(0,T)\mathbb{E}_0\left[(S_T-K)^+\right],$$

where we assume deterministic interest rates and $P(0,T)$ is the deterministic discount factor (risk-free bond price), and an even simpler deal where C promises to pay an amount K to I at maturity T. In this case the risk-free price to the bond holder I is

$$NPV^0(0) = K\ P(0,T).$$

We will often refer to "I" as the lender and to "C" as the borrower. The second payoff is particularly relevant because it is the "derivative equivalent" of a bond or loan or deposit contract, therefore when we introduce risk of default we will have an established market standard to compare with, in order to understand which assumption about close-out is more consistent with market practice. Here the comparison with a bond-style payoff is interesting for a further reason: when bilateral counterparty risk was introduced for derivatives, it was pointed out in the market that this approach, involving a bank to include its own risk of default in valuation, already existed for bonds through the *fair value option*, and this analogy dominated the discussion on its appropriateness. Thus we will analyze here a payoff that has already been used as the reference to understand the implications of different methodologies for the computation of the counterparty risk adjustment.

We now introduce risk of default for both parties. Notice that in the above deals I is the option or bond holder, thus it is the lender in the deal, with no further obligation after the payment of the premium at inception, while C is in the position of the borrower, the party which commits to execute payments at a future time. If we consider an underlying stock independent of the risk of default by the parties, the above formulas for risky price under the two possible close-out assumptions reduce to:

$$NPV_I^{Repl,I,C}(0) = NPV^0(0)[\mathbb{Q}(\tau_C > T) + REC_C\mathbb{Q}(\tau_C \le T)],$$

where the "Repl" superscript denotes the replacement close-out, whereas for the risk-free close-out we obtain:

$$\begin{aligned} NPV_I^{Free,I,C}(0) &= NPV^0(0)[\mathbb{Q}(\tau_C > T) + \mathbb{Q}(\tau_I < \tau_C < T) + REC_C\mathbb{Q}(\tau_C \le \min(\tau_I, T))] \\ &= NPV^0(0)[\mathbb{Q}(\tau_C > T) + REC_C\mathbb{Q}(\tau_C \le T) + LGD_C\mathbb{Q}(\tau_I < \tau_C < T)] \end{aligned}$$

or also

$$NPV_I^{Free,I,C}(0) = NPV_I^{Repl,I,C}(0) + NPV^0(0)\ LGD_C\mathbb{Q}(\tau_I < \tau_C < T)]$$

where $\mathbb{Q}$ is the risk-neutral probability measure. We see an important oddity for the risk-free close-out in this case. The adjusted price of the bond or of the option depends on the credit risk of the lender "I" (bond holder or option holder) if we use the risk-free close-out. This is counterintuitive since the lender has no obligations in the deal, and it is not consistent with market practice for loans or bonds. From this point of view the replacement close-out is preferable.

The bizarre evidence about the dependence of the price with risk-free close-out on the risk of default by the party with no obligations in a deal can be properly appreciated in the following numerical example, where we consider the option-style payoff with $S_0 = 2.5$, $K = 2$, and a stock volatility equal to 40% in a standard Black and Scholes framework. We assume independence between equity and defaults. Set the risk-free rate and the dividend yield at $r = q = 3\%$, and consider a maturity of 5 years. The price of an option varies with the default risk of the option writer, as usual, and here also with the default risk of the option holder, due to the risk-free close-out. In Figure 14.1 we show the price of the option for default intensities λ_I, λ_C going from zero to 100%. We consider $R^C = 0$ so that the level of intensity

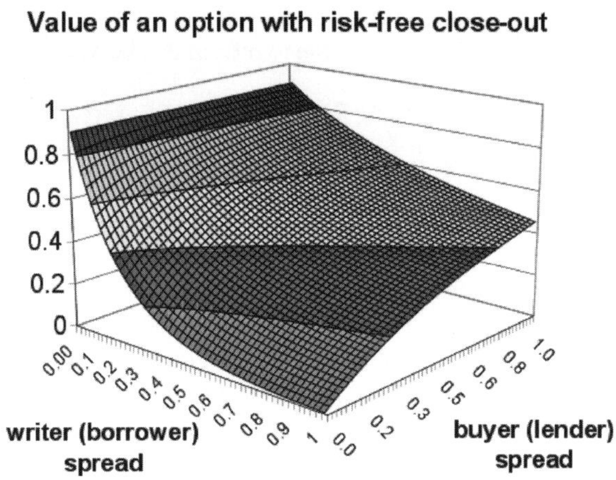

Figure 14.1 Pricing under risk-free close-out

coincides approximately with the market CDS spread on the 5 year maturity. We also assume that default of the entities "I" and "C" are independent of each other.

We see that the effect of the holder's risk of default is not negligible, and is particularly decisive when the writer's risk is high. Similar patterns are shown for a bond payoff in [52]: with a risk-free close-out there is a strong effect of the default risk for the bond holder, an effect which becomes higher the higher the risk of default by the bond issuer. The results of Figure 14.1 can be compared with those of Figure 14.2, where we apply the formula that assumes a replacement close-out. This is the pattern one would expect from standard financial principles: independence of the price of the deal from the risk of default by the counterparty which has no future obligations in the deal.

We can also consider a special case where, at first sight, the picture appears different. We assume the default of "I" and "C" to be co-monotonic, and the spread of the lender "I" to be larger, so we have that the lender "I" defaults first in all scenarios (e.g. "C" is a subsidiary of

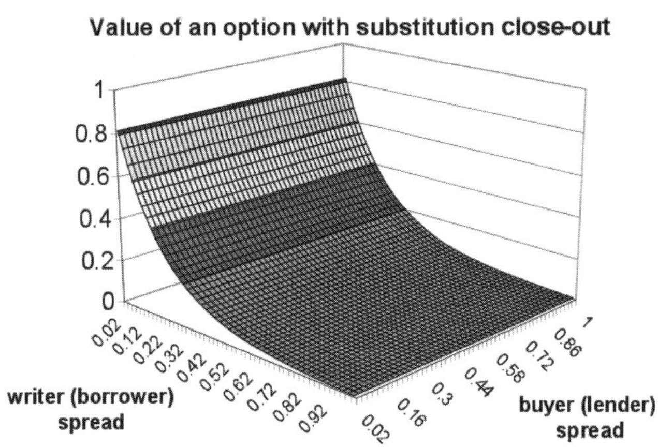

Figure 14.2 Pricing under substitution close-out

"I", or a company whose well being is completely driven by "I": "C" is a tyre factory whose only client is car producer "I"). In this case the two formulas become:

$$NPV_I^{Repl}(0, K, T) = NPV_I(0, K, T)[\mathbb{Q}(\tau_C > T) + REC_C\mathbb{Q}(\tau_C \leq T)],$$
$$NPV_I^{Free}(0, K, T) = NPV_I(0, K, T)[\mathbb{Q}(\tau_C > T) + \mathbb{Q}(\tau_C < T)] = NPV_I(0, K, T).$$

We see that the replacement close-out price does not change, as expected from the fact that the payout does not depend on τ_I, so that changing the dependency between τ_I and τ_C does not change the price under the replacement close-out. The result we obtain with a risk-free close-out coincides with the default free price $NPV_I(0, K, T)$, showing no counterparty risk for "C" either. The risk-free close-out is giving the more logical result in this case. Indeed, either "I" does not default, and then "C" does not default either, or if "I" defaults, at that precise time "C" is solvent, and "I" recovers the whole payment. Credit risk for "C" should not impact the deal. This happens with the risk-free close-out but not with the replacement close-out. However, one may argue that this result is obtained under a hypothesis which is totally unrealistic: the hypothesis of perfect default dependency with heterogenous deterministic spreads (comonotonicity), that can imply that company "C" will go on paying its obligations, maybe for years, in spite of being doomed to default at a fully predictable time. For a discussion on the problems that can arise when assuming perfect default dependency with deterministic spreads see [43], which we discussed at the end of Chapter 7 here, and [153] and [155].

In an example like the one described above, where the borrower is so linked to the lender, the realistic scenario is that the default by the borrower will happen not simultaneously to the default by the lender, but in any case, before the settlement of the lender's default. The borrower, while required to pay the risk-free present value of the derivative, will be in a default state and will pay only a recovery fraction of it. This makes the payout exactly the same as in a replacement close-out, making the valuation under this assumption appear more logical also in the special case of co-monotonic companies. Standard formulas for counterparty risk cannot capture this reality because they make the simplification that default is settled exactly at default time, as we pointed out above.

14.4.1 Contagion Issues

We now analyze contagion issues. We write the price at a generic time $t < T$, and then assume the lender defaults between t and $t + \Delta t$, $t < \tau_I < t + \Delta t$, checking the consequences in both formulas:

$$NPV_I^{Repl}(t, T) = NPV_I(t, T)[\mathbb{Q}_t(\tau_C > T) + REC_C\mathbb{Q}_t(t < \tau_C \leq T)],$$
$$NPV_I^{Free}(t, T) = NPV_I^{Repl}(t, T) + NPV_I(t, T)LGD_C\mathbb{Q}_t(t < \tau_I < \tau_C < T). \quad (14.1)$$

Here the subscript t on the probabilities means that we are conditioning on the market information at time t. This conditioning will be crucial in the co-monotonic case. Indeed, we focus on two cases:

- τ_I and τ_C are independent. In this case the default event τ_I alters only one quantity: we move from

$$\mathbb{Q}_t(\tau_I < \tau_C < T) < \mathbb{Q}_t(\tau_C < T).$$

to

$$\mathbb{Q}_{t+\Delta t}(\tau_I < \tau_C < T) = \mathbb{Q}_{t+\Delta t}(\tau_C < T) \approx \mathbb{Q}_t(\tau_C < T) \text{ for small } \Delta t$$

so that from $NPV_I^{Free}(t, T)$ given in (14.1) we move to

$$NPV_I^{Free}(t + \Delta t, T) = NPV_I(t + \Delta t, T)$$

whereas the replacement close-out price does not change. Under a risk-free close-out, a previously risky derivative turns suddenly into a risk-free one at default by the lender. Its value increases suddenly, automatically increasing the liability of the borrower (bond issuer or option writer). The higher the risk of default by the borrower, the stronger is this effect. It is a form of contagion that affects debtors of a defaulted entity and adds to the standard contagion affecting creditors. Under a replacement close-out we have no discontinuity and no contagion towards the debtors.

- τ_I and τ_C are co-monotonic. Take an example where $t < \tau_I < t + \Delta t$ implies that $t + \Delta t < \tau_C < T$. Then, using $A \mapsto B$ with the meaning of "we go from A to B", we have with $t < \tau_I < t + \Delta t$:

$$\mathbb{Q}_t(\tau_C > T) > 0 \mapsto \mathbb{Q}_{t+\Delta t}(\tau_C > T) = 0,$$
$$\mathbb{Q}_t(\tau_C \leq T) < 1 \mapsto \mathbb{Q}_{t+\Delta t}(\tau_C \leq T) = 1,$$
$$\mathbb{Q}_t(\tau_I < \tau_C < T) < 1 \mapsto \mathbb{Q}_{t+\Delta t}(\tau_I < \tau_C < T) = 1$$

This means that from $NPV_I^{Repl}(t, T)$ given in (14.1) we move to

$$NPV_I^{Repl}(t + \Delta t, T) = REC_C NPV_I(t + \Delta t, T),$$

In the co-monotonic case, under a replacement close-out the default of the lender sends the value of the contract to its minimum value, the value of a defaulted contract. The borrower will see a strong decrease of its liabilities towards the lender. This is a positive fact for debtors, but the contagion increases towards the creditors of the defaulted company, which will see the recoverable amount reduced. This does not happen in the case of a risk-free close-out. This example is under the extreme hypothesis of co-monotonicity, but in this case the main conclusions do not hinge on the unrealistic elements of this hypothesis. We can see it as the extremization of a realistic scenario: the case when the defaulted company has a strong systemic impact, leading the spreads of the counterparties to very high values, deflating the liabilities of the debtors under a replacement close-out. We cannot deny this is realistic: it is what we saw in the Lehman case.

Let us consider a numerical example, using this time the loan/bond/deposit payoff, with counterparty C (borrower) promising to pay $K = 1$ to I (lender). We start from the above $r = 3\%$ and maturity 5 years, for a 1 bn notional. Now we take $R^C = 0$ and two risky parties. We suppose the borrower has a very low credit quality, as expressed by $\lambda_C = 0.2$, that means a probability to default before maturity of 63.2%, while $\lambda_I = 0.04$, that means a default probability of 18.1%. An analogous risk-free "bond" would have a price

$$P(0, 5y) = 860.7mn,$$

while taking into account the default probability of the two parties, which are supposed independent, we have:

$$NPV_I^{Free}(0, 5y) = 359.5mn, \quad NPV_I^{Repl} = 316.6mn.$$

The difference between the two valuations is not negligible but not dramatic. More relevant is the difference in the case of a default. We have the following risk-adjusted probabilities on the happening of a default event:

$$\min\left(5y, \tau^{I}, \tau^{C}\right) = \begin{cases} \tau^{C} \text{ with prob } 58\% \\ \tau^{I} \text{ with prob } 12\% \\ 5y \text{ with prob } 30\% \end{cases}$$

The two formulas diasagree only when the lender defaults first. Let us analyze in detail what happens in this case. Suppose the exact day when default happens is $\tau^{I} = 2.5y$. Just before default, at 2.5 years less one day, we have for the borrower C the following book value of the liability produced by the above deal, depending on the assumed close-out:

$$NPV_{C}^{Free}\left(\tau^{I} - 1d, 5y\right) = -578.9\text{mln},\ NPV_{C}^{Repl}\left(\tau^{I} - 1d, 5y\right) = -562.7\text{mln}$$

Now default of the lender happens. In case of a risk-free close-out, the book value of the bond becomes simply the value of a risk-free bond,

$$NPV_{C}^{Free}\left(\tau^{I} + 1d, 5y\right) = -927.7\text{mln}.$$

The borrower, which has not defaulted, must pay this amount entirely – and quickly. He has a sudden loss of 348.8mln due to default of the lender. With the substitution close-out we have instead:

$$NPV_{C}^{Repl}\left(\tau^{I} + 1d, 5y\right) = -562.7\text{mln}.$$

There is no discontinuity and no loss for the borrower in case of default by the lender. This is true, however, only in the case of independence. If default by the lender leads to an increase of spreads for the borrower, the liability can jump to figures even lower in absolute value, lowering also the expected recoverable amount for the liquidators of the defaulting lender. The situation is summarized in Figures 14.3 and 14.4, and in Table 14.1.

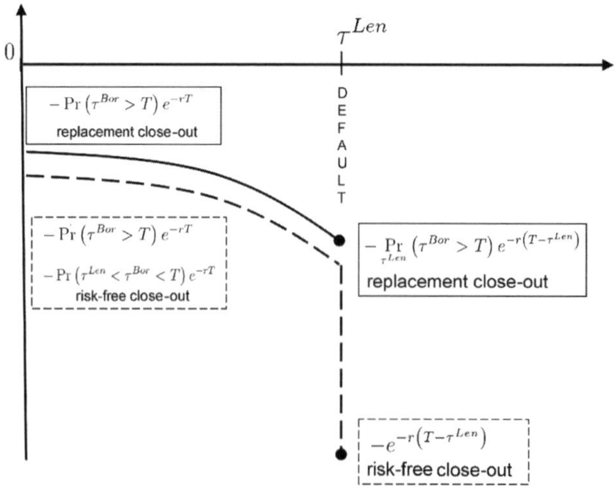

Figure 14.3 The loss for the borrower at default by the lender under risk-free close-out: the value of the risky liability jumps since it becomes risk-free

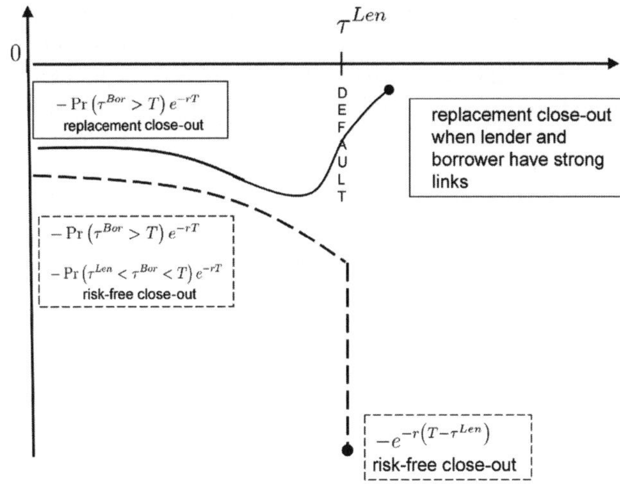

Figure 14.4 Lower recoverable amount for creditors at systemic default under replacement close-out: the value of the risky liability jumps down because of deflation by the increase of spreads

The issue of how to treat the two close-out conventions for the case of collateralized deals, when the final outcome should always be that, irrespective of close-out, collateral and exposure match at default, is covered by [52].

14.5 CONCLUSIONS

In this chapter we have analyzed the effect of assumptions about the computation of the close-out amount on counterparty risk adjustments of derivatives. We have compared the risk-free close-out assumed in the earlier literature with the replacement close-out we introduced here, which is inspired by recent ISDA documentation on the subject.

We have provided a formula for bilateral counterparty risk when a replacement close-out is used at default. We reckon that the replacement close-out is consistent with counterparty risk adjustments for standard and consolidated financial products such as bonds and loans. On the contrary the risk-free close-out introduces at time 0 a dependence on the risk of default by the party with no future obligations.

Table 14.1 Impact of default by the lender under risk-free or replacement close-out and under independence or co-monotonicity between default by the lender and by the borrower. Ideally, default by the lender should lead to "no contagion", since the lender has no further payment obligations in the deal

Dependence→ Close-Out↓	Independence	Co-monotonicity
Risk Free	Negatively affects borrower	No contagion
Substitution	No contagion	Further negatively affects lender

We have also shown that in the case of risk-free close-out a party that is a net debtor of a company will have a sudden loss at default of the latter, and this loss will be higher the higher the debtor's credit spreads. This does not happen when a replacement close-out is considered.

Thus, the risk-free close-out increases the number of operators subject to contagion from a default, including parties that currently seem not to think they are exposed, and this is certainly a negative fact. On the other hand, it spreads the default losses on to a higher number of parties and reduces the classic contagion channel affecting creditors. For the creditors, this is a positive fact because it brings more money to the liquidators of the defaulted company.

The close-out issue should be considered carefully by market operators and ISDA. For example, if the risk-free close-out introduced in the previous literature were to be recognized as a standard, banks would have to understand the consequences of this. In fact banks usually perform stress tests, and set aside reserves for the risk of default of their net borrowers, but do not consider any risk related to the default of net lenders. The above computations, and the numerical examples, show that, should a risk-free close-out prevail, banks had better set aside important reserves against this risk. On the other hand, under replacement close-out, banks can expect the recoverable amount to be lowered when their net borrowers default, compared to the case where a risk-free close-out applies. In the case of a replacement close-out, in fact, the money collected by liquidators from the counterparties will be lower, because of deflation by the default probability of the counterparties themselves, and this will be even more evident if they are strongly correlated to the defaulted entity.

The reader will probably guess how we are going to conclude this chapter.

We have seen many times in past chapters that counterparty credit and debit risk pricing is a very complex, model intensive task. Regulators and part of the industry are desperately trying to standardize the related calculations in the simplest possible ways but our conclusion is that such calculations are complex and need to remain so to be accurate. The attempt to standardize every risk to simple formulas is misleading and may result in the relevant risks not being addressed properly. The subtleties of the close-out we analyzed in this chapter are yet another illustration that one has to do the job properly and make hard choices. The industry and regulators should acknowledge the complexity of counterparty risk pricing and risk management and work to attain the necessary methodological and technological prowess rather than trying to bypass it. As the close-out issues illustrate, there is no easy way out. Or rather, for the specific close-out case, the easy way out would be to ban DVA, reducing to unilateral CVA, which then features no credit risk for the surviving party. However, as we have seen in Chapter 10 it is all but clear that DVA has to go. More generally, replacement close-out might also involve credit risk for the new party with whom the surviving party has restarted the trade. We do not analyze this here, but we have given all the instruments to extend the analysis on this aspect.

15

Bilateral Collateralized CVA and DVA for Rates and Credit

This chapter is based on Brigo, Capponi, Pallavicini and Papatheodorou (2011) [41] and Brigo, Capponi and Pallavicini (2011) [40].

In this chapter we develop some applications of the bilateral collateralized CVA and DVA equation we presented in Chapter 13. We will see two opposite examples:

- A case where collateralization is quite effective in reducing counterparty risk: interest rate swaps.
- A case where collateralization is almost completely ineffective in reducing counterparty risk, namely the case of a credit default swap as an underlying instrument.

We focus on interest rate and credit derivatives. First, we consider interest rate swaps (IRS) and try to highlight the dependency of the total Collateral-inclusive Bilateral (credit and debit) Valuation Adjustment (CBVA) on model parameters and market data. In particular, we examine the impact of margining frequency, re-hypothecation, correlation parameters, and credit spread volatilities. We conclude that in our examples collateral is quite effective in reducing counterparty risk.

Then, we apply our general analysis of Chapter 13 to Credit Default Swaps (CDS) as underlying portfolio. Featuring a CDS as underlying of the trade between two defaultable parties, a third default time enters the picture, namely the default time for the CDS reference credit. We assume a doubly stochastic or Cox processes reduced-form framework to model the default times of all three entities involved in the contract, namely the investor "I", counterparty "C" and the reference credit name (see Chapter 3 for reduced form models). We show that even a continuous collateralization scheme, where the two parties agree on posting collateral on a continuous mark-to-market basis, does not eliminate counterparty risk (credit contagion risk) and is rather ineffective. This is because the computation of the pre-default exposure, which determines the collateral to be posted at each time, is computed by conditioning on the filtration excluding the sigma algebra generated by the default time in the very last minute, whereas the computation of the on-default close-out amount is done on the enlarged filtration including the default time. In practice, this is interpreted by saying that the collateral process cannot take into account the very last minute contagion due to a sudden default. Since the last posting of collateral is at least one minute in the past, it has been done via a mark-to-market that did not take into account the sudden default of the counterparty. This sudden default impacts instantaneously the market information and variables, and the new mark-to-market including that information will be very different from the one corresponding to the last collateral update. Thus, collateral may be completely inadequate to cover the mark-to-market at default, even if updated a few minutes earlier.

We present a numerical study to evaluate the resulting CBVA formula, and show the impact of different collateralization strategies, re-hypothecation and default correlation on the resulting credit and debit valuation adjustments.

The rest of the chapter is organized as follows: Section 15.1 shows applications to interest rate swaps, where we find collateralization to be quite effective in reducing counterparty risk. Section 15.2 shows the detailed contagion calculations that will be necessary in order to compute CBVA for a CDS. These calculations highlight the complicated contagion calculations one has to face even in quite stylized and simplistic dependency models. Section 15.3 deals with credit default swaps and illustrates the application of the previous section's results to CDS. Section 15.4 concludes the chapter.

15.1 CBVA FOR INTEREST RATE SWAPS

In this section we extend the analysis of Chapter 12 (based on [59]), by presenting some numerics on the collateralized CVA and DVA according to the theory developed in Chapter 13. We consider a model that is stochastic both in the interest rates (underlying market) and in the default intensities (investor and counterparty defaults). Joint stochasticity is needed to introduce correlation between rates and credit. We use a G2++ model for the interest rates as in Section 5.1.1 which we calibrate to the ATM swaption volatilities quoted by the market on 26 May 2009 as in Section 12.2.1, while credit spreads are modelled according to CIR++ models as in Section 5.1.2, and default times are coupled via a Gaussian copula as in Section 12.2.2. The Brownian shocks of interest rate and credit spread processes are correlated as in Section 5.1.4. Hence, we have as free correlation parameters only the correlations $\bar{\rho}_C$ (correlation between interest rates and credit spread of "C"), $\bar{\rho}_I$ (correlation between interest rates and credit spread of "I"), and ρ_G (default correlation between "I" and "C"). The first two parameters are defined by Equation (5.8), and they represent the correlation between the short rate and the default intensity of each name. The third term is the Gaussian copula parameter between default times. We recover the other correlations from them.

We use the collateralization mechanism through margining described in Section 13.5. We assume zero minimum transfer amount and thresholds $M = K_I = K_C = 0$. Under this collateralization mechanism, we consider the behaviour of the bilateral credit valuation adjustment as a function of δ, where $\delta := t_i - t_{i-1}$ is the time between two consecutive collateral update times. We consider both the case when received collateral cannot be re-hypothecated by the collateral taker (CBVA given by Equation 13.4) and and the case when it can be re-hypothecated and the surviving party always faces the worst case (CBVA given by Equation 13.5).

15.1.1 Changing the Margining Frequency

First, we consider the margining frequency δ ranging from one week up to six months. Notice that we are considering interest rate swaps (IRS) with a 1-year payment frequency for the fixed leg and a six-month frequency for the floating leg (as usually found in the Euro market). By keeping the frequency δ below six months, we avoid jumps in CBVA occurring at the times when cash flows are exchanged.

In Figure 15.1 we show the sensitivity of the CBVA = CDVA − CCVA for an IRS with a 10 years maturity to the update frequency of collateral margining, which ranges from one week to six months. We see that the case of an investor riskier than the counterparty leads to positive value for CBCVA, while the case of an investor less risky than the counterparty has the opposite behaviour. In order to better explain that, we also plot separately the −CCVA and CDVA terms contributing to the adjustment. It is evident from the figure that, when the investor

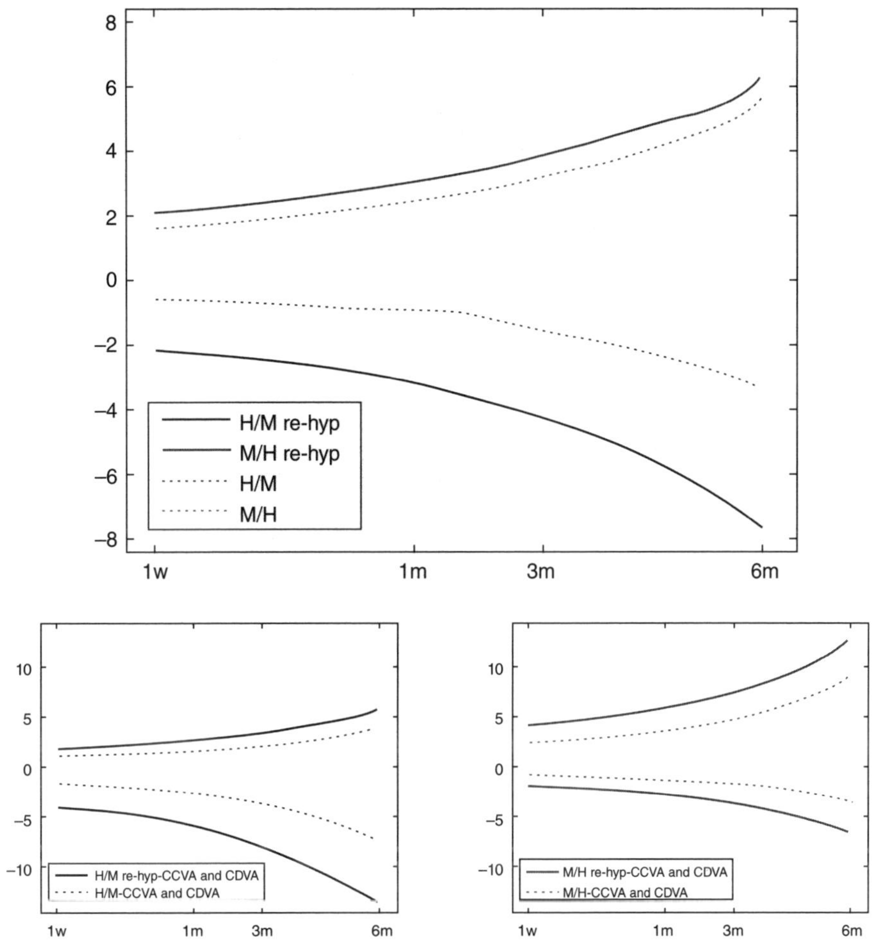

Figure 15.1 CBVA for a 10-year IRS under collateralization through margining as a function of the update frequency δ with $\bar{\rho}_C = \bar{\rho}_I = \rho_G = 0$. Update frequencies under six months. Continuous lines represent the re-hypothecation case, while dotted lines represent the opposite case. The top line of the main figure represents an investor riskier than the counterparty (mid-risk counterparty and high-risk investor, or M/H), while the bottom line represents an investor less risky than the counterparty (high-risk counterparty and mid-risk investor, or H/M). The upper panel plots the CBVA, while the bottom left and right panels plot respectively the −CCVA and CDVA components. All values are in basis points

is riskier the CDVA part of the correction dominates, while when the investor is less risky than the counterparty the adjustment has the opposite behaviour. The effect of re-hypothecation is to enhance the absolute size of the correction, a reasonable behaviour, since, in such a case, each party has a greater risk because of being unsecured on the collateral amount posted to the other party in case of default.

Although realistic update frequencies are usually weekly or daily, and only in exceptional cases reach the order of some months, we also plot all the cases from 1 to 10 years (namely no margining at all) as a tool to discuss collateral re-hypothecation effects.

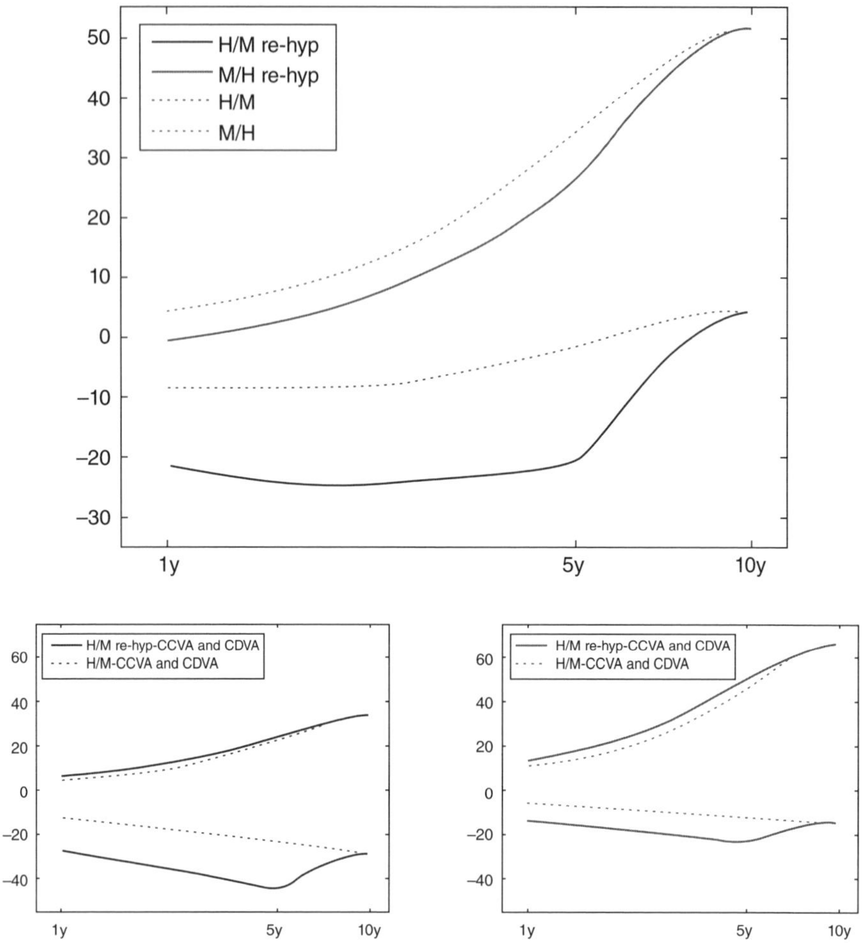

Figure 15.2 CBVA for a 10-year IRS under collateralization through margining as a function of the update frequency δ with $\bar{\rho}_C = \bar{\rho}_I = \rho_G = 0$. Update frequencies from 1 to 10 years. Continuous lines represent the re-hypothecation case, while dotted lines represent the opposite case. The top line in the main graph represents an investor riskier than the counterparty (mid-risk counterparty and high-risk investor, or M/H), while the bottom line represents an investor less risky than the counterparty (high-risk counterparty and mid-risk investor, or H/M). The upper panel plots the CBVA, while the bottom left and right panels plot respectively the −CCVA and CDVA components. All values in basis points

15.1.2 Inspecting the Exposure Profiles

If we look at Figure 15.2, namely, collateral update periods greater than one year, we observe that the case of an investor riskier than the counterparty has a greater CBVA without re-hypothecation. The opposite occurs for frequency under six months. Our explanation is as follows. Our preceding reasoning holds separately for CCVA and CDVA, but not for their difference CBVA. Indeed, when the update frequency is equal to one year or greater, the investor has a greater probability of posting collateral, as shown in Figure 15.3. This leads to an increase in CCVA when re-hypothecation is allowed, while CDVA is little affected.

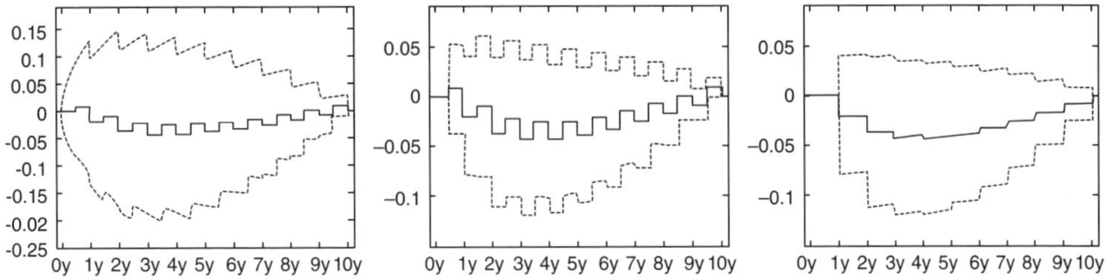

Figure 15.3 Left panel: mark-to-market density of a 10-year IRS uncollateralized exposure through time. Mid panel: collateral density for 6-month update frequency through time. Right panel: collateral density for 1-year update frequency through time. Continuous lines are distributions' mean values, while dotted lines are 95th percentiles

Further insights can be gained by looking at the expected exposure profiles which contribute to the CBVA adjustment. Here, we differentiate between

- the positive part of the (uncollateralized) exposure V_u^+ and its negative part V_u^-;
- the collateralized expected exposure without re-hypothecation contributing to the CCVA adjustment $(V_u^+ - C_u^+)^+$ and the corresponding term $(V_u^- - C_u^-)^-$ contributing to the CDVA adjustment.
- the collateralized expected exposure with re-hypothecation contributing to the CCVA adjustment $(V_u - C_u)^+$ and the corresponding term $(V_u - C_u)^-$ contributing to the CDVA adjustment.

15.1.3 A Case Where Re-Hypothecation is Worse than No Collateral at All

We can clearly see from the right panel in Figure 15.4 that, when assuming re-hypothecation, the collateralized expected exposure may exceed the uncollateralized one. This is a very curious example.

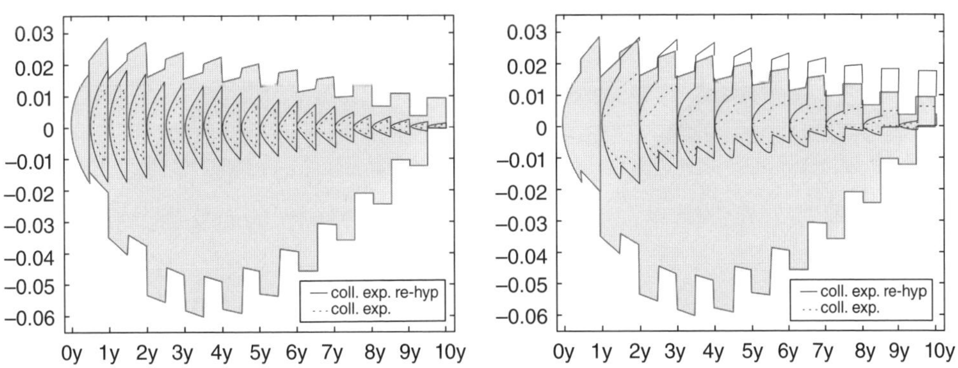

Figure 15.4 Expected exposure profiles for a 10-year IRS through time. The borders of the shaded area are the mean values of the positive and negative parts of the uncollateralized exposures (i.e. $\mathbb{E}[V^+]$ and $\mathbb{E}[V^-]$), while the dark lines within that area are collateralized exposures (continuous line is re-hypothecation case, namely $\mathbb{E}[(V_u - C_u)^+]$ and $\mathbb{E}[(V_u - C_u)^-]$; dotted line the opposite case, namely $\mathbb{E}[(V_u^+ - C_u^+)^+]$ and $\mathbb{E}[(V_u^- - C_u^-)^-]$). Left panel: expected exposure profiles for six months collateral update frequency. Right panel: expected exposure profiles for a one year collateral update frequency

This is the case because we may have $(V_u - C_u)^+ > V_u^+$, which holds in scenarios where at time u it is more likely that $C(u) < 0$, i.e. that collateral is posted by the investor and re-hypothecated by the counterparty. Therefore, this means that the investor is now exposed to the counterparty both in terms of the mark-to-market value of the transaction, that may have an inverted sign since the last posting and gone in the investor's favour, and also in terms of the earlier pre-inversion posted collateral, which is an unsecured claim and may not be returned in full in case of the earlier counterparty default.

15.1.4 Changing the Correlation Parameters

A second example is investigating the effects of correlations (both interest rate/credit spread and default time correlations) for different frequencies for collateral update.

First of all, a direct comparison between Figures 15.5 and 15.6 shows that increasing the collateral update frequency increases the magnitude of the CBVA adjustment (larger update periods imply larger on-default exposures and thus larger CBVAs), but it does not substantially change the dependence pattern of the CBVA on the correlation parameters. Further, we notice that we get similar results both by allowing or not allowing re-hypothecation, or by changing the market set from M/H to H/M.

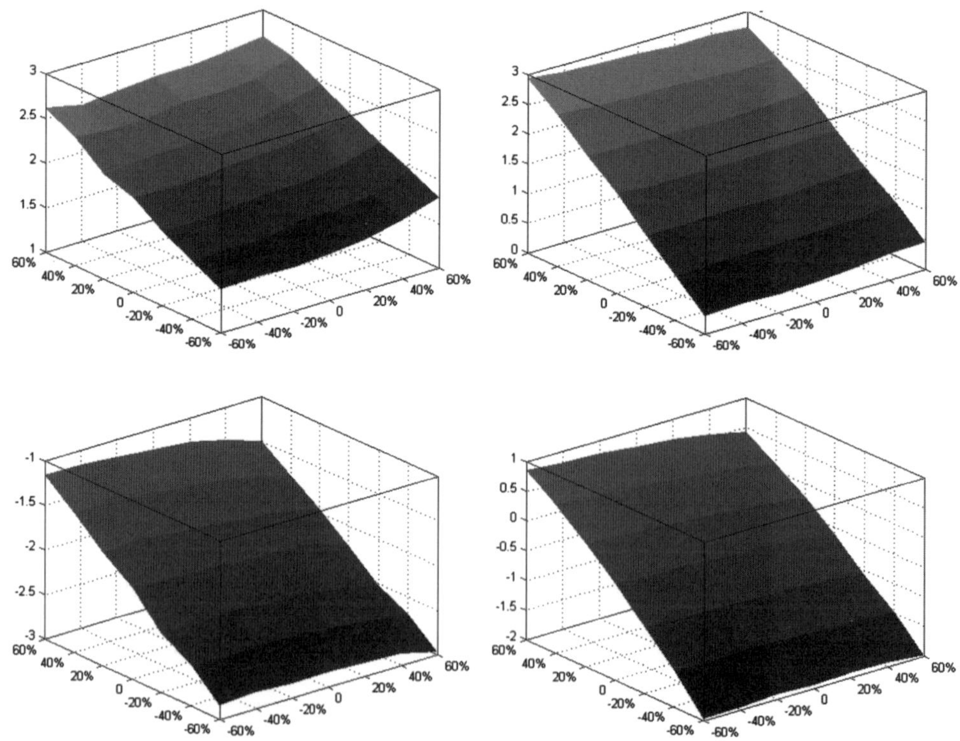

Figure 15.5 CBVA with collateral update frequency of one week for a 10-year IRS (mid to high (M/H) market settings in upper panels, high to mid (H/M) market settings in the lower panels) with different choices of interest rate/credit spread correlation ($\rho_C = \rho_I$ parameters, left-side axis) and default time correlation (ρ_G Gaussian copula parameter, right-side axis). The left panels show values with re-hypothecation, while the right panels show values without re-hypothecation. All values in basis points

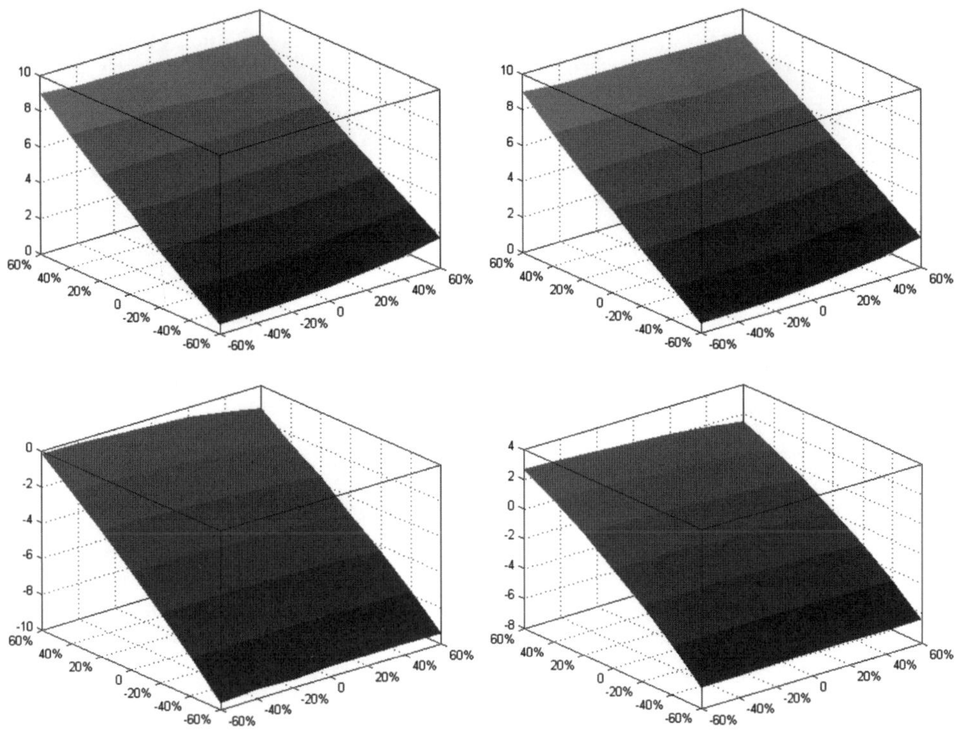

Figure 15.6 CBVA with collateral update frequency of three months for a 10-year IRS (mid to high (M/H) market settings in upper panels, high to mid (H/M) market settings in the lower panels) with different choices of interest rate/credit spread correlation ($\rho_C = \rho_I$ parameters, left-side axis) and default time correlation (ρ_G Gaussian copula parameter, right-side axis). The left panels show values with re-hypothecation, while the right panels show values without re-hypothecation. All values in basis points

We can see that for a given level of default time correlation parameter $\bar{\rho}_G$, a common increase in credit/interest rate correlation parameters $\bar{\rho}_C$ and $\bar{\rho}_I$ leads to higher CBVA adjustments. This is because higher interest rates will correspond to higher credit spreads, thus putting the receiver swaption embedded in the CCVA term of the adjustment more out-of-the-money. This will cause the CCVA term of the adjustment to diminish in absolute value, so that the final value of the CBVA = CDVA − CCVA will be larger for high correlations. As we are considering a counterparty more risky than the investor, the CCVA term will be dominating in the adjustment over the CDVA term. This is just an example of the complexity of patterns in bilateral collateralized CVA and DVA calculations. Model-dependent dynamic parameters, such as volatility and correlations, can change the profile of the bilateral CBVA calculation even in presence of collateral.

15.1.5 Changing the Credit Spread Volatility

A third example involves changing the volatility of the credit spread and monitoring the impact of wrong way risk for different collateral update frequencies, and for different values of interest rate/credit spread correlations.

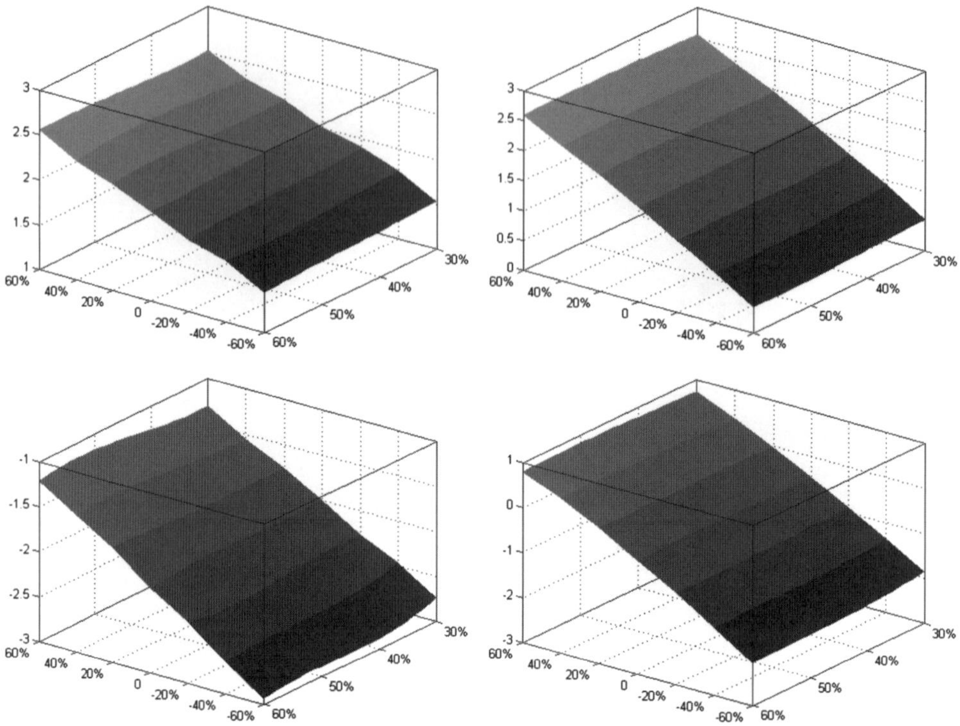

Figure 15.7 CBVA with collateral update frequency of one week for a 10-year IRS (mid- and high (M/H) market settings in the upper panels, high- and mid (H/M) market settings in the lower panels) with different choices of interest rate/credit spread correlation ($\rho_C = \rho_I$ parameters, left-side axis) and counterparty's credit spread volatility (ν^C parameter, right-side axis). The left panels show values with re-hypothecation, while the right panels show values without re-hypothecation. Default time correlation $\rho_G = 0$. All values in basis points

As in the preceding case we notice in Figures 15.7 and 15.8 that, for a given level of the counterparty's credit spread volatility parameter ν_C, the dependency of CBVA on the credit/interest rate correlation parameters $\bar{\rho}_C$ and $\bar{\rho}_I$ leads to higher adjustments for higher correlations. Regardless of the collateral update frequency, the credit-spread volatility has only a small impact on the CBVA adjustment, which is affected much more by the interest rate/credit spread correlations. However, it is worth noticing that for different choices of $\bar{\rho}_C$, the dependence pattern of the adjustements on the credit spread's volatility may be reversed (see for instance the case when $\bar{\rho}_C = 60\%$ where the adjustment is decreasing in ν_C and the case when $\bar{\rho}_C = -60\%$ where the adjustment is increasing in ν_C).

We present a fourth example where we change the volatility of the credit spread and monitor the impact of wrong way risk for various collateral update frequencies, and for different values of counterparty default correlations. We assume flat hazard rate structures, obtained as follows: we take the maximum CDS spread in the high risk name, let us call it CDS^H, and the maximum CDS spread in the medium risk name, let us call it CDS^M. We use the shift ψ in the CIR++ model (see Chapter 3) to match a flat hazard rate curve $h_H = CDS^H/\text{LGD}$ and $h_M = CDS^M/\text{LGD}$. We can see from Figure 15.9 that the adjustments tend to become higher

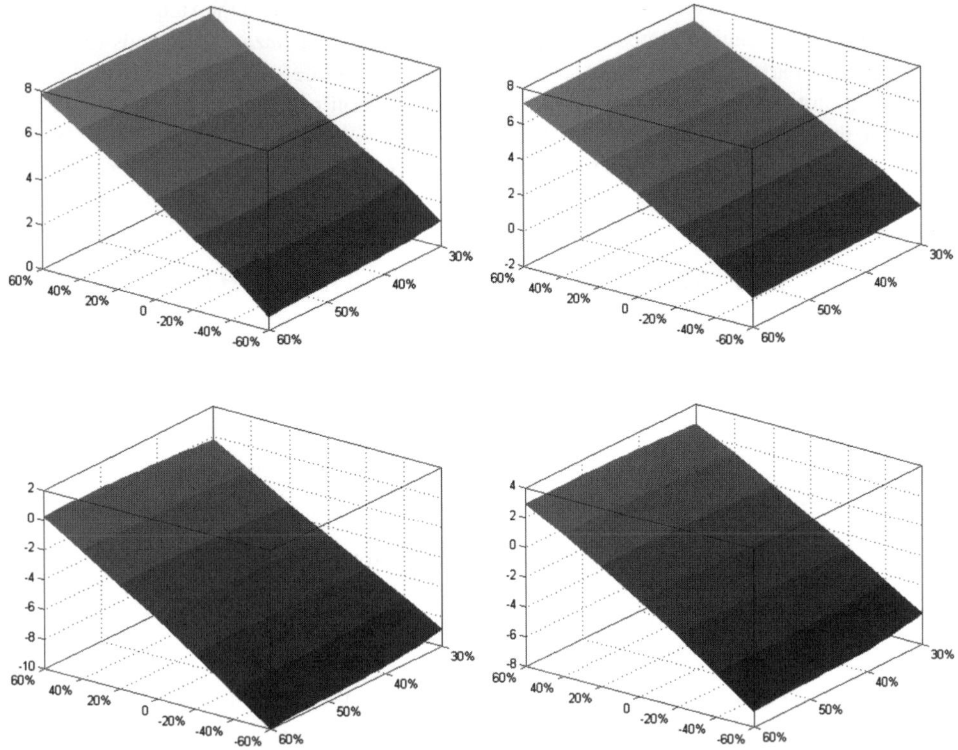

Figure 15.8 CBVA with collateral update frequency of three months for a 10-year IRS (mid to high (M/H) market settings in the upper panels, high to mid (H/M) market settings in the lower panels) with different choices of interest rate/credit spread correlation ($\rho_C = \rho_I$ parameters, left-side axis) and counterparty's credit spread volatility (ν^C parameter, right-side axis). The left panels show values with re-hypothecation, while the right panels show values without re-hypothecation. Default time correlation $\rho_G = 0$. All values in basis points

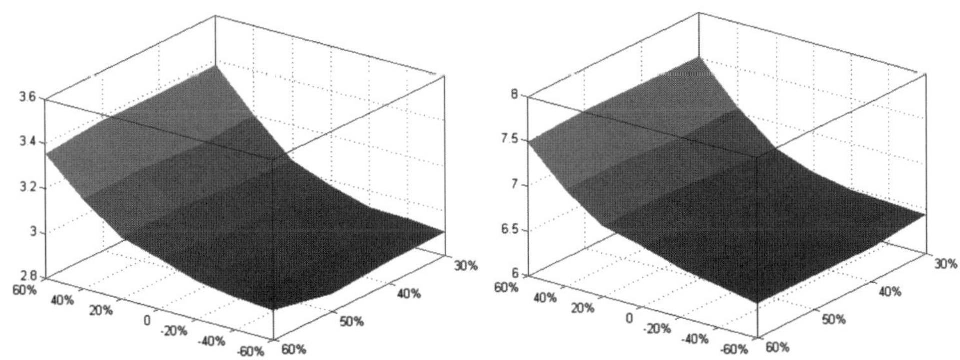

Figure 15.9 CBVA with re-hypothecation for a 10-year IRS with different choices of counterparty default correlation (ρ_G parameter, left-side axis) and counterparty's credit spread volatility (ν^C parameter, right-side axis). We assume $\rho_C = \rho_I = 0$. The left graph refers to a collateral update frequency of one week, while the right graph refers to a collateral update frequency of three months. All values in basis points

when the default correlation is positive. This is expected because when the value of ν_C is close to zero and the correlation is positive, the party with the higher hazard rate tends to default earlier than the party with the lower hazard rate, in almost all default scenarios. Similarly to Figure 15.8, notice that depending on the default correlation parameter ρ_G, the dependence pattern of the credit adjustments on the credit spreads volatility may be reversed (see for instance the case when $\rho_G = 60\%$ where the adjustment is increasing in ν_C, and compare it with the case when $\rho_G = -60\%$ where the adjustment is decreasing in ν_C).

15.2 MODELLING CREDIT CONTAGION

In this section we use the formula developed in Section 13.2 to evaluate CBVA in credit default swap contracts (CDS). Subsection 15.2.1 recalls the CDS price process. Subsection 15.2.2 presents explicit formulas for the conditional survival probability appearing in the counterparty risk adjustment.

15.2.1 The CDS Price Process

The price process CDS_t for a Underlying CDS selling protection LGD_U at time t for default of the reference entity between times T_a and T_b, with $t \leq T_a < T_b$, in exchange for a periodic premium rate S_U is given by

$$
\begin{aligned}
\text{CDS}_t(T_a, T_b; S_U, \text{LGD}_U) := {} & \mathbb{E}_t\left[S_U \sum_{i=a+1}^{b} D(t, T_i)\alpha_i \mathbf{1}_{\{\tau_U > T_i\}}\right] \\
& - \mathbb{E}_t\left[S_U \int_{T_a}^{T_b} D(t, u)(u - T_{\beta(u)})\, d\mathbf{1}_{\{\tau_U > u\}}\right] \\
& + \mathbb{E}_t\left[\text{LGD}_U \int_{T_a}^{T_b} D(t, u)\, d\mathbf{1}_{\{\tau_U > u\}}\right]
\end{aligned}
\tag{15.1}
$$

where α_i is coupon's accrual period and τ_U is the default time for the CDS reference name. If we assume deterministic interest rates, and deterministic recovery rates, then the price process may be written as

$$
\begin{aligned}
\text{CDS}_t(T_a, T_b; S_U, \text{LGD}_U) = {} & \mathbf{1}_{\{\tau_U > t\}}\, S_U \sum_{i=a+1}^{b} D(t, T_i)\mathbb{Q}\{\tau_U > T_i | \mathcal{G}_t\}\, du \\
& - \mathbf{1}_{\{\tau_U > t\}}\, S_U \int_{T_a}^{T_b} D(t, u)(u - T_{\beta(u)})\, d\mathbb{Q}\{\tau_U > u | \mathcal{G}_t\} \\
& + \mathbf{1}_{\{\tau_U > t\}}\, \text{LGD}_U \int_{T_a}^{T_b} D(t, u)\, d\mathbb{Q}\{\tau_U > u | \mathcal{G}_t\}\,.
\end{aligned}
\tag{15.2}
$$

We next proceed to the valuation of the CBVA adjustment for the case of a CDS contract. We use the collateralization rules we saw in Chapter 13, and recall that $\beta(\tau)$ is the last time when collateral was updated before the default event of one of the two parties (in case of continuous collateralization the β function is simply the identity function).

If we apply the formulas in Equation (13.4), (13.5) and (15.2) for ε for the case of the CDS contracts, then it is easily seen that when collateral re-hypothecation is not allowed, the adjustment for a receiver CDS contract (protection seller) running from time $t = T_a$ to time $T_b = T$ is given by

$$\begin{aligned}\text{CBVA}(t, T; C) = &-\mathbb{E}_t\left[\mathbf{1}_{\{\tau=\tau_C<T\}}D(t, \beta(\tau))\text{LGD}_C\left(D(\beta(\tau), \tau)\text{CDS}^+_\tau - \text{CDS}^+_{\beta(\tau)-}\right)^+\right]\\ &- \mathbb{E}_t\left[\mathbf{1}_{\{\tau=\tau_I<T\}}D(t, \beta(\tau))\text{LGD}_I\left(D(\beta(\tau), \tau)\text{CDS}^-_\tau - \text{CDS}^-_{\beta(\tau)-}\right)^-\right]\end{aligned} \tag{15.3}$$

where we recall that our notation $X^- = \min(X, 0)$ is not standard and $\tau = \min(\tau_C, \tau_I)$. In case re-hypothecation is allowed we obtain

$$\begin{aligned}\text{CBVA}(t, T; C) = &-\mathbb{E}_t\left[\mathbf{1}_{\{\tau=\tau_C<T\}}D(t, \beta(\tau))\text{LGD}_C\left(D(\beta(\tau), \tau)\text{CDS}_\tau - \text{CDS}_{\beta(\tau)-}\right)^+\right]\\ &- \mathbb{E}_t\left[\mathbf{1}_{\{\tau=\tau_I<T\}}D(t, \beta(\tau))\text{LGD}_I\left(D(\beta(\tau), \tau)\text{CDS}_\tau - \text{CDS}_{\beta(\tau)-}\right)^-\right].\end{aligned} \tag{15.4}$$

Finally, if we remove collateralization, then we obtain

$$\text{BVA}(t, T) = -\mathbb{E}_t\left[\mathbf{1}_{\{\tau=\tau_C<T\}}D(t, \tau)\text{LGD}_C\text{CDS}^+_\tau\right] - \mathbb{E}_t\left[\mathbf{1}_{\{\tau=\tau_I<T\}}D(t, \tau)\text{LGD}_I\text{CDS}^-_\tau\right]. \tag{15.5}$$

From 15.2 and (15.3, 15.4, 15.5), we can see that the only terms we need to know in order to be able to numerically compute the credit valuation adjustments are the *on-default survival* probabilities

$$\mathbf{1}_{\{\tau=\tau_C\leq T\}}\mathbf{1}_{\{\tau_U>\tau_C\}}\mathbb{Q}\left\{\tau_U > t|\mathcal{G}_{\tau_C}\right\}, \quad \mathbf{1}_{\{\tau=\tau_I\leq T\}}\mathbf{1}_{\{\tau_U>\tau_I\}}\mathbb{Q}\left\{\tau_U > t|\mathcal{G}_{\tau_I}\right\}.$$

Let us assume that $t > \tau_C > u$. Then, in the presence of collateralization, we can see from Equations (15.3) and (15.4) that we need to evaluate the *pre-default survival* probabilities

$$\mathbf{1}_{\{\tau=\tau_C\leq T\}}\mathbf{1}_{\{\tau_U>u\}}\mathbb{Q}\left\{\tau_U > t|\mathcal{G}_u\right\}, \quad \mathbf{1}_{\{\tau=\tau_I\leq T\}}\mathbf{1}_{\{\tau_U>u\}}\mathbb{Q}\left\{\tau_U > t|\mathcal{G}_u\right\}.$$

Let us define

$$\varphi_u(w, x, v) := \mathbb{Q}\left\{\tau_I > w, \tau_U > x, \tau_C > v|\mathcal{F}_u\right\}. \tag{15.6}$$

15.2.2 Calculation of Survival Probability

Before proceeding with the computation of the survival probability, we recall the following lemma from [18].

Lemma 15.2.1 (key lemma). *If τ is a $\mathcal{G}$ stopping time and Y a $\mathcal{G}$-measurable random variable, then we have that for any $t \in \mathrm{R}_+$,*

$$\mathbb{E}^{\mathbb{Q}}[\mathbf{1}_{\{\tau>t\}}Y|\mathcal{G}_t] = \mathbf{1}_{\{\tau>t\}}\frac{\mathbb{E}^{\mathbb{Q}}\left[\mathbf{1}_{\{\tau>t\}}Y|\mathcal{F}_t\right]}{\mathbb{Q}(\tau > t|\mathcal{F}_t)}. \tag{15.7}$$

Then, we prove a second lemma also useful for the computation of survival probability.

Lemma 15.2.2 *Let ς be a finite $\mathcal{G}$-stopping time, and X an integrable random variable. Then, it holds that*

$$\mathbb{E}_{\varsigma}[X] = \lim_{u \downarrow \varsigma} \mathbb{E}_u[X] \tag{15.8}$$

Proof. Define ς_n to be the value of ς rounded upwards to the nearest multiple of 2^{-n}. Clearly, ς_n decreases to ς as $n \to \infty$, and each ς_n is a finite stopping time, because we rounded up. For countable-valued stopping times ι, we have that

$$\mathbb{E}_{\iota}[X] = \sum_u \mathbf{1}_{\{\iota = u\}} \mathbb{E}_u[X]. \tag{15.9}$$

The above equality follows from the definition of stopped filtration, as $A \in \mathcal{G}_{\iota}$ implies $A \cap \{\iota = u\} \in \mathcal{G}_u$. From Equation (15.9), we obtain $\eta_{\varsigma_n} = \mathbb{E}_{\varsigma_n}[X]$, for each stopping time ς_n. Letting $n \to \infty$, and using the right continuity of η_t, along with the martingale convergence theorem, we obtain

$$\lim_{n \to \infty} \eta_{\varsigma_n} = \eta_{\varsigma}$$

which yields Equation 15.8.

Proposition 15.2.3 *Assume $\varphi_u(u, x, y)$ and $\varphi_u(y, x, u)$ are differentiable with respect to y. If $t > \tau_C$, we have*

$$\mathbf{1}_{\{\tau = \tau_C \le T\}} \mathbf{1}_{\{\tau_U > \tau_C\}} \mathbb{Q}\left\{\tau_U > t | \mathcal{G}_{\tau_C}\right\} = \lim_{u \downarrow \tau_C} \mathbf{1}_{\{u \le T\}} \mathbf{1}_{\{\tau_U > u\}} \frac{\frac{\partial}{\partial y} \varphi_u(u, t, y)\Big|_{y = \tau_C}}{\frac{\partial}{\partial y} \varphi_u(u, u, y)\Big|_{y = \tau_C}} \tag{15.10}$$

Similarly, if $t > \tau_I$, we have

$$\mathbf{1}_{\{\tau = \tau_I \le T\}} \mathbf{1}_{\{\tau_U > \tau_I\}} \mathbb{Q}\left\{\tau_U > t | \mathcal{G}_{\tau_I}\right\} = \lim_{u \downarrow \tau_I} \mathbf{1}_{\{u \le T\}} \mathbf{1}_{\{\tau_U > u\}} \frac{\frac{\partial}{\partial y} \varphi_u(y, t, u)\Big|_{y = \tau_I}}{\frac{\partial}{\partial y} \varphi_u(y, u, u)\Big|_{y = \tau_I}} \tag{15.11}$$

Proof. We only prove Equation (15.11), as the proof of Equation (15.12) is analogous and omitted here. Application of Lemma 15.2.2 yields

$$\mathbf{1}_{\{\tau = \tau_C \le T\}} \mathbf{1}_{\{\tau_U > \tau_C\}} \mathbb{Q}(\tau_U > t | \mathcal{G}_{\tau_C}) = \lim_{u \downarrow \tau_C} f(u)$$

where

$$f(u) = \mathbf{1}_{\{u \le T\}} \mathbf{1}_{\{\tau_U > u\}} \mathbb{Q}\left\{\tau_U > t | \mathcal{G}_u\right\}.$$

Notice that on the set $u > \tau_C$, we have $\mathcal{G}_u \supseteq \mathcal{G}_{\tau_C} \supseteq \sigma(\tau_C)$. Therefore, using the key lemma, we have

$$\begin{aligned} f(u) &= \mathbf{1}_{\{u\le T\}}\mathbf{1}_{\{\tau_U>u\}}\frac{\mathbb{E}^{\mathbb{Q}}\left[\mathbf{1}_{\{\tau_U>t\}}\mathbf{1}_{\{\tau_U>u\}}|\mathcal{F}_u \vee \mathcal{H}_u^I \vee \sigma(\tau_C)\right]}{\mathbb{E}^{\mathbb{Q}}\left[\mathbf{1}_{\{\tau_U>u\}}|\mathcal{F}_u \vee \mathcal{H}_u^I \vee \sigma(\tau_C)\right]} \\ &= \mathbf{1}_{\{u\le T\}}\mathbf{1}_{\{\tau_U>u\}}\frac{\mathbb{E}^{\mathbb{Q}}\left[\mathbf{1}_{\{\tau_U>t\}}|\mathcal{F}_u \vee \mathcal{H}_u^I \vee \sigma(\tau_C)\right]}{\mathbb{E}^{\mathbb{Q}}\left[\mathbf{1}_{\{\tau_U>u\}}|\mathcal{F}_u \vee \mathcal{H}_u^I \vee \sigma(\tau_C)\right]} \end{aligned}$$

Further application of the key lemma yields

$$\mathbb{E}^{\mathbb{Q}}\left[\mathbf{1}_{\{\tau_U>t\}}|\mathcal{F}_u \vee \mathcal{H}_u^I \vee \sigma(\tau_C)\right] = \mathbf{1}_{\{\tau_I>u\}}\frac{\left.\frac{\partial}{\partial y}\varphi_u(u,t,y)\right|_{y=\tau_C}}{\left.\frac{\partial}{\partial y}\varphi_u(u,0,y)\right|_{y=\tau_C}} \tag{15.12}$$

and

$$\mathbb{E}^{\mathbb{Q}}\left[\mathbf{1}_{\{\tau_U>u\}}|\mathcal{F}_u \vee \mathcal{H}_u^I \vee \sigma(\tau_C)\right] = \mathbf{1}_{\{\tau_I>u\}}\frac{\left.\frac{\partial}{\partial y}\varphi_u(u,u,y)\right|_{y=\tau_C}}{\left.\frac{\partial}{\partial y}\varphi_u(u,0,y)\right|_{y=\tau_C}} \tag{15.13}$$

Plugging the expressions in Equations (15.12) and (15.13) into the above equation for $f(u)$, we obtain

$$f(u) = \mathbf{1}_{\{u\le T\}}\mathbf{1}_{\{\tau_U>u\}}\frac{\left.\frac{\partial}{\partial y}\varphi_u(u,t,y)\right|_{y=\tau_C}}{\left.\frac{\partial}{\partial y}\varphi_u(u,u,y)\right|_{y=\tau_C}}$$

and the desired result follows.

Notice that, in general, the on-default and pre-default survival probabilities have a different term structure. However, in some special cases, they turn out to be the same, as stated in the next corollary.

Corollary 15.2.4 *Assume*

$$\varphi(w,x,v) = \mathbb{Q}\{\tau_I > w|\mathcal{F}_u\}\,\mathbb{Q}\{\tau_U > x|\mathcal{F}_u\}\,\mathbb{Q}\{\tau_C > v|\mathcal{F}_u\}.$$

Then

$$\mathbf{1}_{\{\tau_U>\tau\}}\mathbb{Q}\{\tau_U > t|\mathcal{G}_\tau\} = \mathbf{1}_{\{\tau_U>\tau\}}\mathbb{Q}\{\tau_U > t|\mathcal{F}_\tau\} \tag{15.14}$$

The proof follows immediately using the independence assumption and the fact that simultaneous defaults are excluded.

Remark 15.2.5 ***(Continuous Collateralization and Contagion)*** *If the default events are not conditionally independent given the reference filtration, it is no longer true that on-default and pre-default survival probabilities are the same when $u = \tau_C^-$. In financial terms, this means that in the case of a credit default swap contract, continuous collateralization ($\beta(\tau) = \tau$) does not fully eliminate counterparty risk. It does so only if the default times of the counterparties and of the reference entity are conditionally independent. Moreover, observe that this is a feature of products such as credit default swaps, where the mark-to-market price of the residual* *transaction, if taken as defining the exposure V_τ, may experience a jump at τ. The same would not occur if the product were, for instance, an interest rate swap, as discussed in Section 15.1. In that case the adjustments, which depend on the collateral account via the following terms $V_\tau^+ - C_{\tau-}^+$ and $V_\tau^- - C_{\tau-}^-$, would drop to zero, thus eliminating completely the counterparty risk.*

In the following sections, we specify credit and default correlation models, and then present numerical simulations to evaluate the bilateral CVA of credit default swap contracts. In order to keep the computation tractable, we consider a square root diffusion model driving the intensity of investor, counterparty and CDS reference credit, and correlate the default events through a copula structure. We measure the impact of default correlation on the resulting adjustment.

15.2.3 Modelling Default-Time Dependence

For the stochastic intensity models we use three CIR++ models as in Section 5.1.2, one model for each name: investor (I), reference (U), and counterparty (C). We focus on two different sets of CDS quotes: a mid-risk and a high-risk setting, which are both defined in Tables 12.3, 12.4 and 12.5. We then calibrate the parameters of the CIR model to these quotes by assuming that recovery rates are at the 40% level.

The default-time correlation between the three names is defined through a dependence structure on the exponential random variables characterizing the default times of the three names. Such dependence structure is modelled using a trivariate copula function.

Let us denote by λ_t^i and $\Lambda^i(t) = \int_0^t \lambda_s^i ds$ respectively the default intensity and cumulated intensity of name i evaluated at time t. Thus, by following the credit spread model presented in Section 5.1.2 we write

$$\lambda_t^i := y_t^i + \psi^i(t; \beta^i), \quad t \geq 0,$$

with $i \in \{I, U, C\}$, and ψ^i is a deterministic function, depending on the parameter vector β^i (which includes y_0^i), that is integrable on closed intervals. We take each y^i to be a CIR process as given by

$$dy_t^i = \kappa^i(\mu^i - y_t^i)\,dt + \nu^i \sqrt{y_t}\,dZ_{3,t}^i.$$

Jumps could be added as in Chapter 3, but we keep the structure simple since the number of parameters is already high and discussion would become cumbersome. We assume λ^i to be independent of λ^j for $i \neq j$, and we assume each of them to be strictly positive almost everywhere, thus implying that Λ^i is invertible. Thus, we place ourselves in a Cox process setting, where

$$\tau_i = \left(\Lambda^i\right)^{-1}(\xi_i),\ i \in \{I, U, C\} \tag{15.15}$$

with ξ_I, ξ_U and ξ_C being standard exponential random variables whose associated uniforms $\Upsilon_i := 1 - \exp\{-\xi_i\}$ are connected through a Gaussian trivariate copula function

$$C_{\mathbf{R}}(\upsilon_I, \upsilon_U, \upsilon_C) := \mathbb{Q}\{\Upsilon_I < \upsilon_I, \Upsilon_U < \upsilon_U, \Upsilon_C < \upsilon_C\}$$

where $\mathbf{R} = [r_{i,j}]_{i,j=I,U,C}$ is the correlation matrix parameterizing the Gaussian copula. Notice that a trivariate Gaussian copula implies bivariate Gaussian marginal copulas. More specifically, the pairs of default times τ_i and τ_j, $i \neq j$, are connected through the bivariate Gaussian copula $C_{\mathbf{R}_{i,j}}(u_i, u_j)$, where $\mathbf{R}_{i,j}$ denotes the $2 \cdot 2$ sub-matrix formed by the intersection of row i and row j with column i and column j.

15.3 CBVA FOR CREDIT DEFAULT SWAPS

In order to simulate the three $y^i(t)$, we use the well-known fact that the distribution of $y^i(t)$ given $y^i(u)$, for some $u < t$ is, up to a scale factor, a non-central chi-square distribution, see [83] or, for example, [48]. More precisely, the transition law of $y^i(t)$ given $y^i(u)$ can be expressed as

$$y^i(t) = \frac{(\nu^i)^2(1 - e^{-\kappa^i(t-u)})}{4\kappa^i} \chi'_d \left(\frac{4\kappa^i e^{-\kappa^i(t-u)}}{(\nu^i)^2(1 - e^{-\kappa^i(t-u)})} y^i(u) \right)$$

where

$$d = \frac{4\kappa^i \mu^i}{(\nu^i)^2}$$

and $\chi'_u(v)$ denotes a non-central chi-square random variable with u degrees of freedom and non centrality parameter v. In this way, if we know $y^i(0)$, we can simulate the process $y^i(t)$ exactly on a discrete time grid by sampling from the non-central chi-square distribution. Let us denote by $\Phi^{t,u}_{CIR,i}(x)$ the cumulative distribution function of the integrated shifted CIR process $\Lambda^i(t)$ conditional on $\mathcal{F}_u$ evaluated at x. Such distribution may be obtained through inversion of the characteristic function of the integrated CIR process, which is well known from the work of [83], and from the literature on Brownian motion, since it is closely associated with the Lévy's stochastic area formula, see also [195]. Moreover, let $\Xi(z) := -\log(1 - \Phi(z))$, where $\Phi(\cdot)$ denotes the cumulative distribution function of the univariate Gaussian. Under the copula model, we have that

$$\varphi_u(v, s, w) = \mathbb{E}^{\phi_R}\left[\Phi^{v,u}_{CIR,0}(\Xi(z_I))\Phi^{s,u}_{CIR,1}(\Xi(z_U))\Phi^{w,u}_{CIR,2}(\Xi(z_C))\right] \tag{15.16}$$

where (z_I, z_U, z_C) is a standard Gaussian vector with density ϕ_R, and R denotes the correlation matrix.

15.3.1 Changing the Copula Parameters

We consider an investor trading a 5-year CDS contract on a reference name with a counterparty. Both the investor and the counterparty are subject to default risk. We consider two different levels of credit risk (mid and high). We measure the counterparty adjustments under three different collateralization strategies, i.e. (i) continuous collateralization, (ii) collateralization with three-months margining frequency, and (iii) no collateralization at all.

We consider two sets of simulations. In both cases, investor and counterparty have a mid credit-risk profile, while the reference entity has high credit-risk profile. Moreover, all three names are equally correlated to each other. We consider a five-year CDS. In the first set of simulations, (a), we set the CDS spread S_U in the premium leg to 100 basis points, while in the second set of simulations (b), we set it to 500 basis points. The break-even or fair spread value for S_U that would make the total value of the CDS equal to zero at time zero is 251 basis points. In this numerical investigation we implement a proper quarterly spaced premium leg, rather

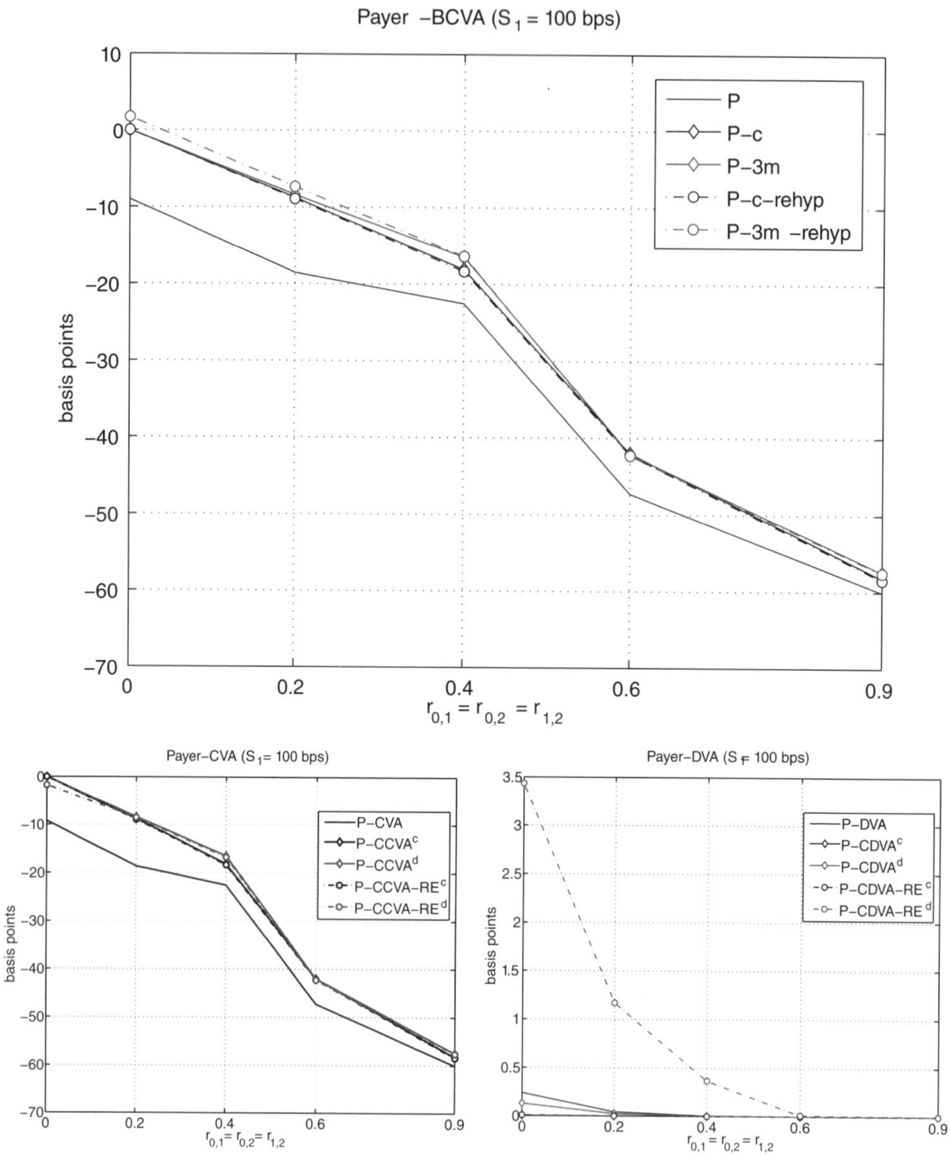

Figure 15.10 Collateral-inclusive Bilateral Valuation Adjustments CBVA, and CCVA and CDVA components, versus default correlation under the different collateralization strategies for the 5-year payer CDS contract. The 5-year CDS spread is set to 100 basis points

than the idealized continually paying premium leg. Results are displayed in Figures 15.10 and 15.12, respectively.

Let us begin by analyzing our results in the case where the protection payment is 100 basis points, case (a). Given that the fair spread is 251, in this setup the payer CDS has a markedly positive initial value, whereas the receiver CDS has a markedly negative one. The case of (b), a protection payment of 500 basis points is discussed in Section 15.3.3.

We discuss the results for the payer CDS contract, as the results for the receiver exhibit a specular pattern. If the investor holds a payer CDS, it is buying protection from the counterparty, i.e. it is a protection buyer. Given that the payer CDS will be positive in most scenarios, when the investor defaults it is quite unlikely that the net present value (NPV) will be in favour of the counterparty. Hence, one expects the DVA to be small or null in most cases due to out-moneyness of the related option. This is what we see from the middle panel of Figure 15.10, except in the case with zero correlation and under re-hypothecated collateral, where the DVA for zero correlation is about 3.5 basis points rather than zero. This can be explained as follows. Under collateralization with re-hypothecation, since the NPV is in most cases in favour of the investor, the counterparty will post collateral to the investor. However, if the investor is allowed to re-hypothecate and then defaults, the counterparty will get back only a recovery fraction of the collateral, and the investor will have a discount on the collateral she needs to give back to the counterparty. This discount generates a non-zero, albeit small DVA. However, when default correlation goes up, it becomes more unlikely that the investor defaults alone and first, without the counterparty and the underlying CDS defaulting as well, and therefore there will be fewer scenarios where the DVA payoff term will be activated by the first default of the investor.

15.3.2 Inspecting the Contagion Risk

We now analyze the CVA term. Again, given that the payer CDS will be positive in most scenarios, we expect the CVA term to be relevant, given that the related option will be mostly in-the-money. This is confirmed by our outputs. We see in the figure a relevant CVA term starting at about 10 and ending up at 60 basis points when under high correlation. We also see that, for zero correlation, collateralization succeeds in completely removing CVA, which goes from 10 to 0 basis points. However, collateralization seems to become less effective as default dependence grows, in that collateralized and uncollateralized CVA become closer and closer, and for high correlations we still get 60 basis points of CVA, even under collateralization. The reason for this is the instantaneous default contagion that, under positive dependency, pushes up the intensity of the survived entities, as soon as there is a default of the counterparty. Indeed, we can clearly see from Figure 15.11 that the term structure of the on-default survival probabilities lie below that of the pre-default survival probabilities conditioned on $\mathcal{G}_{\tau^-}$. Moreover, we can see that for larger values of default correlation (see the case when the default correlation is 0.9), the on-default survival curve lies significantly below the pre-default curve. The result is that the default leg of the CDS will increase in value due to contagion, and instantaneously the payer CDS will be worth more. This will instantly increase the loss to the investor, and most of the CVA value will come from this jump. Given the instantaneous nature of the jump, it is clear that the value after the jump will be quite different from the value at the last date of collateral posting, before the jump, and this explains the limited effectiveness of collateral under significantly positive default dependence.

15.3.3 Changing the CDS Moneyness

We now turn to the case where the premium leg running spread is at 500 basis points, thus roughly twice as much as the equilibrium CDS spread. Hence, in this setup, the payer CDS has a markedly negative initial value, whereas the receiver CDS has a markedly positive one. Let us focus first on the payer CDS.

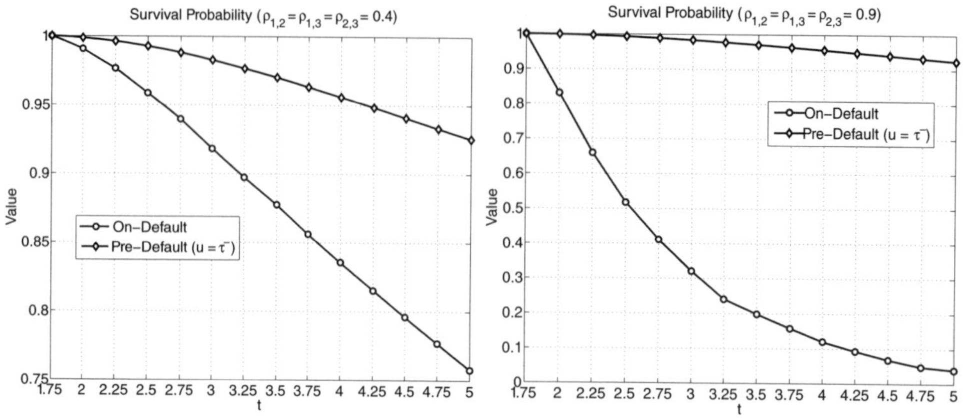

Figure 15.11 On-default survival probability and pre-default survival probability. The default time is $\tau = \tau_I = 1.75$

If the investor holds a payer CDS, he is a protection buyer. Given that the payer CDS will be negative in most scenarios, when the investor defaults it is quite likely that the NPV will be in favour of the counterparty, and therefore we should expect a relevant DVA term. On the other hand, for the same reason, we should expect a small or even zero CVA term. This is what can be seen from Figure 15.12, for the case of uncollateralized DVA under small values of default correlation. However, as we increase correlation, we can see that, even uncollateralized DVA decreases whereas the CVA becomes relevant. Again, this can be explained in terms of contagion. When the investor defaults, under positive dependence the default leg of the underlying CDS jumps up, increasing the value of the payer CDS. This will increase the option moneyness embedded in the CVA term and decrease that for the DVA term, leading to the observed effects. Moreover, notice that the higher the dependence, the higher the effect. We can also notice the impact of collateral and of re-hypothecation. More specifically, collateral makes the DVA term very small even for zero default correlation, where there is no contagion. Under low or zero correlation the underlying CDS spread will not move much upon default by the investor, so that the last posted collateral will be close to the on-default value of the underlying CDS, bringing the loss due to sudden default by the investor near zero. As for the CVA term, we see that for all the values of the correlation parameter there is mostly a difference between the re-hypothecated case and all other cases. In fact, in most scenarios with a largely negative value for the underlying CDS, it will be the investor who will have to post collateral as a guarantee towards the counterparty. If the counterparty defaults first, as in the CVA term, it will give back only a fraction of the collateral received by the investor, increasing the loss for the investor and, consequently, the related CVA term. Without re-hypothecation this does not happen as the counterparty will give all the collateral back to the investor. We also notice that in the CVA term, collateralization does almost nothing to reduce CVA. This is because the moneyness of the contract is always in favor of the DVA term. Thus collateral posted will be coming almost never from the counterparty as a guarantee to alleviate the CVA term. On the contrary, in most scenarios the moneyness will cause the investor to post collateral in favour of the counterparty, thus reducing the DVA term. The bilateral counterparty risk adjustments in Figures 15.10 and 15.12 can be explained exactly in terms of the embedded CVA and DVA.

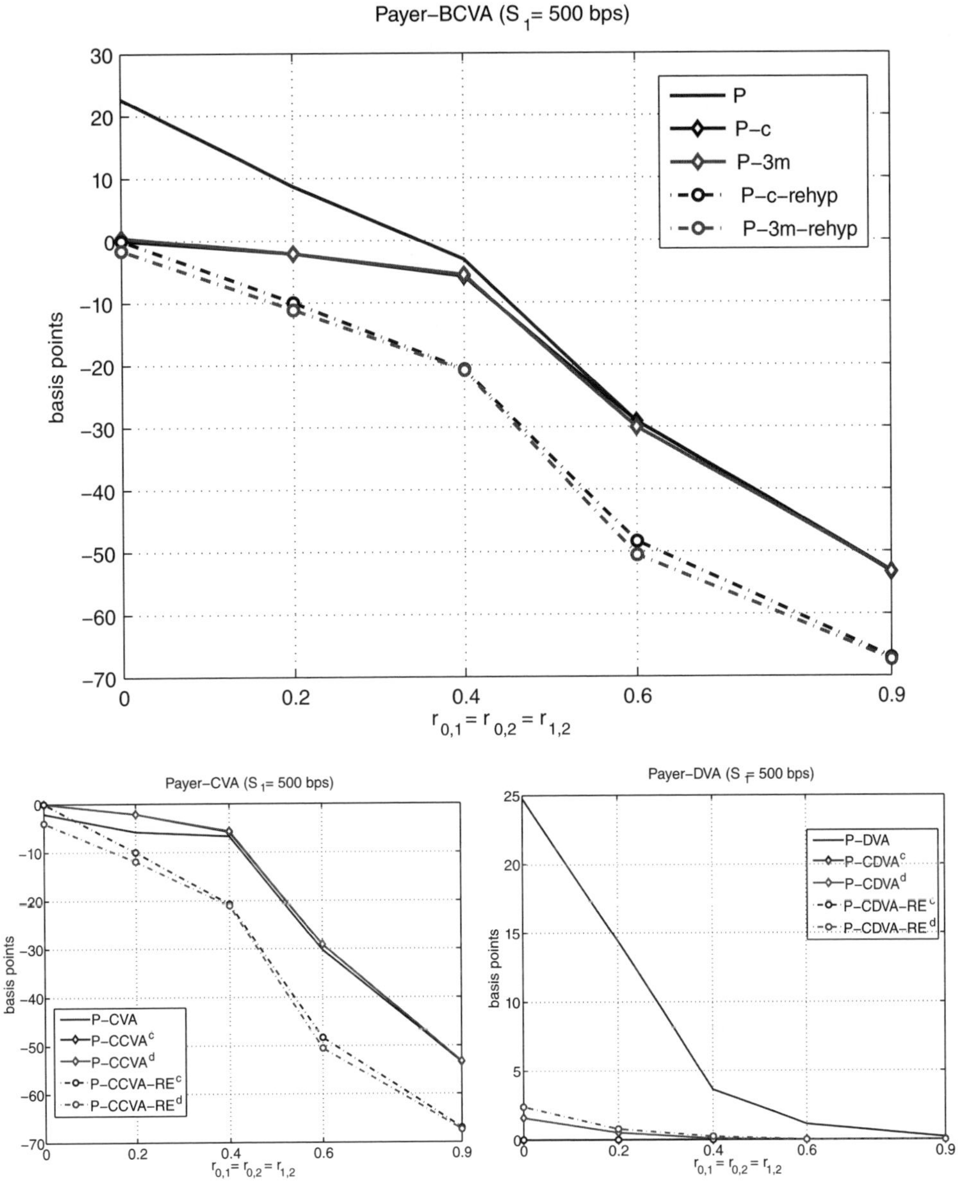

Figure 15.12 Counterparty value adjustments versus default correlation under the different collateralization strategies for the 5-year payer CDS contract. The 5-year CDS spread is set to 500 basis points

15.4 CONCLUSIONS

In this chapter we have considered interest rate swap contracts and, we have shown the impact of collateralization frequency on the bilateral CVA via numerical simulations.

Further, we have specialized our analysis to the case where the underlying portfolio is sensitive to a third credit event, and in particular a credit default swap written on a third reference entity. Through a numerical study, we have analyzed the impact of collateralization frequency, collateral re-hypothecation, and default correlation on the resulting counterparty adjustments.

The results obtained confirm that the adjustments are monotonic with respect to the level of default correlation. Moreover, higher frequency of collateralization reduce counterparty exposure, while re-hypothecation enhances the absolute size of the adjustment due to the possibility that the collateral provider can only recover a fraction of his posted collateral. Finally, contagion effects play a key role in limiting the effectiveness of collateral in the CDS case.

From the analysis above for CDSs one may argue that, in some instances, the effect of contagion is so dramatic as to change CVA and DVA patterns even in the presence of a strong and adverse moneyness in the underlying option terms. This is a feature of copula models that is worth keeping in mind when modelling bilateral counterparty risk. On the other hand, it is easy to simulate and easily allows for decomposing block dependence into pairwise dependence; it is also largely used and understood in limitations by practitioners, even if it is used in an extremely stylized and simplistic way when dealing with synthetic CDO's, see for example the analysis in [60], leading to a number of problems. The situation is however less dramatic when the number of entities who can default is small. Even then, care must be taken in assessing the size of contagion effects, in order to make sure that the model gives realistic contributions.

All these aspects and the complexity of the patterns we analyzed (and we gave up jumps in credit spreads, which should rather be there) point us to reiterate our closing message for our earlier chapters.

Counterparty risk pricing, especially in presence of collateral and contagion, is a very complex, model intensive task. Regulators and part of the industry are desperately trying to standardize the related calculation in the simplest possible ways but our conclusion is that such calculations are complex and need to remain so in order to be accurate. A precise valuation of Gap risk, the residual counterparty risk coming from the fact that the collateral posting is in the past and may be rather misaligned with current mark to market, calls for quite some modelling effort, as we have seen in detail. The attempt to standardize every risk to simple formulas is misleading and may result in the relevant risks not being addressed properly. The industry and regulators might adopt a more realistic approach by acknowledging the complexity of counterparty risk pricing, even under collateralization, and work to attain the necessary methodological and technological prowess rather than trying to bypass it.

There is no easy way out.

16 Including Margining Costs in Collateralized Contracts

This chapter is based on Pallavicini, Perini and Brigo (2011, 2012) [165, 196].

In Chapters 13 and 15 we analyzed many features of trading under the ISDA Master Agreement. In particular, we introduced collateral management procedures. Yet, we did not deal with margining costs. Indeed, CSA agreements force the counterparties to accrue the collateral account at a specific rate, which is usually linked to some market rates.

Here, we develop a risk-neutral evaluation methodology for Collateral-inclusive Bilateral (credit and debit) Valuation Adjusted (CBVA) price which we extend to include margining costs as done in [165]. We refer the reader to Chapter 13 for an extensive discussion of market considerations and of collateral mechanics, and to [41] and Chapter 15 to view an analysis of credit valuation adjustments on interest rate swaps in the presence of different collateralization strategies.

In order to price a derivative, we have to discount all the cash flows occurring after the trading position is entered, and, in particular, we have to include all cash flows required by the collateral margining procedure. Notice that we discount cash flows by using the risk-free discount factor $D(t, T)$, since all costs are included as additional cash flows rather than ad hoc spreads.

As in previous chapters, we refer to the two names involved in the financial contract and subject to default risk as the *Investor* (also called "I", or at times the Bank "B") and the *Counterparty* (also called "C" or at times the Corporate). In cases where the portfolio exchanged by the two parties is also a default sensitive instrument, we introduce a third name referring to the underlying reference credit of that portfolio (also called name "U").

We denote by τ_I, and τ_C (and τ_U) respectively the default times of the investor and counterparty (and underlying entity). We fix the portfolio time horizon $T \in \mathbb{R}^+$, and fix the risk-neutral pricing model $(\Omega, \mathcal{G}, \mathbb{Q})$, with a filtration $(\mathcal{G}_t)_{t\in[0,T]}$ such that τ_C, τ_I (and τ_U) are $\mathcal{G}$-stopping times. We denote by $\mathbb{E}_t$ the conditional expectation under $\mathbb{Q}$ given $\mathcal{G}_t$, and by $\mathbb{E}_{\tau_i}$ the conditional expectation under $\mathbb{Q}$ given the stopped filtration $\mathcal{G}_{\tau_i}$. We exclude the possibility of simultaneous defaults, and define the first default event between the two parties as the stopping time

$$\tau := \tau_C \wedge \tau_I.$$

The main result for the present chapter is the pricing equation (CBVA price) for a deal inclusive of counterparty credit risk (CVA and DVA) *and margining costs.*

The CBVA-adjusted price $\bar{V}_t$ of a derivative contract, which is derived in the following sections, is given by

$$\begin{aligned}\bar{V}_t(C) = \mathbb{E}_t\left[\Pi(t, T \wedge \tau) + \gamma(t, T \wedge \tau; C)\right] \\ +\mathbb{E}_t\left[\mathbf{1}_{\{\tau<T\}} D(t, \tau)\theta_{\tau}(C, \varepsilon)\right]\end{aligned} \tag{16.1}$$

where:

- $\Pi(t, T)$, as in previous chapters, is the sum of all discounted payoff terms in the interval $(t, T]$ when neglecting credit risk of "I" and "C", collateral, and margining costs;
- $\gamma(t, T; C)$ are the collateral margining costs within such interval, C being the collateral account,
- $\theta_\tau(C, \varepsilon)$ is the on-default cash flow, ε being the value of the underlying payoff to the surviving party at the default event by the other party (close-out amount), as seen from "I".

The margining procedure dictates the dynamics of the collateral account C_t, while the close-out amount ε_t is defined by the specific Credit Support Annex (CSA) holding between the counterparties. Common strategies, as we will see later on, may link the values of such processes to the price of the derivative itself, transforming the previous definition into a *recursive* equation. This feature will be crucial also in Chapter 17 when funding and investing rates will be introduced.

In the following sections we re-derive and extend the pricing equations from Chapter 13 by introducing margining costs.

16.1 TRADING UNDER THE ISDA MASTER AGREEMENT

We saw in Chapter 13, the ISDA Master Agreement lists two different tools to reduce counterparty credit risk: collateralization by a margining procedure and close-out netting rules. Both tools are ruled by the CSA holding between the counterparties of the deal.

Collateralization means the right of recourse to some asset of value that can be sold, or the value of which can be applied as a guarantee in the event of default on the transaction. Close-out netting rules apply when a default occurs, and force multiple obligations towards a counterparty to be consolidated into a single net obligation before recovery is applied.

Here, we briefly describe these tools to analyze the margining costs required by the collateral posting procedure, and to integrate their price within our subsequent funding costs model, leading eventually to calculate the Collateral-inclusive Bilateral Valuation Adjusted (CBVA) price $\bar{V}_t(C; 0)$, where 0 means we are not including funding costs yet. In the next chapter we will indeed derive a pricing equation for $\bar{V}_t(C; F)$, inclusive of funding costs.

16.1.1 Collateral Accrual Rates

A margining procedure consists in a pre-fixed set of dates during the life of a deal when both parties post or withdraw collateral amounts, according to their current exposure, to or from an account held by the collateral taker. A realistic margining practice should allow for collateral posting only on a fixed time-grid ($\mathcal{T}_c := \{t_1, \ldots, t_n\}$), and for the presence of independent amounts, minimum transfer amounts, thresholds, and so on, as described in [41]. Here, we extend the framework of Section 13.2 to include collateral accrual rates.

We recall that the collateral account C_t is held by the investor if $C_t > 0$ (the investor is the collateral taker), and by the counterparty if $C_t < 0$ (the counterparty is the collateral taker). If at time t the investor posts some collateral we write $dC_t < 0$, and the other way round if the counterparty is posting.

The CSA agreement holding between the counterparties ensures that the collateral taker remunerates the account at a particular accrual rate. We introduce the collateral accrual rates,[1] namely $c_t^+(T)$ when collateral assets are taken by the investor, and $c_t^-(T)$ in the other case, as adapted processes. Furthermore, we define the (collateral) zero-coupon bonds $P_t^{c^\pm}(T)$ as given by

$$P_t^{c^\pm}(T) := \frac{1}{1 + (T - t)c_t^\pm(T)}.$$

It is also useful to introduce the effective collateral accrual rate $\tilde{c}_t$ defined as

$$\tilde{c}_t(T) := c_t^-(T)\mathbf{1}_{\{C_t<0\}} + c_t^+(T)\mathbf{1}_{\{C_t>0\}}, \tag{16.2}$$

and the corresponding zero-coupon bond

$$P_t^{\tilde{c}}(T) := \frac{1}{1 + (T - t)\tilde{c}_t(T)}.$$

16.1.2 Collateral Management and Margining Costs

We assume that interest accrued by the collateral account is saved in the account itself, so that it can be directly included into close-out and margining procedures. Thus, any cash flow due to collateral costs or accruing interests can be dropped from our explicit list, since it can be considered as a flow within each counterparty.

We start by listing all cash flows originating from the investor and going to the counterparty if default events do not occur:

1. The Investor opens the account at the first margining date t_1 if $C_{t_1} < 0$ (the counterparty "C" is the collateral taker);
2. The Investor posts to, or withdraws from, the account at each t_k, as long as $C_{t_k} < 0$ (i.e. as long as the counterparty is the collateral taker), by considering a collateral account's growth at CSA rate $c_{t_k}^-(t_{k+1})$ between posting dates;
3. The Investor closes the account at the last margining date t_m if $C_{t_m} < 0$.

The counterparty considers the same cash flows for opposite values of the collateral account at each margining date. Hence, we can sum all such contributions. If we do not take into account default events, we define the sum of (discounted) margining cash flows occurring within the time interval A with $t_a := \inf\{A\}$ as given by

$$\begin{aligned}
\Gamma(A; \mathcal{T}_c, C) := {} & \mathbf{1}_{\{t_1\in A\}} C_{t_1}^- D(t_a, t_1) - \mathbf{1}_{\{t_n \in A\}} C_{t_n}^- D(t_a, t_n) \\
& - \sum_{k=1}^{n-1} \mathbf{1}_{\{t_{k+1}\in A\}} \left(C_{t_k}^- \frac{1}{P_{t_k}^{c^-}(t_{k+1})} - C_{t_{k+1}}^- \right) D(t_a, t_{k+1}) \\
& + \mathbf{1}_{\{t_1\in A\}} C_{t_1}^+ D(t_a, t_1) - \mathbf{1}_{\{t_n \in A\}} C_{t_n}^+ D(t_a, t_n) \\
& - \sum_{k=1}^{n-1} \mathbf{1}_{\{t_{k+1}\in A\}} \left(C_{t_k}^+ \frac{1}{P_{t_k}^{c^+}(t_{k+1})} - C_{t_{k+1}}^+ \right) D(t_a, t_{k+1}),
\end{aligned}$$

[1] With a slight abuse of notation we use plus and minus signs to indicate which rate is used to accrue collateral according to the collateral account sign, and *not* to indicate that rates are positive or negative parts of some other rate.

We can rearrange the previous equation by summing, when possible, positive and negative parts to obtain

$$\Gamma(A;\mathcal{T}_c,C)=\sum_{k=1}^{n-1}\mathbf{1}_{\{t_k\in A\}}\left(C_{t_k}D(t_a,t_k)-C^-_{t_k}\frac{D(t_a,t_{k+1})}{P^{c^-}_{t_k}(t_{k+1})}-C^+_{t_k}\frac{D(t_a,t_{k+1})}{P^{c^+}_{t_k}(t_{k+1})}\right)$$
$$+\sum_{k=1}^{n-1}\left(\mathbf{1}_{\{t_k\in A\}}-\mathbf{1}_{\{t_{k+1}\in A\}}\right)\left(C^-_{t_k}\frac{D(t_a,t_{k+1})}{P^{c^-}_{t_k}(t_{k+1})}+C^+_{t_k}\frac{D(t_a,t_{k+1})}{P^{c^+}_{t_k}(t_{k+1})}\right).$$

Now we calculate the previous expression in the following case: we consider the time interval $A(t,T;\tau)$ which goes from t to $\tau\wedge T$, it contains t, and if $T<\tau$ it is closed on the right, thereby containing T, otherwise it is open on the right, thereby not containing τ. Such intervals can be expressed in formula by

$$A(t,T;\tau):=\{u:t\le u\le T<\tau\}\cup\{u:t\le u<\tau\le T\}=[t,\ \min(\tau^-,T)]$$

with $t\le t_1$. The last representation is meant to be informal. We focus on the margining cash flows within $A(t,T;\tau)$, and we define $\bar{\Gamma}$ by

$$\begin{aligned}\bar{\Gamma}(t,T;C)&:=\Gamma(A(t,T;\tau);\mathcal{T}_c,C)\\&=\sum_{k=1}^{n-1}\mathbf{1}_{\{t_k<\tau\}}\left(D(t,t_k)C_{t_k}-D(t,t_{k+1})\mu(t_k,t_{k+1})\right)\\&\quad+\sum_{k=1}^{n-1}\mathbf{1}_{\{t_k<\tau\le t_{k+1}\}}D(t,t_{k+1})\mu(t_k,t_{k+1}),\end{aligned}\tag{16.3}$$

where $\mu(t_k,t_{k+1})$ is the value of the collateral account accrued from date t_k to date t_{k+1} as required by the CSA holding between the investor and the counterparty, namely

$$\mu(t_k,t_{k+1}):=\frac{C^-_{t_k}}{P^{c^-}_{t_k}(t_{k+1})}+\frac{C^+_{t_k}}{P^{c^+}_{t_k}(t_{k+1})}.$$

Hence we can take the risk-neutral expectation of both sides of the Equation (16.3) to calculate the price of all margining cash flows, and we obtain

$$\mathbb{E}_t\left[\bar{\Gamma}(t,T;C)\right]=\mathbb{E}_t\left[\gamma(t,T\wedge\tau;C)+\mathbf{1}_{\{\tau<T\}}D(t,\tau)C_{\tau^-}\right],$$

where the margining costs $\gamma(t,T\wedge\tau;C)$ are defined as

$$\gamma(t,T\wedge\tau;C):=\sum_{k=1}^{n-1}\mathbf{1}_{\{t_k<T\wedge\tau\}}D(t,t_k)C_{t_k}\left(1-\frac{P_{t_k}(t_{k+1})}{P^{\tilde{c}}_{t_k}(t_{k+1})}\right),\tag{16.4}$$

and we introduce the pre-default value C_{τ^-} of the collateral account as given by

$$C_{\tau^-}:=\sum_{k=1}^{n-1}\mathbf{1}_{\{t_k<\tau\le t_{k+1}\}}C_{t_k}\frac{P_\tau(t_{k+1})}{P^{\tilde{c}}_{t_k}(t_{k+1})}.\tag{16.5}$$

In the following, to simplify notation, we usually write $\mathbf{1}_{\{\tau<u\}}$ instead of $\mathbf{1}_{\{\tau\le u\}}$, since we are assuming that the probability that the default event happens at a particular time is zero. More specifically, we assume the distribution of the random variable τ to be continuous so that $\mathbb{Q}(\tau=u)=0$ for all $u\ge 0$.

Notice that we can safely assume that $t \leq t_1$ in the present derivation of margining costs, since we are evaluating the price adjustment due to the whole collateralization procedure, comprising all margining dates. In the following, when calculating the price of the contract at a future time following t_1, we will not need to consider $t > t_1$ and repeat the current derivation. It will be enough simply to adjust the contract's price for the margining costs defined in (16.4) and occurring after t.

Remark 16.1.1 ***(Pre-default collateral account and re-hypothecation)*** *The pre-default value C_{τ^-} of the collateral account is used by the CSA to calculate close-out netted exposures, and it can be different from the actual value of the collateral account at the default event, since some collateral assets (or all) might be re-hypothecated. Indeed, according to section 13.1.3, when applying close-out netting rules, first we will net the exposure against C_{τ^-}, then we will treat any remaining collateral as an unsecured claim.*

16.2 CBVA GENERAL FORMULA WITH MARGINING COSTS

The occurrence of a default event gives the parties the right to terminate all transactions that are included under the relevant ISDA Master Agreement. The ISDA Master Agreement sets forth the mechanism of close-out netting to be enforced. The surviving party should evaluate the terminated transactions to claim for a reimbursement after the application of netting rules consolidating the transactions, inclusive of collateral accounts.

Thus, if we follow the same line of reasoning of Section 13.2, but we consider also the margining costs, we obtain after straightforward manipulations the sum of discounted cash flows due to the derivative contract and to the margining procedure,

$$
\begin{aligned}
&\bar{\Pi}(t,T;C) := \\
&\quad \Pi(t,T\wedge\tau) + \bar{\Gamma}(t,T;C) \\
&\quad + \mathbf{1}_{\{\tau=\tau_C<T\}} D(t,\tau) \mathbf{1}_{\{\varepsilon_{I,\tau}<0\}} \mathbf{1}_{\{C_{\tau^-}>0\}} (\varepsilon_{I,\tau} - C_{\tau^-}) \\
&\quad + \mathbf{1}_{\{\tau=\tau_C<T\}} D(t,\tau) \mathbf{1}_{\{\varepsilon_{I,\tau}<0\}} \mathbf{1}_{\{C_{\tau^-}<0\}} ((\varepsilon_{I,\tau} - C_{\tau^-})^- + \mathrm{REC}'_C(\varepsilon_{I,\tau} - C_{\tau^-})^+) \\
&\quad + \mathbf{1}_{\{\tau=\tau_C<T\}} D(t,\tau) \mathbf{1}_{\{\varepsilon_{I,\tau}>0\}} \mathbf{1}_{\{C_{\tau^-}>0\}} ((\varepsilon_{I,\tau} - C_{\tau^-})^- + \mathrm{REC}_C(\varepsilon_{I,\tau} - C_{\tau^-})^+) \\
&\quad + \mathbf{1}_{\{\tau=\tau_C<T\}} D(t,\tau) \mathbf{1}_{\{\varepsilon_{I,\tau}>0\}} \mathbf{1}_{\{C_{\tau^-}<0\}} (\mathrm{REC}_C \varepsilon_{I,\tau} - \mathrm{REC}'_C C_{\tau^-}) \\
&\quad + \mathbf{1}_{\{\tau=\tau_I<T\}} D(t,\tau) \mathbf{1}_{\{\varepsilon_{C,\tau}>0\}} \mathbf{1}_{\{C_{\tau^-}<0\}} (\varepsilon_{C,\tau} - C_{\tau^-}) \\
&\quad + \mathbf{1}_{\{\tau=\tau_I<T\}} D(t,\tau) \mathbf{1}_{\{\varepsilon_{C,\tau}>0\}} \mathbf{1}_{\{C_{\tau^-}>0\}} ((\varepsilon_{C,\tau} - C_{\tau^-})^+ + \mathrm{REC}'_I(\varepsilon_{C,\tau} - C_{\tau^-})^-) \\
&\quad + \mathbf{1}_{\{\tau=\tau_I<T\}} D(t,\tau) \mathbf{1}_{\{\varepsilon_{C,\tau}<0\}} \mathbf{1}_{\{C_{\tau^-}<0\}} ((\varepsilon_{C,\tau} - C_{\tau^-})^+ + \mathrm{REC}_I(\varepsilon_{C,\tau} - C_{\tau^-})^-) \\
&\quad + \mathbf{1}_{\{\tau=\tau_I<T\}} D(t,\tau) \mathbf{1}_{\{\varepsilon_{C,\tau}<0\}} \mathbf{1}_{\{C_{\tau^-}>0\}} (\mathrm{REC}_I \varepsilon_{C,\tau} - \mathrm{REC}'_I C_{\tau^-}).
\end{aligned}
$$

We define the CBVA adjusted price in the presence of margining costs $\bar{V}_t(C;0)$, but without considering funding and investing costs, by taking the risk-neutral expectation of the previous equation, and we get:

$$
\begin{aligned}
\bar{V}_t(C;0) :&= \mathbb{E}_t\left[\bar{\Pi}(t,T;C)\right] \\
&= \mathbb{E}_t\left[\Pi(t,T\wedge\tau) + \gamma(t,T\wedge\tau;C) + \mathbf{1}_{\{\tau<T\}} D(t,\tau)\theta_\tau(C,\varepsilon)\right]
\end{aligned} \tag{16.6}
$$

where we define the on-default cash flow $\theta_\tau(C,\varepsilon)$ as given by

$$
\begin{aligned}
\theta_\tau(C,\varepsilon) :=\; & \mathbf{1}_{\{\tau=\tau_C<\tau_I\}} \left(\varepsilon_{I,\tau} - \mathrm{LGD}_C(\varepsilon^+_{I,\tau} - C^+_{\tau^-})^+ - \mathrm{LGD}'_C(\varepsilon^-_{I,\tau} - C^-_{\tau^-})^+\right) \\
& + \mathbf{1}_{\{\tau=\tau_I<\tau_C\}} \left(\varepsilon_{C,\tau} - \mathrm{LGD}_I(\varepsilon^-_{C,\tau} - C^-_{\tau^-})^- - \mathrm{LGD}'_I(\varepsilon^+_{C,\tau} - C^+_{\tau^-})^-\right)
\end{aligned}
$$

namely to price a deal (without funding costs) we have to sum up three components: (i) deal cash flows, (ii) margining costs, and (iii) close-out amount reduced by the CVA/DVA contribution.

The above derivation can be found in [165], and it is consistent with Equation (13.2). Indeed, we can recover the CBVA expression if we remove margining costs, namely if we set γ equal to zero.

16.2.1 Perfect Collateralization

As an example of the CBVA pricing formula we consider the case of perfect collateralization, which we define as given by collateralization in continuous time, with continuous mark-to-market of the portfolio at default events, and with the collateral account inclusive of margining costs at any time u, namely

$$C_u \doteq \mathbb{E}_u\left[\Pi(u,T) + \gamma(u,T;C)\right],$$

with close-out amount evaluated as the collateral price, so that

$$\varepsilon_{I,\tau} \doteq \varepsilon_{C,\tau} \doteq C_{\tau}.$$

Then, from the CBVA price Equation (16.6) we get

$$\begin{aligned}\bar{V}_t(C;0) &= \mathbb{E}_t\left[\Pi(t,T\wedge\tau) + \gamma(t,T\wedge\tau;C) + \mathbf{1}_{\{\tau<T\}}D(t,\tau)C_\tau\right]\\ &= \mathbb{E}_t\left[\Pi(t,T) + \gamma(t,T;C)\right]\\ &= C_t.\end{aligned}$$

We thus obtain that under perfect collateralization, namely collateralization in continuous time, with continuous mark-to-market of the portfolio in time (and at the default event in particular, i.e. without instantaneous contagion), and with collateral account inclusive of margining costs at any time, we obtain

$$\bar{V}_t(C;0) = C_t.$$

In this perfect collateralization case, we aim at characterizing the value of the deal in terms of the collateral rate and instrument cash flows. In order to do this, we take a brief detour in discrete time and then take the limit. Consider two margining dates t_k and t_{k+1}. By substituting the expression for margining cash flows we get (up to maturity)

$$\bar{V}_{t_k}(C;0) = \frac{P^{\tilde{c}}_{t_k}(t_{k+1})}{P_{t_k}(t_{k+1})}\mathbb{E}_{t_k}\left[D(t_k,t_{k+1})\bar{V}_{t_{k+1}}(C) + \Pi(t_k,t_{k+1})\right], \quad \bar{V}_{t_n}(C;0) = 0.$$

leading to, with $t_1 = t$,

$$\bar{V}_t(C;0) = \mathbb{E}_t\left[\sum_{k=1}^{n-1}\Pi(t_k,t_{k+1})D(t,t_k)\prod_{i=1}^{k}\frac{P^{\tilde{c}}_{t_i}(t_{i+1})}{P_{t_i}(t_{i+1})}\right].$$

Then, taking the limit of continuous collateralization, and using Equation (16.2), we obtain

$$\bar{V}_t(C;0) = \mathbb{E}_t\left[\int_t^T \Pi(u,u+du)\exp\left\{-\int_t^u dv\,\tilde{c}_v\right\}\right]. \tag{16.7}$$

We derive as an important special case that, in the case of perfect collateralization, we observe that valuation is obtained by discounting cash flows at the collateral rate $\tilde{c}_t$. In particular, the short rate r_t has disappeared from our discounted payout. Note that we had to assume total lack of contagion at default, and this is a quite unrealistic assumption.

Remark 16.2.1 ***(Alternative derivation)*** *The preceding example may be derived by taking the limit of continuous collateralization on the price equation without writing it in an iterative way. Indeed we can write:*

$$\bar{V}_t(C;0) = \mathbb{E}_t\left[\int_t^T D(t,u)\left(\Pi(u,u+du) + \bar{V}_u(C;0)(r_u - \tilde{c}_u)\,du\right)\right]$$

where r_t is the risk-free rate. Now, if we search for a solution for the form

$$\bar{V}_t(C;0) = \mathbb{E}_t\left[\int_t^T \Pi(u,u+du)\,\exp\left\{-\int_t^u dv\,x_v\right\}\right]$$

with x_t an adapted process, we obtain by direct integration a solution that is found for $x_t = \tilde{c}_t$, so that we obtain Equation (16.7).

16.2.2 Futures Contracts

Futures contracts are settled daily by requiring the investor to hold a margin account which is marked-to-market according to the daily gains or losses on the contract, but the counterparties do not accrue interests on the margin account. Thus, if we do not consider other peculiarities of the contract, such as the initial and maintenance margin, we can apply Equation 16.7 with $\tilde{c}_t = 0$, and we get

$$\bar{V}_t^{\text{futures}}(C;0) = \mathbb{E}_t\left[\int_t^T \Pi(u,u+du)\right],$$

which reproduces the usual formula used to price Futures contracts.

16.3 CHANGING THE COLLATERALIZATION CURRENCY

In this section we modify the CBVA master equation to deal with collaterals in foreign currency. We name the collateral account expressed in domestic currency as before with the symbol C_t, while we define the collateral account expressed in foreign currency as C_t^e, so we get

$$C_t := \chi_t C_t^e$$

with χ_t the exchange rate process that converts the foreign currency into the domestic one.

16.3.1 Margining Cost in Foreign Currency

We can safely substitute the collateral account C_t with such expression wherever we find it within the CBVA pricing equation, except in the expression for the collateral costs, where we have to take care of cash flow payment dates. Indeed, we have to rewrite Equation (16.3) as

$$\bar{\Gamma}(t,T;C) = \sum_{k=1}^{n-1} \mathbf{1}_{\{t_k<\tau\}}\left(D(t,t_k)\chi_{t_k}C_{t_k}^e - D(t,t_{k+1})\chi_{t_{k+1}}\mu^e(t_k,t_{k+1})\right)$$
$$+\sum_{k=1}^{n-1} \mathbf{1}_{\{t_k<\tau\le t_{k+1}\}} D(t,t_{k+1})\chi_{t_{k+1}}\mu^e(t_k,t_{k+1}), \qquad (16.8)$$

where we define $\mu^e(t_k, t_{k+1})$ as the value of the collateral account in foreign currency accrued from date t_k to date t_{k+1} as required by the CSA holding between the investor and the counterparty, namely

$$\mu^e(t_k, t_{k+1}) := \frac{C^{e,-}_{t_k}}{P^{c^-}_{t_k}(t_{k+1})} + \frac{C^{e,+}_{t_k}}{P^{c^+}_{t_k}(t_{k+1})}.$$

We can change the fixing time of the exchange rate by moving to the foreign risk-neutral measure, namely

$$\mathbb{E}_{t_k}\left[\chi_{t_{k+1}} D(t_k, t_{k+1})\right] = \mathbb{E}^e_{t_k}\left[\chi_{t_k} D^e(t_k, t_{k+1})\right] = \chi_{t_k} P^e_{t_k}(t_{k+1}),$$

where $D^e(t, T)$ and $P^e_t(T)$ are respectively the foreign risk-free discount factor and zero-coupon bond, and $\mathbb{E}^e_t[\,\cdot\,]$ is the foreign risk-neutral expectation. Thus, we can introduce the margining costs in domestic currency due to a collateralization in foreign currency as given by

$$\gamma(t, T \wedge \tau; C) := \sum_{k=1}^{n-1} \mathbf{1}_{\{t_k < T\wedge\tau\}} D(t, t_k)\chi_{t_k} C^e_{t_k}\left(1 - \frac{P^e_{t_k}(t_{k+1})}{P^{\tilde{c}}_{t_k}(t_{k+1})}\right) \tag{16.9}$$

and use such expression in place of (16.4) in our CBVA pricing equation.

In the case of perfect collateralization we can follow the approach as in the previous section, and after a straightforward calculation we obtain the result of [109], as a particular case of our framework. Indeed, we obtain the price of a claim under perfect collateralization in a foreign currency. This is given by

$$\bar{V}_t(C;0) = \mathbb{E}_t\left[\int_t^T \Pi(u, u+du)\exp\left\{-\int_t^u dv\,(\tilde{c}_v - r^e_v + r_v)\right\}\right] \tag{16.10}$$

consistently with [109]. Notice that we could obtain the above equation in a simpler way. First, we can apply Equation (16.7) to the foreign-currency contract $\bar{V}^e_t(C;0) := \bar{V}_t(C;0)\chi^{d,e}_t$, then we can change measure to the domestic risk-neutral one, and obtain (16.10).

16.3.2 Settlement Liquidity Risk

The pricing Equation (16.10) is valid for contracts collateralized in foreign currency, and it is based on the possibility of changing measure from the foreign risk-neutral measure to the domestic one. From a practical point of view this means that each counterparty can fund itself in foreign currency in the spot FX market without additional costs.

Yet, most domestic financial institutions cannot hold accounts directly with Central Banks of foreign states, so are forced to use the services of one or more custodian agents to hold their government and agency securities, see [15]. Moreover, domestic financial institutions may suffer constraints on borrowing in the uncollateralized foreign inter-bank market, if foreign financial institutions are less willing to lend money, due to increased counterparty risk or liquidity needs, see [9].

Thus, an additional basis due to such settlement liquidity risk should be added to discount factors appearing in the pricing Equation (16.10). Alternatively, as explained in [164], it is possible to model directly funding in foreign currency by using quoted FX swaps without introducing a foreign risk-neutral measure.

16.3.3 Gap Risk in Single-Currency Contracts with Foreign-Currency Collaterals

Counterparty credit risk may be mitigated by margining practice (CSA agreements), namely by using a collateral account as insurance against the counterparty's default. Yet, there are contracts that cannot be completely collateralized even with risk-free assets, since their mark-to-market value jumps at a default event. See Section 17.5.2 in the next chapter for details.

In particular, this happens for cross currency derivatives, e.g. cross currency swaps (CCS), if we allow the FX rate to jump when one of the counterparties has defaulted, as in [105]. Yet, even in the case of a single-currency contract, if collateral assets are expressed in a foreign currency, we can encounter such a problem, which might invalidate the possibility of a perfect collateralization.

16.4 CONCLUSIONS

We discussed how to introduce margining costs within CBVA pricing equations. We analyzed relevant examples and re-derived in our framework some facts already known in the literature. In particular, we studied the problem of perfectly collateralized contracts between risky counterparties, and we obtained as a consequence the pricing equation for future contracts. We covered also the issues of foreign-currency collateralization. This is the case of perfectly collateralized contracts between two risky counterparties when the collateral's currency is different from the deal's currency.

We continue in the next chapter with the last element of our framework that we need to complete the picture: the Funding Valuation Adjustment.

17

Funding Valuation Adjustment (FVA)?

This chapter is based on Pallavicini, Perini, and Brigo (2011, 2012) [165, 196].

We approach the conclusion of the book by presenting the results of [165] and [195]. Here we derive a collateral-inclusive counterparty credit and debit valuation adjusted pricing equation, which allows us to price a deal while taking into account credit and debit valuation adjustments (CVA, DVA) along with margining and, finally, funding costs, all in a consistent way. We find that the equation has a recursive form, making the introduction of a purely additive funding valuation adjustment (FVA) to be added on top of CVA (and possibly DVA) difficult. Yet, we can cast the pricing equation into a set of iterative relationships which can be solved by means of standard least-square Monte Carlo techniques. As a consequence, we find that identifying funding costs FVA and debit valuation adjustments DVA is not tenable in general, contrary to what has been suggested in the literature in simple cases. We will say more on this important point shortly, and we will discuss also the claim "FVA = 0".

We define a comprehensive framework that allows us to derive earlier results on funding or counterparty risk as a special case, although our framework is more than the sum of such special cases. We derive the general pricing equation by resorting to a risk-neutral approach. We consider realistic settings and include in our models the common market practices suggested by ISDA documentation, without assuming restrictive constraints on margining procedures and close-out netting rules. In particular, we allow for asymmetric collateral and funding rates, and exogenous liquidity policies and hedging strategies. Re-hypothecation liquidity risk and close-out amount evaluation issues are also covered. Finally, relevant examples of non-trivial settings illustrate how to derive known facts about discounting curves from a robust general framework and without resorting to ad hoc hypotheses.

We need to warn the reader that this is possibly the most advanced part of the book, and the one we developed most recently. As such, it is still in evolution, and we are researching this area further right now.[1] Hence this chapter should be read with the attitude that it is still very much a work in progress, even though, as we mentioned above, we will derive most of the known facts on funding as special cases.

A final note is that we will also consider funding costs in Chapter 18, although we will do so in the special case of longevity swaps as underlying instrument.

17.1 DEALING WITH COSTS OF FUNDING

Cost of funding has become a paramount topic in the industry. One just has to look at the number of presentations and streams at modelling conferences of 2011–2012 that deal with this topic to realize how much research effort is being put into it. And yet literature is still in its infancy and there is very little published material, which is mostly anecdotal and not general.

[1] This is for example the reason why the paper [196] in the bibliography does not follow the alphabetical order in the list of references.

Funding costs are linked to collateral modelling, which in turn has a strong impact on credit and debit valuation adjustments (CVA and DVA). While there are several papers that try to deal with these effects separately, very few try to build a consistent framework where all such aspects can exist together in a consistent way. Our aim in this chapter is to build such a framework.

17.1.1 Central Clearing, CCPs and this Book

We are witnessing a relevant debate on the expected impact of central clearing, especially following the current regulatory pressure stemming from BASEL III, EMIR and Dodd-Frank. It is natural that CCPs will impact the themes of this book. However, the theory we develop can be applied also in presence of CCPs to value aspects such as contagion, Gap risk, concentration risk, finding the right initial margins, haircuts, and so on. We only devote simple specific examples to pricing funding costs with CCPs in this chapter, but the general theory of the book is much more powerful than what can be seen in that example. In any case, initial and variation margins are not a panacea, as our past examples on Gap risk and wrong way risk highlighted, and dealing with several potential CCPs will be all but trivial, setting the scene for analytics similar to those we develop in this book.

17.1.2 High Level Features

We list the high level features of the approach of [165] and [196]. Then, we move on introducing more specific aspects of their theory.

17.1.2.1 A Risk-Neutral Approach

We adopt a risk-neutral approach.[2] Our theory is essentially risk neutral and we do not add other bank accounts, i.e. other locally risk-free assets that evolve according to different rates (see for example [85]). In a free market this would immediately lead to arbitrage, but one can live with different bank accounts if one assumes market segmentation. Rather than assuming that funding risk is embedded into different discounting and measures paradigms from the start, we add collateral, treasury and hedgers funding fees as explicit cash flows (such as for example φ below). Different discounting and different measures (such as for example $\mathbb{E}^{\tilde{f}}$ below) may emerge later, but simply as computational tools, not as real financial issues. Our approach offers a clear explanation of the fact that we do not need to change the pricing theory, that remains the classical risk-neutral theory, to account for funding costs. Our key message is that one does not need to change the theory but just the payout.[3]

17.1.2.2 Overnight Rates are not Risk-Free Rates

Another high level feature of our approach is that the risk-free instantaneous spot rate r_t associated with the bank account is not forced to be an approximate market rate. Our distinction

[2] We are grateful to Stéphane Crépey for helpful correspondence on this issue.

[3] This implicitly responds also to the FVA debate on the press, see for example "The FVA debate continues: Hull and White respond to their critics", Risk Magazine, October 2012 issue. In the light of our general result, already published in 2011 in [165], this looks like a storm in a teacup. We will show that a hypothetical FVA vanishes only under very special and unrealistic assumptions, including a quite inert role of the treasury in the bank, see Section 17.5.4.

between market and theoretical quantities is sharp and we never claim the (false) fact that overnight rates (such as EONIA) are risk free. The risk-free rate is always r_t and is just an instrumental variable that vanishes if funding and hedging are accomplished through concrete market instruments, as we shall see.

17.1.2.3 Keeping Treasury and Trading Activities Distinct

A different high-level aspect of our approach is that we clearly distinguish trading desk operations and treasury operations and we do not mix up such terms at close-out level (at the first default event if this happens before the final maturity of the deal) without discussing how the treasury rate emerges. The Trading and Treasury worlds are clearly connected only through the treasury rates $\tilde{f}_t$, depending in particular on the bank liquidity policy.

17.1.2.4 Funding a Trade Means Funding its Hedging Strategy

An important high level feature of our approach is that for us a price is real only if it is backed by a hedge, and the hedge is the concrete object to the trader. This is not to say that no arbitrage necessarily needs replication to be defined, since there are approaches to no-arbitrage that do not require replication. However, to back a price in practice one needs a hedge. Hence funding a product means, in our opinion, really funding its hedging strategy. This is why we put emphasis on the hedging portfolio in this chapter. Of course the case where the trader has an almost perfect hedge is rare. In some cases, when the trader is not sure, she will try an approximate hedge but in general will not stand still and wait. This is why we focus on hedging.

17.1.2.5 Pricing and Perspective

Because one entity cannot know in detail the funding policy of another entity, inclusion of funding cannot be bilateral in a valuation procedure. This means that the price of a deal between two parties will be different for the two parties. Our master formula, inclusive of funding costs, can be applied, with different funding inputs, by different parties involved in the deal, for example the bank treasury or the specific trading desk. An important point to realize is that, in general, the trader will not be able to charge its funding costs to the counterparty in the deal, and this is a further reason why the price becomes perspective-dependent. In general the trader may include funding costs into the analysis and obtain a price she may book in her system, and this price also contains the treasury costs of setting up and maintaining the deal, but the actual price that will be charged to the counterparty will not be this price. Similarly, the trader treasury may compute a different price, where the funding component is not present since this is charged to the trading desk. This is a simplistic example but helps clarifying the perspectival nature of the price we obtain. If debit valuation adjustment represents the (dubious) possibility to maintain agreement on the price of a deal when including credit risk, with funding the symmetry breaks for good and there is no longer a point in pursuing a unique price for the two parties. Different approaches can be used, but a general characterization of the relevant equilibrium is beyond the scope of this book.

17.1.3 Single-Deal (Micro) vs. Homogeneous (Macro) Funding Models

When dealing with funding costs, one has to first make a decision on whether to take a single deal (micro) or homogeneous (macro) cost view.

The micro approach can deal with funding costs that are deal specific. It is also an approach that distinguishes between funding and investing in terms of returns since in general different spreads will be applied when borrowing or lending. This is not the unique possibility, however, and typically treasury departments in banks work differently. One could assume an average cost of funding (borrowing) to be applied to all deals, and an average return for investing (lending). This macro approach would lead to two curves that would hold for all funding costs and invested amounts respectively, regardless of the specific deal, but depending on the sign of the exposures.

One can go further with the homogeneity assumption and assume that the cost of investing and the cost of funding match, so that spreads are not only the same across deals, but are equal to each other, implying a common funding (borrowing) and investing (lending) macro spread. In practice the spread would be set by the treasury at a common value for borrowing or lending, and this value would match what is expected to go on across all deals on average. This homogeneous average approach would look at a unique funding/lending spread for the bank treasury to be applied to all products traded by capital markets. The homogeneous approach is assumed for example in initial works such as [108] and [168].

In this chapter we stay as general as possible and therefore assume a micro view, but of course it is enough to collapse our variables to common values to obtain any of the large pool approaches.

We also point out that the micro *vs.* macro approaches view the treasury department in very different ways. In the micro model the treasury takes a very active role in looking at funding costs and becomes an operations centre. In the homogeneous model the treasury takes more the role of a central supporting department for the bank operations. The second view is prevailing at the moment, but we point out that it is more difficult to implement absence of arbitrage in that framework.

17.1.4 Previous Literature on Funding and Collateral

The fundamental impact of collateralization on default risk and on CVA and DVA has been analyzed in [79] and more recently in [41] and [40]. The works [41] and [40] look at CVA and DVA Gap risk under several collateralization strategies, with or without re-hypothecation, as a function of the margining frequency, with wrong way risk and with possible instantaneous contagion. Minimum threshold amounts and minimum transfer amounts are also considered. We cite also Chapter 1 of this book for a list of frequently asked questions on the subject.

Funding implications in presence of default risk have been considered in [157] and [74]. These works focus on particularly simple products, such as zero coupon bonds or loans, in order to highlight some essential features of funding costs.

The paper [109] analyzes implications of currency risk for collateral modelling. Their results are also derived in a different framework in [165, 196].

An initial stylized analysis of the problem of replication of derivative transactions under collateralization but without default risk and in a purely classical Black and Scholes framework has been considered in [168] and [169]. Introduction of collateral modelling in a world without default risk is questionable, since the main role of collateral is indeed serving as a guarantee against such risk.

The above references constitute a beginning for the funding cost literature but do not have the level of generality needed to include all the above features in a consistent framework that can then be used to manage complex products. A general theory is still missing. The only exceptions so far are [65, 66], who however do not deal with the hidden complexities of collateral modelling and mark-to-market discontinuities at default. Furthermore, by resorting to a PDE approach, [65] and [66] are unrealistically constrained to low dimensional situations. The other general result is [85] and is more promising and general, although it does not allow for credit instruments in the basic portfolio.

Our approach to introducing a general framework follows [165, 196], and it takes into account our past research on bilateral counterparty risk, collateral, re-hypothecation and wrong way risk across asset classes. We then add cost of funding consistently, completing the picture and building a comprehensive general framework that includes earlier results as special cases. In particular, we present four examples to highlight the properties of the general pricing equation we have derived. We analyze in particular

1. Default risk but perfect collateral. This is the case of a perfect collateralized contract between two risky counterparties in presence of funding costs;
2. CCP. This is the case of a central counterparty (CCP) pricing a collateralized contract between two risky counterparties, possibly in presence of Gap risk; and
3. No collateral. This is the case of a risky investor evaluating counterparty credit risk on a uncollateralized deal.
4. No collateral for positive payoffs. This is the case studied in [157] and [74].

17.1.5 Including FVA along with Credit and Debit Valuation Adjustment

When including funding costs one has to make a number of choices. We already pointed out above that the first choice is whether to take a bottom-up view at single deal level or a large pool view. We adopt the former because it is more general, but most of the initial literature on funding takes the latter view, in line with current operational guidelines for treasury departments. Clearly the latter view is a particular case of the former, so that we are actually dealing with both views.

When we try and include the cost of funding in the valuation of a deal we face a difficult situation. The deal future cash flows will depend on the funding choices that will be done in the future, and pricing those cash flows today involves modelling the future funding decisions. The dependence in not additively decomposable in the same way as credit valuation and debit valuation adjustments are in the case with no funding costs.

This leads to a recursive valuation equation that is quite difficult to implement, especially when dealing with products that are path dependent, since one needs at the same time backward induction and forward simulation. The recursion has been found also with different approaches, see for example [85] and [65].

17.1.6 FVA is not DVA

In this sense it is too much to expect that funding costs can be accounted for by a simple Funding Valuation Adjustment (FVA) term. Such a term can be defined formally but would not add up with CVA and DVA terms in a simple way. A further consequence of the recursive nature of funding costs is that it is in general wrong to identify FVA and DVA. While this happens in some very special cases, see for example [157], it does not hold in general.

17.2 COLLATERAL- AND FUNDING-INCLUSIVE BILATERAL VALUATION ADJUSTED PRICE

Here, we develop a risk-neutral evaluation methodology for the Collateral-inclusive Bilateral Valuation Adjusted (CBVA) price which we extend to cover the case of Collateral- and Funding-inclusive Bilateral Valuation Adjusted (CFBVA) price by including funding costs as done in [165, 196]. Here "Bilateral" refers to having default times for both parties in the formula, and not to the price being symmetric. Along the way, we highlight the relevant market standards and agreements which we follow to derive such formulae. We refer the reader to [41] for an extensive discussion of market considerations and of collateral mechanics, which also includes an analysis of credit valuation adjustments on interest rate swaps in presence of different collateralization strategies.

In order to price a derivative, we have to discount all the cash flows occurring after the trading position is entered. We can group them as follows:

1. derivative cash flows (e.g. coupons, dividends, etc . . .) inclusive of hedging instruments;
2. cash flows required by the collateral margining procedure;
3. cash flows required by the funding and investing procedures;
4. cash flows occurring on default events.

Notice that we discount cash flows by using the risk-free discount factor $D(t, T)$, since all costs are included as additional cash flows rather than ad hoc spreads.

We refer to the two names involved in the financial contract and subject to default risk as *investor* (also called name I) and *counterparty* (also called name C). In cases where the portfolio exchanged by the two parties is also a default sensitive instrument, we introduce a third name referring to the underlying reference credit of that portfolio (also called name U).

We denote by τ_I,and τ_C respectively the default times of the investor and counterparty. We fix the portfolio time horizon $T \in \mathbb{R}^+$, and fix the risk-neutral pricing model $(\Omega, \mathcal{G}, \mathbb{Q})$, with a filtration $(\mathcal{G}_t)_{t\in[0,T]}$ such that τ_C, τ_I are $\mathcal{G}$-stopping times. We denote by $\mathbb{E}_t$ the conditional expectation under $\mathbb{Q}$ given $\mathcal{G}_t$, and by $\mathbb{E}_{\tau_i}$ the conditional expectation under $\mathbb{Q}$ given the stopped filtration $\mathcal{G}_{\tau_i}$. We exclude the possibility of simultaneous defaults, and define the first default event between the two parties as the stopping time

$$\tau := \tau_C \wedge \tau_I.$$

The main result of the present chapter is the pricing equation (CFBVA price) for a deal inclusive of counterparty credit risk (CVA and DVA), margining costs, and funding and investing costs.

The CFBVA price $\bar{V}_t$ of a derivative contract, which is derived in the following sections, is given by

$$\begin{aligned} \bar{V}_t(C; F) = \mathbb{E}_t\left[\Pi(t, T\wedge\tau) + \gamma(t, T\wedge\tau; C) + \varphi(t, T\wedge\tau; F)\right] \\ +\mathbb{E}_t\left[\mathbf{1}_{\{\tau<T\}} D(t,\tau)\theta_\tau(C,\varepsilon)\right] \end{aligned} \tag{17.1}$$

where

- $\Pi(t, T)$ is the sum of all discounted payoff terms in the interval $(t, T]$,
- $\gamma(t, T; C)$ are the collateral margining costs within such interval, C being the collateral account,

- $\varphi(t, T; F)$ the funding and investing costs within such interval, F being the cash account needed for trading, and
- $\theta_\tau(C, \varepsilon)$ the on-default cash flow, ε being the amount of losses or costs the surviving party would incur upon a default event (close-out amount).

The margining procedure and the liquidity policy dictate respectively the dynamics of the collateral account C_t and of the cash account F_t, while the close-out amount ε_t is defined by the CSA holding between the counterparties. Common strategies, as we will see later on, may link the values of such processes to the price of the derivative itself, transforming the previous definition into a *recursive* equation. This feature is hidden in simplified approaches based on adding a spread to the discount curve to accommodate collateral and funding costs. A different approach is followed by [85] and [65] where the usual risk-neutral evaluation framework is extended to include many cash accounts accruing at different rates. Yet, a similar structure for the derivative price is obtained as a solution of a backward SDE.

In the following sections we re-derive the pricing equations of Chapter 13 by introducing margining and funding costs. In particular, we expand all the above terms to allow the calculation of the CFBVA price.

17.3 FUNDING RISK AND LIQUIDITY POLICIES

We start our discussion by referring to a working paper of the Basel Committee, *"International Framework for Liquidity Risk Measurement, Standards and Monitoring"* of December 2009, that investigates market and funding liquidity issues. We will not proceed with its level of generality here, since we will be dealing mostly with pricing and funding as related to CVA. In pricing applications, modelling consistently funding costs with bilateral CVA-DVA and collateral margining is a complex task, since it includes modelling the bank's liquidity policy, and to some extent the banking system as a whole.

In this respect, realistic funding liquidity modelling can be found in the literature, see for instance [97], or [64] and references therein. Yet, here we resort to risk-neutral evaluation of funding costs by following [165, 196], but see also for a similar framework [85]. More examples can be found in [65], [157], [108], or [162].

In practice, this means that while not addressing the details of funding liquidity modelling, we can simply introduce risk-neutral funding costs in terms of additional costs needed to complete each cash-flow transaction. We may add the cost of funding along with credit (and debit) valuation adjustments by collecting all costs coming from funding the trading position, inclusive of hedging costs, and collateral margining. We may have some asymmetries here, since the prices calculated by one party may differ from the same ones evaluated by the other party, as each price contains only funding costs undertaken by the calculating party.

17.3.1 Funding, Hedging and Collateralization

Without going into the details of funding liquidity modelling, we can introduce risk-neutral funding costs by considering the positions entered by the trader at time t to obtain the amount of cash ($F_t > 0$) needed to establish the hedging strategy, along with the positions used to invest cash surplus ($F_t < 0$). If the deal is collateralized, we include the margining procedure into the deal definition, so that we are able to evaluate also its funding costs. Notice that, if collateral re-hypothecation is allowed, each party can use the collateral account C_t for funding, and, if the collateral account is large enough, we could drop all funding costs. See [109]. The extent of re-hypothecation as a market practice is investigated in [184] and [185].

In order to write an explicit formula for cash flows we need an expression for the cash amount F_t to be funded or invested. Such a problem is faced also in [168], [65] and [85]. In this chapter, to the best of our knowledge, we face this problem in the most general setting. We also point out that there are issues with the self financing condition used in [168] and [65] to derive the results, see for example [38].

We notice that the hedging strategy, perfectly replicating the product or derivative to be priced, is formed by a cash amount, namely our cash account F_t, and a portfolio H_t of hedging instruments, so that, if the deal is not collateralized, or re-hypothecation is forbidden, we get

$$F_t = \bar{V}_t(C, F) - H_t \,,$$

where $\bar{V}_t(C, F)$ is the product risky price at time t, inclusive of funding, investing and hedging costs.

In the classical Black and Scholes theory, as illustrated for example in [99] when resorting to gain processes, dividend processes and price processes, the account H_t would be the delta position in the underlying stock, whereas the hedging position F_t would be the position in the risk-free bank account.

On the other hand, if re-hypothecation is allowed we can use collateral assets for funding, so that the amount of cash to be funded or invested is reduced and given by

$$F_t = \bar{V}_t(C, F) - C_t - H_t \,,$$

where $\bar{V}_t(C, F)$ is the product risky price inclusive of funding, investing and hedging costs.

Notice that we obtain a *recursive* equation, since the product price at time t depends on the funding strategy $F((t, T])$ after t, and in turn the funding strategy after t will depend on the product price at subsequent future times. This will be made explicit in the following sections.

17.3.2 Liquidity Policies

The positions entered by the trader for funding or investing depend on his liquidity policy, namely we assume that any cash amount $F_t > 0$ needed by the trader, or any cash surplus $F_t < 0$ to be invested, can be managed by entering a position with an external party, for instance the treasury or a lender ("funder") operating on the market.

In particular, we assume that the trader enters a funding position according to a time-grid $t_1, \ldots, t_m$. More precisely, between two following grid times t_j and t_{j+1} we have that

1. at t_j the trader asks the funder for a cash amount equal to F_{t_j};
2. at t_{j+1} the trader has to reimburse the funder for the cash amount previously obtained and has to pay for funding costs.

Moreover, we assume that funding costs are established at the starting date of each funding period and charged at the end of the same period. We can follow the same line of reasoning also for investing cash amounts ($F_t < 0$) not directly used by the trader, and consider investing periods along with funding periods.

The price of funding and investing contracts may be introduced without loss of generality as an adapted process $P_t^{f^+}(T)$, measurable at t, representing the price of a funding contract where the trader pays one unit of cash at maturity date $T > t$, and the price $P_t^{f^-}(T)$ of an investing contract where the trader receives one unit of cash at maturity date. We introduce also the funding and investing rates

$$f_t^{\pm}(T) := \frac{1}{T-t}\left(\frac{1}{P_t^{f^{\pm}}(T)} - 1\right).$$

It is also useful to introduce the effective funding and investing rate $\tilde{f}_t$ defined as

$$\tilde{f}_t(T) := f_t^{-}(T)\mathbf{1}_{\{F_t<0\}} + f_t^{+}(T)\mathbf{1}_{\{F_t>0\}}, \tag{17.2}$$

and the corresponding zero-coupon bond

$$P_t^{\tilde{f}}(T) := \frac{1}{1+(T-t)\tilde{f}_t(T)}.$$

Hence, we can define the product or derivative price $\bar{V}_t(C, F)$ inclusive of funding costs and collateral management as given by

$$\bar{V}_t(C, F) := \mathbb{E}_t\left[\bar{\Pi}(t, T; C) + \varphi(t, T \wedge \tau; F)\right],$$

where $\varphi(t, T \wedge \tau; F)$ is the sum of costs coming from all the funding and investing positions opened by the investor to hedge its trading position, according to his liquidity policy up to the first default event. This is going to be defined more precisely in a minute. Instead, $\bar{\Pi}(t, T; C)$ is the sum of the discounted cash flows coming from the product payout and inclusive of the collateral margining procedure and close-out netting rules, as given in the previous section.

Before defining $\varphi(t, T \wedge \tau; F)$, we describe a few examples of liquidity policies, in order to better illustrate our approach to funding and investing costs.

(A) In the first case, we distinguish between funding and investing in terms of returns since there is no reason why funds lending and funds borrowing should happen at the same rate in general, so that P^{f^-} and P^{f^+} will be different. Moreover, the rates may also differ across deals, depending on the deals' notional, maturities structure, counterparty client relationship implications of a single product, etc. We may call this approach the "micro" approach to funding, or possibly the bottom-up approach. This approach is deal specific and changes rates depending on whether funds are borrowed or lent.

(B) A second possibility sees one assuming an average cost of funding borrowing to be applied to all deals, and an average return for lending or investing. This would lead to two curves for P^{f^-} and P^{f^+} that would hold for all funding costs and invested amounts respectively, regardless of the specific deal, so that this approach would still distinguish borrowing from lending but would not be deal specific.

(C) On the other hand, in a third approach one can go further and assume that the cost of investing and the cost of funding match, so that P^{f^-} and P^{f^+} are not only the same across deals, but are equal to each other, implying common funding borrowing and investing (lending) spreads. In practice the spread would be set at a common value for borrowing or lending, and this value would match what goes on across all deals on average. This would be a "large-pool" or homogeneous average approach, which would look at a unique funding spread for the bank to be applied to all products traded by capital markets.

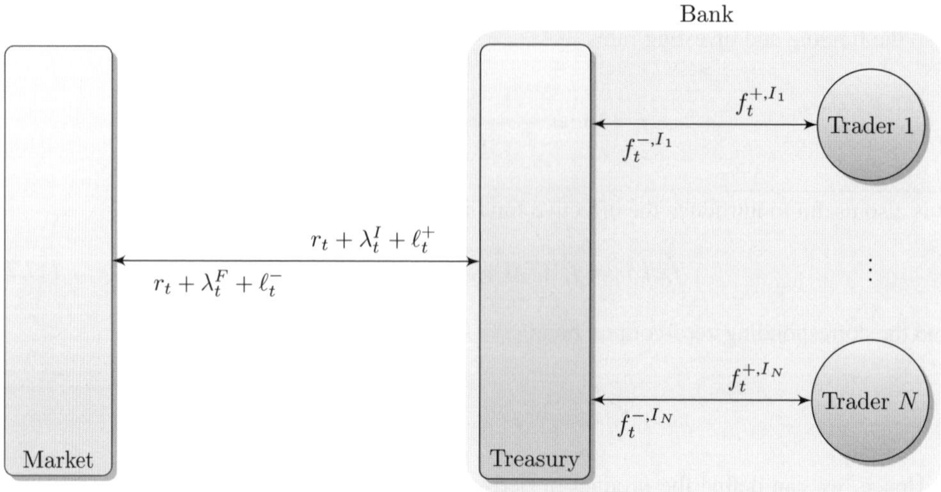

Figure 17.1 Traders may fund and invest only by means of their treasury. Thus, average rates $f^{\pm}$ are applied. The funding and investing trades closed by treasury are not seen by the traders

17.3.2.1 Funding via Bank's Treasury

As a first example, we can consider that the counterparty of funding and investing cash flows is the treasury, which in turn operates on the market. Thus, funding and investing rates $f_t^{\pm}$ for each trader are determined by the treasury, for instance by means of a funds transfer pricing (FTP) process which allows us to measure the performance of different business units. A pictorial representation is given in Figure 17.1.

From the point of view of the investor the following (discounted) cash flows occur when entering a funding or investing position Φ_j at t_j:

$$\Phi_j(t_j, t_{j+1}; F) := -N_{t_j} D(t_j, t_{j+1}),$$

with

$$N_{t_j} := \frac{F_{t_j}^-}{P_{t_j}^{f^-}(t_{j+1})} + \frac{F_{t_j}^+}{P_{t_j}^{f^+}(t_{j+1})}.$$

whose price at time t_j is given by F_{t_j}.

The investor "I" does not operate directly on the market, but only with her treasury. Thus, in case of default, both the parties of the funding/investing deal disappear, without any further cash flow. In particular, in such a case the treasury, and not the trader, is in charge of debit valuation adjustments due to funding positions, so that we can consider the case where funding/investing is in place only if default events do not happen, leading to the following definition of the funding borrowing/lending (investing) cash flows when default events are considered:

$$\bar{\Phi}_j(t_j, t_{j+1}; F) := \mathbf{1}_{\{\tau > t_j\}} \Phi_j(t_j, t_{j+1}; F).$$

Thus, the price of cash flows coming from the j-th funds borrowing and lending positions is

$$\mathbb{E}_{t_j}\left[\bar{\Phi}_j(t_j, t_{j+1}; F)\right] = -\mathbf{1}_{\{\tau > t_j\}}\left(F_{t_j}^{-}\frac{P_{t_j}(t_{j+1})}{P_{t_j}^{f^-}(t_{j+1})} + F_{t_j}^{+}\frac{P_{t_j}(t_{j+1})}{P_{t_j}^{f^+}(t_{j+1})}\right).$$

Then we obtain that funding borrowing and lending costs in case of a treasury-mediated activity can be considered as a sequence of operations to enter into a funding, borrowing and lending position at each time t_j within the funding time-grid, we can define the sum $\varphi(t, T \wedge \tau; F)$ of costs coming from all the funding and investing positions opened by the investor "I" to hedge her trading position according to her liquidity policy up to the first default event. Such sum is given by the formula

$$\varphi(t, T \wedge \tau; F) := \sum_{j=1}^{m-1} \mathbf{1}_{\{t \le t_j < T \wedge \tau\}} D(t, t_j)\left(F_{t_j} + \mathbb{E}_{t_j}\left[\bar{\Phi}_j(t_j, t_{j+1}; F)\right]\right) \tag{17.3}$$

$$= \sum_{j=1}^{m-1} \mathbf{1}_{\{t \le t_j < T \wedge \tau\}} D(t, t_j)\left(F_{t_j} - F_{t_j}^{-}\frac{P_{t_j}(t_{j+1})}{P_{t_j}^{f^-}(t_{j+1})} - F_{t_j}^{+}\frac{P_{t_j}(t_{j+1})}{P_{t_j}^{f^+}(t_{j+1})}\right).$$

This is, strictly speaking, a payout. The cost at t is obtained by taking the risk-neutral expectation at time t of the above cash flows.

17.3.2.2 Funding Directly on the Market

As a second example of liquidity policy, we can consider that each trader operates directly on the market to enter funding and investing positions (see [85]). Here, the treasury no longer has an active role, and it could be dropped from our scheme, as shown in Figure 17.2

The investor operates directly on the market. Thus, her mark-to-market should include the default debit valuation adjustments due to funding positions. Here, we consider the funder

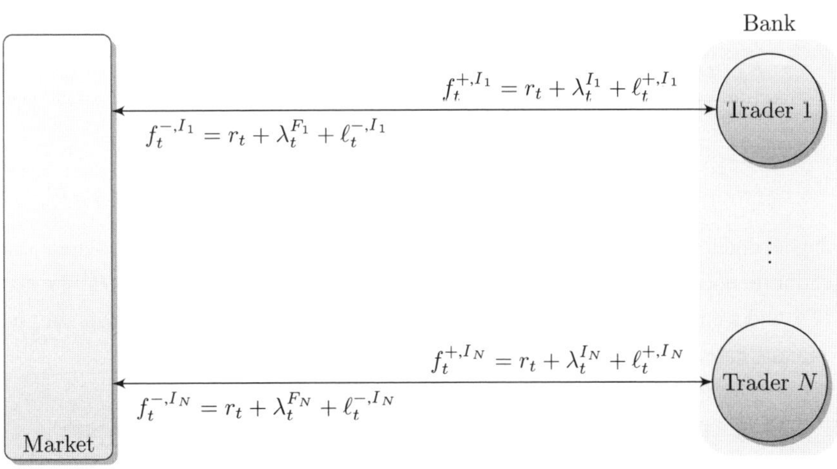

Figure 17.2 Traders may fund and invest directly on the market. Thus, funding and investing rates $f^{\pm}$ must match the market rates. Here λ are the default intensities of traders or funder, and $\ell^{\pm}$ the liquidity (bond/CDS) basis for buying or selling

to be default free. Furthermore, we consider, as in the previous example, the case where the funding procedure is closed down if any default event happens.

By using the CBVA pricing formula without collateralization, we obtain the sum of the funding (discounted) cash flows inclusive of debit valuation adjustments as given by

$$\begin{aligned}\bar{\Phi}_j(t_j, t_{j+1}; F) &:= \mathbf{1}_{\{\tau>t_j\}}\mathbf{1}_{\{\tau_I>t_{j+1}\}}\Phi_j(t_j, t_{j+1}; F) \\ &\quad -\mathbf{1}_{\{\tau>t_j\}}\mathbf{1}_{\{\tau_I<t_{j+1}\}}(\text{LGD}_I\varepsilon^-_{F,\tau_I} - \varepsilon_{F,\tau_I})D(t_j, \tau_I),\end{aligned}$$

where $\varepsilon_{F,t}$ is the close-out amount calculated by the funder on investor's default event, which we assume to be

$$\varepsilon_{F,\tau_I} := -N_{t_j} P_{\tau_I}(t_{j+1}).$$

Notice that, by following [85], we could assume a recovery rate for the investor different from the one we use as recovery rate for trading deals, since the seniority could be different. It is straightforward to extend the present case in such a direction.

Thus, the price of cash flows coming from the j-th funding and investing strategy is given by

$$\mathbb{E}_{t_j}\left[\bar{\Phi}_j(t_j, t_{j+1}; F)\right] = -\mathbf{1}_{\{\tau>t_j\}}\left(F^-_{t_j}\frac{P_{t_j}(t_{j+1})}{P^{f^-}_{t_j}(t_{j+1})} + F^+_{t_j}\frac{P_{t_j}(t_{j+1})}{\bar{P}^{f^+}_{t_j}(t_{j+1})}\right),$$

where the risk-adjusted funding zero-coupon bond $\bar{P}^{f^+}_t(T)$ is defined as

$$\bar{P}^{f^+}_t(T) := P^{f^+}_t(T)\left(\mathbb{E}^T_t\left[\text{LGD}_I\mathbf{1}_{\{\tau_I>T\}} + \text{REC}_I\right]\right)^{-1}$$

with the expectation on the right side being taken under the T-forward measure.

Hence, we can consider funding borrowing and lending costs in case traders fund directly on the market as a sequence of operations to enter into funding borrowing and lending (investing) positions at each time t_j within the funding time-grid. The sum $\varphi(t, T\wedge\tau; F)$ of costs coming from all the funding and investing positions opened by the investor to hedge its trading position according to his liquidity policy up to the first default event is given by

$$\begin{aligned}\varphi(t, T\wedge\tau; F) &:= \sum_{j=1}^{m-1}\mathbf{1}_{\{t\le t_j<T\wedge\tau\}}D(t, t_j)\left(F_{t_j} + \mathbb{E}_{t_j}\left[\bar{\Phi}_j(t_j, t_{j+1}; F)\right]\right) \\ &= \sum_{j=1}^{m-1}\mathbf{1}_{\{t\le t_j<T\wedge\tau\}}D(t, t_j)\left(F_{t_j} - F^-_{t_j}\frac{P_{t_j}(t_{j+1})}{P^{f^-}_{t_j}(t_{j+1})} - F^+_{t_j}\frac{P_{t_j}(t_{j+1})}{\bar{P}^{f^+}_{t_j}(t_{j+1})}\right)\end{aligned} \tag{17.4}$$

where the dependency of φ on τ_I is not explicitly shown to avoid cumbersome notation.

Furthermore, notice that, if we set $\text{REC}_I = 1$ (so that $\text{LGD}_I = 0$) we get that $\bar{P}^{f^+}_t(T)$ is equal to $P^{f^+}_t(T)$, and we recover the previous example. Thus, in the following we will simply write $P^{f^\pm}_t(T)$ in any case.

17.4 CBVA PRICING EQUATION WITH FUNDING COSTS (CFBVA)

In this chapter we stay as general as possible and therefore assume the micro view, but of course it is enough to collapse our variables to common values to obtain any of the large-pool approaches. By the previous examples we understand that a sensible choice for funding and investing cash flows could be

$$\varphi(t, T; F) := \sum_{j=1}^{m-1} \mathbf{1}_{\{t \le t_j < T\}} D(t, t_j) \left(F_{t_j} - F_{t_j}^- \frac{P_{t_j}(t_{j+1})}{P_{t_j}^{f^-}(t_{j+1})} - F_{t_j}^+ \frac{P_{t_j}(t_{j+1})}{P_{t_j}^{f^+}(t_{j+1})} \right)$$

whatever the definition of funding and investing rates may be.

Hence, the CFBVA price $\bar{V}_t(C; F)$, inclusive of funding and investing costs, can be written in the following form:

$$\begin{aligned} \bar{V}_t(C; F) = & \ \mathbb{E}_t \left[\Pi(t, T \wedge \tau) + \gamma(t, T \wedge \tau; C) + \varphi(t, T \wedge \tau; F) \right] \\ & + \mathbb{E}_t \left[\mathbf{1}_{\{\tau < T\}} D(t, \tau) \theta_\tau(C, \varepsilon) \right] \end{aligned} \tag{17.5}$$

The above formula, when funding and margining costs are discarded, collapses to the formula of CBVA adjusted price found in [41], while, when we consider only margining costs, the formula is equal to the formula presented in the collateral section of this chapter. In the following we consider some simple examples to highlight its meaning.

17.4.1 Iterative Solution of the CFBVA Pricing Equation

In the previous sections, we derived the collateral-inclusive credit and funding valuation adjusted price equation (17.5) which allows us to price a deal by taking into account counterparty risk, margining and funding costs. We also built some relevant examples to highlight the recursive nature of the equation and its link with discount curves.

Now, we describe a strategy to solve the equation without resorting to simplifying hypotheses. We try to turn the recursion into an iterative set of equations which eventually are to be solved via least-square Monte Carlo techniques as in standard CVA calculations, see for instance [57].

We start by introducing thc following quantities as building blocks for our iterative solution

$$\begin{aligned} \bar{\Pi}_T(t_j, t_{j+1}; C) := & \ \Pi(t_j, t_{j+1} \wedge \tau) \\ & + \gamma(t_j, t_{j+1} \wedge \tau; C) + \mathbf{1}_{\{t_j < \tau < t_{j+1}\}} D(t_j, \tau) \theta_\tau(C, \varepsilon) \end{aligned}$$

where θ is still defined as in Equation (16.6). The time parameter T points out that the exposure ε inside θ still refers to a deal with maturity T. From the above definition it is clear that $\bar{\Pi}_T(t, T; C) = \bar{\Pi}(t, T; C)$.

We solve Equation (17.5) at each funding date t_j in terms of the price $\bar{V}$ calculated at the following funding time t_{j+1}, and we get

$$\begin{aligned} \bar{V}_{t_j}(C; F) = & \ \mathbb{E}_{t_j} \left[\bar{V}_{t_{j+1}}(C; F) D(t_j, t_{j+1}) + \bar{\Pi}_T(t_j, t_{j+1}; C) \right] \\ & - \mathbf{1}_{\{\tau > t_j\}} \left(F_{t_j}^- \frac{P_{t_j}(t_{j+1})}{P_{t_j}^{f^-}(t_{j+1})} + F_{t_j}^+ \frac{P_{t_j}(t_{j+1})}{P_{t_j}^{f^+}(t_{j+1})} - F_{t_j} \right) \end{aligned}$$

We recall that $F_{t_j} = \bar{V}_{t_j}(C; F) - H_{t_j}$ if re-hypothecation is forbidden, or $F_{t_j} = \bar{V}_{t_j}(C; F) - C_{t_j} - H_{t_j}$ if it is allowed. Furthermore, we have

$$\bar{V}_{t_n}(C; F) := 0 .$$

Hence, by solving for positive and negative parts, we obtain for $\tau < t_j$ that $\bar{V}_{t_j}(C;F) = 0$, while for $\tau > t_j$:

(i) if *re-hypothecation is forbidden*, we have

$$\left(\bar{V}_{t_j}(C;F) - H_{t_j}\right)^{\pm}$$
$$= P_{t_j}^{f^{\pm}}(t_{j+1}) \left(\mathbb{E}_{t_j}^{t_{j+1}} \left[\bar{V}_{t_{j+1}}(C;F) + \frac{\bar{\Pi}_T(t_j, t_{j+1}; C) - H_{t_j}}{D(t_j, t_{j+1})} \right] \right)^{\pm} \quad (17.6)$$

(ii) if *re-hypothecation is allowed*, we have

$$\left(\bar{V}_{t_j}(C;F) - C_{t_j} - H_{t_j}\right)^{\pm}$$
$$= P_{t_j}^{f^{\pm}}(t_{j+1}) \left(\mathbb{E}_{t_j}^{t_{j+1}} \left[\bar{V}_{t_{j+1}}(C;F) + \frac{\bar{\Pi}_T(t_j, t_{j+1}; C) - C_{t_j} - H_{t_j}}{D(t_j, t_{j+1})} \right] \right)^{\pm} \quad (17.7)$$

When the investor implements a specific hedging strategy H_t, he may experience additional costs if he is not directly accessing the (spot) market to hedge his position in the underlying risk factors, but he is forced (or he chooses) to lend and borrow via an intermediate entity, as in the case of stock-lending and repo markets, or to trade other derivative contracts, for instance trading forward contracts on the underlying risk factors.

Indeed, prices of contracts quoted on the market may be different from prices calculated by the investor when funding and investing costs are taken into account, since investor's costs may be different from costs experienced by other market participants.[4] Thus, when evaluating derivative contracts, the investor has to take into account such differences in prices by including them as additional costs.

As usual we can change the drift of the price processes of underlying risk factors to include such costs. For instance, in the case of stock-lending and repo stock markets, we can use as growth rate for stock prices the quoted repo rate. Yet, if we assume that hedging costs are handled by a change of measure, we have also to drop the term depending on H_t in our pricing equation.

We present in the next section a sketchy proof of the above statement in the simpler case of funding and hedging in continuous time. We leave as further work a more rigorous derivation in a more general setting.

17.4.2 Funding Derivative Contracts in a Diffusion Setting

Here, we assume funding and hedging in continuous time. In particular, we start with a discrete time-grid, and at the end of the calculation we take the limit to a continuous time.

We start with the case of re-hypothecation. The same approach applies also when re-hypothecation is forbidden, We solve recursively pricing Equation (17.7), and we get up to maturity or first default event

$$\bar{V}_t(C;F) - C_t - H_t$$
$$= \mathbb{E}_t \left[\sum_{j=1}^{m-1} \mathbf{1}_{\{t_j < \tau\}} \prod_{i=1}^{j} \frac{P_{t_i}^{\bar{f}}(t_{i+1})}{P_{t_i}(t_{i+1})} D(t, t_j) \bar{\Pi}_T(t_j, t_{j+1}; C) \right]$$

[4] Arbitrages may appear only if market imperfections do not prevent market participants to exploit them. We consider differences in funding and investing costs as a component of usual bid-ask spreads observed on the market.

$$+\mathbb{E}_t\left[\sum_{j=1}^{m-1}\mathbf{1}_{\{t_j<\tau\}}\prod_{i=1}^{j}\frac{P_{t_i}^{\tilde{f}}(t_{i+1})}{P_{t_i}(t_{i+1})}D(t,t_j)(D(t_j,t_{j+1})C_{t_{j+1}}-C_{t_j})\right]$$

$$+\mathbb{E}_t\left[\sum_{j=1}^{m-1}\mathbf{1}_{\{t_j<\tau\}}\prod_{i=1}^{j}\frac{P_{t_i}^{\tilde{f}}(t_{i+1})}{P_{t_i}(t_{i+1})}D(t,t_j)(D(t_j,t_{j+1})H_{t_{j+1}}-H_{t_j})\right].$$

By taking the limit of funding in continuous time, and integrating by parts the hedging term, we get

$$\begin{aligned}\bar{V}_t(C;F) &= C_t + \mathbb{E}_t\left[\mathbf{1}_{\{\tau<T\}}\left(\theta_\tau(C,\varepsilon)-C_{\tau^-}\right)D(t,\tau;\tilde{f})\right]\\&+\int_t^T \mathbb{E}_t\left[\mathbf{1}_{\{u<\tau\}}\left(\Pi(u,u+du)+dC_u-\tilde{c}_u C_u\,du\right)D(t,u;\tilde{f})\right]\\&+\int_t^T \mathbb{E}_t\left[\mathbf{1}_{\{u<\tau\}}D(t,u;\tilde{f})H_u(\tilde{f}_u-r_u)du\right]\end{aligned}\qquad(17.8)$$

where we define the funding discount factor as $D(t,T;\tilde{f}) := e^{-\int_t^T du\,\tilde{f}_u}$.

We split Equation (17.8) into four terms to highlight the role of different cash flows. The first term is the collateral price. The second and third terms are formed by the cash flows which are not considered by collateralization, such as the cash flows payed on default event of one of the two counterparties, by mark-to-market movements which are not followed by an immediate reset of the collateral account, and by margining costs not included into the collateral price. The fourth term represents the funding costs of the hedging strategy.

In Equation (17.8) expectations are taken under the risk-neutral measure. Now, we wish to select a different pricing measure which allows us to drop the fourth term in the above equation. We can accomplish such goal if we consider a delta-hedging strategy and we assume that the Itô pricing equation for diffusive processes holds. As we stated before we leave as further work a more rigorous derivation in a more general setting.

Now, we go into details. We start by considering the defaut-free market filtration $\mathcal{F}$ that one obtains implicitly by assuming a separable structure for the filtration $\mathcal{G}$, where $\mathcal{G}$ is generated by the pure default-free market filtration $\mathcal{F}$ and by the filtration generated by all the relevant default times (see for example [18] or the earlier Chapter 7, where the latter is called $\mathcal{H}$). Then, we switch to the market filtration $\mathcal{F}$, leaving the time variable in the expectation (i.e. $\mathbb{E}_t[(\cdot)|\mathcal{F}] \doteq \mathbb{E}[(\cdot)|\mathcal{F}_t]$):

$$\begin{aligned}\bar{V}_t(C;F) &= \mathbf{1}_{\{\tau>t\}}\int_t^T du\,\mathbb{E}_t\left[\left(\partial_u\pi_u+\lambda_u\theta_u(C,\varepsilon)\right)D(t,u;r+\lambda)\middle|\mathcal{F}\right]\\&+\mathbf{1}_{\{\tau>t\}}\int_t^T du\,\mathbb{E}_t\left[(\tilde{f}_u-\tilde{c}_u)C_u D(t,u;r+\lambda)\middle|\mathcal{F}\right]\\&+\mathbf{1}_{\{\tau>t\}}\int_t^T du\,\mathbb{E}_t\left[(r_u-\tilde{f}_u)\left(\bar{V}_u(C,F)-H_u\right)D(t,u;r+\lambda)\middle|\mathcal{F}\right]\end{aligned}$$

where $d\pi_u := \Pi(u,u+du) = \partial_u\pi_u\,du$, λ_t is the first-default intensity, and

$$D(t,T;x) := \exp\left\{-\int_t^T du\,x_u\right\}.$$

We can write the corresponding pre-default PDE if we assume that the hypotheses of the Feynman-Kac theorem are holding, in particular that the underlying market risk factors are Markov with infinitesimal generator $\mathcal{L}_t$. In such case we get for $\tau > t$

$$\left(\partial_t - \tilde{f}_t - \lambda_t + \mathcal{L}_t\right) \bar{V}_t(C;F) - (r_t - \tilde{f}_t)H_t + (\tilde{f}_t - \tilde{c}_t)C_t + \partial_t \pi_t + \lambda_t \theta_t(C,\varepsilon) = 0 \quad (17.9)$$

with boundary condition

$$\bar{V}_T(C;F) = 0.$$

If we consider a diffusive dynamics, and we assume delta-hedging, we can expand the generator $\mathcal{L}$ in term of first and second order operators, and we get

$$\mathcal{L}_t \bar{V}_t(C;F) \doteq \left(\mathcal{L}_t^1 + \mathcal{L}_t^2\right) \bar{V}_t(C;F) \doteq r_t H_t + \mathcal{L}_t^2 \bar{V}_t(C;F)$$

Hence, the pre-default PDE becomes

$$\left(\partial_t - \tilde{f}_t - \lambda_t + \mathcal{L}_t^{\tilde{f}}\right) \bar{V}_t(C;F) + (\tilde{f}_t - \tilde{c}_t)C_t + \lambda_t \theta_t(C,\varepsilon) = 0$$

where

$$\mathcal{L}_t^{\tilde{f}} \bar{V}_t(C;F) := \tilde{f}_t H_t + \mathcal{L}_t^2 \bar{V}_t(C;F).$$

Notice that the above equation does not depend any more on the risk-free rate. The pre-default PDE equation can be numerically solved as in [85]. On the other hand, we can apply again the Feynman-Kac theorem and we obtain the CFBVA pricing equations in case of funding and delta-hedging in continuous time when re-hypothecation is allowed

$$\begin{aligned}\bar{V}_t(C;F) = C_t &+ \mathbb{E}_t^{\tilde{f}}\left[\mathbf{1}_{\{\tau<T\}}\left(\theta_\tau(C,\varepsilon) - C_{\tau^-}\right) D(t,\tau;\tilde{f})\right] \\ &+ \int_t^T \mathbb{E}_t^{\tilde{f}}\left[\mathbf{1}_{\{u<\tau\}}\left(\Pi(u,u+du) + dC_u - \tilde{c}_u C_u\,du\right) D(t,u;\tilde{f})\right] \quad (17.10)\end{aligned}$$

where the expectations are taken under the pricing measure $\mathbb{Q}^{\tilde{f}}$. A similar reasoning holds also when re-hypothecation is not allowed.

Thus, we can conclude this section by stating the following proposition.

Proposition 17.4.1 ***(CFBVA pricing equations in case of funding and delta-hedging in continuous time)*** *In case of funding and delta-hedging in continuous time we may drop the term containing explicitly the hedging strategy from Equation (17.8) provided that we take expectations under the pricing measure* $\mathbb{Q}^{\tilde{f}}$.

Remark 17.4.2 ***(No explicit dependence on r).*** *An important point about our pricing equation (17.10) is that it does not depend on the risk-free rate* r_t*, which does not need to enter the modelling framework. The equation is entirely governed by market rates.*

Remark 17.4.3 ***(Not a real additive decomposition unless $f^+ = f^-$ and further conditions hold).*** *Another important point about our pricing equation (17.10) is that it may appear to have achieved an additive decomposition in different adjustments if one remembers the CVA-DVA terms implicit in the close-out cash flows, including* θ*. However, it is very important to keep in mind that the treasury rates* $\tilde{f}$ *future paths depend on the future signs of the account* F*, which in turn is equal to* $F = \bar{V} - C - H$*. This implies that future paths of treasury rates* $\tilde{f}$ *depend on future paths of the adjusted price* $\bar{V}$ *we are trying to calculate. This keeps the recursion alive and shows there is no real decomposition. One condition to move towards an additive* *formula is for example $f^+ = f^-$, since in such case $\tilde{f}$ would no longer need to know the sign of F (and hence the value of $\bar{V}$). This corresponds to the unrealistic setting where borrowing and lending can occur at the same rates. However, this is not the only complication. One needs to understand how collateral is linked to $\bar{V}$ and how the collateral rate $\tilde{c}$ may need to "know" the sign of C. In the end, to really simplify the picture, one really needs to make sure that no quantity on the right-hand side of Equation (17.10) needs to "know" the future paths of $\bar{V}$.*

17.4.3 Implementing Hedging Strategies via Derivative Markets

In the previous section we considered the possibility to implement a delta-hedging strategy by trading directly on the spot market, If the investor chooses, or is forced, to trade the underlying asset by entering into derivative positions, we should add any additional cost to the CFBVA pricing equation. For instance, this situation may happen when the investor accesses the lending/repo market to implement his hedging strategy, or if he uses synthetic forward contracts built on the European call/put market.

In general, we introduce the adapted processes $h_t^+(T)$, as the effective rate for asset lending from t to T, and $h_t^-(T)$, for asset borrowing. Furthermore, we define the (hedging) zero-coupon bonds $P_t^{h^\pm}(T)$ as given by

$$P_t^{h^\pm}(T) := \frac{1}{1 + (T - t)h_t^\pm(T)} .$$

It is also useful to introduce the effective lending/borrowing rate $\tilde{h}_t$ defined as[5]

$$\tilde{h}_t(T) := h_t^-(T)\mathbf{1}_{\{H_t<0\}} + h_t^+(T)\mathbf{1}_{\{H_t>0\}} ,$$

and the corresponding zero-coupon bond

$$P_t^{\tilde{h}}(T) := \frac{1}{1 + (T - t)\tilde{h}_t(T)} .$$

Hence, if we assume that the hedging strategy is implemented on the same time-grid as the funding procedure, we can sum the funding and hedging costs in a unique term, and we can re-define φ by explicitly taking into account its dependency on the hedging strategy.

$$\begin{aligned}\varphi(t, T \wedge \tau; F, H) \doteq & \sum_{j=1}^{m-1} \mathbf{1}_{\{t \le t_j < T\wedge\tau\}} D(t, t_j) F_{t_j} \left(1 - \frac{P_{t_j}(t_{j+1})}{P_{t_j}^{\tilde{f}}(t_{j+1})}\right) \\ & - \sum_{j=1}^{m-1} \mathbf{1}_{\{t \le t_j < T\wedge\tau\}} D(t, t_j) H_{t_j} \left(\frac{P_{t_j}(t_{j+1})}{P_{t_j}^{\tilde{f}}(t_{j+1})} - \frac{P_{t_j}(t_{j+1})}{P_{t_j}^{\tilde{h}}(t_{j+1})}\right) . \qquad (17.11)\end{aligned}$$

If we repeat the calculation of previous sections, by taking the limit of funding and delta-hedging in continuous time, we obtain, in case that re-hypothecation is allowed, that the CFBVA price is given by

$$\begin{aligned}\bar{V}_t(C; F) = & C_t + \mathbb{E}_t^{\tilde{h}}\left[\mathbf{1}_{\{\tau<T\}}\left(\theta_\tau(C, \varepsilon) - C_{\tau^-}\right) D(t, \tau; \tilde{f})\right] \\ & + \int_t^T \mathbb{E}_t^{\tilde{h}}\left[\mathbf{1}_{\{u<\tau\}}\left(\Pi(u, u + du) + dC_u - \tilde{c}_u C_u \, du\right) D(t, u; \tilde{f})\right] \qquad (17.12)\end{aligned}$$

[5] In case of many risky assets within our hedging strategy, we can introduce a different pair of lending/borrowing rates for each asset.

where the expectations are taken under a pricing measure $\mathbb{Q}^{\tilde{h}}$ under which the underlying risk factors grow at rate $\tilde{h}$.

Thus, we can extend Proposition 17.5.4 in case of hedging strategies implemented by trading on a derivative market where the lending/borrowing rate is $\tilde{h}$, and we obtain:

Proposition 17.4.4 ***(CFBVA pricing equations in case of funding and delta-hedging in continuous time)*** *In case of funding and delta-hedging in continuous time, when the hedging strategy is implemented by trading on a derivative market where the lending/borrowing rate is $\tilde{h}$, we may drop the term containing explicitly the hedging strategy from Equation (17.8) provided that we take expectations under the pricing measure $\mathbb{Q}^{\tilde{h}}$.*

Remark 17.4.5 ***(No explicit dependence on r).*** *An important point about our pricing equation (17.12) is that it does not depend on the risk-free rate r_t, which does not need to enter the modelling framework. The equation is entirely governed by market rates.*

Remark 17.4.6 ***(Not a real additive decomposition in general).*** *A remark completely analogous to Remark 17.4.3 applies here.*

17.5 DETAILED EXAMPLES

Here, we present four relevant examples to highlight the properties of the CFBVA pricing equation. We analyze

- the case of a perfect collateralized contract between two risky counterparties in presence of funding and hedging costs;
- the case of a central counterparty (CCP) pricing a collateralized contract between two risky counterparties, possibly in presence of Gap risk;
- the case of a risky investor evaluating counterparty credit risk on a uncollateralized deal; and
- the case already discussed in the literature of [157] and [74].

In all the following examples we consider funding and delta-hedging in continuous time, so that, according to Proposition 17.4.1, we can drop any explicit dependency on the hedging strategy if we take all of the expectations under a pricing measure $\mathbb{Q}^{\tilde{f}}$ under which the underlying risk factors growth at funding rate is $\tilde{f}_t$. Notice that the growth rate may be corrected for hedging costs when delta-hedging is accomplished by trading on a derivative market as stated in Proposition 17.4.4.

17.5.1 Funding with Collateral

If re-hypothecation is allowed, we assume that we can fund with collateral assets, so that the cash amount $F_t = \bar{V}_t(C, F) - C_t$. This choice for F_t leads to a recursive equation which can be solved backwards starting from the final maturity. Notice that the collateral account value C_t is defined only at margining dates, but we are taking the limiting case of perfect collateralization, so that every time is a margining date (we recall also that our definition of perfect collateralization requires that the mark-to-market of the portfolio is continuous and there is no instantaneous contagion at default in particular). Moreover, being in the re-hypothecated case, we consider recoveries as given by $\text{REC}'_C = \text{REC}_C$ and $\text{REC}'_I = \text{REC}_I$.

We assume, as in the perfect collateralization case, that we have collateralization in continuous time, with continuous mark-to-market of the portfolio in time, and with collateral account inclusive of margining costs. We recall that expectations are taken under pricing measure $\mathbb{Q}^{\tilde{f}}$. Thus, we must also price the collateral account under the same measure, otherwise hedging costs must be added explicitly. Such conditions can be fulfilled by defining the collateral price as given by

$$C_t \doteq \mathbb{E}_t^{\tilde{f}}[\,\Pi(t,T) + \gamma(t,T;C)\,]\,. \tag{17.13}$$

Furthermore, close-out amount is set equal to collateral price, so that

$$\varepsilon_{I,\tau} \doteq \varepsilon_{C,\tau} \doteq C_\tau\,.$$

Then, if we plug the above definitions into the CFBVA pricing equation (17.10) we obtain the following proposition:

Proposition 17.5.1 ***(Funding with collateral)*** *In the case where we may fund with collateral, under the assumptions of the present Section, the CFBVA pricing formula is given by*

$$\bar{V}_t(C,F) = C_t = \mathbb{E}_t^{\tilde{f}}\left[\int_t^T \Pi(u,u+du)\exp\left\{-\int_t^u dv\,\tilde{c}_v\right\}\right], \tag{17.14}$$

where the last equality is given by Equation (16.7), and expectations are taken under $\mathbb{Q}^{\tilde{f}}$ pricing measure. Hence, in case of perfect collateralization, there are no funding costs, since we are funding with collateral and this has no extra cost, as shown in Equation (17.14).

17.5.2 Collateralized Contracts Priced by a CCP

Here, we apply our CFBVA master formula to unfunded instruments, such as interest-rate swaps or credit default swaps, which can be funded with collateral (we assume re-hypothecation is holding).

We interpret CFBVA adjusted prices as the prices calculated by a risk-free central counterparty (CCP), who interposes herself between the two counterparties of the deal. Cash flows coming from the investor to the counterparty are first payed to the CCP, which, in turn, gives them to the counterparty, and similarly for cash flows coming from the counterparty to the investor. Further, we assume that the CCP can fund herself on the money market at

$$\text{overnight rate} \quad e_t$$

plus a

$$\text{liquidity spread} \quad \ell_t^{\pm}$$

(cash flows positive for the investor are negative to her). Then we define

$$f^{\pm} \doteq e_t + \ell_t^{\mp}\,.$$

In the present example we recall that expectations are taken under the pricing measure $\mathbb{Q}^{\tilde{f}}$, and we assume that, on a continuous time-grid, collateral is posted or withdrawn, according to the risk-free price augmented with margining given by (see (17.13))

$$C_t \doteq \mathbb{E}_t^{\tilde{f}}[\,\Pi(t,T) + \gamma(t,T;C)\,]\,.$$

This leads, in the limit of continuous collateralization, because of Equation (17.14), to

$$C_t = \mathbb{E}_t^{\bar{f}}\left[\int_t^T \Pi(u, u+du) \exp\left\{-\int_t^u dv\, \tilde{c}_v\right\}\right].$$

where expectations are taken under the $\mathbb{Q}^{\bar{f}}$ pricing measure.

Furthermore, we consider that upon a default event, the close-out amount is calculated by both the counterparties as they perform the calculations for collateral assets.

$$\varepsilon_{I,\tau} \doteq \varepsilon_{C,\tau} \doteq C_\tau\,, \quad C_\tau := \mathbb{E}_\tau^{\bar{f}}[\,\Pi(\tau, T) + \gamma(\tau, T; C)\,]\,.$$

Moreover, we consider funding and investing operations are entered into on a continuous time-grid.

Then, if we plug the above definitions into the CFBVA pricing equation (17.10) we obtain the following proposition:

Proposition 17.5.2 ***(Pricing with an intermediating CCP)*** *Under the assumptions of an intermediating CCP as in this Section, the adjusted product's price is given by*

$$\begin{aligned}
\bar{V}_t(C, F) = &\int_t^T \mathbb{E}_t^{\bar{f}}\left[\Pi(u, u+du) \exp\left\{-\int_t^u dv\, \tilde{c}_v\right\}\right] \\
&-\mathbb{E}_t^{\bar{f}}\left[\mathbf{1}_{\{\tau=\tau_C<T\}} \mathrm{LGD}_C (C_\tau - C_{\tau^-})^+ \exp\left\{-\int_t^\tau dv\,(\ell_v^+ + e_v)\right\}\right] \\
&-\mathbb{E}_t^{\bar{f}}\left[\mathbf{1}_{\{\tau=\tau_I<T\}} \mathrm{LGD}_I (C_\tau - C_{\tau^-})^- \exp\left\{-\int_t^\tau dv\,(\ell_v^- + e_v)\right\}\right]
\end{aligned}$$

where the last equality is given by Equation (16.7), and expectations are taken under the $\mathbb{Q}^{\bar{f}}$ pricing measure.

17.5.3 Dealing with Own Credit Risk: FVA and DVA

Here, we apply our CFBVA master formula to funded instruments, such as an uncollateralized equity option or a corporate bond, which cannot be funded with collateral. We interpret CFBVA prices as the prices calculated by the investor. We assume that the investor can fund himself at the $f_t^\pm$ rate according to her liquidity policies.

In the present example we recall that expectations are taken under the pricing measure $\mathbb{Q}^{\bar{f}}$, and we assume that no collateral is posted or withdrawn, namely

$$C_t \doteq 0$$

We consider the case where funding and investing operations are entered into on a continuous time-grid. Furthermore, we assume that the close-out amount is calculated as given by

$$\varepsilon_{I,\tau} \doteq \varepsilon_{C,\tau} \doteq \mathbb{E}_\tau^{\bar{f}}[\,\Pi(\tau, T) + \varphi(\tau, T; F)\,]$$

namely we consider a risk-free close-out amount comprehensive of funding costs. We assume the same funding costs for both the counterparties.

Then, if we plug the above definitions into the CFBVA pricing equation (17.10) we obtain the following proposition:

Proposition 17.5.3 ***(Non-collateralized pricing with defaultable counterparties)*** *Under the assumptions of funding and investing operations entered into on a continuous time-grid with risk-free close-out without collateralization, as in this Section, and with the assumptions that the two counterparties have the same funding costs, the adjusted product's price is given by*

$$\bar{V}_t(0,F) = \int_t^T \mathbb{E}_t^{\tilde{f}}\left[\Pi(u,u+du)D(t,u;\tilde{f})\right]$$
$$-\mathbb{E}_t^{\tilde{f}}\left[\mathbf{1}_{\{\tau=\tau_C<T\}} LGD_C \varepsilon_\tau^+ \exp\left\{-\int_t^\tau dv\, f_v^+\right\}\right]$$
$$-\mathbb{E}_t^{\tilde{f}}\left[\mathbf{1}_{\{\tau=\tau_I<T\}} LGD_I \varepsilon_\tau^- \exp\left\{-\int_t^\tau dv\, f_v^-\right\}\right]$$

where

$$\varepsilon_\tau = \int_\tau^T \mathbb{E}_\tau^{\tilde{f}}\left[\Pi(u,u+du)D(\tau,u;\tilde{f})\right]$$

According to the examples of liquidity policies we have presented in Section 17.3.2, we have two possible choices for the investor's "I" funding rate f_t^+.

1. If the investor is funding by means of his treasury, which applies some form of funds transfer pricing (FTP), we have that the funding rate f_t^+ is selected by the treasury, and it may depend (indirectly) on the investor's credit risk.
2. On the other hand, if the investor is able to directly fund himself on the market, then the funding rate f_t^+ is given by the market itself.

17.5.4 Deriving Earlier Results on FVA and DVA

We consider the simpler case of a positive payoff without first-to-default effect. Thus, only the counterparty's default event is relevant, so that we have only the CVA term. Furthermore, we assume zero recovery rate. We obtain, by switching to the default-free market filtration $\mathcal{F}$ (again $\mathbb{E}_t[(\cdot)|\mathcal{F}] \doteq \mathbb{E}[(\cdot)|\mathcal{F}_t]$)

$$\bar{V}_t(0,F) = \mathbf{1}_{\{\tau>t\}} \int_t^T \mathbb{E}_t^{\tilde{f}}\left[\Pi(u,u+du)D(t,u;f^+)|\mathcal{F}\right]$$
$$-\mathbf{1}_{\{\tau>t\}} \int_t^T du\,\mathbb{E}_t^{\tilde{f}}\left[\lambda_u^C D(t,u;\lambda^C+f^+)\int_u^T \mathbb{E}_u^{\tilde{f}}\left[\Pi(v,v+dv)D(u,v;f^+)|\mathcal{F}\right]\Big|\mathcal{F}\right]$$
$$= \mathbf{1}_{\{\tau>t\}} \int_t^T \mathbb{E}_t^{\tilde{f}}\left[\Pi(u,u+du)\exp\left\{-\int_t^u dv\,(\lambda^C+f^+)\right\}|\mathcal{F}\right]$$

where λ_t^C is the counterparty's default intensity.

Then, if we choose the second case above for the investor's funding rate, namely we assume that the investor is able to directly fund himself on the market, and he can adjust the funding rate to include the DVA term entering the deal opened with the funder (funding benefits), as we described in the relevant part of Section 17.3.2, then we have

$$f_t^+ \doteq e_t + \ell_t^+,$$

(where we recall that e_t is an overnight rate) and we obtain a result similar to [157], see also our earlier Chapter 11. Notice that adjusting the funding rate for funding benefits means that the investor is able to hedge his own credit risk in funding positions. If at this stage one further assumes the funding liquidity spread (basis) ℓ^+ to be zero, then one has

$$f_t^+ = e_t.$$

If one further (and mistakenly) identifies OIS with r_t, one has

$$f_t^+ = r_t$$

so that one can fund at the risk-free rate and there are no funding costs.

Remark 17.5.4 *(FVA = 0?) This is the setup for the claim by Hull and White, reported in part of the press, as we pointed out in the introduction of this chapter, that there is no funding valuation adjustment. We hope it is clear by now under how many special and unrealistic assumptions this happens.*

Going back to $f_t^+ \doteq e_t + \ell_t^+$, on the other hand, since we have only the CVA term, we may assume we are dealing only with CVA, thus we can choose not to adjust the funding rate, and we get

$$f_t^+ \doteq e_t + \ell_t^+ + \lambda_t^I ,$$

a result usually found in the literature when funding benefits are disregarded or deliberately left aside, see for instance [74].

17.6 CONCLUSIONS: FVA AND BEYOND

We have seen above that when we try and include consistently funding, credit, (debit) and collateral risk we obtain a highly non-linear and recursive pricing equation. While we derived our equations in the most possible general context under arbitrage freedom, and while we detailed the analysis of funding policies, our results are in line with other recent findings in the literature, such as [85], [86] and [87].

The first outcome of our analysis is that it is difficult to think of funding costs as an adjustment to be added to existing pricing equations, in the sense that something like

$$AdjustedPrice \quad = \quad RiskFreePrice + DVA - CVA + FVA$$

cannot be obtained in a naïve way. This is highlighted for example in Remark 17.4.3 for the continuous time case with delta-hedging, but holds more generally for our most general funding-inclusive equations. In the same remark we highlight under which conditions a really additive decomposition is possible.

Our message is that, similarly to how the CVA and DVA analysis made in [41] and thoroughout this book shows that CVA and DVA cannot be considered simply as a spread on discounting curves, in the same way this book warns against considering FVA as a mere additive term of the pricing equation, let alone a mere discounting spread.

Yet, this long journey has not reached its destination, since integrating funding costs into the pricing equations leads to a side effect that has relevant consequences for the very notion of "price". Indeed, the funding-inclusive price is different for each institution, since each institution has different funding and investing rates depending on her own funding liquidity policy. Even inside the same bank, the treasury and the trading desk may be applying the equation with different inputs. This is why CFBVA prices cannot be agreed upon between two entities. Even collateralized deals, which have an accrual rate defined by the CSA contract, do not have a unique price, since the underlying risk factors grow at a funding rate that can be different for different calculating parties. Hence a deal price will be reached through negotiation and perhaps an equilibrium approach should be adopted to frame part of the funding costs problem in order to compute the price at which the deal will be actually closed among parties, but this would go beyond the scope of this book.

We conclude this chapter by stressing the need to go beyond the results we presented here. We have analyzed the mechanics of funding, collateral and hedging to derive the modifications of the general arbitrage-free pricing framework in a way that is consistent with credit and possible debit adjustments. However, we have not yet started analyzing the implications on specific dynamics in financial modelling across asset classes. Most current financial models have to be re-thought to incorporate such notions from scratch. We leave this (greater) task to future work.

A final remark that may be worth considering concerns Central Counterparty Clearing Houses (CCPs). CCPs will not be the end of the credit and funding pricing problem, but just a special case of the general theory we developed here. A bank may be interested in pricing the same deal under different scenarios, when clearing it through different CCPs, and seeing how the specific margins she is charged would cover Gap risk and wrong way risk. For sensitive deals this can still be a relevant issue.

18

Non-Standard Asset Classes: Longevity Risk

This chapter is based on Biffis, Blake, Pitotti and Sun (2011) [21], from which we borrow heavily.[1]

So far, we have dealt with the very complex task of properly embedding traditional asset classes in new risks such as counterparty default, own default risk, collateral and funding, with all the subtleties that may show up.

However, while the new complex risks are quite innovative, in terms of asset classes we have been quite traditional, dealing with interest rate products, credit derivatives products, commodities, FX cross currency swaps, and equity return swaps.

We now turn to a rather unusual asset class. The purpose of this chapter is to show that not only traditional asset classes of finance are impacted by counterparty credit risk, collateral and funding, but also emerging asset classes such as longevity swaps may be heavily affected by counterparty risk.

18.1 INTRODUCTION TO LONGEVITY MARKETS

We follow the introduction of Biffis, Blake, Pitotti and Sun (2011) [21].

18.1.1 The Longevity Swap Market

The longevity-linked securities and derivatives market has recently experienced an increase in transactions for longevity swaps. Longevity swaps are hedging instruments whereby two parties, typically a re-insurer or investment bank on one side, and a pension fund or annuity provider on the other side, agree to exchange fixed payments against variable payments, as in other swaps. The hedge provider is typically the investment bank or re-insurer, that pays variable and receives fixed payments, whereas the hedge buyer is the pension fund or annuity provider, that pays fixed and receives variable payments. Here payments are indexed to the number of survivors in a reference population [94]. Table 18.1, from [21], presents a list of longevity swap deals.

In looking at Table 18.1, we see that we have bespoke and indexed longevity swaps. Let us explain what is meant by bespoke and indexed.

At the moment, transactions have been mostly tailored to pension funds and annuity providers. The variable payments in such longevity swaps are designed to match precisely the mortality experience of each individual hedger: hence the name bespoke longevity swaps.

[1] Brigo and Pallavicini are grateful to Enrico Biffis for meeting them at Imperial College in September 2012 and for helping to reconcile the original paper [21] with this book.

Table 18.1 Publicly announced longevity swap transactions 2008–2011, reproduced with permission from [21]

Date	Hedger	Size	Term (yrs)	Type	Interm./supplier
Jan 08	Lucida	Not disclosed	10	indexed	JP Morgan ILS funds
Jul 2008	Canada Life	GBP 500m	40	bespoke	JP Morgan ILS funds
Feb 2009	Abbey Life	GBP 1.5bn	run-off	bespoke	Deutsche Bank ILS funds/Partner Re
Mar 2009	Aviva	GBP 475m	10	bespoke	Royal Bank of Scotland
Jun 2009	Babcock International	GBP 750m	50	bespoke	Credit Suisse Pacific Life Re
Jul 2009	RSA	GBP 1.9bn	run-off	bespoke	Goldman Sachs (Rothesay Life)
Dec 2009	Berkshire Council	GBP 750m	run-off	bespoke	Swiss Re
Feb 2010	BMW UK	GBP 3bn	run-off	bespoke	Deutsche Bank Paternoster
Dec 2010	Swiss Re (Kortis bond)	USD 50m	8	indexed	ILS funds
Feb 2011	Pall (UK) Pension Fund	GBP 70m	10	indexed	JP Morgan

In other words the number of survivors that underlies the swap is the exact number of survivors in a given pool that is of specific interest to the hedger.

The case of indexed swaps, as opposed to bespoke, is the case where the variable survival (or mortality) rates underlying the swap are taken from some published index. Examples are represented by the LifeMetrics index developed by J.P. Morgan, the Pensions Institute and Towers Watson, see www.lifemetrics.com, or the Xpect indices developed by Deutsche Boerse, see www.xpect-index.com.

If the hedger were to adopt the indexed swap solution, the hedger would be exposed to the difference between the mortality rate of the index, that he/she is going to receive, and the mortality rate of his/her bespoke pool, whose risk he/she will have to bear. This mismatch is called basis risk. While the bespoke swap may be less liquid, it will spare basis risk to the hedger.

The bespoke longevity swap is essentially a form of longevity risk insurance, similar to annuity reinsurance in reinsurance markets. Indeed, most of the longevity swaps executed to date have been bespoke, indemnity-based swaps of the kind familiar in reinsurance markets. This is true even though some of the swaps listed in Table 18.1 have been arranged by investment banks. The banks have worked with insurance companies (in some cases subsidiaries) in order to deliver a solution in a format that was familiar to the counterparty.

18.1.2 Longevity Swaps: Collateral and Credit Risk

As pointed out in [21], a fundamental difference from other forms of reinsurance is that longevity swaps are usually collateralized, whereas typical insurance/reinsurance transactions are not.[2] The main reason for collateral in longevity swaps is that these instruments are often part of a wider strategy to lower risk. Such strategies involve other collateralized instruments (interest-rate and inflation swaps, for example, see Chapter 15), and also the fact that hedgers have been increasingly concerned with counterparty risk[3] in the wake of the global financial crisis which started in 2007. In this chapter, following [21], we provide a framework to quantify the trade-off between the exposure to counterparty risk in longevity swaps and the cost of credit enhancement strategies such as collateralization, similarly to what we have done in Chapter 15 for interest rate swaps and CDS. We will also consider funding costs as in Chapters 16 and 17.

Since there is no accepted framework as yet for marking-to-market/model longevity swaps, hedgers and hedge suppliers look to other markets to provide a reference model for counterparty risk assessment and mitigation they can emulate. In interest rate swap markets, for example, the most common form of credit enhancement is the posting of collateral, as we have seen at different levels of technicality in Chapters 1, 2, 13, and 15.

Related to our discussion in Chapter 13 in particular, according to the International Swap and Derivatives Association (ISDA), almost every swap at major financial institutions is 'bilaterally' collateralized, [127 (2010)], meaning that either party is required to post collateral depending on whether the market value of the swap is positive or negative.[4] The vast majority of transactions are collateralized according to the Credit Support Annex to the Master Swap Agreement introduced by [127 (1992)]. The global financial crisis highlighted the importance of bilateral counterparty risk and collateralization for over-the-counter markets, spurring a number of responses we have seen in Chapters 13, 15 and 17, see also [127, 39, 8, 41]. The Dodd-Frank Wall Street Reform and Consumer Protection Act (signed into law by President Barack Obama on 21 July 2010) and the Basel III agreement with its CVA VaR charges (see Chapters 1 and 2) are likely to have a major impact on the way financial institutions will manage counterparty risk in the future, and we have already seen industry deals for counterparty risk restructuring in Chapter 10, besides the earlier CCDS and Novation type of deals, see Chapters 1, 5 and 9.

As pointed out in [21], the recently founded Life and Longevity Markets Association (LLMA) [5] has counterparty risk at the centre of its agenda, and will certainly draw extensively from the experience garnered in fixed-income and credit markets we have developed in the earlier chapters.

The design of collateralization strategies is intended to address the concerns aired by pension trustees regarding the efficacy of longevity swaps, but introduces another dimension in the traditional pricing framework used for insurance transactions. The "insurance premium" embedded in a longevity swap rate reflects not only the aversion (if any) of the counterparties to the risk being transferred and the cost of regulatory capital involved in the transaction, but also the expected costs to be incurred by margining and funding, stemming from

[2] One reason for this difference is diversification: reinsurers aggregate several uncorrelated risks, so that pooling/diversification benefits offset the lack of collateral [138, 89]. Insurers/reinsurers are, however, required by their regulators to post capital, which plays a similar role to collateral but at an aggregate level.

[3] As we have seen earlier and in Chapters 1 and 2 in particular [12] defines counterparty risk as "the risk that the counterparty to a transaction could default before the final settlement of the transaction's cash flows". The recent Solvency II proposal makes explicit allowance for a counterparty risk module in its 'standard formula' approach; see [75].

[4] 'Unlike a firm's exposure to credit risk through a loan, where the exposure to credit risk is unilateral and only the lending bank faces the risk of loss, counterparty credit risk creates a bilateral risk of loss: the market value of the transaction can be positive or negative to either counterparty to the transaction. The market value is uncertain and can vary over time with the movement of underlying market factors' [12].

[5] See http://www.llma.org.

posting collateral and funding the cash flows during the life of the swap. We have seen in Chapter 17 how complicated the complete pricing algorithm is when accounting for counterparty risk, collateral and funding. At a simplified level, roughly speaking, the fact that collateral is costly simply reflects the costs entailed by credit risk mitigation. To quantify the impact of collateral on swap rates, one needs to include the collateral margining process and funding costs into the picture, so as to be able to examine the relative sensitivity of the counterparties to its cost.

Following [21], let us first take the perspective of a hedge provider (typically a reinsurer or investment bank) issuing a collateralized longevity swap to a counterparty (typically a pension fund or annuity provider). Whenever the swap is sufficiently out-of-the-money to the hedge supplier, the hedge supplier is required to post collateral, which can be used by the hedger as a guarantee to mitigate losses in case of early default of the hedge supplier. Although interest on collateral is typically rebated, i.e. paid back to the collateral provider[6] (say the hedge supplier), there is both a funding cost and an opportunity cost, as the posting of collateral depletes the resources the hedge supplier can use to meet his/her capital requirements at aggregate level, as well as to write additional business. This is related to the funding policy of the hedge supplier, and it is related to our discussion on different models for the treasury department we have discussed in Chapter 17, looking at different possible funding policies of the hedge supplier.

On the other hand, whenever the swap is sufficiently in-the-money to the hedge supplier, the hedge supplier will receive collateral from the counterparty, thus benefiting from capital relief in regulatory valuations and freeing up capital that can be used to sell additional longevity protection. The benefits can be far larger if collateral can be re-pledged for other purposes, as in the interest rate swaps market.[7]

The same considerations can be made from the viewpoint of the hedger, but the funding needs and opportunity costs of the two parties are unlikely to offset each other exactly. This is particularly relevant for transactions involving parties subject to different regulatory frameworks. In the UK and several other countries, for example, longevity risk exposures are more capital intensive for hedge suppliers, such as insurers, than for pension funds.[8]

In the absence of collateral, and ignoring longevity risk aversion, swap rates, if defined as the rates in the fixed leg such that the total net present value of the product at inception is zero, depend on the best estimates of survival probabilities for the hedged population and on the degree of covariation between the floating leg of the swap and the term structure of interest rates and credit spreads facing the hedger and the hedge supplier (wrong way risk). We may call such swap rates endogenous, meaning that they incorporate credit (and funding when considered) costs. We have seen how to price counterparty risk for several asset classes in the past chapters of the book, mostly as a total additive adjustment, and without looking for an endogenous swap rate, except for the specific case of equity returns swaps, for which we derived in Chapter 8 the endogenous swap rate, inclusive of counterparty risk and wrong way risk.[9] In the presence of collateralization, longevity swap rates are also shaped by the expected collateral costs, and swap valuation formulae involve default risk, the cost of collateral and

[6] One may make the choice of reabsorbing the collateral interest in the collateral account, so as to decrease the next posting that will be needed, or to pay the collateral interest explicitly to the collateral provider. In this chapter we follow the second formulation.

[7] According to [127 (2010)], the vast majority of collateral is re-hypothecated for other purposes in interest rate swap markets, see also [184] and Chapter 13.

[8] This asymmetry is, in part, a by-product of rules allowing, for example, pension liabilities to be quantified by using outdated mortality tables or discount rates reflecting optimistic expected returns.

[9] Along related lines, [126] show how the discount rate for the valuation of pension liabilities should reflect funding risk.

funding. As a result, default-free valuation formulae are not appropriate even in the presence of full collateralization and the corresponding absence of default losses, because funding costs would still be there,[10] see the framework in Chapter 17 with perfect collateralization and continuous mark-to-market at default for Π: in that situation we discount at collateral total return, namely the risk-free rate plus the spread of collateral over the risk-free rate, and not at the risk-free rate itself.

By specializing in our earlier chapters and by applying them to the longevity swaps asset class, obtaining an approach that is essentially the same as the earlier work of [21], we quantify collateral costs in two ways:

(i) in terms of funding costs that are incurred or mitigated when collateral is posted or received, and
(ii) as the opportunity cost of selling additional longevity protection.

In both i) and ii), [21] find that, for typical interest rate and mortality parameters, the impact of collateralization on swap rates is modest when default risk and collateral rules are symmetric. There are two opposing effects at play:

a) On the one hand, the payer of the variable survival rate (the hedge supplier) posts collateral when mortality is lower (survival is higher) and hence longevity exposures are more capital intensive. On the other hand, he/she receives collateral when mortality is higher and longevity protection less capital intensive. The overall effect is to push (fixed) swap rates higher, to compensate the hedge supplier for the positive dependence between collateral flows and capital costs.
b) When the swap hedger or hedge supplier is out-of-the-money, collateral outflows are larger in low interest rate environments (i.e. when liabilities are discounted at a lower rate), hence there is a negative relationship between the amount of collateral posted and the counterparties' funding costs. This mitigates the overall impact of collateralization on longevity swap rates.

When default risk and/or collateral rules are asymmetric, as in the general theory we developed in Chapter 17, the offsetting effects are of different magnitudes and, as a result, the impact of collateral costs on longevity swap rates is larger. For example, [21] find that swap rates increase substantially when the hedger has a lower credit standing and collateral rules are less favourable to the hedge supplier.

At this stage it may be important to clarify a key assumption in the work of [21], that makes their analysis slightly less general than our treatment in Chapters 13, 15, 16, and 17.

Remark 18.1.1 ***(Limits of Duffie and Huang [101]. Pricing dependence between default of the hedger and the hedge supplier and Gap risk)*** *Biffis et al. [21] resorts to a framework à la Duffie and Huang [101], that adopts a weak model for dependency between default of the hedge supplier and of the hedger, in that it assumes conditional independence between the two defaults, the only correlation being spread correlation, and no jump to default dependency. We have seen in past chapters and in Chapters 12 and 15 in particular, that default correlation between the two parties in the deal also has an important impact on the credit (and collateral) adjustment. Jump to default correlation is typically much stronger than spread correlation*

[10] See [130] for the case of symmetric default risk and full collateralization in interest rate swaps, and more generally see Chapters 13, 16, and 17.

in connecting the two defaults. In this sense, correlation risk and systemic risk are likely to be underplayed to some extent in the Duffie and Huang approach. Our approach in the past chapters is general. However, for the specific case of longevity risk, it may make sense to assume the default correlation between the hedge provider and the hedger to be limited, so that the results of [21], that we report below, may be considered to be realistic, and the conditional independence assumption may be appropriated, as long as one does not aim at running scenarios of strong systemic risk. Gap risk in bilateral counterparty risk calculations may also be affected by the conditional independence assumption. On the difference between the full default filtration $\mathcal{G}$ and the pre-default (also known as default free) or spread filtration $\mathcal{F}$; see also Remark 11.3.1.

18.1.3 Indexed Longevity Swaps

While most of what we summarized above concerns bespoke longevity swaps under counterparty risk collateral and funding, as [21] point out investment banks have sold index-based longevity swaps, which have a structure that would be more familiar to capital markets investors. Despite this, indexed longevity swaps have so far been less popular than bespoke solutions, that are more suited to the specific pools and needs of the hedger. Nevertheless, for the longevity swaps market to really take off, it is necessary to expand beyond the limits of the reinsurance market and attract new investors, who are most likely to be attracted by a more liquid and standardized underlying survival rate, such as an index one. The analysis in [21] can be extended to examine the costs of collateral in index-based swaps.

18.1.4 Endogenous Credit Collateral and Funding-Inclusive Swap Rates

The authors of [21] show how longevity swap rates must be determined endogenously from the dynamic marking-to-market of the swap and the collateral rules specified by the contract, similarly to what we did (without collateral) in Chapter 8 for equity return swaps. We also priced adjustments for interest rates and credit under collateralization in Chapter 15, but without computing an endogenous swap rate.

To see why the dynamics of mark-to-market is needed, note that the market value of the swap at each valuation date depends on the evolution of the relevant state variables (mortality, interest rates, credit spreads, collateral mechanics), as well as on the swap rate locked in at inception. On the other hand, the swap's market value will typically affect collateral amounts and, in a setting where collateral is costly, will embed the market value of the costs associated with future collateral flows. Hence, the swap rate can only be determined by explicitly taking into account the marking-to-market process and the dynamics of collateral posting. This is related to the recursion we pointed out in Chapter 17. To avoid the computational burden of nested Monte Carlo simulations, [21] resort to an iterative procedure based on the least-squares Monte Carlo approach.[11] The authors of [21] provide several numerical examples showing how different collateralization rules shape longevity swap rates inclusive of collateral funding and credit, as we shall see below.

[11] A similar approach is used by [10] for surrender guarantees in life policies and by [11] for the computation of capital requirements within the Solvency II framework, while [56, 57, 58] use it for counterparty risk pricing.

As there is essentially no publicly available information on swap rates, the approach of [21][12] has the advantage of using publicly available information on credit markets and regulatory standards, without having to rely exclusively on calibration to primary insurance market prices, approximate hedging methods or assumptions on agents' risk preferences (see [94, 145, 11, 19, 77, 84]).

The remaining part of this chapter is organized as follows: in the next section, we introduce longevity swaps and formalize their payoffs. We consider the case of both bespoke and index-based swaps, but, in the latter case, we ignore the issue of basis risk[13] to keep the chapter focused.

In Section 18.3, we examine the marking-to-market of a longevity swap during its lifetime, to demonstrate the impact of counterparty risk on the hedger's balance sheet.

Section 18.4 recalls the master formula for bilateral counterparty and debit valuation adjustment inclusive of collateral and funding from Chapters 16 and 17, and explains how this can be applied to the specific case of longevity swaps, trying to re-obtain the framework of [21] as a special case.

In Section 18.5, we explain the dynamics that have been adopted in [21], and finally in Section 18.6 we discuss the result of the numerical examples and case studies in [21], where several stylized examples are provided to understand how different collateralization rules may affect longevity swap rates.

18.2 LONGEVITY SWAPS: THE PAYOFF Π

We follow again [21].

Consider a hedger investor (insurer selling annuities, pension fund), referred to as party "I", and a hedge supplier (reinsurer, investment bank), referred to as counterparty "C". Agent "I" has the obligation to pay amounts $X_{T_1}, X_{T_2}, \ldots$, possibly dependent on interest rates and inflation, to each survivor at fixed dates $0 < T_1 \leq T_2, \ldots$ of an initial population of n individuals alive at time zero (annuitants or pensioners). As in [21], we are clearly restricting our attention to homogeneous liabilities for ease of exposition, more general situations requiring obvious modifications. Party "I"'s liability at a generic payment date $T > 0$ is given by the random variable

$$(n - N_T)X_T,$$

where N_T counts the number of deaths experienced by the population during the period $[0, T]$. Assuming that the individuals' death times have common intensity[14] $(\mu_t)_{t\geq 0}$, the expected number of survivors at time T can be written as

$$\mathbb{E}^{\mathbb{P}}[n - N_T] = np_T,$$

with the survival probability p_T given by

$$p_T := \mathbb{E}^{\mathbb{P}}\left[\exp\left(-\int_0^T \mu_t \mathrm{d}t\right)\right]. \tag{18.1}$$

[12] Similarly, [20] endogenize longevity risk premia by introducing asymmetric information and capital requirements in a risk-neutral setting.

[13] See, for example, [82], [178], and [187] for some results related to this risk dimension.

[14] For tractability we restrict our attention to the case of doubly stochastic (or Cox, conditionally Poisson) death times. This is very similar to the Cox processes framework we have seen for credit risk in Chapter 3

Here and in the following, $\mathbb{P}$ denotes the real-world probability measure. The intensity could be modelled by using, for example, any of the stochastic mortality models considered in [67]. For our examples, we will rely on the simple Lee-Carter model that we will detail below.

Let us now consider a financial market and introduce the risk-free rate process $(r_t)_{t\geq 0}$, these days, typically, approximated by an overnight indexed swap rate. We assume that a market-consistent price of the liabilities can be computed by using a risk-neutral measure $\mathbb{Q}$, equivalent to $\mathbb{P}$, such that the death times have the same intensity process $(\mu_t)_{t\geq 0}$ with different dynamics, in general, under the two measures; see [19]. The time-0 market value of the aggregate liability can then be written as

$$\mathbb{E}^{\mathbb{Q}}\left[\exp\left(-\int_0^T r_t \mathrm{d}t\right)(n - N_T)X_T\right] = nE^{\mathbb{Q}}\left[\exp\left(-\int_0^T (r_t + \mu_t)\mathrm{d}t\right)X_T\right].$$

For the moment, we take the pricing measure as given: we will give it more structure later on.

We consider two instruments which "I" can enter into with "C" to hedge its exposure: a bespoke longevity swap and an index-based longevity swap, with tenor structure T_i. As explained in [21], in these swaps, in contrast with interest rate swaps, the fixed leg will be a series of fixed rates each one pertaining to an individual payment date T_i. The reason is that mortality increases substantially in old age and a single fixed rate would introduce a growing mismatch between the cash flows provided by the swap and those needed by the hedger. However, as with interest rate swaps, we can treat a longevity swap as a portfolio of forward contracts on the underlying variable (survival) rate.[15]

Remark 18.2.1 ***(Longevity Swap as a portfolio of longevity FRAs)*** *The value of a swap across payment dates $T_{initial}, \ldots, T_i, \ldots, T_{final}$ is the sum of the values of swaps with single payment dates T_i, which we could call longevity Forward Rate Agreement (FRA) for T_i. However, when adding credit, collateral and funding, this is no longer true, since such effects are highly nonlinear. Hence we need to decide whether to add such effect to each single FRA separately, and adjust the related FRA rate for funding and credit effects, or to apply the effects to the whole swap, and adjust the overall swap rates. Since, as we just mentioned above, longevity FRAs embedded in a swap have different fixed rates over different T_i's, [21] decide to apply the credit and funding analysis to each FRA separately. We shall do the same, but we need to keep in mind that this is not the same as applying the credit and funding analysis to the swap as a whole.*

In this section, we ignore default risk, collateral, and funding, and focus on individual payments at maturity $T > 0$, detailing what was called Π in earlier chapters. Throughout the chapter, we always assume the perspective of the hedger "I".

A *bespoke longevity swap* allows party "I" to pay a fixed rate $\bar{p}^N \in (0, 1)$ against the realized survival rate experienced by the population between time zero and time T. Assuming

[15] With a slight abuse of terminology, we use the term "swap rate" for individual forward rates underlying embedded longevity Forward Rate Agreements as well as for swap curves (a series of swap rates). We note that swap curves are often summarized by the improvement factor applied to the survival probabilities of a reference mortality table/model.

a notional amount equal to the initial population size, n, the net payout to the hedger at time T is[16]

$$n\left(\frac{n-N_T}{n}-\bar{p}^N\right),$$

i.e. the difference between the realized number of survivors and the pre-set number of survivors $n\bar{p}^N$ agreed at inception. Letting S_0 denote the market value of the swap at inception, we can write

$$\begin{aligned} S_0 &= n\mathbb{E}^{\mathbb{Q}}\left[\exp\left(-\int_0^T r_t \mathrm{d}t\right)\left(\frac{n-N_T}{n}-\bar{p}^N\right)\right] \\ &= n\mathbb{E}^{\mathbb{Q}}\left[\exp\left(-\int_0^T (r_t+\mu_t)\mathrm{d}t\right)\right]-nP(0,T)\bar{p}^N, \end{aligned} \tag{18.2}$$

with $P(0, T)$ denoting, as usual, the time-zero price of a zero-coupon bond with maturity T. By setting $S_0 = 0$, we obtain the swap rate as

$$\bar{p}^N = \widetilde{p}_T + P(0,T)^{-1}\mathrm{Cov}^{\widetilde{\mathbb{P}}}\left(\exp\left(-\int_0^T r_t \mathrm{d}t\right), \exp\left(-\int_0^T \mu_t \mathrm{d}t\right)\right), \tag{18.3}$$

where the risk-adjusted survival probability $\widetilde{p}_T$ is defined as in (18.1) with expectations taken under $\mathbb{Q}$:

$$\tilde{p}_T := \mathbb{E}^{\mathbb{Q}}\left[\exp\left(-\int_0^T \mu_t \mathrm{d}t\right)\right]. \tag{18.4}$$

Expression (18.3) shows that if the intensity of mortality is uncorrelated with bond market returns (a reasonable first-order approximation), the longevity swap curve just involves the survival probabilities $\{\widetilde{p}_{T_i}\}$ relative to the different maturities $\{T_i\}$. Several studies have recently addressed the issue of how to quantify risk-adjusted survival probabilities, for example, by calibration to annuity prices and books of life policies traded in secondary markets, or by use of approximate hedging methods. As there is essentially no publicly available information on swap rates, for their numerical examples [21] suppose a baseline case in which

$$\widetilde{p}_{T_i} = p_{T_i}$$

for each maturity T_i and focus on how counterparty default risk and collateral requirements might generate a positive or negative spread on best estimate survival rates. Although in what follows, [21] mainly concentrate on longevity risk, in practice, the floating payment of a longevity swap might involve an interbank (e.g. LIBOR) rate component or survival indexation rules different from the ones considered above. To keep the setup general, [21] at times consider instruments making a generic variable payment, P, and write the corresponding swap rate $\bar{p}$ as

$$\bar{p} = \mathbb{E}^{\mathbb{Q}}[P] + P(0,T)^{-1}\mathrm{Cov}^{\widetilde{\mathbb{Q}}}\left(\exp\left(-\int_0^T r_t \mathrm{d}t\right), P\right). \tag{18.5}$$

[16] For ease of exposition, here and in the following sections, we consider contemporaneous settlement only. Other settlement conventions (e.g. in arrears) have negligible effects, but make valuation formulae more involved when bilateral and asymmetric default risk is introduced.

This setup can easily accommodate the index-based longevity swaps we mentioned above, i.e. standardized instruments allowing the hedger to pay a fixed rate $\bar{p}^I \in (0, 1)$ against the realized value of a survival index $(I_t)_{t\geq 0}$ at time T. The latter might reflect the mortality experience of a reference population closely matching that of the liability portfolio. Examples are represented by the LifeMetrics index developed by J.P. Morgan, the Pensions Institute and Towers Watson,[17] or the Xpect indices developed by Deutsche Boerse.[18] The relative advantages and disadvantages of index-based versus bespoke swaps are discussed, for example, in [22]. Assuming that the index admits the representation $I_t = \exp(-\int_0^t \mu_s^I \mathrm{d}s)$, with $(\mu_t^I)_{t\geq 0}$ the intensity of mortality of a reference population, the swap rate $\bar{p}^I$ is given again by Expression (18.3), but with the process μ replaced by μ^I, and with $\widetilde{p}_T$ replaced by the corresponding risk-adjusted survival probability $\widetilde{p}_T^I$.

18.3 MARK-TO-MARKET FOR LONGEVITY SWAPS

As [21] point out, longevity swaps are not currently exchange traded and there is no commonly accepted framework for counterparties to mark-to-market/model their positions.[19] The presence of counterparty default risk and collateralization rules, however, makes the mark-to-market procedure a very important feature of these transactions for at least two reasons. First, at each payment date, the difference between the variable and pre-set payment generates a cash inflow or outflow to the hedger, depending on the evolution of mortality. In the absence of basis risk (which is the case for bespoke solutions), these differences show a pure "cash-flow hedge" of the longevity exposure in operation. However, as market conditions change (e.g. mortality patterns, counterparty default risk, funding costs), the impact of the swap on the hedger's balance sheet can evolve dramatically. For example, even if the swap payments are expected to provide a good hedge against longevity risk, the hedger's position will weaken considerably if the expected present value of the net payments shrinks due to deterioration in the hedge supplier's credit quality. Second, for solvency requirements, it is important to value a longevity swap under extreme market/mortality scenarios (stress testing). This means that even if a longevity swap qualifies as a liability on a market-consistent basis, it might still provide considerable capital relief when valued on a regulatory basis.

To illustrate some of these points, let us consider the hypothetical situation of an insurer "I" with a liability represented by a group of ten thousand 65-year-old annuitants drawn from the population of England and Wales in 1980. We assume that party "I" entered a 25-year pure longevity swap in 1980 and we follow the evolution of the contract until maturity. The population is assumed to evolve according to the death rates reported in the Human Mortality Database (HMD) for England and Wales.[20] We assume that interest rate risk is hedged away through interest rate swaps, locking in a rate of 5% throughout the life of the swap. The role of collateral is examined later on; here, we show how the hedging instrument operates from the point of view of the hedger. We write the discounted payout as a sum of single swap payments. As before, we may call each T_i longevity swap payment a Forward (longevity) Rate

[17] See www.lifemetrics.com.
[18] See www.xpect-index.com.
[19] At the time of writing, LLMA was working on this issue.
[20] See www.mortality.org.

Agreement (FRA), since this simplifies exposition. A full swap is a set of FRAs. We assume the tenor of the swap is given by maturities

$$T_{\text{initial}}, \ldots, T_i, \ldots, T_{\text{final}}.$$

For this bespoke swap solution, the sum of the discounted cash flows at time t, up to the final maturity $T = T_{\text{final}}$, when neglecting default risk of both "I" and "C" and funding costs of both, is given by the expression

$$\Pi(t,T) = \sum_i \Pi_i(t,T),$$

$$\Pi_i(t,T) = n\left[\exp\left(-\int_t^{T_i} r_s \mathrm{d}s\right)\left(\frac{n-N_t}{n}\exp\left(-\int_t^{T_i}\mu_s \mathrm{d}s\right)\right)\right] - nD(t,T_i)\bar{p}^N_{T_i}, \quad (18.6)$$

where D is the stochastic discount factor at time t for maturity T_i corresponding to the risk-free rate (typically approximated with an overnight indexed rate).

The market value of each floating-for-fixed payment occurring at a generic date T can be computed by using the valuation formula $\mathbb{E}_t^{\mathbb{Q}}\Pi(t,T)$, leading to

$$S_t = n\mathbb{E}_t^{\mathbb{Q}}\left[\sum_i \exp\left(-\int_t^{T_i} r_s \mathrm{d}s\right)\left(\tfrac{n-N_t}{n}\exp\left(-\int_t^{T_i}\mu_s \mathrm{d}s\right)\right)\right] - n\sum_i P(t,T_i)\bar{p}^N_{T_i}, \quad (18.7)$$

for each time t at which no default has yet occurred, with $P(t, T_i)$ denoting the market value of a zero-coupon bond with time to maturity $T_i - t$, and $\mathbb{E}_t^{\mathbb{Q}}[\cdot]$ the conditional expectation under a pricing measure $\mathbb{Q}$, given the information available at time t. As a simple benchmark case, we assume that market participants receive information from the Human Mortality Database (HMD) and use the Lee-Carter model to value longevity-linked cashflows. In other words, at each mark-to-market (MTM) date (including inception), longevity swap rates are based on Lee-Carter forecasts computed using the latest HMD information available.[21] Figure 18.1 illustrates the evolution of swap survival rates for an England and Wales cohort tracked from age 65 in 1980 to age 90 in 2005. It is clear that the systematic underestimation of mortality improvements by the Lee-Carter model in this particular example will mean that the hedger's position will become increasingly in-the-money as the swap matures. This is shown in Figure 18.2. In practice, the contract may allow the counterparty to cancel the swap or re-set the fixed leg for a non-negative fee, but we ignore these features in this example. Figure 18.2 also reports the sequence of net cash flows generated by the swap. As interest rate risk is hedged – and again ignoring default risk for the moment – cash inflows/outflows arising in the backtesting exercise only reflect the difference between the realized survival rates and the swap rates locked in at inception. On the other hand, the swap's market value reflects changes in market swap rates, which by assumption follow the updated Lee-Carter forecasts plotted in Figure 18.1 and differ from the realized survival rates. As is evident from Figure 18.2, the credit exposure of a longevity swap is close to zero at inception and at maturity, but may be sizeable in between, depending on the trade-off between changes in market/mortality conditions and the residual swap payments (amortization effect). The credit exposure is quantified by the replacement cost, i.e. the cost that the non-defaulting counterparty would have to incur at the default time to replace the instrument at market prices then available. As a simple example which anticipates the next section, let us introduce credit risk (but no default – see

[21] See [95, 96, 68] for a comprehensive analysis of alternative mortality models; see also [117].

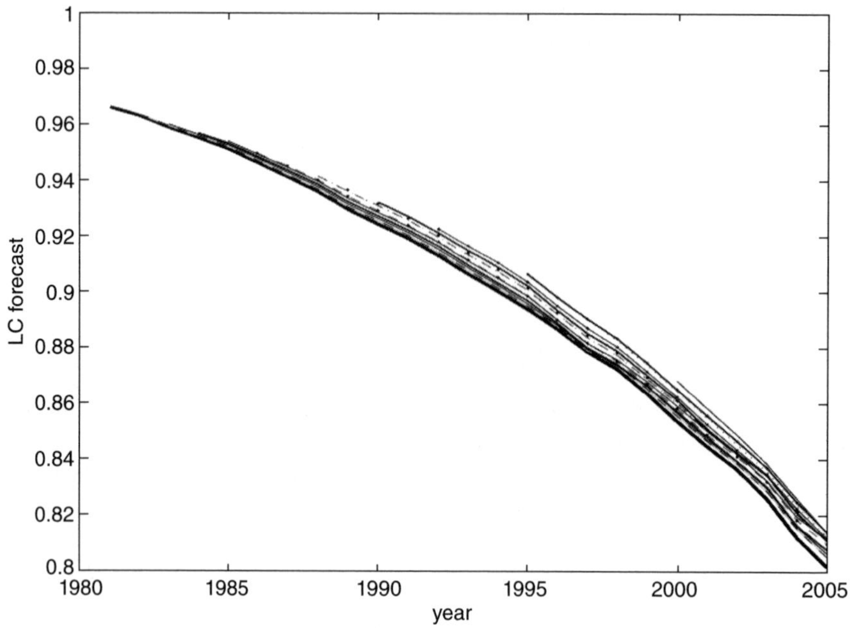

Figure 18.1 From [21]. Survival curves computed at the beginning of each year $t = 1980, \ldots, 2004$ for England and Wales males aged $65 + t - 1980$ in year t. Forecasts are based on the Lee-Carter model using the latest Human Mortality Database data available at the beginning of each year t

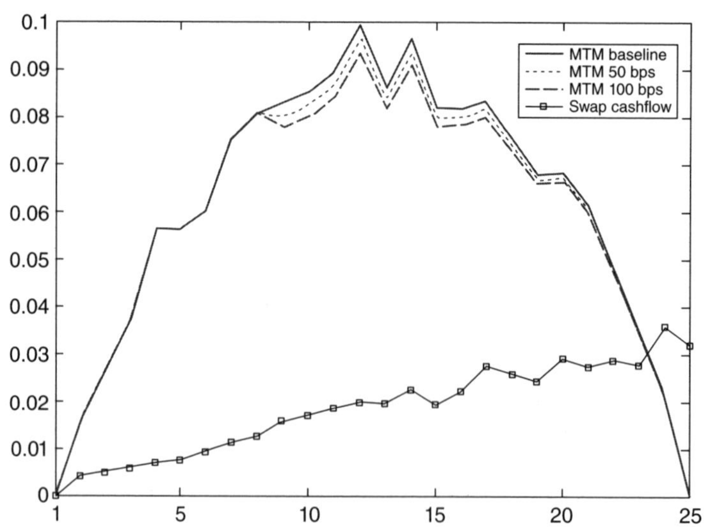

Figure 18.2 From [21]. Mark-to-market value of the longevity swap in the baseline case and with counterparty C's credit spread widening by 50 and 100 basis points over 1988–2005. In the absence of default, the net payments from the swap are insensitive to credit spread changes

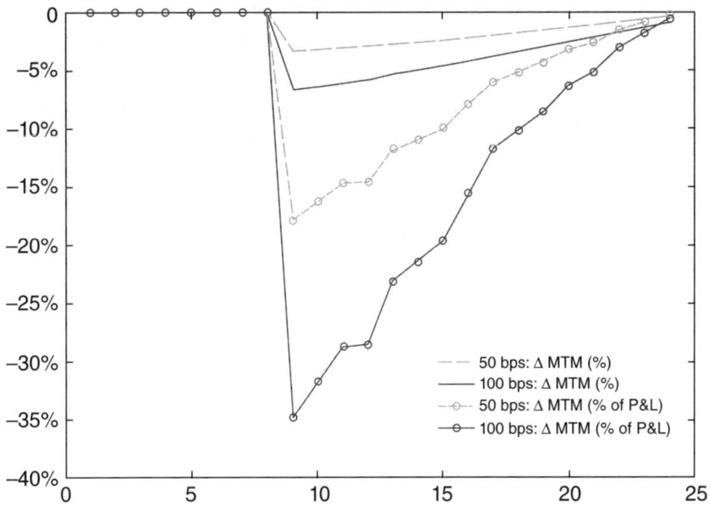

Figure 18.3 From [21]. Change in mark-to-market value of the longevity swap (MTM) relative to the baseline case and the net payments from the swap, when counterparty C's credit spread widens by 50 and 100 basis points over 1988–2005

Remark 11.3.1) and assume that in 1988 the credit spread of the hedge supplier widens across all maturities by 25 and 50 basis points. The impact of these two scenarios on the hedger's balance sheet is dramatic, as shown in Figures 18.2 and 18.3, demonstrating how MTM profits and losses can jeopardize a successful cash-flow hedge.

18.4 COUNTERPARTY AND OWN DEFAULT RISK, COLLATERAL AND FUNDING

We can apply our master equation inclusive of credit risk, collateral and funding, as developed in Chapter 17, to the initial payout $\Pi(t, T)$, and derive the adjusted payout inclusive of all such aspects, for a given exogenous set of swap rates $\bar{p}^N_{T_i}$. While we could go general with the funding model and collateral, we try to establish a setup that is as close as possible to Biffis et al. [21]. This is obtained by assuming that collateral and funding are accounted for continuously, rather than at discrete time instants, leading to the funding-inclusive equation of Chapter 17, that we report here:

$$\begin{aligned}\bar{V}_t(C;F) = C_t &\\ &+\mathbb{E}_t\left[\mathbf{1}_{\{\tau<T\}}\left(\theta_\tau(C,\varepsilon) - C_{\tau^-}\right)D(t,\tau;\tilde{f})\right]\\ &+\int_t^T \mathbb{E}_t\left[\mathbf{1}_{\{u<\tau\}}\left(\Pi(u,u+du) + dC_u - \tilde{c}_u C_u\,du\right)D(t,u;\tilde{f})\right]\\ &+\int_t^T \mathbb{E}_t\left[\mathbf{1}_{\{u<\tau\}}D(t,u;\tilde{f})H_u(\tilde{f}_u - r_u)du\right] \qquad (18.8)\end{aligned}$$

where we had defined the funding discount factor as $D(t,T;\tilde{f}) := e^{-\int_t^T \tilde{f}_u\,du}$ and where Π is the longevity swap payoff. We also recall that τ is the first default time, namely $\tau := \tau_I \wedge \tau_C$.

We recall the decomposition in four terms: The first term C is the collateral price. The second and third terms are formed by the cash flows which are not considered by collateralization, such as the cash flows payed on default event of one of the two counterparties, by mark-to-market movements which are not followed by an immediate reset of the collateral account, and by margining costs not included into collateral price. The fourth term factoring $\tilde{f}_u - r_u$ represents the funding costs of the hedging strategy that is implemented for the instrument, H being the price of the hedging portfolio.

We assume also, as in Section 17.4.2, that we may write

$$\bar{V}_t(C;F) = \int_t^T \mathbb{E}_t^{\tilde{f}}\left[\mathbf{1}_{\{u<\tau<u+du\}} D(t,\tau;\tilde{f})\,\theta_\tau(C,\varepsilon)\right]$$
$$+ \int_t^T \mathbb{E}_t^{\tilde{f}}\left[\mathbf{1}_{\{u<\tau\}} D(t,u;\tilde{f})\left(\Pi(u,u+du) + C_u(\tilde{f}_u - \tilde{c}_u)\,du\right)\right]$$

where we have also partly integrated the collateral term.

In order to review the results of Biffis et al [21], we start by detailing their assumptions on collateralization and close-out amount evaluation:

- Collateral C is a fraction α_t of the mark to market value, namely

$$C_t \doteq \alpha_t \bar{V}_t(C;F);$$

  in [21] the authors illustrate the two extreme cases where collateral matches the full mark to market ($\alpha_t = 1$) and where collateral is not there, or is zero ($\alpha_t = 0$), although they derive a formula for the general case.
- Collateral is posted continuously.
- Collateral re-hypothecation is allowed.
- For simplicity we assume that the recovery rate is zero for both counterparties, but this is not necessary ([21] has the general case).
- Close-out amount is equal to the pre-default deal's price, so that, if we use notation ε_I and ε_C to denote the on-default exposure as priced by I and C respectively, we have

$$\varepsilon_{I,\tau} \doteq \varepsilon_{C,\tau} \doteq \bar{V}_{\tau^-}(C;F).$$

  Notice that this assumption is much more restrictive than our earlier framework: $\bar{V}$ needs to be continuous at default, or else we would not be able to ensure a full collateralization when $\alpha_t = 1$. Moreover, with reference to our earlier Chapter 17, we are assuming that $\varepsilon_{I,\tau} = \varepsilon_{C,\tau}$. As we have seen in that chapter, this symmetric assumption is quite common in the early funding literature. While in this book we deal with the more general theory, in this longevity chapter, to match the theory in [21], we need to assume symmetry.

  More precisely, we are assuming that we are able to see the funding costs of the counterparty, and that

$$f_t^+ \equiv f_t^{+,I} \doteq f_t^{-,C}, \quad f_t^- \equiv f_t^{-,I} \doteq f_t^{+,C}$$

  where $f_t^{I,+}$ (or simply f_t^+) is the funding rate of the investor, $f_t^{I,-}$ (or simply f_t^-) is the investing rate of the investor, $f_t^{C,-}$ is the funding rate of the counterparty, $f_t^{C,+}$ is the investing rate of the counterparty.

One more implicit assumption is that the common funding and investment rates are $\mathcal{F}_t$ adapted or even predictable, meaning that they are observed as spreads at time t by all market parties in the deal.

Under these assumptions we get (still resorting to $\mathcal{G}$ expectations)

$$\begin{aligned}\bar{V}_t = &\int_t^T \mathbb{E}_t^{\tilde{f}}\big[\,\mathbf{1}_{\{u<\tau\}} D(t,u;\tilde{f})\left(\Pi(u,u+du) + \alpha_u \bar{V}_u(\tilde{f}_u - \tilde{c}_u)du\right)\big] \\ &+ \int_t^T \mathbb{E}_t^{\tilde{f}}\big[\,\mathbf{1}_{\{u<\tau<u+du\}} D(t,\tau;\tilde{f})\left(\mathbf{1}_{\{\tau_I<\tau_C\}} + \alpha_u \mathbf{1}_{\{\tau_C<\tau_I\}}\right)\bar{V}_u^+\,\big] \\ &+ \int_t^T \mathbb{E}_t^{\tilde{f}}\big[\,\mathbf{1}_{\{u<\tau<u+du\}} D(t,\tau;\tilde{f})\left(\mathbf{1}_{\{\tau_C<\tau_I\}} + \alpha_u \mathbf{1}_{\{\tau_I<\tau_C\}}\right)\bar{V}_u^-\,\big]\end{aligned}$$

where we dropped the explicit dependency on C and F of the deal's price for better readability. Now, we can define

$$\lambda_u^{C<I}\,du := \mathbb{E}_u^{\tilde{f}}\big[\,\mathbf{1}_{\{u<\tau<u+du\}}\mathbf{1}_{\{\tau_C<\tau_I\}}\,\big]$$

and

$$\lambda_u^{I<C}\,du := \mathbb{E}_u^{\tilde{f}}\big[\,\mathbf{1}_{\{u<\tau<u+du\}}\mathbf{1}_{\{\tau_I<\tau_C\}}\,\big]$$

(both intensities embed a survival indicator at u) so that we obtain

$$\bar{V}_t = \int_t^T \mathbb{E}_t^{\tilde{f}}\big[\,\mathbf{1}_{\{u<\tau\}} D(t,u;\tilde{f})\left(\Pi(u,u+du) - \bar{V}_u(\tilde{\zeta}_u - \lambda_u)\,du\right)\big]$$

where

$$\lambda_t\,dt := \left(\lambda_t^{I<C} + \lambda_t^{C<I}\right)dt = \mathbb{E}_t^{\tilde{f}}\big[\,\mathbf{1}_{\{t<\tau<t+dt\}}\,\big]$$

and

$$\tilde{\zeta}_t = (1-\alpha_t)(\lambda_t^{C<I}\mathbf{1}_{\{\bar{V}_t>0\}} + \lambda_t^{I<C}\mathbf{1}_{\{\bar{V}_t<0\}}) - \alpha_t(\tilde{f}_t - \tilde{c}_t).$$

The above recursive equation can be solved starting from the terminal condition $\bar{V}_T = 0$, and we get

$$\bar{V}_t = \int_t^T \mathbb{E}_t^{\tilde{f}}\big[\,\mathbf{1}_{\{u<\tau\}} D(t,u;\tilde{f}+\tilde{\zeta}-\lambda)\Pi(u,u+du)\big] \tag{18.9}$$

which is an explicit solution if we have a symmetric problem ($f_t^+ = f_t^-$), otherwise a numerical solution is required (e.g. by means of a least-squares Monte Carlo).

We now move from the full default-inclusive filtration $\mathcal{G}_t$ implicit in the last formula to the spread filtration $\mathcal{F}_t$, obtaining through standard filtration switching formulas

$$\bar{V}_t = \mathbf{1}_{\{\tau>t\}}\int_t^T \mathbb{E}_t^{\tilde{f}}\big[\,D(t,u;\tilde{f}+\tilde{\zeta})\Pi(u,u+du)\big|\mathcal{F}\,\big]. \tag{18.10}$$

In the paper by Biffis et al. [21] a particular market setting is assumed when considering longevity swaps. While the examination of funding and collateral in longevity swaps consistently with our earlier chapters is under investigation, for the time being in this book we report the results in the setup of [21].

The authors assume

- the reference currency is USD;
- funding rates are set equal to Treasury rates for both the counterparties, and are in particular equal to each others, so that we are in the symmetric case;
- collateral accrual rates are specified in the "exotic" CSAs of the longevity swaps type markets. We only assume that they are specified in the CSA so as to be adapted and left continuous, essentially meaning that they are predictable in the probabilistic sense. Examples of the concrete type of rules one has are available in [21]. The reason why the CSA collateral accrual rate is not fully specified in this chapter as a deterministic function of relevant market variables is because rules may indeed be "exotic", for example collateral rates may depend on the underlying mortality experience, they may involve path dependence (with respect to mortality experience/expectations for example), and can be monitoring different variables at different frequencies (for example, the CSA may allow for daily adjusted collateral for financial conditions, quarterly adjusted for death experience, and annual adjustments for changes in future improvements, etc).
- there is no default correlation between the two parties I and C, but at most spread correlation, see again Remark 18.1.1. In this case we may write

$$\lambda_u^{C<I}\,du = \mathbb{E}_u^{\tilde f}\big[\,\mathbf{1}_{\{u<\tau_C<u+du\}}\big] = \mathbf{1}_{\{\tau>u\}}\lambda_u^C\,du$$

and

$$\lambda_u^{I<C}\,du = \mathbb{E}_u^{\tilde f}\big[\,\mathbf{1}_{\{u<\tau_I<u+du\}}\big] = \mathbf{1}_{\{\tau>u\}}\lambda_u^I\,du$$

where it is understood that λ_u^C and λ_u^I are the $\mathcal{F}_u$ measurable components of the intensities. In such settings Equation (18.10) can be cast in the following form

$$\bar V_t = \mathbf{1}_{\{\tau>t\}}\int_t^T \mathbb{E}_t^{\tilde f}\big[\,D(t,u;r+\tilde\zeta^B)\Pi(u,u+du)\big|\mathcal{F}\big] \tag{18.11}$$

with r_t the treasury rate, and

$$\tilde\zeta_t^B = (1-\alpha_t)(\lambda_t^C\mathbf{1}_{\{\bar V_t>0\}} + \lambda_t^I\mathbf{1}_{\{\bar V_t<0\}}) - \alpha_t\tilde\delta_t \tag{18.12}$$

with

$$\tilde\delta_t := \tilde c_t - r_t, \quad \delta_t^{\pm} := c_t^{\pm} - r_t. \tag{18.13}$$

For the definition of $c_t^{\pm}$ and the related $\tilde c$ see Chapter 16.

This setting leads indeed to a formula that is equivalent to the one given in [21]. In particular, the final formula for the total discounting spread over r_t coincides with the spread Γ given in [21].

One comment we need to make here is that in [21] the rate $r+\tilde\delta$ is the cost of borrowing the collateral (either externally or from the treasury) that needs to be posted. We instead defined $\tilde c$ as interest that is either earned on collateral that has been posted from the other party in the deal, or as interest that is paid on collateral that is received from the other party in the deal.

We make the assumption that the funding costs of the other party are visible, and thus we may charge the other party the cost of funding the collateral. This means that we may charge the other party precisely $r+\tilde\delta$ on the collateral we post, so that we obtain with out notation

$$\tilde c_t = r_t + \tilde\delta_t.$$

This implies that

$$\tilde{\delta}_t = \tilde{c}_t - r_t$$

consistently with what we assumed above in (18.13).

In [21] the authors continue by modelling the five quantities r_t, $\lambda_t^{I,C}$ and $\delta_t^{\pm}$. They use a two-factor model for the treasury rate and mean-reverting one-factor models for the other four rates. Thus, they use six underlying processes.

So far we have discussed the payout adjustment to account for credit, collateral, and funding, but we have not populated the dynamics of the relevant quantities with specific models. While we could do that consistently with the earlier chapters of the book, as this is a work in progress we report here the analysis that has been already carried out by Biffis et al. [21].

18.5 AN EXAMPLE OF MODELLING SPECIFICATION FROM BIFFIS ET AL. (2011)

An important element that is in [21] and that we have not dealt with, except for equity return swaps in Chapter 8, is the search for a credit-debit-collateral-funding inclusive equilibrium swap rate rather than for a total additive price adjustment. In other words, we may look for a new swap rate that sets the price of the deal to zero when this price includes counterparty credit and debit risk, collateral and funding. To clarify this, we note that the payout of the longevity swap (18.6) depends on the swap rate $\bar{p}^N$, so that we write $\Pi(t, T, \bar{p}^N)$, $\bar{\Pi}(t, T, \bar{p}^N)$ and $\bar{V}_t(C; F, \bar{p}^N)$ to highlight the dependence on the swap rate $\bar{p}^N$. Finding the endogenous fair swap rate means finding $\bar{p}^N$ such that

$$\bar{V}_t(C; F, \bar{p}^N) = 0. \tag{18.14}$$

We may implement a root search in our framework, where the solution of Equation (18.14) is obtained by iterating a complex Monte Carlo simulation for several different values of $\bar{p}^N$.

We now specify a little more the modelling choices in [21].

The authors of [21] use a continuous-time model for the risk-free yield curve, the LIBOR and mortality rates, as well as for the cost of collateral. The credit risk of party "C" (the hedge supplier) is assumed to be equal to the average credit quality of the LIBOR panel (Interbank market), so that the Interbank/Treasury (TED) spread would be party "C"'s default intensity if there were zero recovery upon default.[22] They then set $\lambda^I = \lambda^C + \Delta$ and consider two cases: party "I" is either of the same credit quality as party "C" ($\Delta = 0$) or is more credit-risky ($\Delta > 0$). They consider a Markov setting, and describe the evolution of uncertainty by a six-dimensional state variable vector X with Gaussian dynamics.

The components are:

- the short rate, $r = X^{(1)}$, assumed to revert to
- the long-run central tendency factor $X^{(2)}$, representing the slope of the risk-free yield curve;
- the TED spread $X^{(3)}$, so that the LIBOR rate is given by $X^{(1)} + X^{(3)}$;
- and the net yield on collateral in the interest rate swap market, $X^{(4)}$, namely the quantity $\delta_t^I = \delta_t^+$.

[22] [21] was written before the LIBOR rigging scandal came out in 2012.

- The remaining two components describe the yield on collateral attached to longevity risk business, $X^{(5)}$, namely the other quantity $\delta_t^C = \delta_t^-$, in the application considering the opportunity cost of collateral, namely b) below,
- and the log-intensity of mortality of a given population, $\log \mu = X^{(6)}$.

The Gaussian dynamics of X (under $\mathbb{Q}$) in [21] is given by

$$\begin{aligned}
dX_t^{(1)} &= \left(k_1(X_t^{(2)} - X_t^{(1)}) - \eta^1\right) dt + \sigma_1 dW_t^1 \\
dX_t^{(2)} &= \left(k_2(\theta_2 - X_t^{(2)}) - \eta^2\right) dt + \sigma_2 dW_t^2 \\
dX_t^{(3)} &= \left(\kappa_3(\theta_3 - X_t^{(3)}) + \kappa_{3,1}(X_t^{(1)} - \theta_2) + \kappa_{3,4}(X_t^{(4)} - \theta_4) - \eta_3\right) dt + \sigma_3 dW_t^3 \\
dX_t^{(4)} &= \left(\kappa_4(\theta_4 - X_t^{(4)}) + \kappa_{4,1}(X_t^{(1)} - \theta_2) + \kappa_{4,2}(X_t^{(2)} - \theta_2) - \eta_4\right) dt + \sigma_4 dW_t^4 \\
dX_t^{(5)} &= (\kappa_5(\theta_5 - X_t^{(5)}) + \kappa_{5,1}(X_t^{(1)} - \theta_2) + \kappa_{5,2}(X_t^{(2)} - \theta_2) + \kappa_{5,3}(X_t^{(3)} - \theta_3) \\
&\quad + \kappa_{5,4}(X_t^{(4)} - \theta_4) + \kappa_{5,6}(X_t^{(6)} - E_0[X_t^{(6)}]) - \eta_5) dt + \sigma_5 dW_t^5 \\
dX_t^{(6)} &= \left(A(t) + B(t)(X_t^{(6)} - a(t))\right) dt + \sigma_6(t) dW_t^6,
\end{aligned}$$

where $W = (W^1, \ldots, W^6)^\mathsf{T}$ is a standard $\mathbb{Q}$-Brownian motion, the constants η^i represent market prices of risk and the functions $A(\cdot)$, $B(\cdot)$, $\sigma_6(\cdot)$ are defined below. The $\mathbb{P}$-dynamics are obtained by removing the market prices of risk from the drifts of the relevant factors and replacing the innovations with the corresponding $\mathbb{P}$-Brownian innovations.

A key assumption in [21] is that $X^{(6)}$ has the same dynamics under the physical and the pricing probability measures, consistent with the baseline case of a swap rate equal to p_T for each T in the absence of collateral. Recall also that there are no instantaneous jumps in the mark-to-market upon default in the model X.

The Brownian innovations are uncorrelated, with the exception of the pair W^1, W^2, whose instantaneous correlation is denoted by $\rho_{1,2}$.

Under the assumption of independence between the interest rate and mortality rates, Biffis et al. [21] can estimate separately the dynamics of the two groups of factors $(X^{(1)}, X^{(2)}, X^{(3)}, X^{(4)})$ and $X^{(6)}$.

a) In particular, as a first example, [21] disregard $X^{(5)}$, and focus on funding costs. They simply take $\delta^C = X^{(3)}$ and $\delta^I = X^{(3)} + \Delta$ meaning that net collateral costs coincide with each party's borrowing rate net of the risk-free rate (assuming it is rebated). In the case of asymmetric default risk, they consider values of 100 and 200 basis points for Δ. Here in particular there is an assumption on the funding policy of the other party to be known to the calculating party.
b) In a second example, [21] focus on the opportunity cost of selling additional longevity protection and simulate the capital charges arising from holding a representative longevity-linked liability to estimate the dynamics of $X^{(5)}$. In other words, they 'synthesize' the dynamics of $X^{(5)}$ by using information on regulatory requirements to quantify the capital charges accruing to the counterparties during the life of the swap. For details on this second approach we refer to their original paper.

Table 18.2 From [21]: Parameter values for the dynamics of X. The estimates for $X^{(5)}$ are based on the assumption that capital increases are funded by counterparties at 6% plus the LIBOR rate

κ_1	0.969	η_1	−0.053	σ_1	0.008	UK	
κ_2	0.832	η_3	−0.014	σ_2	0.155	δ_K	−0.888
κ_3	1.669	η_4	0.007	σ_3	0.009	σ_K	1.156
κ_4	0.045	η_5	0.055	σ_4	0.010	US	
κ_5	0.990	$\kappa_{5,1}$	0.147	σ_5	0.690	δ_K	−0.761
$\kappa_{3,1}$	−0.163	$\kappa_{5,2}$	1.340	θ_2	0.046	σ_K	1.078
$\kappa_{4,1}$	0.114	$\kappa_{5,3}$	2.509	θ_3	0.003		
$\kappa_{3,4}$	0.804	$\kappa_{5,4}$	−0.133	θ_4	0.007		
$\kappa_{4,2}$	−0.038	$\kappa_{5,6}$	−0.002	θ_5	0.115	$\rho_{1,2}$	−0.036

Summing up:

- For the first four factors ($X^{(1)}, X^{(2)}, X^{(3)}, X^{(4)}$), [21] use data from [130] who rely on a two-stage maximum likelihood procedure based on weekly data sampled on Wednesdays, from 1990 to 2002, and set the long-run mean of $X^{(3)}$ equal to the average of the 3-month TED spread over the sampling period. This procedure leads to the parameter values of Table 18.2.
- For the log-intensity $X^{(6)}$, they use the mortality model described below, and assume that the Brownian component W^6 is uncorrelated with the other ones. The intensity of mortality is modelled using the following continuous-time version of the Lee-Carter model [19]: first use the annual central death rates $\{m_{y,s}\}$ for US and UK males from the Human Mortality Database to estimate the model

$$m_{y,s} = \exp(\alpha(y) + \beta(y)K_s)$$

for dates $s = 1961, 1962, \ldots, 2007$ and ages $y = 20, 21, \ldots, 89$ with Singular Value Decomposition. The resulting estimates for K are then fitted with the process

$$K_{s+1} = \delta_K K_s + \sigma_K \varepsilon,$$

with $\varepsilon \sim N(0, 1)$. For fixed age $x = 65$, the estimates for $\{\hat{\alpha}(x+h), \hat{\beta}(x+h)\}_{h=0,1,\ldots}$ are interpolated with differentiable functions $a(t), b(t)$.

Table 18.3 Sensitivity with respect to parameter σ_5: we compute 25-year swap rates and spreads (in basis points) under full collateralization by setting $X^{(1)}, X^{(2)}$ equal to their long run means. The baseline estimated parameter values for the dynamics of $X^{(5)}$ are $\theta_5 = 0.000254$, $\kappa_5 = 1.005073$, $\sigma_5 = 0.000542$, $\eta_5 = 0.000269$, $\kappa_{53} = 0.003648$, $\kappa_{54} = 0.000018$, $\kappa_{56} = 0.000261$

σ_5	p_{25}	$\bar{p}^c$	spread (bps)
0.0005	0.201425	0.201469	2.15
0.0100	0.201425	0.201822	19.68
0.0150	0.201425	0.202009	28.96
0.0200	0.201425	0.202196	38.26
0.1000	0.201425	0.205237	189.24
0.1500	0.201425	0.207184	285.90

The functions A, B, σ_6 are finally obtained by setting

$$A(t) = a'(t) + b(t)\delta_K,$$
$$B(t) = b'(t)b(t)^{-1},$$
$$\sigma_6(t) = b(t)\sigma_K.$$

The expectation appearing in the drift of $X^{(5)}$ ensures that the longevity capital charges react to departures of realized mortality from the term structure of survival rates estimated at inception.

- How do we estimate the dynamics of $X^{(5)}$? This is the component of collateral costs related to longevity risk. [21] set the duration $\bar{T}$ of the representative liability equal to 15. They simulate forward all of the other state variables, and at each time step, they compute the opportunity cost of capital arising from the capital charges accruing to the hedge supplier based on the simulated mortality and market conditions, and they assume that funding occurs at the LIBOR rate plus a fixed spread of 6%, a reasonable value for the cost of internal capital. To obtain the net cost of collateral, [21] take into account the rebate of the risk-free rate. They estimate the dynamics of $X^{(5)}$ on each simulated path, setting the parameter θ_5 equal to the average of $X^{(5)}$ along the simulated path. The parameter estimates are computed for each simulated path and then averaged across all simulations. The estimates are reported in Table 18.2.

Based on this framework, [21] compute the longevity swap rates for a 25-year swap written on a population of 10,000 US males aged 65 at the beginning of 2008.

18.6 DISCUSSION OF THE RESULTS IN BIFFIS ET AL. (2011)

In Figure 18.4, we plot the swap curves obtained for different collateralization rules against the percentiles of survival rate improvements based on Lee-Carter forecasts. We see that margins are positive and increasing with payment maturity in the case of symmetric default risk, for both uncollateralized and fully collateralized transactions. As soon as we introduce asymmetry in default risk ($\Delta > 0$), however, margins widen in the case of no collateralization, reflecting the fact that the hedger needs to pay an additional premium on account of its higher credit risk. In the case of full collateralization, the hedge supplier benefits from the negative dependence between funding costs and collateral amounts: equilibrium swap rates are pushed lower and produce a negative margin on best estimate swap rates. In Figure 18.5, we examine the swap margins induced by one-sided collateralization in the case of asymmetric default risk. When only the hedge supplier has to post full collateral, swap rates are higher than best estimate survival probabilities, meaning that the hedger has to compensate the hedge supplier for bearing both the cost of risk mitigation and the hedger's default risk. The opposite is true when it is the hedger who has to post full collateral when out-of-the money. In this case, swap margins are clearly negative, and decreasing in payment maturity. These effects are amplified when the asymmetry in counterparties' credit quality is greater, as can be seen from the swap spreads reported in Table 18.4 for some key maturities and collateralization rules.

Plotting the swap rate *margins* against best estimate mortality improvements allows one to interpret the swap rates as outputs of a pricing functional based on adjustments to a reference mortality model (which is common practice in longevity space). On the other hand, longevity

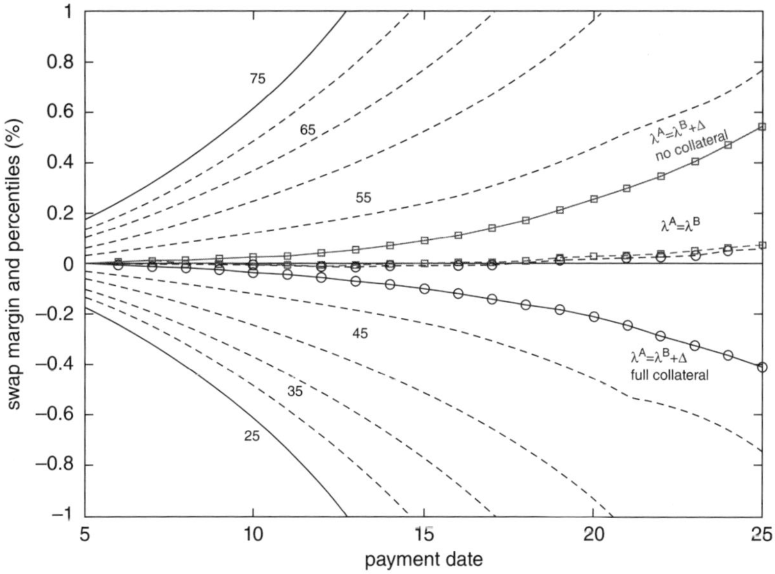

Figure 18.4 From [21]. "A" is our "I", and "B" is our "C". Swap margins $\bar{p}^c_{T_i}/p_{T_i} - 1$ computed for different maturities $\{T_i\}$ and collateral rules, with $\delta^A = \lambda^A$ and $\delta^B = \lambda^B$: no collateral (squares), full collateralization (circles); $\lambda^A = \lambda^B + \Delta$, with $\Delta = 0$ (dashed lines) and $\Delta = 0.01$ (solid lines). p_{T_i} is the risk-free swap rate with the same tenor and maturities as $\bar{p}^c_{T_i}$. The underlying is a cohort of 10,000 US males aged 65 at the beginning of 2008. Swap rates are plotted against the percentiles of improvements in survival rates based on Lee-Carter forecasts

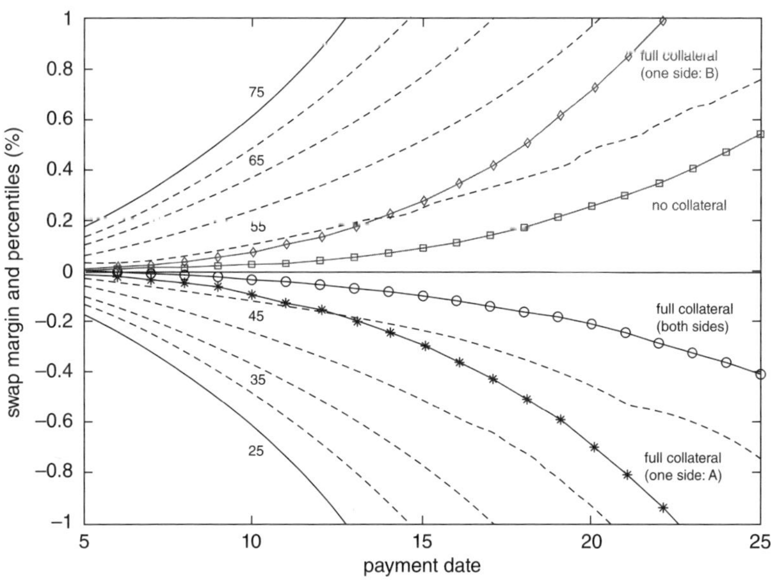

Figure 18.5 From [21]. Swap margins $\bar{p}^c_{T_i}/p_{T_i} - 1$ computed for different maturities $\{T_i\}$ and collateral rules, with $\delta^I = \lambda^I = \lambda^C + 0.01$ and $\delta^C = \lambda^C$: no collateral (squares), full collateralization (circles), full collateral posted only by party "I" (stars) or party "C" (diamonds). The underlying is a cohort of 10,000 US males aged 65 at the beginning of 2008. Swap rates are plotted against the percentiles of improvements in survival rates based on Lee-Carter forecasts

Table 18.4 From [21]. "A" is our "I", and "B" is our "C". c^A and c^B are the fractions of mark to market that constitute collateral at each point in time. Hence $c = 1$ denotes full collateralization, whereas $c = 0$ means no collateral at all. Second example in Section 17.5: swap spreads $\bar{p}^c_{T_i} - p_{T_i}$ (in basis points) for different collateralization rules, maturities and credit spread $\Delta \in \{0, 0.01, 0.02\}$. The LSMC procedure uses 5,000 paths over a quarterly grid with polynomial basis functions of order 3, and is repeated for 100 seeds

	Maturity payment (yrs)	$c^A = 0$ $c^B = 0$ (bps)	$c^A = 0$ $c^B = 1$ (bps)	$c^A = 1$ $c^B = 0$ (bps)	$c^A = 1$ $c^B = 1$ (bps)
$\lambda^{A,B} = \lambda,$	15	0.03	11.34	−11.76	0.05
$\delta^{A,B} = \delta,$	20	1.11	19.93	−17.94	0.86
$\delta = \lambda$	25	1.50	21.25	−18.35	1.24
$\lambda^A = \lambda^B + \Delta,$	15	5.45	16.79	−17.29	−5.84
$\delta^i = \lambda^i,$	20	10.16	28.95	−27.08	−8.23
$\Delta = 0.01$	25	10.96	30.75	−27.76	−9.19
$\lambda^A = \lambda^B + \Delta,$	15	11.30	22.29	−22.90	−11.25
$\delta^i = \lambda^i,$	20	19.26	38.06	−36.16	−17.42
$\Delta = 0.02$	25	19.46	40.27	−37.02	−18.38

swap *spreads* are easier to compare with those emerging in other transactions. In Table 18.5, we make a comparison with the interest rate swap spreads implied by our parameterization of the state vector $(X^{(1)}, X^{(2)}, X^{(3)}, X^{(4)})$. In particular, we report the difference between interest rate futures prices (obtained by considering full collateralization and setting the cost of collateral equal to the risk-free rate) and interest rate swap rates for collateralized transactions with collateral costs equal to the funding costs of the counterparties. Spreads are negative, in line with the intuition that interest rate risk leads to a discount for the payer of the fixed rate,

Table 18.5 From [21]. "A" is our "I", and "B" is our "C". c^A and c^B are the fractions of mark-to-market that constitute collateral at each point in time. Hence $c = 1$ denotes full collateralization, whereas $c = 0$ means no collateral at all. Second example in Section 17.5: comparison of interest rate swaps (IRSs) with longevity swaps. The IRS spreads represent the difference betweeen the futures prices (the opportunity cost of collateral coincides with the risk-free rate for both parties) and the swap rate for the collateralized IRS (for different collateralization rules, maturities, and credit risk)

		IRSs			Longevity swaps		
	Maturity payment (yrs)	$c^A = 0$ $c^B = 1$ (bps)	$c^A = 1$ $c^B = 0$ (bps)	$c^A = 1$ $c^B = 1$ (bps)	$c^A = 0$ $c^B = 1$ (bps)	$c^A = 1$ $c^B = 0$ (bps)	$c^A = 1$ $c^B = 1$ (bps)
$\lambda^{A,B} = \lambda,$	15	−7.96	−44.97	−52.86	11.34	−11.76	0.05
$\delta^{A,B} = \delta,$	20	−12.68	−42.64	−56.22	19.93	−17.94	0.86
$\delta = \lambda$	25	−17.94	−40.98	−58.92	21.25	−18.35	1.24
$\lambda^A = \lambda^B + \Delta,$	15	−8.00	−67.87	−75.23	16.79	−17.29	−5.84
$\delta^i = \lambda^i,$	20	−12.65	−63.84	−77.42	28.95	−27.08	−8.23
$\Delta = 0.01$	25	−17.65	−60.63	−77.64	30.75	−27.76	−9.19

and are of a magnitude consistent with the findings of [130]. The results show that longevity swap spreads are comparable with, and often much smaller in absolute value than, those found in the interest rate swap market. For example, in the case of bilateral full collateralization, longevity swap rates for 15- to 25-year maturities embed a spread substantially smaller than that of interest rate swaps of corresponding maturity. In the case of one-sided collateralization on the hedger's side, in interest rate swap rates we find a discount (negative spread) that turns into a premium (positive spread) of comparable size in the corresponding longevity swap, due to the additional and opposite effect of longevity risk on swap rates. Our findings are robust to the choice of maturity, collateralization rules, and counterparty credit quality, and are mainly driven by the fact that interest rate risk and longevity risk impact longevity swap margins in opposite directions, thus diluting the overall effect of collateralization on longevity swap rates.

Then we consider choice b) above, in the previous section, thus including the process $X^{(5)}$. In the case of symmetric collateralization, we find results comparable with those obtained by using the counterparties' funding costs for the process δ. However, Figure 18.6 shows that margins increase (decrease) considerably when one-sided collateralization on the hedge supplier's (hedger's) side is considered. This is because the party required to post collateral explicitly takes into account tail events in computing collateral costs, whereas in Figure 18.5 based on choice a) for $X^{(5)}$, funding costs were computed on the basis of the market value of the longevity swap.

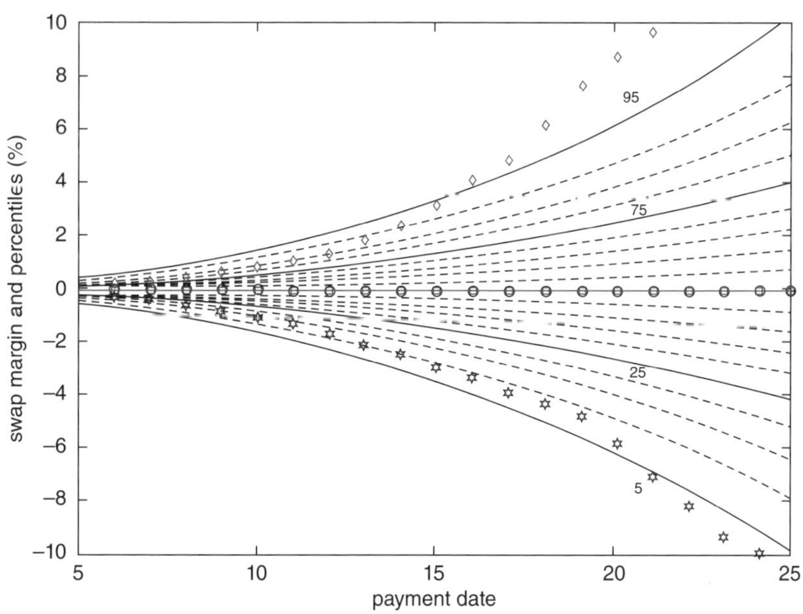

Figure 18.6 From [21]. Swap margins $\bar{p}^c_{T_i}/p_{T_i} - 1$ computed for different maturities $\{T_i\}$ and collateral rules, with $\lambda^I = \lambda^C$ and $\delta = X^{(5)}$, where the parameter estimates of X are given in Table 18.2. Collateral rules: no collateral (squares), full collateralization (circles), full collateral posted only by party "I" (stars) or "C" (diamonds). Swap rates are plotted against the percentiles of improvements in survival rates based on Lee-Carter forecasts

Finally, we study the sensitivity of longevity swap spreads to the volatility of the net collateral cost $X^{(5)}$. To close off the interest rate risk channel, we fix the factors $X^{(1)}$, $X^{(2)}$ equal to their long-run means. Table 18.3 reports the results obtained for different values of the volatility parameter σ_5 in the case of symmetric default risk and bilateral full collateralization. We see that spreads increase dramatically for large values of the volatility parameter, but are comparable with those found in the previous examples for reasonable volatility levels (i.e. below 5%).

19 Conclusions and Further Work

This chapter concludes the book. In the strict context of the book's themes, the conclusion can actually be found in Chapter 1, which gives a dialogue summary of the book, and in Chapter 10, which summarizes Part III, the advanced part of the book. A view of the general situation has been presented in the preface, "Ignition". In this final chapter we take the opportunity to try and enlarge the picture and reason on the role of modelling in today's market landscape. It should be clear to the reader who has navigated through the book thus far that this is not just a book on credit risk, collateral, and funding, it is a first book on what we could call a new "holistic" theory of valuation. In this sense we feel a general conclusion where we reason on the large-scale implications of current and future modelling is appropriate.

We close then with a reprise of the initial question and answer dialogue in Chapter 1, where a few years later the ex-rookie analyst meets the senior colleague again . . .

19.1 A FINAL DIALOGUE: MODELS, REGULATIONS, CVA/DVA, FUNDING AND MORE

Q: [The junior colleague looks more confident and mature, and is holding a book in his right hand.] Good to see you again, Alice. I am here to thank you for the good start you gave me few years ago. Now I feel much more confident, both because of my experience and because I practically wore out the book you gave me, this volume I am holding by Brigo, Morini and Pallavicini (BMP). It was very timely for me, in that "counterparty risk, collateral and funding with pricing cases from all asset classes" dealt precisely with many of the questions I had to face on the job.

A: [Senior colleague, she looks less tired and stressed] I am happy about that, Lewis. I re-read the book myself recently. As you say, in that book there are all the most relevant problems in today's financial landscape, all the interesting discussions on credit and debit valuation adjustments, close-out, first to default, re-hypothecation, plus collateral modelling and consistent inclusion of funding costs. In fact, everything we discussed some time ago.

Lewis: The book also discusses the two "solutions" to the counterparty risk pricing problem: either collateral, that is believed to completely kill counterparty risk . . .

Alice: Wrongly believed, it is said . . .

Lewis: Yes . . . wrongly believed to completely kill counterparty risk, wrongly because Gap risk can be quite significant, and contagion can be quite surprising. And if collateral is not used, the other "solution" is based on capital reserves to be held against this risk following Basel III. So we can have either collateral, or capital, or CVA pricing and hedging, or even better a mix of the three, plus funding. Do you think that's all modern financial modelling is about?

Alice: All? No, of course not. There are still a few things that must be said. Think of the LIBOR rate rigging scandal by some top banks, showing not only that the "risk-free interbank benchmark rate" of the past has never really been credit-risk free or liquidity-risk free, but also that it has not been fraud-risk free either. What is the point of working on twenty different extensions of the LIBOR market model with smile for exotics when the very underlying rate is being manipulated to the verge of illegality? Indeed, are models relevant at all? [Leans forward]

Lewis: I didn't think you were that passionate about your job! Look, now I understand more about this world of finance, and while I sympathize with your irritation – having also read your past papers on LIBOR market model implementation (I did a lot of reading!!) – I think models are still relevant. Back in 2009 one of the authors of the book you gave me, Morini, wrote in a paper that LIBOR fixings in the crisis were tweaked by banks, and incorporated this fact in modelling the basis between different LIBOR tenors, a topic also mentioned in the BMP book you suggested to me. We cannot prevent the market from committing frauds, but we can avoid making our models fraudulent. We can avoid making them represent a fictitious world but try to describe as much as possible the real one. Although, I have to admit, the size of the fraud, and the way it was used against the public, still surprises me.

Alice: But this is the real point. Finance is being perceived more and more by people on the street as a virtual reality. Preying on the real economy, dealing with a fictional universe, removed from real economics and fundamentals, and based on complicated, obscure, and unnecessarily global instruments whose purpose is not helping the real economy but simply maximizing the profits stemming from those virtual worlds. In a world like this can modelling really make a difference? I gave my best efforts to this job for many, many years, and sometimes I really feel I have been betrayed by the industry and its top managers.

Lewis: Well, please forgive me for saying so, but it's almost funny. After we quants were somehow accused of being the cause of the crisis, with some absurd and amusing accusations in the press, as again Brigo, Pallavicini and one more Italian guy, Torresetti, have shown in another book, models are now almost at the opposite end. To the point that sometimes models seem to be irrelevant in the face of frauds and market manipulations we read about in the newspapers, and the political decisions that seem to condition the markets. And yet, after what I have seen in the market and in the literature, even if I think we were not the cause of the crisis, and no formula "killed Wall Street", as part of the press would have it, I still think we had some responsibility. As Morini wrote in his book on Model Risk, too often in the past models have been designed as complex sets of equations with little relation to the real world, which has led to them being used like mathematical black boxes to create a false sense of confidence rather than really increasing our understanding.

Alice: Well, it seems you have learnt a lot in these few years! These years have been very intense for our industry. You have touched on a good point. Are models really objective tools or just sophisticated justifications? I also think models are relevant, but only to the extent where the market culture does not try to use models to justify dubious, greedy, or even illegal decisions a posteriori, and genuinely considers model outputs as a component of a decision process. A discourse of intellectual honesty in the industry is important here. The constant attempts to dumb down, standardize, and simplify the modelling apparatus for very complex problems seems to show that this fact has not been appreciated . . . complexity is the key here.

Lewis: So you are saying, if modelling is to be used, let modelling be used in its entirety and honestly, with an attitude of acceptance for what the models have to say, without trying to simplify models to the point of castration or to twist their outputs to match a pre-assigned plan. And yet, from what I have seen, simplifying too much is not the only way to make models prone to manipulation. There is another way that was abused before the crisis: making them over-complex, increasing the sophistication of the mathematical details to hide ignorance of the underlying system. This is an abuse of the power and beauty of mathematics, which should, instead, be an efficient way of translating the unavoidable complexity of financial problems into reasonably manageable tools.

Alice: Still, a balance is very fundamental here. Too much simplification is not good either. Even regulators who are certainly in good faith, such as the Basel Committee, have been trying to simplify and standardize the Credit Valuation Adjustment calculations beyond reasonable limits. BMP make that quite clear in the book I gave you.

Lewis: I am with you on this one. I have realized that such regulatory toy models fuel clever exploitation of model weaknesses – that is often called regulatory arbitrage. They hide the need for substantial risk management behind formal compliance, worst of all, they make banks herd together favouring procyclicality . . .

Alice . . . Procyclicality?? Have you become an economist too?? Well . . . you must have learnt that you need a lot of skills in our job . . .

Lewis: On the contrary, model research with a variety of competing models is a crucial way to evaluate and diversify away model risk . . .

Alice: Yes, I agree. If doing serious modelling means that a completely specified standard cannot emerge, so be it. This is another fundamental point.

Lewis: We talked about model risk and model diversification. I think this book you advised me to read is an attempt to follow this difficult road. In fact they do not propose "the model", the final definitive solution. Actually, BMP illustrate quite a variety of models.

Alice: True. You did read it! They have a variety of reduced-form approaches, playing the lion's part, and also one structural approach and one BGM approach (you already know I liked that). But which models should be chosen in the end, in practice?

Lewis: I may be an enthusiastic young analyst, but I think now the community of readers will help in model selection and improvement. In any case, after so many books and advisory reports on CVA that mention models continually but never show even one in detail, this book and the models it describes have been really useful. Model risk awareness should not be an excuse for not proposing models.

Alice: I am happy this book was a good starting point. They show how one can use methods that are already much more advanced than most of what the market and software vendors have been doing for a while for counterparty risk and funding. They do this across asset classes. Part of the research BMP summarize in this book dates back to 2004–7, before the crisis. I remember reading the related papers. But, having said that, there is still much more to do.

Lewis: I got the impression that advanced models such as those in BMP have been there for a while but they have been ignored by counterparty risk people for a long time.

Alice: We can no longer afford that. The gap that had traditionally existed between counterparty risk people, derivatives pricing, and hedging people needs to be closed. On one side, it does not make sense to consider derivatives as platonic instruments living in a world of their own without being affected by credit, default, liquidity, funding, and collateral. Once upon a time this would have been the attitude of derivatives quants, who had better things to do than model collateral. But when even a vanilla instruments portfolio is embedded in such risks, it becomes the most formidable derivative to be priced or managed.

Lewis: Yes. I think the crisis has been like a microscope. In the past spreads and bases were so small that the approximation using one single interest rate curve was acceptable. The crisis has transformed irrelevant details into crucial points, and in changing the scale of our observation it has forced us to change our whole approach to the problem.

Alice: Of course, and if the consistent inclusion of funding costs properly modelled leads to a complicated nonlinear recursive algorithm, we can no longer hide behind the hope that it all boils down to applying different spreads to simple discount functions. It's not an easy problem at all.

Lewis: And, again, not so difficult as to be completely secluded in over-complex papers either. In fact, in the book BMP have one chapter where funding is analyzed in its full complexity, and one where the crucial weaknesses of a trivial discount approach are shown, with simple examples that can be explained even to senior management. Considering that we are touching crucial issues for the management of financial institutions, we have to commit to making our discussion of their results understandable to a wider audience, otherwise our job will be wasted.

Alice: At least, one has to try. On the other hand, it is quite wrong to pretend that such complex risks for such portfolios can be captured by toy measures such as Credit VaR or Expected Shortfall, by multipliers or granularity factors, as traditional counterparty risk people would have done. Hard work needs to be done properly and shortcuts simply do not work. Besides the numerical examples for the failure of multipliers given in the book by BMP for pricing space, and the fact that the pricing of credit risk has been twice as damaging as actual defaults, go a long way towards how dangerous a poor modelling apparatus can be when everyone believes it.

Lewis: I seem to recall BMP have illustrated some such points with numerical examples in the book. This is far from conclusive though.

Alice: We need to make our colleagues realize that complex problems are... complex. A financial institution where the front office holds all the power may convince the risk department that they have all the tools needed: "apply discounting here and there, tweak this and that, and let's go out with a price and some greeks, after all it is a big business and we can't miss it, and we'll be paying your bonus too, by the way".

Lewis: It's not just because now I work in banking... [smiles] But I don't really think that bonuses are an issue... well they can be, when they distort the decision process of an institution, as they have often done in the recent past. But they can also be a virtuous management tool. Management is the real issue. Obviously, if the head of risk management is three levels below the head of the derivatives division of an investment bank, the poor risk manager will be hardly listened to when he says that a position or a model are dangerous...

Alice: And "closing the deal" will remain the only thing that matters. I think that sometimes if one is honestly aware of the fact that the methodological apparatus is simply not adequate for a product or a risk to be modelled, the deal should be dropped rather than pursued with dubious methodological instruments. In this sense, the standards of the financial industry are lower than those of other industries. Yes, I know, I still work in a bank too... [laughs]

Lewis: Remember also that the shuttle exploded, and I say this with pain as someone who loves space exploration. True, we should be talking more about standard industry aircraft like Boeing or Airbus rather than aerospace prototypes, but I still feel that many industries do not take into account externalities like the effect of pollution or climate change. At times, unfortunately, there is the idea that in any case "finance does not kill anyone", but when it favours an incredibly fast economic growth, and it helps by dragging the world into a global economic crisis, people realize that finance is not a harmless game! It can contribute to destroying lives, companies, or even countries.

Alice: Now, however, after years where privatization and liberalization have been endorsed by governments, Keynesian ideas are coming back with a vengeance. Or maybe even Marxist ideas...

Lewis: Let's not get too entangled in politics! You are already at the top of your career, but I do not want to harm my promotion [smiles]. In any case, yes, markets left to themselves do not self-regulate. Intervention is now unavoidable, with the understanding that regulation must become as global as the financial market. And certainly now we cannot afford the same mistake as in the Thirties, when lack of intervention deepened the economic depression after the financial bubble burst. But be careful, once again equilibrium is important. In the past, regulations have not been the solution to prevent the crisis, or to change the bad habits of institutions during the crisis. At times I think we would have been better without simplistic regulations allowing banks to claim they were safe when they were not, but just with real control of shareholders on the risk-taking of banks, in a really free market...

Alice: Now it's you getting political... remember your promotion! [Laughs].

Lewis: Talking seriously, let me try to conclude with a summary of what I understood of the events of the last years, and then you'll tell me if you agree.

As BMP said many times in their book, counterparty and funding risk pricing is a very complex, model-dependent task and requires a holistic approach to modelling that challenges the ingrained culture in most investment banks and in most of the financial industry, and even of western science to some extent. Even in their book BMP have not been fully on a par with such a holistic approach. Regulators and the industry are desperately trying to standardize the related calculations in the simplest possible ways but our conclusion, like BMP's, is that such calculations are complex and need to remain so to be accurate. The attempt to standardize every risk to simple formulas is misleading, and may result in the relevant risks not being addressed at all. The industry and regulators should acknowledge the complexity of this problem and work to attain the necessary methodological and technological prowess rather than bypass it, with help from academia and private research. Until the methodology is sufficiently good, we should refrain from proposing inadequate solutions that may only worsen the situation. As BMP say, there is no easy way out.

Alice: Gosh! You have understood even too much. I would say this would even have been a great sentence for BMP to conclude their book! It has been great to meet you again and . . . Hey!!

Lewis: What . . . what's happening?

Alice: I am feeling a strange pull . . . this BMP book I am holding in my hand, I feel a pull . . . sounds crazy, I know . . . I am seeing the formulas and text in the sky, out of the window . . . what's this? What's this???

Lewis: I . . . I see it as well, oh my goodness, we are surrounded by formulas and acronyms on the wall, and I bet they are this book's formulas . . . I recognize them!!! And someone is looking at me right now . . .

Alice: Aaahhh . . . Oh my . . . I see what's going on. If I am right . . . there's only one way out. There's no time . . . Close that BMP book, Lewis, quickly, close it NOW!!!

Lewis: But I want to know . . .

Alice: There's no time . . . We are vanishing . . . Close IT!!!

Lewis: OK!!!

[SLAM]
(To be continued . . .)

Bibliography

[1] Alavian, S., Ding, J., Whitehead, P., and Laudicina, L. (2008). Credit valuation adjustment (CVA). Available at http://ssrn.com

[2] Albanese, C., Bellaj, T., Gimonet, G., and Pietronero, G. (2011). Coherent Global Market Simulations and Securitization Measures for Counterparty Credit Risk. SC 2008 November 2008, Austin, Texas, 11(1): 1–20.

[3] Albanese, C., Brigo, D., and Oertel, F. (2011). Restructuring counterparty credit risk. Deutsche Bundesbank, Working Paper, forthcoming.

[4] Albanese, C., Pietronero, G., and White, S. (2011). Optimal funding strategies for counterparty credit risk liabilities. Working paper available at http://www.level3finance.com

[5] Alfonsi, A., and Brigo, D. (2005). New families of copulas based on periodic functions. *Communications in Statistics: Theory and Methods*, 34(7).

[6] Allen, F., and Gale, D. (2000). Bubbles and Crises, *Economic Journal*, 110: 236–55.

[7] Arvanitis, A., and Gregory, J. (2001). *Credit: The Complete Guide to Pricing, Hedging and Risk Management*, Risk Books, London.

[8] Assefa, S., Bielecki, T. R., Crépey, S., and Jeanblanc, M. (2009). CVA Computation for counterparty risk assessment in credit portfolios. In: T. R. Bielecki, D. Brigo, and F. Patras, (eds.), *Credit Risk Frontiers: Subprime Crisis, Pricing and Hedging, CVA, MBS, Ratings and Liquidity*, John Wiley & Sons.

[9] Baba, N., and Packer, F. (2009). From turmoil to crisis: Dislocations in the FX swap market before and after the failure of Lehman Brothers. BIS Working paper, 285.

[10] Bacinello, A., Biffis, E., and Millossovich, P. (2010). Regression-based algorithms for life insurance contracts with surrender guarantees. *Quantitative Finance*, 10: 1077–90.

[11] Bauer, D., Benth, F., and Kiesel, R. (2010). Modeling the forward surface of mortality, Tech. rep., Georgia State University.

[12] BIS, Basel Committee on Banking Supervision International convergence of capital measurement and capital standards a revised framework comprehensive version (2006). Strengthening the resilience of the banking sector (2009). Available at http://www.bis.org.

[13] BIS, Basel Committee on Banking Supervision (2010). Basel III: A global regulatory framework for more resilient banks and banking systems. Available at http://www.bis.org.

[14] Cannabaro, E., Picoult, E., and Wilde, T. (2005). Counterparty risk. *Energy Risk*, May issue.

[15] Bech, M., Martin, A., and McAndrews, J. (2012). Settlement liquidity and monetary policy implementation – lessons from the financial crisis. FRBNY Economic Policy Review, 3.

[16] Bielecki, T. R., Jeanblanc, M., and Rutkowski, M. (2008). Hedging of credit default swaptions in a hazard process model. *Annals of Applied Probability*, 18(6).

[17] Bielecki, T. R., and Crépey, S. (2010). Dynamic hedging of counterparty exposure, http://www.maths.univ-evry.fr.

[18] Bielecki, T. R., and Rutkowski, M. (2001). *Credit Risk: Modeling, Valuation and Hedging*, Springer-Verlag.

[19] Biffis, E., Denuit, M., and Devolder, P. (2010). Stochastic mortality under measure changes. *Scandinavian Actuarial Journal*, 2010: 284–311.

[20] Biffis, E., and Blake, D. (2010). Securitizing and tranching longevity exposures. *Insurance: Mathematics & Economics*, 46(1): 186–97.

[21] Biffis, E., Blake, D. P., Pitotti L., and Sun, A. (2011). The cost of counterparty risk and collateralization in longevity swaps. Available at http://ssrn.com.

[22] Biffis, E., and Blake, D. (2010). Mortality-linked securities and derivatives. In: M. Bertocchi, S. Schwartz and W. Ziemba (eds.), *Optimizing the Aging, Retirement and Pensions Dilemma*. John Wiley & Sons.

[23] *BIS Quarterly Review* (December 2007), International banking and financial market developments, http://www.bis.org/publ/qtrpdf/r_qt0712.pdf.

[24] Black, F., and Cox, J. C. (1976). Valuing corporate securities: Some effects of bond indenture provisions. *Journal of Finance* 31(2): 351–67

[25] Black, F., and Scholes, M. (1974). The effects of dividend yield and dividend policy on common stock prices and returns. *Journal of Financial Economics*, 1(1): 1–22.

[26] Blanchet-Scalliet, C., and Patras, F. (2008). Counterparty Risk Valuation for CDS. http://www.defaultrisk.com.

[27] Blundell-Wignall, A., and Atkinson, P. (2010). Thinking beyond Basel III. Necessary solutions for capital and liquidity, *OECD Journal: Financial Market Trends*, 2, 2010(1): 9–33. Available at http://www.oecd.org/dataoecd/42/58/45314422.pdf.

[28] Beumee J., Brigo D., Schiemert D., and Stoyle G. (2009). Charting a course through the CDS big bang. Fitch Solutions research report.

[29] Boenkost, W., and Schmidt, W. M. (2005). Cross currency swap valuation. Available at http://ssrn.com/abstract=1375540.

[30] Brace, A., Gatarek, D., and Musiela, M., (1997). The market model of interest rate dynamics. *Mathematical Finance*, 7(2), 127–47.

[31] Brigo, D. (2005). Market models for CDS options and callable floaters. *Risk*, January issue.

[32] Brigo, D. (2006). Constant maturity CDS valuation with market models. *Risk*, June issue. Earlier extended version available at http://ssrn.com/abstract=639022.

[33] Brigo, D. (2011). Credit risk management. King's College FM10 Master Course Lecture Notes.

[34] Brigo, D. (2011). Counterparty risk FAQ: Credit VaR, PFE, CVA, DVA, Closeout, Netting, Collateral, Re-hypothecation, WWR, Basel, Funding, CCDS and Margin Lending. Available at http://arxiv.org/abs/1111.1331.

[35] Brigo, D., and Alfonsi, A. (2005). Credit default swaps calibration and derivatives pricing with the SSRD stochastic intensity model. *Finance and Stochastic*, 9(1): 29–42.

[36] Brigo, D., and Bakkar I. (2009). Accurate counterparty risk valuation for energy-commodities swaps, *Energy Risk*, March issue.

[37] Brigo, D., Buescu, C., and Morini, M. (2011). Impact of the first to default time on bilateral CVA, http://arxiv.org/pdf/1106.3496.pdf. To appear in updated format in *International Journal of Theoretical and Applied Finance*.

[38] Brigo, D., Buescu, C., Pallavicini, A., and Liu, Q. D. (2012). Illustrating a problem in the self-financing condition in two 2010–11 papers on funding, collateral and discounting. Working paper available at http://papers.ssrn.com/sol3/papers.cfm?abstract_id=2103121.

[39] Brigo, D., and Capponi, A. (2008). Bilateral counterparty risk valuation with stochastic dynamical models and application to CDSs. Working paper available at http://arxiv.org/abs/0812.3705. Short updated version in *Risk*, March 2010 issue.

[40] Brigo, D., Capponi, A., and Pallavicini, A. (2011). Arbitrage-free bilateral counterparty risk valuation under collateralization and application to credit default swaps. Accepted for publication in *Mathematical Finance*.

[41] Brigo, D., Capponi, A., Pallavicini, A., and Papatheodorou, V. (2011). Collateral margining in arbitrage-free counterparty valuation adjustment including re-hypotecation and netting. Working paper available at http://arxiv.org/abs/1101.3926.

[42] Brigo, D., Capponi, A., and Predrescu, M. (2010). Credit default swaps liquidity modeling: a survey, In: T. R. Bielecki, D. Brigo and F Patras (eds.), *Recent Advancements in Theory and Practice of Credit Derivatives*, Bloomberg Press.

[43] Brigo, D., and Chourdakis, K. (2009). Counterparty risk for credit default swaps: impact of spread volatility and default correlation. *International Journal of Theoretical and Applied Finance*, 12(7): 1007–26.

[44] Brigo, D., and Chourdakis, K. (2012). Consistent single- and multistep sampling of multivariate arrival times: a characterization of self-chaining copulas. Available at http://arxiv.org, http://ssrn.com, http://www.defaultrisk.com.

[45] Brigo, D., and Cousot, L. (2006). A comparison between the SSRD model and the market model for CDS options pricing. *International Journal of Theoretical and Applied Finance*, 9(3).

[46] Brigo, D., and El-Bachir, N. (2010). An exact formula for default swaptions pricing in the SSRJD stochastic intensity model. *Mathematical Finance*, 20(3): 365–82.

[47] Brigo, D., and Masetti, M. (2005). Risk-neutral pricing of counterparty risk. In: M. Pykhtin (ed.), *Counterparty Credit Risk Modelling: Risk Management, Pricing and Regulation*, Risk Books, London.

[48] Brigo, D., and Mercurio, F. (2001). *Interest Rate Models: Theory and Practice with Smile, Inflation and Credit*, second edition 2006, Springer-Verlag, Heidelberg.

[49] Brigo, D., and Morini, M. (2006). Structural credit calibration, *Risk*, April issue.

[50] Brigo, D., and Morini, M. (2006). Efficient analytical cascade calibration of the LIBOR market model with endogenous interpolation, *The Journal of Derivatives*, Fall issue.

[51] Brigo, D., and Morini, M. (2009). A structural model for investigating the relation between equity and credit and the possibility of model arbitrage. Working paper.

[52] Brigo, D., and Morini, M. (2010). Dangers of bilateral counterparty risk: the fundamental impact of closeout conventions. Preprint available at http://ssrn.com or at http://arxiv.org.

[53] Brigo, D., and Morini, M. (2010). Rethinking Counterparty Default, Credit flux, 114: 18–19.

[54] Brigo, D., and Morini, M. (2011). Close-out convention tensions, *Risk*, December 2011 issue.

[55] Brigo D., Morini M., and Tarenghi M. (2011). Equity return swap valuation under counterparty risk. In: T. R., Bielecki, D. Brigo and F. Patras (eds.), *Credit Risk Frontiers: Sub-prime crisis, Pricing and Hedging, CVA, MBS, Ratings and Liquidity*, John Wiley & Sons, 457–84.

[56] Brigo, D., and Pallavicini, A. (2006). Counterparty risk and contingent CDS valuation under correlation between interest rates and default. http://ssrn.com/abstract=926067. Published later in [57] and [58].

[57] Brigo, D., and Pallavicini, A. (2007). Counterparty risk under correlation between default and interest rates. In: Miller, J., Edelman, D., and Appleby, J. (eds.), *Numerical Methods for Finance*, Chapman & Hall, London.

[58] Brigo, D., and Pallavicini, A. (2008). Counterparty risk and contingent CDS under correlation, *Risk*, February issue.

[59] Brigo, D., Pallavicini, A., and Papatheodorou, V. (2011). Arbitrage-free valuation of bilateral counterparty risk for interest-rate products: impact of volatilities and correlations, *International Journal of Theoretical and Applied Finance*, 14(6): 773–802.

[60] Brigo, D., Pallavicini, A., and Torresetti, R. (2010). *Credit models and the crisis: a journey into CDOs, copulas, correlations and dynamic models*. John Wiley & Sons, Chichester.

[61] Brigo, D., and Tarenghi, M. (2004). Credit default swap calibration and equity swap valuation under counterparty risk with a tractable structural model. Working paper, available at www.damianobrigo.it/cdsstructural.pdf. Reduced version in *Proceedings of the FEA 2004 Conference at MIT, Cambridge, Massachusetts, November 8–10* and in *Proceedings of the Counterparty Credit Risk 2005 C.R.E.D.I.T. conference*, Venice, 22–3 September, Vol 1.

[62] Brigo, D., and Tarenghi, M. (2005). Credit default swap calibration and counterparty risk valuation with a scenario-based first passage model. Working paper, available at www.damianobrigo.it/cdsscenario1p.pdf. Also in: *Proceedings of the Counterparty Credit Risk 2005 C.R.E.D.I.T. conference*, Venice, 22–3 September, Vol 1.

[63] Broadie, M., and Kaya O. (2006). Exact simulation of stochastic volatility and other affine jump diffusion processes. *Operations Research*, 54(2): 217–31.

[64] Brunnermeier, M., and Pedersen, L. (2009). Market liquidity and funding liquidity. *The Review of Financial Studies*, 22(6).

[65] Burgard, C., and Kjaer, M. (2010). Partial differential equation representations of derivatives with counterparty risk and funding costs. *The Journal of Credit Risk*. 7(3): 1–19.

[66] Burgard, C., and Kjaer, M. (2011). In the balance. *Risk*. October issue.

[67] Cairns, A., Blake, D., Dowd, K., Coughlan, G., Epstein, D., Ong, A., and Balevich, I. (2009). A quantitative comparison of stochastic mortality models using data from England and Wales and the United States. *North American Actuarial Journal*, 13(1): 1–35.

[68] Cairns, A., Blake, D., Dowd, K., Coughlan, G., Epstein, D., and Khalaf-Allah, M. (2011). Mortality density forecasts: An analysis of six stochastic mortality models. *Insurance: Mathematics & Economics*, 48: 355–67.

[69] Canabarro, E., and Duffie, D. (2004). Measuring and marking counterparty risk. In: *Proceedings of the Counterparty Credit Risk, 2005 C.R.E.D.I.T. Conference*, Venice, 22–3 September, Vol 1.

[70] Canabarro, E., Picoult, E., and Wilde, T. (2005). Counterparty risk, *Energy Risk*, May issue.

[71] Carr P., and Chou, A. (1997), Breaking barriers: static hedging of barrier securities, *Risk*, October issue.

[72] Carrière, J. (1996). Valuation of the early-exercise price for options using simulations and nonparametric regression. *Insurance: Mathematics and Economics*, 19(1): 19–30.

[73] Carver, L. (2011). Quants call for ISDA to clarify close-out values. *Risk*, December issue.

[74] Castagna, A. (2011). Funding, liquidity, credit and counterparty risk: links and implications. Available at http://ssrn.com/abstract=1855028.

[75] CEIOPS (2009). SCR Standard Formula: Further advice on the counterparty default risk module. Tech. rep., Committee of European Insurance and Occupational Pension Supervisors' Consultation Paper no. 51.

[76] Cesari, G., Aquilina, J., Charpillon, N., Filipovic, Z., Lee, G., and Manda, I. (2010). *Modelling, Pricing, and Hedging Counterparty Credit Exposure: A Technical Guide*, Springer-Verlag, Heidelberg.

[77] Chen, H., and Cummins, J. (2010). Longevity bond premiums: The extreme value approach and risk cubic pricing, *Insurance: Mathematics & Economics*, 46(1): 150–61.

[78] Cherubini, U., Luciano, E., and Vecchiato, W. (2004). *Copula Methods in Finance*. John Wiley & Sons.

[79] Cherubini, U. (2005). Counterparty risk in derivatives and collateral policies: the replicating portfolio approach. In: L. Tilman (ed.), *ALM of Financial Institutions*, Institutional Investor Books.

[80] Collin-Dufresne, P., and Goldstein, R. (2001). Do credit spreads reflect stationary leverage ratios? *Journal of Finance* 56, 1929–58.

[81] Collin-Dufresne, P., Goldstein, R., and Hugonnier, J. (2004). A general formula for valuing defaultable securities. *Econometrica*, 72(5): 1377–407.

[82] Coughlan, G., M. Khalaf-Allah, Y. Ye, S. Kumar, A. Cairns, D. Blake and K. Dowd (2011). Longevity hedging 101: A framework for longevity basis risk analysis and hedge effectiveness. Tech. rep., to appear in *North American Actuarial Journal*.

[83] Cox, J. C., Ingersoll, J. E., and Ross, S. A. (1985). A theory of the term structure of interest rates. *Econometrica*, 53(2): 385–407.

[84] Cox, S., Lin, Y., and Pedersen, H. (2010). Mortality risk modeling: applications to insurance securitization. *Insurance: Mathematics & Economics*, 46(1): 242–53.

[85] Crépey, S. (2011). A BSDE approach to counterparty risk under funding constraints. Available at grozny.maths.univ-evry.fr/pages_perso/crepey.

[86] Crépey, S. (2012). Bilateral counterparty risk under funding constraints – Part I: Pricing. Forthcoming in *Mathematical Finance*.

[87] Crépey, S. (2012). Bilateral counterparty risk under funding constraints – Part II: CVA. Forthcoming in *Mathematical Finance*.

[88] Crouhy M., Galai, D., and Mark, R. (2000). A comparative analysis of current credit risk models. *Journal of Banking and Finance* 24: 59–117.

[89] Cummins, J., and Trainar, P. (2009). Securitization, insurance, and reinsurance. *Journal of Risk and Insurance*, 76(3): 463–92.

[90] Danziger, J. (2010). Pricing and hedging self counterparty risk. Presented at the conference "Global Derivatives", Paris, 18 May 2010.

[91] Davis, M., and Lo, V. (2001). Infectious default. *Quantitative Finance* 1: 382–7.

[92] Dehapiot T., and Patry, C. (2012). Calculating CVA and DVA, BNP Paribas working paper.

[93] De Prisco, B., and Rosen, D. (2005). Modelling stochastic counterparty credit exposures for derivatives portfolios. In: M. Pykhtin (ed.), *Counterparty Credit Risk Modelling: Risk Management, Pricing and Regulation*, Risk Books, London.

[94] Dowd, K., Blake, D., Cairns, A., and Dawson, P. (2006). Survivor swaps. *Journal of Risk and Insurance*, 73(1): 1–17.

[95] Dowd, K., Cairns, A., Blake, D., Coughlan, G., Epstein, D., and Khalaf-Allah, M. (2010a). Backtesting stochastic mortality models: An ex-post evaluation of multi-period-ahead density forecasts. *North American Actuarial Journal*, 14(3): 281–98.

[96] Dowd, K., Cairns, A., Blake, D., Coughlan, G., Epstein, D., and Khalaf-Allah, M. (2010b). Evaluating the goodness of fit of stochastic mortality models. *Insurance: Mathematics & Economics*, 47: 255–65.

[97] Drehmann, M., and Nikolaou, K. (2009). Funding liquidity risk defintion and measurement. ECB working paper series 1024 (3).

[98] Duffee, Gregory. (1998). The relation between treasury yields and corporate yield spreads, *Journal of Finance*, 53: 2225–43.

[99] Duffie, D. (2001). *Dynamic Asset Pricing Theory*, third edition. Princeton University Press.

[100] Duffie, D., and Garleanu, N. (2001). Risk and valuation of collateralized debt obligations. *Financial Analysts Journal*, 57(1): 41–59.

[101] Duffie, D., and Huang, M. (1996). Swap rates and credit quality. *Journal of Finance*, 51(3): 921–50.

[102] Duffie, D., Pan, J., and Singleton, K. (2000). Transform analysis and asset pricing for affine jump diffusions. *Econometrica*, 68: 1343–76.

[103] Duffie, D., and Singleton, K. J. (1999). Modeling term structures of defaultable bonds. *The Review of Financial Studies*, 12: 687–719.

[104] Duffie, D., and Zhu, H. (2010). Does a central clearing counterparty reduce counterparty risk? Working paper, Stanford University.
[105] Ehlers, P., and Schoenbucher, P. (2006). The influence of FX risk on credit spreads, ETH working paper, available at http://www.defaultrisk.com.
[106] Embrechts, P., Lindskog, F., and McNeil, A. (2001). Modelling dependence with copulas and applications to risk management. ETH working paper.
[107] Facchinetti, G., and Morini, M. (2009). Modelling correlations for forward exchange rates. Working paper.
[108] Fries, C. (2010). Discounting revisited: valuation under funding, counterparty risk and collateralization. Available at http://ssrn.com.
[109] Fujii, M., Shimada, Y., and Takahashi, A. (2010). Collateral Posting and Choice of Collateral Currency. Available at http://ssrn.com.
[110] Fujii, M., and Takahashi, A. (2011a). Choice of collateral currency. *Risk*, January issue.
[111] Fujii, M., and Takahashi, A. (2011b) Clean valuation framework for the USD silo. Available at http://ssrn.com
[112] Geman, H., and Ohana, S. (2000). Forward curves, Scarcity and price volatility in oil and natural gas markets. *Energy Economics*, 31(4): 576–85.
[113] Genest, C., and Rémillard, B. (2006). Discussion of copulas: tales and facts, by Thomas Mikosch. Available at http://neumann.hec.ca/pages/bruno.remillard/Papers/mikosch–response.pdf.
[114] Gibson, R., and Schwartz, E. S. (1990). Stochastic convenience yield and the pricing of oil contingent claims, *Journal of Finance*, XLV(3): 959–76.
[115] Giesecke, K. (2002). Correlated default with incomplete information. *Journal of Banking and Finance*, 28(2004): 1521–45.
[116] Giesecke, K. (2004), Credit Risk Modelling and Valuation. An Introduction, to appear in *Credit Risk: Models and Management*, 2, Riskbooks, London.
[117] Girosi, F., and G. King (2008). *Demographic Forecasting*. Princeton University Press.
[118] Gregory, J. (2009). Being two faced over counterparty credit risk, *Risk* 22(2): 86–90.
[119] Gregory, J. (2010). *Counterparty Credit Risk: The New Challenge for Global Financial Markets*, John Wiley & Sons, Chichester.
[120] Gregory, J. (2012). Closing out DVA? Working paper.
[121] Gupton, G. M., Finger, C. C., and Bathia, M. (1997). CreditMetrics technical document. Available at http://www.defaultrisk.com.
[122] Hull, J., (2006). *Options, Futures, and other Derivatives*, sixth edition. Prentice Hall.
[123] Hull, J., and White, A. (2000). Valuing credit default swaps II: Modeling default correlations. Working paper, University of Toronto.
[124] Hull J., Nelken, I., and White, A. (2004). Merton's model, credit risk, and volatility skews. *Journal of Credit Risk* 1, 1–27.
[125] Hull, J., and White, A. (2012). Is FVA a cost for derivatives desks? Working paper. Available ar http://www.defaultrisk.com.
[126] Inkmann, J., and Blake, D. (2012). Managing financially distressed pension plans in the interest of beneficiaries. Tech. rep., Pensions Institute Discusson Paper PI-0709.
[127] ISDA. Credit Support Annex (1992), Guidelines for Collateral Practitioners (1998), Credit Support Protocol (2002), Close-Out Amount Protocol (2009), Big Bang Protocol (2009b), Margin Survey (2010), Market Review of OTC Derivative Bilateral Collateralization Practices (2010). Available at http://www.isda.org.
[128] ISDA (2009). Big Bang protocol. Available at http://www.isda.org.
[129] Jamshidian, F. (2002). Valuation of credit default swap and swaptions, *Finance and Stochastics*, 8: 343–71.
[130] Johannes, M., and Sundaresan, S. (2007). The impact of collateralization on swap rates. *Journal of Finance*, 62(1): 383–410.
[131] Joe, H. (1997). *Multivariate Models and Dependence Concepts*. Chapman & Hall, London.
[132] Jones, E. P., Mason, S. P., and Rosenfeld, E. (1984). Contingent claims analysis of corporate capital structure: an empirical investigation. *Journal of Finance* 39, 611–25.
[133] Jorion, P. (2007). *Value at Risk*, third edition, McGraw Hill.
[134] Jouanin J.-F., Rapuch G., Riboulet G., and Roncalli T. (2001). Modelling dependence for credit derivatives with copulas. Groupe de Recherche Opérationnelle, Crédit Lyonnais, France.
[135] Keenan, J. (2009). Spotlight on exposure. *Risk* October issue.
[136] Kenyon, C., and Stamm, R. (2012). *Discounting, Libor, CVA and Funding*. Palgrave Macmillan.
[137] Kenyon, C. (2010). Completing CVA and liquidity: firm-level positions and collateralized trades. Available at http://arxiv.org.

[138] Lakdawalla, D., and Zanjani, G. (2007). Catastrophe bonds, reinsurance, and the optimal collateralization of risk transfer. Tech. rep., RAND Corporation and Federal Reserve Bank of New York.

[139] Lando, D. (1998). On Cox processes and credit risky securities. *Review of Derivatives Research* 2: 99–120.

[140] Leung, S. Y., and Kwok, Y. K. (2005). Credit default swap valuation with counterparty risk. *The Kyoto Economic Review*, 74(1): 25–45.

[141] Lipton, A., and Sepp, A. (2009). Credit value adjustment for credit default swaps via the structural default model, *The Journal of Credit Risk*, 5: 123–46.

[142] Lo, C. F., Lee H.C., and Hui, C.H. (2003). A simple approach for pricing barrier options with time-dependent parameters. *Quantitative Finance* 3: 98–107.

[143] Longstaff, F. A., and Schwarz, E. S. (2001). Valuing American options by simulation: a simple least-squares approach. *Review of Financial Studies*, 14: 113–47.

[144] Lord, R., Koekkoek, R., and Van Dijk, D.J.C. (2006). A Comparison of Biased Simulation Schemes for Stochastic Volatility Models. Working paper.

[145] Ludkovski, M., and Young, V. (2008). Indifference pricing of pure endowments and life annuities under stochastic hazard and interest rates. *Insurance: Mathematics and Economics*, 42(1): 14–30.

[146] Marshall, A., and Olkin, I. (1967). A multivariate exponential distribution. *Journal of the American Statistical Association*, 62(317): 30–44.

[147] McNeil, A. J., Frey, R., and Embrechts, P. (2005). *Quantitative Risk Management: Concepts, Techniques, and Tools*. Princeton University Press.

[148] Merton R. (1974). On the pricing of corporate debt: the risk structure of interest rates. *The Journal of Finance* 29: 449–70.

[149] Mikosch, T. (2005). Copulas: tales and facts. Available at http://www.math.ku.dk/~mikosch/Preprint/Copula/s.pdf.

[150] Mikulevicius, R., and Platen, E. (1988). *Time discrete Taylor approximations for Ito processes with jump component*. Mathematische Nachrichten 138: 93–104.

[151] Moreni, N., and Pallavicini, A. (2010). Parsimonious HJM modelling for multiple yield-curve dynamics. Submitted to *Quantitative Finance*. Available at http://ssrn.com.

[152] Moreni, N., and Pallavicini, A. (2012). Parsimonious multi-curve HJM modelling with stochastic volatility. Forthcoming in M. Bianchetti and M. Morini (eds.), *Interest Rate Modelling After the Financial Crisis. Risk Books*.

[153] Morini, M. (2009). One more model risk when using Gaussian copula for Risk Management. Available at http://ssrn.com/abstract=1520670.

[154] Morini, M. (2010). Can the default of a bank cause the default of its debtors? The destabilizing consequences of the standard definition of bilateral counterparty risk. Working paper.

[155] Morini, M. (2011). *Understanding and Managing Model Risk*. John Wiley & Sons.

[156] Morini, M., and Brigo, D. (2011). No-armageddon measure for arbitrage-free pricing of index options in a credit crisis, *Mathematical Finance*, 21(4): 573–93.

[157] Morini, M., and Prampolini, A. (2010). Risky funding: a unified framework for counterparty and liquidity charges, *Risk*, March issue.

[158] Morini, M., and Prampolini, A. (2011). A unified framework for counterparty and liquidity charges. Working paper available at http://papers.ssrn.com/sol3/papers.cfm?abstract_id=1669930.

[159] Nathanaël, B. (2010). The Basel Committee's December 2009 Proposals on Counterparty Risk. Federal Reserve/FSA presentation at the International Workshop on Counterparty Risk Management and Application of CVA, Bank of Japan, 14 June 2010.

[160] Nelsen, R. (1999). *An Introduction to Copulas*. Springer, New York.

[161] Pallavicini, A. (2010). Modelling wrong way risk for interest-rate products. Presented at the 6th Fixed Income Conference, 23–24 September 2010, Madrid.

[162] Pallavicini, A. (2010). Counterparty risk evaluation for interest rate derivatives. Presented at the Risk and Modelling in Fixed Income Interest Rates conference, 15 April 2010, London.

[163] Pallavicini, A. (2011). Pricing counterparty credit risk: a realistic simulation framework. Presented at the Risk Credit Summit conference, 28 June 2011, London.

[164] Pallavicini, A. (2012). HJM modelling in collateralized markets: multiple-curve calibration to swaption smiles. Presented at the Quant Congress, 10 October 2012, London.

[165] Pallavicini, A., Perini, D., and Brigo, D. (2011). Funding valuation adjustment: a consistent framework including CVA, DVA, collateral, netting rules and re-hypothecation. Available at http://ssrn.com and http://arxiv.org.

[166] Parker, E., and McGarry, A. (2009). The ISDA master agreement and CSA: close-out weaknesses exposed in the banking crisis and suggestions for change. *Butterworths Journal of International Banking Law*, 1.

[167] Picoult, E. (2005). Calculating and hedging exposure, credit value adjustment and economic capital for counterparty credit risk. In: M. Pykhtin (ed.), *Counterparty Credit Risk Modelling*, Risk Books, London.

[168] Piterbarg, V. (2010). Funding beyond discounting: collateral agreements and derivatives pricing. *Risk*, February.

[169] Piterbarg, V. (2012). Cooking with collateral. *Risk*, August.

[170] Pollack, Lisa (2012). Barclays visits the securitisation BISTRO. *Financial Times*. Alphaville Blog, Posted by Lisa Pollack on 17 January 2012 at 11:20.

[171] Pollack, Lisa (2012). The latest in regulation-induced innovation – Part 2. *Financial Times*. Alphaville Blog. Posted by Lisa Pollack on 11 April 2012 at 16:50.

[172] Pollack, Lisa (2012). Big banks seek regulatory capital trades. *Financial Times*. Alphaville Blog, Posted by Lisa Pollack on 29 April 2012 at 7:27.

[173] Pykhtin, M. (ed.) (2005). *Counterparty Credit Risk Modelling: Risk Management, Pricing and Regulation*, Risk Books, London.

[174] Rapisarda, F. (2003). Pricing barriers on underlyings with time-dependent parameters, Working paper.

[175] Rebonato, R. (1998). *Interest Rate Option Models*. Second Edition. John Wiley and Sons, Chichester.

[176] Rebonato, R. (1999) On the simultaneous calibration of multifactor lognormal interest rate models to black volatilities and to the correlation matrix. *The Journal of Computational Finance*, 2: 5–27.

[177] Rosen, D., and Pykhtin, M. (2010). Pricing counterparty risk at the trade level and CVA allocations. *Journal of Credit Risk*, 6 (Winter 2010): 3–38.

[178] Salhi, Y., and Loisel, S. (2010). Joint modeling of portfolio experienced and national mortality: A co-integration based approach. Tech. rep., ISFA Lyon.

[179] Schaefer, S., and Strebulaev, I. (2008). Structural models of credit risk are useful: evidence from hedge ratios on corporate bonds. *Journal of Financial Economics*, 90: 1–19.

[180] Schoenmakers, J., and Coffey, C. (2003). Systematic generation of correlation structures for the LIBOR market model. *International Journal of Theoretical and Applied Finance* 6(4): 1–13.

[181] Schönbucher, P., and Schubert, D. (2002). Copula-dependent defaults in intensity models. Working paper available at http://ssrn.com.

[182] Schwartz, E., and Smith, J. (2000). Short-term variations and long-term dynamics in commodity prices. *Management Science*, 46(7) July: 893–911.

[183] Senior Supervisors Group. (2009). Risk management lessons from the global banking crisis of 2008. Available at www.newyorkfed.org/newsevents/news/banking/2009/SSG_report.pdf.

[184] Singh, M., and Aitken, J. (2010). The (sizable) role of rehypothecation in the shadow banking system. IMF Working Paper, WP/10/172.

[185] Singh, M. (2011). Velocity of pledged collateral: analysis and implications. IMF Working Paper, WP/11/256.

[186] Sorensen, E. H., and Bollier, T. F. (1994). Pricing swap default risk. *Financial Analysts Journal*, 50: 23–33.

[187] Stevens, R., De Waegenaere, A., and Melenberg, B. (2009). Longevity risk and hedge effects in a portfolio of life insurance products with investment risk. Tech. rep., Tilburg University.

[188] Tilley, J. (1993). Valuing American options in a path simulation model. *Transactions of Society of Actuaries*, 45: 83–104.

[189] Torresetti, R., Brigo, D., and Pallavicini, A. (2006). Implied correlation in CDO tranches: a paradigm to be handled with care. Available at http://ssrn.com, later included in [60].

[190] Torresetti, R., Brigo, D., and Pallavicini, A. (2009). Risk-neutral versus objective loss distribution and CDO tranche valuation. *Journal of Risk Management in Financial Institutions*. 2(2): 175–92.

[191] Tuckman, B., and Porfirio, P. (2003). Interest rate parity, money market basis swaps, and cross-currency basis swaps. Lehman Brothers, Fixed Income Liquid Markets Research.

[192] Watt, M. (2011). Corporates fear CVA charge will make hedging too expensive. *Risk*, October issue.

[193] Weeber, P., and Robson E. S. (2009). Market practices for settling derivatives in bankruptcy. *ABI Journal*, 9: 34–5, 76–8.

[194] Yi, C. (2009). Dangerous knowledge: credit value adjustment with credit triggers. Bank of Montreal research paper.

[195] Yor, M. (1992). *Some Aspects of Brownian Motion, Part I: Some Special Functionals. (Lectures in Mathematics ETH Zurich)*, Birkhauser Verlag, Berlin.

[196] Pallavicini, A., Perini, D., and Brigo, D. (2011). Funding, collateral and hedging: uncovering the mechanics and the subtleties of funding valuation adjustments. Available at http://ssrn.com and http://arxiv.org.

Index